MW00563298

The Sulu Zone, 1768–1898

PARAO MERCANTE

A heavily armed trading *prahu* employed in the Philippine coasting trade. Vessels such as this were prime Iranun targets at the end of the 18th century.
(courtesy of the Museo Naval, Rafael Mouleon, *Construccion Naveles*)

The Sulu Zone
1768–1898
(Second Edition)

The Dynamics of External Trade, Slavery, and Ethnicity in the
Transformation of a Southeast Asian Maritime State

JAMES FRANCIS WARREN

NUS PRESS
SINGAPORE

© NUS Press
National University of Singapore
AS3-01-02, 3 Arts Link
Singapore 117569

Fax: (65) 6774-0652
E-mail: nusbooks@nus.edu.sg
Website: http://www.nus.edu.sg/npu

First edition 1981
Second Edition 2007

ISBN 978-9971-69-386-2 (Paper)

National Library Board Singapore Cataloguing in Publication Data

Warren, James Francis, 1942–
    The Sulu zone, 1768–1898 : the dynamics of external trade, slavery, and ethnicity
in the transformation of a Southeast Asian maritime state / James Francis Warren.
— 2nd ed. — Singapore : NUS Press, 2007.
    p. cm.
    First ed. 1981.
    Includes bibliographical references and index.
    ISBN-13 : 978-9971-69-386-2 (pbk.)

    1. Slave trade – Philippines – Sulu Archipelago – History.   2. Ethnology –
Philippines – Sulu Archipelago.   3. Sulu Archipelago (Philippines) – History.
4. Sulu Archipelago (Philippines) – Commerce – History.   I. Title.

DS688.S9
959.9902 – dc22   SLS2007017940

Typeset by: International Typesetters Pte Ltd
Printed by: Vetak Services

For

My Daughter,
Dr. Kristin Warren
and
my grand-daughters
Rusmah, Masniah and Paridah

Contents

List of Tables

List of Maps

List of Illustrations

Page ii: A heavily armed merchant *prahu* of the late 18th century

Between pages 178 and 179

List of Appendices

Abbreviations

AGI   Archivo General de Indias
AHN   Archivo Historico Nacional
AMAE   Archivo Ministerio Asuntos de Exteriores
ANRI   Arsip Nasional Republik Indonesia
AR   Algemeen Rijksarchief
ASJ   Archive Society of Jesus, Philippine Province
AUST   Archive University of Santo Tomas
BH-PCL   Beyer-Holleman collection of Original Sources in Philippine
             Customary Law
BIA   Bureau of Insular Affairs
BKI   Bijdragen tot de Taal-land-en Volkenkunde van Nederlandsch-
             Indie
BMGN   Bijdragen en Mededelingen Betreffende de Geschiedenis der
             Nederlanden
BRB   Borneo Research Bulletin
BRPI   Emma Blair and James A. Robertson, *The Philippine Islands,
             1493–1898* (Cleveland, 1903–1909), 55 vols.
CO   Colonial Office, London
FO   Foreign Office, London
GCG   Governor Captain General
HDP   Historical Data Papers, Republic of the Philippines, Bureau of
             Public Schools
IOL   India Office Library
JIAEA   Journal of the Indian Archipelago and Eastern Asia
JMBRAS   Journal of the Malaysian Branch Royal Asiatic Society
JSEAS   Journal of Southeast Asian Studies
MN   Museo Naval
NBH   British North Borneo Herald and Official Gazette
PNA   Philippine National Archive
P.P.H.C.   Parliamentary Papers House of Commons
PRO   Public Records Office, London
SSJ   Sabah Society Journal
TBG   Tijdschrift voor Indische Taal-, Land-en Volkenkunde, uitge-
             geven door het (Koninklijk) Bataviaasch Genootschap van
             Kunsten en Wetenschappen

Weights, Measures, and Currencies

Weights

Tahil(tahel)	— 1.33 ounces
Kati (16 tahel)	— 1.33 pounds
Picul (100 kati)	— 133.33 pounds (Manila = 137.50 lb)
Bahar (3 picul)	— 400 pounds
Koyan (40 picul)	— 5,333.33 pounds
Quintal	— 100–110 pounds

Measures

Gantang (4 kati)	— 3.1 kilogrammes of rice
Cavan (25 gantang)	— 44 kilogrammes of rice
Arroba	— 25.36 pounds (5½ arroba = picul)

Currencies

100 Spanish dollars (pesos, duros)   — 224½ Company Rupees
£26.50
252.27 Dutch Guilders
$366.97

Alungi Bisalla Alenyap na Bangsa—
Lost Language, Vanished People

—an old Samal Bajau Laut adage—

Foreword

Since it was first published a quarter of a century ago, *The Sulu Zone* has been one of the most important books in the field of Southeast Asian history. Having known Jim Warren for forty years and closely followed his lifelong preoccupation with Sulu, I am delighted to accept his invitation to write the foreword to this new edition of the book. This gives me a welcome opportunity to highlight a few of the ways *The Sulu Zone* has changed understandings of the Sulu sultanate.

First of all, by creating "the Sulu zone" the book produced a new way of conceptualizing the sultanate itself. A fundamental principle of the book is that historians must not allow the boundaries of contemporary nation-states to shape the way they look at the past. Instead, they must map out the connections people actually had with one another. Thus, much of the book is devoted to a painstaking reconstruction of the trade in opium, guns, bird's nests, *tripang* (*bêche-de-mer*), and slaves centered on Jolo, the seat of the sultan of Sulu. The zone expanded and contracted according to the sultan's ability to command the obedience of outlying chiefs, who were fairly autonomous within their own realms. At its peak it included much of the east coast of Borneo as well as the Sulu Archipelago and the western and southern coasts of Mindanao. Its reach even extended upriver into the interior of Borneo, where tribal leaders were quick to take advantage of the ever increasing demand for jungle products at Jolo. The zone therefore extended far beyond the area actually controlled by the sultan to encompass all the places oriented towards Jolo.

In addition to mapping out the Sulu zone, the book presented a vision of the zone as part of a larger world. Specifically, it challenged the widely held view that the sultanate was a decaying backwater by portraying it as a fragmented but nevertheless thriving polity vigorously taking advantage of the growth of the China trade. As the British demand for Chinese tea grew in the late 1700s, country traders based in India looked for alternatives to silver to pay for the tea. Selling Indian opium to the Chinese provided part of the answer, but these traders also exploited the great demand in China for the sea and jungle products of the Malay Archipelago. Thus, on their way to China the country traders could stop at Jolo to exchange opium, firearms, and Indian textiles for pearl shell, tripang, bird's nests, and other local products that they could sell in China. Soon, Chinese traders based in Manila and Singapore as well as Bugis traders from the south began to arrive as well.

But who collected all the sea and jungle products traded at Jolo? The key to the whole book is the argument that Sulu's booming economy depended on the labour of people captured by Iranun and Balangingi raiders and put to work in the zone as slaves. In short, the people collecting *tripang*, pearl shell, and other products in various parts of the Sulu zone were part of a larger economic system along with the sultan and his chiefs, slave raiders, powerful merchants in London and India, country traders, and consumers of opium and fine food in China. I can still recall the excitement I felt when reading *The Sulu Zone* for the first time and saw how it tied together so many phenomena and groups that previously had appeared to be quite unconnected.

The book also changed the common view of the slave raiders. Like earlier books, *The Sulu Zone* portrays them as brutal marauders, describing in great detail how the Iranun and Balangingi scoured the coasts of the Philippines, Borneo, Celebes, and even the Malay Peninsula in search of their prey. Unlike its predecessors, however, *The Sulu Zone* demonstrates that they were an integral part of the whole economic system, for they procured the labour on which this system depended. The Balangingi in particular had a powerful motivation to become raiders. Inhabitants of a small barren island in the Sulu archipelago, they braved the seas and colonial navies in a search for captives they could hand over to the sultan and chiefs in exchange not only for opium and guns but also for rice and other necessities of life. Understanding these circumstances does not make their brutality any more palatable, but it goes a long way towards explaining it.

Most of all, *The Sulu Zone* presented a new view of the captives and slaves. More precisely, it brought into view people who had been barely visible except as anonymous victims of the raiders. In this respect *The Sulu Zone* is part of a larger project. Jim has seen it as his mission to bring to life people forgotten by later generations and ignored by other historians: the voices of the "little people" deserve to be heard as much as those of sultans, governors, captains, and tycoons. In all his major books Jim has shown not only how they endured discomfort, cruelty, death, loss, and injustice but also how they had some mastery over their own fates, whether they decided to endure, to adapt, to run away, to resist, or in extreme cases to escape by ending their lives. These people may have been victims but they were also individual human beings with their own pasts, dreams, and fears. This outlook is most pronounced in Jim's later books on the rickshaw pullers and prostitutes of Singapore, but it certainly comes through as well in the final chapters of *The Sulu Zone*, where he presents the stories of the many thousands of people taken into captivity and put to work collecting sea and jungle products for their masters.

The great challenge Jim faced was to find a way to tell these stories. His urge to give voice to members of the underclass has long driven him to go to extraordinary lengths to find new sources. Perhaps most notably, his discovery of the coroner's records for colonial Singapore launched his books on rickshaw pullers and prostitutes. In the case of *The Sulu Zone*, he set himself the task of tracking down as many statements by slaves as he could, and eventually located a multitude of such statements in the records of interviews of former slaves who had been picked up by European naval patrols. In order to make sense of this material, Jim employed and adapted, as he would in his later books, the techniques of collective biography. Using these techniques, he presents a general picture of the lives led by slaves, but he also provides remarkable insights into the great variety in these lives. Most slaves were put to work collecting sea and jungle products, but some became traders making a good living, while others became raiders and preyed on the villages from which they or their parents had originally come. Some never gave up the hope of returning to their home villages, but others came to regard their new lives as no worse than those they had left behind. Some never forgot their origins, but many, particularly those captured when fairly young, readily adopted new ethnic identities. Indeed, we learn, the "Balangingi" included people who had originally been brought to Sulu from places throughout the island world. All of these observations have a historiographical purpose, whether it is to show how slavery in the Sulu zone differed from that in other parts of the world or to shatter common preconceptions about the enduring nature of ethnic categories. More subtly, they offer an insight into the adaptability of human beings in the most trying circumstances.

All this leads to a question I have often asked myself: where does the passion that permeates Jim's work come from? In his introduction to this new edition Jim writes that he became aware of the direction his life's work might take when he was living in a Samal Bajau Laut village on the east coast of Sabah as a Peace Corps Volunteer. This experience may account for Jim's focus on Southeast Asia, particularly the area where present-day Malaysia, Indonesia, and the Philippines meet, but it hardly accounts for the passion itself. Likewise, the intellectual influences Jim identifies may help to explain the particular shape of his work, but they explain little about what has made him so receptive to them. Perhaps, as he suggests in the introduction, his passion has to do with his family background and heritage. Fortunately, readers of *The Sulu Zone* and Jim Warren's other books can safely disregard E.H. Carr's injunction to study the historian before studying the history. The important point is simply to appreciate that this passion, whatever its origins, is integral to the work itself. It helps to define the questions Jim asks, it sustains the task of compiling and collating mountains of evidence, it drives the analysis, and it is the source of the empathy that informs the description.

No historical work goes unchallenged forever. Indeed, it is a mark of important books that they push other scholars to adopt new perspectives and ask new questions. Some historians have criticized Jim's reluctance to describe the slave raiders as "pirates". Others have argued that Jim has overestimated the extent to which the export economy of the zone relied on slave labour and therefore overestimated the number of people the Iranun and Balangingi captured and brought to Sulu. Jim responds to this second point in his new introduction by referring to a source he recently discovered that allows him to approach the issue in a new way. No doubt the debate will continue. I certainly hope so. But one thing is clear: the elegant structure of the book, the power of the argument, the vivid description of the island world, the ease with which Jim draws on other disciplines, the immense range of sources, the imaginative use of these sources, the lucid prose, and, most of all, Jim's passion for his subject all combine to make *The Sulu Zone* a brilliant work of historical scholarship. Its broad vision of the scope and methods of historical research has taught historians of my generation much about the practice of our craft. May this new edition of *The Sulu Zone* go on to enlighten, inspire, and challenge a new generation of readers.

John Butcher
Department of International Business and Asian Studies
Griffith Business School, Griffith University
Australia

February 2007

Preface

It seems to me inaccurate to dispose of such Indonesian states as Palembang, Siak, Achin, or Johore with the qualifications corrupt-despotisms, pirate states, and slave states, hotbeds of political danger and decay. Inaccurate, if for no other reason, because despotism, piracy and slavery are historical terms, and history is not written with value judgements. To choose examples from the field of Dutch history, the town of Flushing based its existence in the seventeenth and eighteenth centuries in no small measure on privateering and smuggling, and Middleburg's renowned trading company of 1720 occupied itself with privateering, smuggling to and from Spanish America and slave trade.... The chief point is something else; what was the power-political-maritime-economic of the harbour principalities.

J.C. van Leur

Of the many topics in the history of modern Southeast Asia, more attention should be drawn to those which concern the sociocultural evolution of the maritime world. Despite the stress Jacob van Leur gave in the 1930s to illuminating the study of the region's numerous maritime traditions,[1] few since then have looked beyond the European experience to the broader stream of Southeast Asian development.[2] The maritime populations that were dependent on the sea for their economic pursuits—trading, raiding, collecting, and fishing—remain largely caricatures in the historiography of the region; their culture and social organization have been little studied by historians of the region. Much of the history of the eastern archipelago continues to be written around a set of traditional assumptions and unchallenged postulations about the essential "nature" and historical development of the sea-oriented peoples and communities. Historians continue to pursue the "trade and empire" approach, while the region's separate history remains, in Van Leur's words, "grey and undifferentiated".[3] Significant among the neglected aspects of the history of the eastern archipelago is a reconstruction of the character of commerce and power in the maritime community. Essential developments in the region's economic structure and social and cultural evolution, in particular the expansion of external trade and the growing incidence of slave raiding in the latter part of the eighteenth century among maritime peoples, have claimed the attention of most historians only when those activities conflicted with or were affected by European policy.[4] Most histories of the region have been political and administrative in preference to social and economic. As a result of this bias, the complex interrelationship of commerce, marauding, and servitude and their broader sociocultural implications have been virtually ignored.

To seriously take up Van Leur's challenge and vision, historians and anthropologists of Southeast Asia must divest themselves of the shipboard view of the eastern archipelago encountered in European sources of the period and willingly enter the looking glass to "examine history from the *other side*—since we are still used to thinking of the European point of view as the right side of history".[5] This book is an attempt to piece together the view "from the other side" and to understand how a maritime "frontier" region responded to Western expansion. It also documents the independent activities of several seafaring peoples in a large trading region who were stimulated by European expansion and commerce, but who developed their own patterns of trade often in defiance of the interests of three European empires: the Spanish, the Dutch, and the British. It is a very complicated story of diverse but interrelated uses of the sea by peoples and communities who have remained shadowy in European sources, despite the many accounts of Western contact with them.

The book focuses specifically on the world of the Sulu trading zone situated on the margins of three empires in the late eighteenth and nineteenth centuries and the relationship of the trading zone with China during a period when the China trade was still strong and profitable. A basic interpretation of the history of the Sulu Sultanate, the heart of the zone, must focus on the place of the slave, or "acquired person",[6] in Sulu society and the decisive importance of slaves in the functioning of Sulu's economic structure.

This turned out to be a research topic of remarkable richness but one that would not be served by the objectives of conventional historiography. An ethnohistorical research strategy proved an absolute necessity for the study of inter-ethnic relations, external trade, and slavery. The Sulu Sultanate in the late eighteenth and nineteenth centuries provided an ideal basis for such an investigation on several grounds. Solid anthropological fieldwork had been done over the course of the last two decades among the Taosug of Jolo, the Balangingi Samal, the Samal Bajau Laut, and the Yakan of Basilan in the Sulu archipelago and northeast Borneo, and among the Maranao and the Subanun of Mindanao.[7] Without the ethnographic materials that have been published as a result of this fieldwork, it would have been difficult for me to assess the value of European historical sources and place them in context.

There were ample sources for the study of the commercial-marauding patterns of the Sulu Sultanate in the period 1768–1898, but they were still scattered, even unrecognized, in several European archives, and in Manila and Jakarta. While much of the material in English on Sulu had been exploited, primary source material in Spanish and Dutch archives had yet to be systematically investigated. There remained then a need for extensive and thorough archival research to present a coherent picture of Sulu's commercial position from the mid-eighteenth to the late nineteenth century.

I have drawn upon anthropological concepts, European documents in several languages with excerpts and examples from official reports, diaries, letters, journals and newspapers, and local accounts to examine the economic vitality of the independent Sulu Sultanate, in its role as entrepot for European and Asian commerce in the China trade from the late eighteenth to the late nineteenth century. Among the most important sources I have used are the manuscripts in the archives of Spain (principally the Archive of the Indies) on trade from Manila to the Sulu Sultanate between 1768 and 1848. When compiled and ordered as a time series, these documents (particularly the *estados* and the *almojarifazgo*) suggest the overall level of commercial activity, shifts in market preferences, and the economic interdependence of Manila and Jolo in the period (see Appendix F). A careful reading of these documents reveals the level of economic integration achieved by Sulu and its Bornean dependencies in the wider island economy, the magnitude of the change that occurred after 1768, and possible reasons for shifts in the trade patterns over time. This data goes far towards rounding out the detailed evidence which Van Leur saw to be lacking for maritime powers in the eastern archipelago.

In the late eighteenth and nineteenth centuries, the population of Sulu was heterogeneous and changing—socially, economically, and ethnically. This was a direct result of external trade. The populating of the Sulu zone by captives from the Philippines and various parts of the Malay world and their role in the redistributional economy centred at Jolo cannot be underestimated. Previous historical studies of the Sultanate depended largely on published colonial records and accounts to understand the economic and social role played by slaves in the economy rather than on records produced by the slaves themselves. Slavery in Sulu was observed through the eyes and preconceptions of European observers and writers who viewed Sulu as the centre of a world fundamentally hostile to their interests—an Islamic world whose activities centred about piracy and slavery.

A unique alternative to this Eurocentric perspective is presented by the scattered statements of fugitive captives from the Sulu Sultanate. From over one hundred and eighty fugitive slave accounts, manuscript sources, and travel literature, clear patterns of social life and economic activity can be constructed. As a historical source the published and unpublished testimonies of the fugitive slaves of the Sulu Sultanate are invaluable. The testimonies tell us much about the experience of slavery in Sulu that could never be found in more traditional sources. Indeed without them much of the inside view of everyday life in the Sultanate would have been lost. The experience of captives from the moment of seizure, and their passage in the slave *prahus,* to their settlement, life and labour in Sulu, emerges from anonymity in the slave testimonies. The total effect of these individual lives and cases of fugitive slaves is to throw very considerable light on the internal processes, the ethnic and social transformations, in the Sulu trading zone during the nineteenth century (see Appendix R).

The trade data and the statements of the fugitive slaves complement one another, and together enable us to resolve many fundamental questions about the size of Sulu's indigenous trade, about its flourishing slave population, and about how these changed over time as a consequence of the impact of external trade.

Two perspectives have dominated the historiography of the Sulu zone and have tended to obscure the complex but integrated patterns of external trade, raiding, and slavery. On the one hand, there is the persistent theme of the advent of piracy in the Malay world in the eighteenth and nineteenth centuries and the decline of indigenous maritime power—the "decay theory". Among historians concerned with the European advance in the region, Nicholas Tarling is the most notable exponent of this perspective.[8] He has argued that the monopolistic trade practices of the Europeans in the eighteenth century tore away the props that supported the economic foundations of many of the indigenous coastal and island realms such as Sulu; severely weakened by the loss of revenue and commerce these states turned to piracy. Though Tarling recognized the functional importance of piracy in *Piracy and Politics in the Malay World*, and questioned the use of the term "piracy" to describe the slaving activities of the Iranun and Balangingi, and though his overall interpretation of the decline of traditional pristine political systems is not given exclusively in terms of that "decay", he nevertheless has adopted uncritically the assumptions about Sulu and the rise of slave raiding made by European writers of the period, especially Sir Stamford Raffles. As a consequence, he has concentrated much of his attention upon British efforts to suppress Sulu "piracy", rather than on significant indigenous initiatives.

An earlier approach to Sulu history has been to emphasize the rivalry between Catholic Spaniards and the Muslim population of the Sultanate. In the pioneering histories of Sulu by Najeeb Saleeby and Cesar Majul, raiding is interpreted within the framework of the "Moro Wars" as retaliation against Spanish colonialism and religious incursion.[9] I have discarded this approach for several reasons. Saleeby and Majul provide some insight into the role of Muslim raiding and slaving in the sixteenth to eighteenth centuries and its commercial, military, and administrative consequences for the Spanish colonial regime in the Philippines, but there is a clear historiographical problem in their writings on piracy. They do not always clearly differentiate between Muslim ethnic groups engaged in these activities in different periods. While the Sulu (Taosug) did conduct raids in the earlier period the printed chronicles of the sixteenth to eighteenth century point to the Magindanao as the principal slave raiders. More importantly, if this is so, there is a real discontinuity between early and later slaving and raiding pursuits, its composition and organization, and the reasons for the accentuated tempo of these activities in Southeast Asia in the post-1768 period. In the earlier period, "Magindanao" raiders seem to have been from Mindanao, and their marauding was then viewed as an extension of *jihad*, with political, not simply economic motives. This sort of activity was far less common after the advent of European trade in the Sulu archipelago in the late eighteenth century when raiding was more organized and slaves were the prime object of wealth. Both approaches have underestimated the relationship of slavery and raiding activity to the economy of the Sulu Sultanate in the late eighteenth century.

This book attempts to use the maritime history of the Sulu Sultanate revolving around the interrelated themes of external trade, slave raiding, and state formation as the key to the general history of the zone. The first part of the book (Chapters 1–6) examines Sulu's response to the need for its maritime products in the China trade. By fitting into the patterns of European trade with China, the Sultanate established itself as a powerful commercial centre. The maritime and jungle products to be found within the Sulu zone and in the area of its trading partners—*tripang*, bird's nest, wax, camphor, mother of pearl, tortoise shell—were new products for redressing the British East India Company's adverse trade balance with China.

To Sulu went textiles and other imported manufactures, opium, and, of crucial importance, guns and gunpowder which contributed to the Sultanate's physical power. Taosug merchants on the coast and their descendants developed an extensive redistributive trade in which they wrested the function of the collection and distribution of commodities from traditional competitors, the Sultanates of Brunei and Cotabato. This commerce involving trade with the Bugis of Samarinda and Berau to the south, with Manila to the north, with Singapore and later Labuan, formed a complex set of interrelationships through which the segmentary state of Sulu was able to consolidate its dominance over the outlying areas of the zone along the northeast Borneo and western Mindanao coasts.

Taosug *datus* forged trade pacts with tribal peoples of East Borneo and Bugis traders to the south to obtain *tripang*, bird's nest, wax, and camphor for Chinese consumption. Captives and trade commodities were introduced along the rivers by Taosug and their trading partners. Taosug who intermarried with tribal people and lived at the middle reaches of the rivers on Borneo's northeast coast formed a commercial link between ethnic groups at the periphery of the zone and their Taosug kindred at the centre.

As the Sultanate organized its economy around the collection and distribution of marine and jungle produce, there was a greater need for large-scale recruitment of manpower in Sulu's economy to do the labour-intensive work of procurement. Slaving activity developed to meet the accentuated demands of external trade. Jolo became the nerve centre for the coordination of long-distance slave raiding. The second part of the book (Chapters 7–9) analyses the technical aspects of the seasonal raiding programmes in search of additional manpower to service the procurement of trading produce.

Driven by the desire for wealth and power, the Iranun and Balangingi Samal surged out of the Sulu archipelago in search of slaves. Within three decades (1768–98), their raids encompassed all of insular Southeast Asia. Their well-armed *prahus* scoured the coasts of the Indonesian world and sailed northwards into the Philippines. They joined with other Iranun and Samal speakers living at satellite stations on the coasts of Borneo, Celebes, and Sumatra in the course of these raids. Navigating with the monsoon, their *prahus* returned to Jolo loaded with captives to be exchanged to Taosug for rice, cloth, and luxury goods. The raiding system enabled the Sultanate to incorporate vast numbers of people from the Philippines and eastern Indonesia into the Sulu population. Traffic in slaves reached its peak in Sulu in the period 1800–1848, founded on the basis of trade with China and the West.

The last section of the book (Chapters 10–11) delineates the parameters of slavery as an institution in the Sulu Sultanate and describes in some detail how captive "slaves" served as dependants of the Sulu elite and were able to better their condition and end up, at least in the second generation, as assimilated members of the Taosug and Samal population. The object of the final chapter is to depict the everyday experience of the slaves and, to some extent, glimpse the working of the social structure into which they were incorporated.

Acknowledgements

This book grew out of a doctoral dissertation submitted to the Australian National University in 1975. I wish to express my gratitude to the University for its generosity and support and to the Department of Pacific and Southeast Asian History for sponsoring my fieldwork. To my supervisor, Dr. A.J.S. Reid, I owe a debt of gratitude, both personal and professional, that is difficult to express. His incisive questions and exhaustive commentary have strengthened the overall interpretation of the thesis and the book.

I am indebted to the following colleagues for their valuable comments, criticisms, and encouragement over the years both in helping me revise the thesis for publication, and, the re-issue of this book — Jeremy Beckett, Carolyn Brewer, John Butcher, Bruce Cruikshank, Shinzo Hayase, David Henley, Reynaldo Ileto, Tsuyoshi Kato, Adrian Lapian, John Legge, Alfred McCoy, Anne L. Reber, Norman Owen, John Schumacher, S.J., Heather Sutherland, William Henry Scott, Kurt Stenross, Eric Tagliacozzo, Nicholas Tarling, Esther Velthoen and O.W. Wolters.

Many people have contributed to this study. Major sources of inspiration have been the thought of John Smail and Anne Lyndsey Reber's thesis on the Sulu world. I am indebted to Dr. Terry Hull for assisting me to "translate" my data on slave raiding and demography for the computer and to Mrs. Gloria Robbins, the programmer. I am grateful to Dr. Bruce Cruikshank for having copied much of the trade data in the period 1820–30 as well as the censuses for 1793, 1796, 1797, 1798, and 1799 that he encountered in the course of his own research at the Archive of the Indies. In this context, I wish to thank my research assistant in Manila, Miss Shirley Madrid, who flagged items on Muslim raiding for me to investigate in the Ereccion del Pueblo bundles and in the Historical Data Papers. Thanks are also due to Mr. Keith Mitchell, cartographer, Research School of Pacific Studies, Australian National University, for his assistance and advice in the Laboratory, and for rendering a base line map of the Sulu zone.

I also wish to thank Mary-Anne Spalding, Leonie Pimm, and Leanne Blackwell for their intelligent and efficient assistance in preparing the final draft of the manuscript.

Finally, I want to express my gratitude to my wife, Carol—friend, intellectual companion, and critic—who has invested considerable time on this subject over the years, time which has necessarily been taken away

from her own research. The book is a better study because of her help and
encouragement.

Some parts of the present book have been printed in articles which
appeared in the *Journal of the Malaysian Branch Royal Asiatic Society* 50
(1977), *Philippine Studies* 25 (1977), the *Journal of Southeast Asian Studies*
8 (1977), the *Journal of Asian Studies* 38 (1978), and *Archipel* 18 (1979).
I am indebted to the editors of these journals for permission to reproduce
material.

Introduction to the Second Edition

Some Reflections on
Researching and Writing
"The Sulu Zone"

Passing Over

I would like to begin by simply stating that it has been 40 years since I first "passed over" into a world that I would later dub "The Sulu Zone". The process of "passing over" from one culture to another, from one way of life to another, and, the equal and opposite process—"coming back", returning with new insights about other people and places, and possible pasts and futures, gave birth to the ideas behind this book in 1967, on the east coast of North Borneo. What I will be doing in this new preface, therefore, is to briefly attempt to map the life of a book on time.

New York-born to second generation Irish and northeastern European Jewish parents I never intended to end up in Southeast Asia. While teaching African history at a suburban upper Westchester County High School north of New York City in the mid-1960s, and passing over once a week, under the auspices of the Afro-American College Assistance Programme at Columbia University, into the street wise world and emotional milieu of the black revolution sweeping Harlem, I had my future mapped out: finish my Master's thesis on the slave trade between West Africa and Brazil, and then join the Peace Corps in Peru. I wanted to learn Quechua and pass over the cultural frontier of the altiplano, the high plateau, to live with the vanquished Indian descendants of the great empire builders, the Incas. But when the United States Government cut Corps funding to that area, my wife and I—we were then newly married—were given a choice of destination(s): initially only Liberia, but several months later also either Korea or Malaysia. We chose the latter.

I (we) lived for two years as Peace Corps volunteers in Semporna, on the east coast of Borneo (1967–69). The period from January to November 1969, spent in Kampong Bangau Bangau, a Samal Bajau Laut village consisting of a flotilla of boat dwellers and a semi-sedentary population of Bajau Laut in varying stages of adaptation to a house-dwelling way of life, was particularly memorable. It was the rapid abandonment of sea nomadism—a life-style which has characterized the Samal Bajau Laut as a people that has a long history and from which they drew their sense of identity—which first motivated my interest in Southeast Asian history. Hence, the actual origin of this book began in personal experience rather than with books and formal training.

My subsequent experience of attempting to write my Master's thesis on the Samal Bajau Laut under North Borneo Chartered Company rule, a history involving a non-western people based primarily on written (British) records, pointed out the extreme difficulty of presenting a balanced interpretation, using only traditional historiographical methods and sources.[1] It impressed upon me the vital importance of oral traditions and an ethnohistorical perspective, in any future effort to investigate changes in identity, cultural values, social organization, economic systems and political patterns of the maritime people of Southeast Asia; transformations and transitions initiated by the world capitalist economy, colonialism and modernity. There remained the need then to attempt to integrate my small-scale investigation of the problems of cultural ecological adaptation of the Samal Bajau Laut with the study of world historical events and experiences, and to show how they were linked together as a world historical process. I felt the necessity too, to expand the temporal reach of analysis to better understand the response of a loosely structured port polity—centred around the Sulu Sultanate and the nearby areas of northern Celebes (Sulawesi), northeastern Borneo (Sabah) and the central and western territories of Mindanao— to the ascendance of global capitalist expansion and the imperialism of European dominance. While lying behind it all there was still the pre-war challenge and vision of the Dutch sociological historian, J.C. Van Leur, to see the past through the eyes of those subject and subordinate people who became mere objects of conventional post-war Southeast Asian history. This book was meant to be a powerful response to Van Leur and a stunning record of witness to the intractable problem of the link between desire and displacement on a remarkable scale, focussing on the economic and cultural encounters and conflicts between European colonisers and non-European people, and attempting to reconstruct the experiences of both sides, ranging from Canton and Jolo, to London and Salem, and from the extraordinary voyages of Orang Kaya Kullul and Panglima Taupan to those of Captains Thomas Forrest and Jose Marie Halcon, as well as from the banquet tables of the Qing Dynasty to the decaying stone watchtowers and churches scattered along the coastline of the Philippines—crumbling monuments to the export of tripang and bird's nest to China.

Seeing the Sulu Zone

In contemporary ethnohistorical studies of Southeast Asia the "zone" and/or "border" have recently become chosen metaphors for theorizing the historically complex and contradictory ways in which cultural difference and ethnic diversity have been articulated in social relations and in political and economic practice across time. Thirty-six years ago the doctoral research on which this book is based explored global cultural interconnections and interdependencies in insular Southeast Asia in the late eighteenth and nineteenth centuries with particular reference to a polity and world that I dubbed the "Sulu Zone".[2] This book aimed to enhance critical understanding of historiographical methods and models used in problematizing and investigating economic and cultural "border zones" in a changing global-local context. My emphasis was on a "zone" created through the intersections of geography, culture and history centred around the Sulu and Celebes seas, as well as China's and the West's complicated place within its long history of globalization that can be readily traced back to the eighteenth century, if not earlier. Hence my approach to framing and representing the ethnohistory of the Sulu Zone on its own terms, rather than merely as a corollary of the history of Western imperial expansion in East Asia from the end of the eighteenth century, was to tease out and, albeit, unravel the economic, cultural and ecological interconnections embedded in the world capitalist economy, with particular reference to the evolution and transformation of the "zone": namely, globalized connections that have non-Western as well as Western origins. This broad conceptual schemata also aimed to enhance understanding of these global systemic links and interactions between geo-political core areas, notably China and Europe, and strategically positioned "zones" or places with loosely structured polities, strong trading bases and thin populations like the Sulu Sultanate, which encompassed a variety of economic sub-regions and extremely specialized territories.

My initial thinking about how the late eighteenth century global economy created a "borderless world" or "zone", both spatially and historically in the area of the Sulu and Celebes seas, owes much to the influence of John Smail's thought about autonomous histories and perspective in historical writing.[3] Smail, in turn, had been strongly indebted to the writings of Van Leur and the hemispheric cross-regional historical orientation of Marshall Hodgson, who attempted to locate the history of Islamic Civilization and situate the history of European modernity in a parallel move within a world historical framework. Templates for the "zone" and possible core-periphery and trade-process models, were provided by the path-breaking works of E.R. Leach, Fernand Braudel and Andre Gunder Frank. The inherent advantages of such a conceptual-theoretical, evolutionary-ecological approach for framing and interpretation in a shifting upland agricultural context were already apparent to me in Leach's pioneering work on the political systems of highland

Burma. In the context of the Sulu Zone, however, insular Southeast Asia was a region in which the sea served as a major means of communication for a wider inter-regional economy in which national boundaries were fluid and by no means fixed.[4] Following in the footsteps of Leach and Braudel, I abandoned the blinkered geographic perspective of earlier historians of the Philippines, Indonesia and Borneo for a more dynamic diagrammatic representation and definition of the Sulu Sultanate's boundaries. It was based on larger scale processes of social-cultural change and a "borderless" history of a global maritime trade network oriented towards China, Europe and North America. A history without borders was about entangled commodities and patterns of consumption and desire, which were linked to slavery and slave raiding, the manipulation of ethnically diverse groups, the formation and maintenance of ethnicity, the meaning and constitution of "culture", and state formation, as all part of the same system of world commerce and economic growth. To be released from the conceptual constraints of conventional historical geography, I called this wide-ranging web of economic influence and interpersonal relations that centred on the polity of the Sulu Sultanate a "zone".

My framing and interpretation of the "zone" as a spatial system rested on the axiom that it was "inherently unstable and generally dynamic"[5] and that it was thrust on the global stage at a specific moment or era in "regional time". Leach's remarkable work on state and community structures in highland Burma aimed at tracing the pattern of the shifting balance between two representations of political order and social phenomena over some 150 years. Similarly, for me, the "zone" was also a process in time:[6] a recognition that all ethnic groups and communities were being shaped and reshaped by the interplay between internal social and cultural forms and ongoing, external courses of action and extrinsic factors. In a very real sense, the peoples of the zone—the Taosug *datus*, Iranun and Balangingi slavers, and the huge numbers of displaced captives or slaves—were in fact "products" of large-scale processes of global socio-economic change which had made them what they were and which continued to shape their responses in reaction to the uncontrollable and rapid impact of these globalizing forces. The holism of the zone as a "spatial system" was posited, both as a model and a necessary analytic schema, not a given. The invisible connections linking the processes of structural change and the dynamic movement of local systems and networks of this complex, albeit difficult to see, "zone" to the wider economic and political world(s) of colonial capitalism and free trade, of which it was fast becoming a part, had to be traced and explained in "regional time". To rectify the pre-suppositions of earlier studies, I developed an ethnohistorical research strategy, utilizing a global, cultural-ecological perspective and framework where the inter-dependence of all states and societies could be seen at once, and their inter-connectedness to one another within the framework of the world economic system was readily apparent.[7] It is crucial to an understanding of the more flexible trans-disciplinary approach required to write The Sulu Zone that it was based on devising a new conceptual, analytical framework guided by the assumption that history and ethnography are inextricably linked. It was a conceptual framework and a paradigm of sorts to enhance our understanding of crucial economic and social processes in insular Southeast Asia—a broad, loose but nonetheless coherent explanation and model about the nature of a Southeast Asian polity and economic region that responded to a set of interdependent connections and relationships fostered by the modern world system from the end of the eighteenth century. Apart from offering a panoramic perspective and a means of explanatory power for understanding these global-regional inter-relationships, the diagrammatic "model" and role of the zone provided the major principle for framing and organization of the narrative; it was the essential backdrop or stage against which to begin the fascinating task of unravelling the main strands in the development of these separate but increasingly related inter-regional and local histories of various societies and cultures in East and Southeast Asia, and beyond.

The Sulu Zone—The Meaning and Constitution of "Culture"

By arguing for a broader interconnected global economic perspective interesting complex questions were raised about what constitutes our conception of "culture" and ethnicity. While thousands of captive people were allocated throughout the zone each year as slaves in the period under consideration, the borderlines of race, "culture", and ethnicity were increasingly blurred by the more inclusive practices of incorporation and pluralism in a traditional Muslim social system. I maintained in The Sulu Zone that the Taosug, Iranun and Samal not only lived in an increasingly interdependent world but that they also lived in an emergent multi-ethnic polity and society, the multicultural inhabitants of which came from many parts of Asia and elsewhere in the world. How are identities—single or multiple—forged? What symbols, rituals and perceptions create a strong sense of collective identity? The traditional assumption of a "culture" as enduring over time despite outward changes in people's lives and value orientations is both "empirically misleading and deeply essentialist".[8]

As Roger Keesing noted, there is no part of Eastern Asia where both the production and reproduction of "culture" and cultural meaning can be characterised as unproblematic, without glossing over or disguising radical changes in relation to ethnicity, power and hierarchy that have differentially affected states like the Sulu Sultanate and marginal settings like the zone.[9] In terms of questioning the ethnic boundedness and cultural homogeneity of an emergent way of life unfolding in the zone at the end of the eighteenth century, I gradually recognized the power of language, commodities and memory as key elements and symbols in the construction of new ethnic identities and communities. Filling a conspicuous gap in the literature this aspect of the book's ethnohistorical research explored the accomplishment, or re-invention, of ethnicity as a consequence of developing ties to world commerce and economic growth, and to the expanding world of *Darul* Islam. The question of the conditions under which these new identities were formed and the ethnicity accomplished throughout the zone, especially in the first half of the nineteenth century, has aroused considerable subsequent interest. I stressed in *The Sulu Zone* the inextricable relationship between slave raiding, displacement and forced migration on the one hand, and "homeland" and identity on the other, as absolutely critical factors that led to the emergence of new communities and diasporas. This way of historically conceptualising the "ethnicity" and "culture" of maritime communities leads us to consider a new way of framing and representing a sense of kinship, group solidarity, common culture and conflict, particularly political struggles, in the history of Southeast Asia. By stressing the problems of self-definition and the reconstruction of identities, and the meaning of homeland and lost places, as revealing social and psychological processes in their own right, *The Sulu Zone* challenged lineal notions of history with their origins in Western Europe and bounded static conceptions of "culture" and ethnic groups that were imposed, imagined and maintained by Europeans both before and after colonization.

This expedient reinvention of ethnicity resulting from the interconnected force of circumstance generated by the China trade also compels us to think about related notions of society and "culture" in more processual ways.[10] Historians and ethnographers of the region need to locate the emergence, maintenance and abrogation of populations and the "cultures" they encompass within the framework of a series of historically changing, imperfectly bounded, multiple and branching integrated sets of local, regional, and global social and economic alignments. Here, some of the questions posed about the birth and accomplishment of ethnicity and identities in *The Sulu Zone* for understanding both the recent and more distant past, especially on the margins of states, and beyond the frontier(s), in Southeast Asia are far-reaching, particularly if one considers the contemporary complex theoretical cultural implications of the nature of "ethnicity" (often associated with economic and political conflict in developing societies) as a key factor for unravelling the development and history of the terms "Indonesian", "Malay", "Thai", "Burmese" and "Vietnamese". These labels have been successfully manufactured as part of a national imaginary by modern states in the interest of forging national unity and to mythologise history.[11] This case-based discussion, of the concept of

Asian "cultures" and the creation of "imagined communities" of nationalities as problematic, and recognition of the crucial factors which led, as part of one inter-connected and inter-dependent process, to the accomplishment of ethnicity in the Sulu Zone, provides some of the basic building blocks for future comparative and theoretical analyses of the interpretation of culture.

The Sulu Zone—In Search of "Evidence"

The chronic problem facing ethnohistorians of Asia, Africa and Latin America is the uneven nature of the source material available for certain people, places and times. How can one provide a well detailed historical reconstruction and measure change if the documents as "instruments of measurement" are scarce, non-existent, or themselves changing?[12] The effort has to be made to bring to bear as wide a range of evidence as possible, on critically specific points, to emphasize the global interconnections and interdependencies of particular societies and regions, in order to frame a holistic or "total" explanation of their mutual encounters, interactions and conflicts in a contemporary "borderless world"; a world that has a long history, created in part by an evolving world capitalist economy. Hence, it proved necessary, to research and write this book, to seek out as much evidence wherever it could be found, especially because of the accidental generation and destruction of historical records concerning the ethnohistory of the Sulu Zone. Consequently, I used an extremely varied, in fact eclectic, body of documentation, from 26 different archives, libraries and repositories around the world, to resolve the problem of explaining the profound significance of the China tea trade in the transformation of Taosug society and culture in the late eighteenth and nineteenth centuries. I went in search of all forms of evidence—archaeological, anthropological, historical and oral testament—and not a page was meant to be left unturned along the way.

In the late eighteenth and nineteenth centuries, the population of Sulu was heterogeneous and changing—socially, economically, and ethnically. This was a direct result of global trade. The populating of the Sulu Zone by captives from the Philippines and various parts of the Malay world and their role in the redistributive economy centred at Jolo, the capital of the Sultanate, cannot be under-estimated. The perennial problem confronting the historian has always been to achieve a balance in the historical record. Frequently this record is written by the empowered. As such, their observations are, naturally enough, laden with their own preconceptions, social bias and self-interest. Their accounts have often been employed to provide a "contrast" and sometimes justification for a particular policy or historical attitude. However, in colonial and national archives sometimes there are misplaced or forgotten documents and neglected objects of material culture that have survived the passage of time to tell a different story: the deeds and even the authentic speech of the captives of the Iranun and Balangingi recounting their stories of the middle passages; the letter of a Balangingi female prisoner of war asking to join her incarcerated husband on death row; the harrowing report of a Spaniard captured and sentenced to a Balangingi prahu as a galley slave; an artist's sketch here, a misplaced oil painting there—all awaiting rediscovery and analysis by a young ethnohistorian, searching after the fact(s) in order to understand various enigmatic processes in the Sulu Zone.

To understand the economic and social role played by slaves in the economy previous historical studies of the Sultanate depended largely on published colonial records and accounts rather than on records inadvertently produced by the slaves themselves. Slavery in Sulu had been observed through the eyes and preconceptions of European observers and writers who viewed the Sulu Sultanate as the centre of a world fundamentally hostile to their interests—a traditional Islamic world whose activities centred on piracy and slavery. A unique alternative to this Eurocentric perspective was presented to me by the discovery, and, subsequent compilation, of the scattered statements of the fugitive captives of the Sulu Sultanate. Carlo Ginsburg, a gifted Italian historian, whose classic works have challenged us to retrieve social worlds that more conventional history does not record, describes particular types of legal-juridical documentation, as "written records of oral speech".[13] For example, according to Ginsburg's way of thinking, the written proceedings and statements of the fugitive captives, which proved so essential to writing *The Sulu Zone*, could be considered comparable in certain respects to the notes or notebook of an ethnographer, who had studied a cultural system where slavery and ethnogenesis were a common occurrence; or to put it another way, the handpicked naval commanders of various colonial powers struggling to rid Southeast Asia of Iranun-Balangingi raiding and the slave trade, momentarily transformed on the deck of a gunboat, as anthropologist and inquisitor, performing a deadly type of "fieldwork" in the waters of the zone, several centuries ago.

What the direct testimony of the fugitive captives contained was "life": a freshness and wealth of small-scale detail that could be used to explore the mentalities and material world of several generations of slaves; an exceptionally rich source, containing singularly invaluable textured accounts around which to base on a cultural level a historical ethnography, case studies and a collective biography. I made extensive use of this neglected source of social history in the book to reconstruct the social organisation of Sulu slave raiding, slave life in the zone and to attempt to make slave voices speak.[14] The macro-empirical trade data based on the shipping returns of the port of Manila (particularly the *estados* and the *almojarifazgo*) and the statements of the fugitive slaves complemented one another, and together enabled me to resolve a number of fundamental questions about the scope and magnitude of the Sulu Zone's global-regional trade, its flourishing slave population, and how these changed over time as a consequence of the impact of the China trade and the machinations of the world capitalist economy. The methodological search for a way to link the experience of individuals and related events in their lives, to larger, impersonal systems, as described and analyzed in *The Sulu Zone*, was most tenable at the intersection(s) bridging the "narrative space of ethnography",[15] the use of quantitative methods by the prosopographer, and the study in depth of the small scale. In this way, I adapted the methods of social anthropology and historical computing to do historical research and ethnography in the archives, in order to understand the "otherness" of a previous era and place the Sulu Zone, or, as the French social historian Robert Darnton phrased it, to do "history in the ethnographic grain".[16]

A key problem in focussing on the collective identity of particular social groups in the book—slaves and Iranun and Samal Balangingi raiders— was to choose a sample which represented the total regional and social population(s) of the zone. Spanish naval officers, specialists in "contemporary Sulu affairs", interrogated the fugitive slave informants, and more than a century and a half later, I used both content and statistical analysis, to create a multi-source, integrated database, as a prosopographer. The difficulties that attended an analysis of the social and ethnic complexity of the historical situation(s) of the slaves and their Taosug and Samal masters could only be depicted through a prosopography: a collective biography, resting on a scaffolding of empirically integrated fragments of life histories. The effort entailed to recover their stories from abstruse sources for this book, the raw material for both history and anthropology, is based on the capacity of a creative imagination to evoke the everyday life of a "little people"—namely captives and slaves—and the conviction that carefully accumulated detail or "thick description", emphasizing both experience and explanation, is the best way to reconstruct a sense of their time and place.

The Sulu Zone: Some Conclusions: Slavery, Transformations and Rethinking Globalization

My understanding and discussion of global economic-cultural interconnections and interdependencies linking the Sulu Zone and the China trade was based on the premise that these intersections were governed by particular economic systems and set in a specific era and locality. The Taosug lived in a singular time and time meant change. They also lived in a singular place and geography meant destiny. The zone was a place where borders were becoming ever more porous, less bounded, less fixed, stimulated in large measure by global-regional flows of commodities, people and ideas; a kind of powerful magnet whose force European and Chinese traders were drawn to because that was where a lot of the exotica for Chinese cuisine and medicine and other commodities for the Canton market were being collected and processed. What then is the importance of *The Sulu Zone*'s thesis, about the China tea trade's complicated place within its "borderless" history? It is a central argument of this book that we cannot think of societies and cultures in isolation, as self-maintaining, autonomous, enduring systems.[17]

In the pages of this volume the world has changed through the intersections of the global trade economy centred on the Sulu and Celebes seas, as well as the Sultanate's critical place within it. Here, ordinary Southeast Asian farmers and fishers were traumatically uprooted and forced to live in a distant economic region. This world was comprised of winners responding to new economic opportunities of "globalization" and losers, who were those forced to live in ways unanticipated before that moment of capture and enslavement. Trade debts in Jolo were paid off by slaves serving Taosug masters in the fisheries and forests of the zone. The point is that tens of thousands of ordinary Southeast Asians lived among maritime peoples completely removed from those with whom they had been born and grown up. They found themselves abroad in the seascape of the zone. Firstly, because advanced technologies and new social alignments made long distance slave raiding easier and secondly, because revolutionary economic historical developments forcefully landed them in an unintended place—the Sulu Zone. European traders joined with Taosug *datus* to spark one of the largest population movements in recent Southeast Asia history with hundreds of thousands of individuals sent into slavery across the zone. Turnover in Iranun-Samal slave trafficking was in excess of several million dollars a year: human cargo and Chinese tea then were as profitable as drugs and guns. Hence, all these commodities became inextricably entangled with one another in a deadly global trade. One of the most intractable problems facing the Southeast Asian world in the eighteenth and nineteenth centuries was connected with the huge number of captive people being taken to the Sulu Zone, never to return. However, displacement need not necessarily always be equated with social death.

Let us briefly contemplate here the force of circumstance and fate of the indigenous women of the Visayas and Luzon, who were unmercifully targeted by the Iranun and Balangingi slave raiders. Strand gatherers, these women were picked off from the beaches in the grey light of dawn as they fossicked along the shoreline. Their husbands were often slaughtered on the spot and the bodies left as a grim warning to others. In their time, these women of Luzon, the Visayas and other coastal stretches of Southeast Asia knew something of fear and real despair. For women around the region seized as captives, life in the middle passage could look like a valley of dry bones with no signs of hope of a new life. Yet out of such a tragic reality, the traditional Muslim social system could inspire new life, new beginnings and new hope—if captives were prepared to cross the line and renounce their previous ways of life and faith. The newly widowed women (sometimes with their children) were transported as slaves to the powerful sultanate(s) in the south of the archipelago where they were expected to work on providing lucrative goods to be traded with the English, Chinese and Americans—or where they became concubines or secretaries (if they could read and write) of the already rich and powerful. By the start of the nineteenth century, slave identities in the zone were being shaped and changed by the forces of "globalization" as distinctions of ethnicity and culture blurred and were broken down; thousands of "outsiders" were being incorporated into the lower reaches of a rapidly expanding Islamic trading society. The Sulu Sultanate provided an outstanding example of how a collective identity was established, made real, and assumed a particular cultural content.[18]

There are no statistics on the overall number of slaves imported into Jolo between 1768 and 1878, except the estimates of European observers and local informants. In this book, I have argued that slave imports to the Sulu Sultanate during the first 65 years probably averaged around 2,000 to 3,000 annually. The steepest rise in the estimated number of slaves annually brought to Sulu—from 3,000 to 4,000—occurred in the period 1836 to 1848 and slackened considerably in the next several decades, with imports ranging between 1,200 and 2,000 slaves a year until the external trade collapsed in the 1870s. The figures appeared to show that between 200,000 and 300,000 captives were transported in Iranun and Samal Balangingi vessels to become slaves in the Sulu Sultanate in the period from the late eighteenth to late nineteenth centuries. However, now, earlier estimates of the scale of the slave traffic described and analyzed in *The Sulu Zone* have to be revised further upward for the first half of the nineteenth century, especially as the trade with China reached its zenith in the decades between the 1820s and 1840s. In July 2004, I discovered a hitherto unknown confidential report on the number of slaving vessels entering the port of Jolo, with detailed data provided by a Spanish merchant captain on the numbers captured and brought to be sold there. The stunning findings of the confidential log or "census" suggests that between 4,000 to 6,000 Visayans—expert divers and seafarers—alone were being enslaved on an annual basis by the Iranun and Balaningi by 1845.[19]

Certain lessons and examples from history about global economic-cultural interconnections and interdependencies in this book also tended to explain patterns and events which have been formally glossed over. For example, sugar "demanded" slaves and the Atlantic slave trade. Similarly, tea, inextricably bound to sugar as product and fate, would also inadvertently "demand" slaves in the Sulu Zone and thus lead to the advent of Iranun-Balangingi, long distance, maritime slave raiding. Since the Europeans and Americans primarily wanted sea cucumber, sharks fin, pearls and birds' nests for the trade in China tea, the issue of the nature of productive relations in the Sulu Sultanate—slavery—suddenly became of primary importance. The soaring demand for certain local commodities in return for foreign imports affected the allocation and control of labour and the demand for fresh captives throughout the Sulu Zone. In this globalizing context, tea was more than simply the crucial commodity in the development of trade between China and the West. In this history of the Sulu Zone, filled with so many deals and intrigues and such geographical scope, tea was also a plant that was instrumental in the stunning systematic development of commerce, power and population in the Sulu Zone which changed the regional face and history of insular Southeast Asia. Nevertheless, in a comparative diasporic context, the statistics on the explosion of displacement and production in *The Sulu Zone*, to satisfy the trajectory of a craving and taste, are small when compared with eleven million Africans who endured the middle passage to the new world during the three and half centuries of the Atlantic slave trade.

The Sulu Sultanate was also an exceptional case for ethnohistorical investigation, because the history of the zone demonstrated clearly the links between large economic and cultural systems and social mechanisms and institutions, on the one hand, and, on the other, the making of collective worlds of more localised smaller communities. In short, as Kenneth Prewitt puts it: "The global-local notion is not a metaphor invented by social theorists."[20] Rather, it was the lived experience of millions of people in the zone and on several continents, inextricably bound to one another as product and fate. Part of the challenge for me had been to identify and connect broad patterns and variations in interactions of the global economy and macro-historical trends with the "autonomous-local history" of a barely recognized economic region in Southeast Asia. The long-term changes that occurred in these patterns and trends, based on economic interconnections and imperatives of the world capitalist economy and colonialism, had to be explained and understood through their interdependent effects on the environment, on ideas, on events, on human nature, and on the social and cultural transformation of the world(s) of the "Zone".

The patterns revealed by the book threw up some unavoidable conclusions. The first was that the implications of the framing and analysis of the economy, culture and society of the Sulu Zone perhaps, could be applied in a wider framework not only to elucidate the development of states and the elaboration of ethnic diversity in insular Southeast Asia, but also to develop a comparative framework with mainland states and cultures, concerned namely with the impact of foreign trade, the rise and demise of populations, the rapid and expansive circulation of commodities, ideas and genes and colonial interventions.[21] A second conclusion concerns an observation that can be made about the nature of researching and writing Southeast

Asian modern history. Namely, it is the trans-historical, trans-cultural, trans-disciplinary methodological approach, linking detailed research of a local situation to wider global-regional economic systems and issues that underpins the work in this book.

Finally, a third inescapable conclusion of *The Sulu Zone* entailed something more: the making of this ethnohistory not only involved an extension of the content and meaning of ethnicity and "culture", in the pursuit of history, it also implied a revision of that content. What I first suggested in this volume, more than a quarter of a century ago, was that in a new history of insular Southeast Asia, the "little people"— fishers, "raiders", divers, traders, highlanders, forest dwellers, "squatter" agriculturalists, refugees, asylum seekers and slaves—both men and women, should be prominent and visibly present, as part of the cultural landscape and complex geographical environment of a series of regional-economic "zones"—areas often on the margins of states, enmeshed in the hemispheric framework of the larger changing contemporary globalized world of cultural flows and economic interactions, replete with their relentless painful accounts of intrigue, displacement, paradox and insights into the human condition about courage and the will to survive. This methodological approach is especially relevant today, in a world where globalization has become critically important in the first decade of our new century. So much controversy filled history, so much research and analytical-storytelling skills required. The fundamental problems of North-South intersections and interactions encountered in the everyday lives of peasants, maritime and tribal peoples, making their livings and losing them, entangled in globalizing events beyond their own local geographic borders and worlds, is the work of future concerned historians of Asia.

James Francis Warren
Murdoch University

January 2007

Notes

[1] Warren, James Francis, *The North Borneo Chartered Company's Administration of the Bajau, 1878–1909* (Athens: Ohio University Press, 1971).

[2] Howard Dick, "Indonesian Economic History Inside Out", *Review of Indonesian and Malaysian Affairs* 27 (1993): 1–12, p. 6; Warren, *The Sulu Zone 1768–1898: The Dynamics of External Trade, Slavery, and Ethnicity in the Transformation of a Southeast Asian Maritime State* (Singapore: Singapore University Press, 1981).

[3] Laurie Sears (ed.), *Autonomous Histories Particular Truths Essays in Honor of John Smail* (Madison: University of Wisconsin, Center for Southeast Asian Studies, 1993).

[4] Dick, "Indonesian Economic History Inside Out", p. 1; John Comaroff and Jean Comaroff, *Ethnology and the Historical Imagination* (Boulder: Westview Press, 1992), p. 22.

[5] Comaroff and Comaroff, *Ethnology and the Historical Imagination* (Boulder: Westview Press, 1992), p. 22.

[6] E.R. Leach, *Political Systems of Highland Burma, A Study of Kachin Social Structure* (London: London School of Economics and Political Science, 1954), pp. 4, 212.

[7] Warren, *The Sulu Zone 1768–1898*, pp. xi–xvi, 252–55.

[8] Roger M. Keesing, "Asian Cultures?" in *Southeast Asian Review* 15(2) (1991): 43–50, p. 46.

[9] Ibid.

[10] E.R. Wolf, *Europe and the People Without History* (Berkeley: University of California Press, 1982), p. 387.

[11] Benedict Anderson, *Imagined Communities* (Manila: Anvil, 2003).

[12] P. Burke, *History and Social Theory* (Oxford: Polity Press, 1992), pp. 38–39.

[13] Carlo Ginsburg, *Clues, Myth and the Historical Method* (Baltimore: Johns Hopkins University Press, 1989), p. 156.

[14] Warren, *The Sulu Zone 1768–1898*, pp. 299–315.

[15] George Marcus, "Problems of ethnography in the modern world system", in *Writing Culture. The Poetics and Politics of Ethnography*, ed. J. Clifford & G. Marcus (Berkeley: University of California Press, 1986), pp. 165–93, 190.

[16] Robert Darnton, *The Great Cat Massacre and other Episodes in French Cultural History* (New York: Vintage Books, 1985), p. 3.

[17] Wolf, *Europe and the People Without History*, p. 390.

[18] Comaroff and Comaroff, *Ethnology and the Historical Imagination*, p. 44.

[19] Warren, "The Port of Jolo and the Sulu Zone Slave Trade: An 1845 Report" (unpublished paper), 2005.

[20] Kenneth Prewitt, "Presidential items", in *Items Social Science Research Council* 50(1) (1996): 15–18.

[21] Victor Lieberman, "An age of commerce in Southeast Asia? Problems of regional coherence — a review article", *The Journal of Asian Studies* 54(3) (1995): 796–807.

References

Anderson, Benedict. *Imagined Communities*. Manila: Anvil, 2003.

Braudel, Fernand. *The Mediterranean and the Mediterranean World in the Age of Philip II*, 2 vols. New York: Harper Row, 1972.

Braudel. *Civilisation Materielle, economic et capitalisme, Xve-XVIIIe Siecle*. Paris, 1979.

————. *On History.* London: Weidenfeld and Nicolson, 1980.

Burke, Peter. *History and Social Theory.* Oxford: Polity Press, 1992.

Comaroff, John, and Jean Comaroff. *Ethnology and the Historical Imagination.* Boulder: Westview Press, 1992.

Darnton, Robert. *The Great Cat Massacre and other Episodes in French Cultural History.* New York: Vintage Books, 1985.

Dick, Howard. *"Indonesian Economic History Inside Out"*, *Review of Indonesian and Malaysian Affairs* 27 (1993): 1–12.

Frank, Andre Gunder. *World Accumulation, 1492–1789.* London: Macmillan Press, 1978.

Ginnsburg, Carlo. *Clues, Myths and the Historical Method.* Baltimore: John Hopkins University Press, 1989.

Hodgson, Marshall G.S. *The Venture of Islam 3.* Chicago: The University of Chicago Press, 1974.

Hodgson. *Rethinking World History: Essays on Europe, Islam and World History.* Cambridge: Cambridge University Press, 1995.

Keesing, Roger M., "Asian Cultures?" *Asian Studies Review* 15(2) (1991): 43–50.

Leach, E.R. *Political Systems of Highland Burma: A Study of Kachin Social Structure.* London: London School of Economic and Political Science, 1954.

Lieberman, Victor. "An Age of Commerce in Southeast Asia? Problems of Regional Coherence — A Review Article", *The Journal of Asian Studies,* 54(3) (1995): 796–807.

Marcus, George. "Problems of Ethnography in the Modern World System", in *Writing Culture. The Poetics and Politics of Ethnography*, ed. James Clifford and George Marcus. Berkeley: University of California Press, 1986, pp. 165–93.

Prewitt, Kenneth, "Presidential Items", *Items Social Science Research Council* 50(1) (1996): 15–18.

Sears, Laurie (ed.). *Autonomous Histories Particular Truths Essays in Honor of John Smail.* Madison: University of Wisconsin, 1993.

Van Leur, J.C. *Indonesian Trade and Society.* The Hague: Van Hoeve, 1967.

Warren, James Francis, *The North Borneo Chartered Company's Administration of the Bajau, 1878–1909.* Athens: Ohio University Press, 1971.

————. *The Sulu Zone 1768–1898 The Dynamics of External Trade, Slavery, and Ethnicity in the Transformation of a Southeast Asian Maritime State.* Singapore: Singapore University Press, 1981.

————. "The Port of Jolo and the Sulu Zone Slave Trade: An 1845 Report" (unpublished paper), 2005.

Wolf, Eric R. *Europe and the People Without History.* Berkeley: University of California Press, 1982.

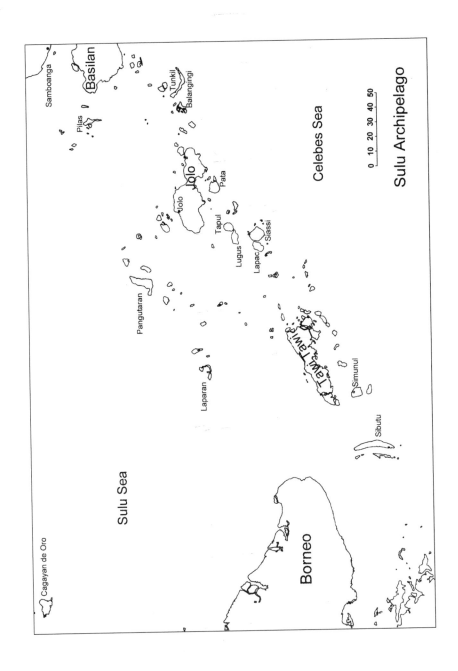

Samboanga

Basilan

Pilas

Tunkil

Balangingi

Jolo

Jolo

Pata

Tapul

Lugus

Siassi

Lapac

Pangutaran

Laparan

Tawi Tawi

Simunul

Sibutu

Celebes Sea

0 10 20 30 40 50

Sulu Archipelago

Sulu Sea

Cagayan de Oro

Borneo

Introduction to the First Edition

The Sulu archipelago bridged two worlds and lay at a most strategic point for the maritime trade of the nineteenth century. China, the Philippines and Mindanao were situated to the north. Borneo to the southwest, and to the southeast, the Celebes and Moluccas. A watershed on the landscape of insular southeast Asia, the Sulu chain of islands separated the autonomous Muslim maritime world of the eastern archipelago in the eighteenth and nineteenth centuries from the Philippine archipelago to the north— agrarian, Christianized, and administered by Spanish colonial authorities from Manila.

The crystallization of Jolo, the capital of the Sulu Sultanate, at the end of the eighteenth century as the focal point of a broad system of trade, and centre for the marketing of slaves, outfitting of marauders, and defiance of Spanish incursion, was in large measure attributable to its location astride the arterial trade routes near the centre of the eastern Malaysian seas. The geopolitical and commercial advantages inherent in the Sultanate's location were both enviable and unique.

The zone encompassing the Sulu Sultanate is the historic home of peoples, languages, and cultures as varied as its landscape. The Taosug ("people of the current"), the dominant ethnic group in the Sulu archipelago, are the sole residents of Jolo island, the historical seat of the Sultanate.[1] Linguistic analysis links the Taosug language which has no marked dialectical variation to the Visayan language group. This lends support to the hypothesis that both the Taosug and their language were alien to Sulu. Seafaring immigrant Taosug from the north arrived on the island of Sulu no earlier than the eleventh century.[2] Originally fishermen and traders with martial skills and a flair for organization, many of them adopted agriculture. With the introduction of Islam, about the fifteenth century, they evolved a well-articulated political and economic system.[3] The institution of the Sultanate established formal dominance of the Taosug over indigenous Samalan-speaking peoples and later migrants to Sulu.

Unquestionably, the sea played an important role in the evolution of the Sulu Sultanate at the end of the eighteenth century, but this does not imply that the Taosug were predominantly a seafaring people. While also found scattered in villages throughout the archipelago, on Borneo's east coast and in southern Palawan by 1800, most of the Taosug still resided inland as agriculturalists on the volcanic high islands of the Tapul group and on Pata and Siassi. The Tau Gimba ("people of the interior")[4] lived in small dispersed settlements and cultivated cassava, maize, and a wide assortment of fruits and vegetables. The Tau Higad ("people of the coast"), who were far more dependent on the sea for a livelihood, took a direct interest in the pearl and shell fisheries, interinsular trade, and slave raiding. After 1768, the efforts of *datus* among the Tau Higad to participate in the growing external trade altered regional market patterns, neighbourhood relations, and, equally important, their own world view.

The Samal, strand dwellers with close ties to the sea,[5] possessed of highly developed boat-building techniques and sometimes practising simple garden agriculture, are the most widely dispersed of all ethnolinguistic groups in the Sulu chain. Manifesting the greatest degree of internal linguistic and cultural differentiation, Samal communities predominate on the corraline island clusters of the northern and southern part of the Sulu archipelago, as well as on north Borneo and on Celebes. The Samal distinguish among themselves by dialect, locality, and cultural-ecological factors (principally between sedentary Muslim shore-dwellers and nomadic animistic boat-dwellers).[6]

Samals tend to identify themselves with a particular island, island cluster, or regional orbit. In the late eighteenth and early nineteenth centuries, they comprised several groups which occupied non-contiguous territories along the southern Mindanao shore, on the south coast and in the near interior of Basilan, and on the islands of the Tapian Tana group, Cagayan de Sulu, and the Balangingi cluster. Expert voyagers at sea, particular Samal groups had fixed bases of operation on a series of low coral-and-sand islands flanking the northeastern side of Jolo. This group of islands, named Los Samales by the Spanish, was a springboard for launching seasonal raids against coastal villages from Luzon to Celebes. The most important island was Balangingi, dwelling place and organizational centre of the major slave-retailing group for the Sulu Sultanate in the first half of the nineteenth century.

The fertile Cotabato basin is the traditional home of the Magindanao, an inland dwelling agricultural people. The valley and its inhabitants have historically been divided between the Sa-ilud, the lower valley or flood plain, and the Sa-raya, the upper valley or highland area. The former was the seat of the Sultanate of Cotabato while the latter was the residence of the Sultanate of Buayan.[7] At the apogee of its power towards the middle of the eighteenth century, most of the western part of Mindanao and Zamboanga were dominated by the Sultanate of Cotabato. In later years, the Cotabato basin became a rice bowl for neighbouring realms and provided Sulu with large quantities of paddy and hulled rice annually.

Fundamental to understanding Sulu's ascendancy after 1768 is the necessity of interpreting the Sultanate's historical experience within a wider regional framework. Essential to Sulu's hegemony was an expansive trade. A commercial marauding pattern of regional dimension developed after 1768, involving munitions, natural produce, and slaves, and conducted by Taosug *datus,* Samal raiders, Magindanao chiefs, and adventurous Europeans.

To explain social interaction between ethnic groups within the region I have used the framework of a "centre-periphery" concept. "Hinterland" refers not only to the interior of a large land mass such as Mindanao or Borneo but also includes island clusters within the Sulu archipelago that depended on the port Sultanate at Jolo.[8] This mode of analysis provides a means of interpreting the tensions prevalent in a region where traditional states were defined by varying relationships to the centre rather than fixed geographical frontiers. Ethnic interrelations then can be viewed in terms of a single "cultural ecosystem" in which the parts "are bound together by alternating bonds of antipathy and symbiotic relations".[9]

I am arguing that in the late eighteenth and nineteenth centuries there existed in the zone comprising the Sulu archipelago, the northeast coast of Borneo, the foreland of southern Mindanao, and the western coast of Celebes a loosely integrated political system that embraced island and coastal populace, maritime, nomadic fishermen, and slash and burn agriculturalists of the coastal rim and interior foothills. The zone provided a sociocultural context for intersocietal relations and commerce within the Taosug state and beyond. *Datus* forged political links and trade pacts with riverine swidden cultivators on Borneo's east coast. Upland tribes, hunters and gatherers, and nomadic boat people formed subject groups who performed procurement roles for Sulu's export trade with China and the West. This network of interpersonal relations which was fluid across time and subject to disruption was integrated by the commercial-marauding patterns which came to be focused on the Sulu Sultanate as the prime redistributive centre for the zone in the late eighteenth century.

A Segmentary State

The small states of the Sulu and Celebes seas crystallized in the fifteenth and sixteenth centuries. These Muslim realms were situated on sparsely populated islands, coasts, and rivers and were reliant on trade as a resource. Lacking recognized boundaries, the political systems of these traditional polities linked widely disparate communities and groups who were not organically united above the village level in a larger, complex, dynamic web of social and political loyalties to the state.[10] "State" is defined as the entire social system, rather than a particular aspect of the social structure.[11] Territorial dominion, a system of specialized offices, and a political hierarchy exercising some control over the use of force in the area of alleged dominion were implicit in the genesis of such traditional states (Sultanates) as Sulu, Cotabato, Brunei, and Kutai.[12]

Within the typology of states and political systems devised by political anthropologists, the segmentary state is the model which approximates the traditional Taosug polity.[13] Pyramidal in form, a segmentary state is composed of sub-units which are structurally and functionally equivalent at every level of the political system. In a traditional segmentary state, territorial sovereignty waxed at the centre and waned at the periphery. The Sulu Sultanate was a centralized political system whose territorial sovereignty was recognized most strongly at the centre, in the environs of Jolo town, and shaded off into ritual hegemony in distant areas.

Taosug society is dyad centred. "Rather than beginning with a permanent group", as Thomas Kiefer notes, "the Taosug begin with a dyadic bond between two males and treat the larger group as an extension of it...."[14] In the late eighteenth and nineteenth centuries, the primary loyalties of a Taosug were to his immediate leader rather than towards a higher superordinate authority or the state. Power remained diffuse within the political system, and governance in the traditional Taosug state was predicated on factional politics and revolved around highly variable leader-centred groups.

Power and wealth in Sulu were defined only secondarily in terms of territory. A leader's power and status was based more on his control over personal dependents, either retainers or slaves, that he could mobilize at a given moment for what was deemed to be commercially or politically expedient, than on the formal state structure. A report expressly prepared in 1812 for Sir Stamford Raffles, the Lieutenant-Governor of Java, by J. Hunt, who lived in Jolo for six months, recognized the significance of such dependent relationships, which vertically cross-cut class divisions:"the power and weight of the chiefs arise solely from their wealth, or like the Barons of old amongst us, from the number of *ambas* (slaves) or retainers each entertain".[15]

Institutionalized friendship linked smaller groups to larger and larger ones in a ramified series of alliances encompassing the entire state. The kinship system was unimportant in Taosug society except as one of several modes of recruitment for fostering alliances.[16] Traditional Taosug society was a precarious network of shifting affiliations articulating kindred, nonkindred, *datus*, and ultimately the Sultan. In the Taosug polity, actual power flowed upwards in a changing network of alliances while the titles, which conferred authority and were symbols of that power, reached ever downwards to ritually integrate even distant headmen within the domain of the state.

Critical to understanding the centrifugal nature of the Sulu Sultanate is the fact that it lacked an effective means of centralizing rights associated with the legal, political, and administrative spheres of the state.[17] In the Sultanate the rights and duties of authority figures were duplicated at different levels of the traditional political system. The primary rights associated with the traditional political system among the Taosug were: (1) rights to perform legal functions; (2) rights to appoint and regulate religious officials; (3) rights to control over territory; (4) rights to control over subject people; (5) rights to wage external warfare; (6) rights to tribute and legal fees; (7) rights to control over markets; and (8) rights to mediate private warfare and feud.[18]

In discussing the performance of rights and duties associated with political office in the Taosug State, Kiefer stresses the importance of considering the Sultan and the village headmen as "mirror images of each other",[19] though aligned at the opposite extremities of the traditional political spectrum. Differences then between the upper and lower levels of the political system were reflected solely in terms of the degree of authority exercised and the extent of its influence. In the period under consideration, it was not uncommon for strong leaders to use raw power in the appropriation of rights theoretically attached to the Sultan in order to further their personal interests and prestige. The Sultan, however, by the very nature of his office, did exercise certain unique ritual and religious functions as the symbolic head of an Islamic state.

Stratified prestige in Taosug society was perpetuated through a system of ranked social categories. The three legally defined segments of the population were the aristocrats, privileged and powerful yet numerically small, the village dwelling commoners comprising the broad mass of the Sultanate's population, and the *banyaga* or slaves who were numerous and mostly of foreign origin.

The aristocratic *datus* formed the most significant group at the top of the estate system. They were principally royal *datus*, the Sultan's kindred and those who claimed descent from the first Sultan, and others recruited through appointment by the Sultan.[20] High ascribed status assured social prestige in Taosug political culture, but not power. For the scions of "royal blood", wealth and leadership talents were essential to attain political office. They attracted and retained followers, acquired prestige symbols, and established themselves in the political hierarchy through administration of some of the more important Samal inhabited islands in the archipelago, vigorous participation in the procurement trade, and promotion of slave raiding.

Commoners were simply "people without ascribed status".[21] They neither possessed heritable titles nor the wealth and prestige to attract followers. Although they were eligible for and did occasionally achieve minor titles of headmanship, they were dependent for their security and material well-being on the *datus* who contended for their allegiance as clients. The salient characteristics of a commoner were his dependence upon the aristocracy and the invaluable obligations that he performed as a retainer. *Datus* employed commoners and their families in agriculture, commerce, and marauding, as farmers, artisans, fishermen, and mariners.

At the bottom of the Sulu hierarchy were the *banyaga*. The testimonies of fugitive slaves and historical accounts leave no doubt that slavery was an essential element in determining the economic, military, and social patterns of the Sulu state. In large measure it was the *banyaga* who held the fabric of Taosug society together.

The Sultan, invested with an aura of sanctity and charisma, symbolically legitimized the social system. As the head of a consciously defined Islamic state, he was at the centre of the organization of its worldly aspects, between God and man. Ideally a Sultan (as well as a *datu* or any person vested with the responsibility of leadership), should be virtuous, generous, and courageous. Majul's analysis of *khutbahs* and *kitabs* strongly affirms the historic expectation that Taosug leaders epitomize certain ideal qualities— wisdom, religiosity, and charity.

The pre-eminent position of the Sultan at the apex of the political system was expressed by certain rites and symbols which validated his authority. Social distance was rigidly maintained between the Sultan and his subjects. Although court ritual was highly elaborate, the Taosug never evolved a system as formalized as those of other Southeast Asian states.[22] While his commercial and administrative involvement rendered him something of a "public" figure at the port centre, as the negotiation of foreign trading treaties was the prerogative of the Sultan alone, he was often perceived as withdrawn and sacrosanct by the larger society over which he reigned.

In Sulu, Sultans traditionally have lacked the administrative framework necessary to exercise soverign power to the degree that the ideology of the state might have permitted. The realities of power which were embedded in the segmentary character of the political system and mirrored in the personalistic-autocratic traditions of *datu* independence classified the Sultan as merely the "highest *datu*, the highest religious official, and the highest legal authority" within the Sultanante.[23] To the extent that his participation at the centre—the economic and organizational focus for the zone— was active and control effective, the Sultan held in check the centrifugal tendencies of the segmentary Sulu state. The prestige of his office, the force of his personality, and his ability to manipulate powerful factions and foster alliances were critical factors determining the limits of a Sultan's actual authority. The ability of a Sultan to maintain the loyalty of his following was crucial to the preservation of his political power. When accredited with foresight and character, the Sultan's personal opinions and decisions were more often than not supported. The Sultan generally did seek the advice of prestigious Taosug aristocrats in matters of state. However it is apparent that on occasions strong *datus* not only rejected his initiatives but were able to force their will on the Sultan.[24] The style of Taosug sovereign leadership varied according to the man and the circumstances of his time. The lack of corporate institutions and the political ethos of the Taosug culture forced the Sultan to rely to a greater extent on personal following, wealth, and clever statecraft than on the prestige of his office to retain effective authority.

The Taosug Sultanate was situated on the eastern periphery of the Islamic world. Acknowledged as the "defender of the faith" and the highest ecclesiastical authority of state, the Sultan symbolized the community of the faithful on earth and their communal membership and participation in Daral-Islam. Islam was the prime legitimizer of the Sultan's authority, and the Sultans of Sulu were expected to be orthodox adherents of Islam. The religious hierarchy paralleled the political hierarchy of the traditional Taosug state. Political and ecclesiastical institutions of the Sulu Sultanate were united in the person of the Sultan. At the state and local level, *kadis* who acted as juridical advisors, administrators of Islamic law and *adat* and catechists, conducted the Sultanate's religious administration and established the Sultan's presence and the strength of Islam even in culturally distant rural communities on Jolo and neighbouring islands.

The essence of the state was bound up in the intimate spheres of politics and religion. Its functions were "ritual or religious in which the Sultanate is the embodiment of the community of the faithful on earth; and legal, in which the Sultanate serves to channel and control conflict".[25] The Sulu Sultanate was characterized by a dialectical tension between the strains of incessant factionalism and the centripetal character of Islamic institutions and ideology.

I

PATTERNS OF TRADING, 1768–1898

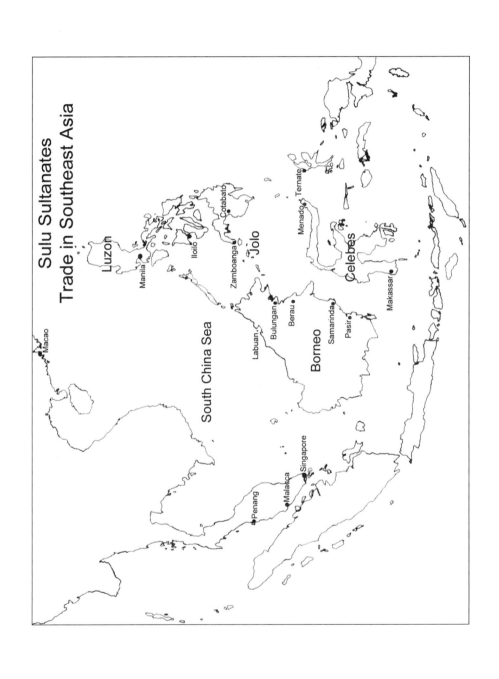

Sulu Sultanates
Trade in Southeast Asia

Macao

South China Sea

Luzon

Manila

Iloilo

Cotabato

Zamboanga

Jolo

Menado

Ternate

Celebes

Makassar

Labuan

Bulungan

Berau

Samarinda

Pasir

Borneo

Penang

Malacca

Singapore

I. PATTERNS OF TRADING, 1768–1898

The economy of the Sulu Sultanate traditionally had a commercial orientation. For more than two hundred years prior to 1768, Sulu participated in the more expansive maritime network of trade in Southeast Asia—though merely as one of the many small autonomous states scattered throughout the eastern archipelago. The Taosug customarily conducted commerce with their then more powerful neighbours, the Magindanao. Expert navigators as well as merchants, they travelled considerable distances in small craft, trading as far as Brunei and Ternate.

The tiny archipelago's critical location between the Asian mainland and the large islands of Mindanao, Borneo, and Celebes, its varied and productive resource base, and its sizeable population early attracted merchants from China and Makassarese-Buginese mariners from Celebes. The annual arrival of Chinese junks and Bugis *prahus* at Jolo reflected a regular demand for local products procured principally from the Sultanate's essential domain—the sea. The foreigners brought in coarse textiles, silk, ceramic, earthenware, and spices. It is important to note, however, that this Asian trade was limited in scale. An examination of the traditional pattern cannot adequately explain Sulu's sudden rise to regional primacy in the period after 1768, but it does provide a necessary prologue to its transformation, largely initiated by international forces.

By 1800, regional redistribution had become the dominant pattern of the economy of the Sulu Sultanate. The advent of this expansive pattern, predicated on ever increasing international demand, inter-insular slave raiding, and the littoral-procurement trade, enabled Sulu within the short span of several decades to establish itself as a pre-eminent market centre and regional power.

Indirectly, it was the insatiable demand for tea that initiated European interest in Sulu's natural products. During the eighteenth century, tea replaced ale as the national beverage in England and was especially popular among the poorer classes. China was almost the sole supplier of tea to England. The incessant English clamour for tea opened China to a wider trade involving both the Indian sub-continent and Southeast Asia. Asian, European and American merchants based in Calcutta, and later Manila, Macao, and Salem, were unable to provide suitable commodities for the burgeoning Canton market. These merchants were quick to recognize the potential of participation in the Sino-Sulu trade as a means of redressing the flow of silver from India. Marine and jungle products highly valued in China were needed to stem it.

Sulu's ascendancy at the end of the eighteenth century developed out of the expanding trade between India, insular Southeast Asia, and China. Commercial and tributary activity became linked to long-distance marauding and incorporation of captive persons in a system which made Jolo the unrivalled centre for extracted produce for the China trade. It is the unique character of the Sulu response and the interdependence of the three factors— external trade, raiding, and slavery—on which it was based that is the central theme of the ensuing study.

1

Traditional Patterns of Trade of the Sulu Sultanate

THE SINO-SULU TRADE

Sulu appears in Chinese sources as early as the Yuan dynasty (1278–1368), and a lengthy account of a tributary mission in 1417 from Sulu to the celestial court is recorded in the Ming Annals. Little appears then to have been written about the Sulu chain of islands for several hundred years until the beginning of the eighteenth century, which witnessed an earnest renewal of diplomatic activity and trade between China and the Sultanate. The Ching Annals refer to five separate tribute-bearing missions despatched by the Sultans of Sulu in the years between 1727 and 1763. The envoys of these missions, which were spaced approximately a decade apart, spent several years in China before returning to Sulu on one of the great junks voyaging to the "tributary lands" bordering the South China Sea with renewed friendship and wealth in gifts. The large number of references to Sulu in the Ching Annals reflect the desire of the Sultans to extend their personal authority and wealth, and to strengthen the State's influence in a politically fragmented region through Chinese recognition and commerce.*

Chinese trading junks annually sailed before the northern monsoon from Amoy and more northerly ports to almost every commercial port in Southeast Asia. One to two hundred large vessels and approximately a thousand smaller craft visited Siam, Cambodia, the Malay peninsula, Sumatra, Java, Borneo, Celebes, the Philippine archipelago, and Sulu each year.[1] The mat sail was a familiar sight on coasts where the European canvas was never unfurled.

---

* These missions were sent to China in the years 1726, 1733, 1754, and 1763, (Majul, *The Muslims in the Philippines,* pp.348–52). As a matter of policy China had traditionally preferred to foster and support strong Malay kingdoms strategically situated at the regional interfaces of insular Southeast Asia to keep vital maritime routes open, encourage local productivity, and sustain trade prosperity. But in the 18th century, trade and imperial policy had become largely independent. By then tribute missions to China were regular only in those periods when other avenues of trade were closed by imperial fiat. The significance of China's tributary system in Southeast Asia's regional history over nearly a millenium is discussed at length in O.W. Wolters, *The Fall of Srivijaya in Malay History,* pp.37, 49–76.

From Amoy the *Tung-Yang* junk route skirted the Formosan coast and extended down the length of the Philippines from the Batanes islands to the Sulu archipelago and beyond as far as Makassar. Junks destined for Sulu could include Manila and Panay on their course.[2] As Chinese coasters from Amoy and Pactow threaded their way down through the various islands of the archipelago to the Sultanate, they were known to have stopped to barter some of their wares in the central and southern Visayas. Lacquered ware, porcelain, earthenware, and other articles from the celestial kingdom were exchanged for such culinary delicacies as beche-de-mer, shark's fin, and bird's nest. Rice, for which there was always a ready demand in the Sulu market, was also taken on in the islands.

Reliable figures for the number of junks which visited Sulu from China's maritime provinces are virtually non-existent for the first half of the eighteenth century. The scant evidence available reveals that although the scale of the trade increased gradually in the years between 1760 and 1840, there was an actual decline in the participation of smaller ships. In 1761, three or four junks were annually employed between Amoy and Sulu.[3] Over a half century later, the number of junks which visited was seldom less than one but rarely exceeded four—each from 3,000 to 7,000 piculs (200–465 tons) burden.[4] By 1830 the conduct of this commerce was limited to two well-laden Amoy junks of the largest type (up to 800 tons).[5]

The Conduct of Trade

Vessels from Chinese waters could arrive in Jolo as early as the first week in March but never later than the middle of April. Junks originating from the same port often voyaged in tandem to minimize the hazards of shipwreck and the risk of piratical attack. Their trading time-table, rigidly determined by the monsoon wind regime, made it imperative for them to leave for the Asian mainland no later than the beginning of August.[6] For the straggler the risks of being lost at sea greatly increased at that time, and further delays meant contending with strong headwinds and heavy seas strewn with rocks and shoals along the ill-defined Palawan coast.[7] The alternative to physical disaster in the treacherous South China Sea was a financial one; "some have been known to have wintered in the Spanish ports and ultimately been compelled to sell their junks and cargoes".[8] The impending arrival of these huge vessels stimulated a flurry of economic activity both in Jolo's sizeable Chinese community and among resident Taosug aristocrats. Upon its arrival, an *ad valorem* duty was not levied upon the junk's cargo. Instead a single impost was negotiated by the Sultan and prestigious *datus* in consultation with the vessel's commander and super-cargo. Arbitrary in character, this customs duty could be influenced by the trade interests of particular *datus*, prevailing market conditions, and later, the political chicanery of rival European competitors—Spanish, Portuguese, and English.

The Sultan collected anything up to 10 per cent on imported Chinese goods.[9] In 1814, the two junks at Jolo paid 4,500 and 5,000 Mexican dollars on their cargoes worth respectively 50,000 and 100,000 dollars.[10] While at Jolo, visiting merchants were habitually obliged to offer trade goods on credit to the Sultan and *datus*. Those *datus* who actually repaid their Chinese benefactors tended to do so in unjustifiably priced goods. The amount of goods that could be feasibly extended on credit was dependent on the size, content, and value of the cargo and the number of *datus* who had an interest in it. Hunt calculated that from 300 to 500 dollars worth of credit was offered, or approximately 0.5 to 1 per cent of the total value of the vessel's cargo.[11] His figures, however, appear to be a conservative estimate when contrasted with the isolated accounts of other reliable observers. Dalrymple wrote that the Chinese visiting Sulu "by exactions and presents, tho there be no port charge or regular customs, pay above 50 per cent".[12]

In 1834 a Chinese junk attempted to trade under the guns of the fortress at the neighbouring Spanish settlement of Zamboanga instead of in Jolo's roadstead. The vessel's commander willingly offered to pay the Spanish authorities a port duty equivalent to 30 per cent of the cargo's value, rather than have to cope with the possible extortions of the Sultan and various influential *datus*. When this request was denied, the commander chose to travel and trade along the Mindanao coast in preference to Jolo.[13]

Nevertheless, the above case appears to have been a rare exception. Sulu's trade was lucrative and the Chinese generally preferred to purchase immunity to ward off arbitrary interference by Taosug. An occurrence in 1761 reveals the vagaries of trade with a segmentary society. There were two Amoy junks in the port:

> ... but the oppression they suffered was a great discouragement to the traders: In one of the junks Sultan Bantilan (Muizzud-Din) had an interest to promote which, on some frivolous pretence, he laid an embargo on the other junk, taking the rudder on shoar: Dato Bandahara and others, remonstrated on this conduct, which was ... injurious to the community; for, if the strangers had not protection and justice it could not be expected that they would frequent the port, and consequently everyone suffer, by having no vent for the produce of their estates: these representations being ineffectual, Dato Bandahara, Oranky Mallick and Panglima Milaham went on board the other junk, in which the Sultan had an interest, and brought the rudder also on shoar, informing the Sultan that when he discharged the one, they would release the other, but not till then: the Sultan was thus compelled to do the Chinese justice....[14]

The acceptance of almost any pecuniary imposition was a worthwhile precaution against such harassments to trade in Jolo.

Before actual trading could begin, the Chinese officers had to distribute
those goods contracted during the previous season, rent space on shore
for a market, and arrange for a *datu* to supply a new mast for the return
trip. A portion of the freight brought for Jolo's resident Chinese was then
distributed to them on credit—tea, drugs, dried fruit, fireworks, and wearing
apparel—to be paid for in natural produce collected towards the return
cargo at fixed rates. The vessel's remaining wares were retailed daily for the
produce of *prahus* from neighbouring islands and small craft arriving from
the east Bornean coast.[15]

The Trade Wares

Junk cargoes consisted principally of Chinese porcelain (thousands of
cups, saucers, dishes, bowls, and plates), tiles, silk and satin garments, bolts
of white and black cotton cloth, muslin and chintz piece goods, brassware,
wrought iron, arms and munitions, rice, sugar, oil, and lard.[16] Raw silk was
brought in considerable quantities only on the Amoy junks. Coarse textiles
and earthenware comprised the most valuable part of the freight. The cargoes
of bigger vessels, which represented the speculative interests of large
numbers of people, were worth from 50,000 to upward of 100,000 pesos and
compared favourably with those of Chinese vessels visiting Manila.[17]*

Return cargoes embraced an incredible variety of marine and forest
products as well as craft goods of the Sultanate and neighbouring realms.
The principle items were pearls, mother of pearl, tortoise shell, seaweed,
and precious shells from the Sulu archipelago, edible nests, beeswax, and
camphor from Borneo's east coast, and pepper, clove bark, betel nut, and
lumber from Basilan and Mindanao.[18]

While the Sino-Sulu trade entailed risks, the profits to be made on such long
voyages by Chinese traders were exceptional. As Thomas Forrest commented,
"the Chinese must gain handsomely by their trade hither; else they would not
put up with the rough usage they sometimes receive from ... the Datoos".[19]
The margin of profit on trade goods from China ranged between 30 and
300 per cent. Primary textiles—*kowsongs*, *kompow*, and *kangans* were sold
in Sulu at up to 30 per cent profit while silk pieces and manufactures were
retailed at prices from 100 to 300 per cent above cost. Manufactured wares,
particularly hardware, were costly, although the seemingly high price
of natural produce in Sulu enabled the Taosug to purchase such articles
readily. Small cast-iron bars, frying pans, cooking vessels, household

---

* In 1795, the cargoes of the six junks that visited Manila from Amoy and Nanking
ranged from 119,425 pesos (Amoy) to 218 pesos (Nanking). In April of 1803 the *Josun* from
Amoy imported 145,891 pesos worth of goods at Manila, Estado, AGI, Ultramar 658.

utensils, and brassware realized a gain of 90 to 100 per cent. Underglaze blue on white and grey porcelain crockery, the bulk of the cargo, sold at double their cost in China and yielded the highest returns, owing to their sheer volume.

The advantages to be earned on the return cargo were generally even greater. Although small in bulk, high quality products such as bird's nest and beeswax realized a profit of 90 to 100 per cent when sold. Mother of pearl, used in the manufacture of beads, furniture, and fans, was marketed in China for nearly three times the original price in Sulu.[20] Homeward bound junks carried cargoes estimated at between 60,000 and 80,000 Spanish dollars.[21] The net profit derived on this freight when unloaded at China's southern ports could be double the original investment. Hunt claimed (with some exaggeration) that if only one out of three junks managed a safe return nothing was lost.[22]

In 1814 an English Naval Officer was informed by Jolo's *Kapitan China* that the annual value of the trade between China and Sulu averaged 150,000 Spanish dollars.[23] The total volume of trade in produce had doubled since 1760, and reached its peak in the early decades of the nineteenth century—at least 12,000 to upward of 25,000 piculs a year. This contention is supported by Spoehr's recent archaeological investigations on Jolo island which have provided another perspective on the historical contours of Chinese trade links with the Sulu Sultanate. The disproportionately large number of fragments of Chinese ceramic produced in the late eighteenth and nineteenth centuries confirm the accelerated tempo of Sino-Sulu trade at this time.[24]

In the face of brisk European competition in the 1830s all but the very large Amoy junks were eliminated from the lucrative trade with the Sulu Sultanate. They alone could anticipate a good market, owing as much to the quality of their cargoes, selected with the tastes of their clientele in mind, as to their size. After 1840 fewer and fewer Amoy junks visited Sulu, as a consequence of the active enterprise of European and Chinese traders resident in Manila and the increased Spanish presence in the Sulu Sea. Much of the Sino-Sulu trade was reoriented towards the Spanish metropole as the principal port for the staging of trade between China and the Sulu Sultanate.

Manila's belated emergence as an entrepot for the Sino-Sulu trade was to be eclipsed by a radical alteration of the Sultanate's trade patterns. Taosug trade began to converge on the newly created English colony of Labuan, adjacent to the Brunei Sultanate on Borneo's west coast, and the thriving port of Singapore. This new commercial pattern which emerged after 1850 contributed to the demise of direct traffic from the maritime province of Fukien to the Sulu archipelago. Within the decade the last of the large bluff ships from China's south coast arrived in the roadstead at Jolo.

BUGINESE TRADE WITH THE SULU SULTANATE

The other important participants in early Taosug commerce were the Makassarese and Buginese, or Bugis, of south Celebes who voyaged to almost every corner of insular Southeast Asia in search of trade in the late eighteenth and nineteenth centuries. The hub of their commercial activity was the port town of Makassar.* From there Bugis *prahus* sailed west across the Java sea to Batavia, Malacca, and beyond; some annually sailed south and east as well.[25] Their *paduakans* frequented the coast of west New Guinea and went to northern Australia where they procured *tripang* and shark's fin to supplement the spices, sandalwood, and rattans which they traded with Chinese and European merchants in colonial capitals and outlying fortified entrepots.[26] Others monopolized the trade of Borneo's southeast coast and their sailing craft reached as far north as Manila.[27] Bugis trade with the Sulu Sultanate was conducted from the Moluccas and by a handful of communities along the southeastern coast of Borneo, primarily Pasir and later Samarinda.

The town of Pasir was situated along the banks of the Kendilo river some forty-five miles from the coast. In 1772, Forrest visited Pasir and described it as a "place of great trade".[28] The town consisted of about three hundred houses, mostly occupied by Bugis merchants, and the Malay Sultan's residence and wooden fort which were located on the opposite bank of the river. The Bugis traders were not considered subjects of the Sultan of Kutai who frequently bestowed titles on them to secure their loyalty and trade.[29] Despite such efforts, the Bugis remained a separate trading community, ethnically distinct and politically autonomous. By contrast, further to the north, in the tiny realms of Berau and Bulungan, immigrant Buginese traders intermarried with prominent families and were assimilated.[30]

By 1800 Pasir was no longer the most important Bugis trading town on the east coast of Borneo. Some Buginese merchants had moved across to Pulau Laut, a large island at the extreme southern tip of Borneo, and established a market town.[31] While others, the traders of Wajo, had shifted the centre of their activity further north, to Samarinda at the mouth of the Mahakam river. The Buginese population of Samarinda was estimated at 5,500 in 1829.[32] Their continued independence of the Sultanate of Kutai and their ability to regulate the movement of trade goods from the mouth of the Mahakam river to the Sultan's residence at Tenggarong and inland across his domain is disclosed in this description of Samarinda:

---

* The few Buginese maps and charts that have survived from the 19th century clearly show the important role Makassar played in their trading patterns despite it being a Dutch monopoly stronghold. See the fascinating map reproduced in L. Tobing, *Hukum Pelajaran Dan Perdagangan Amanna Gappa*.

On approaching Semerindan ... the houses are situated on the right bank and extend about a quarter of a mile in length .... most of the people live in floating houses, called "rooma rackets" ...[which] can be moved up or down the river .... these houses are placed three or four abreast of each other; there are besides, bamboo houses on the land of a superior description inhabited by the anakodas and rich Bugis.... abreast of Semerindan and within one hundred yards of the houses there are ten fathoms of water ... here all the principal Bugis dwell and all the prows which sail from Coti are kept at this place, none going further upriver; the whole of the trade from every part of the country upon a large scale is here transacted; all cargoes arriving are immediately purchased by the Bugis, and sent up the river in small boats to agents whom they have in every part of the country. Semerindan is the grand depot of all exports as well as imports and in point of real strength is able to cope with the Sultan of Coti and all the power he can bring.[33]

The Conduct of the Trade

Before 1760, fourteen of fifteen Bugis *prahus* visited Sulu every year.[34] The number of deep-laden *paduakans** from Pasir that came to Sulu increased when regular trade was established between Bengal and the Sultanate after 1768. Not all Bugis trade went directly from the Moluccas or Pasir to Jolo. Some Bugis merchants chose to restrict their commercial intercourse with the Sulu Sultanate to its trading enclaves in Berau and Bulungan. Others chose to sell their trade wares and raw materials to the Taosug at traditional meeting places situated near islands at the edges of the zone. The two most important sites in the first half of the nineteenth century were Sarangani island south of Mindanao, and the small channel which separated Tambesan island from the northeast coast of Borneo.[35] The Bugis of Pasir remained in Jolo from six to eight months, leaving for the Moluccas in January and February to collect cloves, nutmeg, and black pepper. This gave them sufficient time to return to Jolo with another cargo before the monsoon changed.[36]

---

* The Bugis *paduakans* were between 20 and 50 tons burden, broad beamed with high sides. A Dutch naval officer described these "workhorses" of the eastern archipelago:

A paduakan has only one sail, and is steered by two rudders (one on each quarter) which can readily be raised out of the water. The two cables, each from thirty to fifty fathoms long, are made of twisted rattans, and the anchors are composed of hardwood, having the flukes a little sharpened, and a large stone fastened to the stocks. A small canoe is carried on the deck. The bottom of the vessels is covered with a composition of lime, and the top sides are painted with a black mixture made from burnt rattans and husks of cocoanut. Some pots of fresh water, a little salt, a quantity of sago bread, and some fishing hooks and lines, complete their equipment, *Kolff, Voyages of the Dutch Brig of War Dourga*, pp.307–8.

Spices, Captives, and Munitions

Buginese imports to Sulu at the time of Forrest's visit in 1775 consisted of spices, bird's nest, sugar, and rice from Menado.[37] Gunpowder was a main trade item.[38] The Bugis exchanged their own woven cotton cloth and *lontar,* a dyed papyrus made from the leaves of the palmyra palm, which was used as writing material and for wrapping.*

Spices were among the most important items the Bugis traded with Sulu. Buginese *nakodahs* from Pasir gave Dalrymple an account of the spices they brought to Sulu every year: 400 piculs of cloves, 50 piculs of nutmeg, and 200 piculs of black pepper.[39] They were the only merchant traders who could deliver these goods to the Taosug. All the cloves brought to Manila in the late eighteenth century were carried first to Sulu by the Bugis at considerable risk.[40] The Dutch asserted that a great part of the Bugis trade, especially the traffic in spices, was illegal. The Bugis evaded the severe laws and regulations, spreading their commerce over wide areas in which the Dutch claimed a monopoly.†

The *datus* of Jolo purchased gunpowder and arms from the larger Bugis *prahus* which frequented Batavia, Malacca, and Penang.[41] The Buginese brought slaves, spices, wax, cotton cloth, and coffee to the European market to pay for bar iron, saltpetre, muskets, and gunpowder. The Dutch attempted to prevent the export of war stores from their ports through the registration of Bugis vessels, the issuance of a restricted trading pass (only valid for a single voyage, a specific period, and a certain destination) and their export cargoes were subject to the inspection of customs agents.‡ While such

---

* Bugis cotton cloth in checquered patterns, especially red against blue, were ordinarily sold for six to ten Spanish dollars a piece. They were handwoven from imported Balinese cotton, durable and of fine craftsmanship. The more expensive pieces of cloth were wrapped in *lontar,* an important trade item in itself—"they often dye this paper of various colours and export much of it even to Manilla, and various other places...." Forrest, *A Voyage from Calcutta to the Mergui Archipelago,* p.80.

† For example, the authorities at Batavia declared in 1767 that "all persons whatever are prohibited under pain of death from trading in the four kinds of spices, unless such spices shall be first bought from the Company". Abstract orders relating to the trade and navigation that is permitted with places to the Eastward of Batavia, as proclaimed and established in the year 1767, in Mr. Raffles to Gilbert Elliot, 1st Earl of Minto, Governor-General of India, 18 Feb. 1811, IOL, Raffles Minto Collection, EUR.F. 148/5, p.111.

‡ The Dutch restriction on *prahus* carrying gunpowder was as follows:
   No prow or vessel shall carry any greater quantity of gunpowder and shot, than may be permitted and regularly entered in the pass under pain of confiscation of the vessel and cargo, and a corporal punishment to the parties similar to that inflicted for theft, and on the arrival of prows and vessels to the eastward at the different residencies or at Timor, the same [gunpowder] must be landed in a place of security until their departure.
Mr. Raffles to 1st Earl of Minto, Governor-General of India, 18 Feb. 1811, IOL, Raffles Minto Collection, EUR. F. 148/5, p.114.

measures were a hindrance they did not deter the Bugis from getting arms from Dutch ports to trade to the Sulu Sultanate.

The tempo of the Buginese trade in war stores increased after 1820. Only several years after the free port of Singapore was founded, the Bugis had already established their own trading quarter in the city—Kampong Bugis—and *nakodahs* from Samarinda, who no longer visited Batavia, freely obtained arms and supplies for export to Jolo.[42] In 1835, the number of *prahus* that visited Singapore from Bugis communities involved in trade with the Sulu Sultanate, Berau, and Bulungan were: Kutai, fifteen *prahus*; Pasir, ten *prahus*; Kylie, eight *prahus*.[43] The Buginese from the east coast of Borneo and the west coast of Celebes made no more than one voyage a year to Singapore. The journey, which took between twenty-five and forty days, was considered long and tedious.[44]

The Taosug exchanged captives, opium, and Bengal cloth for the gunpowder and spices brought by the Bugis of Pasir and Berau. In the 1770s the Bugis annually transported several hundred Filipinos from Sulu to slave markets at Batavia, Malacca, Bantam, Chirebon, Banjarmasin, and Palembang.[45] In these cities they were sold to long-established Dutch families and Chinese as servants, boatmen, labourers, and concubines. The Filipinos sold into slavery by the Bugis on Java or at ports in the straits of Malacca were never returned to the Philippines.*

On more than one occasion, the Spanish ambassador to the Netherlands formally protested that the colonial authorities in Batavia tolerated the sale of Filipinos taken to Dutch possessions by the Buginese.[46] As a result of these protests, the importation of Spanish subjects was prohibited in the Netherlands Indies in 1762,† but enforcement of the measure proved difficult if not impossible for the Dutch. The law was not vigorously enforced in Batavia and was ignored for years in outlying settlements. In

---

* In 1773, two Filipino women were taken off a Portuguese packetboat en route from Batavia to Macao that was forced to put into Manila for provisions. The women (who were the concubines of two Chinese passengers) had been captured by Magindanao in 1761. One had been sold in Batavia for the equivalent of 90 pesos and the other, 112 pesos. They testified that there was a thriving trade in Filipino slaves at Batavia and that there were a large number of them in the city. No.9, 19 Dec. 1775, AGI, Filipinas 359.

† For a copy of the decree of 16 June 1762 forbidding the retailing of Spanish subjects in the Netherlands Indies, see AR, Kolonien Archief 2922, p.667; No.2, 9 May 1767, AGI, Filipinas 669. Part of the decree reads:

No slaves are permitted to be brought from the eastward above the age of 14 years, and the names and number of all slaves that may be brought from the eastward must be inserted in the pass. The importation of slaves belonging to the king of Spain is prohibited under a penalty of 500 Rix dollars, and the annulment of the purchase.

Mr. Raffles to 1st Earl of Minto, Governor-General of India, 18 Feb. 1811, IOL, EUR. F.148/5, p.114.

1766 and 1776, the Spanish again objected in vain against the continued
Buginese traffic in war stores and Filipino captives.[47]

Interestingly, Bugis traffic in Filipino slaves declined with the growth of
external trade to the Sulu Sultanate. In the first half of the nineteenth century,
there is no mention in the Spanish documents of Filipinos being exported
from Sulu to Singapore—this, despite the fact that slaves remained one of
the Bugis'principal stock in trade. Abdullah Munshi depicts the Buginese as
herding droves of slaves through the streets in the early days of Singapore
and selling them to Chinese, Indian, and Malay customers from their *prahus*
moored in the harbour.[48]

There were several factors responsible for the scaling down of long
distance Buginese slave traffic with the Sulu Sultanate. First and most
important, the Taosug were faced with an acute manpower problem because
of the demands created by external trade. Increasingly, *datus* chose to
retain the majority of the captive people brought to Sulu for the littoral
procurement trade rather than barter them to professional slave traders.
But in a limited sense, Sulu remained a constant source of slaves for the
Buginese communities on Celebes and Borneo until 1860.

Secondly, as a consequence of the growth of international commerce, the
Taosug were able to provide the Buginese traders with alternative exports,
particularly opium and Bengal cloth, which were labelled contraband by the
Dutch.* For the Bugis this traffic was as lucrative as the slave trade, and
Jolo offered the simple advantage of being much closer to their trading orbit
than either Malacca or Penang. By 1800, the Buginese were as interested
in obtaining cloth and opium at Sulu as captives. Sulu continued to be an
alternative source of opium and Indian textiles for neighbouring Buginese
traders long after Singapore was established.

Taosug Trade with Bugis Entrepots

The Taosug aristocracy of Jolo, Sandakan, Bulungan, and Berau carried
on a complementary trade with the Dutch ports of Menado and Ternate,[49] the
Buginese villages of Kylie and Pasir, and Samarinda. Trading expeditions
were either led by *datus,* their kindred, or trusted retainers—usually a *sherif,*
Chinese trader, or Bugis slave. Taosug trading vessels frequenting Menado

---

* The articles relating to the Dutch prohibition of opium and Indian cloth are as follows:
"All trade in opium is in a like manner prohibited [under pain of death] unless the same is first
purchased from the company at Batavia", and "the import and export of Surat silks and of
Indian cloths and muslins is strictly prohibited under the penalty of confiscation and a fine of
4 times the value of the articles tended in and if the party holds any office under the company
he shall be dismissed therefrom". Mr. Raffles to 1st Earl of Minto, Governor-General of India,
18 Feb. 1811, IOL. EUR.F. 148/5, p.111.

and Ternate exchanged Chinese commodities for rice, bird's nest, shark's fin, tortoise shell, lorikeets, and spices. Because of the prohibition of direct junk trade from China to the outer islands, the Taosug experienced no difficulty in exchanging their wares with the Dutch burghers, Buginese traders, and Chinese inhabitants.* Most of their imported articles were Chinese manufactured in contrast to their exports which consisted of cereals and marine jungle produce.

Until 1850, one of the most frequent Sulu exports to Samarinda was captives (men, women, and children) which had been bartered to the Taosug by Iranun and Balangingi Samal. Forrest noted in 1776 that *datus* in Jolo "sometimes ... purchase whole cargoes, which they carry to Pasir, on Borneo; where, if the females are handsome, they are bought up for the Batavia market".[50]

Assessments of the total volume and value of Bugis trade with the Sulu Sultanate from 1800 to 1850 vary considerably. The Manila-Chinese traders estimated that 50,000 pesos was the value of the traffic conducted each year between Sulu, Singapore, Sarangani island, and Sandakan Bay by Buginese traders and the *sherifs* of northeast Borneo.[51] I think this figure is probably too low. The value of a single import cargo often ranged between 10,000 and 40,000 dollars,[52] and at least twenty *prahus* traded on an annual basis with the Taosug till 1848. A more accurate estimate of the trade's worth would have to be almost 250,000 pesos a year.[53]

Buginese traffic to Jolo waned after the mid-nineteenth century, but trade along the southern periphery of the zone persisted for another two decades. The opening in 1846 of the port of Makassar to free trade allowed the Bugis access to formerly prohibited trade goods. For some traders there was no longer any need to resort to either Singapore or Sulu to obtain opium and cloth. The continued efforts of the Manila Government to control

---

   * The following articles are examples of the prohibitive Dutch trade laws of 1767 which were intended to make the *Buitengewesten,* "the outer islands" as dependent as possible on Batavia:

   Article 19—At Amboyna, Banda, Ternate, Macassar, and Timor the pass from Batavia ceases and another becomes necessary; Article 20—The China junks are not permitted to trade except to Batavia and Banjar [Bandjermasin]; Article 21—Vessels from Amboyna, Banda, Ternate and Timor cannot enter at any port except Batavia but the inhabitants of Amboyna and Banda are permitted to trade with Macassar for rice the same permission being granted to the people of Macassar to go to Amboyna, but all other navigation from Amboyna, Banda and Ternate to the Celebes is prohibited; Article 22—From Timor navigation cannot be carried on to the Southward islands, and the inhabitants of the southeast islands must carry on trade through the inhabitants of Banda.

   Mr. Raffles to 1st Earl of Minto, Governor-General of India, 18 Feb. 1811, IOL, Raffles Minto Collection, EUR.F. 148/5, p.116.

the Sultanate's trade after 1850 further discouraged other Buginese from coming to Jolo. Spanish naval steamers now patrolled the waters of the Sulu archipelago and the southern Mindanao coast in an effort to intercept all unlicensed trading craft bound for Jolo. The Bugis also had to contend with the enterprise of merchant venturers like John Ross and William Lingard as well as the hostility of Samal raiders on Tawi-Tawi who, no longer loyal to the Sultan, were bent on disrupting Bugis trade with Taosug communities north of Bulungan. In this unsettled atmosphere, direct Buginese participation in the Sulu Sultanate's trade ended by 1870.

2

Balambangan and the Rise of the Sulu Sultanate: The Formative Years, 1772–1775

The source of Sulu's hegemony after 1768 was its role as a regional emporium in the commerce between European traders, Southeast Asian realms, and China. The increasing magnitude of this external trade made regional redistribution the dominant pattern of the economy of the Taosug state and established its ascendancy in the region.

The commercial interests of the English East India Company and private country traders in India provided the initial catalyst for the transformation of Sulu in the late eighteenth century. It was from the trade in tea with China that the Company derived the bulk of its profits. The need to find British goods exchangeable for Chinese tea became a chronic problem as the importance of the beverage increased in England. English commodities did not sell in China, and the drain of silver to purchase the Chinese supplies threatened financial ruin for the Bengal administration.[1]

This predicament drove officials and merchants in Calcutta, European and Asian, to look to the islands of Southeast Asia. The region provided a vast new market for English manufactures and India's trade commodities, especially opium and piece goods.[2] An account written in 1795 expressed the potential importance of insular Southeast Asia for Britain:

> The produce of the archipelago, dependent and independent of the Dutch, consists of an infinity of items; of which the most prominent are diamonds, pearlshells, gold, spices, pepper, tin and bird's nests. This produce ever has and probably ever will draw specie from China, as the demands of the Chinese for these items is great and the wants of the archipelago from China small. The archipelago wants much from Bengal and India and has little wanted in Bengal and India to give in return.[3]

The Company sought a substitute to specie payment in the establishment of factories or trading posts strategically situated throughout the Malay world for attracting and warehousing trade produce for China.[4] In its search for suitable sites, the East India Company chose Balambangan, an island adjacent to North Borneo, within the domain of the Sulu Sultanate, for the establishment of a trading post on the way to China. This decision of 1768 was to have an important impact on the Taosug aristocracy of Jolo.

A Man with a Vision

Alexander Dalrymple, a Madras civil servant, was the principal architect of the scheme to establish a trading station at Balambangan.[5] He came to Fort St. George at Madras in 1752 as a Company writer and was appointed as deputy secretary five years later. Described as a man of "capacity, integrity, and unwearied application",[6] Dalrymple in his new role thoroughly familiarized himself with the Company's ledgers, correspondence, and trade returns. His research convinced him that the Company could not only recover its share of the eastern trade but extend it to further areas that were neither under Dutch control nor within effective Spanish jurisdiction. Dalrymple appears to have been especially interested in the zone wedged between Spanish and Dutch colonial interests comprising the Sulu archipelago, the east coast of Borneo, southern Mindanao, and the north coast of Celebes. The personal encouragement of George Pigot, president of the Madras settlement, and the timely English invasion of Manila enabled Dalrymple to undertake a series of voyages to the Sulu archipelago between 1759 and 1764. He entered into several treaties with the Sultans of Sulu and obtained the cession of Balambangan island and a considerable part of the north Borneo coast.*

On 22 January 1763, Dalrymple took possession of Balambangan and hoisted the British flag. Five years elapsed, however, before official approval was granted by a committee of the Company's Board of Directors in London for the establishment of a trading station on the island.[7] Although barren and only fourteen miles in length, Dalrymple thought the small island ideally situated as a market for trade with China and the areas surrounding Sulu; he wrote: "if a circle of 2,000 miles be drawn round the East Indies the middle point will be found at Balambangan ... betwixt the northeast coast of Borneo and Palawan".[8] In his mind this unimposing, uninhabited island could

---

* Alexander Dalrymple arrived at Sulu on 18 August 1762 and obtained the cession of Balambangan from sultan Bantilan (Muizz ud-Din) on 12 September 1762. A year later he returned to Sulu for a third time and Alimuddin II, the son of the deceased Sultan, made a grant of the northern part of Borneo, the southern part of Palawan, and all the intermediate islands to the Company. However, the official cession, which was not agreed to until the following year, was solely restricted to Sulu's Bornean dependencies and authorized by the elderly Sultan Alimudin I (Azim-ud Din) who had been returned recently to Sulu from Manila with Dalrymple's assistance. Alexander Dalrymple to the Court of Directors of the United East India Company, 30 Oct. 1769, IOL, H/Misc/771/12, pp.190–91; see also Fry, *Alexander Dalrymple and the Expansion of British Trade*, pp.67–73; Quiason, *English "Country Trade" with the Philippines*, pp.122–31.

become a regional trade centre through Chinese immigration and settlement, diversion of the junk trade from Batavia and Manila, and provision of a local market for Bengal manufactures especially to the enterprising Bugis traders to the south.

When troops, stores, and large quantities of trade goods were finally sent from India in 1772 on the *Britannia*, Alexander Dalrymple had already been dismissed from the Company's service for more than a year because of a protracted salary dispute.[9] Belatedly established in 1773, the trading station was deprived of his judicious leadership, extraordinary knowledge of Asian trade, and personal experience among the Taosug. In his place Madras appointed John Herbert, a functionary at Benkulen, as the chief of the Balambangan factory.[10] Subsequent events were to prove their choice mistaken.

Opium, Gunpowder, and Raiding

The East India Company's relations with Sulu have been widely interpreted within the framework of Alexander Dalrymple's career and British policy and trade in Southeast Asia in the late eighteenth century.[11] At the same time, the impact of the short-lived Balambangan factory on regional commerce and politics from the Taosug perspective has been largely ignored.

Balambangan's trade with the Taosug and Magindanao was a trade in opium, munitions, and piece goods. Opium was only widely introduced among the Taosug as a consequence of the trade dealings of John Herbert's regime. Ill-disposed towards the Balambangan venture, the self-seeking Englishman was able to convince the distant Fort St. George authorities that the prospects for the profitable development of the settlement's commerce were dismal unless opium was retailed on a large scale. Shortly before his departure for Balambangan, Herbert wrote to his superiors:

> ... you will easily conceive the disadvantage of going on this expedition with piece goods alone, ... I cannot but strenuously recommend ... the provision of a very large supply of ophium which may well be considered as a necessary of life; all the manufactures on the west of India will not have half the attraction that this single article will have, it will effectually operate on every other sort of goods, wanting that alone the undertaking will wear a dreary prospect.[12]

He concluded his lengthy letter:

> ... the Dutch have in great measure absorb'd the profits of the circle described by Mr.Dalrymple for two hundred years, and can we suppose them such bad merchants as to come merely for the want of foregoing an inconsiderable loss annually for the space of three years only; this period being the published avowed time when experience is to demonstrate the utility or inutility of the under-taking ... the ophium investment being the pivot on which the success of the expedition to Balambangan will most immediately and principally turn

exceeds every apology, I should make either for the repitition of the subject or
for any impropriety that may appear in the manner of my treating it.[13]

He further requested Madras to enforce the ban which prohibited private
country traders from carrying opium to the east. This would enable
Balambangan to act as an entrepot for trade to the Chinese territories which
annually consumed 750 to 1,000 chests of opium.[14]

In the short space of eighteen months, a sizeable trade in opium was
inaugurated between Balambangan and Jolo. The cargoes of the *Britannia,
Carlisle, Phoenix,* and *Syren* all contained opium on the account of the
Company. In August 1773, the *Phoenix* alone delivered 300 chests of opium
to the Balambangan settlement.[15] This huge consignment was, however,
adulterated, and Herbert reminded Company officials that "the credit of a new
establishment in this quarter essentially depends on being supplied (particularly
at the commencement) with the best of that commodity", and requested that a
large quantity of the finest Patna opium be freighted to the settlement.[16]

By June of 1774, the Court of Directors had become apprehensive of
their principal factor's personal ambitions among the Taosug and refused to
honour any further requests for increases in the quantity of opium exported
to Balambangan.[17] This did not deter Herbert from ordering fifty chests of
the best Patna opium in December of the same year.[18] Herbert did not find
the market he had expected at Jolo, and handed over seventy-three chests of
opium on extended credit from twelve to eighteen months to coastal *datus* at
an apparent loss to the Company.[19] Although expressly forbidden to dispose
of the opium in such a speculative manner at Jolo except for "ready money
or immediate and advantageous barter", he sold it at 550 dollars a chest on
Company account (50 dollars less than the amount at which he resold the
same opium to his employers) and embezzled the mere 1,570 dollars in cash
that was received on the trade investment.[20] Herbert was too incompetent
to assume the responsibility for so precarious an undertaking. The chief
factor lacked the sincerity of purpose, tact, and force of authority necessary
to oblige the *datus* to pay their debts (mostly for opium) and instead
charged them to the Company's account. Equally important was his lack of
experience of the conduct of Sulu's regional trade.

It is evident from Herbert's official correspondence that he never
considered the social and political consequences of the introduction of
opium among various segments of Sulu's population. It was those aristocrats
involved in external trade who first acquired a taste for the habit-forming
drug. Within two decades, opium smoking was considered integral to the
life style of the *datus* near the coast. In the nineteenth century, it was to be
still more widely used and few among the wealthier *datus* avoided addiction.
Opium had a severe debilitating effect on the Jolo aristocracy and prevented
some among its ranks from exercising leadership. European observers who
commented on the impact of opium use and addiction among the Taosug

included Charles Wilkes, Edward Belcher, Melchior Yvan, and Spenser St. John.[21] Alexander Dalrymple as an astute observer of Taosug society had expressly forbidden the introduction of opium as a trade commodity in Sulu. He foresaw the tragic physical and psychological consequences that would ultimately accompany its advent:

> ... we never saw any appearance of drunkenness amongst them and what is very remarkable and much to their honour is that ... ophium is in no estimation amongst them and never used. I thought it but just that this should be made a contraband commodity tho the Sultan said it might be imported to vend to the Buggese but the hazards of corrupting the Sooloos seemed a sufficient reason to forgoe any pecuniary consideration of this nature.[22]

Thomas Forrest, who travelled with Herbert on the *Britannia* to Jolo, confirmed what Dalrymple had written a decade earlier, when he briefly noted that in Sulu, "opium is not in great demand, Celebes being its great mart".[23]

As a result of the opium dealing instigated at Balambangan between 1773 and 1775, the drug became a profitable article of trade by the end of the eighteenth century. Taosug merchants began to barter it to neighbouring Magindanao and Samal for Canton goods such as wax and bird's nest as well as to Iranun marauders for Filipino captives. In 1788, however, the Taosug trade in opium was still limited in scope and was hardly worth note in the Cotabato basin. John Meares, a British merchant, observed, "The people of Magindanao universally chew the betal and areka but make a more moderate use of opium than any other inhabitants of the Eastern Seas."[24] Most of the local exchange traffic was in Taosug hands, but the Bugis remained the large-scale indigenous distributors of opium within the inter-regional trade network beyond Sulu. As a market for opium was gradually created at Jolo, it proved an invaluable trade item worth its weight in gold, pearls, and edible nests. It was estimated that a cargo of Gujerat opium would at least afford a profit in excess of 100 per cent.[25]

Balambangan's ultimate failure in no way diminished the ability of Taosug aristocrats to obtain opium. From 1780 to 1805, the traffic in opium continued between English country traders and Jolo's nobility.[26] Unfortunately, the shipping records and logs of the East India Company provide little statistical or written material which could clarify the activities of these independent traders at Sulu. After 1780 we have no way of knowing precisely in what numbers they frequented Jolo's roadstead.* In the first two

---

* The manifests of country traders may well be found in the Calcutta Port Commission records from which a time series could potentially be created for trade from Bengal to the Moluccas and Sulu. The East India Company records became somewhat more explicit after 1796 when Britain occupied the Moluccan Archipelago and the Government's commercial interest directly conflicted with the activities of the country traders. Official correspondence at this point carefully outlines their dealings in opium, piece goods, and spices, particularly at Ceram and Ambon.

decades of the nineteenth century, the Taosug were also supplied with the drug by Chinese and Bugis traders, and Iranun who obtained it from native vessels they captured among the Dutch islands.[27] By 1839, the trade in opium at Sulu annually averaged twenty-five to thirty chests which weighed between 100 and 120 pounds each.[28]*

The settlement at Balambangan contributed towards the assertion of regional dominion by the Taosug and also increased Iranun raids through the large-scale introduction of lead, iron, shot, gunpowder, and cannon to the regional exchange network. From its inception, the contest to gain control of this aspect of Balambangan's trade, the supply and distribution of a vital resource—superior weapons—was a primary concern of the Taosug. They were eager to purchase gunpowder and arms from Herbert and his council in their emerging role as regional resource controllers, but reacted swiftly when the English factors attempted to undermine their political authority by trading in armaments with their Magindanao rivals. The successful destruction of Balambangan in 1775 must be seen as an expression of interregional political strife and trade competition for advanced technology.

Prior to 1768, the Taosug and Magindanao were technically unfamiliar with the use and maintenance of large ordinance for their raiding vessels. Previously, they employed *rantanka*, *lantanka*, and *lella*, small imported portable brass swivel cannons, for artillery on board their sailing craft. During the 1760s, the lack of heavy ordinance and skills in the manufacture of firearms among the Taosug and Magindanao had been observed by several European traders and travellers. A memoir, probably written by Dalrymple, cites the small proportion of Magindanao raiding craft that actually carried heavy ordinance *circa* 1765: "The Magindanaos are at present at war with the Spaniards and fitted out last year against the Philippines 317 fighting vessels, *several of which carry artillery*."[29] Three years later, Captain Pierre Marie Francois de Pages, an adventurous French naval officer on a private trip around the world, wrote that the Taosug and Magindanao were:

> but little acquainted with the use of firearms and have only a few guns which have accidentally fallen into their hands in the course of their wars with Europeans. In this respect they are widely different from their bretheren in the neighbourhood of the Dutch settlements (Bugis) who have established a rude manufacture of muskets on several of their islands and are in general ahead in improvement.[30]

In 1761, in his effort to establish regular commercial intercourse with the Sulu Sultanate, Dalrymple, assisted by Sultan Bantilan (Muizz ud-Din),

---

* By contrast, Sulu's consumption of the narcotic drug in 1814 had been six chests of Benares opium. Hunt, "Some Particulars Relating to Sulu", p.46.

drew up a list of European manufactures and Bengal commodities highly desired by the Taosug. While opium was conspicuously absent from this list, Dalrymple recognized their need for iron, lead, and munitions, including six-pound cannon, and he was not at all averse to establishing a trade in war stores at the proposed settlement.[31] Nearly a decade later, he wrote to the Court of Directors discussing the future prospects of this traffic:

> in this indent they desired arms and ammunition to the amount of 10,000 dollars. Small swivel guns are much wanted for their boats in all those ports. Crisses would be a very considerable article both amongst the Sooloos and Bugguese, the latter are very fond of blunderbusses. If the Company should make Balambangan a mart for arms and ammunition the demand would be very great and nothing would bring strangers thither sooner.[32]

Dalrymple felt from both a commercial and political viewpoint that an arms trade coordinated from Balambangan would serve the best interests of the East India Company against their rival European competitors, particularly the Dutch whom he openly despised. In his opinion, aside from the highly profitable potential, well-armed Taosug and Magindanao allies would provide the fledgling settlement with the necessary strength to stave off possible attack from either the neighbouring Spanish or Dutch settlements. He undoubtedly had this in mind when he wrote: "they who have heard of the Ladrone proas will easily conceive how excellent these would become when instructed by the English".[33]

Heavy ordinance and gunpowder were the key articles of exchange in the early munitions traffic between the East India Company and the Sulu Sultanate. The demand for imported gunpowder is understandable in light of the fact that for more than a century, the Taosug and Magindanao had manufactured a coarse, weak powder with inadequate raw materials. Saltpetre, an essential ingredient, was obtained in a cave near Taviran on Mindanao and from three large open pits on Pata island.[34] This local saltpetre compared unfavourably with the Bengal saltpetre used in the manufacture of English gunpowder.

Even less is known about the magnitude of the munitions traffic at Balambangan during Herbert's brief administration than about the opium trade. The demand for arms and the highly competitive role played by the country traders in its early stages is revealed however in a singular letter written in February of 1774 by the chief council to the governing authorities at Bengal. Herbert initially commented on the high value of gunpowder as a trade item, and provided his superiors with several implausible reasons to justify his request for a hundred barrels. In a visible effort to establish exclusive control of its supply in the regional market, he concluded the letter with a plea for the colonial Government to prohibit Bengal country traders from shipping gunpowder to Sulu:

The expence of powder is great all over the East being used on all sorts of entertainments as well as at burials; we therefore request your Honour and Council will be pleased to send us by every opportunity that offers 100 barrels; we are centrally situated among pyratical states who carry on no other commerce but in goods, vessels and slaves, obtained by force of arms. The fair merchant must be equipped in such a manner as to repel an enemy he is almost sure to encounter with; it becomes therefore absolutely necessary for us to assist him otherwise none wou'd dare to navigate to and from this port. We were short fitted out with this article and arms for the expedition and on that account availed ourselves of some brought thither by the *Syren* and private traders but on a future occasion we desire that it may be made known to all sailing from your port that they must not bring any for sale to the Eastward as we are determined to put the act of Parliament in force against such as do, for we hope it will seldom happen again that the Company will be distressed for these articles; then the private traders will seek to vend them underhand to such as may use them to the prejudice of their Honour's affairs and our own safety.[35]

At the end of the year he wrote again: "no gunpowder having been received by the *Jason* we are distressed for the article, and request it may not be omitted in the next consignments".[36] Within a short time, his regime had amassed a vast quantity of munitions. According to the information given to the *alcalde mayor* of Calamianes by five Filipinos who had fled in a small sailing craft from Balambangan, there were at least 340 barrels of gunpowder which weighed 75 pounds each, more than 1,900 muskets in seventy cases, and a large crate of pistols and sabres, stored at the settlement.[37]

There is an apparent correlation between intensified Magindanao/Iranun raiding in the Philippine archipelago and the munitions traffic which was conducted at Jolo by the factors of the East India Company and country traders from Bengal. While the historian is hampered by the lack of empirical data, from 1768 to 1775, the bold and relentless character of raiding activity, concentrated on southern Luzon and the central Visayas and extending even to the confines of Manila Bay, was an indication of the accelerated tempo of the English weapons trade at Jolo. Spanish ecclesiastical authorities, helpless and dismayed by the precision and strength of these raids, were especially vociferous and repeatedly drew the attention of Manila to the increasing social and economic dislocation produced by the marauding.

The Provincial of the Recollect Order, Father Sebastion de la Assumpcion, was one of the first to observe the basic relationship between increased Iranun raiding, the English munitions trade, and the Taosug's emergent role in controlling the necessary resources for raiding activity:

From the Calamianes and Palawan I have not received any news. I am inclined to believe because of the inordinate delay in the mail that grave hostilities have been committed in these provinces. The Sultan of Jolo, apostate of our faith, is the arch enemy of his excellency in this archipelago because not only does he commit hostilities against your Majesty's dominions, but also encourages the Sultans of Mindanao to do likewise, and supplies the Ylanos [Iranun] with weapons and gunpowder of which he has large stocks that have been obtained from the English who trade there.[38]

The following year, the governing officials in Manila noted with equally grave concern the raiders' newly acquired skill in the use of firearms and the presence of heavy artillery on their vessels. Governor Simon de Anda wrote to the Crown:

the English have established a settlement in the islands of the Jolo archipelago where they not only openly trade warstores but instruct and discipline the inhabitants in the use of cannon and other firearms of which they have had no prior knowledge up until now.[39]

The Governor Captain General advised Madrid that the Balambangan settlement's policy of selling large quantities of war stores was intended to foster raiding against the Philippine provinces and create unbearable expenditures for his already faltering government. This new and dangerous practice had the potential of forcing Spain to abandon the islands.[40] While Simon de Anda's political paranoia may have been justifiable in the aftermath of the English invasion and occupation of Manila a decade earlier, it ignored the fundamentally economic motives of both English trade and Taosug raiding. The complementarity of English commercial interests and the evolving redistributive role of the Sultanate were responsible for the intensified pattern of raid, rather than any conspiratorial design on the Philippine colony. It was another example of Spanish failure to perceive the essential nature of Sulu's evolving role in the region.

In 1772 Simon de Anda reiterated in an official despatch the crippling effect of Iranun raiding on the local shipping of the archipelago. He observed that the trade of the Madras Company had strengthened and encouraged Muslim raiding at sea because ill-equipped Filipino and Chinese craft could not defend themselves against vessels mounting large calibre ordinance—six to eighteen pound cannon.[41] The Spanish found ample evidence of the introduction of war stores by private traders and Company agents among the Taosug even prior to the founding of the Balambangan settlement. Manuel Alvarez, the Sergeant Major of the Spanish fortress at Zamboanga, taking inventory of Taosug artillery in Jolo towards the end of 1772, noted in the Sultan's stockade a large number of three, two, and one pound cannon and smaller portable *lantanka*; one 36-pounder, two 18-pounders, five 8-pounders, and four 6-pounders, but he was unable to provide an estimate of the remaining number of cannon stored in the houses of influential datus.[42] A Mexican gunner in the service of the Sultan of Sulu, who had deserted his post in Zamboanga,* informed Alvarez that the Sultan also had an adequate

---

* The significant role played by such deserters in providing technical assistance vital to the use and maintenance of large ordinance is noted by Barrantes:

number of rifles but lacked shot, especially for large ordinance, and had only a limited stock of English gunpowder.[43] The deserter mentioned the poor quality of the locally manufactured powder, which must also have been apparent to Herbert and the other factors upon their arrival at Jolo. In accordance with Dalrymple's advice, however, the trade in war stores was not limited to gunpowder and firearms; it also attempted to satisfy the Taosug preference for blade weapons of superior quality. In July 1774, Anda caustically noted that:

> the most recent English shipment from Europe contained a large quantity of a type of short dagger with a wavy blade, which in the east is called a Kris. Since it is widely used here, they have manufactured them in England.[44]

In the same despatch, the Governor Captain General again brought the recent establishment of the English within the dominion of the Sulu Sultanate to the attention of the home government and stressed the extent to which its trade with the Taosug and Magindanao had jeopardized the welfare of the archipelago. Anda's urgent plea for a quick resolution to the problem did not fall on deaf ears at Madrid. The Spanish Ambassador to the Court of St. James formally protested against the "illicit" trade of the East India Company's distant outpost.[45] Ironically, the fate of the Balambangan settlement had already been sealed by a faction of the Taosug aristocracy in Jolo when belatedly, the Court of Directors expressly forbade any further traffic in munitions there.*

Inter-Ethnic Rivalry and Outpost Intrigue

Access to foreign trade in the region after 1768 had significant bearing on the rise and fall of traditional states. At stake was the exclusive control

---

... although incapable of strict discipline, they already had a rudimentary understanding of military science thanks to the English and the deserters from our infantry and artillery at that time who instructed them in mounting artillery, repairing gun carriages, and in vastly improving the standard of Jolo's defences ...

Barrantes, *Guerras Piraticas,* p.100.

    * The Court of Directors (unaware of the destruction of Balambangan) wrote to Herbert's replacement:

> It has been signified to us from the Secretary of State that his most Catholic Majesty's Ambassador to the crown of Great Britain has complained that our late chief and council have furnished certain vessels, employed for piratical purposes, with arms, ammunition and other assistance, which have been used against the subjects and vessels of the Spaniards navigating the eastern seas to their great prejudice, contrary to that good faith and amity which should subsist between the two nations, we therefore require you, if it shall appear that the irregularities in question have been practical, to put an absolute and effectual stop to them, and, as you value a continuance in our service, to maintain inviolate that good harmony and understanding which ought ever to be maintained with his majesty's allies.

Court of Directors to the Balambangan Council, 25 Oct. 1775, IOL, H/118/12, p.609.

of European trade articles and commodities within the local exchange network. In particular, to monopolize the supply of European weapons and military stores, which could either confer or deny political, economic, and symbolic might, became the paramount objective of the Taosug of Jolo in the formative years of this external trade. While the Sultan and his close supporters encouraged the English to do business at Jolo's strategically located regional market, they fought aggressively to curtail the personal influence, private trade, and intrigue of Herbert and his council with other Taosug, and with the Magindanao and Iranun.

Sulu's ideal commercial position was offset by a precarious strategic situation in the struggle to gain effective control over the region's trade until the advent of sophisticated European weaponry. Any effort to assert its hegemony in the zone was resisted by the neighbouring Sultanates of Brunei and Cotabato and the Spanish maritime settlements on the southern Visayan frontier. Until the latter part of the eighteenth century, these three competitors had been able to circumscribe the Sulu Sultanate.

Sultan Bantilan expressed Taosug anxiety regarding Sulu's indigenous neighbours to Alexander Dalrymple in 1761: "he was more inclined to peace than war with the Spaniards as guarding against them prevented him from reducing to obedience the Borneons and opposing the Magindanaoe". When Dalrymple informed him that England was presently at peace with Spain, the Sultan said "he did not regard them [Spain] so much as the other two [Magindanao and Brunei] against either of whom he could not go to war without leaving Sooloo exposed to the attacks of the other".[46] Notably absent in this period was the low opinion in which the Brunei Sultanate would later be held in the first decades of the nineteenth century when it was on the defensive and its role in the regional exchange network drastically curtailed.

The trading settlement at Balambangan was established in the same year that the elderly Sultan Alimudin I (Azim-ud-Din) abdicated his authority in favour of one of his sons, Mohammad Israel. The new Sultan, who spoke Spanish and had spent a considerable period of time in Manila during his father's exile, was felt to be sympathetically inclined towards the Spaniards, and government officials in Manila believed the orderly transition of authority at Jolo to be a favourable sign.* Israel, however, recognized the primacy of external trade in the politics and economy of the region, as well as the threat it posed to himself and his people. His accession and the commencement of trade at Balambangan witnessed an increase not only of

---

* In 1773, Israel sent letters to both the English and the Dutch informing them that the legitimacy of his claim as the Sultan of Sulu had been recognized by all Taosug. See Sultan Mahamed Isreil to President and Council, 4 Dec. 1773, IOL, P/341/39, pp.718–19: AR, Kolonien Archief 3281, p.166.

raiding in the Philippine provinces but also of interethnic conflict between Taosug and the Magindanao with their Iranun mercenaries. Initially, a strategy of manipulating the conflicting interests of the Spanish and English to his best advantage enabled Sultan Mohammad Israel to prevent regional consolidation by the Magindanao through purchase of large quantities of English arms. In the end the Taosug resorted to the calculated use of raw power to resolve the region's political future.

Israel viewed with apprehension the independent activities of the factors at Balambangan who were determined to make the settlement an alternative market for the Chinese and Bugis traders who visited Jolo. His anxiety was not unwarranted. The trading outpost was in fact intended to be a conduit for the East India Company's trade to China through which Herbert and his council were supposed to rechannel the trade flow of the area, entering into commercial contracts with the captains of junks and the *nakodahs* of *prahus*.[47] Israel feared that if such an enterprise prospered, it would ultimately erode the basis of his authority over the traditional commerce of the Sultanate and hence undermine his support. Even before Balambangan was founded, a Company agent perceived Israel's distaste for the project:

> he behaves very civilly to the English, but I believe I may venture to say that, he does not approve of having them for such near neighbours as they are likely to be, for he always speaks with great reserve upon the subject.[48]

From his point of view, it became critical that the traffic in opium and arms be centred at Jolo instead of Balambangan. While the Sultan was adamant in not allowing the English to transfer their establishment from the inhospitable island to the mainland of Sulu,* he insisted that the inexperienced English factors conduct their trade at the market in Jolo, over which he exercised control. Asserting the Sultan's monopoly of control over foreign commerce, Israel also imposed a customs charge on all imports and exports of country trade vessels as well.

> ... the present Sultan seems to rather shew a jealousy of so near an English establishment as that of Balambangan, and has insisted that a duty of 5 per cent ad valorem on all commodities should be paid by private traders in his dominions ....[49]

The Magindanao had already proposed a unilateral treaty of friendship and alliance with the East India Company before Balambangan was

---

* Alimudin I told a Spanish officer from Zamboanga that Israel and the datus of Jolo informed the English that they ought to be satisfied with the site that had been chosen for the settlement at Balambangan or abandon the venture. While they refused to allow the English a piece of land on Jolo proper, they suggested that the English might occupy several of the many uninhabited Spanish islands. No.228, 18 July 1772, AGI, Filipinas 492; No.380, AGI, Filipinas 686.

established.* They saw in the Company a powerful ally who could assist them in maintaining their regional influence over against the Taosug, Spanish, and Dutch. In 1755 they had renewed in earnest their "war" against the Spanish, with devastating effect. In the Visayas, coastal trade stopped for years at a time, huge tracts of cultivable land were left fallow, and many villages on the coast were destroyed in raids or abandoned in fear. In the course of their desultory conflict against the Philippine archipelago, the Magindanao solicited aid from the English. In 1769, when Captain Savage Trotter visited Balambangan and Jolo on behalf of the East India Company, he conditionally offered assistance to the Sultan of Cotabato on behalf of his employers because he was convinced of the riverine realm's natural wealth in products for the China trade.[50] These plans received a severe setback in 1771, however, when the British Government issued a stern warning to the East India Company against assisting the Magindanao in their "war":

> ... I am ordered to recommend to you, that you give strict injunctions to your servants in India not to offer any violence to the Spaniards settled on Palawan, where they evidently had a footing in 1659 ... and likewise that they abstain from giving assistance to the Sultan of Mindanao in the war which he is represented as he allej to carry on against the Spaniards, who might justly look on such assistance as an act of hostility to the crown of Spain.[51]

As a result, the Magindanao were temporarily denied the direct assistance and recognition that linked the British Government in India to the Sulu Sultanate. The British were officially precluded from settling near or trading in munitions to the Cotabato Sultanate. The instructions, however, proved less than compelling on the spot and were ignored by the chief of Balambangan and private merchants who found it in their interest to deal with the Cotabato Sultanate. The friendship and business of the Magindanao and their Iranun congeries provided Herbert and his council with a useful foil against the apparent enmity of the Taosug.

It would appear that the Magindanao were principally supplied from Balambangan rather than by country traders. Herbert did not keep an official account of his contracts and purchases, and none of the actual settlement records which could detail the subtle shifts of political fortune involving the Taosug and Magindanao with Balambangan have survived.[52] It is known though that a large quantity of war stores, weapons, and trade goods were left by the British Company at the residence of the Sultan of Cotabato in 1772.[53]

---

* An early overture from the Sultan of Cotabato was made through an emissary who travelled to Manila during the English occupation. See explanation of the treaty with the king of Sooloo, 24 Mar. 1765, IOL. H/Misc/771/2, p.73.

The growing Taosug fear of their Muslim neighbours was linked to a corresponding disenchantment with the traders of Balambangan. While the young Sultan wanted to impede the development of Balambangan, he knew at the same time that he could not afford to alienate either the British Government in India or the occasional Calcutta merchant venturer in the growing conflict with the Magindanao.

Israel's talent for statecraft is evident in a letter he wrote in December 1773 announcing his accession and simultaneously requesting the governing authorities in Bengal to provide him with arms and technical assistance to combat the Brunei and Iranun of Southern Mindanao whom he labelled the "common enemies" of the East India Company and the Sultanate.

> ... I have to acquaint you of my coming to the government with the general consent of the heads of all the people here, and I hope the same will prove to the satisfaction and for the good of the Honourable Company, I do solicit your news as my greatest friend and allys. Shortly after having entered into the exercise of the government, I was embarrassed by frequent complaints of the Borneos and Mallaroes, enemys who cause a thousand distructions and barbarities to the subjects of the Honourable Company's possession as well as mine, which lays me under an absolute necessity of applying to your excellencies for a succour and assistance of military stores and ammunition, to enable me to establish a lasting peace with them. What I want is fifty barrels of gunpowder, two cannons, shot for the same and one hundred musquets and on my receiving the favour of these things, I shall remitt you its cost by the first ship that will sail for your place ....[54]

The request for such a large stock of gunpowder lends support to its reported shortage in Jolo during the previous year when Sergeant Major Manuel Alvarez compiled his profile of the community's defences.

Israel also portrayed the Magindanao and Iranun as being opposed to the interests of the Dutch in a letter the same year to the Governor of the Moluccas, reaffirming the friendship and trade of the Taosug with the Dutch "who have lived from the beginning in good relations with our forefathers":[55]

> We will further explain our attitudes as well as that of the Rulers of the Magindanao and Illanun which our esteemed friend should be well aware of; as it is the custom of the rulers of the Magindanao and Illanun to rob any people they meet either ashore or at sea. We are not of that kind and remain like our ancestors true to our friends ....[56]

The Sultan's diplomacy should be interpreted as an effort on his part to gain access to the technology and political support of the British and Dutch by establishing alliances which would involve the major European powers in Taosug political intrigue. His efforts proved unsuccessful for several reasons. While it was almost impossible for the factors and traders at Balambangan and Jolo to remain indifferent to shifts of fortune in regional politics,* this did not prove to be the case for distant governments. The benefits of such political involvement seemed more than dubious to the East India Company. Any reservations that the Company had concerning Israel's intentions towards its settlement were compounded by Herbert and his council, who deliberately portrayed the Sultan as a Spanish sympathizer who had established relations with the *presidio* of Zamboanga and encouraged trade between the fortress and his port. The British authorities did not grant his official request.

The Dutch, with greater experience in Southeast Asia, expressed interest in the prospects of commerce between Sulu, Menado, and Ternate but remained unconvinced of the sincerity of Israel's offer of friendship. From a letter written by the Governor of the Moluccas to the Resident of Menado, it is apparent that Israel was unable to allay completely their fear of the Taosug:

> We approve of the measures you have taken to totally prohibit the smuggling of these people [the Taosug]. Further, you are to encourage them to engage in friendly commerce, which ultimately if the Sultan were inclined towards could only benefit the Company. Meanwhile you must be extremely cautious of the Magindanao and Sulu who arrived in Manado ....[57]

It was at this point, when his authority was seriously threatened by Datus Alimudin and Sarapudin,† who were secretly supported by Herbert's regime, that Israel turned to the Spaniards for assistance against the Magindanao and Iranun. The leading members of Israel's faction, including his father, Alimudin I, and the Datus Molok, Teteng, and Mamancha, hoped that by enlisting the support of the *presidio* at Zamboanga in their conflict against the Magindanao, they might be able to sever the trade connection between Balambangan and Cotabato.[58] The Spanish at Zamboanga, who were long-standing antagonists of the Sultan of Cotabato, and who privately engaged in trade with Jolo, felt obliged to assist Israel against his more powerful

---

* The dilemma of Europeans attempting to engage in trade without becoming caught up in local politics was forcefully expressed by a Company agent at Jolo: "Merchants experienced in the Eastern trade say, that it is impossible to make any new establishments in these parts where the natives are in a constant state of war with one another, under their respective chiefs, without embracing the party of some one or other and it is upon such conditions only that any advantages can be obtained from them. That the countenance of a few Europeans is generally sufficient to throw the balance into any scale; and to give security to the reigning chief. That when the trade of those parts was in private hands they have been frequently obliged to give assistance to the person who called himself King against his enemies, or no trade could have been carried on." Intelligence from Xolo and Balambangan received from Mr.Majendei, 16 Oct. 1772, IOL, H/Misc/107/3, pp.34–35.

† Alimudin and Sarapudin, the "esteemed friends of the English", were the Company's agents in Jolo. The former was a nephew of Sultan Alimudin I while the latter was his son and a brother of Israel. No.3, Memorandum, Papers relating to the loss of Balambangan, IOL, H/Misc/165/28, p.315; No.380, 16 July 1774, AGI, Filipinas 686.

neighbours, if only to encourage the Taosug to act against the British settlement and the latent threat it posed to Spain's political influence in the region. Captain Udin, a Magindanao serving the Spanish garrison, told a superior officer at Zamboanga that in his opinion,

> ... the Datu and Joloanos ... strongly desire our friendship because presently they have incurred the enmity of the Magindanao, Iranun, and Brunei and are also fearful of the English. Now, they have no other source of protection, but the Spanish.[59]

The founding of an English trade centre within the dominion of the Sulu Sultanate had been cause for great alarm among the Spaniards. Highranking officials felt this sudden presence to be audacious in itself and the possible harbinger of a more ambitious political scheme that would endanger the future security of the colony. The possibility of exploiting a rift between the Taosug and British was very attractive, but the Manila authorities were less than convinced of Israel's posture towards the Spanish Crown.[60]

Hampered by the fact that his sole knowledge of the settlement had been assembled from secondary informants, fugitive captives or Taosug traders,[61] the Governor-General instructed the military Governor of Zamboanga to open a secret dialogue with the new Sultan. Sergeant Major Manuel Alvarez was a good choice for this delicate diplomatic mission.* Alvarez spent fifty-three days in Jolo exploring with Sultan Israel and other influential aristocrats the threat posed by the English settlement's trade and intrigue to the already waning authority of the Taosug, and to the security of the *presidio* at Zamboanga.

The Sultan made it clear to Alvarez that he lacked the strength to expel the British from his dominion. In exchange, however, for Spanish assistance to destroy the settlement, Israel implied that he would allow their troops to be garrisoned at a prearranged site within his jurisdiction. He also offered to free Taosug vessels and crews to sail with Spanish ships from Zamboanga against the Iranun of Mindanao and to allow the Spanish to manufacture patrol craft at Jolo on a large scale. Israel made this latter concession because the Sulu Sultanate was suddenly confronted with the task of constructing a sizeable number of vessels if it was to adequately protect its trade with China† which had been severely disrupted by Iranun raiding.[62]

---

* While skilled in the art of negotiation, the indefatigable Zamboangueono also managed to find time in the evening to provide lessons in the minuet which was extremely popular among the Taosug men and women of high birth. No.29, 28 Feb. 1773, AGI, Filipinas 687.

† Chinese traders were liable to be attacked within the region during periods of intense interethnic conflict. Majul has written, "Although in their wars or raids, the Sulus and Iranuns did not spare those Chinese settled among the native inhabitants in Spanish-held territories, they never captured or enslaved Chinese traders going to or coming from Sulu." Majul, *Muslims in the Philippines*, p.252. Chinese vessels in fact had been prevented from trading at Sulu *circa* 1773 because they feared being seized by Magindanao-provoked Iranun raiders.

Israel emphasized to Alvarez the need for immediate military assistance from Zamboanga to combat particular recalcitrant groups of Iranun that he had recently banished from islands within his dominion because they had been attacking his followers. In a letter to Simon de Anda, the Sultan labelled these maritime people allies of the Magindanao and emphasized the need for the Spanish to support the Taosug in their struggle with the Cotabato Sultanate.[63] Herbert was painfully aware of Alvarez's protracted stay in Jolo. He saw the implications of Spanish technical assistance and arms for extending Israel's personal authority at the expense of his current political rivals whether Taosug kindred, Magindanao-Iranun marauders, or European merchants.[64]

The Spanish Governor, acting on the advice of the commander of the *presidio* at Zamboanga, who was in close and sympathetic touch with Israel, was hopeful of concluding a treaty of friendship and commerce with the Sulu Sultanate that would allow the conditional introduction of Catholicism in the Taosug realm, the establishment of free trade between Manila and Jolo, and provision for a Spanish military presence.[65] In early 1774, a sizeable military expedition under the command of Colonel Juan Cencelli was despatched from Manila to establish friendly relations with Israel's Government, reconnoitre the Balambangan settlement, and carry out operations against Iranun communities on the south coast of Mindanao. The Governor instructed this seasoned veteran, whose career in the imperial army had spanned thirty years on several continents, to assist the Taosug against the Magindanao.[66] Simon de Anda was aware that the menacing circumstances compelling Sulu to negotiate directly with Manila could suddenly disappear if the English agents decided to provide Israel with munitions to curb Iranun raiding.[67]

The expedition was a dismal failure. It proved unsuccessful, not because of English interference but rather because of the spirit in which it was conducted by Cencelli who considered himself an exemplary professional soldier in the service of the crown and the cross.[68] He felt the expedition to be "quixotic" and, on this basis, summarily attempted to wreck the mission beyond all hope of a successful outcome in a series of deliberate moves. His unannounced arrival with a large well-equipped force in the Jolo roadstead, where he failed to provide the customary salutes, created an uproar among the Taosug which threatened violence. Israel's confidence in the Spanish was considerably shaken, and only partially restored through the offices of Espanol, the Governor of Zamboanga, whose belated message to the Sultan explained the untimely arrival of Cencelli's squadron at Jolo.[69]

Cencelli, however, viewed Jolo as the centre of a world fundamentally hostile to the interests of Spain and Catholicism—an Islamic world whose activities centred about piracy and slavery—and questioned the motives behind Israel's diplomatic overtures in a series of bitter exchanges with Espanol.[70] In his damning report to Spain he revealed not only that particular groups of Iranun traded at Jolo but also that the Governor and officers of the *presidio* of Zamboanga were involved intimately in the trade and politics of the Sulu Sultanate to the detriment of Manila's interests.[71] His unwillingness to commit troops, war vessels, and technical assistance on behalf of the Taosug and his ill-mannered behaviour further contributed towards the deterioration and ultimate collapse of the negotiations between the Taosug and Spanish. Cencelli's mission of "goodwill" had accomplished nothing on Israel's behalf. It further weakened the basis of his local support and heightened the tension in Jolo between the pro-Spanish faction that continued to follow the Sultan and the increasingly restive aristocratic element which was inclined towards the English of Balambangan.

By the end of 1774, the Sultan may well have determined to destroy Balambangan. Although his efforts to secure direct assistance from Manila had failed, Israel was secure in the knowledge that neither the Dutch nor the Spanish would interfere if the Taosug attacked the settlement. His political survival in Jolo, and the contest to gain control over the region's resources and trade network required nothing less. The incident responsible for precipitating the destruction of Balambangan in February 1775 was an angry dispute between Herbert and Datu Teteng, whom Cencelli described as "being between twenty and twenty-two years old, handsome, confident, extremely intelligent and possessed of a valorous reputation for which he [was] held in high esteem at Jolo".[72] The young *datu*, a first cousin of Israel, had been contracted by Herbert along with his followers and slaves to build houses and cut timber for the island's settlers. Teteng was indebted to Herbert and the factor insisted that he leave his slaves as security when he prepared to return to Sulu. He objected strongly to this demand, and in the ensuing argument was disarmed and humiliated in front of his followers by being placed in stocks.* Although released shortly afterwards and allowed to return with his slaves to Jolo, Teteng prepared to take revenge.[73]

Herbert carelessly chose to ignore the repeated warnings of possible Taosug reprisal and enabled Datu Teteng and Datu Timongon with several hundred followers and slaves to destroy the defenceless settlement with ease. Alimudin had sent Orang Kaya Bassal Udin from Sulu to Balambangan to inform Herbert of Teteng's plan several weeks prior to the attack. Herbert paid little attention to what he had been told and did nothing to improve

---

* He would later state to the Sultan and influential *datus* "that he had no other inducement for perpetrating the act against the English than their demanding his arms, which he thought was not only a reflection on his honour as an individual but a general one on that of the Sooloans". Extract of a letter from Mr.John Jesse resident at Borneo proper, 3 May 1775, IOL, H/Misc/165/28, p.355; a similar account is provided by Israel to the Dutch—see AR, Kolonien Archief 3337, pp.314–15.

Plan of the Settlement of Balambangan
When Taken by Surprise

A. The stockade mounting 9 guns, about 60 yards
   distance from the beach.
B. The military officers' house, about 200 yards
   distance from the guns.
C. The Sepoy Barracks, between which and the
   magazine enemy rushed in and seized the guns.
D. Thick bushes and fern, where the enemy are
   supposed to have lodged in the night.
E. The Secretary's offices.
F. Sulu prahus, hauled up on the beach from
   which the signal was made.
G. Bugis House, distant about 60 or 70 yards
   from the stockade.
H. Mr. Coles' house, and one of the Company's
   godowns.
I. The Company's large Godown.
J. Chinese Houses.
K. The chief's house.
L. The house at the point is distant about
   1 3/4 to 2 miles.
M. The road leading to the houses about 3/4 mile to
   back of the stockade.
N. Where the enemy, from the boats entered.

From a M.S. at the East-India Office Library.

the lax security of settlement. On the evening of 25 February 1775, one of Teteng's slaves graphically detailed the manner in which the attack was to be executed in the early hours of the following morning to a servant of an English factor in the settlement. This intelligence, though alarming, was ignored. Early the following morning after the Sepoys had grounded their arms and retired to the well to wash, the attack occurred:

> ... at gunfire in the morning the troops was ordered to lay down their arms ..., except the customary centinels, about ten minutes after the gun fired the soolooans imagined everybody was gone to sleep ..., when they made the signal, one of them run out of his boat with a fire-brand and set fire to the house, at the same time ... both partys run to the stockade and seized the guns those in ambush at the back got possession first, the centinel at the magazine discharged his piece ... they lanced him, the military officers was then in their houses and the Sepoys seeing themselves without their officers run off the hill ... the soolooans ..., immediately discharged the cannon ... down on the houses and the inhabitants on the beach: by this time the chief [Herbert] and some gentlemen ... had got down to the beach ... when one of the military officers came running from the stockade, calls out, all lost the soolooans are in possession of the guns ... upon this the inhabitants got on board the vessels as fast as possible, and the soolooans then directed their cannon against the vessels ...[74]

Significantly the demise of Balambangan also witnessed the beginning of a rapid decline of Magindanao influence in the region. The Cotabato Sultanate's power in the years between 1772 and 1775 had been precariously supported by the English Company trade and the loyalty of coastal dwelling Iranun. Subsequently unable to obtain trade goods directly, the riverine realm had to subordinate its economic interests and regional ambitions to those of the Taosug, upon whom they developed dependence in matters of foreign commerce. In this connection, the rapidly expanding external trade, with a proliferation of trading outposts in the Sulu Sultanate's sphere of influence, strengthened the Sultan's authority.

The military stores captured at Balambangan, which included 45 cannon of the calibres 8, 10, and 12 200 quintales of gunpowder, 22 000 rounds of ammunition, 228 rifles, 35 pistols, and 45 swords, fuelled the Taosug's drive to establish themselves decisively as the region's principal resource controllers and promoters of raiding related activities.[75] In retrospect this was recognized by Herbert,

> as you know it is no difficult matter to bribe which the soolooans now have in their power to do any of the pyratical tribes which infect those seas many of whom are intermarried with the different sects ....[76]

In the aftermath of Teteng's daring victory, the Cotabato realm was further weakened over the next several decades by the gradual movement of sizeable communities of Iranun who, attracted by the prospects of trade and the outfitting facilities provided by the Taosug at Sulu, shifted their residence and political affiliation from within the Magindanao orbit to islands within Sulu's domain.

The evolution of the Sulu Sultanate's dominion in the regionally fragmented world of the Magindanao, Iranun, and Brunei Malays is directly linked to the destruction of the Balambangan settlement and the expulsion of its British agents. The downfall of the trading station marked a critical turning-point in the development of Sulu, after which it evolved as the established centre for trade in the zone. The munitions traffic which continued to emanate from Bengal and Celebes despite the attack, would enable the Taosug leadership to consolidate wealth and power in their favour by 1800.

3

The External Trade of the Sulu Sultanate: Florescence, 1768–1848

THE COUNTRY TRADE

The significance of the country trade* as the principal source of the Canton remittance in the China trade from 1768 to 1800 was underscored in the works of Furber, Parkinson, and Greenberg decades ago.[1] Since then little has been added to our knowledge of this unofficial branch of Asian trade and the impact of its enterprising practitioners beyond the Straits of Malacca.[2] A considerable obstacle to this task remains the lack of documentation on their activities. The country trade was highly competitive, private, and often illicit; captains were rarely inclined to reveal details of either their cargoes or their trading locales when they put into the harbours of colonial capitals like Batavia and Manila. Memoirs, detailed logs, or private journals are virtually non-existent for the country trade to Brunei, Cotabato, Pasir, and Sulu, as few of these men wrote at any length of their trading experiences.

The arrival of country traders in the Sulu archipelago was related to events in India and North America which compelled Company servants, independent merchants, and the free mariners of Bengal to seek their fortunes in the development of private commerce in island Southeast Asia. A small number of British residents began to promote the country trade as a result of the abolition of the lucrative privileges of the inland trade of India in 1767, and the advent of the American War of Independence when free merchants and Company employees were prohibited from lending money or granting bills of exchange to foreign companies and traders.[3] By 1790 there were over fifteen agency houses in Calcutta whose wharfs and warehouses were described as "a sink of corruption and iniquity". One of these firms, Farley and Ferguson and Company, owned nine large sailing vessels and five other trading houses had at least two vessels each.[4]

In the absence of accurate statistics for country commerce from Calcutta to Jolo, we can only sketch the parameters of its development from fragmentary

---

* Private commerce between India, insular Southeast Asia, and China from the end of the seventeenth centruy until 1850 was known as the country trade.

archival sources. The country trade experienced unprecedented growth throughout Southeast Asia, and it is not unreasonable to assume that before 1800 the specific trend for the Sulu zone approximated the overall pattern. The Dutch shipping records for Batavia contain little documentation on the country trade at Sulu. Among the few examples of country vessels that put in at Batavia, known to have come from Jolo, were the 200 ton brigantine *King George* in 1769 and the small heavily armed brig *Hanna* which traded in the Sulu archipelago during the following year.[5] Neither ship provided cargo manifests to the local authorities, since no offloading took place.

We also learn of country ships at Jolo through East India Company despatches relating incidents between private traders and the Taosug. In 1771 Captain William Mercer,* the commander of a Bengal merchant vessel, was involved in a serious altercation with the Sultan of Sulu. Upon his return to Calcutta, he was cautioned by the Government "to avoid in any of his future dealings giving the Sultan or his people the least cause of dislike or dispute".[6] In the same year, Mohammed Israel discussed in a letter to the Company's agent at Balambangan the charge he intended to levy on the cargoes of vessels of "the captains and other private traders who come here from time to time".[7]

Information regarding country traders at Sulu was occasionally provided by fugitive captives who had fled from Jolo to the *presidio* at Zamboanga. It was in this fashion that the Spanish learnt of the presence of a heavily armed, triple-masted merchantman at Sulu. The large vessel, which had arrived on 27 September 1780, had a mixed crew of upward of a hundred men, mainly Lascars, with a sizeable number of "Manila men" (Tagalogs), and several deserters from Zamboanga. It was accompanied by a small single-masted sailing vessel equipped with sixteen swivel guns which was used to transship trade goods and to procure produce among the adjacent islands.[8] During the course of a three-month stay, its captain traded with the Taosug of Jolo and transacted business from the deck of his ship with Iranun vessels. When the ship left for an unknown destination in December, another one already had arrived to take its place.[9]

While it appears the majority of the vessels were private, ships' logs reveal that even East India Company vessels stopped in the Sulu archipelago on their homeward journey to replenish their supply of fresh water and beef and conduct private trade. The Company packet *Fox* spent five days in the

---

* William Mercer, who arrived in India in 1767 and quickly established a good reputation as a ship captain, was perhaps related to Thomas Mercer the captain of several country ships between 1772 and 1774 to Kedah, Selangor, and Pasir. See AR, Kolonien Archief 3283, 605; Bassett, "British Commercial and Strategic Interest in the Malay Peninsula During the Late Eighteenth Century", p.138.

Jolo roadstead in May of 1782 while in passage from Macao to Calcutta.[10]
During the following year, the *Antelope* spent a month trading among the
Samal inhabited islands of Tapian Tana and Cagayan de Sulu.[11]

Between 1768 and 1785, the scant evidence culled from harbour reports,
official despatches, ships' logs, and the testimonies of fugitive captives
suggests that a continuous flow of country vessels visited Sulu. In these
years, private traders also conducted considerable commerce with the Bugis
at Pasir who annually traded English wares to immigrant Taosug settled at
river mouths on the east Bornean coast and at Jolo and Sarangani island.* In
the course of the next two decades, brigantines, barques, and larger country
vessels sailing from Calcutta and Penang visited the Sulu Sultanate with
some regularity, although their number in any one year would appear to have
seldom exceeded four.

The Conduct of the Country Trade

Sulu's trade attracted country captains with their square-rigged boats
year round. However, in an age when the science of hydrography was still
in its infancy, the route between Calcutta and Canton via Sulu was long
and hazardous. It took country traders into a labryinthine world of islands
and seas unsurveyed by European navigators. The available charts were
of little assistance, failing to note even the most prominent reefs, shoals,
and headlands to be encountered. This factor, coupled with the uncertain
character of winds and currents in the Celebes Sea, the Makassar strait, and
the Palawan passage, made it almost impossible to complete an average
journey in less than a year.

Country vessels appear to have frequented Sulu either early in March or
late in the year after the junks had already left for the main land. The timing
of their arrival at Jolo was critical. Captains preferred not to trade there
at the same time as other merchants because of the stiff competition then
offered by the Chinese, Spanish, and Portuguese. Instead they attempted to
preempt the demand for Sulu produce. They arrived early to trade a month
or two before the formal season began or visited the port after all business
had ceased, to acquire the remaining stocks of sea cucumber, pearl shell,
and bird's nest and encourage the local collection of produce in the outer
islands. Thus, by trading out of season, country captains arrived in Canton
at a critical time when the supply of Sulu produce in the local market had
begun to dwindle and would not be replenished for another four to five

---

* The harbour records for Batavia list the following English vessels as having visited
Pasir in the short span of three years: *Fortunate* (1773), *Dolphin* (1773), *Crescent* (1773),
Royal Admiral (1775), *Devonshire* (1776). See AR, Kolonien Archief 3259, 3283, 3315, 3341.

months. Their cargoes were bargained for at higher prices and quickly sold to Chinese merchants.

When a country vessel arrived at Jolo, a port duty was immediately laid upon the cargo by the Sultan in consultation with the *ruma bichara*. Since these vessels were transient and could not be relied upon to return and since they carried goods coveted by the Taosug—war stores, opium, and textiles— their hosts were liable to extort as much as they possibly could from the itinerant captains. An impost of at least 5 per cent was levied on the cargoes of private vessels after 1771 as a result of the dissatisfaction of leading *datus* in Jolo over the custom duties captains had been willing to pay up until then.[12] Efforts to impose higher imposts were a common cause for conflict between the Sultan and country traders, who often owned or had a partial interest in the ship and its cargo, and therefore personally stood to lose a great deal.[13] This was a traffic which entailed high risks and high gains for the trader, but more so for his customers, since the political careers of Taosug on the coast and ultimately the survival of the state depended upon their monopolizing the purchase of war stores. The *datus'* economic role as the redistributors of vital resources—arms, powder, and lead—was essential to the maintenance of their hegemony in the region. Under such circumstances, the masters of country vessels were obliged to deal almost exclusively with the Sultan and several aristocratic officials who controlled external trade. Because of their efforts to limit the range of market opportunities available to country traders at Jolo by price fixing and restricting their accessibility to rival Taosug and Chinese in trade, the Sultan and *datus* incurred the resentment and wrath of these merchant-venturers. It has already been noted that in 1771, Captain William Mercer had an acrimonious dispute with the Sultan and was "so conscious of his bad behaviour that he never afterwards ventured on shore".[14]

In a controversial testimony which purported to defend his commercial transactions at Sulu in July 1797, the commander of the *Gloucester,* George Smith, revealed the extreme difficulty Sultan Sharaf ud-Din had in restraining private trade between the English and other inhabitants of Jolo, who were at once his subjects and chief rivals in commerce:

> At the island of Sooloo I certainly had transactions both with the Sultan, and with one Laxamana a merchant. Those with the former were finally concluded before I left the island with the latter my intercourse was confidential. But as, in a case of this kind, everything must be told: I do not conceal that his intention was to smuggle some goods which I had to deliver to him and that for this purpose he put off receiving them, until I should be about to sail.[15]

As is evident in Smith's statement, an important part of the trade was conducted by captains from the security of their heavily armed vessels. They neither contracted a permanent market on shore nor distributed much of their freight on extended credit towards a return cargo for the following year. Trade was limited to the direct exchange of high quality produce for European and Bengal manufactures. By trading out of season, with no advance notice and sometimes remaining for only a week or two, country captains could not realistically expect to obtain either the variety or the volume of certain kinds of natural produce, which were more readily available at other times of the year. The unusually brief duration of some merchants' visits, the frenetic pace at which such trade must have been conducted, and the unpredictable availability of local produce in Jolo, is disclosed in a single sentence written by Smith to Roebuck-Abbot and Company, who financed several vessels in the country trade to the Moluccas and Sulu after 1795: "I remained eleven days here [Jolo] and sold a great part of the goods, and got bird's nest in return, but not any wax to be procured, it being too early in the season."[16]

Since cargoes could not always be furnished at Jolo, country traders had to be prepared to risk accompanying *datus* to their districts in other parts of the archipelago. In 1821, Lieutenant William Spiers, an officer of the Royal Navy on leave of absence, conducted a trading voyage in the *Seaflower* from Bengal to Sulu. On 2 August, several weeks after his arrival at Jolo, he left for the Tawi-Tawi group with one of the *datus* "for a large quantity of eastern produce [tortoise shell, pearl shell, wax, and brass guns] which he said he had collected at the islands of which he was rajah".[17]

Country Freight: Ironmongery and Textiles

The cargoes of country vessels were made up of a variety of English manufactures and Bengal commodities catering to the needs of the Taosug, and to a lesser extent Jolo's Chinese community and Bugis traders who had settled along the rim of the Celebes sea. The earliest detailed information on the freight that country vessels carried to Sulu is provided in the indent compiled by Dalrymple when he visited Jolo in 1761. Besides war stores, the Taosug nobility professed to him a particular interest in British manufactured brassware, ornamental cloth, fine lace, yellow, blue, red, and green broadcloth, small carpets, glassware, and some iron, steel, and soft white lead.[18] In drawing up this order of goods, expanded upon by country traders over the next several decades, Dalrymple added that the introduction of the boat compass "would be a very acceptable commodity and if well made not only every prow and boat would be glad of them but perhaps even the Chinese junks"—"Our compasses in their construction are better adapted for use than the Chinese compasses which almost all the Sooloo boats and Bugguese prows now have."[19] When Captain Trotter visited Jolo eight years later, he added knives, hatchets, and ordinary articles of cutlery to the growing list of manufactured items which were readily saleable to the Taosug.[20]

Apart from opium, textiles (fine muslins, madras chintz, coloured long cloth, and coarse cotton stuffs) were the single most valuable items to be obtained in Bengal by country traders bound for the Sulu archipelago. Dalrymple's list of 1761 included fourteen different types of Indian cloth for which there was already a potential market at this early stage of trade. The textiles he mentioned varied in quantity from a few pieces to several hundred and in value from as little as two dollars per piece to twenty dollars.[21] In the opinion of Captain Trotter it was blue linens that could account for the bulk of Sulu's textile consumption.[22] Forrest provided a brief but comprehensive list of the fabrics that were marketable among the Magindanao. Their tastes were not dissimilar to the Taosug upon whom they had come to rely for obtaining textiles by the end of the eighteenth century. At Cotabato in 1775, "all kinds of Indostan cloth answer well ..., especially long cloth ordinary, white, blue, and red handkerchiefs of all kinds; chintz preferably, with dark grounds; [and] Surat goods of most sorts".[23]

In the several decades following Dalrymple's involvement with the Sulu Sultanate, imports were gradually modified as private traders adapted to Taosug preference for particular Western manufactures and Indian commodities. By 1792 the following articles were recommended to be carried for trade to Sulu: "Bengal chintz, white cloth, palempores, any coarse piece of goods of India, opium, cutlery of the cheap kinds, knives, scissors, razors, small looking glasses, spy-glasses for day and night, perfumes, essence of lavender, essence of lemon, curious toys, and a few fine goods."[24] Although war stores were conspicuously absent from the above list, in Milburn's *Oriental Commerce,* published two decades later, they are openly acknowledged as staple articles of trade between India and Sulu.[25]

The exports of country traders from Sulu were chiefly natural produce, small in bulk and highly prized by the Chinese. Their cargoes consisted of marine-jungle products, spices, and locally handcrafted goods. Sultan Bantilan (Muizz un-Din) furnished Dalrymple with a list of thirty-seven products of Sulu and its immediate dependencies that English traders could expect to purchase at Jolo. Among the more important items mentioned, for which there was a constant demand in China between 1760 and 1840, were: "pearls, tortoise shell, *tripang,* mother of pearl, shark's fin, bird's nest, wax, camphor, cinnamon, pepper, cocoa, rattans, and ebony".[26] For private traders these were to remain the principal items in their traffic from Sulu to Canton and Singapore until well beyond 1850.

High Risks, High Gains

The conduct of private trade with the Taosug involved risks, and personal fortunes could be won or lost during the course of a single voyage. The hazards of the trade demanded that country vessels be swift, heavily armed, and competently manned. Parkinson described the ideal country ship as between 200 and 300 tons, carrying eighteen to twenty-two guns on a flush deck, with a fighting complement of one sergeant, two corporals, two drummers, a fifer, and twenty sepoys in addition to its crew.[27] A captain who chose to undertake a journey to Sulu in a small, ill-manned and illequipped vessel, was liable to be attacked by Taosug bent on seizing the ship's cargo.

In later years, captains were cautioned regarding the conditions of trade at Sulu in Horsburgh's *India Directory*, an indispensable, but biased, reference for country traders:

> Bullocks are plentiful, of good quality, and at a moderate price. Poultry and livestock of all kinds, with abundance of vegetables and fruits may be procured; also food and water. But the inhabitants are a treacherous race, and must be carefully watched: it is not adviseable to touch here in a small ship to procure supplies or to trade unless well armed, and prepared to resist any attack that may be made by the natives.[28]

Horsburgh labelled the Taosug a "dangerous people" with whom to conduct trade, yet he failed to include any guidelines of conduct for country captains in their dealings at Jolo, some of whom were aptly described as "men of desperate fortune".[29]

The trade was indeed hazardous, but the profits to be made by those who freighted war stores, opium, and textiles, were uncommonly high. It is not difficult to see why private traders were willing to expose themselves to a long, perilous voyage in trade to the Sultanate. A Company agent at Balambangan and Jolo wrote:

> the natives of Xolo, ... love finery, have all the appearance of riches, and will give any price for such goods as is fit for that market; [and] ... the large profit is a temptation for the merchant to run all risk.[30]

The net profit on muskets, flints, shot, gunpowder, and saltpetre was well in excess of 100 per cent. Flat iron and soft white lead also yielded at least double their original cost.[31] The Spanish crown had prohibited trade in iron and lead in the Philippine archipelago; these metals could purchase gold from the Magindanao.[32] Brassware, glassware, hardware, and other manufactured articles, whether scissors, pins and needles, or mirrors, were frequently purchased by Taosug at 100 per cent above cost.[33] The profit to be earned from traffic in opium at Sulu was liable to be in excess of 100 per cent.[34]

Beginning with Dalrymple's visit, there was a continuous demand in the Sulu Sultanate for textiles manufactured in India. Coarse Madras piece goods in a variety of colours, especially blue and white, and finer fabrics from the Coromandel coast, particularly brightly coloured handkerchiefs, when exchanged at Jolo brought returns of between 100 and 200 per cent on investment.[35] These percentages should not be construed as exceptional.They show the average net gain derived on imported articles but do not illustrate the extraordinary fortunes that were sometimes made at Sulu. Hunt reveals the risks and the potentially high profit margin in the trade between Bengal and Sulu. Forced to sell his cargo at a loss, he observed:

> ... the competition excited in the market by the arrival of three Chinese junks, three vessels from Manilla and Olo-Olo (Iloilo) and subsequently by the brig *Thainstone,* captain Peters from Penang, not only considerably retarded the sales of the honourable Company's cargo, but the latter vessel importing direct from Bengal and thus being able to undersell us ... compelled me to buy produce at rates proportionately high to stand the competition; our cargo was likewise ill assorted much too small a proportion of blue and white cloths and these from Bengal instead of Madras, in some cases we have been compelled ... to pay the Datoes an unreasonable price for their produce [and] on other occasions forced to give credit and receive whatever they chose to pay us in return ... notwithstanding these obstacles, had the goods been laid in at Bengal and Madras instead of Batavia, the profits on the voyage must have turned out considerable; for by a comparative view of the Bengal, Madras and Europe prices the whole of the goods sold by me bear an advance of *400 to 600 per cent* on the original prime cost ....[36]

Success in the country trade required exceptional seafaring skills as well as familiarity with the Malay language and local custom. It was a trade for neither the foolhardy nor the novice. The indispensable knowledge and experience these veterans acquired was rarely divulged to others even within the same trading firm. William King, who traded in Lombok and Kutai, and whose name is still remembered after a century and a quarter in the oral traditions of Bali, described some of the essential attributes of a successful country trader:

> [to] be well acquainted and on good terms with the Rajahs, conversant with the trade, laws, particularities of the natives and their method of doing business as well as being well aclimatized (as the climate is at times very fatal to European constitutions) and another great requisite in a person trading in these countries is an endless stock of patience without which all other qualities are of no avail.[37]

The favourable outcome of a venture at Jolo depended on how thoroughly a captain had prepared his ship for the voyage, and the extent to which he avoided incident, once on the spot. In the atmosphere that existed at Sulu, patience was often strained to breaking-point, and both parties were capable of fraud, deception, and violence in the conduct of trade. Mercantile activities between English merchants and Taosug were notable for their lack of restraint because of the vested interests—commercial and political—at stake.

There were numerous casualties in the trade. The number of attempted seizures of private vessels at Sulu reflected not only the audacity of *datus* rising in power and personal fortune but their justifiable suspicions of traders, whose belligerence and indiscretion in their dealings with Taosug was sufficient provocation.

It is worth examining at some length the attempted seizure of the English country vessel, *Gloucester*, for what it reveals about the conduct of private trade at Jolo. In May of 1798 its captain, George Smith,* who had made at least two journeys to Sulu prior to 1797 on behalf of Roebuck, Abbot and Company, had serious charges brought against him by his chief officers. They accused him of defrauding a considerable sum of money from the *Laxamana*, a leading Taosug merchant.[38]

During the first nine days the *Gloucester* was in Jolo, the trade had been brisk. The captain, in his dealings with the Sultan and the Laxamana, received a great quantity of nests in addition to three valuable pearls belonging to the latter as a deposit, one of which was reputedly worth 2,500 Spanish dollars. In the initial week of trade, the Taosug had "behav'd to us in an unexampled attentive manner, supplying us with all our wants, and shewing us every attention in their powers".[39] According to the sworn testimonies of Smith's officers, matters dramatically changed over the following days. During the next two evenings when the *Laxamana* was on board the *Gloucester* with a fresh supply of bird's nest, the captain was alleged to have told him that he did not intend to sail for several days. Shortly after the *Laxamana* left the vessel, on the evening of the eleventh day, Smith suddenly gave the order to hoist the anchor and set sail. The vessel made little headway during the night and was almost becalmed several miles from Jolo when the *Laxamana* approached with two or three heavily armed vessels. A writer sent with the ship by Mr. Roebuck to Ambon describes what ensued.

> ... when near enough, he [Laxamana] demanded payment of the goods he had given the captain, the restitution of the three pearls all of which I think he valued at about 10,000 Spanish dollars. At first the captain seemed unwilling to part with his booty, and prepared the guns, muskets, etcetera, but a few prows being seen offshore, and Laxamana preparing his lances ... as I suppose to engage the ship, and Mr. Porter representing to the captain the danger he exposed the ship and her company to, he at last was induced to give up the pearls and two or three bales of cloth with a written paper for the Sultan the contents of which none of us knew, he telling Mr. Porter it was wrote in

---

* George Smith, a resident of Calcutta, briefly held partial Spanish contracts for the Philippine Company with the Bengal firm of Graham & Mabroys. He went bankrupt in 1787. Cheong Weng Eang, "Changing the Rules of the Game: The India-Manila Trade: 1785–1809", p.5.

Spanish; and with this Laxamana went away ...; your ship was very near cut off, and I much fear for the fate of any other English vessel that may hereafter happen to touch at that port.[40]

Captain Smith admitted having conducted private trade with the *Laxamana* (at the expense of his employers) but denied the more serious charge of having attempted to rob him. In Smith's version the confrontation was described as follows:

What accidents prevented Laxamana from coming at the time appointed I do not know. He came in the morning, but ... under suspicious circumstances. I could easily suppose that having been prevented from landing the goods in the way he meant, it might be necessary to cloak his design under the appearances alluded to; but I did not think it safe to trust him, and therefore as in the eastern trade is always usual, I prepared for the defence; however when his canoe came up, I delivered the goods agreed upon, and also a pearl of his which ... the deponents have multiplied into three pearls and they have magnified the deposit from 1,500 dollars ... to several thousands.[41]

Under threat of prosecution, he subsequently admitted to his employers that there were in fact some errors in his accounts but was reticent on the subject of his private trade activities at Sulu.[42] The impression remained that part of Smith's debt to the Taosug *datu* remained unsatisfied.

Other country captains were less fortunate than Smith. Three years after Smith's visit, while the country ship *Ruby* was at anchor in Jolo's roadstead with a cargo of gunpowder, cloth, and spices, her captain and several crew members were killed in an obscure incident on shore. The vessel managed a safe exit but not before shelling several large *prahus* in the roadstead. Five Taosug were killed in the incident on shore and ten in the subsequent cannonade including the son of one of the leading *datus*.[43]

A similar scenario, in which the Taosug were the apparent assailants, involved the *Seaflower*, a vessel of sixteen guns, which visited Sulu from Bengal in July of 1821. During the ten days the vessel was at Jolo, Lieutenant Spiers, its commander, formed the opinion that the atmosphere was relaxed and calm. He was repeatedly told by Taosug that his "countrymen who had visited that place, had in every instance behaved with the strictest good faith in all their dealings there".[44] When Spiers left for Tawi-Tawi to procure a cargo that he had contracted for with a *datu* in Jolo, and which was to be paid for by him upon delivery in the islands, he was anxious about his reception there. Sultan Ali ud-Din allayed his fear and provided him with a letter addressed to his subjects, which directed them to "treat us as friends wherever we went and render us all the assistance in their power if we stood in need of it".[45]

The *datu* who accompanied the vessel remained on board the *Seaflower* for nearly two weeks, and Spiers developed considerable confidence in him. Ten days after leaving Jolo, the country trader reached the environs of Tawi-Tawi. The Datu Molok arrived from Jolo shortly afterwards with several large *prahus*. The *Seaflower* was anchored near Boona-Boona, where brass cannon and other cargo were being brought to the vessel. Spiers described what ensued when the Taosug boarded his ship:

> Datto Mollok the Raja Bander of Sooloo ... was most lavish in his protestation of friendship embracing me .... He even called for the Sultan's letter and shewd it all around. He purchased a number of articles, etc. and drank at my table in the most friendly way; all appeared to be best of friends; our people had just sat down to dinner when at a signal by Datto Mollok, those on board drew their cresses, those alongside jumped on board .... after a short but very desperate conflict, it pleased the Almighty God to give us the victory, ... their loss could not have been less than 40 to 50 killed among whom was the Datto Mollok and two of the headmen of the Orang Bajoos who I believe were forced into the Villainous attempt much against their will.[46]

Four of the crew were killed.

The Volume of Country Trade to Jolo

It was "not easy to ascertain the exact quantum of the cargoes [from Bengal] that [found] their way into the islands in the vicinity of Felicia [Sulu zone]".[47] Several sources, spanning three-quarters of a century can be used however to illustrate the increased Taosug demand for European manufactures and Indian commodities and provide at least an approximate measure of the rapid growth of the country trade between 1760 and 1840.[48] These figures also betray the powerful impact of the country trade on the material culture of the Taosug and their growing dependence on the free traders.

A comparison of the indent provided by Sultan Bantilan (Muizz un-Din) to Dalrymple in 1761 with Hunt's published figures for Sulu in 1814, and a list of goods for Jolo's market given to an American mariner from Salem by Datu Emir Bahar, *circa* 1835, provides a useful index of the rate of growth of war stores, opium, textiles, and other imported articles in the country trade at Sulu.*

The Taosug requested ten thousand dollars worth of arms and ammunition from Dalrymple in 1761. This included heavy ordinance (four 6-pound cannon) but no other items were specified in detail. Hunt provides no figures for war stores and states simply that they "[would] sell, but these [were]

---

* There are difficulties involved in undertaking a comparison of such disparate sources. The omission of particular articles or their lack of differentiation, particularly the failure to distinguish between various types (i.e., iron—flat iron, bolts, bars, and balls) and the innumerable varieties of woven cotton stuffs which were variously labelled at different times by both traders and the Taosug, has made a meaningful comparison especially difficult in some cases. See Appendix D.

dangerous articles of traffic and ought to be discouraged".[49] Two decades later, Gamaliel Ward, captain of the Spanish brig *Leonidas,* reveals the extent to which the arms trade had been expanded at Jolo since Dalrymple's time. The *datus'* request included: "1,000 25-pound kegs of gunpowder, 6 swivel guns, 6 large cannon preferably brass, 600 muskets, 100 pistols, 4 bags of shot of varying sizes, gun flints, 2 dozen boxes of percussion caps and 8 dozen matchlets".[50] By 1835, gunpowder and muskets were the principal items desired by Taosug *datus.* These figures must be considered as only a partial estimate of the volume of war stores furnished at Sulu's market, because large quantities of gunpowder and firearms reached the Taosug as a consequence of Bugis enterprise.

Between 1761 and 1835, there was a reduction in the amount of crude iron and lead used in Jolo. The Taosug preferred by 1835 finished cast iron and lead articles in the form of small bars, bolts, and shot. This trend does not mean that the volume of these imported metals decreased. On the contrary, there is evidence which suggests that Spanish traders from Manila obtained English iron at Sulu in quantities which exceeded the amount regularly used by the Taosug.*

It has already been mentioned that opium was not among the articles the Taosug desired from Bengal in 1761. By the time of Hunt's visit, annual consumption had risen to six chests of Benares opium, and the import of this article was to increase fivefold over the next twenty years. The Tau Gimba scornfully observed that the rapid spread of the opium eating habit among the coastal populace was responsible for their declining martial spirit.[51]

A comparison of Dalrymple's figures for Indian textiles with those of Hunt's list (Appendix D) reveal that by 1814 the variety and the volume of woven cotton fabrics imported to Jolo was at least twice as great. Although the volume of muslins showed no sizeable increase, and the consumption of fine bleached moores cloth was drastically reduced, the importation of Madras chintz had increased by 100 per cent, long blue cloth by 150 per cent, and white Surat cloth (caftas) twentyfold—from 200 pieces in 1761 to 4,000 pieces in 1814.

The Taosug demand for imported cloth had increased considerably and had become remarkably discriminating by 1814. Fourteen types of cloth from Coromandel, Bengal, and Surat, which had not been included in Dalrymple's indent, and four sorts of handkerchiefs were differentiated in

---

* In 1817 the following Spanish vessels exported nearly twice the volume of iron listed by Hunt as Sulu's annual consumption in 1814; the brigantine *Vigilante,* 300 piculs of iron valued at 1,200 pesos; the pontin *Nuestra Senora del Carmen,* 20 piculs of iron, valued at 277 pesos; and the pontin *San Pascual,* 71 piculs of bar iron valued at 277 pesos. Hunt, "Some Particulars Relating to Sulo", p.47; Estado, no.77, AGI, Filipinas 511.

Hunt's list. Eight of these fabrics, and Pulicat, Madras, and Ventepollam handkerchiefs were each imported in quantities of a thousand or more pieces a year. The growth in the textile trade must have continued to increase at least in proportion to its development from 1761 to 1814. Ward's 1835 list of potential consumption of American cloth alone indicated increases in demand for certain types of cloth. The total level of commerce in textiles in that period must have doubled if we assume a sustained volume for Indian fabrics exported on native *prahus* and European sailing ships from Singapore and Penang to Sulu.

The Inheritors: Salem Traders and Merchant-Venturers

By the second decade of the nineteenth century, a substantial portion of the country trade had been taken over by rival Spanish, Portuguese, and American traders. Bengal vessels continued to visit Sulu, but without a trading outpost in the region they were at a severe disadvantage and had to leave the full potential of Jolo's commercial development to other traders who not only brought arms and textiles but sugar, rice, tobacco, and other staples for Sulu's expanding population. This trend was already discernible within the zone by 1804: "a great part of ... [this] trade ... [say one half] has of late years been engrossed by the Dutch, the Portuguese, the Spaniards and Americans, in consequence of the English not possessing any commercial depot, or port of exchange in those countries".[52] These competitors did not rearrange the conditions of the country trade at Jolo but simply increased the tempo of external trade with the Sultanate and extended its commercial pattern to Manila, Macao, and Singapore.

I would like to examine briefly here American private commerce at Jolo which gave further impetus to the importance of Sulu in regional trade. For Sulu, the role of American commerce was analogous to that of the English country trade and should be interpreted within the framework of the wider pattern of private trade with the Sultanate which had its origins in Bengal. The munitions traffic to the Sulu Sultanate, pioneered by the free traders of Calcutta, was broadened by Yankee maritime activity after 1820. It was the island-hopping Salem vessels which traded along the periphery of the Malay world at Ceram, Ceram Laut, and Goram that later included Sulu on their route to Canton. In 1811, Stamford Raffles described these "commercial interlopers" who threatened British political influence and commercial interests in the outer islands:

> The Americans wherever they go, as they have no object but commercial adventure, are by no means scrupulous how they acquire their profits, and as firearms are in the highest request especially among the more easterly isles these would be considered as the most profitable articles. They have already filled the different clusters of islands in the South seas with firearms, and they would not fail to do the same in the different eastern islands.[53]

It was well known that Americans had little to offer in Canton except furs, agricultural and domestic implements, articles of coarse cutlery, and dollars. Desperately in need of products more attractive on the Chinese market, such as bird's nest, *tripang*, and tortoise shell, the New England traders supplied powder, shot, and rifles to the Taosug and Magindanao. By 1829 firearms had become their stock in trade. According to an article published in the *Singapore Chronicle:*

> Almost all the vessels leaving the ports of the U.S. for China, convey muskets, pistols, swords and gunpowder, which they sell on their outward passage to the natives and other inhabitants of Palawan and Magindano.[54]

The article went on to assert, although there is little direct evidence to support the allegation, that

> there are Americans living on both these islands who make the necessary arrangements, and who have several small native vessels, constantly sailing about the usual tracks of ships to China in the proper season, for the sole purpose of meeting American vessels and taking from them their cargoes of warlike stores....[55]

It was not uncommon in this period to find adventurous American and English mariners in the employ of European agency houses, sailing in native craft and small brigs and schooners throughout the archipelago. G.W. Earl mentions one of them:

> A small Spanish brig from Manilla, owned and commanded by an American, touched at the Sulus in 1834 and brought a valuable cargo of pearl shell to Singapore. She made the same voyage again the following year....[56]

The vessel that Earl was referring to was undoubtedly the Spanish brig *Leonidas* of Manila. In 1836 the *Leonidas* visited Zamboanga and traded at Jolo from the beginning of March to the end of August.[57] Her captain, Gamaliel Ward, was given a letter signed by the Datu Emir Bahar soliciting private trade and a treaty of friendship and commerce with the United States.[58] Ward still was trading privately in Sulu six years later when Wilkes visited Jolo for several days and managed to negotiate a treaty on behalf of the U.S. Government for trade and protection of American commerce with the Sulu Sultanate:

> Besides the trade with China, there is a very considerable one with Manilla in small articles and I found one of our countrymen engaged in this traffic, under the Spanish flag. To him I am indebted for much information that his opportunities for observation had given him.[59]

William Wyndham, an English mariner, firmly established Sulu's trade link with Singapore during these same years. He began his career in the Philippine archipelago as a mate on a Spanish brig trading from Manila to the Moluccas and subsequently sailed as the commander of various vessels which traded throughout the eastern archipelago but particularly to Sulu.[60] By 1842 the shrewd, self-educated trader owned his own schooner, the *Velocipede,* and had settled at Sulu.[61] From his commercial establishment in Jolo's Chinese community, he frequented the pearl banks near Tawi-Tawi and navigated as far as the Aru islands to procure tortoise shell and mother of pearl for customers in Singapore. Married to a *mestiza* from Iloilo, Wyndham spoke fluent Taosug and had acquired considerable status and authority in Jolo. He was described by Spenser St.John in 1848 as being "dressed in Malay costume and from long residence among them, he had assumed much of both the appearance and manner of a native".[62]

After 1820, it was the Salem skippers and men like Ward and Wyndham who dealt almost exclusively in firearms, cloth, and opium at Sulu. Export manifests rarely disclosed whether their vessels were carrying munitions. It is possible that listings such as "sundries", "ironmongery", "ballast" or "hardware" were conveniently used to mask arms shipments.[63] American captains were adamant in their refusal to provide detailed freight lists to their own consular representatives in the Philippines. The American consul in Manila noted their lack of cooperation in a letter to the State Department in 1823:

> I find it extremely difficult to ascertain the exact amount of the importation and exportation from this island. The commanders and supercargoes of American vessels are very unwilling to give me a list of their cargoes and I have no instructions to compel them to give me the exact amount....[64]

An identical letter was written again towards the end of the following year. In March of 1829, the Salem brig *Quill* called at Manila. Among the articles declared were: 290 barrels of gunpowder, 144 shotguns, 24 large boxes of axes, 150 pounds of shot for the shotguns, 120 dozen axe handles.[65] Although the ship's destination was not stated, the inclusion of these items in the cargo and the fact that March was the beginning of the official trading season at Sulu suggest that the Sultanate may well have been included on its itinerary.

For more than a quarter of a century, Wyndham was to be one of the Taosug's most reliable suppliers of munitions, opium, and cotton cloth. He made one and sometimes several trips to Singapore each year where he traded natural produce of Sulu. In January 1848, the following note appeared under the heading "Tortoise shell" in the weekly market report of the *Straits Times* and *Singapore Journal of Commerce:* "The importation of 4 piculs from Sooloo per Velocipede had been taken in barter for Benares Opium; the latter at Duros 550 per chest and the shell at Duros 425 per picul".[66] Wyndham was repeatedly accused of trafficking in munitions and saltpetre by Spanish captains who traded at Jolo, and the Spanish consul in Singapore was convinced that on more than one occasion he freighted firearms from the port to Sulu.[67]

The country traders from Bengal, the Yankee mariners from the New England seaboard, and a handful of merchant venturers like Wyndham and Ward performed an indispensable role in transforming Taosug economy and society. The participation of these Europeans and Americans in Sulu's trade stimulated the economic, demographic, and political development of the Sultanate. Their trade at Jolo between 1768 and 1848 enabled the Taosug to expand control over the supply and distribution of firearms as well as woven fabrics, opium, and an ever-increasing catalogue of European domestic manufactures and luxury items desired throughout the zone.

The rate of growth of the Sultanate's population had not kept pace with its expanding commercial economy. The Western traders' insatiable demands for produce acceptable in Chinese markets promoted the intensification of Taosug-sponsored Iranun-Samal raiding expeditions to obtain captives. It would be Visayan, Minahassan, and Buginese captives as well as flotillas of nomadic Samal Bajau laut that would gather the *tripang*, mother of pearl, and tortoise shell for the European traders to take to China. The gunpowder and firearms supplied by the traders allowed the coastal dwelling Taosug to promote slave raiding on a large scale and keep the zone free of intruders and competitors until 1840.

THE MANILA-JOLO TRADE

Not the least important axis of external trade between 1768 and 1848 was that from Manila to Jolo. In the late eighteenth century, the junks from Amoy and the country traders from Calcutta shared Sulu's trade with brigantines, frigates, and large sailing *prahus* belonging to Manila's Spanish traders and Chinese merchants. It took the Spanish authorities in Manila over a decade after 1768 to establish a permanent basis for commercial relations with Sulu. Governor Simon de Anda first suggested the possibility of trading Philippine manufactures to the Sultanates of Sulu and Cotabato in 1772.[68] He felt that the trade would not only be profitable but would also have important bearing on the future security of the islands. The establishment of permanent commerce and friendly relations with Sulu, he hoped, would check English influence and the traffic in arms.[69]

In 1773, the question of direct trade between Manila and Jolo was discussed at length during Alvarez's mission to Sulu. The officer stressed the commercial advantages the Taosug would derive from a treaty with Spain. Certainly the Taosug were attracted by the possibilities of acquiring not only trade goods but Mexican silver as well. Sultan Mohammed Israel was anxious to inaugurate free trade with Manila and Zamboanga and also informed Alvarez that he would open several mines and pay the Government one-fifth of the output if adequate technical assistance were made available to him.[70]

Encouraged by Alvarez's report, Simon de Anda notified Israel towards the end of 1773 that Taosug *nakodahs* would be welcome in Manila to freely barter their produce.[71] On the eve of the departure of Cencilli's expedition for Sulu, the Captain General stated that he would consider it a major triumph if the Taosug began to participate in Manila's commerce.[72] These trade negotiations collapsed in the aftermath of Cencelli's botched mission and were not resumed until after Israel's death in 1778.

Israel's successor was his former rival and cousin Azim ud-Din II. In 1779, the new Sultan sent a mission to Manila to establish a treaty of friendship and commerce, but the Taosug craft never reached its destination. The vessel was intercepted by a Magindanao raiding Flotilla and Azim ud-Din's emissaries perished.[73] The newly appointed Spanish Governor, Jose Basco, did not learn about the incident until a year later when some Bugis arrived in Manila with a letter and gifts for the Governor-General from the Sultan of Sulu. Azim ud-Din's letter informed the Governor of the loss of the previous mission and solicited a new treaty with Spain.

The Sultan apologized for having sent a Bugis merchant to convey such an important letter. He had chosen the *nakodah*, Supdia Alidia, because few Taosug vessels had frequented Jolo since the Magindanao had murdered his ambassadors. Although open conflict had broken out between his realm and the Sultanate of Cotabato, he promised that several Taosug of high status would be sent to Manila as his representatives the following year.[74] The Governor-General took advantage of the rivalry between the Taosug and Magindanao to encourage Sultan Azim ud-Din II to send an ambassador to Manila, but indicated that he lacked the necessary authority to ratify a treaty on behalf of the Spanish Government. He knew the treaty would have to be deferred (ratification would take the Crown several years because of Spain's current involvement in the Anglo-American conflict), but he nevertheless stressed the need for permanent friendship and trade between Manila and Jolo.[75]

The Governor-General's attitude was shared by influential Spaniards who comprised the tribunal of the Philippine Company. In classified instructions sent from Madrid to Manila in 1785, the tribunal recognized the singular importance of peace and commerce with Jolo and Mindanao and advocated trade agreements with these states.[76] The efforts of Governor Basco and other high-ranking Spaniards to attract Taosug *nakodahs* to Manila proved successful after 1785. The arrival of a Taosug *vinta* with more than 8,000 pesos worth of produce the following year marked the beginning of continuous commerce between Manila and Jolo for more than half a century.[77]

The Growth of Trade

The information available on trade from Manila to the Sulu Sultanate between 1786 and 1848 reveals the invaluable nature of Spanish source material for reconstructing indigenous trade patterns.[78] When compiled and ordered as a time series these documents (particularly the *estados* and *almojarifazgo*) suggest the overall level of commercial activity, shifts in market preferences, and the economic interdependence of Manila and Jolo in the period.[79] The data reveals both the growth in trade between the two centres and the growing importance of Sulu as a commercial entrepot in the larger context.

In the earliest years of the new trade, Manila was visited annually by a Taosug *vinta,* but before 1787 no Spanish or Chinese coasting vessels regularly went to Jolo.[80] By 1792 several Chinese coasters were trading to the Sultanate, and two years later two well-armed Spanish vessels visited it.[81] As the trade increased from the Manila end, fewer Taosug sailed to the colonial capital and the *datu*'s direct participation in the trade receded after 1795. The *Juat* and the *Chan* which brought cargoes of Canton produce to Manila in 1818 were the last recorded Taosug-sponsored sailing craft to have made the journey from Jolo.[82] Sulu *prahus* and schooners, however, would continue to make occasional voyages to Manila from the distant Bornean dependencies of Bulungan and Berau until as late as 1830.[83] An average of four to five Spanish vessels were already engaged in trade to Jolo at the end of the first decade.

During the period 1796–1803, Spain was at war with England and Manila was closed to British traffic. There was a decline in the number of Spanish craft trading to the south, but the Spaniards did not entirely relinquish their share of the commerce. They were content instead to sponsor Manila Chinese in trade to Jolo rather than risk losing their vessels to an English naval squadron or the privateers which harried Spanish shipping throughout the archipelago. After 1798, Chinese participation grew in the Manila-Jolo trade. Cargoes of sugar and indigo were brought to Jolo that year by three Chinese coasters, *Guing Fin, Gua Jap,* and *Sing Yap Di,* and the junk *Sin Sin Tay.*[84] Spanish enterprise continued this indirect method of trade after the war ended in 1803.

In the twenty years after 1807, the number of Spanish vessels involved in the trade doubled. Spanish efforts to encourage commerce with Sulu grew as successive colonial administrations struggled to make the Philippines economically self-sufficient.[85] Native sailing craft were replaced by brigantines and frigates as Spanish vessels in increasing numbers returned to Sulu. This condition was reflected in the steady growth of commerce between Manila and Jolo prior to 1840. There was a notable increase in the tempo of the traffic after 1820. A Spanish frigate, five brigantines, and two smaller sailing craft visited Jolo in 1823.[86] Three years later, seven Spanish brigantines as well as five Portuguese merchant ships traded in Sulu.[87] An average of six to eight Spanish sailing ships visited the sulu archipelago each year. The *estado* for 1835 listed the arrival in Manila of the English barque *Elizabeth* and six Spanish brigantines.[88] Statistical material on the ships' voyages is scarce for the ensuing decade, but as late as 1848 Robert Mac-Micking, an English merchant, observed that "occasionally as many as eight small [Spanish] vessels are seen there [Jolo] at a time".[89]

Manila-based brigs and schooners began their voyages between December and April, and often visited the provinces of Antique and Iloilo on their way to Sulu.* The island of Panay, situated on the main route for ships bound to Jolo and the Moluccas, was where the Manila traders ordinarily completed their sulu cargoes. Sugar, rice, tobacco, coconut oil, locally woven fabrics, and other handcrafted items, were purchased there at a saving. At Iloilo, on 17 February 1836, the following entry was recorded in the log of the Spanish brig *Leonidas* destined for Sulu: "completed our cargo here with sugar, [and] rice it being cheaper than at Manila".[90]

The practice of avoiding the export duties at Manila by trading locally was long-standing, despite severe penalties imposed by Spanish law for stopping at any other place in the Philippine archipelago. Chinese captains continued to export staples profitably from the central Visayas to Jolo, and by 1828 there were indications that the Government openly acknowledged this clandestine practice. In the *estado* for 1828, the destination of the *Nuestra Senora de la Merced* is listed as Iloilo and Jolo, and in 1829 Negros and Jolo appear as the destination of the brigantine *San Juan Nepomuceno*. The following year the Government attempted to regulate and encourage the trade by rescinding the restrictive legislation and establishing a customs house at Zamboanga, but the Manila traders evaded Zamboanga as well whenever possible.

They arrived at Jolo by June or July, which was the height of the trading season, when the *prahus* from the outer islands and the Bornean coast brought in their produce.[91] Travelling alone or in small expeditions, the vessels returned to Manila between September and November, and new voyages were not undertaken until the following year.[92]

Merchants and Peddlers

It was the Chinese merchants of Manila who carried out most of the voyages to Sulu. In 1838, the Governor Captain General remarked. "... up to the present time, [almost] no Spanish merchant has himself had direct dealings with the inhabitants of Sulu; the Chinese alone being engaged in this trade...."[93] Spanish commercial houses chartered brigs and schooners

---

* It has been generally assumed that vessels left for Jolo in March and April. The tables show that while many ships did leave Manila at that time, others had departed several months earlier or as late as June. See MacMicking, *Recollections of Manila and the Philippines,* p.148; Wickberg, *The Chinese in Philippine Life,* p.89; Jose Maria Halcon a GCG, 31 Dec. 1837, AUST, section Folletos, Tomo 117, pp.50–52.

to Chinese. Some prosperous Chinese also hired out sailing craft for the seasonal trade. The ships were let for between 600 and 700 pesos a month, and the voyage from Manila to Jolo and back generally occupied six to eight months.[94] In addition to investing heavily in the cargo, the Spanish shipowner provided the Chinese with a loan of between 10,000 and 20,000 pesos at interest rates of 20 to 30 per cent.[95]

The Spanish or Manila Chinese shipowner, the Chinese captain and supercargo, and a number of merchants all had an interest in a vessel's cargo. The "peddlers" of Van Leur also added their wares. The commercial statistics on the *almojarifazgo,* the import export tax, provide details by voyage on the kind and quantity of trade.*

In March 1811 the brigantine *San Luis* exported a small cargo of rice and rusk to Sulu. In addition to its declared cargo, four private traders freighted a total of over 8,000 pesos worth of merchandise to Jolo.[96] Lu Cong Fuang shipped twelve boxes of trade stores valued at 1,022 pesos, including over 650 pieces of assorted Bengal textiles and coarse red and blue cotton cloth of varying lengths. Besides the cloth the Chinese trader also brought some flour, biscuits, and noodles. A Manila merchant, Jose Maria Fernandez, took four boxes of fine Indian fabrics and fifty yards of blue cotton cloth worth 1,651 pesos. Pedro Cruz de los Santos freighted 2,876 pesos worth of cloth in four boxes and fourteen large bundles. Con Suy exported five boxes of cloth and six bundles of Indian fabric, as well as seventy piculs of sugar and twelve jars of biscuits.†

Manila Chinese traders sometimes sent trade goods to Jolo on several vessels during the same year. In January 1812, the trader Juan Ausero sent 638 pesos worth of cloth, shoes, quill pens, and fans on the junk *Guing Fin Le* and freighted several hundred pieces of textiles, thirty-four piculs of sugar, and three jars of duck's eggs on the pontin, *San Josef,* a few months later. The shipment of the *San Josef,* which belonged to the charterer Jose San Tiang, the captain Thomas Acong, and six others, reveals the disparity in the value and volume of goods carried by the various parties. The Chinese shipowner freighted over 8,500 pesos worth of trade goods for the venture. Even the captain's investment, 3,345 pesos, was more than the

---

* This information was not provided in the *estado* which listed the overall value and volume of the export cargo declared by the captain but did not necessarily include the value of trade goods accompanying independent traders who travelled as passengers to the Sultanate. The total export values cited in the *almojarifazgo,* in which the cargoes are broken down by trader, are therefore much more inclusive than those provided in the *estados.*

† The traders also brought personal effects and a stock of provisions for the journey and their stay in Sulu. Pedro Cruz de los Santos took a box of clothes and a bed. Con Suy carried eight boxes of clothes, a box of Chinese notebooks, eight jars of rusk, quantities of fried meat, Chinese noodle, soybean cakes, chocolate, and sugar as well as crockery for the crew.

combined value of the goods of all the remaining traders.* The value of their merchandise was as follows: the Chinese Juan Ausero, 996 pesos; the Chinese Tin Guan, 458 pesos; the Chinese Joo, 223 pesos; the Chinese Quim Fe, 383 pesos; and Pedro and Francisco Navarro, 226 pesos.[97]

The captain was not held liable if the ship and cargo were lost, but had to pay for the routine expenses of the trip, negotiate the payment of the Sultan's tariff, and cope with the exorbitant demands of the *datus*. When a trader returned from a successful voyage, the shipowner received his share of the profits and his loan with interest. From the standpoint of profit and personal security, the practice was widely adopted by Spanish shipowners and merchants as traffic from Manila to the Sultanate accelerated in the first half of the nineteenth century.

Small expeditions of Spanish vessels generally arrived in Jolo several weeks to a few months in advance of the Amoy junks. Upon arrival, the Manila Chinese captain had to pay the sultan's trade tariff. A certain amount of scheming sometimes accompanied the settlement of the trade impost. Philippine traders often curried favour with the Sultan† and encouraged the imposition of inordinate charges on the cargoes of their competitors:[98] successful intrigue seriously damaged the commercial prospects of rivals.[99] The arbitrary character of the impost and the rivalry that surrounded their mercantile activities at Jolo exacerbated the antipathy that existed among the Manila Chinese in Sulu's trade.

Once the Sultan's fee had been paid, the captain acquired a market-place on shore from the *ruma bichara* in return for a nominal amount of trade goods. The trader was then free to unload the freight, tally his imports, and begin to trade. Since Manila ships returned annually to the Sultanate, a portion of either the shipowner's or captain's trade stores was disposed of on consignment to Chinese agents resident in Jolo. Those small traders who had no contacts peddled their cloth bundles and wares at Jolo and in outlying areas.

The difficult market conditions at Jolo tested the reputation of the Manila Chinese as traders with skill, perseverence, and patience. Once an exchange had been agreed upon and the price of the articles established, it was customary for Chinese merchants to deliver their trade goods to Taosug *datus*. As the trade grew and the competition increased for Sulu's leading articles of export, the practice of delivering large quantities of merchandise before the

---

* Over 237 separate entries in small and large boxes, barrels, chests, and bundles are listed as the captain's and traders' cargo on the *San Joseph*. It was principally textiles and some foodstuffs.

† In 1837 it was conservatively estimated that the Sultan received 50,000 pesos annually in harbour and market fees from the Manila traders. See Jose Maria Halcon, a GCG, 31 Dec.1837, AUST, Seccion Folletos, Tomo 117, p.43.

articles to be taken in exchange were received became indispensable. Some *datus* complied with their obligations and paid for all goods bartered to them by Philippine traders, but the majority rarely paid the total amount owed. Their outstanding debts were carried over to the following year but seldom were recoverable.[100]

A case in point was the experience of Jose Maria Dujiol, the commander and supercargo of the brigantine *Lingayen*. In 1836, several of Jolo's leading *datus* owed debts to him. Dujiol had delivered a cargo to the Datu Molok the previous year without having demanded a written contract. In an apparent effort to gain a competitive advantage over other Manila merchants, he had given the *datu* a number of silver pesos and six ounces of gold in Spanish currency.[101] Datu Molok did not fulfil his verbal agreement. In 1836, the amounts owed by Molok and other *datus* to Dujiol were as follows: Datu Molok, 5,174 chapas, 222 piculs, 43 cates of pearl shell, and 136 silver pesos; Datu John, 43 piculs of pearl shell, and 25 cates of bird's nest; Datu Bandahara, 19 piculs, 28 cates of pearl shell; and Datu Bulok, 17 piculs of pearl shell, 17,000 chapas, and 2 silver pesos.* The following year the *Lingayen* was delayed at Jolo until late September as its Chinese passengers had not sold all their wares, the captain was still waiting for the promised arrival of a *sherif* from Sandakan with a large amount of trade produce, and because Datu Emir Bahar and Datu Molok still owed outstanding debts to the vessel's Chinese traders.[102] When the net results of a trading venture to Sulu were good, the expenses incurred in harbour and market fees, gifts, and unfulfilled contracts were written off as inevitable costs.[103] The Manila-Sulu commerce was lucrative and net returns of fifteen-and twentyfold on a merchant's investment were common.† This especially seems to have been so prior to 1820, even when trade goods were given as gifts to powerful *datus* and/or sold without payment being received.

Between 1820 and 1830, the Taosug took full advantage of the increased commercial competition at Sulu to force the level of the Manila merchant's profit down. Depending on the prevailing market conditions in sulu, *datus* either demanded and received more trade goods for less Sulu produce at inflated prices or insisted that Manila traders reduce their prices before

---

* In 1836, Dujiol, who was unable to redress his loss, attempted to undermine Datu Molok's authority through trade and intrigue with his principal rival Datu Bulok. A chapa was a small Chinese brass coin with a hole in the centre (also called pitlis or laxa), used as a form of currency in Jolo for small market exchanges. It fluctuated in value. In 1814, 450-500 chapas were worth one Spanish duro. Hunt, "Some Particulars Relating to Sulo", p.46.

† The import-export statistics declared by the merchants were registered and converted to values on the basis of prices current in Manila. The quality of these official figures is marred by the fact that they do not always account for changes in the price level, and for the purposes of analysis must be considered as estimates of the real value.

bartering. The net gains were far more variable in this period, and a merchant sometimes did not realize a profit until he ultimately shipped his investment in Sulu goods to Macao or Canton.

The Focus of Exchange, Food Staples, and Exotic Produce
The assistance of an experienced Chinese was indispensable in compiling the cargo invoice for a Manila vessel.[104] There was a wide variety of goods appropriate for the Taosug market, and a thorough knowledge of current prices and demand in Sulu was a skill which few Spaniards possessed. Covering many pages, a suitable list included cotton textiles and opium from India; porcelain crockery, crystal, iron and hardware from Europe; rice, cheap sugar, rusk, salt, and a myriad of small handicraft items from the Philippines; and nankeens, chapas, coarse earthenware, and silk goods from China.

Basically, it was a bulk trade in staples. Rice, sugar, rusk, salt, and indigo were all retailed on a large scale. Of the articles directly exported from Manila and the central Visayas to Jolo, rice and sugar were the most important. MacMicking noted that "rice is generally taken from its being always in demand by the Sooloomen".[105] The constant flow of this staple from a region of rice surplus, the Philippines, to an area of chronic rice shortage, Sulu, is disclosed in the data on Spanish export cargoes between 1786 and 1830. Information is provided on the export cargoes of 68 out of the 134 vessels that went to Sulu. The *estados* list 52 of these vessels as departing from Manila with cargoes of rice and/or sugar prior to 1830. The remaining sixteen vessels could have completed their cargoes with these staple commodities at Panay or Negros. The statistics also depict a steady growth in the average volume of rice and sugar annually carried on Spanish vessels. These staples were among the fastest growing section of the Philippines export trade to Sulu. Total cargoes were sometimes worth between 20,000 and 30,000 pesos.*

The Manila traders received *tripang*, shark's fin, pearl shell, wax, bird's nest, Chinese porcelain, Bengal textiles, and European manufactures from the Taosug in exchange for their rice, sugar, and cloth. *Tripang* (also known as beche-de-mer or sea slug) was one of Sulu's most valuable exports in trade with Manila. It was taken in large quantities by visiting traders for use in Chinese cuisine. Over thirty-three varieties of *tripang* were distinguished and each type required grading as first, second, or third quality.[106] Selecting among various kinds and preparing the *tripang* for shipment required Chinese proficiency.

* These figures show the inaccuracy of Montero y Vidal's statement that the most important cargoes sent from Manila to Sulu never exceeded 2,500 pesos. Jose Montero y Vidal, *Historia general de Filipinas desde el descubrimiento de dichas Islas hastu nuestros dias,* vol.2, p.557.

Hunt observed: "A Chinese sorter and a few China and Bugis coolies are positively necessary to choose and pack the *tripang* and produce, for it is death to any settler or native to give information on this head...."[107]

The prime importance of *tripang* in the Manila-Sulu trade is shown by the variety and volume shipped in Spanish coastal vessels between 1786 and 1830. For the period before 1805, we lack specific information on articles imported at Manila from Sulu. Often the label "Canton goods" (natural produce of Sulu) was recorded on the *estado* rather than detailed statistical data from the vessel's import manifest.* Still, it is not unreasonable to assume that *tripang* was freighted on the majority of the *prahus* and ships trading at Jolo before 1800. Details are provided on imported Sulu cargoes for 67 voyages between 1805 and 1830. *Tripang* was included in 48 of these cargoes. It was not unusual for vessels to freight as many as fifteen different types of sea cucumber in varying amounts up to fifty tons.† The Spanish pontin *Nuestra Senora del Rosario* and the brigantine *San Jose* alone imported a total of one hundred tons of *tripang* to Manila in 1821.[108]

Wax collected in the hills and valleys of Mindanao and Borneo was exported in large amounts at Jolo and is listed in the Manila import manifests of 52 out of 67 vessels. Used in the manufacture of candles in the Philippines, this was one of the few primary products of Sulu that was not

---

* *Tripang* was divided into three basic groups by the Manila Custom House. These categories are used in the *estado* for recording a vessel's cargo. The first sort were Bacalungos, Monang, and Talipong; the second sort, Tactacong and Anguinang; and the third sort Mani². Dias Arenas, *Memoria*, p.13.

† The *tripang* imported in the cargo of one spanish *galiot*, the *San Antonio* in 1808, was comprised of the following sorts:

Type	Volume		Value
First sort:	(arroba)	(lb)	(pesos)
Bacalungan	74	14	135
Munang	57	7	104
Talipong	69	14	202
Second sort:			
Munang	78	10	71
Tactacong	32	3	79
Combata	20	3	18
Blanco	116	13	84
Third sort:			
Combata	6	6	5
Munang	138	15	113
Tarip	270	5	171
Blanco	335	18	122
	1,195	97	1,104

The Spanish arroba was approximately 25 lb. See Estado, No.61, AGI, Filipinas 506.

re-exported from Manila to China. Cacao was another export used for local manufacture and consumption within the Philippines. The cacao of Sulu was preferred in Manila to the South American variety and Spanish vessels exported from 100 to 200 piculs of cacao annually.[109]

The most valuable article was bird's nest, procured primarily from limestone caves on the east coast of Borneo. The tiny swallow nests were of two sorts. White nests were worth their weight in silver and a kati was sold for between twenty and twenty-five pesos or more. Sandakan nests and other off-colour varieties were of lesser value. Black bird's nest were inferior and commanded about one-tenth the price of white nests. In 1837, they were valued at between 200 and 250 pesos per picul.[110] Bird's nest was sent exclusively to China, where it was esteemed both as a delicacy and as a medicinal broth. Bird's nest was included in 49 out of 67 import cargoes between 1805 and 1830, and was shipped by vessels in amounts varying from less than fifteen katis to upward of 100 piculs.*

Much of Sulu's natural produce was re-exported from Manila to Macao or Canton. The Manila-Sulu trade was a vital link in a broader pattern of Spanish-Philippine trade with China. In the late eighteenth century, none but Portuguese and Spanish vessels were permitted, by Chinese regulations, to trade at Macao. This exclusive privilege encouraged Manila to develop commerce with the Sulu archipelago on a large scale.

The Sulu Sultanate's important role in the trade economy of the Philippines is shown by the following figures. In 1836, the Manila Chinese traders estimated the real value of their trade with Jolo to be worth 300,000 pesos a year.[111] An additional 150,000 pesos must be added to these figures as the estimated annual value of the Sino-Sulu traffic whch was channelled through Manila in the years between 1840 and 1848.[112] By then Manila's trade with Sulu was worth nearly half a million pesos.

Manila-Singapore-Jolo

The founding of Singapore in 1819 was to provide an alternative axis of Spanish mercantile activity with the Sulu Sultanate. Manila Chinese bound for Sulu began to voyage to Singapore as early as 1829.† In the next two decades, at least one or two Spanish vessels and several Portuguese ships from Macao were liable to touch at Singapore each year before sailing to the Sultanate.

---

* For example, in 1808 the junk *Jap Son* exported 123 piculs of bird's nests. A decade later, a Taosug sailing craft commanded by Jua, exported 5 piculs of white bird's nest and 80 piculs of black bird's nest. See Estados, No.61, AGI, Filipinas 506; and No.77, 13 Aug. 1819, AGI, Filipinas 511.

† On 25 September 1829 the brigantine schooner *Soledad* arrived in Manila from Singapore and Jolo. See No.329, GCG a Senor Secretario de Estado, AGI, Ultramar 664.

In this period the competition was especially keen for Sulu's exports. The smaller Chinese carriers from the mainland could no longer compete with the Manila Chinese and Portuguese merchants at Sulu, and withdrew from the traffic. The impact of their commerce between 1830 and 1840 was to weaken the direct trade connection from China to Sulu. In the next decade, the Amoy junk traffic was diverted to Manila.

The chief rivals of the Manila Chinese were the Portuguese of Macao. In 1836, a Portuguese trading expedition flooded the Taosug market with Chinese manufactures. The Manila Chinese, who had previously carried identical trade wares to Jolo at a profit, could not compete and temporarily lost their market among the Taosug. In exchange for their cheap wares, the Portuguese insisted on being paid in pearl shell, which was the only product that had a higher preferred market value in Manila than Macao. They then bartered the pearl shell to the Manila Chinese at Jolo at an even greater margin.[113]

Manila Chinese captains faced with declining profits at Sulu and rising costs for their Manila investments were the first to be attracted to Singapore. They were able to purchase European manufactures and textiles more cheaply in the open stalls and bazaars of the British emporium than in Manila. In this way, some of them were able to retail their wares profitably at cut-rate prices to the Taosug.

Not all goods purchased at Singapore could be legally traded in the Philippines. The unauthorized introduction of Indian fabrics and wine and spirits was considered harmful to the interests of local manufacturers and national commerce.[114] War stores including cannon, muskets, and English gunpowder were freely sold to traders in Singapore. There is a real probability that arms were freighted by Manila merchants to Sulu. While officially disclaiming Spanish involvement in the arms trade with Sulu, the Governor-General nevertheless issued the following order on 23 July 1836:

> I decree with all their authority the laws that prohibit the carrying of gunpowder and arms to the Indies, as well as taking them to enemy territories to trade, and thereby rendering liable to confiscation those that may be found on native [Philippine] boats destined for Jolo or to any of those states whose datus are engaged in Piracy in the [Philippine] islands to the detriment of the commerce and tranquility of their towns.[115]

Singapore assumed a more important role in the Sultanate's economy as political relations grew worse between Manila and Jolo after 1845.

The End of an Era of Trade

Manila's trade with Jolo continued to expand until 1830. Sulu's role in the export economy of the Philippines was less significant in the next twenty years with the advent of the rice trade to China.* The rice economy of the Philippine archipelago boomed after 1830. This sector of the Philippine's economy was rapidly developed and rice became the colony's principal export to China.[116] Rice proved an adequate item of exchange with the mainland and the flow of trade from Manila to Sulu did not increase much beyond the level of 1830. The number of Manila trading ships visiting the Sultanate and the volume of produce exported on them remained fairly constant between 1830 and 1848. The fact that Spanish investments in the trade did not decline attests to Sulu's continued importance to Manila as the basic source of certain staple commodities for export to China.[117]

The decline of trade between Manila and Sulu was linked to Anglo-Spanish commercial rivalry over the Sultanate. In the first half of the nineteenth century, the Taosug tried to diversify Sulu's commercial relations with the West to gain political allies, and enhance the trade prospects of their state. Their skill as diplomats and traders in negotiating treaties and commercial conventions with the United States in 1842, France in 1845, and Great Britain in 1849, created considerable anxiety in Manila. The Sultanate's autonomy in trade led the Spanish Government to organize a series of expeditions against the Sulu archipelago in 1845 and 1848. These expeditions were ostensibly mounted to destroy Sulu's piratical strongholds. In fact, their underlying purpose was to thwart the regional ambitions of the Dutch and English. The Spanish wanted to demonstrate through a series of swift, successful military campaigns that they were capable of controlling the Sultanate, which Spain considered to be located within its sphere of influence. All trade between Manila and Sulu ceased in the aftermath of these expeditions.

The Sulu Sultanate experienced rapid economic growth between 1768 and 1848. New commercial relations with country traders, Manila Chinese, and Portuguese merchants caused alterations in Sulu's economy and society. The appearance of foreign traders in Jolo and the subsequent introduction of war stores, cotton cloth, and opium among the aristocratic Taosug stimulated the procurement of natural produce on an unprecedented scale. As the demand in Jolo increased for trade goods from outside the zone, principally powder and shot, but also porcelain crockery and textiles, an annually larger surplus of marine-jungle products became an economic requisite. After 1768 the volume of produce that the Sultanate exported rose well beyond previous levels.

---

* As a direct consequence of the rice trade the Spanish merchant fleet experienced unprecedented growth. In 1856, 44 Spanish vessels were employed in trade with the Asian mainland: 2 frigates, 6 barques, 5 brigantines for Amoy; 7 barques, 5 brigantines, 3 schooners, 1 brigantine schooner for Hong Kong; 1 barque, 2 brigantines for Shanghai; 2 barques, 4 brigantines for Macao; 1 barque, 1 brigantine for Whampoo; 1 barque, 3 brigantines for Chanchue. *Cuadro General del Comercio Exterior de Filipinas,* p.145.

A comparison of the figures for the volume of Sulu exports cited by Sultan Bantilan (Muizz ud-Din) to Dalrymple with those in the Datu Emir Bahar's list provides an approximate measure of the intensity of Taosug efforts in the development of the littoral-procurement trade between 1761 and 1836.

TABLE 1

MARINE-JUNGLE PRODUCE ANNUALLY EXPORTED FROM JOLO

Produce	Sultan Bantilan 1761	Datu Emir Bahar 1835
	(piculs)	(piculs)
Tripang	1,000–10,000	10,000
Pearlshell	2,000	12,000
Tortoise Shell	100	600
Shark's Fin	100	600
Bird's Nest	70	100
Wax	300	1,000
Camphor	2	100
Dammar	1,000	6,000
Cinnamon	150–200	10,000
Cacao	100	500

Notes: The volume and diversity of produce collected and redistributed at Jolo varied. Factors such as the changing preferences of foreign traders and interethnic conflict and trade rivalry within the zone affected the annual volume of produce available at Sulu. The figure for bird's nest in the table is especially low when compared with the detailed statistics on cargo information in the *estados*. Hunt listed 500 piculs of black bird's nest and thirty piculs of white bird's nest as having been already exported from Sulu by the middle of the trading season in 1814. Hunt, "Some Particulars Relating to Sulo", p.48.

Source: The figures for the table have been compiled from the following sources: "List of Products of Sulu and Its Immediate Dependencies", 26 Feb. 1761, PRO, Egremont Papers, 30/47/20/1; "List of Goods to be Had at Sooloo", MS, included with the log of the ship *Albree*, 656/1833A, Peabody Museum.

The prosecution of the procurement trade affected interethnic relations throughout the region as the Taosug strove to coordinate the collection, movement, and provision of produce for external trade. The Magindanao and Brunei, as well as other groups in the zone, desired the war stores, cloth, ceramic, and other articles from Bengal, Manila, and Macao. Critical to the Taosug's dominance over these ethnic groups was their control of the volume and diversity of trade in imported goods by the end of the eighteenth century.

The demands of external commerce reinforced the need for slave raiding as the labour of captives was essential to Sulu's expanding littoral-procurement trade. The advent of long-range slave raiding in this period became a decisive factor in Sulu's economic growth. The interdependence of the patterns of external trade contributed towards the Sultanate's ability to promote raiding, and hence its rise to power. The country traders provided the Taosug with the sinews of marauding—shot, powder, ball, and large cannon. The Manila Chinese supplied staples in bulk. The Taosug needed a reliable source of foodstuffs for the archipelago's expanding population if they were to employ their human resources in procurement and raiding rather than in agriculture. From the Taosug viewpoint, the opening of trade with Manila provided the necessary complement to the country trade in Sulu's burgeoning economy.

Jolo became the nerve centre for the coordination of slave raiding. The French navigator Pierre Sonnerat has left one of the earliest published references to Jolo after it became the common market of Iranun/Samal raiders: "... the harbour serves as a retreat for the moors, who roam over the seas as pirates, molesting the navigation of the Spaniards, and sometimes carry off with them the people of the colonies, in their incursions, whom they make slaves".[118] In 1795, the Portuguese captain, Juan Carvallo, informed the Governor that: "... the outfitting of Iranun vessels [by the *datus*] can be arranged quickly because there is a surplus in Jolo of both small cannon and heavy ordinance...."[119] In return for providing security, equipment, vessels, and sometimes crew to maritime people, the Taosug received wealth in natural produce and manpower for the Sultanate.

External trade strengthened the political influence and wealth of the Taosug state. Sulu's emergence in the region in the late eighteenth century with a commercial net extending over the Celebes sea cannot be divorced from the activities of private merchants in Calcutta, Salem, and Singapore, the Manila Chinese, and the Portuguese of Macao. These traders supplied the Taosug with what they needed to advance their mercantile interests in the intersocietal exchange network and strengthen their hegemony in relations with the Magindanao and Iranun, the riverine agriculturalists of northeast Borneo, and the Bugis of Samarinda, Kylie, and Berau.

4

The Internal Trade of the Sulu Zone

MARINE GARDENS

The sea played a major role in the Sultanate's procurement trade. The Taosug drew heavily upon the resources of Sulu's fisheries for some of the products most sought after in China and the West—*tripang*, pearl, and mother of pearl bearing oyster. These resources, concentrated in the coral reefs of Tawi-Tawi or in the waters around the Sibutu cluster and the tidal flats of the low dry islands near Jolo and Basilan, were procured largely by Samal-speaking peoples. For the Samal of Balangingi, who participated in seasonal raiding expeditions, marine procurement was seldom a full-time occupation. *Tripang* and pearl fisheries, however, were the hub of community life for the majority of Sulu Samal, and *tripang* procurement was the main subsistence pursuit. The task of collecting *tripang* and diving for pearls, which was of immense importance to the Taosug aristocrats, fell to their retainers, slaves, and the "sea people" or Samal Bajau Laut.*

The Boat People

As a pariah group under the Sulu Sultanate, the Samal Bajau Laut were distinguished from the larger sedentary population by their boat-dwelling habit, animistic faith, and certain physical features which directly stem from their unique way of life.[1] Scattered in small flotillas throughout the Sulu Archipelago and along the Celebes rim, they were often found near

---

* There is considerable confusion regarding the ethnic nomenclature of maritime people in the Sulu-northeast Borneo region. In the Sulu archipelago, Samal principally refers to the sedentary coastal *Sama* populations, while "Bajau" is used to describe maritime, nomadic boat-dwelling *Sama* (Samal). Since 1878, with the advent of the North Borneo Chartered Company, the term "Bajau" has been used in North Borneo (Sabah) to refer to all Samal speakers irrespective of cultural-ecological differences. I will follow the usage Samal Bajau Laut to identify the maritime nomadic boat-dwellers of Sulu, northeast Borneo, and Celebes. This follows usage in G. N. Appel, "Studies of the Taosug (Suluk) and Samal Speaking Populations of Sabah and the Southern Philippines", pp.21–22.

the strand, in inlets, and on the sea among the reefs adjacent to Taosug and Samal communities.*

Sea nomadism, a way of life which has characterized the Samal Bajau Laut as a people and from which they have derived their sense of identity, tended to inhibit the crystallization of cohesive kinship groups. The nuclear family was the only discrete kinship unit recognized by these nomadic fishermen. Each boat household comprised a family. These families formed temporary alliance units when residing at traditional mooring sites. A *panglima*, generally an older man, assumed a nominal degree of authority over the several boat clusters or "family alliance units" within the moorage only when an arbiter was required.[2] The Governor of Zamboanga described them as:

> devoted to fishing with no other lodging than their *vintas* [outrigger boat-houses] in which they all live, one family per *vinta*. They pass years without setting foot on the land except to collect kinding wood .... the extensive shallows and reefs provide them with an abundance of fish which is practically their only source of food and with which occasionally they can obtain some rice and the scant pieces of cloth they use to cover themselves on especially hot days. Ordinarily, they are naked and fully exposed to the sun and the spray of the sea.[3]

He reported that they were prohibited from bearing arms (indicative of their low status in a militant society) and that there were proscriptions against their entering villages.[4] Scorned by land-dwelling Taosug and Samal, and held to be physically and socially repugnant, their inferior status as a pariah group was reflected in the pejorative terms *luwaan*† and *pala'u* and denigrating etiological myths.

The Samal Bajau Laut possessed neither a territorial base nor the internal political structure necessary to weld localized kindred groups into viable political communities. Landless and destitute, these fishermen were dependent on Taosug and strand-dwelling Samal headmen for their security and meagre material benefits. However, reliance on movement and the

---

* The Samal Bajau Laut were a small population in the 19th century. The remnant of these nomadic subsistence fishermen, approximately 2% of Sulu's population, is found today, still clients of land-dwelling Taosug near the major islands of Jolo, Pata, Lungus, Siassi, and Tapul, but are particularly concentrated in the Tawi-Tawi region. For an excellent discussion of the Samal Bajau Laut as a client group, see Kiefer, *The Tausug*, pp.22–24; and Clifford Sather, "Sulu's Political Jurisdiction over the Bajau Laut", *Traditional States of Borneo and the Southern Philippines*, ed., Clifford Sather, pp.58–62.

† Kiefer notes that the word *luwaan*, literally means "that which was spat out", referring to God's rejection of their way of life—*The Tausug*, p.22. See also Richard L.Stone, "Intergroup Relations Among the Tausug, Samal and Badjaw of Sulu", pp.114, 124, 125. Balandier's assertion of the political significance of myth is relevant in the Samal Bajau Laut context. Recorded myths and origin tales of these maritime boat people invariably stress their outcaste and alien status. Georges Balandier, *Political Anthropology* (London, 1970), p.190; see also James F.Warren, *The North Borneo Chartered Company's Administration of the Bajau, 1878–1909*, pp.17–20.

ability to offer their allegiance and services to other political contenders in the face of unreasonable authority prevented their absolute subordination and distinguished them from slaves.

The maritime nomadic fishermen had limited scope for interaction with the majority of the population, and played only a marginal role in the life of the zone. Yet as fishermen and gatherers of sea produce, they performed an invaluable service to the Sultanate. Among the best of pearl divers, they were mobilized as clients of coastal Taosug and Samal to procure *tripang,* mother of pearl, and other sorts of shells for Sulu's overseas markets.

Tripang, Salt, and Pearls

More than sixty species of *tripang* (principally *holothuria spp.*) are found in the Sulu and Celebes seas.[5] At the beginning of the nineteenth century, *tripang* fisheries were found throughout the whole of the Sulu chain, but especially near the islands of Pangutaran, Panducan, Siassi, Tawi-Tawi, and Sitangkai. Hunt mentions that Samal Bajau Laut were dependent on collecting and processing *tripang* for their livelihood in all these localities as well as in Sandakan Bay, Sabahan, and places further south along the coast.[6] To encourage flotillas of boat dwellers to tap the rich fishing and collecting grounds of Maratua island, in Tirun district, the Taosug built several wells to sustain Samal Bajau Laut populations that seasonally went "thither to collect sea slug which is in great plenty on the banks near it".[7]

The reefs, islets, and bays of the southeast coast of Borneo have long been places of rendezvous and encampment for the Samal Bajau Laut. As early as 1773, Forrest encountered nomadic Samal fishermen along the southern edge of the zone.* In Tirun, communities of these fishermen were retained in clientage relationships by the rulers of the states of Gunung Tabor and Sambaliung. In 1843, the following boating populations were situated at river mouths beginning in the north of Tirun and extending south along the coast: Taballar, Talysian, Dumaring, Sungai Dua, Tapian Durian, and Batu Putih.[8] Here too, Samal Bajau Laut interaction was limited to their procurement role, in this case with the Buginese of Gunung Tabor, Kutai, and the west coast of Celebes.[9]

---

* Forrest's concise observations (*Voyage to New Guinea,* pp.372–74) predated by almost a century anything of a similar nature in European literature. The earliest accounts of Samal boat dwellers in Celebes had been written by Dutch officials. Francois Valentjin, writing at the beginning of the 18th century at Amboina, quotes two manuscript reports on the Bajau fishermen in his encyclopedic work on the East Indies. The manuscripts were written in the 1670s, one by a cleric and the other by a Dutch colonial official. These two accounts (*c.* 1675) provide an early picture of Bajau peoples inhabiting eastern Celebes who were at that time pursuing nomadic and semi-nomadic ways of life. Valentjin, *Oud en Nieuw Oost-Indien,* vol.1, p.61 in Sopher, *The Sea Nomads,* p.300.

The "sea people" employed various techniques in collecting edible *holothuria*. Expertly seeking out new sources of *tripang*, Samal fisherfolk would either spear them in shallow water or dive for the larger sort on the coral bottoms at considerable depths. The techniques involved in cleaning and curing *tripang* varied. A general formula was:

> ... washing, eviscerating by squeezing the animal if this has not already been done by spearing, boiling, rubbing off the hard shell-like outer skin with some abrasive substance like coral flowers, [and] drying either in the sun or over a smoke fire.[10]

Tripang collecting went on year round in the zone, but the most important activity in the Sulu archipelago was concentrated in the months of May, June, and July.*

The expansion of Western commercial activity to include China at the end of the eighteenth century stimulated the production of *tripang* and other strand commodities on an unprecedented scale. The statistics in the *estados* for Manila harbour show that the *tripang* trade developed rapidly after 1768. Perhaps the significance of the figure of ten thousand piculs of sun-dried *tripang* being marketed from Jolo in 1835 can be best appreciated in terms of the labour required to deliver such a prodigious quantity.[11] *Tripang* procurement and curing was labour intensive. It was not uncommon for a Taosug *datu* to employ several hundred fisherfolk (Samal retainers, slaves, or Samal Bajau Laut) in flotillas of fifty to one hundred small *vintas,* to collect *tripang.*† I have estimated that some twenty thousand men must have been involved in *tripang* procurement in any one year at the height of Sulu's trade.

The commercial production of salt was also important in Samal and Iranun settlements dedicated to *tripang* fishing. Certain communities in the Samalese

---

* In May 1781, Sultan Azim ud-Din II acknowledged the receipt of forty pesos from the Governor of Zamboanga for the redemption of a Spaniard. The Sultan wanted to send him two red-crested cockatoos and several lorikeets, but he could not send his gift because it was the height of the *tripang* collecting season:

> I have been unable to find anyone [for the task] because it is an extremely busy time of the year. None of the datus who could assist me are presently in Jolo. They are engaged in collecting tripang to sell to the Chinese.
> Sultan Mujamed Alimuden a Gobernador Juan de Mir, 13 May 1781, PAN Mindanao/ Sulu 1769–1898.

† For example, in a period of three consecutive days in May 1866, Sultan Jamal ul-Azam granted 73 licences to the inhabitants of Parang to procure *tripang* and mother of pearl in an equal number of small boats throughout the Sulu archipelago. He also granted fishing licences to Panglima Anzanudin and Buiti, a Muslim from Balabac, whose *sapit* was accompanied by a large number of small sailing craft from Patean island. El Secretario de la Sultania de Jolo a el Gobernador Militar y Politico de Mindanao, 27 Feb. 1867, PNA, Mindanao/Sulu 1839–1898.

group and on the Cotabato coast developed superior skill in manufacturing salt from seaweed and salt water. The method most commonly practised by the strand people (Samal, Samal Bajau Laut, Kalibugan) is described by Forrest who saw it at the salt sheds of Kabug near the mouth of the Pulangi in the 1770s:

> They cut down a quantity of wood always near the sea side, and rear over it a sort of shed, of the leaves of the trees of the palm kind, such as the sago, the nipa, or others. This pile is then set on fire; but as any flame issues, they throw on salt water, to check it. In this manner they continue, till the wood be consumed, there remaining a quantity of ashes strongly impregnated with salt ... These ashes they put into conical baskets, point downwards; and pour on fresh water, which carries off the salt into a trough. The lye [residue] is then put into earthen pots, and boiled till it becomes sometimes a lump of salt, [and] sometimes salt in powder. They often burn in this manner seaweed, of which the ashes make a bitter kind of salt.[12]

The ideal conditions for the production of salt by this method were found at Sipac on Balangingi island, Tunkil island, and on the north Borneo coast in the vicinity of Marudu Bay.* Dalrymple also speaks of the Bolod islands to the north of Jolo as being "low and flooded, which affords a conveniency for making much salt."[13]

The Taosug conducted an extensive trade in salt with the hinterland areas of the zone where there was a perpetual salt shortage. Considerable quantities of this coarse bitter salt were taken in cakes by Taosug traders and exchanged for hill rice, wax, bird's nest, and camphor with inland people who were not able to make it for themselves, on Jolo, Basilan, Palawan, Mindanao, and the northeast coast of Borneo.†

Sulu's pearl fisheries were renowned in Asia. Chinese records as early as 1349 mention the pearls found in the "marine gardens" of the Sulu archipelago as important objects of trade:

> The Su-lu pearls, which are better than those produced at Sha-li-pa-chou, Ti-san-kan (third port) and other places, are white and round. Their price is very high. The Chinese used them for head ornaments. Their colour never fades, and so they are considered the most precious rarities. There are some about

---

* For references to salt manufacture at Balangingi, Sipac, and Tunkil, see the statements of the fugitive captives Angel Custodio and Juan Sabala. Interestingly, the latter mentioned the founding of the Samal settlement of Catamar on Balangingi, *circa* 1832, which had no more than 30 homes and a total population of 400 employed exclusively in raiding and salt manufacture, Exp. 12, 4 Oct. 1836, PNA, Mindanao/Sulu 1803–1890; see also the statements of Benonko, Abdulla, and Pedro Juan in Verklaringen van ontvlugten personen uit de handen der Zeeroovers van 1845–1849, ANRI, Menado 37; Forrest, *Voyage to New Guinea*, p.369.

† Interior people could not become directly involved in salt manufacture because they were denied access to the coast by the dominant state society. Taosug and Samal control over coastal mangrove and islands where salt was made, placed saltless areas in an economically dependent situation.

an inch in diameter. Even in the place of production the large pearls cost over seven or eight hundred "ting". The medium ones cost two or three hundred "ting", the small ones ten or twenty "ting".[14]

Dalrymple's more recent account of Taosug trade and society is the clearest exposition of the economy of Sulu's pearl fisheries. His well-researched "Account of Some Natural Curiosities at Sooloo" describes the various types of mother of pearl bearing oysters found in Sulu waters, the *panglooroorak*, or divers, who performed the perilous task of collecting them, and the location of the pearl beds.[15] He was amazed by the richness and extent of Sulu's pearl banks which spanned nearly the entire archipelago in an uninterrupted track—in places over twenty-five miles wide—from the Sangboy islands in the north to Tawi-Tawi in the south. Numerous pearling sites in the Laparan, Pangutaran, and Pilas groups were recorded by him in addition to the pearl beds near Balabac and Maratua, but it was the fishery at Tawi-Tawi which attracted a host of Samal-speaking people, their kindred, and slaves.[16] Dalrymple noted that the shoals and reefs in the environs of Tawi-Tawi were "extremely intricate and narrow", but invaluable to the commerce of the Sultanate—"These guts [the intricate and narrow channels] are the most valuable pearl fishery in the world."[17]

While most sedentary Samal speakers procured *tripang*, tortoise shell, and agar-agar, the collection of pearls demanded the exceptional diving skills of boat-dwellers and trained slaves. Certain Taosug communities claimed the services of these local "specialists" solely for the procurement of pearls and mother of pearl shell. The Samal Bajau Laut of Parang, Maimbung, Tulayan island, and Tawi-Tawi were all pearl divers.[18] The majority of these nomadic boat people were the subjects of the Sultan of Sulu and his kindred.

In the Sulu archipelago, procurement activity in the pearl fisheries was seasonal—fixed by the rhythm of the semi-annual monsoon. There were two collecting periods; the first began with the termination of squally weather at the end of the southwest monsoon and lasted from the middle of September to the middle of December, when there were frequent calms; the second covered February to May. But at Tawi-Tawi, where the surrounding sandy islands, shoals, and reefs created an inland sea, pearl fishing was a year-round pursuit.[19]

Diving trips, involving hundreds of small *vinta* and lasting several months at a time, were organized and led by Taosug *datus* and allied kindred. In 1880, a Spanish naval officer alluded to the size of the groups employed in Jolo's mother of pearl fisheries: "In order to collect mother of pearl shell, they [the Taosug] assemble innumerable expeditions which are often led by a datu (I guarded one [expedition] of 2,200 fishermen and 3 datus)."[20] Customarily, the crew of a *vinta* numbered up to ten. All were young and exceptionally fit, as Dalrymple's description of the *panglooroorak* demonstrates:

> The divers never use any expedient to facilitate their continuing under water, but drawing up their breath in the hollow of their hands; and even this scarce ever is practised by professed divers, who commonly go down in the depths of seven or eight to twelve or fifteen fathoms; but though a few can dive in 20 fathoms, that is too great a depth for the fishery. They swim to the bottom, tumbling when they first plunge into the water, and then making long strokes, get out of sight in three or four. They rise a considerable distance from the place where they go down, but this distance is merely accidental, from the direction they go along the bottom, their fortune in finding shells, and the time the diver continues under water; they generally remain from one to two minutes, but in warm sunshine they can stay, perhaps longer.*

Two to three experienced divers could procure in a day "about forty or fifty shells, sometimes even one hundred, and sometimes scarce any".[21] Success depended to a large extent on being able to dive in clear water and calm weather. Dalrymple noted that the mother of pearl shell found in the waters of the Sulu archipelago yielded the best pearls,† but perhaps only one shell in a thousand had a pearl.[22]

Pearl diving was difficult and dangerous work. Occupational hazards included sight impairment, "... even professed divers have, after diving, their eyes much inflamed; in some this goes off, but in others it always remains"—and death from the shark and giant stingray which infested the Sulu sea.[23] The reluctance of the Samal Bajau Laut to exploit some of Sulu's richest pearl banks stemmed from their dread of sharks. Hunt wrote of the Sangboy islands:

> The tepoy (mother of pearl shell) is of remarkably large size. There are also pearls of a large size and extremely valuable, but from want of Bajows, the depth of water and innumerable sharks and sea monsters, the fishery is not carried to that extent its importance would warrant.[24]

---

* From an anecdote provided by Dalrymple it is apparent that the talents of some pearl divers were required on rare occasions for salvage operations: "There is one [pearl diver] now an old man his name Bantura, who cut down the main-mast of a large Chinese junk under water, though this was not at once diving; the time of his continuance under water, he described to me to be, 'so long as it required to make a dish of chocolate'. But he is reckoned the best diver that ever was at Sulu." "Account of Some Natural Curiosities at Sooloo", pp.11–12; see also Comision Reservada a Borneo y Jolo 1881–1882, p.39.

† The pearls yielded by these oysters were often large and if jet black were considered to be very rare. Sultan Badar ud-Din I, who reigned from 1718 to 1732, was reputed to have received a shell containing twelve pearls.

In the nineteenth century, the *palit*, a bamboo dredge,* was used by some divers to minimize the risks involved in collecting mother of pearl.[25]

The Sultan and *datus* claimed any pearl of value.[26] In return for a very large pearl a slave diver was entitled to his freedom, and they rarely delivered any to their masters without some form of compensation.[27] Forrest noted that if a diver attempted to defraud his master and sold a pearl of great worth to the Chinese merchants, he received more, but never its full value.[28] All pearls under a penny weight belonged to the divers, and to evade the proprietary rights of their *datus*, the *panglooroorak* "frequently rub off the outer coat of the pearl till they reduce them to the size of which they are entitled".[29]

Mother of pearl shell became a more profitable export for the Taosug than pearls at the beginning of the nineteenth century. Mother of pearl had previously been sought for the China market only on a limited scale.† The trade increased from 2,000 piculs in 1760 to an estimated 12,000 piculs a year by 1835. Once the Manila Chinese and country traders realized the shell's value to manufacturers of jewellery, cutlery, and furniture in Ceylon and Europe, they became the chief customers of this commodity,‡ which, with *tripang*, was among the most important items of export from Sulu's market.

The Sulu Sultanate's demand for additional labour, on which the success of the mother of pearl industry and strand exploitation in general depended, increased at the end of the eighteenth century. The need for a reliable supply of manpower was met by the Iranun and Balangingi. It was the Balangingi Samal—slave raiders from May to November and fishermen and manufacturers of salt during the west monsoon—who annually brought several thousand captive people to Sulu to be trained to work alongside the Samal Bajau Laut in the *tripang* and mother of pearl fisheries.[30] It can be roughly estimated from trade statistics that some 68,000 fishermen must have been engaged in diving for mother of pearl and fishing for *tripang* by hundreds of Taosug *datus* and Samal headmen during the 1830s.§

---

* This rake-like instrument, which was weighted with a stone, was employed extensively by the Taosug who "do not practice diving at all, ... and only comprehend the slow method of dredging for the tipy, with a thing like the fluke of a wooden anchor". Hunt, "Sketch of Borneo", p.21

† The Chinese manufactured mother of pearl articles in the form of beads, fish counters, fans, and combs. Milburn, *Oriental Commerce*, vol.2, p.513.

‡ In 1859 the Singapore price of a picul of mother of pearl shell varied according to the quality between $300 to $600. It was not unusual to pay up to $850 to re-export it to Ceylon. No.83, El Consul de Espana en Singapore a el primer Secretario de Estado, 3 July 1860, AMAE, Correspondencia Consulados Singapore 2067.

§This estimate has been arrived at by using the few examples in the literature, archival documents, and private manuscripts to provide ratios between the number of people involved

THE LITTORAL AND RIVERINE PROCUREMENT TRADE OF EAST BORNEO

Northeast Borneo was the core of the Sulu Sultanate's procurement trade. Fronting on the Sulu Sea, its highly irregular coastline was seasonally accessible from the Sultanate. So valuable were the products of the sea and the land along the coast stretching from Marudu Bay to Bulungan that *datus* settled at river mouths, in bays, and on coastal islands to "harvest" them. *Tripang*, bird's nest, and wax were obtained in abundance by Taosug from the reefs, beaches, caves, and forests of North Borneo. It was principally from this environment that the Sultanate was supplied with specialities for the external trade.

Rivers were the only major arteries linking the coastal areas and hinterlands. East coast rivers were difficult to enter even at high tide, because of the shifting sand bars across their mouths; but they provided the only means of access to the resources of Borneo's interior. Taosug entered the forest valleys and foothills of this heartland from their settlements on the Paitan, Sugut, Labuk, Kinabatangan, and Bulungan rivers.

Most of the indigenous inhabitants were Ida'han speakers,* living in

---

in marine procurement and their annual output at small collecting centres in the zone. I have used these figures in conjunction with the statistic for the estimated volume of *tripang* (10,000 piculs) and mother of pearl (12,000 piculs) exported from Jolo in the 1830s to establish the relative size of the labour force. For example, Hunt wrote that at Towson Duyon in Sandakan Bay, "*A hundred bajow or fishermen* [are] employed in catching and curing tripang; they obtain about *fifty piculs annually*", and at Loo-Loo, "there are ... thirty to forty Bajow fishermen employed in catching tripang; *twenty or thirty piculs* are cured here annually". On Tawi-Tawi there were "*eight hundred Islams*, chiefly the slaves [clients?] of Datu Mulut Mondarasa and Datu Adanan. They produce annually for the Sulo market *three hundred piculs of Kulit tepoy* [*mother of pearl*], *forty piculs of beche de mer* ... and some very valuable pearls...." At Basilan, *fifteen hundred Islams produced twenty piculs of black birds'* nest, *three hundred piculs of Kulit tepoy*, a few pearls, some tortoise shell, and twenty or thirty prows of paddy for annual export. Hunt, "Some Particulars relating to Sulo", pp.54–55, 59 (emphasis added). These figures tend to support the conclusion that the collecting and curing of a picul of *tripang* or a picul of mother of pearl shell required the average annual labour of two men for *tripang* and four men for mother of pearl. This means that in the first half of the 19th century an estimated 68,000 men laboured in Sulu's fisheries.

* The ethnic nomenclature traditionally applied to populations on the east coast of North Borneo is particularly unreliable. Observers and writers frequently failed to recognize the ethnolinguisitc distinctions perceived by the various indigenous populations. D.J.Prentice cites several reasons for the current confusion: (1) indiscriminate use of a foreign label (i.e., "Murut" or "Dusun") applied to widely divergent groups; (2) a local genuine name for a particular ethnic group is wrongly used and applied outside its original referent; (3) an ethnic group is referred to by several different names by neighbouring people, none of which necessarily need coincide with the antonym; (4) the group has no name for itself other than that of the village where they reside, a toponym, which can change if the community moves to another site; (5)

noncontiguous settlements, practising swidden agriculture or hunting and gathering among the foothills at the upper reaches of the rivers. The Taosug established a variety of relationships with these ethnically fragmented peoples. Some were the subjects of the Sultan and paid yearly tribute in produce. Others formed part of the following of a particular riverine *datu* or *sherif*. As clients, they worked beside slaves to procure bird's nest, fish for pearls, and collect *tripang* when it was demanded by their Sulu overlords. Certain powerful tribal groups at the headwaters of the various rivers were autonomous but developed stable trade relationships with the Taosug.

The Taosug river chiefs were the key links in Sulu's littoral procurement system. They channelled the flow of produce to Sulu to be redistributed to foreign traders. A significant number of Sulu *datus*, attracted by the bird's nest, *tripang*, camphor, and timber, emigrated with their clients and slaves and established settlements on or near river mouths along the east coast. Others founded communities further inland at the confluence of several rivers. The most valuable river basins were controlled by the Sultan's kindred or his representatives, who often were *sherifs* or talented slaves. Speculative mercantile considerations motivated many other *datus* to establish seasonal residence in this outlying area of the Sultanate. From their fortified stockades, these Taosug attempted to coordinate the coast-inland trade, exact tribute from dependent people, and control the movement of riverine tribal populations.

No record is extant of *datus* ruling over large areas. It is doubtful whether Sulu overlords could have exercised authority outside their local districts. Taosug exercised authority only as the representatives of their minor lineages, over against other such traditional leaders. The *datus* were sufficiently distant from Jolo to have considerable autonomy, and their rights to control over territory and dependent people were rarely contested from the centre. These rights were more apt to be appropriated by competing communities on the east coast. The entrances to rivers and the inland trading settlements as well as the bird's nest caves and *tripang* fisheries were the persistent focus of economic and political strife between Taosug *datus*, Buginese traders, and Kenyah chiefs.

---

a people have accustomed themselves to being labelled in a particular fashion, in response to government and other authorities, who have ignored ethnolinguistic distinctions and expect populations to place themselves in one of the official categories. However, all the indigenous languages of North Borneo seem to be members of the Ida'han family (the language family Ida'han is not to be confused with the coastal dwelling ethnic group Ida'an situated near Lahad Datu). For an excellent discussion of the present state of linguistic analysis in North Borneo and the related problems of ascription and ethnic nomenclatures, see D.J.Prentice, "The Linguistic Situation in Northern Borneo", pp.369–407; also see G.N. Appell, "Social and Medical Anthropology of Sabah: Retrospect and Prospect", pp.246–86; Frank M.Le Bar, ed. and comp., *Ethnic Groups of Insular Southeast Asia*, vol.1, pp.147–48.

Marudu District

Three districts were recognized by the Taosug towards the end of the eighteenth century—Marudu, Mangindora, and Tirun.[31] They correspond broadly to natural provinces divided by rivers. The three districts differed not only physically but also in resources, ethnic composition, and political character. As this region was vital to the development of the Sultanate, it is important to discuss its internal dynamics in some detail.

Marudu district comprised the north end of the island, as well as the Paitan, Sugut, and Labuk rivers, and extended as far as the west end of Sandakan Bay.[32] The Taosug had not always exploited this district. Marudu Bay supplied only small quantities of pearls and rice for Sulu's market in 1761.[33] *Datus* did not begin to develop trade with this area on a large scale until over a decade later when the Sultanate's international commerce began to grow. It was the desire to gain control over the abundant resources in this region that brought the Sultanate of Sulu into direct conflict with the Sultanate of Brunei in the last quarter of the eighteenth century.

The historical record is slight on this contest to control the trade and resources of southern Palawan, Balabac, and the north end of Borneo. It is clear though that the Taosug assumed the offensive. In 1771, Mohammed Israel led a fleet of one hundred and thirty large *prahus* against the Bornean Sultanate.[34] Taosug-sponsored raids directed at the trading boats and settlements of Brunei *pengirans* increased with the establishment of Balambangan. The Brunei Malays responded to the challenge. In 1774, the Sultan of Brunei attempted to redress the regional balance of power by concluding a treaty with the English at Balambangan. He offered them the exclusive trade in pepper on the stipulation that they protect Brunei's interests from the depredations of the Iranun of Sulu and Mindanao.[35] Neither party was able to fulfil its agreement and the raiding continued unabated. By the early 1780s, immigrant Iranun had firmly established themselves at Tempasuk on the northwest coast of Borneo. This powerful community, linked to the Sulu Sultanate through kinship and trade, further weakened Brunei's influence in the Marudu district.[36]

The Sultan of Brunei sought the assistance of the Spanish as his fortunes continued to decline over the course of the next several decades. Two large *prahus* and two smaller vessels were sent to Manila in 1802.* The Sultan's secretary, Bandajari, expressed Brunei's desire for renewed friendship and trade with Spain. He explained that Brunei *nakodahs* were no longer able to visit Manila as they once had done because of their unending conflict with the Sulu Sultanate.[37] The Governor Captain General sent a gracious reply

---

* The arrival of these *prahus* is noted in Appendix H. The *estados* demonstrate the extent to which the once brisk commercial intercourse had declined by the beginning of the 19th century.

to the Sultan of Brunei but offered him no assistance against the Taosug.[38]
The cautious policy adopted by the Spanish in this instance reflects the
importance they placed on Manila's already substantial trade with Sulu.
The failure of the mission meant that Brunei could not hope to recover its
influence and trade beyond Marudu Bay.

Brunei nobles continued to oppose the Taosug and murdered several
ambassadors in 1804. The *pengirans*

> alleged that the northern parts of Borneo and the circumjacent islands were
> their right, and had been treacherously snatched from them by the Sooloonese,
> and that they were endeavouring to recover their hereditary possessions by
> force of arms.[39]

Their trade, nevertheless, was circumscribed by the constant raiding of the
Iranun and Balangingi, sponsored by the Sultan of Sulu. In 1813,

> the Sultan [of Brunei] complained of a total stagnation of trade and hoped the
> British government would do all in their power to cause vessels to trade with him.[40]

In rapid decline, the Brunei Sultanate's authority was limited to a few
districts in the vicinity of the capital, although it nominally extended as far
as the west side of Marudu Bay. By 1820, the Taosug had eliminated Brunei
as a competitor in the littoral procurement trade of the zone.[41]

Among the Sultan of Sulu's river chiefs in the Marudu district were
several powerful traders of Arab descent who possessed religious charisma,
physical prowess, and a marked degree of political acumen. The most
important of these men to acquire authority from the Sultan in the first half
of the nineteenth century was Sherif Usman. His family represented the Sulu
Sultanate in the Marudu district *circa* 1830–86.

Sherif Usman was married to a sister of Datu Mohammed Buyo, the
Raja Muda of Sulu.[42]* Described after his death as a "man of character
and energy",[43] Usman controlled the littoral procurement trade of Marudu
district, Balabac, and southern Palawan. Accustomed to wielding authority,
he crushed resistance on Balabac and reduced the population of the island by
nearly half when its Samal inhabitants refused to pay the Sultanate tribute
any longer.[44]† This occurred in the late 1830s. He also promoted raiding
against the Brunei Sultanate on a sizeable scale. His town was a staging
centre for the Balangingi, who repaid him in captives for the food and
arms that he advanced at the outset of each cruise.[45] Usman's following of

---

*A captive who escaped to a Spanish vessel in the Jolo roadstead in 1837 described his
former master as a very powerful sherif from Borneo who was married to the sister of Datu
Buyo, No.8, 9 Nov.1837, PNA, Mindanao/Sulu 1816–1898.

†Many Samal communities must have moved away in their boats rather than continue to
pay tribute.

1,500 to 2,000 fighting men equalled those of Brunei's most prestigious nobles. The *pengirans* of Brunei feared the power and influence that he had acquired.

Usman's career was cut short by a man of similar temperament and talent. The moribund Brunei Sultanate brought charges of piracy against him to the English adventurer James Brooke. This white Rajah with the assistance of a strong British naval expedition under Sir Thomas Cochrane attacked Usman's large *kota* on the Marudu river in 1845. Sherif Usman was killed and his community dispersed. In the absence of Usman's leadership, the Sulu Sultanate's authority in the Marudu district was decentralized and internal dissension became increasingly evident. The Taosug, Datu Alimuddin,* gained control over the trade of southern Palawan and Balabac.[46] After Usman's death, his son Sherif Yassin fled to the Labuk river. There he levied tolls and delivered produce to Jolo from 1851 to 1869.† Sherif Yassin returned to Marudu Bay in 1870 and formed a settlement at the mouth of the Tandik river, where he collected

> ... a considerable revenue in tortoise shells and pearls from the sea, and camphor, rattan, and beeswax from the interior ... every other year ... for the Sultan and himself as well.[47]

Sherif Hussin, the grandson of Usman, was the overlord of the Sugut river until his death in 1886.[48]‡

At the beginning of the nineteenth century, the Taosug considered Marudu to be the "most fruitful, populous, and valuable district on all Borneo".[49] The principal town, Sungai Besar, was strategically situated at the entrance of Marudu Bay. Neighbouring settlements with smaller populations were Bawengun, Tandik, Malasingin, Sipuni, Kudat, Tambalulan, Panglian, and Malubang.[50] These communities were inhabited by Muslim merchants and settlers who moved towards the coast from the interior, attracted by the fish, tortoise shell, salt, cloth, porcelain, and metal utensils the Taosug offered in trade.

The *sherifs* of Marudu Bay acquired the district's rice, pearls, and interior products. Large quantities of hill rice were exported to Sulu from Marudu Bay as well as from Taosug settlements on the Paitan and Sugut rivers.[51] Rattans and pearls were the most important local products. The forests surrounding the bay abounded with rattans. Dalrymple estimated that

---

* In 1874, Datu Kassim, Alimudin's son, represented the Sulu Sultanate in southern Palawan.

† Sherif Yassin was married to the sister of Sultan Jamal ul-Azam who ruled Sulu from 1862 to 1881. Spenser St.John to Viscount Palmerston, 19 Feb. 1852, enclosure 95 in P.P.H.C., vol.31, p.484; "Diary during a Visit to Marudu Bay", Mr.Witti, 7 May 1881, CO, 874/74.

‡ Hussin's wife was the daughter of the Sugut river chief Sherif Datu Muhammed Israel.

4,000 tons could be cut annually for the China trade without exhausting the supply.[52] They were collected by non-Muslim people for trifling sums. As late as 1879, rattan collectors* in Marudu Bay exchanged five bundles of a hundred pieces each for a piece of cotton cloth.[53]

Pearls were obtained from the *kapis,* a mollusk found almost exclusively in the shallow waters along the west side of Marudu Bay near Sungai Besar.† The *kapis* shell was not collected by divers as in the Sulu archipelago. It was procured by large numbers of women from client communities within the bay who gathered them in water up to their waists or at low tide in the sand beaches.[54]

Besides rattans, clove bark, and rice, the Paitan river was renowned for its camphor. Forests of camphor trees flourished on hillsides near the Paitan. It was the finest sort in the world and preferred in China to the camphor of Sumatra. The quantity collected was immense, and Taosug traders were able to acquire it at extraordinarily cheap rates because it was so abundant. In 1814, riverine people gave the Taosug a bamboo of camphor‡ for a bamboo of salt.[55] Few Taosug had lived on the Paitan in 1760.[56] Within half a century, there were three major Sulu trading settlements on the river: Pitan, Kinarubatan, and Kulepan.[57] The continued importance of camphor in Sulu's procurement trade was attested to by Spenser St. John, some forty years later, when he wrote that on the Paitan "there are above a thousand Islams ... and the Ida'an in the interior are represented to be as numerous as the leaves on the tree ...."[58]

Sugut was a leading trading settlement for the Taosug towards the southern part of the Marudu district. Situated on the river of the same name, it had achieved widespread notoriety on the east coast by 1800. Hunt described it as a "considerable town" administered by *orang kaya* from Sulu. As an important market centre, Sugut employed six to eight large *prahus* in sending rattans, wax, and camphor to Jolo.[59] At mid-century Sugut was still a rich and populous area with a thriving trade.[60]

The personal and ethnic ties of the *sherifs* that held the procurement network of the Marudu district together ended beyond the Sugut river in Labuk Bay. The shore of Labuk Bay was a point of embarkation for Taosug trade and for receiving produce from the neighbouring hinterlands. The upriver settlements of Camburcan, Labuk, Songsohi, and Ano supplied the same forest produce as the Paitan as well as clove bark and bird's nest for Sulu's external trade.[61] In

* Rattan collecting was despised by those who were forced to cut it because of its great bulk.

† The oyster known as *melegrina margarifera,* which yielded the finest shell, was also the one in which seed pearls were found. The placuna of this oyster, known as *selisip,* was pounded or ground up into powder for use in Chinese pharmocopoeia.

‡ Camphor is a tough gumlike compound obtained from the wood and bark of the evergreen camphor tree. The Chinese used it for medicinal purposes.

1814, Ano, which had an estimated population of five hundred Muslims and one hundred Ida'an, exported to Sulu 15 piculs of cotton wool, 10 piculs of beeswax, 1,000 bundles of rattans, and 20 katis of lime.[62]

Labuk also had a seed pearl fishery, Lingkabo, located twenty miles off the entrance to the Bay. It was a mangrove-covered islet which was almost completely submerged at high tide.[63] The seed pearl industry was controlled by the Sultan. In direct contrast to the rest of the Marudu district, this appanage was solely administered by Taosug until the late 1870s. Sherif Datu Mohammed Israel, the Taosug mandarin of the Sugut river and father-in-law of Sherif Hussin, was the Sultan's administrator of Lingkabo from about 1860 to 1878. Procurement activity at Lingkabo lasted from January to the end of March. In 1878, two hundred people were employed by the Sultan, who paid them a nominal amount in goods before they began shell collecting.[64]

Mangindora District

The district of Mangindora centred on Sandakan Bay and the Kinabatangan river. Sandakan figured importantly in the Sulu Sultanate's development of the littoral procurement trade for several reasons. First, it had an excellent harbour. Hunt assessed the bay as "one of the finest harbours in the world or rather an assemblage of harbours with soundings and shelters for the whole navy of Great Britain".[65] Moreover, Sandakan possessed considerable natural wealth, including varieties of bird's nest, wax, rattans, gold, and *tripang*.[66] Sultan Sharaf ud-Din considered the produce of this district so important that he appointed his son to govern Sandakan from 1791 to 1808.[67]

Within Sandakan Bay at the beginning of the nineteenth century, Taosug settlements were located at Towson Duyon, Pulau Loobukon, Domendung, Segalihud, and Tong Luly Luku. Varying considerably in size and population, some of these settlements were governed by Taosug and others by local *panglimas*. Hunt described a fortified Sulu settlement within the bay, situated near the mouth of the Sandakan river, as follows:

> The chief is named tuan Abandool with a hundred Islams and there are many orang idan in the interior parts. There is a small mud fort mounting 3 large guns, 5 smaller of brass, 30 rantakas, and 60 muskets. Its annual products, when the Sulo people come over in numbers and chuse to exert themselves are 50 piculs of white birds' nest, ... 200 piculs of black, of different qualities ... 3 piculs of camphor first sort ... 3 piculs of wax, capis pearls in abundance, 5 catties yearly if looked for, and 50 piculs of tripang ....[68]

Towson Duyon, a similarly fortified bay outpost, is described as

> ... another small population hereabouts under the command of a panglima; it has a nakile or fort of 3 guns and is peopled with a hundred Bajow fishermen, employed in catching and curing tripang ....[69]

The steady development of the littoral-procurement trade in Sandakan Bay and the presence of several of these Taosug communities until as late as the 1880s was linked to the obvious trading importance of the Kinabatangan.

The Kinabatangan, the largest Bornean river and most important to the Sulu Sultanate, rose in the southern part of the mountain range that divides north central Borneo. This mighty river, three hundred and fifty miles long, winds and flows most of the distance until it empties into Sandakan Bay. Taosug *datus*, in search of trading opportunities, visited the Kinabatangan every year. The river provided openings for their economic pursuits which ranged from bird's nest collecting in the mammoth Gomantan caves behind Sandakan Bay* to the collection of wax procured at their behest by Ida'an people further upriver. Hunt described the efforts of the "visitors" to exploit the bird's nest caves of the Kinabatangan and its numerous tributaries:†

---

* The Gomantan caves were situated in the vicinity of the Kinabatangan some two days' journey from Sandakan Bay. The caves and shelters were part of a sheer limestone cliff over 900 feet high. The entrance to the largest cave was "over 100 feet wide by 250 feet high, and the roof slopes upward 110 feet more, forming a magnificent natural cathedral some 360 feet in height ... the nests were attached to the sides and roof in incredible quantities, and in seemingly inaccessible spots, but the nest gatherers had nevertheless planted everywhere the light stages [scaffolds] and ladders of cane and bamboo with which they pursue their hazardous occupation...." W.Medhurst, "British North Borneo", Royal Colonial Institute, XVI (1884/85), p.288. According to oral traditions of the Segalud Buludupy, a coastal people, the cave complex was discovered at the beginning of the 18th century. They claim that, "Datoh Bandar Betau, grandfather of the late Pangeran Temanggong and chief of the Segalud Buludupies, first found the Gomantan caves. He informed Sandukur [grandfather of Pangeran Samah, a powerful river chief of the Kinabatangan in 1882] and invited him to assist in collecting the nests, Sandukur however cheated him and collected [them] by himself, several battles were fought but the matter was eventually arranged and when the Buludupies evacuated the Sapu Gaya river, where they were much harassed by people from Sulu and Marudu, who used [to] periodically come to steal nests, the Datu Bandar shifted [their place of residence] to the Kinabatangan. To stop the raids continually being made on the caves by people who had no right to them Sandukur gave the then Sultan of Sulu Bubung Bulud cave. The Sultan then issued an edict prohibiting others from collecting there. The Sultan's sister afterwards came over and got Derhaus [cave] and his son got [the one called] Kuris ...." The Taosug exercised authority over the Gomantan caves, which annually yielded $25,000 worth of nests, by the middle of the 18th century. C.A. Bampfylde to William Treacher, 23 Sept. 1883, CO, 874/233; see also William Pryer to Alfred Dent, 18 June 1880, CO, 874/192.

† Bird's nest collecting on the Kinabatangan lasted from February to June, at whch time Sulu *prahus* returned to Jolo in the midst of the trading season. The nests from the Kinabatangan were divided among the cave owners (who collected them at great risk), the river chief, and the Sultan. In 1878, one half of the nests went to the men who procured them, and the remaining shares were divided equally between their Sulu overlord and the Sultan. Diary of William Pryer, 21 Mar. 1878, CO, 874/67; Tom and Barbara Harrison, *The Prehistory of Sabah*, pp.229–36.

It is the practice of the industrious datus and chiefs to proceed to this place with all their slaves for the season; in which case they are sure to make great profits; formerly the birds' nests caves in this district were considered royalties, and the produce immense, at the present time they are plundered ad libitum and the quantity decreases every year.[70]

Even in 1814, 380 piculs of bird's nest were taken to Sulu despite this disregard for its conservation.

The Kinabatangan was one of two rivers (the other was the Sibuco) that large trading *prahus* could ascend. This enabled Taosug to collect their own rattan at distances no greater than a mile or two from the banks of the river for a stretch of more than 150 miles above Sandakan. The small but powerful market town of Kinabatangan, which was a rendezvous for such traders, linked Sandakan Bay to a vast hinterland that was divided among various Ida'an tribes as far as the headwaters of the river. This community, seven days' journey from the coast, was defended by a stockade with twenty-four large cannon and administered by a river chief who was appointed by the Sultanate. The population of the town was thirty Muslims and one hundred Ida'an[71] The Taosug never succeeded in establishing their own trading outposts beyond this point on the Kinabatangan for any length of time. Instead, they were obliged to rely on Ida'an villages further upriver to supply them with the produce they could not procure themselves. It was estimated that thirty large *prahus* traded on the Kinabatangan from Sulu each season.[72]

In the second half of the nineteenth century, Taosug trade on the Kinabatangan declined. Several factors were responsible. One of these was the decline of Sulu strength overall. After 1852, trading *prahus* from Sulu visited less frequently because their *nakodahs* feared being attacked by the independent Samal of southern Tawi-Tawi (see Chapter 8). Further, the mandarins of the Kinabatangan were unable to prevent the flight of tribal populations from their jurisdiction in the face of either the incursions of the Segai-i, a headhunting people from the Kuran/Berau region to the south, or the contagion of diseases such as smallpox. Nevertheless, the extreme importance of the Kinabatangan produce was confirmed, even in a period of decline, by the fact that numerous high-ranking *datus* were still transacting "traditional" business on the river when the Sultan of Sulu thwarted Spanish territorial designs, and ceded the east coast to the North Borneo Chartered Company in 1878.

Sabahan was situated well up a small but navigable river in Darvel bay, on the southern periphery of Sulu's "sphere of influence". It owed its existence to the inland riverine network which linked the mercantile activity of the Bugis in southeast Borneo to hinterland communities in the north as far as the Kinabatangan. Hunt described this remote but flourishing market centre on the interior trade route:

... not marked on any chart, is the grand port of the Suloo on Borneo called
Sabahan, situated upon a small river of considerable length and it is five days pull
up to the negri. The chief here is Datu Sapindin, a nephew to the present Sultan
of Sulo. There are 1,000 Islams, 800 orang idan and cafir; [and] a fort of piles
mounting 45 large guns; ... The Islams here, being for the most part Buguese,
give this place more of a commercial turn than those [further to the north].[73]

It was here that the gap between the Bugis-dominated southern area and the
Taosug north was closed. While Bugis settlement did not extend beyond
Sabahan, they were unable to prevent the Taosug from moving south and
establishing small trading stations at Giong and Madai* as well as market
towns in Tidong and Bulungan.[74]

The last town of commercial consequence in Magindora was Tidong.
Its location is unclear from Hunt's description. We only know that it was
situated on a large, densely populated river in the region between Sabahan
and Tirun.[75] It could have very well occupied a coastal site on either the
Tingkayu or Apas rivers.† A fort was located at the river mouth which
formed the basis of a trading town under the Sulu Sultanate with two
thousand Muslim inhabitants, none of whom were Buginese. It was a short-
lived settlement compared to others. Whether the community chose to
move upriver to exercise more effective control over trade in the interior, or
departed when the Ida'an villages along the river bank withdrew because of
the destructive effects of raids mounted by the Segai-i, is not known. It is
certain though that Tidong had disappeared from the river by 1850.

Tirun District

Tirun, the final district, lay at the southern extremity of the Sulu zone.
At the beginning of the nineteenth century, it included four major river
systems—the Sibuco, Sambakong, Bulungan, and Berau.[76] Tirun was
inhabited by vigorous, predatory swidden agriculturalists of the Kenyah-
Kayan-Kayang culture complex who lived in villages and long-house units
along the banks of the rivers as far as the interior highlands.[77] Until the end
of the nineteenth century, all groups were labelled Dayak in official Dutch

---

   * In the northwest corner of Darvel Bay near Madai are the limestone cliffs of *bud* Silam.
Situated only a few miles from the coast, the 2,000-foot peak is riddled with more than 25
caves which were owned and worked by Islamized Ida'an people (Era'an and Sabahan) under
the protection of Sulu *datus*. In the bay on Gaya island, there was to be found a kind of bird's
nest like "driven snow".
   † According to Hunt, Tidong annually exported to Sulu, "50 catties of superior white
birds' nests, which fetch 75 dollars the catty in China and is expressly reserved for a bonne
bouche for the Chinese emperor, [and] one to two hundred piculs of blacknest"—ibid. The
largest known source of bird's nest in this region were the Baturong caves which are situated
near the Tingkayu river.

despatches and occasional travel accounts, whether they were actually
Tidong of the Sibuco and Sambakong, Bahau, Wahau, Long Wai, and Tring
of the middle Mahakan river, or Segai-i of the upper reaches of the Berau.[78]
Upland, moving in small bands throughout the southern region, were the
nomadic Punan.[79]

The political character and population of Tirun differed from Mangindora
and Marudu in a number of important ways. First, there were several small
semi-autonomous riverine states with large Buginese populations within
the district. Gunung Tabor and Sambaliung were situated at the confluence
of the Segah and Kelai rivers.[80] Further north was the realm of Bulungan.
These trade centres were sometimes tributary to the Buginese, sometimes
to the Taosug, and when occasion permitted sometimes independent of the
authority of their stronger overlords.

Most of the district fell more effectively within the Buginese than the
Taosug sphere of influence.[81] The Sulu Sultanate experienced in Tirun some
of the problems that confronted Brunei in its struggle to retain control over
the Marudu district. The problems of inadequate communication with Sulu
and a sparse migrant population that could not be forcefully supported by
the Sultanate were complicated by stubborn Buginese resistance to the
establishment of Taosug trading settlements in the southern area of the
district. In the latter part of the eighteenth century, the Bugis of Kutai, Pasir,
and Kylie moved their frontiers north into Tirun in the absence of Taosug
authority and trade in the area. Their commercial penetration of Tirun
blocked the Taosug from spreading further south along the east coast than
Bulungan. Nevertheless, despite Bugis-Taosug conflict and trade rivalry
there developed a lively commercial traffic between these contested areas
within Tirun as well as with Sulu and Makassar.[82]

On the Sibuco, Sambakong, and Bulungan rivers the Sultanate's hegemony and trade were still plainly visible. Taosug travelled long distances into
the interior on these rivers to barter tradewares for forest produce with Tidong
people. Many permanently settled in estuarine and upriver Tidong communities where they acted as intermediaries in the coast-hinterland trade. Their
islamized descendants, often chiefs or headmen, continued to function as
principals in the barter trade between Taosug merchants from Sulu and non-
Muslim forest people such as the Punan. The Sultanate relied on these chiefs
as political agents to control the river trade and maintain Sulu's influence
among the larger heterogeneous population at the edge of the frontier.

Long-distance trade, Islam, and slavery modified the traditional culture
of these interior peoples especially on the Sibuco and Sambakong rivers. In
the 1770s, Forrest described the Tidong as a pagan riverine people who then
frequented the outer islands of the Sulu archipelago to barter Filipino slaves
and booty they had acquired from raids on Spanish coastal communities and
shipping:

Even the small mangaio prows of the orange tedong ... a barbarous piratical
people, who live up certain rivers on the northeast coast of Borneo, are
admitted here [Cagayan de Sulu] .... These orang Tedong, are not mohametans;
this circumstance, and their country being under the dominion of Sooloo, may
be the reason why Sooloos will not permit them to come into any of their ports
on that island [Jolo] ....[83]

Their way of life had changed by 1800.* The Tidong turned from slave
raiding in the seventeenth and eighteenth centuries to agriculture and the
exploitation of local resources at the beginning of the nineteenth century.
They concentrated on supplying the Taosug with foodstuffs for Sulu's
expanding population besides rattans, wax, and nests for its international
market.[84] The Tidong, who comprised a large number of independent
riverine tribes, underwent a process of gradual conversion to Islam through
protracted contact with Taosug trading partners, which began towards
the end of the eighteenth century when the Sulu Sultanate established its
commerce through kinship and patronage in Tirun.

Conflicting claims to the rivers below the Sambakong flared up frequently
between the Taosug and Buginese in the last quarter of the eighteenth
century, and were a constant source of opposition and frontier adjustments.
The Sulu Sultanate forcefully wrested political influence and much of
the trade of Bulungan from the Buginese of Pasir in the late eighteenth
century.[85] For the Taosug, control over the trade of Bulungan, which
claimed jurisdiction over the Sibuco, Sambakong, Sesajap, and Sembawang
rivers, was fortuitous; for the Buginese it was a galling loss. Nevertheless
Bulungan remained an integral albeit less important part of the Buginese
trade network which centred on Pasir. Bulungan's market-place continued
to be linked through kinship ties to the Buginese settlements of southeastern
Borneo and merchants from Berau, Kutai, Pasir, and Pulau Laut both traded
in Bulungan[86] and passed through the community on their way to Taosug
settlements further north along the coast or in the Sulu archipelago.

Sulu's political role was confined to the administration of the upriver
settlement of Bulungan. According to Hunt, the settlement was ruled by a
Taosug aristocrat in 1812.[87] In ensuing decades, the Sultanate turned the
governance of Bulungan over to carefully selected local leaders. These *rajas*
relied for prestige and authority on titles conferred by the Sultanate.

The efforts of Sulu *datus* to monopolize trade on rivers tributary to
Bulungan were less successful where they attempted to exercise their
prerogative as alien overlords forcefully. When the Taosug adopted large-

---

* References to raids being conducted by Tidong on Philippine settlements disappear
from the Spanish record after 1760. Although the Tidong no longer mounted large expeditions,
they continued to make desultory attacks on Spanish islands for at least another two decades,
but these raids appear to have ended by 1790.

scale raiding as a tactic to establish their authority on certain rivers they encountered resistance. In the first decade of the nineteenth century, a large flotilla of Sulu and Iranun vessels staged an attack on the settlements of the Sembawang river. The villagers defended themselves well and forced the invading fleet to withdraw with heavy losses. Where overt force had failed the attraction of the prosperity to come with trade succeeded, ultimately giving the Taosug commercial entrees up the Sembawang.[88] Such events demonstrated to the Taosug that no control could be exercised on the rivers surrounding Bulungan without the support of indigenous political agents.

Until 1860, Bulungan's trade was dominated by the Sulu Sultanate. The island of Tarakan off the mouth of the Sesajap river was the rendezvous for Taosug *prahus* when they arrived from the Sulu archipelago.[89] From there, *nakodahs* went up the different rivers in search of forest produce and to trade with the Tidong. Bulungan furnished wax, bird's nest, *tripang*, gold (collected by the Punan), and some saltpetre.[90] Rattans and gutta-percha had not yet entered into the trade and were only delivered on request.[91]

The heart of Bulungan's trade with Sulu, however, was sago and rice. In Tidong and Kenyah villages situated along various river systems, subsistence was based on dry rice agriculture. After 1768, sago and rice became the main commercial crops of these swidden cultivators (who supplemented their economy by gathering forest produce) when Sulu could no longer provide the necessary food reserves to keep pace with its expanding population. Dalrymple wrote, "There is one vegetable production in the Sooloo dominions of great consequence ... sago ... no place has greater abundance, or more excellent sago trees than the coast of Tirun."[92] Conservation practices in sago cropping enabled the Tidong to make it a stable trade item to the food-short Sultanate. The Tidong exchanged granulated sago to the Taosug for as little as a dollar a picul.[93]

Hunt noted the importance the Taosug placed on Tirun as a source of rice. It is not surprising that a large part of Sulu's stockpile was obtained in Bulungan through tribute. The Raja of Bulungan received tribute in rice, bird's nest, and wax. In 1848, he received an estimated 3,300 piculs of rice in tribute from the Segai-i and one other neighbouring Kenyah group. Islamized Tidong villages paid tribute in rice and provided the use of their long canoes and *prahus* for transporting it to Bulungan for export to Sulu.[94]

Bulungan's bird's nest was collected in the rocks at the headwaters of the Secatak and Sembawang rivers. These caves were subject to raids by the Wahau, a Kenyah people, who were encouraged by Buginese on the coast to dispute Bulungan's tributary rights to the nests, to stem the flow of this precious commodity to Sulu. Bird's nest and wax were also collected in the remote highlands by the Tinggallan who only traded with the Taosug and Islamized Tidong of the Sambakong and Sesajap rivers.[95]

In exchange for forest products, riverine tribal people received salt, tobacco, salted fish, coconut oil, cotton cloth, and slaves from the Taosug.[96] Although salt was an important trade item on the east coast, it was not commonly used by the more distant upland tribes of Tirun, it being too dear for them.[97]

Forest produce arrived by water from the interior and was for the most part transported from Bulungan to Sulu in time to meet the vessels from Manila and China. The *estados* show that Taosug craft occasionally voyaged directly from Bulungan to Manila. This trade was carried on in *prahus* between thirty and thirty-five tons burthern. In 1818, a large *vinta* brought 6,236 pesos worth of wax, bird's nest, *tripang*, pearl shell, camphor, gold, and diamonds.[98] There are descriptions of Bulungan *pancos, pontins,* and a schooner arriving in Manila with similar cargoes in 1820, 1821, 1823, and 1830 (see Appendix F).

Berau, just to the south of Bulungan, was another focal point of trade. The Berau realms of Gunung Tabor and Sambaliung linked northern Celebes and Kutai to the Sulu Sultanate. As traders, the Taosug formed a small but influential community in these market centres. What is striking about Berau is the nature of the relationship between the Taosug and Buginese. The Taosug exacted tribute and trade from Gunung Tabor for over a half of a century. Nevertheless Berau remained a predominantly Buginese trading enclave. The Taosug of Gunung Tabor tended at times to identify more closely with the ruling Buginese of Kutai than with Sulu traders and political agents further north on the coast.

Gunung Tabor and Sambaliung were independent states at the time of Dalrymple's first visit to Sulu in 1761. The Sultanate did not attempt to subjugate them until about the year 1770. Forrest wrote that the Taosug were able to take advantage of an internecine struggle to intervene:

> While these two princes [of Gunung Tabor and Sambaliung] were at war, one of them called the Sulos to his assistance. The Sulos seized the opportunity, making both princes prisoners, and after ravaging the country carried them both to Sulo, where they were released on condition of becoming tributary to Sulo, and confirming their trade to that nation.[99]

Despite Forrest's account, we can surmise from the oral traditions of Gunung Tabor that the Taosug encountered resistance for several decades. The rulers of Gunung Tabor shifted their place of residence from one river to another rather than submit to the Taosug. In the years between 1770 and 1800, they lived successively on the Kuran, Uluk, Pujut, and Bangun rivers, before finally settling at the confluence of the Segah and Kelai.[100] During this period, there was a rapid decline in Gunung Tabor's traditional trade. The settlements on the Uluk, Pujut, and Bangun were destroyed by Taosug

fleets.* The Taosug were only able to force a grudging acknowledgement
of their dominion from the people of Gunung Tabor because they controlled
the sea—depriving the inhabitants of access to the coast and their trade with
Darvel Bay.

The trade of Gunung Tabor fell into the hands of the Taosug by the start of
the nineteenth century. This is clear from Hunt's description in 1812:

> ... it [Gunung Tabor] has a wooden fort with 30 guns of different sizes, they
> acknowledge the government of Sulo; the chief is named Raja Allum; there
> are 3,000 Buguese, 500 Malays, 10 Chinese, and an immense number of orang
> idan in a whole string of negris [villages].[101]

Neither the Raja nor the local populace owned trading vessels of any
consequence.[102] The Buginese of Kutai imported salt, tobacco, cotton cloth,
opium, *chapa,* and other staples against bird's nest, *tripang,* gold, and
rattans. They also brought firearms and gunpowder for transhipment to
Sulu. *Prahus* from the Bugis settlement of Kylie, on the northwest coast of
Celebes, brought coconuts, salt, and sugar. From Sulu came salt, cloth, and
slaves. The main export commodities from Gunung Tabor to Sulu were wax
and bird's nest. *Tripang* and gold ranked second and third.[103]

Kutai was a principal source of wax for Berau's trade with Sulu. Between
1823 and 1828, it was estimated that 2,500 piculs of wax were annually
collected in the hinterlands surrounding Kutai. An 1831 description noted:

> Beeswax may be procured in almost any quantity; it is amazing to see the
> immense quantities brought down by the Diaks ... the quality found here
> [Kutai] is very superior; that found in many parts of the Diak Rajah Selgie's
> country being perfectly white, and of beautiful transparency. In every part of
> Coti, wax is taken by the Bugis assisted by their slaves ... Selgie, the great
> [Wahau] Rajah, has at least 900 men in the vicinity of Marpow [immediately
> north of Tengorrang] alone, employed solely in procuring wax. Already this
> year [c.1828] he has accumulated 1,430 piculs and expects 1,000 more; 1,735
> piculs have already been sent to Brawe [Berau]....[104]

The wax was brought to Tengarrong in August and September when the
Wahau came down the Mahakam river on rafts and dug-out canoes to trade
their cargoes of forest produce. Much of this wax was taken by Buginese to
Gunung Tabor for barter with the Taosug.

---

* In the raid against Bangun, the Taosug vessels were led by Datu Camsa and the
Buginese Tusa. Although Van Dewall cannot provide a date for this event, the Spanish
records of the early 1790s describe Camsa as one of Sulu's most enterprising marauders
who was related by marriage to both the Sultans of Sulu and Cotabato. See No.7, GCG a
Senor Secretario de Estado, 4 June 1806, AGI, Filipinas 510; Barrantes, *Guerras Piraticas,*
pp.159–61.

Segai-i Raiding for Bird's Nest

The "gentleman's agreement" that apparently emerged between Taosug and Buginese with regard to trading rights for jungle produce did not apply to bird's nest. There was vicious competition between Taosug and Buginese to obtain bird's nest because of the uncommon value put on them by the Chinese. Muslim traders in Berau rarely had direct access to the hundreds of small caves located in upland regions, and were wholly dependent for their bird's nest supply on powerful Kenyah groups such as the Wahau and Segai-i. The efforts of the Buginese of Kutai to control this resource was a primary cause for early Kenyah raids north of Berau after 1800.[105] I have already mentioned Wahau raiding on the Secatak and Sembawang rivers stemming from the rapid development of Bulungan's procurement trade in bird's nest.

The manifest prosperity brought to such Kenyah groups through trading and raiding for bird's nest was most evident among the Segai-i.* Their long-houses and stockaded settlements were located at the headwaters of the Segah and Kelai rivers and on the banks of their tributaries and streams. Van Dewall, the first Dutch administrator on the southeast Bornean coast, estimated the male Segai-i population of the region at ten thousand in 1848.[106]† Political integration between Segai-i communities and other groups was maintained through marriage alliances between members of the aristocratic chiefly class.

These slash-and-burn cultivators were among the most ardent headhunters in Borneo. The veneration of heads was central to the Segai-i way of life. Fresh heads were required for *mamat*, recurrent head feasts, which accompanied purification, funeral, and initiation ceremonies.[107] Traditionally, small parties led by chiefs participated in organized raids against other long-house groups, such as the Wahau, for this purpose.[108]

---

* Frank Marryat, who accompanied Edward Belcher, described the Segai-i of Gunung Tabor as "the very perfection of savage warriors". He wrote:

> We here [Gunung Tabor] fell in with a most remarkable tribe of Dyaks; they wore immense rings in their ears, made of tin or copper, the weight of which elongated the ear to a most extraordinary extent. On their heads they wore a mass of feathers of the argus pheasant. They wore on their shoulders skins of the leopard and wild cat, and necklaces of beads and teeth. They were armed with the usual parang, blowpipe, and shield. They were a much larger race of men than the Dyaks of the north coast ....

Frank Marryat, *Borneo and the Indian Archipelago,* pp.134–35.

† If Van Dewall's figure has been underestimated, Capt. Edward Belcher, who visited Bulungan in 1845, overestimated their numbers when he wrote that there were 60,000 males in the Segai-i population of Bulungan. There were six Segai-i settlements on the Kayan river tributary to the Rajah of Bulungan in 1848, and Belcher could have easily confused them with the much larger Tidong population who had similar customs and social structure. Belcher, *Voyage of the Samarang,* vol.1, p.230.

The intrusive effects of external trade were felt among the Segai-i, for whom bird's nest became the key to the cloth, salt, and slaves (an alternative source of heads) offered by Muslim traders of Kutai and Gunung Tabor.* The Segai-i responded by organizing raiding parties to gather nests belonging to tribes hundreds of miles away. As external trade continued to grow in the 1830s, there was a corresponding increase in tribal warfare for control of bird's nest sites. The powerful Segai-i Kelai asserted their superiority, and became feared throughout the interior of northeast Borneo.[109]

The Segai-i Kelai frequently went as far as the headwaters of the Kinabatangan† seeking bird's nest, heads, and a predominant position in the procurement trade.[110] In preceding decades they had repeatedly head-hunted and pillaged the bird's nest caves further south along the Secatak, Sembawang, and Sambakong watersheds.[111] Their raiding forced the Tidong to abandon their villages (which numbered over thirty in 1810) on the Sibuco River and seek refuge to the north. The Sibuco was reportedly uninhabited in 1845.[112]

They did not limit themselves to tribal groups as Taosug were not spared during the course of these expeditions. The Sultanate's southern outposts on the Langas and Atas rivers were assaulted by the Segai-i during the same period. Evidence of such incursions are the ruins of several old forts on the Langas and Atas rivers which had been built by Ida'an people under the

---

* For a discussion of the slave trade and ritual sacrifice, see Chapter 9; items symbolic of ritual wealth such as Chinese jars and brassware were also desired by the Segai-i in exchange for nests, gold, and wax. Copper or brass coinage was not used in trade with the Segai-i, and cloth frequently served as a money object in barter. Exchange equivalencies were stipulated in cloth in terms of the *kayu,* the standard unit of value of the Segai-i. According to Van Dewall, ten fathoms of plain or red chintz, three fathoms of red or yellow chintz with flowered prints, a common Buginese sarong, or an ordinary betelnut box were all the equivalent of a *kayu.* A Buginese sarong of fine craftsmanship was worth one and a half *kayu.* The principal money used by the Segai-i was gold, "said to be the purest in Borneo", wax, and of course bird's nest. In 1827, the standard exchange was a small bamboo of gold for the value of twenty guilders in trade goods and a picul of wax for ten to fifteen guilders worth. The value of bird's nest was determined on a pro-rata basis. It was not unusual for Buginese traders to make profits in excess of 800% when trading with the inland tribes. Copie verslag van C. Notte, 24 Feb. 1827, AR, Kolonien Archief 3200; Van Dewall, "Aanteekeningen Omtrent de Noordoostkust", pp.450–51; Belcher, *Voyage of the Samarang,* vol.1, pp.122–23; ibid., pp. 232–33.

† The Segai-i followed several of the rivers, notably the Bulungan and Kalabakang, to reach the richer territory to the north and the Kinabatangan. The route and time involved in such a journey was described in some detail by inland traders in 1906. From the upper Kalabakang to Teagow was a day's journey. A three-day canoe trip upriver on the Teagow and a three-day trek overland brought one to the headwaters of the Quarmote. From there another three days was required to go downriver to where the Quarmote meets the Kinabatangan. Hastings to A.C. Pearson, 24 Apr. 1960, CO, 874/277.

direction of *datus* to protect themselves from these attacks.[113] Their small isolated trading stations situated near the bird's nest caves at Baturong, Madai, and Segalung were principal targets of Segai-i expeditions.

After 1850, Segai-i raiding crippled the Sultanate's Bornean trade which was predicated on control over populations rather than territory. In the southern districts, the Segai-i gradually deprived the Taosug of an essential resource in the procurement trade—manpower. The period from 1830 to 1881 was characterized by sporadic demographic upheaval or "depopulation" throughout northeast Borneo, but especially in the area below the Kinabatangan.* It was Segai-i aggression that culminated in the virtual expulsion of the Taosug from the Tidong district by 1850. Some of the smaller Ida'an populations disappeared, others were absorbed or enslaved, and those who survived these interior raids were dispersed to the north. Communication ceased between the coast and the upper reaches of the Sembawang, Sibuco, and Segama rivers which the Segai-i passed on their way to harry settlements at the headwaters of the Kinabatangan.[114]

The repercussions of Segai-i raiding on Sulu's procurement trade were also significant in the northern region. The settlement pattern and riverine trade were drastically affected in parts of Mangindora district. It has been noted that at the beginning of the nineteenth century the upper reaches of many rivers in this district were settled. By 1860, the headwaters of even the Kinabatangan were sparsely populated because of the Segai-i. Populations that remained unscathed were pressured to move away from the bird's nest caves and further downriver, rather than risk a confrontation with this dreaded group.

Ida'an on these rivers, who feared for their lives, refused to enter the forest at any great distance to collect nests or wax for their Sulu overlords. Specific knowledge of important caves, the location of which was often known to only one or two people, was lost to weaker tribes as they were scattered and displaced by the Segai-i. In 1885, a river chief on the Kinabatangan stated:

> ... in the old days the largest [bird's nest] cave of all was one named Phang, the whereabouts of which is now lost; but it is somewhere inland behind Segalung ... the Erahaans had to abandon the district it is in years ago owing to it being much exposed to Sagai raids.[115]

To the descendants of migrant Ida'an, the vast area to the southwest of the Kinabatangan was still "Segai country" until as late as 1878.[116]

The economic prosperity and political stability of the Sulu Sultanate from

---

* Other factors responsible for social dislocation and population movement on the northeast coast in the second half of the 19th century were diseases such as small-pox and the raiding of the Samal of Tawi-Tawi, who attacked coastal villages for the purposes of procuring slaves. Warren, *The North Borneo Chartered Company's Administration of the Bajau,* pp. 26–27.

1768 to 1878 were inextricably bound up in the procurement trade on the east coast of Borneo. Economic resources had attracted the attention of the Sultanate in the latter part of the eighteenth century and involved Taosug in littoral procurement relations with north Bornean people.

Dyadic ties and marriage alliances were forged between *datus* and the chiefly families of diverse cultural and ethnic groups. They intermarried with Ida'an and Tidong to ensure their control over bird's nest sites, riverine trade, and the movement of tribal people. These lineage ties reinforced the influence and authority of the Taosug in the autonomous upriver areas and enabled the social participation of Bornean authority figures in Sulu's political system and, hence, the larger life of the zone. In distant river systems, *datus* were able to maintain a *de facto* trading monopoly by bestowing offices of the lowest grade on tribal patriarchs. The system provided a way of organizing and incorporating ethnically fragmented populations within the political and economic framework of the Sultanate.

Nevertheless, it must be stressed that certain tribes were never fully integrated into the Sulu-Bornean social system. The Segai-i, in particular, who traded with the Buginese and Taosug largely on their own terms, and a number of the more remote, upriver Ida'an and Tidong groups maintained a considerable degree of political independence.

Table 2 shows the extent to which the procurement trade provided integration to the zone. The existence of a wide-ranging market network that linked sizeable hinterland riverine settlements (long since vanished) with the Sulu Sultanate is affirmed by the table's trade statistics for the estimated annual volume of natural products.*

Ethnic integration into the procurement trade was no less remarkable than the extent and complexity of the system itself. Samal Bajau Laut and trained slaves specialized in the harvest of sea produce. The Islamized *orang sungai* of the Paitan river were mobilized to procure camphor, while coastal and riverine dwelling Ida'an speakers of Sandakan Bay and the Kinabatangan (Buludoopy, Era'an, Ida'an, and Sabahan) seasonally collected bird's nest for immigrant Taosug. Effective authority at the periphery of the zone was limited. In the Tirun district, the Taosug encountered Segai-i raiding and Bugis trade competition. The Buginese did not allow the Taosug to gain political ascendancy on the southern rivers, but the Taosug managed to coexist with their stronger rivals, and Sulu's trade and political interests were pronounced in Tirun prior to 1850.

---

* The statistic for bird's nest from the Tirun district, which implies a lower level than one would have expected from the reputation of that area as a source of bird's nest, suggests the early signs of Taosug-Bugis discord over the bird's nest trade and the advent of large-scale Kenyah raiding in the interior. Any effort to create a similar table illustrating aspects of Sulu's procurement trade for the second half of the 19th century would have to exclude all the riverine communities below Madai.

TABLE 2

ESTIMATED ANNUAL VOLUME OF MARINE/JUNGLE PRODUCE IMPORTED TO SULU FROM THE NORTHEAST BORNEAN COAST

District & Settlements	Kapis Pearls	Wax	Camphor	Rattans	Bird's Nest	Tortoise Shell	Tripang	Rice	Clove Blark	Cotton	Gold	Ivory
Marudu District												
Marudu Bay	25 katis	200 piculs	20 piculs	considerable quantity	27 piculs	50 piculs		considerable quantity		15 piculs		
Paitan		unspecified quantity	considerable quantity	unspecified quantity		considerable quantity		unspecified quantity	considerable quantity			
Sugut		considerable quantity					considerable quantity	unspecified quantity	unspecified quantity			
Labuck	considerable quantity	unspecified quantity		unspecified quantity	unspecified quantity					15 piculs		
Mangindora District												
Sandakan Bay	5 katis	3 piculs	3 piculs	unspecified quantity	250 piculs		150 piculs				10 katis	
Kinabatangan		600 piculs		considerable quantity	130 piculs							
Giong					unspecified quantity							
Madai					unspecified quantity							
Sabahan	considerable quantity	3 piculs	5 piculs		130 piculs		40 piculs	considerable quantity				unspecified quantity
Tidong		300 piculs	2 piculs	considerable quantity	200 piculs	unspecified quantity	unspecified quantity				1 picul	
Trun District												
Sibuco		100 piculs		100 piculs	50 piculs							
Sambakong					20 piculs			considerable quantity				
Leo & Li Dong					25 piculs						considerable quantity	
Sicatak					100 piculs							
Bulungan											considerable quantity	
Kuran/Berau		400 piculs	unspecified quantity		23 piculs	10 piculs	1,000 piculs				2 piculs	5 piculs

Note: This table was compiled from the following sources: Hunt, "Some Particulars Relating to Sulo", pp.54–57; Dr Leyden, "Sketch of Borneo", pp.29–30; the figures provided to Hunt by Taosug informants seem to reflect optimum rather than average volumes in the case of the less important settlements in Marudu Bay and Magindora District.

RICE IN THE ECONOMY OF THE SULU SULTANATE

The most important article in Sulu's local system of trade and exchange was rice. Supplemented by fish, it was the mainstay of life for most Taosug and Samal. On the volcanic islands of Jolo, Pata, Tapul, and Siassi, rice was cultivated with the plough and carabao in non-irrigated fields. Possessed of numerous short streams at intermediate and high elevations and adequately developed soil covers, cultivable areas extended to the very edge of volcanic craters on some of these islands.* In 1761, the Taosug estimated the archipelago's annual rice production as 15,000 to 20,000 piculs.[117]

Table 3 based on data copied by Hunt from the Sultan's archive specifies the type of economic activity carried on by coastal communities on Jolo and neighbouring offshore islands.† It provides an index to the importance the Taosug placed on rice cultivation in the indigenous economy—thirty-four out of the thirty-seven communities listed planted rice on a large scale. Furthermore, Hunt was unable to supply any data on the hinterland villages of the Tau Gimba which were solely preoccupied in the cultivation of rice, sugar cane, corn, and sago.

Nevertheless, the Sultanate did not produce enough rice for its consumption. The agricultural potential of these islands were never fully exploited by the Taosug because of erratic rainfall. The lack of suitable bottom land for irrigated fields made the Taosug peasant dependent on the heavy rains which occurred during the southwest monsoon from May to October.[118] Drought was not unfamiliar to Sulu. Drought conditions in the archipelago resulting from the late and inadequate arrival of rain were commented on by European observers in the eighteenth and nineteenth centuries.[119] Droughts spanning months and occasionally years turned Jolo island's usually bare self-sufficiency into severe shortage.‡

Equally important, as a mixed economy evolved, many Taosug deliberately chose not to participate in the agricultural sector which conflicted with the trade and procurement activities. Rice was sown in the

---

* Dalrymple described Tapul as "a high island, abounding with fresh water, small cattle, goats and yams, being cultivated to the very top". Dalrymple, *Oriental Repertory*, p.516.

† The fugitive captive Chrishaan Soerma listed the following communities as cultivating rice and having livestock in 1834; Siassi, Maimbung, Lumapiet, Silangkan, Njuik-Njuik, Mubu, Kau Nejan, Taglibie, Hasu, Kausepat, Bual, Tulayan, Karang, and Basilan, Verklaringen van Chrishaan Soerma, 10 Aug.1846, ANRI, Menado 50.

‡ In 1748, Juan Angles, Jesuit Superior of a mission sent to Jolo, described the drought conditions that confronted him on his arrival in the Sulu archipelago. The drought had lasted nine months and one of the worst affected areas was Jolo island where the harvest had been destroyed and the Sultan and populace reduced to eating roots and foliage, GCG a Senor Secretario de Estado, 4 June 1806, AGI, Filipinas 510.

TABLE 3

THE VILLAGE ECONOMY OF JOLO'S COASTAL COMMUNITIES AND OFFSHORE ISLANDS

Political Leaders	Village	Estimated Population in 1812	Rice	Coconuts	Sugar Cane	Cocoa	Cattle	Buffalo	Horses	Tripang	Mother of Pearl Shell	Pearls	Sharks Fin	Tortoise Shell	Birds Nest
Sultan Ali-ud-Din	Jolo	6,800	x			x	x	x	x		x	x			
	Dulbatu	300	x												
	Matanda	1,000	x												
Sherif Hassan	Batu-Batu	1,000	x												
Perkasa Alum	Kanjaia	1,500	x												
Maharajah Pahlawan Damung	Timahow	2,000	x		x										
Panglima Hassan	Sagaugun	4-5,000	x	x	x										
Datu Adanun	Silangkan	4-5,000	x	x	x										
Orang Kaya Kindinga	Alu	5,000	x		x										
Laximana Pala	Bawisan	1,500	x		x	x									
Orangkaya Abu, Palamputla	Tundok Bunga	4,000	x	x											
Datu Adonan, Orang Kaya Sali Bangsawan, Maharajah Buan	Parang	8,000	x							x	x	x			x
Maharajah Pahlawan, Sherif Maharaiah Sali, Bangsawan Imbi	Lagasan	2,000	x							x	x	x			
Datu Majindi	Maimbung	2,000	x							x	x	x			
	Patean Island	1,500	x							x	x	x	x	x	
Panglima Japar	Pata Island	7,000	x											x	
	Talipau	3,000	x												
Maharajah Pahlawan Baizid	Patibulan	2,000	x												
Parkasa Allum, Abdul Hamman	Tapokan	1,000	x												
Daimaowan, Orang Kaya Amil Hamzah	Kadongdong	6,000	x												
Orang Kaya Abdul Samad	Pitoko	1,500	x												
Mamankotara	Tandok	8,000	x												
Laxamana Dahman	Kamingan Is. (Cabingaan Is.?)	15,000	x												
Laxamana Dainan	Bait-Bait	9,000	x				x	x	x						
Tuan Mandangan	Bulit Kutin	3,000	x				x	x	x						
Orang Kaya Abdul Samad	Tulayan Island	3,000	x				x								
Panglima Daud	Bual	6,000	x				x	x	x						
Paduka Tahil, Paduka Atti	Kansipat	4,000	x				x	x	x						
Mamancha Abdulla	Soo	6,000	x							x					
Parkasa Alum	Bun-Bun	1,000	x			x									
	Tuup	1,000	x												
	Lahim	1,000	x												
Tuan Tahil	Taglibi	4,000	x												
Panglima Kamba	Buang Hinan	4,000	x				x								
Panglima Asib	Patikul	5,000	x												
Baiyung	Tandu	1,500	x												
Datu Bandahara	Mubu	1,500	x												

Note: This table was compiled from the following source: Hunt, "Some Particulars Relating to Sulo", pp.41–42.

Sulu archipelago at the beginning of April—precisely the time of the year when the trading vessels from Manila were arriving and *datus* in Jolo, Maimbung, Parang, and other communities were setting out for different parts of the zone to collect *tripang*, pearls, and mother of pearl shell.[120]

The Taosug looked to their neighbour's to solve their problem of chronic food shortage. In addition to the rice brought from Manila and the northeast coast of Borneo, the Taosug relied on rice imported from the Cotabato basin, stapling points on southern Palawan, Basilan, and Cagayan de Sulu, as well as Chinese merchants and Spanish traders from Zamboanga and the southern Visayas.

Favourable circumstances in the first half of the eighteenth century had predisposed the Cotabato Sultanate to maritime marauding and trade as well as subsistence agriculture. This was before the Sulu Sultanate eclipsed its power and prestige. By 1800, the economy of the Magindanao, who occupied the best land in the Cotabato basin, was largely based on the cultivation of rice—both in permanent irrigated fields and swidden plots—and only secondarily on raiding. Heavy seasonal rains and perennial river floods which inundated large areas of the basin floor (comprising more than a thousand square miles of arable land) enabled lowland rice to be extensively cultivated.[121] Forrest observed, "On the banks of the Pelangy [Rio Grande de Mindanao] and Tamantakka, the mohametans grow much rice."[122]

Much of Cotabato's rice for export to Sulu came from the swiddens of the Subanun and Tiruray, animistic tribal groups practising slash-and-burn agriculture in the upriver areas surrounding the triangular basin and the interior of the Mindanao panhandle.* They lived in dispersed settlements as clients of Magindanao who exacted tribute and trade from them in rice and forest produce. Forrest, who spent eight months in Cotabato (1775–76), differentiated between "harafora" and Muslim Subanun in describing the annual tribute or *buhis*:

> The vassals of the Sultan, and of others who possess great estates, are called Kanakan. Those vassals are sometimes mahometans, though mostly haraforas. The latter only may be sold with the lands, but cannot be sold off

---

* Forrest variously refers to the Subanun, who form a distinct cultural and linguistic group, as "Haroforas", "Sunabos", "Kanakan", and "oran Manubo". The Subanuns are believed to have derived their name from the word "Sula" which means river. Ordinarily found at the upper reaches of small rivers, Subanun designates "up-river" people, BH-PCL, vol.6, Paper 162, No. 25, Emerson Christie Brewer, "The Non-Christian Tribes of the Northern Half of the Zamboanga Peninsula". See also E.B.Christie, *The Subanuns of Sindanagan Bay;* John Park Finley and William Churchill, *The Subanu: Studies of a Sub-Visayan Mountain Folk of Mindanao*; Charles Frake, "Social Organization and Shifting Cultivation among the Sindangan Subanun" (Ph.D.diss., Yale University, 1955); Stuart Schlegel, "Tiruray Magindanaon Ethnic Relations: An Ethnohistorical Puzzle", pp.25–30; Ileto, *Magindanao, 1860–1888*, pp.24–25.

the lands.... The Mahometan vassals are bound to accompany their lords, on any sudden expedition; but the haraforas being in great measure excused from such attendance, pay yearly certain taxes which are not expected from the Mahometan vassals. They pay a boiss, [buhis] or land tax. A harafora family pays ten battels of paly (rough rice) 40 pounds each; three of rice about sixty pound; one fowl, one bunch of plantains, thirty roots called clody, or St.Helena yam, and fifty heads of indian corn. I give this as one instance of the utmost that is ever paid. Then they must sell fifty battels of paly, equal to two thousand pound weight, for one Kangan.[123]

Buhis was not always collected in produce. This is evident from Forrest's account of what one of the Sultan's tax gatherers had collected from some five hundred harafora families: "2,870 battels of paly, of forty pounds each; 490 Spanish dollars; 160 Kangans; 6 tayls of gold, [and] ... a cloth made of the plantain tree, three yards long, and one broad".[124]

Rice and other Subanun products were also acquired by the Magindanao through a form of forced trade called *pemuku*. It was conducted as follows: the Sultan or *datu* would send a Subanun village a gift—wooden chests, Chinese jars, brass gongs, bolts of coarse cotton cloth, salt, or tobacco—and the Subanun were obliged to reciprocate, but their gift had to be worth twice as much as the Sultan's trade goods. If they were unable to repay double the value of the gift and preferred to return it, they could do so provided they added half its value in produce to "placate" the Sultan.[125]

The kind of negative reciprocity practised by the Magindanao caused isolated Subanun groups to move beyond the dominion of their wet rice growing masters in the hope of finding security in Sibuguey territory or at makeshift villages near the Zamboanga *presidio*. But their status and social condition remained unchanged. In the 1830s these Subanun were regarded by the Spaniards and the Sibuguey *datus* as socially inferior but skilled in rice cultivation, and for such groups exploitative trade relations were established anew.[126]

Trade between the Sultanates of Sulu and Cotabato was based on rice. That important link in the indigenous system of trade and exchange developed out of differences in the political fortunes and basic economies of the Magindanao and Taosug by the end of the eighteenth century—between a sultanate that had limited contact with the outside world and one which controlled the external trade of the region, and between an area endowed with rice and one which had little.

Forrest recognized that the Sulu Sultanate acquired Magindanao rice through a monopoly of trade with the Chinese:

> This [pearls] is the source of their wealth, and sets them more at ease than any Malays I ever knew, though their island does not generally produce so much rice as they consume. They trade therefore to Magindanao with Chinese articles for that grain, and make a great profit, as no China junks have for a long time gone thither.[127]

The Cotabato traders exchanged rice for "kangans, beads, gongs, China basons with red edges, deep brass plates, five in a set; deep saucers, three and four inches diameter; brass wire and iron".[128] The kangan, thinly woven cloth, nineteen inches broad and six yards long, was a standard measure used by the Taosug in exchanges with the Magindanao. In 1836, four piculs of rice in the Rio Grande was worth one kangan.[129] A documented analysis of the trade flow between Cotabato and Sulu is not possible but we know that it was sizeable. For example, between January and April of 1838, thirty large Taosug *prahus*, laden with Manila goods, arrived at Cotabato to obtain rice* and wax.[130]

Rice was also shipped to Jolo in large quantities from Basilan and the outer islands of Cagayan de Sulu and Palawan.† On Basilan, rice was grown by the Yakan or agricultural Sama, who resided inland on the eastern and northern parts of the largest island in the Sulu chain.[131] As cultivators of upland rice and tubers, and having a rich weaving tradition, they were considered a "subject people" of the Sulu Sultanate.‡ The character of the Sultanate's control over the Yakan was largely ritual, since the Taosug rarely exercised meaningful authority in Basilan's interior.[132] Nevertheless, as agriculturalists, the Yakan were dependent on maritime strand-dwelling Samal and Taosug for trade items vital to their life and culture such as salt, pottery, iron tools, brassware, and opium, which were translated into power and prestige factors in Yakan communities.§ In return, upland rice and forest produce were brought to the Taosug at coastal villages. Basilan's rice export to Jolo was estimated at twenty to thirty large *prahus* year.[133]

There could hardly have been greater contrast between two places in the zone whose fate was so intimately linked than that between Zamboanga and Sulu. The Spanish *presidio,* first established in 1635 to

---

* It is important to note in this instance that the Taosug were insisting on rice even though the Magindanao were in the midst of a drought.

† Farren to Palmerston, 17 Jan. 1851, CO, 144/8. In 1814, 10 koyans of rice and 60 koyans of paddy were collected in tribute from Palawan. On Cagayan de Sulu, which had a smaller Taosug population than Palawan, rice was extensively cultivated for export by the 1790s. Hunt, "Some Particulars Relating to Sulo", pp.58–59; Capt. Savage Trotter to the Court of Directors, 24 Dec. 1769, IOL, H/Misc/102/4, p.343; Amosa Delano, *A Narrative of Voyages and Travels in the Northern and Southern Hemispheres, p.169.*

‡ Yakan *datus* recognized the sovereignty of the Sultan of Sulu until the beginning of the Spanish forward-movement in the region in the middle of the 19th century. Christie, "The Moros of Sulu and Mindanao", p.51.

§ The Yakan's lack of seafaring capability was mentioned as late as 1892, in a Spanish clerical document: "The ... Moros ... called Yacanes, live in the interior of the island, devoting themselves to agriculture ... they are not navigators, as they are scarcely capable of handling boats and many know absolutely nothing." Apuntes sobre la Isla de Basilan, 1892, SJA, XIV—9, pp.33–34; for another contemporary description, see the letter from Father Pablo Cavalleria to Father Francisco Sanchez, 31 Dec. 1886, BRPI, 43, p.256.

contain Muslim raiding, was located deep within the zone, and occupied a position of strategic importance at the southern tip of the Zamboanga peninsula in the westernmost region of Mindanao.[134] Immediately after its reestablishment in 1719, it became one of Spain's most important frontier communities with a large, permanent garrison, and a developed commercial life with Cotabato and China. But in the face of the ascent of the Sulu Sultanate, few ports in the region had less trade than Zamboanga by 1800. As it failed to attract foreign commerce or control trade into interior Mindanao in the latter part of the eighteenth century, Zamboanga itself was placed in a position of economic dependence and became a part of Sulu's trade hinterland.

Zamboanga focused its commercial activity with Sulu around the export of rice.[135] This occurred despite its being situated in an unprosperous agricultural region where even in years of abundant harvest there was not sufficient rice to meet Zamboanga's need. The difference was imported from Manila and Panay.[136] Rice cultivation with the plough and carabao was a full-time occupation for most settlers, who were restricted to living in and near the fortress.

The grain trade, which began in earnest in the 1770s, proved lucrative for the governors of Zamboanga, and they did not hesitate to empty the stocks of the *presidio*'s warehouses in trade with the Taosug.[137] Local rice and even the annual supplement shipped from Manila was furnished under their authority to Taosug for Chinese products. Sulu vessels which plied between Jolo and Zamboanga carried rice in periods when there was not enough to go around in the Spanish fortress and settlement. The result was wealthy governors and hungry people.* Of the trade that the Governor of Zamboanga conducted on his own account, Meares observed:

---

* In a scathing report written fifteen years earlier, Cencelli described in horrified terms the Governor's residence as a "general store", replete with stocks of vinegar, salt, candles, shoes, and Chinese trade wares, and wrote of the officials of Zamboanga: "These Governors have spent their three years solely thinking about making money, and their predecessors, who had abandoned Zamboanga saying 'it is good that another will come', and it has continued in this fashion until present." Diario de la Expedicion del mando de Don Juan Cencelli, 16 Apr. 1774, AHN, Estado 2845, caja 2. The following entry of 22 Jan. 1794 appears in the journal of the *Britannide*, which put into Zamboanga, on a voyage from England to Port Jackson: "Every kind of produce, natural to this clime appeared to be enjoyed by the inhabitants of this place, in abundance, but the Jew-like Governor prohibits any person from assisting us with refreshments, we of course bought every article had of him, and he had the conscience to ask 5 shillings for 20 lbs of rice." Journal of a Voyage from England to Port Jackson, New South Wales in the years 1792, 93, 94, and 95, and in 1795 in the ship *Britannide*, 656/172B, Peabody Museum, Salem.

Inconsiderably, however, as this settlement may appear, the Governor is supposed to clear thirty thousand dollars in the three years of his residence there.[138]

Zamboanga's rice harvest in January and February coincided with the arrival of rice-laden vessels from the Visayas and Manila.[139] The traders, who had to leave before the beginning of the following monsoon in August, were forced to sell their rice in Zamboanga when it was still plentiful and cheap. Much of this imported rice was taken to Jolo in trade to augment Sulu's dwindling grain reserves.

Shortly before November, when the price of unhulled rice rose to as much as twelve pesos a cavan in Zamboanga and provincial trading vessels were unable to sail around the bottom of Mindanao and reach the fortress, the Taosug harvested their own rice crop.[140] For a brief duration in the last four to five months of the year, when Zamboanga's grain stocks were virtually non-existent, Taosug returned to capitalize on the "spoils system" of the governors and sold quantities of their rice at great profit. In November of 1847, the Governor of Zamboanga wrote:

> ... thirty Joloano *pancos* have arrived over several months, nearly all with cargoes of rice and padi which is in short supply throughout the province.[141]

When Taosug merchants were preoccupied with foreign traders in Jolo and chose not to voyage to Zamboanga in the latter part of the year, Zamboanga's condition of scarcity was transformed into one of severe want and soaring prices.[142]

It has been estimated that sixty Taosug *prahus* were trading to Zamboanga from Jolo in 1800.[143] This local trade, which primarily involved Chinese trade pottery (storage jars and porcelain vessels from Macao and Amoy) and rice, was worth between 3,600 and 5,800 pesos a year in the 1830s.[144]

Zamboanga's failure to attract trade troubled Manila. In 1836, Jose Maria Halcon, a naval officer expert in Sulu affairs, suggested that the Taosug stranglehold over the network of local trade and exchange could be broken if Zamboanga could reestablish its commercial life with the Cotabato Sultanate. The key to the resolution of Zamboanga's dilemma was rice:

> The Jolo archipelago cannot cultivate sufficient rice to sustain its large population. This, coupled with the huge number of people employed in the fisheries to procure mother of pearl shell, pearl, and *tripang*, and the sterility of the Samal islands, has made unhulled rice the principle article of trade ....[145]

By centring its trade with the Taosug around the control and distribution of Magindanao rice, and persuading Manila merchants to forsake the Sulu Sultanate and trade at Cotabato, Zamboanga, in Halcon's opinion, could replace Jolo as the region's trade emporium.

In the end nothing changed. The Manila traders intent on their personal fortunes refused to cooperate,* and Halcon's suggestions to reorganize the *presidio*'s administration, to make Zamboanga a free port for vessels calling from nearby islands and from China, and to assist Chinese traders in establishing themselves by a ten-year moratorium on all taxes, were ignored by his superiors.[146] Strategically Zamboanga remained important, but its economy continued to decline and suffered a severe setback in the third quarter of the nineteenth century when the Taosug reduced their trade to the Spanish settlement at the expense of the British colony and free port of Labuan.

---

* These merchants preferred to trade at Jolo, where they knew a full cargo could be obtained before the end of the season, rather than risk a voyage to Cotabato or Sarangani. The captain Don Inocencio Escrivano, in defending his right to trade at Jolo before the Governor of Zamboanga, pointed to the fact that the Manila pontin *San Rufo* had been at Cotabato over four months and was unable to complete her cargo. In 1838, the Manila traders demonstrated their displeasure of government efforts to tamper with their trade, when they deliberately turned a deaf ear to the Governor of Zamboanga's plea to go to the relief of the drought-stricken Cotabato Sultanate and took their rice to Jolo instead. No.4, Manuel de la Cruz a GCG, 25 Apr. 1838, PNA, Mindanao/Sulu 1816–1898; Expediente 591, El Gobierno Military Politico de Zamboanga a GCG, 8 Apr. 1838, PNA, Mindanao/Sulu 1838–1890.

The Sulu Zone

Canipaan ■ Maliud
Panitan

SULU SEA

Tobug ✶ **Mindanao**

Balambangan
▲ Cagayan de Sulu

Zamboanga

Tempasuk ✶
Paitan
Sugut
Labuk
Kinabatangan

Jolo ■ ✶ Balangingi

Segama

Sarangani

Sabahart
Sibuco
Sambakong

CELEBES SEA

Sangir

Bulungan

▲ Berau

Menado ● Bangka

Borneo

Tontoli ✶

Kylie

Makakam
Samarinda ▲ Dongala ▲

Trading Centre
■ Taosug
▲ Bugis
✶ Raiding Centre
  Land above
  500 metres
  Land above
  1500 metres

Pasir

Celebes

Palau
Laut

5

The External Trade of the Sulu Sultanate: Vicissitudes, 1856–1878

LABUAN AND SINGAPORE

By 1850 European powers had begun to play a more direct role in the Taosug state. Sulu was still a major port Sultanate, but increasingly caught between conflicting colonial interests. The Sultanate was entering a perilous period in its history, marked by exposure to superior Spanish naval strength, uneven diplomacy with Manila, and developing trade with Spain's principal colonial rival—Britain.

Fearing possible English or Dutch intrusion in the Sulu archipelago, Spain adopted a hard line along the borders of its southern frontier and destroyed the Samal "pirate nests" on Balangingi with steam gunboats in 1848. This act visibly weakened the Taosug and convinced them of the necessity for English friendship and trade. The Sultanate severed its long-established commercial tie with Manila and welcomed the assistance of James Brooke, the politically ambitious Governor of Labuan, who sought to protect Sulu from the Spanish embrace.

James Brooke was the architect of the Sulu Sultanate's commercial reorientation to Labuan. Taosug trade to the English settlement, which began in 1856, originated in Brooke's efforts to encourage "the countries and rivers from Sarawak to Sulu and Bulungan" to avail themselves of the commercial advantages of the Labuan market.[1] He paid a brief promotional visit to Jolo on board the British warship *Maeander* in December 1848. Sultan Muhammed Fadl, harassed by the Spanish, provided a friendly reception for Brooke, who presented a letter of introduction from the Governor of the Straits Settlements (see Appendix I for the text of the letter). The Sultan professed an interest in friendship with England and the establishment of trade with Labuan. The visit prepared the way for a Treaty of Friendship and Commerce between Britain and Sulu which Brooke negotiated when he returned to Jolo in May 1849 (see Appendix J for the text of the treaty).[2]

The agreement signed, Brooke's mission steamed to Zamboanga. Brooke informed Cayetano Figuerao, the Spanish Governor, that he had concluded a treaty with the Sulu Sultanate which included mutual trading privileges and a number of advantages for British subjects. Figuerao expressed surprise at this sudden turn of events because the treaty of 1836 between Spain and

Sulu (of which James Brooke had no knowledge) stipulated that the Sultan could not enter into a new alliance without the consent of Spain. He formally protested against article seven of the English treaty:

> His Highness the Sultan of Sulu, for purposes of avoiding in the future any occasion for disagreement, promises to make no cession of territory within his dominions to any other nation, nor to subjects or citizens thereof, nor to acknowledge vassalage or feudality to any other power without the consent of her Britannic Majesty.[3]

The treaty was sent to England, approved and ratified by the Queen on 31 October 1849. Brooke's absence from Labuan inadvertently postponed its formalization. The delay proved unfortunate for the Sulu Sultanate. The English Government, under increasing pressure from the Spanish ambassador at the Court of St James, sent instructions to Brooke not to proceed with the exchange of ratifications.[4] England's temporary loss of official interest and Dutch designs on the northeast coast of Borneo led the Spanish to take decisive measures against Sultan Muhammed Fadl for repudiating Spain's claim of sovereignty.*

The raids conducted by the Samal inhabitants of Tunkil, Bukutua, and Bulan in November 1849 provided Don Antonio Urbiztondo, the new Governor of the Philippines, with the pretext to invade Jolo and claim a monopoly of Sulu's trade.[5] After a brief campaign against these islets, in which over a hundred boats and a thousand homes were destroyed, the Spanish force returned to Zamboanga. There, Urbiztondo reinforced his expedition for the invasion of Sulu. The fleet's war vessels—steam and sail, troop transports, and native craft—carried 142 officers, 2,876 soldiers, and 925 volunteers from Cebu, Iloilo, and Zamboanga.†

The assault on Jolo began on the morning of 28 February 1851.[6] The Sultan, who had expressed his resolve to adhere to the Brooke treaty,

---

* Baron Van Hoevell, in an article entitled "Labuan, Sarawak, the Northeast Coast of Borneo and the Sultan of Sulu", in the *Tijdschrift voor Nederlandsch Indie*, published in Jan. 1849, drew the attention of his countrymen to the immediate importance of James Brooke's activities at Sulu and the trade of the northeast coast of Borneo. Hoevell outlined Sulu's tributary relationships with the various districts, listed their products, and pointed out that Sandakan Bay would be the best place to establish a settlement when they took possession of the coast. The Spanish could not allow the Dutch Government to coerce the Sultan into a treaty that would carry out Van Hoevell's views. W.R.Van Hoevell, "Laboean, Serawak, de Noordoostkust van Borneo en de Sulthan van Soeloe", *TNL*, XI, pt. I (1849), pp.66–83.

† At Bulan the Spanish troops burned 250 houses and 20 *vintas*. The Samal of Bukutua surrendered and promised to remain loyal to the Spanish Crown. After a series of skirmishes on Tunkil, about a thousand houses and 106 boats were put to the torch. Saleeby, *History of Sulu*, pp.104–5. Contributions towards the expenses of the expeditions from the *Ayuntamiento*, or municipal government of Manila, the religious orders, and private individuals amounted to nearly 10,000 pounds. Farren to Palmerston, 16 Mar. 1856, CO. 144/8.

received no protection or aid from that quarter. Mohammed Fadl and his *datus* withdrew from their *kotas* into the mountain fastness of the island's interior after a spirited resistance; all the fortifications and villages in the vicinity of Jolo were razed within forty-eight hours. But the Spanish troops, hampered by heavy rains, mud, and dysentery could not leave a garrison to occupy the destroyed town. The result was a treaty concluded between the Military Governor of Zamboanga and the Sultan and his principal *datus*.

If the treaty had been observed it would have made the Sulu Sultanate and its dependencies an integral part of the Spanish Colony of the Philippines.* It nullified the Brooke agreement and stated that no foreign vessel would be allowed to trade in the Sulu archipelago except at a port properly opened for foreign commerce. The treaty called for the establishment of a trading factory and naval station at Jolo to protect Spain's commercial interests and prevent future traffic in munitions.[7]

But neither side upheld the provisions of the treaty. The Spanish quarrelled over the Taosug translation which was interpreted as "the expression of a friendly union with Spain".†[8] The treaty was to have a more important impact in the diplomatic circles of Europe than in Sulu and Zamboanga where the terms remained for years a dead letter. The Sultanate continued to trade in arms, opium, and cloth with other colonial powers, but especially at Labuan and Singapore.

The Labuan-Jolo Entrepot Trade

Labuan Island,‡ on the South China Sea some thirty-five miles from the entrance to Brunei Bay, was made a British colony in James Brooke's expectation that it would serve as an entrepot for the commerce of Borneo and a naval base for the suppression of piracy:[9]

---

* In the treaty of 19 April 1851, the Sultan and his *datus* recognized Spain's sovereignty, promised to assist in eradicating piracy, to fly the Spanish flag exclusively, and not to trade or use firearms without the permission of Spain. The Spanish promised to respect Taosug customs and religion, to confer royalty on them, to confirm rights of succession upon reigning families, to secure the authority of the Sultan and promote trade to the Spanish ports. They allowed the Sultan to issue passports and agreed to pay him 1,500 pesos yearly. (For the text of the treaty, see Appendix K).

† According to Saleeby, the Taosug could not understand "Kunkista", the word transliterated from Spanish for "conquest" in the Sulu text of the treaty. Saleeby, *History of Sulu*, p.110.

‡ Labuan's position relative to the key trade emporiums of Southeast Asia was excellent. Situated between the Philippine archipelago and Dutch possessions, the island was about 650 miles from Manila and 900 miles from Batavia. It was situated 700 miles south of Singapore and 600 miles from the French colony of Cochin-China and Saigon. P. Hennesey to the Duke of Buckingham and Chandos, 18 Nov. 1868, CO, 144/28.

The position of Labuan is central and commands Brunei the capitol. The position, relative to China is good, and the trade with the northern part of Borneo, Sulu, Magindanao, etc., may be opened and encouraged. For the suppression of piracy no place could be preferable, as it would bring us within reach of the Illanun and Balangingi ....[10]

Nevertheless, Labuan's prospects for attracting regional trade proved bleak. The settlement's unhealthy environment deterred influential Chinese and Malay traders from establishing themselves there.[11] The *pengirans* of Brunei viewed the new settlement as a further English intrusion. They feared losing their control over the trade of northwest Borneo to Labuan and did not hesitate to discredit the motives of the new government with subject people up the various rivers. As a result, Labuan lacked the necessary impetus— local capital and enterprise—for creating a trade centre. The small number of Bornean *prahus* that visited the settlement with trade commodities could not provide the stimulus to develop Labuan's market. A British naval officer described the settlement in 1852:

> This place has not advanced one single step since I was here two years ago, and for my own part I scarcely see how or when it is to advance. There is nothing but a boat trade, which never can amount to anything deserving that name, but what I consider a much worse point is I see very few more settlers; two years ago I was told the Chinese were coming over in great numbers but where are they?[12]

Despite a government campaign to improve sanitary conditions and persuade Chinese merchants in Brunei to purchase land and locate themselves within the settlement, the colony's future and modest prosperity were made secure only after the Taosug became involved in Labuan's trade and the export of guns in 1856.[13]

The Manila-Jolo trade collapsed after the bombardment of Balangingi in 1848. From nearly half a million pesos in 1848 it dropped to 68 pesos in 1853.[14] Besides Manila, Singapore had played a prominent part in the Sulu Sultanate's trade in the first half of the nineteenth century, through the supply of weapons and opium. As Sulu's economy recovered, Singapore became the principal market for most of the Taosug goods that formerly had gone to Manila. Labuan, a week to ten days' journey from Jolo, became an entrepot for the Sulu Sultanate's trade with Singapore. Taosug *prahus* from the outer islands that wished to avoid the long voyage to Singapore and risk of Balangingi attack, began to arrive at Labuan.

Lieutenant Governor Scott, writing as early as 1851, reported that the chiefs of Marudu bay had visited the colony to trade,[15] but *prahus* from Palawan, the Kinabatangan and Sulu found their way to the Labuan market for the first time only in 1856.[16] In that year, Datu Alimuddin of Palawan expressed his desire to trade with the settlement in a letter to the English Governor.[17]

The first *prahus* that came from Palawan with beeswax and *tripang* were able to dispose of their cargoes without difficulty; but when the trading vessels from the northeast coast of Borneo began to arrive with pearls, camphor, and rare edible nests, Labuan's few Chinese and Malay shopkeepers with no appreciable capital were unable to take advantage of the opportunity. The Taosug were obliged to carry their most valuable produce to Singapore.[18] Governor Edwardes, who first drew attention to the importance of the trade from northeast Borneo and the Sulu archipelago in Labuan's economy, wrote in 1856:

> From the islands of Sooloo and the northeastern part of Borneo we have had this year several cargoes of too great a value for our trade which had to seek a better market. Were the ill repute of our climate removed, there is no doubt our merchant population would increase ....[19]

Labuan's trade increased in spite of these obstacles. Its market was preferred by the Taosug to those administered by the Spanish at Zamboanga and Balabac and was fortunate to have no other competitors.[20] By 1861 many new shops had been constructed and the island's trade nearly doubled within that year.[21] The growing attraction of the *nakodahs* to the free port induced more enterprising small-scale Chinese traders from Brunei and Singapore to come to Labuan. As their number grew, *prahus* bringing produce from the Sulu zone were increasingly able to dispose of their freight.*

The commerce of Sulu's outer islands was drawn to Labuan after 1860. Many *prahus*, small and great, visited from Maliud, Datu Alimuddin's village, on the southeast coast of Palawan.[22] Each year a trading flotilla was sent to Labuan by Sherif Yassin, the chief of the Bengaya river on the east coast of Borneo. Yassin, who was described by the Governors as a shrewd trader, moved his settlement to Marudu Bay in 1869. From the mouth of the Tandik River, he carried on a thriving commerce with Labuan on one side and Palawan, Banguey, Balabac, and Jolo on the other side.[23] Haji Mansur, a

---

* One of these was Malacca-born Chao Mah Soo. He had emigrated to Brunei where he established a business in sago manufacture and trade with the Sultanate. In 1858, Governor Edwardes persuaded him to open a shop at Labuan and two years later he took up residence. Chao was reported to be worth 4,000 pounds a year at the time of his death in 1872. Four years earlier, Governor Pope Hennesey described Labuan's leading Chinese merchant: "He is the proprietor of the sago manufactory near the town of Victoria ... He has built the four first substantial houses in the town. He is the owner of some of the best trading schooners that bring the productions of the northeast coast of Borneo to this colony. He has recently taken some land at the western side of the harbour where he is about to erect a handsome villa for his children (16 in number) who have just come from Singapore [and] ... his carriage and pair are far superior to those of the governors." Pope Hennesey to the Duke of Buckingham and Chandos, 10 Sept. 1868, CO, 144/28; Bulwer to the Earl of Carnarvon, 9 May 1874, CO, 144/42.

powerful aristocrat on Cagayan de Sulu, was one of the most regular of these traders, who frequently brought precious cargoes to Labuan.[24]

Gutta-Percha, Wax, and Opium

Articles for Chinese consumption generally reached Labuan from the Kinabatangan river, especially bird's nest and camphor. Wax that previously went to the Philippines was imported from Palawan.[25] Marine products—*tripang*, tortoise shell, and shark's fin—were not brought to Labuan in great quantities. The trade in these specialities declined, except for mother of pearl which remained centred at Jolo. In their absence, gutta-percha, used for insulating telegraph cables, was the fastest growing import of the Taosug trade.[26] The demand for gutta-percha in European markets continued unabated for several decades, and Labuan's supply from the northeast coast of Borneo, Tawi-Tawi, and Mindanao steadily increased between 1858 and 1868.[27]

Labuan's exports—opium, cotton textiles, and munitions—were all obtained from Singapore.[28] The settlement's opium traffic with Sulu began in 1860. The drug trade to the Kinabatangan which commenced soon afterwards was initially small but increased year by year.[29] Among Labuan's sixty Chinese traders and shopkeepers, three in particular dealt with large amounts of opium—Chao Mah Soo, Ching Ling, and Wat Sing.[30] The price of opium, usually sold two to three balls at a time, varied with the wholesale price in Singapore. A chest of forty balls of the best quality opium could be purchased in Singapore for $552 to $567.[31] The average price was between $15 and $18 per ball according to market fluctuations, but the price did rise on occasion to as much as $30, owing to scarcity in Bengal.[32] The Taosug received fair rates from the Chinese for their produce. The Labuan traders hoped to make their profit on the value of Sulu produce in the Singapore market rather than on the sale of opium. There was always keen competition to obtain the produce, and some shopkeepers were content to sell their opium at cost price.[33] Seven to eight chests of opium were sold to the Taosug of Sulu each year.[34] The evidence suggests that by 1868 almost as many chests were finding their way to the northeast coast of Borneo as well.

As the trade in piece goods increased, the Taosug took advantage of the rivalry between the Labuan traders to press their demands for superior quality cloth. When their *prahus* anchored opposite Beach Street, their preferences were quickly satisfied:

> The cases run larger than formerly, and there is a decided increase in silks, satins and other expensive fabrics; while the quality of the common piece goods has improved, the native merchants from the Sooloo Sea demanding the very best description of goods, and taking no inferior sorts.[35]

During the first six months of 1868, 317 bales of grey shirting of better quality and 400 cases of piece goods were imported from Singapore. Almost 90 per cent of the textiles, worth £70,000, were re-exported, primarily in trading *prahus* to Sulu, Palawan, and the northeast coast of Borneo.[36]

The unrestricted sale of arms and ammunition in Labuan's market had been permitted by the local government since the founding of the colony. The correspondence of the early governors of Labuan reveals that Taosug traders and Balangingi raiders purchased munitions at the settlement.[37] Until 1862, the Balangingi stripped their vessels of warlike equipment and left the greater part of their crew on nearby islands when they visited as "peaceful traders" to buy gunpowder, shot, and European goods.[38] But by 1865, the raiding activity of the Samal in West Bornean waters had been curbed, and they as well as the Magindanao of Buayan received their arms shipments from Taosug traders who visited Singapore and Labuan.[39]

In June 1862, Governor Callaghan drew the attention of the Colonial Office to the fact that "a large trade for such a small place was carried on ... in these articles", but no effort was made to introduce restrictive measures.[40] The shopkeepers of Labuan felt that legislation would have no practical value as long as similar facilities for the arms trade existed in Singapore. But when the question of Labuan's munition traffic was again brought to the attention of the home government in 1865, a law was passed to regulate "the manufacture, importation, transport and sale of arms and ammunition".[41] The prompt passage of the law allayed the fears of government critics in England. Of course it was not in the interest of the colony's economy to ban the exportation of warstores, and the law was not enforced at Labuan. Firearms brought from Singapore gained in value and became, by virtue of heightened Taosug and Magindanao resistance to Spanish domination, Labuan's most valuable export during the 1870s and 1880s.

The carrying trade between Singapore and Labuan was dominated by Captain John Dill Ross. Arriving at the settlement in 1860 as the master and part owner of a small, heavily mortgaged schooner, Ross began to carry the mail, Taosug and Chinese passengers and their cargoes between Labuan and Singapore.[42] Through industry, sea skill, and the support of the Labuan traders, he built up commerce and firmly established the Sulu Sultanate's vital trade link with Singapore via Labuan. His voyages were especially important to the Taosug because Buginese shipping from Singapore to Sulu declined once Makassar was declared a free port.[43] Ross, whose ability and courage as a master earned the respect of Taosug *nakodahs,* made an average of seven voyages a year between Singapore and the Borneo coast bringing freights of opium and arms.[44]

As Sulu's trade with Labuan grew, his circumstances improved. He managed to save enough money to purchase the schooner and then replace it with a brig, and subsequently, his brig with a barque; he built a number of brick shops at Labuan and lent money, a few hundred dollars at a time at high rates of interest, to the settlement's Chinese merchants.[45] In the 1870s the impact of this pioneer's activity on Sulu's trade was felt all along the Borneo coast. Ross was considered by the coastal populace of northeast Borneo as "first in the earthly classifications of powers, followed by Captain Alejo [meaning Spain] second, and the Sultan of Sulu".[46]

The Decline of Trade

The Sulu Sultanate's commerce with Labuan constituted half of the total trade that the settlement received and forwarded to Singapore.[47] While the port returns for the general trade of Labuan are incomplete,[48] the available lists contain trade statistics and other kinds of detail that provide an indirect measure of its value.

Labuan's trade in the period 1848–56 was limited, only once exceeding £10,000.[49] Although bird's nest and camphor worth £800 first appeared as items of export in the series of returns which commences in 1852, the trade of the colony only radically improved after 1860.[50] The total value imports from the Sulu archipelago and the northeast coast increased from £12,000 in 1860, to £50,000 in 1866, £65,000 in 1867, and £80,000 in 1868.[51]

The steady growth of Labuan's trade with Sulu did not continue beyond 1868. The returns for 1869 show no further progress, and in the following years there was a marked decline.[52] Governor Pope Hennesey's ill-calculated measures to increase the colony's revenues by farming out the tobacco monopoly in 1868 and opium in 1870 were responsible for the falling off in trade.[53] When the opium trade was placed in the hands of the farmers, the average price of opium for export rose from $15 to $18 per ball to $30 to $35 per ball and in some instances even $40.[54] But with the trade no longer free, the opium farmers exported less and less each year. Influential Sulu *datus* on the east coast, such as Israel and Ansurrudin, complained that they could not afford to buy opium at the farmers' rates.[55] Some of them, rather than deal with the farmers, sold their cargoes at Labuan and continued their voyages to Singapore where they could buy opium and tobacco wholesale. Others took their trade directly to Singapore, and a few returned to Sulu and the northeast coast empty-handed, having refused to trade at Labuan.[56] The Chinese trader Chong Siang Kiat stated: "In one instance I remember of Datu Ansurrudin coming here with pearls for sale which he wished to exchange for opium, and the farmers asked him 40.00 a ball. He would not consent to give that price and went away with his pearls."[57]

The high prices of the farm drove many of the small shopkeepers out of business and they quit the island.[58] But the illiberal farmers also experienced hard times when Taosug *nakodahs* went elsewhere. After 1870 less than one and a half chests of Labuan opium were sold to the Taosug of Sulu each year. Chao Bok Song, the partner of Lee Cheng Hok, a leading opium farmer from 1870 to 1873, provided figures on their sales before and after the establishment of the farm: 1865, half a chest; 1866, 1 chest; 1867, 2 chests; 1868, 2chests; 1869, 2½ chests; 1870/73, half a chest a year.[59] The monopoly was abolished by the Governor at the end of 1872, but not in time to prevent enterprising traders from Singapore and Hong Kong from carrying opium directly to Sulu and the northeast coast at lower rates.[60]

Labuan's commerce, like that of its neighbouring rival Zamboanga, was dependent on the relative convenience the settlement's trade offered to Sulu's merchants.[61] Fluctuating levels of stock and capital at Labuan's shops and the establishment of the opium farm discouraged Taosug aristocrats, particularly in Jolo, from further developing their trade there.* The extent of Labuan's dependence upon trade with the Sulu Sultanate was observed by Governor Bulwer in 1874:

> Since the year 1860 ... [there] has been an extensive trade ... [nevertheless] it was only a small portion of the trade of those countries that came into the hands of the Labuan traders. But there were three features observable in it which should be noticed. First: although not a large portion of the Sulu and Northeast coast trade it was a large portion of the Labuan trade for it made up certainly one half of the imports into Labuan .... Secondly: it was in one sense the most valuable portion of the Labuan trade because the products brought thence were not so much of bulk as of value, consisting chiefly of pearls, mother of pearl, the best kinds of edible bird's nest, Bornean camphor and tortoise shell, and it was upon this class of produce that the Labuan traders made their best profit .... Thirdly: it was an increasing trade. It certainly had been so until 1869 and with encouragement and capital it might have developed into a valuable trade.[62]

Conversely, while the Taosug had viewed Labuan as a "conduit pipe of commerce to Singapore",[63] and remained dependent on it for some of their munitions, which they in turn traded to the Magindanao, a large percentage of the Sulu Sultanate's exports reached Singapore directly in country trade vessels and Taosug *prahus* from Jolo.

The Contrabandistas

In the 1850s, when Britain took no interest in the means by which Spanish authority was extended to the Sulu archipelago, the independent

---

* As Labuan's trade with the Sulu Sultanate decreased in the years following 1868, there was a corresponding increase in local traffic from Jolo to Zamboanga. Nevertheless, the volume of this trade was still well below previous levels until 1870. The value of trade from Basilan, the Samalese Islands, and Jolo with Zamboanga from 1865 to 1870 was: 1865/66–4, 061 pesos, 1866/67–2, 226 pesos; 1867/88–6, 534 pesos; 1868/69–4, 941 pesos; 1869/70–10, 429 pesos, Gobierno Politico y Militar de Mindanao a GCG, 8 May 1870, PNA, Mindanao/Sulu 1836–1897.

commercial interests of the Straits Settlements, with over three decades of close commercial contact at Jolo, played a critical role in the conflict against Spanish imperialism. Country traders continued trading with Sulu despite the treaty of 1851. Small vessels—schooners, brigs, barques—captained by men like McKie, Wyndham, Jackson, Ross, and Schuck sailed from Singapore to the Sulu Sultanate more than a decade before Britain's forward movement began in Borneo. The fact that Jolo remained a centre of their activities enabled the Sulu Sultanate to retain control over foreign trade within the zone at a time when its regional prestige had suffered a severe setback.

Again, the statistical information on the shipping activities of British, German, and American merchants, which was rarely revealed to the authorities and very often camouflaged in circulars of current prices, market reports, and the shipping notices of the Straits newspapers (for example, under destination, "Eastern Archipelago" or "unknown"), is scanty.[64] The available evidence suggests that a few country vessels left Singapore every year for Sulu during the 1850s.*

By openly encouraging European traders to visit Jolo, Sultan Muhammed Fadl was instrumental in restoring confidence in the Sultanate's authority. In 1858, Taosug *nakodahs* informed Labuan's harbourmaster that the Sultan was "anxious to see vessels in his port".[65] As a result, one Labuan merchant had sent a vessel from Singapore to Jolo, and another trader arranged to send a schooner to work the pearl banks of the Sulu archipelago.† Indeed, in 1858 there was an unfriendly exchange of correspondence between the Governor Captain General and the Sultan over the presence of the English schooner *Alfred* at Jolo with a cargo of arms. Another vessel reported to be carrying munitions arrived shortly after the *Alfred* left Jolo.[66]

Muhammed Fadl ignored the Spanish protests regarding Jolo's "contraband trade" with foreign vessels, which Manila felt contravened the treaty of 1851.[67] The extent to which the Sultan was a sovereign ruler and not a colonial puppet is revealed in an extract from the journal of the English barque *Osprey* which made several trips from Singapore to Sulu in 1862 and 1863. Captain Jackson wrote:

---

* The Singapore firm of Almeida & Son, which had acted as agents for Wyndham, sent a brig to Jolo in 1852. *The Straits Times* and *Singapore Journal of Commerce,* vol. 8, no.591, 6 July 1852; see also vol.7, no.513, 7 Jan. 1851, which lists the arrival of the English vessel *Syed Khan* from Sulu with a letter from Muhammed Fadl to the British authorities in Singapore.

† The small pearling schooner *Rossatte,* chartered by one W.Rickeridge, a ship chandler, was still lying in the roads of Singapore in March 1859. It has been detained because of a lack of funds. Captain Clure to Admiral Seymour, 1 Mar. 1859, CO, 144/15.

Upon my arrival in Sooloo I enquired if there was anyone living on shore
representing the Spanish government and to whom I could deliver my papers,
to which the Sultan's secretary replied, no, that he would take charge of
them. I then asked him if there was any duties to pay or any formalities to
be observed previous to commencing trade, to which he replied no, nothing
beyond the customary presents of the Sultan.[68]

But Jackson quickly learnt that Sulu was considered the exclusive commercial preserve of Spain:

We had been laying there [Jolo's roadstead] for some seven or eight days,
trading without any trouble or interruption, when three Spanish vessels of war
came in, a twelve gun brig, a steamer, and a small screw boat. The commander
of the brig immediately put a stop to all trading, saying that we must first go to
Samboangan and pay duties there. I strongly remonstrated against this ... he gave
but one answer, that his orders from the government of Manilla were to stop all
vessels trading in any of the smaller Spanish settlements in the China Sea until
they had satisfied the demands at the nearest custom house which in my case
was Samboangan. Of course, having no power to resist and no one to whom to
appeal, I was compelled to go there. [After four days] ... I got at last settled with
by paying an ad valorem duty of 10 percent, upon the whole cargo.[69]

Jackson's unfortunate experience proved the exception rather than the rule.
The Spanish were unable to establish their claim over the Sulu archipelago
and prevent the Sultan from either dealing with Singapore traders or sending
merchant *prahus* to Labuan.

In 1864, William Frederick Schuck, an ex-member of the German consular
service, came to Sulu. Sailing his brig, *Queen of the Seas,* on a trading
trip from Celebes to Singapore, he put in at Jolo for water and provisions.
Schuck met Sultan Jamal ul-Azam, the son of Muhammed Fadl, who
encouraged him to remain at Jolo. The captain continued to sail to Celebes
for a time, but he then decided to establish his headquarters at Jolo after
having made several voyages to Sulu from Singapore.[70] Schuck, recognizing
the prospects of a future there, returned and settled.

Lacking in capital but not imagination, Schuck associated himself with the
Singapore-German trading firm of Schomburg and catered to the interests
of the Sultan and Datu Majenji, the overlord of Tawi-Tawi. As a resident
merchant, the German master had the unique opportunity to extend the intra-
island trade from the southern part of the Sulu archipelago to Jolo. Quantities
of arms, opium, textiles, and tobacco were shipped directly from Singapore
to Tawi-Tawi and exchanged for slaves at the rate of thirty pesos per person.
Schuck then took the slaves and remaining trade goods to Jolo and bartered
them for mother of pearl shell.[71]

The introduction of the opium farm at Labuan led Schuck to recognize
the opening there was for a permanent trading establishment on the

northeast coast of Borneo.[72] In 1872, he not only made several voyages to the northeast coast and Sulu for the trading house of Schomburg but forwarded a letter to Bismarck from the Sultan.* The arrival of the German warship *Nymph* at Sulu in the beginning of the new year enhanced Schuck's local prestige as a trader. Schuck acted as interpreter for the commander of the visiting warship, and the Sultan believed that he had some influence with the German Government; shortly afterwards Schuck was given a grant of land by Sultan Jamal ul-Azam in Sandakan Bay to establish a trading station, and the monopoly of the rattan trade of the northeast coast. The mercantile house of Schomburg, on whose behalf Schuck had acted, constructed warehouses and residences and placed two steamers under the German flag on the trade from Sandakan to the Kinabatangan; a small one for collecting riverine produce and a larger one to carry on trade between Singapore and Sandakan.[73]

The new trading depot was a formidable competitor for Labuan.[74] Rivalry in trade forced Ross to abandon his promotion of general interests in the island's welfare and come to terms with the Sandakan traders. Goods brought out of Sandakan Bay by the Germans of Singapore were transhipped at Labuan to Ross' steamer the *Cleator*.[75] If this powerful combination worried the Governor of Labuan because "no Labuan trader was to be allowed a passage or to send or receive goods by the Sandakan station ships",[76] it aroused fear in the minds of politically astute Spaniards. The process of commercial penetration was precluded to the Spanish at Sulu because of the entrenched position of the German and British merchants of Singapore.

The Sultan's stubborn assertion of autonomy had induced Spain to take even stronger measures to restrain the commercial activities of foreign nations with Sulu. In 1855, when London's protests were not yet firm enough to protect the interests of the Straits traders, the Spanish had established an open port at Zamboanga and issued a decree that all vessels engaged in trade in the Sulu archipelago must first touch at the Spanish *presidio*.[77] The arrival of the first trading *prahus* at Labuan just after the establishment of Zamboanga's customs house was more than coincidental. The introduction

---

* This letter solicited friendly relations with the German Empire, protested against the conduct of the Spanish Government towards Sulu's trade and asked for assistance. It was accompanied by a gift of pearls and Schuck's notes on Sulu and its trade prospects. In a reply written several years later, the German Emperor explained the diplomatic circumstances in Europe which prevented him from championing the Sultan's cause and sent a gift that included a dagger with a silver scabbard, a bust of the emperor, and a crystal vase. Comision Reservada a Borneo y Jolo, 1881–1882, 129; see also Stephen Carl Hunter, "English, German, Spanish Relations in the Sulu Question, 1871–1877" (M. Sc. diss., University of London 1963).

of the customs house and differential duties not only drove away English and American whalers but also most of the Taosug and Samal *prahus* that formerly visited Zamboanga.[78] The Spanish established a garrison on Balabac island in 1858 as a counterbid to Labuan aimed at preventing the growth of the Sulu *prahu* trade that was beginning to reach the English settlement.[79] Spanish gunboats began to divert craft sailing to Labuan and Brunei; in spite of their efforts larger numbers of Taosug trading boats visited Labuan every year.[80] The occupation of Balabac did little to change Zamboanga's situation. Sulu rather than Zamboanga remained the important centre of foreign trade in the region. Taosug continued to act as distributors of imports to the Magindanao and their neighbours.

Even the more prosperous Chinese merchants from the Visayan provinces and Manila were denied the export of Taosug produce from Zamboanga by the frequent visits of the Straits traders, against whom they were unable to compete. A Chinese who traded with Zamboanga lost 4,000 pesos because of the untimely arrival of the English schooner *Alma* at Jolo with a cargo of munitions, tobacco, opium, and cloth. Shortly before the *Alma* left the roadstead of Jolo on 10 January 1859 and hoisted the Sultan's colours, the captain had assured Muhammed Fadl of the return of his vessel and another English one within two months.[81]

The failure of the customs regulations at Zamboanga led the Spanish Crown to interfere directly with the external trade of the Sulu archipelago on 2 July 1860:

> Owing to the repeated infractions of the custom house regulations in force in the Philippines by foreign vessels which have carried to the island of Sulu, illicit merchandise, ammunition and war stores, our gracious lady the Queen has been pleased to order that you be requested to represent to the government of your residence that the ports of Manila, Suals, Iloilo, and Zamboanga alone being open to foreign trade, no direct traffic will be permitted under a foreign flag, with Sooloo and its dependencies which according to the capitulation of 30th April 1851 form an integral part of the Philippine archipelago.[82]

The Spanish prohibition was widely circulated in Singapore but it failed to convince the *contrabandistas* to abandon trade with Sulu.

The Blockade

The Sulu Sultanate became important to Britain during the 1860s because, in the hands of a strong power, the Sulu archipelago could have commanded the southeastern flank of the route between Singapore and China, and because it was the mainstay of the commercial prosperity of Labuan. The Sultanate's trade with Labuan and Singapore and the change of policy on the part of the Foreign Office towards North Borneo and Sulu forced Spain to strengthen its position.[83] An attitude prevailed in

Manila, especially in naval circles, that war with the Sulu Sultanate was inevitable. Spanish leaders wished to delay no longer before a new sense of imperial interest provoked other powers to intervene.[84] They were strengthened in their determination by the British survey of the Sulu sea begun in 1870.[85]

In November 1871, Spain renewed in earnest its efforts to conquer Sulu. Spanish gunboats bombarded Samal villages in the Tawi-Tawi group and blockaded Jolo.[86] As the war in the waters of the Sulu archipelago began to escalate, the Sultanate came to rely almost exclusively on Singapore's market for assistance. Although the movement of foodstuffs was initially disrupted, the Taosug managed to obtain a steady supply of arms and provisions from the blockade runners of the Labuan Trading Company. This Singapore-based firm managed by Schomburg and William Cowie (ex-admiral of the Sultan of Riau Lingga's fleet and a Sumatran coal prospector) established a lucrative business running munitions from Labuan to Sulu.[87]

The Sultan placed great value on the unsanctioned Singapore trade. He gave Schuck the land in Sandakan bay as a safe harbour from which the German firm's ships could operate freely against the blockade.[88] Kampong German, far up Sandakan Bay, served as a base for the running of gunpowder and firearms, the transhipment of goods, and direct trade with Sulu. The Spanish blockade proved ineffective against their astutely handled ships. Ross plied regularly between Singapore and Labuan; the *Cleator* carried over cheap cloth, opium, and munitions which were transferred to Schuck's vessel, the *Augusta,* in Labuan harbour and carried to their outlet at Sandakan. Some of the cargo was then shipped out of Kampong German on the final leg of the journey by several small screw steamers (the *Tony* and *Far East*) rigged as fore and aft schooners.[89] Their small size and speed insured their success against the blockade. When pursued by Spanish cruisers the ships ran into the mouths of small rivers and creeks on Jolo and were hidden under the foliage of mangrove and trees.*

The Labuan Trading Company's boats (half of which flew the British flag and half the German flag and also the flag of the Sultan of Bantam) developed the plan of reaching Jolo after dark and leaving before daylight; a vessel running the blockade tried to reach either Maimbung in the south, or Jolo on the north side of the island at dusk. Through information supplied by company agents, the Sultan, and Taosug, the blockade runners not only were able to communicate and be directed by signals from the shore, but

---

* The *Argyle,* an iron screw steamer, 53 feet long with a 9-foot beam and a registered burthen of 14 tons, was purchased by Schomburg and Cowie; she was thoroughly renovated and overhauled and renamed the *Tony,* after Mr.Schomburg's sister Antonia, before taking up her service as a gun runner. St. John Hart, "The Strange Story of a Little Ship", pp.348, 351.

had a "telegraph" system across the island that warned them of the cruiser's movements.

The cargo was discharged by Sachze, "a tall fair Prussian, and a singularly cool and brave man"[90] or by Cowie with vital and necessary precision:

> The *Tony* with a cargo from Singapore, would put into Tianggi [Jolo] ... the chief port of Sulu, when the Spanish gunboats were absent; or, if they were in port, would hang about outside the three mile limit till they started to patrol the coast. Then she would steam in, discharge her cargo into empty prahus waiting to receive it, and, if possible, whip in her return cargo and be outside again before the Spaniards returned. But at first this rarely happened, and generally there was only time to discharge cargo before a gunboat was signalled, when the *Tony* would steam around the opposite side of the island some forty miles south to a hiding place at Benkawan .... Here the *Tony* would lie with fires banked until darkness fell, when with all lights out and a covering over the binnacle she crept down the creek and round the coast to Tianggi, transshipped her return cargo of pearl shell from prahus awaiting her in the roads, and steamed once more beyond the danger zone before day break.[91]

At the beginning of 1875, a British naval commander was informed by Sachze, the skipper of the *Tony,* that he had made twenty-one trips in fourteen months and had rarely encountered a Spanish warship.[92]

Search and Destroy

After an ineffectual bombardment of Jolo in February 1872, the blockade was temporarily suspended in favour of a more calculated and harsh policy.[93] It was at this time that a small book written by Santiago Patero, a naval commander, first appeared. With insight into the Sultanate's economy and society, Patero made fifteen recommendations to reduce the Taosug to submission and gradually convert them from a trading aristocracy to peasant agriculturalists.[94] Central to his thesis was the role of the *prahu* both for pearl fishing and in the redistributive economy of the Sulu Sultanate. Patero argued that if Spain wanted to insure its occupation of the Sulu archipelago it would have to make greater use of steam power, and introduce a system which would eliminate Sulu craft and the villages which built them.[95]

Shortly after the appearance of Patero's book, Rear Admiral Juan Antequera published a series of regulations for a campaign to destroy systematically all Taosug shipping and with it a long tradition of seafaring and commerce (see Appendix L). A fleet of gunboats, which was insufficient to maintain the blockade but could wreak havoc and fear by destroying everything it met, began to cruise the waters of the Sulu archipelago. When a trading, fishing, or passenger *prahu* was encountered, the boat was seized and the crew sent to Zamboanga or Manila to labour in irons on public works.[96] Traders, fishermen, or voyagers found armed were tried by military courts.[97] On occasion no quarter was given and *prahus* were simply rammed or sunk by gunfire. Minor expeditions were made against coastal villages on Jolo and Tawi-Tawi. Cruisers shelled the villages before dawn, drove their inhabitants inland, and burnt whatever remained to the ground.[98] In this manner, Balimbing, Ubian, and other villages built close to the sea were destroyed.[99] From its inception, the blockade prevented Taosug merchants at Jolo from leaving for Labuan, but the usual number of *prahus* from southern Palawan and Cagayan de Sulu continued to arrive at the British settlement.[100] The greatest amount of trade came from the boats of Maliud, Datu Kassim's community. But the Palawan *prahus* began to meet stiffening resistance from the Spanish in 1873. The new strategy of cruising employed by the steam gunboats succeeded within two years in stopping most of these trading boats from reaching Labuan.

No trade voyages could be made from Maliud, on Palawan's southeast coast, wtihout fear of encountering the Spaniards.[101] One of the cruisers on station attacked the *prahu* of Datu Kassim,* as he was taking his wife from Maliud to Sambilong; they barely reached the safety of the shore before the Spanish plundered the *datu's* boat. To escape the vigilance of Spanish cruisers in the Sulu sea, *prahus* only dared sailed about the coast at night and fishing was necessarily confined to the shelter of coastal mangrove. Trading boats from the western side of Palawan could still reach Labuan by standing straight out to sea, but were unable to take advantage of the coastal route which was the safest passage in the southwest monsoon.[102]

Haji Mansur of Cagayan de Sulu, another leading trader, was also attacked by the Spanish. He left for Cagayan de Sulu in two *prahus* that had been awaiting his return in Labuan harbour from a pilgrimage to Mecca in July1875.[103] It was after calling at one of the trading villages at the southern end of Palawan that his *prahus* met the Spanish war vessel *Santa Lucia,* on its way to Zamboanga. Contrary to the terse account that appeared in the *Commercio* reporting the "extermination by grape shot of two native vessels", Haji Mansur did survive but almost his entire family perished in the incident.†

---

* Kassim was the son of Datu Alimuddin.

† The translation of the paragraph from the Manila newspaper *Comercio* reads:"We are informed that during the voyage the said vessel [Santa Lucia] fell in, near Baneuran Island with two piratical prahus manned by forty men altogether, whom she exterminated with grape shot, but not without their returning the fire although without causing any loss or damage to our vessel." Cutting from Overland edition of the *Singapore Straits Times,* 11 Dec. 1875, in Acting Consul Gen. Low to the Earl of Derby, 3 Jan. 1876, CO, 144/46; Haji Mansur's trading activities are briefly discussed by William Pryer in 1879 when the headman of Cagayan de Sulu visited Elopura. See the Diary of William Pryer, 11 Aug. 1879, CO, 874/69.

In face of such an aggressive policy, the Sultanate's *prahu* trade to Labuan could not survive. Instead, Taosug vessels that chose to run the blockade took their cargoes to the German trading station at Sandakan or to the Chinese of Zamboanga. The 1873 trade returns for Labuan reflect the reluctance of Taosug *nakodahs* on both sides of the Sulu sea to embark on their annual voyages.[104] The returns show the value of imported produce in 1872 as £65,701 against £49,190 for 1873—a decrease of 25 per cent.[105] The adverse effect of the traffic of the German traders on Labuan's commerce with Sulu is also apparent in the decreased imports of marine-jungle produce. The deterioration of the Labuan-Singapore trade was made clear to the Colonial Office in September 1873 by a group of Chinese in Singapore who petitioned the British Government to take action against the Spanish blockade.[106] The branch of their trade had almost disappeared.

In 1874, Labuan's Governor wrote that virtually no marine and forest products were seeping into the settlement's market through Palawan and the northeast coast:

> Their blockade ... stops all regular communication and in great measure hinders the collection of the produce of which the trade thence is composed. What escapes the Spanish ships is all or mostly secured by the Sandakan traders, and as they run the risks no one can grudge them the profit. Were it not for the small steamer with which they successfully run the blockade very little trade would either enter or leave Sulu. What did escape would probably find its way to Labuan, and to that extent our traders are losers both by the blockade and by the rival trading station ... as for the trade of the northern coast of Borneo, that, or three quarters of it at least, we must consider as lost to Labuan, so long as the Sandakan station can hold its own.[107]

Although the cruising system destroyed many of the Sulu *prahus* that could trade with Labuan, the ability of the Taosug to wage a defensive war against the Spanish was undiminished as long as foreign trading ships were able to import munitions to the Sultanate. The Spanish blockading force was inadequate for the task. The squadron was small: a corvette, the *Santa Lucia,* plus three or four steam gunboats, concentrated around Jolo island; only once a fortnight were gunboats able to visit adjacent islands such as Siassi or Lapac.[108] Inefficiently maintained, it had been labelled a paper blockade by an English observer.* The *Tony* made on an average one to two trips per

---

* Capt. Knorr of the German warship *Hertha* described the Spanish vessels and the operation of the blockade: "The flat-decked corvette [*Santa Lucia*] with the flag of command, had, so far as could be seen, nine or ten smooth guns of about the calibre of ... 36 pounders. She is slow and, as I was told, old. The gunboats, of which a fourth is said to be stationed on the south coast of the island, were not much larger than the fire engine steamer of the Kiel dockyard, each of them carried a smooth bowgun ... 24 pounders, and several swivels on the

month to Jolo or Siassi during 1874. When the German warship *Hertha* visited Sandakan Bay, its commander described the activity of Kampong German:

> ... during our stay, two small steamers under the German flag, ostensibly coming from Labuan, ran in; also a third, of about the same size, with a flag of all yellow, the property and flag, as I was told, of the Datu Alum. Judging from the stores in the settlement, cotton goods, arms and especially firearms, appear to be the articles of trade with the natives of Sulu.[109]

The development of the cruising system and the blockade had major significance for Taosug economy and society. When the blockade was first established, there was a severe rice shortage in Sulu, since the Taosug had previously concentrated their activities and labour in the fisheries, and most of their paddy was imported and paid for with *tripang* and mother of pearl shell. In their extreme need, a basket of pearl shell worth about $50 was exchanged for a bag of seed paddy worth about one-tenth that sum,[110] and when mother of pearl shell sold for as much as $250 per ton at Singapore in the 1870s, the return cargo of Straits vessels were often composed of little else.[111] For Sulu, whose fate was tied to the international economy of Singapore, it was a cruel sort of trade.* Cruising made it impossible for many communities to fish for pearl shell and gather *tripang* on the reefs except at the risk of their lives; yet Straits traders insisted on being paid in it.[112] The Sultan took a defiant stance against Spanish pretenses by issuing hundreds of passes for the procurement of shell to armed *prahus*. To Sulu, pearl shell became the mainstay of commercial activity with the Straits traders.[113] Upon it depended the survival of the state.

While the Taosug depended on these traders for munitions and trade goods they could not realistically expect them to supply staples on a large scale. A major shift occurred in the internal economy of the Sultanate in

---

railing. They were all built in the colony, whilst the engines and boilers were brought from England. Their small draught (2 meters) seemed to make them especially suitable for their present purpose and the coast service of the colony ... the crews of almost all the vessels consist almost exclusively of Malay natives of the Philippines, ... each Spanish gunboat serves six weeks in the blockading squadron before Sulu, during which time the fires in the steam boilers of all the vessels are continually kept up; the relief comes from the most southern marine station, Isabella, on the island of Baselan established only for the purpose of the blockade, and depending on the station, Zamboanga, the vessels pass the same length of time at Isabella for repairs and provisions, and then return to the service." Capt. Knorr to the Imperial Admiralty, Berlin, 27 May 1875, in the Earl of Derby to Lord Odo Russel, 12 Feb. 1876, CO, 144/46.

* Datu Harun al Rashid observed: "The people of Sulu are very much in want of cloth, opium, and Chinese tobacco which articles the 'Toney' takes them, but will receive nothing in exchange but pearl shell, which the sulus are obliged to go out and procure. This is the reason that so many of them are captured ...." Statement of Datu Harun al Rashid in Report by Commander Buckle on the State of the Sulu Archipelago, CO, 144/45.

order to correct the long-standing imbalance—from a rice deficit region towards self-sufficiency in grain production. This process, which had actually begun some time before when Sulu was denied Manila's rice trade in 1848, received a real boost in the 1860s when the concerted action of the steamboats of several colonial powers made it all but impossible for most Taosug to promote raid-related activities any longer. Many communities turned towards their island hinterlands and, under the guidance of their *datus,* moved into agriculture to fill the gap in rice production.

This important process of transformation and environmental change was briefly noted in the *Diario de Manila* because the Spanish were obviously satisfied with the success of what they considered the necessary adjustments of the Taosug from a maritime to a sedentary way of life that had resulted from the actions of their steam gunboats:

> Since 1861, ... a degree of peace and prosperity has been maintained in the Sulu archipelago thanks to the small squadron of gunboats stationed there ... their piratical expeditions have met with so many checks that the people numbering in Sooloo and the adjacent islands upward of 200,000 ... have to a considerable extent turned [to] labour and agriculture.[114]

Nevertheless, the Taosug still did not cultivate sufficient rice to cope with the essential needs of their society. The onset of the blockade denied them access to traditional sources of rice and sago—the northeast coast, Palawan, Cagayan de Sulu, and Mindanao—and intensified their drive to coax rice from volcanic hillsides; more and more acreage was brought under cultivation. Less than a decade later, Siassi island was described as "scarcely wooded"—"From the sea until the top of this mountain the land has been completely denuded by the natives whence they cultivate their rice and Chinese yams."[115] In five years, the feat had been more or less accomplished. By 1875, an English naval officer could write:

> When the blockade was first established, the people were in great want and misery ... now the people have abundance of padi, fruit, [and] vegetables ... having been compelled from necessity to cultivate their land, and rely on their own resources.[116]

The Conquest of Jolo

By 1875, the Spanish still did not consider Jolo-Manila interests as irreconcilable. They were in regular contact with the Sultan of Sulu and more distant leaders including Sherif Yassin of Marudu and Datu Kassim of Maliud.[117] The reason the Spaniards could not come to terms with the Sultan and these men was that they insisted on their freedom of trade with foreign nations and refused to "dismantle their forts, deliver up their arms nor consent to their trade being forced into Spanish ports".[118] The failure of the blockade and the negotiations led to a second expedition, which national prestige demanded. The Governor Captain General, Jose Malcampo, felt the occupation of Jolo island to be essential if Spain was to establish its claim to actual possession of the Sulu archipelago. Malcampo personally led the expeditionary force of nine thousand soldiers in eleven transports and twenty-two war vessels.[119] On 30 February the Spaniards attacked and destroyed the town of Jolo from the land and sea, and in ensuing weeks reduced the settlements of Maimbung and Parang to ashes as well as Taosug strongholds on Tapul and Lapac.[120] The Spanish, this time committed to the occupation of the tiny area of Jolo island they had conquered, established a garrison and several forts, and began to rebuild Jolo along European lines as a walled city. They remained there until 1899.

The beleaguered Sultanate was transferred to Maimbung from where the resistance continued against Spain. The Spanish strengthened the blockade and German traders found their task far more difficult than before. They completed fewer and fewer trips. The squadron had already intercepted the German schooner *Minna* at Siassi before it could embark on a trading voyage to Singapore in late 1875.[121] The Spanish seized the ship, which belonged to a German firm, Lind, Asmus and Company, along with $15,000 worth of pearls, and pearl shell personally entrusted to Schuck, the vessel's skipper, by the Sultan.[122] Several other private trading ships were captured and confiscated when Spanish naval authorities acted on information supplied by their agent in Labuan, Father Cuarteron.*

The Sultanate's survival beyond the pale of the Philippines was in part due to the continued rivalry between the colonial powers—Spain, Great Britain, and Germany. But by 1877, the interest of the Germans in the area, a more dangerous power than Spain in the opinion of the Foreign Office, made it seem desirable to Britain that the Spanish should be allowed to occupy the Sulu archipelago.[123] The combination of Berlin's strong representations to the Spanish Government over the illegal seizure of their vessels and

---

* A Spaniard, this Conradian figure arrived in the Philippines in 1830 on the *Santa Ana,* a vessel of the *Real Compania de Filipinas.* He made a fortune by salvaging the cargo of a shipwreck in the China Sea. He was accused of piracy by the Manila Government but the charges were dropped and he returned to Europe and was granted an audience with the Pope. In the Vatican Cuarteron expressed his desire to found a mission in Borneo, and after several years of study was admitted to the Society of the *Propaganda Fide.* He arrived at Labuan in 1857 with four Italian missionaries to build a church and school. Although he attained the rank of prefect apostolic, his mission failed and his assistants were withdrawn, but he remained at his post in Labuan. By the late 1860s as a paid agent of the Manila Government he monitored the movement of the Straits traders. Carlos Cuarteron, Prefecto Apostolico, a GCG, 25 Dec. 1878, PNA, Isla de Borneo (1); Acting Consul General Low to the Earl of Derby, 25 Nov. 1875, CO, 144/45; St. John, *Life in the Forests of the Far East,* vol.2, pp.382–83. Much of Cuarteron's correspondence is found in the Isla de Borneo bundles.

Britain's interest in the legitimacy of Spanish sovereignty in Sulu resulted in the Protocol of 1877. London and Berlin insisted that the Sulu archipelago remain open to world trade, and the Spanish had to give way to the demands of British and German commerce and raise the blockade. In return the two powers signed the Protocol which in effect meant they recognized the Spanish occupation of Jolo.[124]

The signing of the Protocol in a distant European capital was a significant benchmark in the history of the Sulu Sultanate. It did great disservice to the Taosug and the integrity of their state. After several centuries of inconclusive conflict, Spain finally had secured international recognition of its claim to the Sulu archipelago and was free to pursue the war without fear of foreign intervention. Britain did not feel obliged by more than a century of trade with Sulu to take further measures to guarantee the Sultanate's future independence:

> I have already, on previous occasions, had the honour of stating my conviction ... that the security and privileges of our trade, once secured and observed, as they now are, our interest in the differences between Spain and the Sooloo "Sultan" is at an end; except that it would be on the whole more for our advantage, and that of the inhabitants of the Philippines in general that the Sooloo Archipelago should be under Spanish Government than under that of the "Sultan" ... that the present struggle will thus terminate if not interferred with, is almost certain; while we, as bystanders, reap, without trouble on our part, the most substantial advantages of the issue.[125]

Thus the fate of the Sultanate and its relationship to the Philippine archipelago was fixed in the modern world system dominated by Western imperial interests.

In 1878, negotiations were begun with the Spanish Governor of Sulu when Datu Harun al Rashid convinced Sultan Jamal ul-Azam to end formal resistance and restore peace in order to save the state from ruin.[126] In the treaty of 20 July 1878, the Sultan and his *datus* acknowledged Spanish sovereignty. He agreed to assist the Spanish authorities to suppress piracy and was authorized by them to collect duties on foreign vessels in ports occupied by Spain, to issue passports, and provide licences on muzzle-loading cannon. The Sultan also agreed to use the Spanish flag.

While the treaty stressed the submission of Sulu to Spain, the Taosug never considered it more than a *modus vivendi* with the Spanish. The annual payments of 2,400 pesos to the Sultan, 700 pesos to the heir of the Sultanate Datu Badaruddin, and 600 pesos to four other *datus* comprising the Sultan's council were interpreted as a form of "tribute" in exchange for their cooperation.[127] The Taosug were constantly to test the limits of the treaty. Certainly much of the grassroots resistance that was organized around Datu Uto of Buayan in the Mindanao upland and by hinterland communities on

Jolo after 1878 was possible because of the Sultanate's continued autonomy in trade that was to last until almost the end of the Spanish regime in 1899.

Thus far the central theme has been the rise of the Sulu Sultanate and the spread of its trade domination throughout northeast Borneo and western Mindanao. The period 1768–1848 had been characterized by growth and transformation for the Sultanate in response to the impetus of international economic stimuli from the expansion of European commerce into eastern Asia. But the second half of the nineteenth century marked the beginning of a far more difficult period in the Sultanate's history, a period in which, to maintain control over Sulu's external trade and to strengthen his authority, the Sultan was obliged to negotiate a diplomatic treaty with Spain's principal adversary—Britain.

Spain was bent on reducing Sulu's thriving commercial empire, but the Sultanate would not succumb easily. For the Sultan, the trade in natural produce was the source of guns and powder from the English and German private traders; loss of the trade would bring a decline in his authority within the zone and eventually conquest by Spain. The Spanish considered all Taosug who cooperated with the *contrabandistas* to be either "smugglers" or "pirates". A war was inevitable. After 1871 the Spanish navy attempted to sever this connection. For the next eight years, steam gunboats periodically blockaded Jolo and patrolled Sulu waters, destroying all boats sailing across the Sulu sea to and from Jolo and other islands in Sulu. This systematic campaign waged by navy ships against both local and international shipping and coastal settlements led to the Spanish conquest of Jolo in 1879, but Sulu's autonomy in trade was to last until almost the end of the Spanish regime.

6

Trade and Transformation in the Sulu Zone, 1856–1898

THE CHINESE IN SULU'S ECONOMY

Despite their earlier disadvantage as resident traders, the Chinese of the Sulu Sultanate exercised profound influence on events between 1870 and 1886. The Taosug's loss of the redistributive trade of the Sulu zone to the Chinese was not a gradual process; rather it was the sudden and unexpected consequence of a combination of factors—the Spanish cruising system and immigration of Chinese from the Straits Settlements. The Sultanate's effective autonomy after 1870 came to depend on the loyalty and trade of its Chinese inhabitants.

There is little evidence of a sizeable Chinese population in Jolo before the middle of the eighteenth century. The growth of Sulu's Chinese community can be traced to the evolution of the Sultanate as a regional entrepot in the years following 1768. Many of these early Chinese settlers migrated to Sulu on the great Amoy junks.[1] Although there are no available statistics, it can be roughly calculated that between 1770 and 1800 some 18,000 Chinese visited Jolo on the trading junks from South China.* The majority of them, crew members, passengers, and merchants, returned to China on the next monsoon, but many came over to stay, mostly the poor.[2] These Chinese were similar to their countrymen migrating to other parts of Southeast Asia in that nearly all were men and most were prepared to stay only long enough to make their fortune.[3]

In 1803, the Portuguese captain Juan Carvallo reported that there were 1,200 Chinese established in Jolo town.[4] This figure did not include those Chinese in other Taosug communities on Jolo or nearby islands. Hunt estimated the size of their community, administered by three Kapitan China, to be about a thousand in 1814.[5] The significance of over four decades of

---

* I have arrived at this figure by cautiously assuming that during a period of thirty years an average of two junks visited Sulu annually. These vessels with their reinforced iron hulls, up to four fixed masts, water-tight bulkheads, and cabins for more than fifty passengers, carried some 300 or more people per voyage. The figure in fact was probably higher because Chinese from Canton and Macao also travelled to Sulu on Spanish and Portuguese vessels during these years. Van Leur, *Indonesian Trade and Society*, pp.86–87; see also Appendix F.

migration can only be fully realized when compared with similar figures on the Chinese for the whole of the Philippine archipelago; Comyn estimated that there were 7,000 in 1810.[6] The number of Chinese living in Jolo was still far greater than in any of the Spanish cities in the Philippines with the exception of Manila. Sulu attracted them despite the fact that until the 1860s the local Chinese did not dominate the Sultanate's economy and their numbers never exceeded twelve per cent of the population of Jolo town.

When Wilkes visited Jolo in 1842 the town was built along the shore and on three pile bridges extending out into the bay. The Chinese quarter, which was joined to the Taosug community by a bridge and stretched further out into the roadstead—within cannon shot of visiting traders—consisted of some three hundred bamboo and nipa dwellings.[7] The intentional location of this foreign ward by the Taosug, at a great distance from the shore, underlined the atmosphere of insecurity and fear in which the Chinese lived at Jolo. In the event of attack their homes were in the front line of fire while the Taosug settlement at the edge of the bay could be quickly abandoned for an escape to the hills.

The wide variety of occupations in which the Chinese were engaged at Jolo in the first half of the nineteenth century further reflected their inferior status and poverty. They principally worked as craftsmen, skilled and unskilled labourers, and domestic servants for wealthy Taosug and Chinese.[8] Although some Chinese had small shops or operated from trading *prahus,* they failed to gain a foothold and develop substantial trading enterprises for their countrymen within the Sulu archipelago. The marketing of imported articles within the local network of trade and exchange was conducted by Taosug, their clients, and slaves. When Chinese did play an active role in the redistributive trade of the Sulu Sultanate, it was only as clients and middlemen in the dealings of the pre-eminent *datus* of Jolo with other communities. Often, these Chinese had intermarried with Taosug commoners or slaves and accepted Islam to improve their social status.

In this period it was not at all unusual for powerful Taosug to provide Chinese with the wherewithal to trade—the *prahu,* crew (often slaves), and sometimes a large percentage of the trade goods. Speculative in nature, these temporary business alliances were not always successful for the Chinese, who sometimes were obliged to flee Jolo. Zamboanga's small Chinese community, composed largely of impoverished fugitives from Sulu, attests to the high rate of failure of such partnerships.* It was only in the

---

* In 1833, the Governor of Zamboanga wrote that the Chinese of Zamboanga were not from the provinces of the Philippine islands but poor fugitives from Jolo. Among those Chinese that chose to remain at the *presidio* there was a high degree of cultural adaptation to Zamboanga's population as they intermarried with local women and some became Christians. By 1859 there were some three hundred Chinese settled in Zamboanga whose shops occupied

second half of the nineteenth century that the local Chinese were to become indispensable to the trade economy of the Sultanate.

The movement of Chinese traders from the town of Jolo, where they had been mainly confined for more than half a century, to more remote villages began in the 1840s. William Wyndham, an English trader resident in Jolo, informed a member of Brooke's party in 1849 that he found the Chinese:

> very troublesome competitors; as, spreading themselves all over the neighbouring islands, they offered apparently higher prices for produce than he could possibly do, so he obtained from the Sultan an order for their recall to the capital....[9]

The destruction of Jolo two years later by the Spanish hastened the process of internal migration as the *datus* were helpless to prevent Chinese from fleeing to the security of rural villages whose inhabitants, often uncertain allies of the Sultan, encouraged them to stay. By 1856, the pockets of Chinese establishing themselves and developing small shops in villages like Parang, Maimbung, Ka Dong Dong, and Bual were part of the scattered pattern of Chinese settlement that was taking hold in the Sulu archipelago.[10]

Those Chinese who went to the hinterland of the archipelago were the predecessors of a new wave of immigrants from Singapore who came to Jolo as a consequence of the re-orientation of Sulu's trade patterns. The newcomers were seasoned traders when they arrived at Jolo. Mostly from Fukien province, they came to Singapore and learnt the Malay language, gained experience in the marine jungle produce trade and in dealing with Southeast Asian peoples, and adjusted to a tropical climate. In short, Singapore was a training ground where the Chinese experimented and perfected their talents as traders before emigrating to places like Sulu. While the Taosug encouraged their immigration, they were to find it far more difficult to curb the independent trade activities of the Straits Chinese than of their less experienced brethren who had come to Sulu in the past.

It was estimated that there were several hundred Straits Chinese in Jolo in 1863;[11] the number rose to more than a thousand by 1871. How many had gone to the countryside by then is not known. As the Straits Chinese worked their way into the established pattern of Sulu's trade, they built warehouses at Jolo and conveyed marine jungle products by *prahu* from other parts of the archipelago to Jolo to trade with foreign ships that called there.[12] Gradually, more and more European trade goods began to reach the Taosug through Chinese traders. As a larger percentage of the local trade came into their hands, even the Taosug in Jolo were obliged to traffic

---

one entire street of the town. No.5, El Governador Militar y Politico del Zamboanga a GCG, 23 July 1833, PNA, Unclassified Mindanao/Sulu bundle; Sir John Bowring, *The Philippine Islands*, pp.345–46.

directly with them, especially after the Spanish blockade of 1871 increased Sulu's dependence on Singapore's trade. By 1875 Sultan Jamal ul Azam was anxious to have an English merchant establish himself at Jolo to break the Chinese monopoly.[13]

Despite the blockade, the Straits Chinese were able to establish a wide range of contacts that linked Singapore and Jolo with Zamboanga, the interior of Cotabato, and the outer islands of the Sulu archipelago. Prior to 1870, Chinese traders had visited Singapore and Labuan every year and occasionally chartered schooners for trading ventures between Singapore and Sulu.[14] Once the Spanish began the calculated destruction of Sulu shipping, Chinese merchants freighted their goods from Singapore on European-owned vessels through family and business associates, while continuing to operate their *prahus* between certain parts of the archipelago. In this manner they came to occupy the pivotal position in the trade of the Sulu zone. This was most apparent in the case of Zamboanga.

Since Zamboanga's commerce was most adversely affected by a strict blockade of Jolo island, the Spanish had to allow a "smuggling" trade from Zamboanga to Jolo. Chinese trading boats running the blockade from Zamboanga landed their goods on the west coast of Basilan where they were transhipped into Chinese *prahus* from Jolo.[15] The trade was entirely in Chinese hands. When they went directly to Zamboanga, they reported themselves to the Spanish authorities as being from Basilan.[16] From 1870 to 1875, the Spanish cruisers were obliged to allow this breach of the blockade. When the Spanish conquest of Jolo put an end to the trade in 1876, it was too late for the Taosug to prevent the Chinese from gaining control of Zamboanga's market.

The Spanish were far more concerned about Chinese trade with the still unconquered areas of Mindanao, especially in the Sa-raya (upper valley) of the Cotabato basin. Spain had reduced the Sultanate of Cotabato to vassalage by 1860 but in the Sa-raya, Datu Uto of Buayan was to enlarge his political base among the upriver settlements and consolidate his power through the purchase of arms from Sulu in exchange for slaves.[17]

The Chinese traders of Sulu were to play an important part in Uto's rise to power. The English colony of Labuan continued to peddle arms after the Spanish conquest of Jolo, but the pattern of the trade changed.[18] For years Labuan had concentrated on the Jolo market, and the largest percentage of its arms exports went to Sulu. After 1876 Labuan still found its principal customers in the Taosug and Chinese of Maimbung (the *de facto* capital of the Sultanate) but now the Enfield and Spencer rifles, assorted pistols, and gunpowder found their way to the Magindanao of Buayan to support their resistance against Spanish rule.[19] Major arms importers until a few years earlier, the Taosug and Chinese were now re-exporting them as Uto prepared to meet the challenge of the Spanish who had been pressing inland.

In the 1880s it was estimated that there were about a thousand Chinese living on Mindanao.[20] Some resided in garrison towns—Zamboanga, Cotabato, and Misamis. Others were scattered about the coast and in the interior in villages yet self-governing. It was in communities like Lalabuan and Glan and at places of rendezvous in Sarangani Bay that the Maimbung Chinese arranged their sales of new and slightly used weapons at a handsome profit.[21]* Through these same channels came opium, crockery, textiles, and Borneo ivory.† In return the gun-runners received Mindanao goods—wax and gutta-percha—and slaves funnelled to the coast from upland regions.

As a direct consequence of the Spanish cruising system and the blockade, the Maimbung Chinese had become the principal purveyors of weapons and other goods in the Sulu archipelago by the early 1880s. They established traditional commerce at new, alternative market centres in the region and developed the transhipping trade of the outer islands. On the south coast of Mindanao, on Palawan, and in the Tawi-Tawi chain, the local export business was controlled almost exclusively by Chinese who sent the raw products of these areas to the settlements of Elopura and Labuan in North Borneo and to Singapore on small steamers and trading *prahus*.

This process was brought into sharp focus on Mindanao where Maimbung was vying with Manila for the commerce of the Buayan hinterland.[22] There the opposing lines of trade were most clearly drawn between the Chinese from Maimbung who traded with Labuan, Elopura, and Singapore and the Chinese from Spanish-occupied Jolo who tended to rely on Zamboanga and Manila. Maimbung, on the south coast of Jolo island, had become one of the most important centres of resistance to the extension of Spanish rule

---

* In 1903 the Chinese of Glan were still acting as principal agents for the distribution of arms and opium. Diary of Leonard Wood, 26 Oct. 1903, Library of Congress, Leonard Wood papers, container 3; Garin supplied a list of the standard price charged by the Chinese for their exported arms:

"Percussion" type rifles: 3, 4 and 6 duros apiece
"Piston" type rifles:

Carbines	—	20 duros apiece
Smiths	—	32 duros apiece
Spencers	—	60 duros apiece
Each 100 rounds of ammunition	—	4 duros apiece
Apicul(128 1b) of gunpowder	—	24 duros apiece
Lantaka shot(acc. to weight)	—	26 duros apiece

Garin, "Memoria sobre el Archipielago de Jolo", p.206.

† Ivory, brought from the region of the Kinabatangan where elephants were found, was prized by the Bagobo, a hill group who conducted a brisk trade with Muslims and Chinese located on the coast. It was used by them for the manufacture of ear plugs. Va Dewall, "Aanteekeningen Omtrent de Noordoostkust", p.426; Fay Cooper-Cole, *The Wild Tribes of Davao District, Mindanao*, p.60.

on Mindanao. Within the supportive framework created by the Sultan of Sulu, arms brought by foreign steamers were readily purchased there by Magindanao or delivered to their agents by Maimbung Chinese.*

The Spanish realized that if Magindanao resistance in the Sa-raya was to be dampened, Maimbung had to be destroyed. But the Sulu Sultanate's commercial relations with Singapore, Labuan, and southern Mindanao remained unaffected until April 1887 when Colonel Juan Arolas, the military governor of Jolo, bent on establishing political control over all the island, marched on Maimbung. By forcing his troops to advance overland in the rainy season, an unprecedented feat, Arolas surprised Maimbung; he destroyed the new seat of the Sultanate once and for all and seized a large quantity of munitions.[23] The Chinese, who had lived in their own *kampong ayer,* were given twenty-four hours to collect their wares and board a waiting Spanish warship for the journey to Jolo, before their shops were razed.

An immediate consequence of the Spanish success was the almost total collapse of Labuan's trade economy. The munitions traffic had been Labuan's fastest growing business since 1856, and the island's governors stubbornly refused to place an embargo on the colony's arms trade within the region until 1886—just before the Spanish ended the resistance of Datu Uto and destroyed Maimbung. Labuan by the 1890s had become a tropical backwater, a poor island settlement.†

Now in control, the Spanish Government was alarmed at the extent to which the Straits Chinese had become directly involved in the commerce of the region. They found it difficult if not impossible to restrict the Chinese to military centres on Mindanao and Sulu in the years following the destruction of Maimbung, and to prevent them from spreading over the countryside to retail arms, metals(iron, copper, tin) saltpetre, and gunpowder. Nor did the flow of Chinese immigrants from Singapore cease. Their obvious concern to know the precise nature and extent of Chinese economic predominance, as well as to collect tribute, led the Manila authorities to take a yearly census of Jolo's Chinese residents during the 1890s. The *Padrones de Chinos,* which

---

* Naturally European goods were far cheaper in Maimbung than Jolo and the Sultan purchased them directly from Singapore with the steamer *Far East* in which he had a controlling share(two-thirds). The remaining share in the vessel was owned by the brother of his Chinese mestiza concubine. "Comission Reservada Borneo y Jolo", pp.76, 77, 78.

† Although Labuan was to continue to export arms in small amounts well into the 1890s, the Governor of Labuan felt justified in writing an "epitaph" for the colony: "She has albeit with a struggle, played well her part as a pioneer, and introduced directly and indirectly civilization and British commerce along so many hundreds of miles of Bornean coast...." Leys to the Colonial Office, 12 Oct. 1886, CO, 144/61. For references to the arms trade at Labuan in the 1890s, see Beaufort to Martin, 11 Sept. 1891, CO, 874/251; No.48, Consulado de Espana en Singapore a Senor General Governador Politico y Militar de Jolo, 24 Oct. 1896, PNA, unclassified Mindanao/Sulu bundle.

classified Chinese residents into six categories by occupation for purposes of tribute payment, demonstrate the importance of chain migration in the movement of the Straits Chinese to Sulu and Mindanao at the end of the nineteenth century. They also provide information on the migrant's place of origin in China, age, sex, and religion. The Spanish hoped to use registration to force the Chinese to live in predetermined areas and prevent merchants from leaving Jolo for the interior or for Mindanao to trade and possibly settle without having first obtained a special permit.*

In July 1887, several years before the first census, a study was made of 329 Chinese in Jolo.[24] It should be made clear that the survey concentrated only on the Chinese in Jolo and did not include those living in nearby villages who had commercial dealings with the Spanish. Between 1878 and 1887, 325 Chinese had migrated to Sulu from Singapore, of which 292 alone had come in 1886 and 1887.† All but eleven migrants listed their place of origin as Amoy, and all but six were unmarried.

The survey, which classified the migrants into four categories according to a decree of 1839—foreign and wholesale traders, shopkeepers and retailers of dry goods, artisans and apprentices, and unskilled labourers—revealed the extent to which the recent immigrants had thoroughly ensconced themselves at every level of Jolo's economy. In the first category there were listed five foreign traders and forty-eight wholesale dealers. Fifty-eight Chinese considered themselves to be retail traders but this did not include book peddlers(10) and others who hawked their wares on the street corners of Jolo and in neighbouring areas. Among the total of artisans there were represented a wide range of indispensable skills. The Spanish must have welcomed their useful contributions as silversmiths(2), carpenters(3), cobblers(9), clerks(2), barbers(2); a baker, a charcoal maker, and a singer were also listed. The remainder, some 139 migrants, fell into the category of unskilled labourers.‡

---

* Irregular censuses were taken of the Chinese from the 1830s onward, but were confined to the greater Manila area. It was only in the 1890s that annual censuses were begun for the Chinese in the provinces. Edgar Wickberg, "Spanish Records in the Philippine National Archives", p.18.

† The remaining four Chinese came to Jolo from Zamboanga, 1881; Manila, 1882; Patikul, 1887; and Maimbung, 1887. The exact breakdown of the year and the number of Chinese that settled in Jolo is as follows: 1865–1; 1877–3; 1879–4; 1881–2; 1882–9; 1884–4; 1885–7; 1886–225; 1887–67.

‡ The *Padron de Chinos* for Jolo in 1892 listed 442 Chinese of whom 437 declared their place of origin as Amoy—the other five were from Hong Kong. All of them were single and only nine were not Confucian. Fifty Chinese fell into the first occupational category. Among the 58 artisans in category 2 there were notaries(2), tailors(2), gardeners(12), and cooks(16). There were 287 migrants in the last group, of which a large proportion were assistants(139) and day labourers(81), along with a few servants(5). The *Padron* for Jolo in 1893 listed 435 Chinese in Jolo. PNA, *Padron de Chinos—Jolo—*1892, 1893, 1894.

The Spanish in Jolo and Mindanao faced a hopeless task as the rate of internal and external migration increased in the 1890s. New restrictive legislation regarding residence and travel did not prove to be much of a barrier to the Chinese immigrants. They blatantly ignored it and left district centres for remote areas without residence certificates. In 1892, the Manila Government authorized local authorities to undertake a house-to-house search of Jolo in an effort to apprehend unregistered Chinese.* Similar steps were taken in Mindanao where in 1890, and again in 1894, legislation was enacted to prohibit "all persons wearing Chinese dress, whether they be mestizos or not", from trading to the interior in metal products.[25]

Although Jolo was a free port under the Spanish and boasted a garrison, naval station, prison, and a large public market, Spaniards did not care to be commercial pioneers and settle there. The greater part of the trade of Jolo centred around the "Chinese Pier" and was handled by the firm of Hernandez and Company, and the commercial houses of Chuan Lee and Bau Guan.[26] The Chinese were the only ones who really benefited from Jolo's free port status which guaranteed them the support and security to develop local trade throughout the zone. Most of their import and export traffic was with Singapore and it was estimated to be worth a half a million dollars a year.[27]

The trade suffered a serious reverse in 1892 when three steamers that plied between Singapore and Jolo were lost in a series of storms. Their principals in Singapore, upon whom the Chinese in Jolo relied for capital and credit, lost so heavily as a result of this calamity that they refused to meet further orders from Sulu unless these were paid for in cash.[28] This sudden mishap brought many Chinese in Jolo to the verge of ruin. Along with the fear of increased taxation, it was responsible for many Chinese leaving Jolo after 1892 for Maimbung and other parts of the archipelago.† But above all, trade—old and new—had begun to flow along different lines and at different rates when ports in Mindanao such as Zamboanga, Cotabato, and Davao were tied together by steamship lines and regular communication with other islands to

---

* The investigation was to be carried out during the day-time by an official and two Chinese from the community in question so as not to arouse undue suspicion. Intendencia General de Hacienda de Filipinas a Senor Governador Politico y Militar de Jolo, 11 Feb. 1892, PNA, unclassified Mindanao/Sulu bundle.

† This fear was not unwarranted. The small number of Chinese in Zamboanga by 1892 was a result of many having left rather than pay taxes on their shops as the military authorities began to keep a closer watch on their economic activities. Senor Administrator de Hacienda Publica de Zamboanga a Senor Gobernador Politico y Militar de Jolo, 4 Dec. 1876, PNA, unclassified Mindanao/Sulu bundle; GCG a Senor Brigadier Gobernador Politico y Militar de Jolo, 10 Dec. 1889, PNA, unclassified Mindanao/Sulu bundle; Majul, "Chinese Relationships with the Sulu Sultanate", p.157.

the north was established. As Jolo lost its significance as a regional entrepot, the Chinese began to migrate to economically more attractive places.

The trend was to continue. Shortly before the American invasion of the Philippines, the Chinese had come to control the trade between northeast Borneo, the Sulu archipelago, and Mindanao, and were spread over the entire zone.* By the end of the Spanish period Saleeby observed the radical transfer of economic power that had taken place:

> ... [The] Chinese have complete control of the trade of the Sulu Archipelago. They are found everywhere and command all avenues of commerce. The Sulus [Taosug] have abandoned commerce as a trade and apparently have no inclination to resume it on a large scale. This is due to the decline of their power and the present abeyance of their national life.[29]

THE NORTHEAST COAST OF BORNEO

The Chartered Company

To prevent the northeast coast of Borneo from falling into Spanish hands, Sultan Jamal ul-Azam leased his dominions "commencing from the Pandassan River on the east, and thence along the whole coast as far as the Sibuku River on the south",† to Baron Gustavus Von Overbeck, once honorary consul for Austria-Hungary in Hong Kong, who represented a private syndicate headed by the Dent brothers, commercial agents in London and Shanghai. In 1878, the Sultan transferred all his rights in North Borneo to the syndicate in exchange for a promised annual payment of $5,000. Neither the Austrian adventurer nor the

---

* After 1892 there were Chinese traders settled on almost all the well-populated islands of the Sulu archipelago. On Siassi in particular there was a great deal of trade in shark's fin, *tripang*, and pearl shell. This compact little town consisted principally of Chinese stores and warehouses built over the water. The number of Chinese on Siassi began to increase in 1884, and by 1892 numbered 108 adult males. Ranging in age from 15 to 58, they included 58 shopkeepers and retailers of dry goods(by 1895 there were only 20), porters, cooks, bakers, barbers, carpenters, servants, and a gardener. The 1895 census listed 119 Chinese in Siassi town of whom only two either could or would supply information on the vessel that had brought them to the Sulu archipelago and the month and year of their arrival. In the Tawi-Tawi group on Sibuto, Ubian, Tandu Bas, and at Bongao on Sanga-Sanga island, Chinese had settled and were trading with Elopura and other parts of the archipelago. Spanish gunboats attempted in vain to seize Chinese "smugglers" and their *prahus* that traded from these islands to Elopura and Maimbung throughout the 1890s. For references to the Chinese in Siassi, see PNA, Padron de Chinos Jolo 1892; PNA, Chinos, Cotabato, Davao, Jolo, Misamis, 1872–98; Gobierno Politico y Militar de Siassi a Senor Gobernador Politico y Militar de Jolo, 28 Dec. 1887, PNA, unclassified Mindanao/Sulu bundle; Diary of Leonard Wood, 20 Aug. 1903, Library of Congress, Leonard Wood papers, container 3.

† The lease included coastal areas known as Paitan, Sugut, Banggai, Labuk, Sandakan, Kinabatangan, Mumiang, as well as territories within Darvel Bay and all islands situated less than nine miles from the coast.

Dent brothers were at all familiar with the large territory they had acquired. They had speculated, intending to resell it to whatever nation was interested in its commercial or political worth. In London the young brothers quickly found themselves in a predicament, since the British Government wanted neither to annex so vast a territory nor allow it to be sold to a foreign power; nor was England willing to allow Dent and his company the opportunity of governing it under the extensive powers granted by the Sultan, without responsibility to Great Britain.[30]

Unable to sell the territorial acquisition, the English firm began to assess the practicability of developing it on a commercial basis. Alfred Dent made a trip to the territory and engendered considerable interest in the novel venture, especially after a petition was addressed to the Government for a royal charter to rule the country and develop its resources. In 1881, the political and business world of London was startled by the announcement that the Gladstone Cabinet had granted a Royal Charter for the organization of administration and the development of the territory. The revival of this mode of governance in a remote corner of Southeast Asia, although it has been referred to as an imperial fit of "absent mindedness",[31] suited the English Government well. It enabled Britain to leave the burden of the development of this area to an unofficial agency. The British not only could maintain a commercial foothold in a region increasingly dominated by Spanish and Dutch interests, while avoiding heavy financial investments, but at the same time disclaim direct responsibility for any embarrassing political or commercial incidents that might arise.

The new Company, however, lacked the staff and finance to administer a territory as large and diverse as North Borneo. It was both "too weak to be arrogant and too poor to be powerful".[32] In the early years, pioneering officers had to adapt administrative techniques to suit the Company's feeble financial underpinnings.* They learnt to utilize skilfully certain concepts inherent within the traditional Taosug system to establish control without undue expenditure or extensive bureaucracy.

During the three years from 1878 to 1881, a tentative administration was established on the northeast coast by William Pryer, which began to exercise modest control over trade and exploit the exotic produce in the environs of Sandakan. Pryer's first administrative act, to issue regulations and impose duties upon all trade passing through Sandakan Bay, was not well received locally. The four per cent tariff he imposed on both imports and exports was

---

* The Company was able to absorb the traditional system through the recruitment of Taosug *datus* and the use and manipulation of traditional rank titles by its first officers. For a detailed discussion of this process on the northeast coast, see Warren, *The North Borneo Chartered Company's Administration of the Bajau*, pp.99–103.

more than equivalent to the previous duties paid under the Sultan.[33] As a result, trading *prahus* coming from Labuan began to visit Lingkabo instead of Sandakan Bay to avoid paying the duty.[34]

Nevertheless, Pryer's strong personality, the timely use of the limited power at his disposal, and his recognition of the importance of providing security as his Sulu predecessors had done, established his remarkable reputation among the coastal populace and enabled him to overcome the initial disincentives of his tariff policy. It was after he had assisted the people of Timbong, the headquarters of the trading datu Haji Mohammed Ansurrudin, to stave off a small Segai-i raiding party that the first *nakodahs* from Cagayan de Sulu, Palawan, and Sibutu began to call regularly at his isolated trading station. Elopura, the town that he founded in Sandakan Bay, prospered. Captain Johnstone of H.M.S. *Elgeria*, who visited Elopura in 1880, described it as a growing community of some six hundred persons with many shops doing a brisk business.[35] Trade, attracted from Sibutu and islands as far to the north as Sulu itself, but especially from Cagayan de Sulu, increased and expanded by the month.

Cagayan de Sulu and Palawan

The Jama Mapun of Cagayan de Sulu had traded on a seasonal basis along the southern coast of Palawan and in North Borneo before 1850, but their principal trade had been with Sulu.[36] Later the *datus* and *sherifs* from Cagayan de Sulu, because of their location toward the periphery of the Sultanate, were among the first to engage in trade with Labuan. Their traffic in coconuts, oil, edible nests, and mats became an important part of the settlement's trade economy. But in 1868 the Governor of Labuan built a public market in order to raise revenues and forced the sellers of fruits, vegetables, poultry, and fish to lease stalls. Many Cagayan de Sulu traders were driven away by the public market system and went to Brunei.[37] Labuan became even less important to the trade of the Jama Mapun once the Spanish blockade had begun in 1871 because of the hazards of voyaging in the Sulu Sea. Their cargoes were now carried to Sandakan Bay and bartered to local traders and the Germans.

Local products and crafts gave the Jama Mapun the opportunity to enter into a wide range of trading connections and take advantage of seasonal trade. When the southeast monsoon began, an expedition of twenty-five to thirty carvel-built *prahus* of about ten to twenty tons burthen was fitted out to purchase paddy on Palawan. The paddy only recently harvested was bartered for coconut oil and mats of pandanus leaves which the Jama Mapun women had split, dyed, and plaited. These mats were desired trade items throughout the region. When the northeast monsoon set in, their *prahus* carried coconuts and quantities of coconut oil, made on the island, to

Sandakan Bay where by virtue of its scarcity, it fetched a good exchange in firearms, cloth, and brassware.*

The establishment of the Chartered Company administration and the founding of Elopura reinforced the pattern of direct trade from Cagayan de Sulu to Sandakan Bay. One of the earliest *prahus* to arrive—shortly after Pryer introduced his port regulations—was that of Haji Aning laden with coconuts and coconut oil destined for villages at the back of the bay and on the Kinabatangan. The Haji, who claimed to be the grandfather of the Sultan of Sulu, was among the first traders to pay the new tariff. He initially protested that the Governor of Labuan never asked him to pay a customs duty; however, Pryer's determination prevailed, and the tariff was paid in kind on his cargo.[38]

Throughout the 1880s the leading traders of Cagayan de Sulu obtained munitions in either Labuan or Elopura.[39] Taosug and Chinese *prahus* from Maimbung and islands as far south as Simunal and Tawi-Tawi visited Cagayan de Sulu to purchase firearms and gunpowder.[40] A Spanish agent was sent to the island in 1886, but he lacked the force necessary to establish his authority over the *datus* and *sherifs*.[41] He was unable to prevail upon the Government to send a small detachment of soldiers or a steam gunboat,† and his presence was ignored by the islanders who refused to fly the Spanish flag from their *prahus* and continued to stockpile munitions in their villages as late as 1889.[42]

Elopura continued to be the natural oulet for their coconuts. Cagayan de Sulu produced more than 800 piculs of coconuts a month, all of which was sent to Elopura.[43] Coconut imports from the island continued to increase, despite the establishment of numerous plantations in Sandakan Bay during the 1890s, because of the introduction of copra on a large scale as a cash crop.[44] Imported coconuts were eagerly bought up by local copra traders who paid about $12 per 1,000 nuts early in the year and as much as $21 before the end of September when the dry season ended and the trade closed.[45]

Lying across the Sulu Sea to the northwest of Jolo was the great island of Palawan. According to oral tradition, many of the Taosug communities that gained prominence in Palawan in the 1870s were founded in the previous century when the Sulu Sultanate first became an emporium for Europe's trade with China. Early sites appear to have been opened to settlement and

---

* The *prahus* stayed away for three to four months, and it was not unusual for several of them to be lost at sea by being blown away with their crew towards Tawi-Tawi. In 1896, according to Skertchly, there was not a family on Cagayan de Sulu that had not lost someone on one of these trading expeditions. Ethelbert Skertchly, "Cagayan Sulu: Its Customs, Legends and Superstitions"; Casino, *The Jama Mapun*, pp.71–73.

† The Spanish did not have enough troops for the myriad islands that warranted a small outpost, especially on one like Cagayan, that would be difficult to maintain and supply—the island did not have a suitable anchorage for steamers.

trade in the last quarter of the eighteenth century in the area between the Panatian river and Manalut bay by settlers from Jolo, the followers of Datu Kassim's grandfather.[46] There is some oral evidence which also suggests that a number of Taosug trading settlements had been established on Palawan's southwest coast as early as 1778. All of these communities had centred their activities in trade and marauding around Jolo in the first half of the nineteenth century.[47]

By 1857, when Datu Alimuddin, Kassim's father, exercised jurisdiction over much of southern Palawan, and Maliud had become the most important trade settlement on the southwest coast, with Aiu on the opposite side of the island,* fleets of Palawan *prahus* had begun to make annual voyages to Labuan.[48] Certainly the power of Datu Alimuddin on Palawan was directly linked to his family's near monopoly over the island's commerce with the British settlement until the advent of the Spanish blockade.

The Chartered Company was notably less successful in attracting Palawan's trade than Cagayan de Sulu's. Early Company officials thought that Taosug *prahus* from Palawan might be attracted to Kudat in Marudu Bay, but the trade was taken away by Labuan.[49] A vigorous traffic in dammar and rattans was carried on between Palawan, Labuan, and Singapore by the Steamers S.S. *Royalist* and S.S. *Banca.*[50] Some Chinese traders and several itinerant Europeans came to Palawan in the 1880s to seek their fortunes. They were exclusively engaged in the forest product trade and became both the principal agents for and chief rivals of Taosug like Datu Kassim. The initiative passed from the Palawan *nakodahs* to these Chinese and European merchants, who came to control not only the carrying business but, in some instances, the collection and distribution of Palawan's products.[51]

The island's traditional trade was also disrupted for almost a decade by the struggle for power waged between Datu Harun al Rashid, who settled on southern Palawan in 1879 and began to exact tribute in his own name, and Datu Kassim.[52] After Harun al Rashid was proclaimed Sultan of Sulu in 1886 by the Spanish, all vessels trading with southern Palawan villages were first supposed to obtain passes at Jolo.[53] Few vessels bothered to visit Jolo, but not all of Palawan's trade went to Labuan in this period; groups of trading boats, especially from Culasian, traded with Elopura until as late as 1901.[54]

The Nest Trade

The economic inducements and security found at Elopura attracted more Taosug and Samal *prahus* each year, and the trade and settlers they brought

---

* Aiu, situated near the Campan river, was estimated to have a population in excess of 10,000 that included a large number of resident Chinese.

had long-term influence on the development of the territory.[55] The rapid growth of the town, however, did not guarantee the settled conditions necessary for the commercial development of an important local industry—the collection of edible bird's nest. The Chartered Company considered the anticipated royalties from the export and sale of bird's nest to be one of their most promising sources of revenue.* This and the importation of opium were meant to provide a fiscal base for the Company and help to subsidize administrative costs before the plantation sector of the economy became well established.

Although the Chartered Company's paternalistic philosophy and exploitative goals were not at all inconsistent with the pre-existing Sulu social system, the Company proved too weak to prevent traditional leaders from retaining control over the littoral procurement trade. The Taosug-and Samal-inhabited islands scattered in the southeastern corner of Darvel Bay became the major focus of resistance against company measures to control the coast's economy.[56] The incorporation of Borneo into the Sulu zone had begun with the lucrative bird's nest trade. Naturally, Company efforts to prevent the export of nests to Maimbung met resistance from Sulu agents in the region. As the Company attempted to establish a basis for control over one of the Sultanate's richest sources of revenue in the region, reef-girdled Omaddal island assumed major significance in the Company's eyes. Its geographical proximity to Bulungan and its sizeable population enabled it to both harass and attract coastal trade.[57] Omaddal's naturally protected position astride the major trade artery between Elopura and the Kuran/Berau region enabled its inhabitants to develop their economy at Elopura's expense.

The Company received no revenue from the bird's nest caves except the export duty of ten per cent on the small quantity of nests which found their way to Elopura. When the nests were properly harvested by hereditary collectors, the largest proportion was taken to Sulu where the slave crews of trading *prahus* could not escape, where there was no question of the Company's share, and where gunpowder and firearms could be purchased without difficulty.[58] Chinese and Taosug carried out an unknown quantity of nests by way of Omaddal to Maimbung and Jolo. In 1885 Governor Treacher wrote:

> I regret to say that our expectations as regards the birds nests are not so far being fulfilled. From accounts to hand it appears that up to the end of April the value of nests declared to government was black, 3,960 pounds and white,

---

* Baron Van Overbeck had instructed Pryer to cultivate friendly relations with the local authorities and introduce change gradually and in accordance with local custom and stressed that his "principal attention [would] have in the first instance to be directed to the collection of the revenue hitherto paid to the Sultan of Sooloo". Overbeck to Pryer, 10 Feb. 1878, CO, 874/187.

3,724... of what has been smuggled we cannot judge, but we know that nest
has been sold in Sulu, having been taken there from Omaddal.[59]

Along with the Maimbung-Jolo trade, the large traffic conducted in bird's
nest at Bulungan was all from nests collected by trading boats from the south
coast at Omaddal and other spots north of the Sibuco.[60]

The Chartered Company's attempts to prevent the flow of nests to Sulu
and elsewhere, whether via Omaddal or by Taosug and Samal boats which
went straight to the caves, were restricted by its inability to police the
coastal areas adequately. This was to become an acute problem, especially
in the 1890s when the Company was forced to slash its expenditure on
administration because of a failing tobacco market. In 1887, the Company
had placed a clerk on Omaddal to collect custom duties from those who were
prepared to pay them and to record the name of *nakodahs* leaving the island
who had refused to cooperate. The experiment was short-lived; the clerk fled
the island under threat of his life.*

The following year, Pryer took the first effective measure to take over the
Darvel Bay bird's nest caves for the Government.[61] He hoped to channel
all the nests through Silam, the site of the Company's experimental farm
in Darvel Bay, by leasing the right to collect the nests at the Madai and
Segalung cave complexes for one year at a time to the Era'an for the sum of
£1,500, rather than revert to the collector's traditional custom of supposedly
paying a proportion of the harvested nests to the Company. These nests were
to be sold at Silam or in Elopura at which places a twenty per cent duty was
to be charged on them.[62]

Conflict was inevitable once the Company began to organize manpower
to collect the nests of Madai and Segalung. Trade competition led to reprisal.
The Omaddal islanders attacked the Silam station and several Era'an villages
in 1885.[63] These raids which openly challenged the Company's authority and
future prosperity resulted in Governor Treacher's decisive action to end the
political autonomy of the Omaddal islanders.[64] He was able to prevail upon
the naval authorities at Labuan to send a gunboat, the H.M.S. *Zephyr,* in
June 1886 which summarily destroyed villages and *prahus* on Omaddal and
Kuli Babang (Bum-Bum).[65] Shortly afterwards, another British warship, the
H.M.S. *Satellite,* a composite steam corvette, reinforced the British presence
in Omaddal.[66] The visits of these warships enabled the administratively and

---

* The Government notification, presented by the clerk upon arrival at Omaddal, read: "It
is hereby notified to all whom it may concern, that Osman has this day been appointed clerk at
Omaddal. All duties whether imports or exports are to be paid to the said clerk, and any boats,
prahus, etc. leaving the port, the nakoda of such boats, prahus etc. are required to obtain a port
clearance from the said clerk and make a true declaration of their cargoes." Mr.Daly to William
Pryer, 19 Apr. 1884, CO, 874/236; Pryer to Mr. Daly, 19 May 1884, CO, 874/236.

militarily weak Company to claim a temporary monopoly of force in the bay.

Nevertheless, thorough exploitation of east coast resources demanded not the infrequent visits of "borrowed" gunboats but the establishment of a permanent local base of administration to exercise Company jurisdiction over these formidable seafaring people. Essential to the establishment of control in the region would be the reorientation of the Samal towards a surplus productivity, involving them in a cash economy and in a more sedentary way of life. In the months immediately following the *Zephyr*'s visit, Darvel Bay was peaceful. Taking advantage of this security, Treacher took the initial steps towards the Company's eventual consolidation of authority in the Bay—he opened up the Omaddal area to settlement by founding Semporna as a site for a government trading station.[67]

The first settlers of Semporna were the Chinese who had fled to Elopura from Sulu when Maimbung was destroyed by the Spanish.[68] The arrival of these Chinese refugees provided the necessary impetus for creating a trade centre for the exploitation of natural produce under Company auspices. Led by a merchant named Toonah, they asked for permission to settle on the northeast coast.[69] The Company encouraged them to do so and placed Toonah at Semporna to found the trading station. His considerable influence among the Taosug and his own countrymen, it was hoped, would foster peace and prosperity in and near Omaddal.* He was appointed "Kapitan China", and was authorized to settle disputes in his community, to fly the Company flag, and to collect trade duties.[70]

The new settlement made rapid strides. Local traders found it impossible to compete with Toonah, and his construction of a godown and wharf attested to his belief that Semporna would rapidly become the chief market for the nests, rattans, and sea produce of the surrounding areas which had

---

* Toonah was no ordinary trader. He had two Taosug wives and had resided first in Jolo and later Maimbung for 23 years before coming to northeast Borneo. As a consequence of his intermarriage with Taosug, his command of the language and his wealth, Toonah had considerable influence among the Taosug of Maimbung, especially with the mother and family of the deceased Sultan, Jamal ul Azam. The Company could not have had better fortune. Toonah's godown would always be filled with rattans and *tripang* exchanged for his stock in trade: gaudy silk and cotton *sarongs* and piece goods of English manufacture, Chinese tobacco, fish hooks and lines, brass vessel and boxes.

However, his business interests would occasionally clash with those of the Elopura administration. His sale of gunpowder, for example, served to perpetuate the slave trade since one barrel gunpowder was an accepted customary measure of exchange for a slave. He would return to China in 1893 before dying two years later as a wealthy man in Semporna. Indicative of his wealth was the $3,000 worth of goods in gold, clothes, and ornaments claimed by his Taosug wives. Crocker to Sir Rutherford Alcock, 7 May 1887, CO, 874/243; Creagh to Martin, 24 Sept. 1892, CO, 874/253; *NBH*, 1 Apr. 1893, p.100; 1 Sept. 1896, p.261.

previously been taken to Sulu.[71] Toonah's steady development of trade between 1887 and 1895 spurred the settlement of the entire Darvel Bay area.* His market and the security which Semporna and Elopura offered attracted Taosug and Samal from the Sulu archipelago and southern Borneo to settle much of the northeast coast.[72]

In order to prevent jungle produce from being taken out of North Borneo to Bulungan, the Company, encouraged by Toonah's success, sent several Chinese traders from Elopura to settle in Sibuco Bay to establish a new trade centre at Tawao (Tawau) in 1892. A Tidong chief, Puado, was placed in charge of the outstation. Tawao had less than two hundred founding inhabitants, the majority of them being fugitive slaves from Tawi-Tawi, Omaddal, and Bulungan. In six years the population swelled to more than two thousand, including a large number of immigrant Tidong. By then Tawao consisted of a main street with two rows of well-built shops and a planked wharf about one hundred yards long.[73]

At the end of the nineteenth century, the Sulu Sultanate maintained virtually no control over the littoral procurement trade north of Tambesan. The North Borneo Chartered Company had relied on indirect methods of rule to absorb the political system and trade of the Taosug. It fostered a deliberate policy of economic and societal reorientation, but one which remained substantially dependent on the traditional Sulu sysytem based on patron-client relationships.

The success of its policy has to be attributed to the increasing opportunities provided by the Company to participate in commerce and to own land, and to its improved capacity to provide security for an ever-increasing settled population. The thriving produce trade and cheaper traffic in trade goods at Elopura, Semporna, and Tawao attracted the people of Palawan, Cagayan de Sulu, and Tawi-Tawi.

Even before the establishment of Company control along the northeast coast and the Spanish destruction of Maimbung in 1886, radical changes were occurring that weakened the Sultanate's effective jurisdiction over regional trade. The first grave discontinuities in the Sulu system of trade resulted from the Spanish campaign to suppress "piracy". Spain's much

---

* Government census figures for this period are unreliable. The ethnology of the coastal population was often obscured. This was particularly true for the Samal, whose mobility made accurate accounting impossible. The years 1887–92 marked the first period of Samal immigration and settlement from the Tawi-Tawi archipelago to North Borneo. The Tawi-Tawi Samal settled in the following areas along the northeast coast: Tubig Indangan and Simunal Samal at Sandakan Bay; Banaran, Manuk Mangka, and Simunal Samal at Tambesan; Latuan Samal at Tungku; Tuggusang, Simunal, and Balimbing Samal at Semporna; and Monghay Samal at Bulungan. The combined Samal population—Samal and Samal Bajau Laut inhabitants of both east and west coast—in 1891 was cited as 11,150. According to the official figures, the Taosug population nearly doubled in the decade between 1891 and 1901—from 3,733 to 6,373.

superior naval power obliged Taosug to rely on Western traders and the Straits Chinese of Maimbung and the outer islands not only to carry their natural produce but to retail their foreign merchandise within the zone.* Steamships like the *Hong Ann, Banca,* and *Borneo* visited Elopura, the *Royalist* made coasting voyages from Labuan to Maimbung and Silam, and the *Paknam* visited Semporna and occasionally went as far as Bulungan. By 1892, nearly all the trade of Palawan and Sulu was carried in English, Chinese, and North Borneo Company vessels.[74]

External Trade and Transformation, 1768–1898

I have argued in the first part of this book that the social and economic history of the Sulu Sultanate from the late eighteenth century onwards must be interpreted within the framework of the modern world system. The preeminent factor was the effect that the opening of China to Western trade had on Taosug economy and society. The Sultanate's geographical situation in relation to Asian routes of trade and exchange and its abundant natural resources for export to China attracted the attention of the West. The trade which Sulu established with Bengal, Manila, Macao, and Canton, and later with Labuan and Singapore, initiated large-scale importation of weapons, luxury goods, and foodstuffs. It was the Taosug's "spirit of commerce", their success in monopolizing this trade, and control of the exchange of important trade items in the regional network that enabled them to retain their political sovereignty until 1886. The Spanish naval campaign of the 1870s and the large-scale immigration of Straits Chinese provided the formula for the economic and political collapse of the Sulu trading sphere. The Spanish conquest of Sulu and the advent of steam shipping lines on the eve of the twentieth century introduced a new era in which much of the commercial life and trade passed into the hands of immigrant Chinese.

In the second part of this book we shall return to the period of Sulu's economic ascendancy to consider its relationship to the development of Iranun and Balangingi raiding. I will argue that slave raiding became fundamental to the Taosug state as its economy expanded and in the period 1768–1848 contributed significantly towards making the Sultanate one of the most powerful states in Southeast Asia. Indeed, the rapid growth of raiding grew in proportion to the development of Sulu's external trade in order to provide the prime requisite for the continued growth and prosecution of the littoral procurement trade—manpower.

---

* This inexorable process of the fragmentation of Taosug trade through a combination of colonial warfare, capitalist development, and Asian enterprise(Chinese and Arab) was equally pronounced in the Kuran/Berau region where it had been set in motion several decades earlier. See Jim Warren, "Joseph Conrad's Fiction as Southeast Asian History; Trade and Politics in East Borneo in the Late 19th Century", pp.21–34.

II

PATTERNS OF RAIDING, 1768–1898

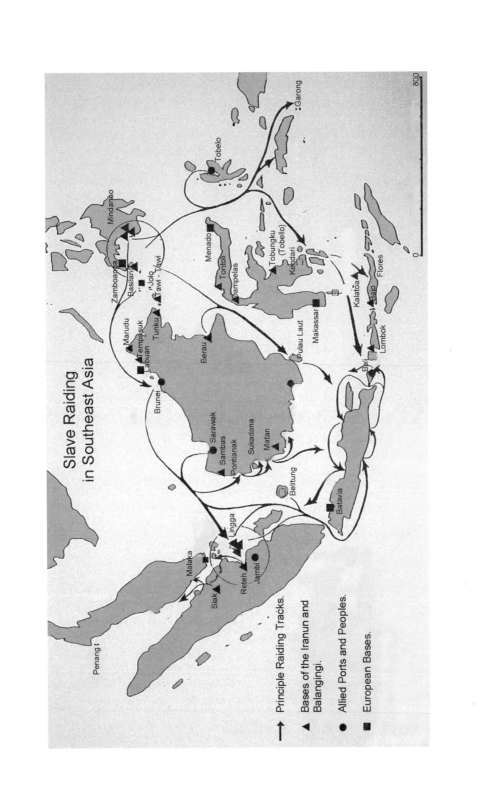

Slave Raiding
in Southeast Asia

Penang

Malaka

Siak

Reteh

Lingga

Jambi

Belitung

Batavia

Matan

Sukadana

Pontianak

Sambas

Sarawak

Brunei

Labuan

Tempasuk

Marudu

Zamboanga

Basilan

Mindanao

Jolo

Tawi-Tawi

Tunku

Berau

Pulau Laut

Makassar

Dampelas

Tontoli

Menado

Tobungku
(Tobello)

Kendari

Kalatoa

Bali

Lombok

Bajo

Flores

Tobelo

Garong

800

0

Principle Raiding Tracks.

Bases of the Iranun and
Balangingi.

Allied Ports and Peoples.

European Bases.

II. PATTERNS OF RAIDING, 1768–1898

From the end of the eighteenth century to the middle of the nineteenth, Southeast Asia felt the full force of the slave raiders of the Sulu zone. Their harsh exploits were carried out on a large scale; manning well-organized fleets of large, swift *prahus*, they navigated along the west coast of Borneo and crossed the South China Sea to the Straits of Malacca and the Bay of Bengal. In the south, their raiding vessels thrust through the Makassar Strait and fanned out over the Indonesian world. They crossed the Banda sea to New Guinea, made raids along the coasts of Java, and circumnavigated Borneo. In pursuit of captives, Iranun and Balangingi terrorized the Philippine archipelago. They preyed on the poorly defended lowland coastal villages and towns of southern Luzon and the Visayan Islands. They even sailed and rowed their warships into Manila Bay, their annual cruises reaching the northern extremity of Luzon and beyond. They earned a reputation as daring, fierce marauders who jeopardized the maritime trade routes of Southeast Asia and dominated the capture and transport of slaves to the Sulu Sultanate.

Historical studies have invariably failed to place Sulu's raiding activity in the proper context. Past and present historians of the colonial period have uncritically adopted the interpretation perpetrated by interests "on the deck of the gunboat". They have relied heavily on sources inherently antagonistic to the nature of the society and values of the raiders: the hostile accounts of the Spanish friars, the printed reports of Dutch and English punitive expeditions, and Sir Stamford Raffles's and James Brooke's influential reports on "Malay piracy".[1]

Anne Reber has shown that Raffles's writings were largely responsible for the genesis of a "decay theory" of Malay piracy; Raffles forcefully argued that the monopolistic trade practices of the Europeans (particularly the Dutch) in the eighteenth century tore away the props that supported the economic foundations of many of the indigenous coastal and island realms; and that, severely weakened, these polities turned to piracy, the "nemesis" of native trade and European commercial involvement in the Malay world.[2] Meant primarily for English consumption, Raffles's and Brooke's writings about the "nefarious activities" of the Iranun and Balangingi relegated the Sulu Sultanate to the status of a mere"pirates' nest" in the 1840s. This propaganda portraying the Sulu world as the scourge of the seas from Singapore to Papua became grist for anti-piracy campaigns mounted to destroy these seafarers whose demonstration of power aroused colonial governments from their lethargy. The decline and decadence interpretation gained currency with the passage of time, and is widely upheld by contemporary historians of the area.[3]

It is inadequate to explain the explosion of the Iranun and Balangingi into the mainstream of Southeast Asian history after 1768 purely in these terms. Imperative to an understanding of the nature and evolution of their marauding activities is a consideration of the relationship of Iranun and Balangingi raiding to the indigenous society and economy of the Sulu Sultanate. Much information can be gleaned from the heretofore virtually ignored statements of captives, and records of trials and interrogations; these provide invaluable detail on the genesis and ethnic identity of particular Samal populations, and on the place of slaves and raiding in the Sulu world, from the perspective of the indigenous participants themselves.[4]

7

Slave Raiding in Southeast Asia, 1768–1830

THE IRANUN, LORDS OF THE EASTERN SEAS

I-Lanaw-en is a word of Magindanao origin meaning "people from the lake".[1] The term *I-Lanaw-en,* popularized by the coastal inhabitants of the Philippine archipelago, the Malay peninsula, Java, Sumatra, and their European rulers as "Illanun" (Iranun, Illanaon, Lanun, Illano)— was erroneously extended to include the non-Maranao speaking people of southern Mindanao, the Taosug of Jolo, and the Samal of the Sulu archipelago. In the correspondence of the commanders of imperial gunboats who hunted them, in colonial gazettes, and in published works, the labels *Moros, Zeeroovers,* and "Illanun"* were still being used as late as 1862 to classify various maritime peoples whose ethnic origins did not always correpond to linguistic and political affiliation.[2] Only Magindanao, Maranao, and Iranun were called "Illanun" by the Taosug of Jolo.[3]

The name *I-Lanaw-en,* is a clue to the origins of the Iranun marauders. It suggests that they were originally Maranao, "people of the lake" from the lofty tableland around Lake Lanao in central Mindanao.[4] In the upland recesses of the lake country, the Maranao lived in a stratified society based on an elaborate system of titles but lacking centralized authority.[5] Their contact with the outside world was via Dansalan (present-day Marawi) and the Magindanao of Cotabato. Walled in by mountains and isolated in their highland fastness, Maranao artisans developed the arts of weaving, woodcarving, and metal work. Wet rice was planted along the southern part of the lake.

---

* The English used *Illanun* indiscriminately to denote simply "Sulu pirates". The Dutch considered the "Illanun" a "vile race", identifying them as the shore-dwelling people of southern Mindanao, Sulu, and several places on the coasts of Borneo and Sumatra. The widespread nature of Iranun activities and their larger, better equipped, and manned *prahus* made them much feared at sea by native traders. In 1838, Sabit, a Malay, stated:"... that he had never heard of Sooloo before, but had heard of the Illanuns and pirates, though he did not know from whence they came, that although there was no formal war between their respective countries, yet the people of his country and the Malays in general ... would always attack Illanuns wherever they met them, because they considered them to be general priates who would plunder not the Malays only but all other people...." Bonham to Maitland, 28 June 1838, PRO, Admiralty 125/133.

Scant documentation is available regarding the migration of the Maranao from the lake region to the southern coast of Mindanao before the end of the eighteenth century. Until then, the Maranao remained little known to Spanish invaders, European travellers, and traders because of their upland agricultural orientation. What descriptions there are of them come from the Magindanao world. In 1686, the English buccaneer Dampier visited Cotabato and described the insularity of the Maranao:

> The Hilanoones live in the heart of the country; they have little or no commerce by sea, yet they have Proe's that row with 12 or 14 oars apiece. They enjoy the benefit of the gold mines; and with their gold buy foreign commodities of the Mindanao people.[6]

Ninety years later, Forrest put his finger on one of the reasons for their migration; ecological factors appear to have caused some Maranao to move to the flood plain of the Pulangi river and the coast. He wrote of a natural catastrophe, an enormous volcanic eruption (*circa* 1765), that destroyed entire villages and cultivated fields. The devastation caused by the Maketering volcano forced groups of Maranao to abandon their heartland and move south and west; some went short distances into Magindanao territory; others settled at considerable distances in Sulu and on the northwest coast of Borneo:

> About ten years ago, one of the mountains, six or seven miles inland from their part of the coast, broke out into fire and smoke, ... It ejected such a quantity of stones and black sand, as covered a great part of the circumjacent country, for several feet perpendicular ... During the eruption of the volcano, the black sand was driven to Mindano, the ashes as far as Sooloo which is about forty leagues distant; and the Illanon districts suffered so much, that many colonies went to Sooloo, even to Tampassook and Tawarran, on the west coast of Borneo, in search of a better country, where many of them live at this day.[7]

Another possible cause for the out-migration of the Maranao was their class system. Some hereditary aristocrats sought strategic marriage alliances with neighbouring Maranao and other communities in order to validate their rank and authority by descent lines. An immigrant Maranao, or *I-lanaw-en*, Raja's claim to rank and privilege established an identity which transcended his own community.[8] His claim to authority was recognized in every community which was defined as Maranao. The ties established through intercommunity marriage linked Maranao-speaking communities and other ethnic groups to form a social network with no clearly defined boundaries. The bond of a common dialect, traditions, and interlocking marriages tied Iranun communities on southern Mindanao with those being established on Jolo, and still others on the coasts of Borneo, Celebes, and Sumatra for purposes of slave-raiding and political assistance. Other discontented and ambitious Maranao sought to escape the pressure of subordination exerted on them by a highly stratified society and left the lake area to seek wealth and power elsewhere.[9] It was these people who were attracted by Sulu's economic expansion, and by the important potential for personal advancement that existed in slave procurement.

The area between Lake Lanao and the coast acted as a buffer or "sanctuary" in the struggle for power between the Sultanates of Cotabato and Sulu. At the end of the eighteenth century, many of the Iranun who were willing to join slaving expeditions and fight either for or against the Magindanao were recruited from within this no-man's-land. Those Iranun who lived contiguous to Cotabato were influenced by Magindanao language and custom.[10] The sources are not explicit, however, on the nature of the jural and political authority exercised by the Cotabato Sultanate over these communities. Marriages were arranged between Magindanao and Iranun of high social standing to provide the Sultanate with political and economic support.[11] Forrest mentions the marriage of the eldest son of an Iranun Raja to a daughter of the Raja Muda of Cotabato; he also witnessed many Iranun *prahus* enter the Pulangi river for a festival sponsored by the Sultan of Cotabato on behalf of his granddaughter.[12] It is clear though that many Iranun settlements were never under the sole jurisdiction of the Sultan of Cotabato.[13] Iranun oral traditions confirm the more or less autonomous character of some immigrant communities whose inhabitants viewed themselves as mercenaries or allies rather than dependents of the Sultan.[14] When Sultan Kibad Sahriyal pledged his support to Spain in 1794, whole villages of Iranun had already willingly shifted their allegiance to the Taosug at Jolo.

The Iranun established settlements and mooring sites along the river mouths of the southeast coast of Illana Bay from Punta Flechas to Polloc and all along the west coast as far as Sindangan Bay.[15] Their cruisers were fitted out in the vicinity of the Bay of Iligan at Larapan in the north, and at Tubug and Tukuran in the south.[16] Along the mangrove-screened coast of Illana Bay and in its innumerable inlets the Iranun lived in, built, and repaired their *prahus* with impunity until well into the second half of the nineteenth century.

The Sulu archipelago witnessed the appearance of Iranun communities that specialized in slave-raiding. These Iranun settled on the north and east coast of Jolo and on Basilan, and established clientage relationships with Taosug. In the 1780s many of these Iranun lived in distinct "colonies" or wards,[17] having their own headmen, *nakodahs*, blacksmiths,* along

---

* Iranun blacksmiths had developed their industrial art to a degree unequalled by their Taosug or Magindanao neighbours. At the beginning of the 19th century, they introduced important changes in the smithing industry and brass manufacture at Jolo. Garin, "Memoria sobre el Archipielago de Jolo", p.193.

with Visayan *renegados*, who had developed the necessary expertise for successful slave-raiding in Southeast Asia.

The Iranun wards at Jolo were responsible to the Datus Camsa and Anti in the last two decades of the eighteenth century. Almost all of the Iranun craft (upward of 100 boats, large and small) that carried captives to Sulu were under the direction of Camsa, the son-in-law of Sultan Sharaf ud-Din.[18] Besides Camsa's family, the nephew of the second wife of the Sultan and two of his sons also had an interest in outfitting Iranun raiding craft.*

The Sultan of Sulu exercised a tenuous authority over the Iranun that settled on Jolo through a carefully spun web of marital and political alliances. Incidents of promiscuous raiding carried out by Iranun—individually and collectively—without the Sultan's sanction were widespread throughout the period under consideration.[19] Still it was in his interest to provide them with a market for their captives. More serious problems occasionally arose when the Sultan's authority was challenged by the independent behaviour of powerful Iranun. In 1772, Mohammed Israel banished a group of them from Jolo because they had endangered the interests (presumably trade) of aristocratic Taosug.[20] Camsa's successful control of Iranun expeditions that used Jolo as a base of operations led other *datus* to league against him and expel him from Sulu before 1795.[21]

At the end of the eighteenth century, the Iranun population of the Sulu Sultanate experienced rapid growth as Taosug *datus* became "silent partners" in raiding endeavours. More interested in the distributive or exchange aspects of raiding, *datus* advanced the outfits and, equally important, provided a market at Jolo for all spoils taken. Rennell in 1762 mentions that "some Illanians are now settled at Basselan and Sooloo from whence they fit out their privateers".[22] Twelve years later, Forrest described many of Jolo's inhabitants as *orang Illano*, "who live in a quarter by themselves".[23] Iranun expansion was in character with changes occurring in the economy of the Sulu Sultanate. Spanish reports in the period 1774–95 show the ever-increasing opportunities for the Iranun to settle, trade, and equip vessels, at Jolo.[24] As the Cotabato Sultanate continued to decline with the growth of

---

* In April 1794, the frigate *Constante,* skippered by the Portuguese master Juan Carvallo, was in the roadstead of Jolo when three large raiders, well armed with 6- and 8-pound cannon, and each one with a crew of more than a hundred men, dropped anchor. Carvallo was obliged to lodge a complaint with the Sultan on behalf of the Manila authorities as it was public knowledge that the three vessels belonged to his son-in-law, Datu Camsa. The Sultan feigned ignorance and the vessels left for Bual that same night and unloaded their human cargo. Several days later, the cruisers returned to Jolo and were beached and careened outside of Datu Camsa's house. One of them had been commanded by Datu Tabuddin, a son of Camsa, and another by a Visayan *renegado* called Impa.

external trade to Sulu, it became a Taosug practice to solicit groups of Iranun to settle in the Sulu archipelago for the purpose of raiding.

In 1814, Hunt listed the Iranun communities in the Sulu archipelago from which attacks were launched against the Visayas and Celebes. By then several thousand Iranun were exclusively engaged in slave-raiding.

TABLE 4
THE IRANUN COMMUNITIES IN THE SULU ARCHIPELAGO (1814)

Location	Kampong/ward	Jurisdiction	Size of Male population	No. of raiding prahus
Jolo town	Subyon	Datu Molok Bilul Datu Bukon (a Magindanao)	600	20
Jolo Island	Bual	Raja Muda Buling Panglima Daud	1,500	30
Tulayan Island			300	
Pilas Island			300	10
Pangutaran Island	Bait-Bait	Orang Kaya Malik	Many Iranun	
Basilan			300	
Balangingi Island			Many Iranun	
Tunkil Island		Datu Timbing	500	10
Tawi-Tawi		A Magindanao datu	300	10
Palawan	Babuyan		600	20

Note: The table is based on information compiled by Hunt for Stamford Raffles. I have only listed those communities designated as Iranun. The other "piratical establishments" mentioned by Hunt were predominantly Samal-speaking communities which could also have had Iranun residents. Hunt, "Some Particulars Relating to Sulu", pp.50–51, 57–60.

From 1820 to 1848 when regional trade was firmly controlled by the Taosug, some of the descendants of these immigrants shifted their ethnic affiliation as their communities grew and became more heterogeneous. They did not call themselves "Iranun" but went by the name of their village or island—a'a Tunkil, "the people of Tunkil". On Jolo some adopted Taosug ethnicity. Other Iranun communities remained discrete, unincorporated; at the beginning of the twentieth century they could still be recognized as a separate element in many localities.[25]

A Nursery for Marauding

The thousands upon thousands of inhabited islands in Southeast Asia, stretching 3,500 miles from the Pacific to the Indian Ocean, and north into the South China Sea, provided a natural setting for Iranun-Balangingi raiding. There was no practical way for the colonial powers to link their respective "dominions" together in an island-wide network of defence and communication, and the Iranun ravaged the populations and commerce of these ill-defended seas. The countless mangrove-fringed islands served as their haunts for attack and concealment. Southeast Asians compared these clustering islands cut by straits and gulfs "to so many spider webs".[26] The Spanish likened them, with their shoals and reefs over which no European vessel dared venture. to an extensive series of rats' nests.[27]

The Iranun and Balangingi relied on the prevailing winds in navigating their *prahus* across Southeast Asia. The semi-annual monsoon winds governed both the direction and duration of their raiding expeditions. Slavers set out from the Sulu archipelago almost year round, but most vessels departed during December, January, and February when the northwest monsoon prevailed for Celebes—a journey of five or six days. Once through the Makassar Strait the fleets separated. One squadron went west-ward to the Moluccas; some to northern Java, Bali, and Timor; and the remaining squadron spread along the shores of Borneo, Banka, and the eastern coast of Sumatra.[28] At the change of the monsoon, the raiding generally ended and most vessels returned to the Sulu archipelago to augment other cruisers about to proceed to the Philippines on the southeast monsoon. The regularity of these sweeps were as predictable as the winds which carried the Iranun boats to their target areas. Customary warnings were issued each year by the Dutch and English to coastal towns and small craft on the approach of the "pirate wind" in August, September, and October that brought the Iranun to the Strait of Malacca.

The raiders were never out of sight of land for long because the islands lay so thickly on the sea. Essential to their navigation was a thorough knowledge of the shores, headlands, and coves. Some Iranun acquired this knowledge by long experience,* but frequently the navigators were assimilated captives or slaves who had an intimate understanding of the area from which they had previously been uprooted and were now returning to as

---

* Dalrymple described the remarkable skill of one such navigator, Bahatol, who was alleged to be more than 90 years old. Dalrymple dismissed as inaccurate the large variety of printed and manuscript charts for the Sulu archipelago and the northern part of Borneo, except for the one drafted for him by Bahatol. Of Bahatol's mental sketch of the islands, coastlines, and rivers Dalrymple wrote:"Amongst the authorities of this kind, I cannot omit mentioning a very extraordinary chart, of the Sooloo Isles, and northern part of Borneo; it was formed by the description of Bahatol, ... from the reflected experience of almost a century: particular observation was made some use of, in limiting the islands adjacent to Sooloo, and mistakes in these, were the source of some confusion: but, though it cannot be supposed a draught, made from memory, and delineated by the hands of another, should be free from very material errors and omissions; I need not be afraid of exceeding, in my applause of so remarkable a work of natural, genius!" Dalrymple, *Oriental Repertory,* pp.500–501; also Rennell, "Journal of a Voyage to the Sooloo Islands and the Northwest Coast of Borneo", pp.21–23.

assailants. To assist navigators, most raiding *prahus* were equipped with a compass,* and many carried a good brass telescope to enable them to make out shoreline features, craft, and communities in detail.[29] Sailing directions of other kinds were used when the Iranun struck off across expanses of open sea: bearings were taken from the direction of the winds, the currents, and position of the sun. At night they were guided by the stars, the moon, and weather signs. A veteran navigator informed Dalrymple that proven weather signs were passed on from one generation to the next. The most important signs were principally from lightning; when lightning flashes upward there will soon be wind; high, tremulous lightning is a sign of rain; low, tremulous lightning indicates a hill; when the lightning is red, it indicates a rocky formation; when yellow, the hill is earth; low flashes upon the surface of the water denote a shoal beneath it; a shoal above water has an atmosphere hanging over it, which appears like an island; low, long lightning, upon the surface, shows an island with trees; when an island is high at one end, the lightning will be in a slanting line that corresponds to the hill.[30]

Fertile, uninhabited islets furnished the Iranun and Balangingi with food, water, and firewood, and served as careening places, where their *prahus* could be dragged up on a beach and turned above ground on logs to be cleaned and repaired. To maintain the overall condition of the vessels when away was of vital concern to the raiders, and their hulls were examined and overhauled every few months during the course of their voyages at these spots. The raiders had their own names for the islands so as not to betray their exact location. Dutch knowledge of these places was largely based on testimonies of escaped captives: the small islands on the northwest coast of Borneo north of Tanjung Datu; the islands to the south of Celebes-Kalatoa, Tana Jampea, and Bonerate; on the northeast coast of Celebes, the islets of Banca and Talisse, and small bays and coastal sites on Sumbawa, Komodo, and Flores.[31] Similarly, in the Philippines carefully selected spots were chosen for replenishing provisions and maintaining their *prahus*. The most important sites, before the nineteenth century, were located in the Sibuyan sea on the islands of Mindoro, Masbate, and Burias.

As the last quarter of the eighteenth century advanced, the length and duration of Iranun voyages made establishment of satellite settlements necessary. The distances between Sulu and the edges of the Malay world were so great that it would have been impossible for the Iranun to have carried on their operations without convenient staging points set up within the target areas or at crossroads along their routes. Nor by the 1790s were all raiders marauding only in the favourable monsoon and returning home annually. Cruises could last several years at a time as Iranun established

---

* Compasses were plundered from European vessels or purchased in European ports.

semi-permanent residence in settlements on the coasts of Borneo, Celebes, and Sumatra.[32] The distance between Sulu and the corners of Southeast Asia was shrunk by a network of communities based on kinship for the purpose of raiding. At these outlying bases, captives could be cared for or traded, vessels repaired, and attacks safely launched against adjacent coastal areas until the raiders were ready to return to Sulu and Mindanao.

The Iranun satellite communities that engaged in raiding were founded by invasion, as a result of social unrest in their homeland, or through political support to a foreign monarch. Although the historical origins of these communities differ they share much in common. In their heyday they maintained a separate Iranun identity and were essentially non-aligned with neighbouring realms. Raiding was at the dentre of their livelihood, but the majority of their inhabitants—women, children, and slaves—were engaged in subsistence agriculture. Located near vital straits and rivers that they commanded, these communities were large and prosperous but historically ephemeral.

The direction of early Iranun marauding and expansion was primarily to the west, along the coast of Borneo and the island and delta areas of east Sumatra. It was from Jolo and the satellite communities of Tempasuk and Reteh that the Iranun systematically raided the Malacca Straits at the end of the eighteenth century.

Iranun Raiding in the Malacca Straits

The *Tuhfat al Nafis*, the Malay-language history of Riau, chronicles the coming of the Iranun to the Malacca Straits, telling of Dutch efforts to wrest control of the valuable tin trade from the Buginese, and of the Malay Sultan Mahmud's decision to summon the Iranun of Tempasuk on West Borneo to assist him in expelling the Dutch from Riau.* Led by Raja Ismail, these raiders crossed the South China Sea in big *prahus*, eighty to ninety feet long between stem and stern, which native and European observers henceforth called *lanongs*, and successfully assaulted the Dutch garrison in May 1787.† Fear of Dutch reprisal led Mahmud to abandon Riau as his residence, but the Iranun remained to settle in discrete

---

* Mahmud sent a mission headed by a man called Talib to Tempasuk with the letter for the Raja of Tempasuk. For a thorough literary historical study of the Tuhfat, see Virginia Matheson, "Tuhfat Al Nafis" (Ph.D. diss., Monash University, 1973) pp.583–87; Stukken Betreffende Riouv, 1787–1788, ANRI, Riouw 20/3.

† According to the Dutch account of the attack, the Iranun deployed their forces in a skilful fashion and surrounded the garrison with their cannon. The Dutch were compelled to surrender and accepted the offer of safe passage to Malacca. Matheson, "Tuhfat Al Nafis", p.1051.

communities on the east coast of Sumatra, and filled the power vacuum created in that part of the archipelago by declining Bugis fortunes. There sprang up between the Jambi and Indrageri rivers large fortified Iranun communities—Reteh and Saba—as well as a number of small villages.*

The desire of the Iranun to exploit the mercantile activity then developing in the South China Sea was a primary reason for the founding of these satellite communities. The burgeoning market in China was creating new trading opportunities on the coasts and islands of the Malay peninsula with the South China Sea acting as the major thoroughfare. For this reason, Reteh was strategically situated across the straits due south of Malacca and Penang, the British trading station. It was an ideal base for attacks upon the nearby islands of Bangka and Billiton with their rich deposits of tin which the East India Company was anxious to procure for sale in China. This expansion of British trade between India and China in the last quarter of the eighteenth century was an important factor behind the Iranun raids in the decades that followed.

Frequently, in sailing from Jolo for the straits the Iranun first visited Tempasuk. The origins of this settlement are not as clear as Reteh. Spanish sources have emphasized that Tempasuk was founded by Taosug, probably towards the middle of the eighteenth century, and heavily settled in the following decades by Iranun from Mindanao.[33] This interpretation suggests that among later immigrants were those who fled the devastation of the Maketering volcano. Oral traditions, on the other hand, explain the arrival of the Iranun at Tempasuk in a different way, stating that the original leaders of the Iranun settlement were sent to Tempasuk under a commission from the Sulu Sultanate.[34] But one thing is certain, the Iranun were strong enough by the 1790s to drive the Taosug out of Tempasuk and establish their own sphere of influence locally.[35]

From Tempasuk, Iranun *prahus* sailed to Karimata where they dispersed in different directions. The raiding began in May. Some scoured the straits and the coasts of Bangka; some the east coast of the Malay peninsula as far north as Siam; others went up the Straits of Malacca northward of Kedah. When cruising in the straits these seaborne raiders relied for support on their countrymen at Reteh.[36] In the middle of October when the monsoon shifted, they recrossed the South China Sea to Tempasuk and the Sulu archipelago.

---

* Besides Reteh and Saba, Toekal [the river Joekal?] and Ayer Itam were important communities. Other Iranun were scattered in small clusters of huts along the branches of the rivers or lived in their *prahus*. Kommisar de Palembang, aan den Gouvenuer General van Nederlandsch Indien, 25 May 1818; No. 115, De Resident van Banka, aan den Gouveneur General over Nederlandsch Indien, 29 Jan. 1831, AR, Archief Kolonien 4168.

That the activities of the Iranun in the Malacca Straits threatened the commercial interests of the English and Dutch there is no question. Official despatches from Penang, founded in 1786 as an entrepot for the trade of Bengal with China, stress the necessity for armed cruisers to protect the hundreds of native *prahus* that frequented its port from the Iranun.[37] These records also show that the Iranun were frequently willing to join forces with, and sell their services to, neighbouring Malay rulers for politically sanctioned raids. Syed Ali, a noble of Siak, with the aid of an Iranun party, attacked Songkhla on the southeast coast of Siam in 1789 and severed overland communication between the Malacca Strait and the South China Sea; they burned the town, seized two Chinese junks, and carried off a large number of people.[38] The following year, an Iranun squadron from the Sulu archipelago, consisting of eighteen *lanongs* with heavy artillery and thirty smaller craft carrying about one thousand men, attacked the Dutch factory at Perak but were repulsed.[39] The Sultan of Kedah, wanting to drive the English out of Penang, sent an emissary to the commander of this fleet when it arrived in Kedah waters. The Iranun Raja agreed to attack Penang at night and massacre the English garrison at the Sultan's behest, in return for $20,000 and a guarantee of assistance if they failed in their attempt to take the fort by surprise.[40] The plan fell through when the English learnt of their movements beforehand, but their formidable presence just opposite Penang created fear and confusion in the port for several days.

The Iranun were active in the south as well. Each year some sailed with their Reteh relations to the Lampongs and the southern coast of Java to harry villages and gather bird's nest among the coastal rocks.[41] When the east wind began to blow, they cruised their favourite hunting ground in the Gelasa Strait for Javan trading *prahus* bound for Malacca, and descended along the coasts of Bangka and Billiton in search of slaves. Bangka, in particular, was subject to repeated attacks between 1792 and 1804 that resulted in the desolation of the eastern part of the island.[42] The Iranun ascended the rivers, destroyed settlements, and reduced the produce of the tin mines by carrying away hundreds of Malays, Chinese, and Javanese.* They established

---

* The first Iranun attack was directed against Sungailiat in 1792. Three years later, the attack was repeated but the community had since built a stockade which the raiders could not overpower. In a third effort, they undertook a siege of the stockade but were repulsed. They abandoned this part of the eastern coast and concentrated their activity on the southern extremity of the island where the population was known to have no forts. They established themselves in the Kapu river and worked their way around the coast from one river mouth to the next towards Toboali. Settlements along the way offered little resistance and their inhabitants were seized as slaves. Villages along the western coast were deserted by their inhabitants before the Iranun could reach them; many families went inland or to the northern part of the island. From the security of the Banko-Kutto, Selan, and Kapu rivers, the Iranun gradually increased their strength and at last attacked and overcame Koba, the nearest

themselves in the rivers on the western and southern coasts and their numbers increased over the years. Many people fled the island and a number surrendered themselves to the Makassar slave dealers who visited Bangka rather than face the famine and disease which followed the repeated raids.[43] There was little left on Banka for the Iranun by the time they withdrew in 1804, but they continued to visit the island on their long cruises until the 1840s.

The establishment of the free port of Singapore in 1819 further lured the Iranun to the Straits Settlements. Singapore's early trade with neighbouring Malay states was threatened by these raiders. By 1830 the lack of security on the east coast of Malaya prevented the *nakodahs* of trading boats from Patani, Kelantan, Pahang, and Trengganu from making their accustomed voyages to Singapore.[44] Bugis traders, on whose traffic Singapore greatly depended, threatened to desert it altogether and seek another port. These *nakodahs* sarcastically criticized English officials for their restraint in dealing with the Iranun and drew their attention to the earnest measures their Dutch counterparts were taking to destroy the "Sulu Zeeroovers".[45]

In order to assist the Dutch to suppress Iranun raiding, native traders willingly supplied information about east Sumatra. What material there is on Reteh and its kindred communities is based on informants' descriptions between 1818 and 1830. The inhabitants of Reteh were depicted in 1818 as a race of people wholly set apart from their neighbours. It was common knowledge that these *orang timor* ("people from the east") were newcomers; descended from the Iranun of Mindanao who had entered into the war between Sultan Mahmud and the Dutch Trading Company. In less than a generation they had built two stockaded settlements: Saba was located six hours from the mouth of the Jambi river and had an estimated eighty houses; Reteh comprised some sixty houses on the river of the same name opposite Singkep island.[46] Opinions on the number of their raiding vessels varied greatly, partly because some of the vessels were transients, while raiding *prahus* used on trips to Jambi and Singapore were easily converted for trading as well. In 1831, the Resident of Bangka supplied what he felt was a conservative estimate: Saba, 15 large *prahus,* 15 small *prahus;* Reteh, 5 large *prahus,* 10 small *prahus;* Toekal, 2 large *prahus,*

---

settlement on the eastern coast. They extended their raids further north commanding the mouths of the rivers Koba, Kuru, and Pangkul and attacked the important interior settlement at Paku. Nor were Pangkalpinang and Tirah spared as several hundred families were taken into captivity; others perished in the interior from malnutrition. The survivors fled to the northern districts where they eked out a precarious living. Horsfield, "Report on the Island of Banca", pp.315–17; Testimony of Pangeran Syed Hassan Habassy, 15 Oct. 1830, AR, Archief, Kolonien 4168.

10 small *prahus*.* When the *prahus* were included as domiciles it was believed that the Iranun could muster two thousand men at arms.[47]

In 1834 the Dutch acted decisively against the Iranun settled in Straits waters. Three government cruisers, together with fifty *prahus* fitted out by the Sultan of Riau, attacked Reteh. Eight *panglimas* were taken prisoner to be executed† or condemned to hard labour for life.[48] The Dutch reinforced their garrison at Riau three years later to make more troops available for service in coastguard boats and strengthened the patrol fleet in that residency.[49] During the same years Singapore's populace, its local authorities, and the Calcutta Chamber of Commerce were calling for admiralty jurisdiction in Singapore's supreme court to try offences committed upon trading *prahus* and other vessels in the straits.[50] The granting of this jurisdiction to its court, and the introduction of armed steam vessels and well-manned cruisers and skiffs by the British after 1836 made it more difficult than ever before for the Iranun to raid in the Straits.[51] Until 1840 the Reteh descendants of the Iranun expedition of 1787 played a vital supportive role in the western raiding pattern that originated from the Sulu archipelago.‡ But as the Iranun and Balangingi tended less and less to concentrate their attacks on the Malacca Straits, an impression emerges that most of the third generation Iranun of Reteh were gradually assimilated with the indigenous population, and became "Lingganese".[52]

Iranun Raiding in the Celebes and Moluccas

The location of Iranun settlements often determined the sphere of their raiding. To the shore-dwellers of Celebes, these seaborne raiders became known as "Magindanao". While they were rarely able to distinguish among the several ethnic groups that brought devastation to their coast every year, the people of the Celebes never forgot whence came the first Iranun marauders—southern Mindanao, opening like a window on Celebes; the

---

* The larger Iranun marauding *prahus* were two-masted and these were employed in pursuit of heavily armed Buginese *paduakans*. Amongst their vessels at Reteh were also several *lamongs*, "beautiful three masted prahus with long sweeps that drew six feet of water and were manned by sixty men" (see Appendix A). The smaller *prahus* ranged up to 30 feet in length. De Resident van Bantam aan der Gouveneur General van Nederlandsch Indien, 16 Oct. 1831, AR, Archief Kolonien 4168.

† Among those beheaded at Lingga were the Iranun Rajas Marasan and Markong from the village of Inok situated just north of the Indrageri river, Personal communication, Virginia Matheson, 1 Apr. 1975.

‡ When Sultan Mahmud was deposed by the Dutch in 1857, all territorial chiefs of Riau-Lingga complied with the change of Government except Panglima Besar [Raja] Sulong of Reteh. He remained loyal to the ex-Sultan who had supplied him with munitions from Singapore. The Dutch destroyed Reteh in October 1858, in a bitter campaign described as "eene schoone bladzidje in de geschiedenis van Nederlandsch-Indie". Matheson, "Tuhfat Al Nafis", vol. 1, pp.441–50; vol.2, pp.1108–10.

label *Magindanao* was still being used in that aggrieved area to describe the Balangingi Samal in the 1850s.[53]

Raiding *prahus* outfitted by Taosug and Magindanao set out from Illana Bay on the northwestern monsoon. They frequently sailed along the coast of Borneo, heading for the satellite port of Tontoli on the northwest corner of Celebes.[54] Here the *nakodahs* decided on the expedition's course. When the *prahus* were numerous, some went through the Makassar Strait while others followed the north coast of the island to reach the Gulf of Tomini and the Moluccas. Still other *prahus* steered directly southeast from Mindanao, down through the Sangir Islands, rounding the northern end of Celebes* and penetrating the Moluccan sea.[55] A fleet that circumnavigated Celebes ordinarily concentrated on roving in the Buton group, the Gulf of Bone, and the Salajar Strait.[56] These areas were heavily populated and in the direct track of Buginese trading vessels. Availing themselves of the southeast monsoon, the homeward journey via the Bangka Strait took less than a week. The bigger *prahus* that chose to remain longer on the southern coast of Celebes had to beat their way up the Makassar Strait, stopping at Pasir for supplies and refitting on Tarakan island on the way north.[57]

It was originally as clients of Magindanao datus that the Iranun waged war against the Dutch in Celebes. In the 1770s, their *prahus* with renegade guides to direct them made raids on Amurang, on Menado, and on Kema.[58] From Forrest we know that some of these forays involved the family of Sultan Pahar ud-Din of Cotabato:

> On the 31st [July 1775], came in a large prow belonging to Datoo Malfalla, Raja Moodo's brother in law, from a cruise on the coast of Celebes. She had engaged a Dutch sloop, and was about to board her, when the Dutch set fire to their vessel, and took to their boat, notwithstanding the fire, the attackers boarded her, and saved two brass swivel guns ... this vessel brought to Mindanao about seventy slaves.[59]

In Forrest's description of Tuan Haji, a lesser noble of Celebes who navigated a small *prahu* through the Sangir islands, the Moluccas, and Sulu for him, we see the Cotabato Sultanate fostering alliances that would unite the Magindanao and their Iranun kindred in Tukurun with Buginese on the Makassar coast, so that they could launch raids with more force against the Dutch:

---

* Forrest gives an account of the passage of a raiding *prahu* from Cotabato to Celebes along the Sangir track. The vessel, which was owned by the brother-in-law of the Raja Muda of Cotabato, touched at the following places after passing Sarangani island: a day to Kawio; another day to Kawalusa near northern Sangir, one day to Karikita. From there the craft navigated to Siao in a day where provisions were obtained; then to Tahulandang in a half a day, then to Banka and the Celebes coast, *Voyage to New Guinea,* pp.303, 319.

... I learnt that Tuan Haji had been at Tukoran, and married Rajah Moodo's wife's sister, daughter to the Sultan there. Before he left Mindanao, and before the coolness arose between him and Raja Moodo, he had ... promised to return to Selangan [Cotabato] by the beginning of the northeast monsoon, and proceed in some vessel of Raja Moodo's, against the Dutch in the Molucca islands.[60]

The garrisons of Menado and Gorontalo were stiffened as a consequence of the losses suffered by the Dutch in the northern part of the island.* In their estimation, this area had to be maintained at all cost for two reasons: firstly, it was the granary of Ternate; and secondly, it produced gold. Further reinforcements were sent to Menado in the form of a sloop of war and six well-armed Ternatan Kora-Kora manned by a thousand local men (taken into Dutch pay) when the alarming discovery was made by the Governor of Ambon in 1778 of a larger political scheme that allied the Iranun of Cotabato with the Sultan of Tidore to expel the Dutch from the Moluccas.†

The newly appointed Governor of Ternate placed too much confidence in his conscripted force and consistently underestimated the Iranun. His bias proved advantageous to the Iranun; shortly after his arrival from Batavia in 1778, the outstation of Kema was destroyed by a fleet of thirty "Magindanao" *prahus* under the command of Haji Omar (the Tuan Hadji of Forrest's *Voyage to New Guinea*). In the next decade the Dutch, who were already hard-pressed to defend their trade and settlements, found it almost impossible to curb Iranun raiding and at the same time suppress the Tidorese rebellion sweeping the Moluccas.[61]

Significantly, during these years the roles that the Sultanates played in the raiding pattern which focused on Celebes changed. The Sulu Sultanate

---

* Prior to 1763, Amsterdam Castle at Menado had a garrison of 80 men and 40 soldiers permanently stationed at Gorontalo. Account of Celebes by Alexander Dalrymple, Apr. 1763, IOL, H/Misc/795/11, p.43; Farquhar to Colonel Oliver, 1 June 1802, IOL, P/255/18.

† When Sultan Jamal ud-Din was questioned by the Dutch at Ternate in 1779 about the intercepted letter, he denied responsibility for its authorship, and alleged that his secretary, a Javanese *ulama*, had abused privilege as he was the only person who had access to his closet and seals and that he, the scribe, was undoubtedly the author of the letter. The *ulama* ably defended himself stating that he had repeatedly warned his sovereign of the consequences of carrying on an "illicit correspondence" contrary to the tenor of the engagements made with the Dutch. Farquhar to Colonel Oliver, 1 June 1802, IOL, P/2–5/18; the Tidorese also appealed to the Taosug for assistance. A letter written in jawi script with the seal of the Sultan of Sulu was found on a beach at Pantani, east Halmahera, among the bodies of Tidorese "rebels" in 1781. It stated that the Sultan of Sulu had acted upon the instructions of his Tidorese brethren and had sent a Spanish deserter (most likely from Zamboanga) in a Dutch vessel to Bengal to contact Captain Farris (Thomas Forrest) through whom they hoped to secure assistance from the English.

began to take a more active part in promoting Iranun raiding against the southern islands. As the trade domain of the Taosug grew in the 1780s, the basis of Magindanao raiding strength—the allegiance of the Iranun—disappeared to a large extent. The Magindanao came to recognize in the Taosug a far more dangerous enemy than the Dutch, and one much closer to home. The decision of the Sultan of Cotabato to send the Raja of Sarangani to Ternate in 1787 to conclude a treaty of friendship, trade, and alliance with the Dutch signalled the curtailment of Magindanao initiatives in slave raids on Celebes and the Moluccas.[62] It was a sign of the extent to which the Cotabato Sultanate was being eclipsed by the economic and military strength of the Taosug.

Because slavery was an integral part of the Sulu Sultanate's economy, the Taosug mounted ever stronger raids against the weaker islands in the Celebes. The Iranun were extremely active in the Moluccas during the short British occupation of the islands.[63] The new masters lacked the resources to administer the Moluccas properly and concentrated their energies almost exclusively on the affairs of Ambon and Ternate.[64] Indeed, the inhabitants of some of the more distant islands were unaware that the Moluccas had changed hands![65] The Iranun took full advantage of this weakness to attack remote settlements.* The force of their raids frequently severed all communication between the outposts and Ambon for months on end.[66] The naval force stationed there was wholly inadequate; there were too few crown warships to police the islands and those on station spent most of their time procuring provisions or lying at anchor in the harbour.[67] Not surprisingly, some of the Iranun attacks in the Celebes at this time were instigated by Dutch emissaries—and strengthened by Dutch military stores—against their former subjects and the British.[68]

Statements of fugitive captives from Celebes show that they were mostly subsistence fishermen or traders (see Appendix R). Their settlements were located on exposed coasts rather than island hilltops and those in the Sangir islands were rendered even more vulnerable to sea-borne attack because of their close proximity to Sulu and Mindanao. In 1801, an Iranun squadron of forty vessels on their way to Celebes put in among the Sangir islands in yet another series of raids which reduced the principal settlement on Sangir to ashes and brought about the death of its Raja and the captivity of nearly

---

* In 1802 Farquhar wrote from Ternate:
I was repeatedly annoyed ... by the ... incursions of the Magindanoe ... on the coast of Celebes where they had rendevoused in great force. These people are a set of rovers of the most daring and desperate kind who have frequently rendered themselves the terror of the small trading vessels in the neighbourhood of Monado and have spread their devestations to a considerable distance in the Molucca seas....
Farquhar to Lord Clive, 1 Jan. 1802, IOL, P/242/42, 2551.

two hundred women.[69] Tontoli served for years as the forward base for large-scale Iranun raids in the Celebes and Moluccas. In 1812 Hunt wrote:

> Tontoli ... is a great piratical establishment, governed by Sultan Mohammed Kubu; the town is fortified with 300 guns and 3,000 Illana (Iranun) ... and 50 or 60 prows. This with the piratical establishments on the island of Magindanao, are intimately connected with the Sulu government, sharing their spoils, disposing of their booty, refitting and obtaining their supplies from the Sulu Datus ....[70]

Most of the Iranun lived in their *prahus* in the harbour of Tontoli on a temporary basis for up to several years at a time.[71]

The Dutch recovered their colonial possessions in 1816, but outside Java and the strongholds of Makassar and Menado their authority remained nominal. They continued to maintain a number of small fortified posts in the Moluccas and the Menado Residency, but on most of the numerous islands east of Celebes there were no Dutch establishments. Systematic slave-raiding directed against the outer islands from the Sulu archipelago increased between 1816 and 1848 for precisely this reason; the Iranun and Balangingi, not the Dutch, were the true lords of the eastern seas.

The efficacy of Dutch authority in the region was little improved by a series of measures meant to suppress "piracy" and restore confidence in the political and commercial life of the islands upon their recovery. One of the most important of these dealt with the improvement of the Colonial Marine. The Netherland's Government commissioned the construction of a large number of inexpensive *prahus* to be used especially against piracy.* It was believed that these vessels, ideally suited for river and coastal warfare, could patrol and protect a much greater expanse of water and territory than the Dutch gunboats.

To increase the size and strength of the Colonial Marine was a necessary first step. In order to plan measures intelligently against the Iranun and Balangingi, Dutch Residents and naval officers were instructed to collect detailed information on "pirate" populations: their size and ethnicity, the location and strength of their principal centres and satellite communities, and the nature of their subsistence economy.[72] Valuable reports on this subject

---

* The use of native *prahus* for patrol work was not new. Some years before, it had been proposed that the Government build a fleet of Kora-Kora but no action was taken on the measure. Subsequently when the plan was approved another kind of cruising *prahu* was chosen for the colonial marine—the Kolek Trengganu. The boat was light and carried a 4-pound cannon and swivel guns. It was manned by 24 men armed with muskets and pikes who were handpicked from maritime communities—Bugis, Madurese, Sumbawa people. The cruising *prahus* were placed under the jurisdiction of the residencies. Testimony of Pangeran Syed Hassan Habassy, 15 Oct. 1830, AR, Archief Kolonien 4168; St. John, *The Indian Archipelago: Its History and Present State,* vol.2, pp.192–93.

were drawn up by Muntinghe in 1818, Kolff in 1831, and Vosmaer in 1833, with the assistance of informants (ex-raiders and captives), local villagers, and regional traders.[73] The information furnished in these reports enabled the Dutch to form an overall picture of the nature of Iranun-Balangingi raiding and its role in the Sulu Sultanate's economy. But on the whole, Dutch efforts to suppress piracy and impose a Pax Neerlandica proved unsuccessful. The cruising *prahus* were only a partial answer at best. Not as swift as the fast sailing, raiding boats, the importance of the cruising *prahus* was limited to protecting shipping in the vicinity of the settlements where they were stationed on the coasts of Java, Borneo, and Celebes.[74]

The failure of the plan to use local vessels to protect coastal communities against slave-raiding was most evident in the Residencies of Menado and Gorontalo which formed the northern area of Celebes. This was an extremely fertile and densely populated region, where irrigated rice was grown on a large scale and gold was mined,[75] but it was not politically integrated by the Dutch. The principal targets of the Iranun and Balangingi were the fishing villages and riverine agricultural settlements of the Minahassans, the Bolaang Mongondow, and the Gorontalo, dotting the extreme northeastern corner of the peninsula and the gulf of Tomini. Gold miners, fishermen, and coasting traders—Bugis, Chinese, and Arabs—were frequently seized within cannon shot of Dutch outposts at Amurang, Belang, and Gorontalo.[76] In 1843 the Governor of the Moluccas observed that piracy was a major factor in the decline in the population of a number of islands in the Moluccas and the Gorontalo area.[77] The annual raids against the Menado residency were to continue for another twenty-five years. The Dutch with their limited resources would be almost as helpless in defending this wealthy but weak area from the Balangingi between 1850 and 1865 as they had been in protecting it against the constant threat of Iranun invasion in earlier years.

Iranun Raiding in the Philippines

The biggest Iranun slave raids in Southeast Asia were directed against the Philippine archipelago. In 1755 raiding began in earnest, and for the next hundred years the coastal towns of southern Luzon, the Visayas, and northwestern Mindanao were the scenes of persistent slave attacks, well organized, on a large scale, and always launched from the sea. The annual reports of the *alcaldes mayores* and friars on these "moro" raids, and the ruins of crude stone towers and forts built as far north as Ilocos are fearful reminders of the power of the slave takers in this period.

The Sultanate of Cotabato—though not the only source—was the springboard for the aggression against the Philippines between 1755 and 1775.[78] For years Magindanao craft hugged the shore from Zamboanga to

Caraga on the northern Mindanao coast* to reach the Visayas.[79] The Dutch
ports were the chief outlet for their Filipino captives who were purchased by
the Bugis and transported.[80] Manila's authority became weaker and coastal
defences in many regions were neglected, but the Spanish were determined
to prevent the Iranun from using Mindanao as a "gateway" to the north. They
slowly closed off this coast to the Iranun of Cotabato by erecting a series
of small *presidios* with fleets stationed along it. This measure to strengthen
defences on the north side of Mindanao was another factor that contributed
to the resettlement of the Iranun of Cotabato at Jolo, Bual, and Balangingi.
Denied easy access to Negros Oriental, Cebu, and Bohol by 1765, the track
of the Iranun from Illana Bay to the Visayas now lay in the direct path of
Taosug settlements to the southwest. They usually set a southerly course for
the islands midway between Jolo and Zamboanga, the Samalese group, and
steered by them past Jolo towards Borneo. Upon sighting Balabac island,
to the south of Palawan, they sailed north along its eastern coast, entered
the narrow strait between Dumaran island and Palawan, from where they
crossed over to the Cuyo islands to obtain food and water before entering the
Visayas.[81]

Once in the Sibuyan sea, raids took place on Romblon island, on
Marinduque island, and on the western coastal towns of the southern
Luzon provinces. Sometimes these assaults were launched from satellite
communities on Mindoro, Burias, and Masbate. Mamburao was for many
years the most important of these Iranun bases. Located some distance up
a river on the coast of Oriental Mindoro, it was well appointed for staging
raids against the greater Manila area. In 1770, its fortified stockade sitting on
a sharp bend in the Mamburao river contained four hundred to five hundred
fighting men. The community owned ten large vessels, several of which
were prizes, including a Canton junk. The fields surrounding the stockade
were cultivated by Filipino captives who were held there until they could be
sold to Brunei traders or transported to Sulu.[82]

While Mamburao and the settlements on Burias were not as large as Reteh
and Tempasuk, they were well established and in close proximity to the
Spanish capital. Forrest mentions the Iranun who operated from Burias:

> These [Iranun] within ten years before 1775, have done much mischief to the
> Spaniards, ... and, at this time, they possess an island in the very heart of the
> Philippines, called Burias, where has been a colony of Illanos, for many years,
> men, women, and children. The Spaniards have often attempted to dislodge
> them, but in vain; the island ... being environed with rocks and shoals to a
> considerable distance.[83]

---

* The other route north was extremely hazardous. It was almost impossible to leave
southern Mindanao and sail east around Cape St. Augustin into the headwind and heavy seas.

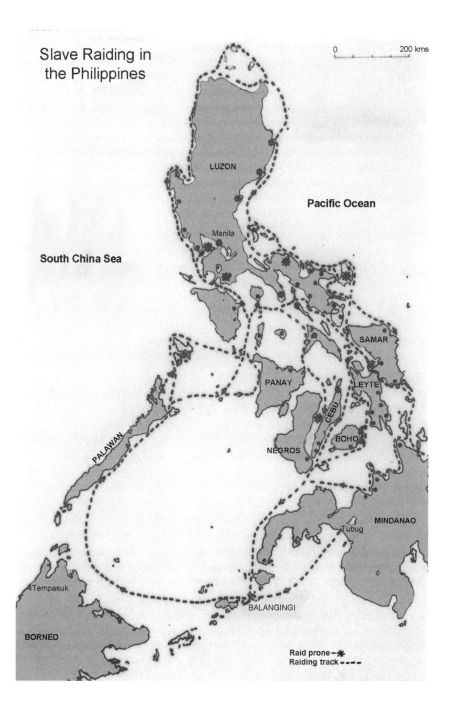

Slave Raiding in the Philippines

Slave raiders from Mamburao and Burias concentrated many of their attacks on coastal villages along the outer rim of Manila Bay. By 1772 some of the more defenceless settlements closest to the entrance were deserted.[84] The village of Mariveles was particularly vulnerable and could not put up effective resistance against attacks in 1774 and 1780.[85] The French navigator de la Perouse described Mariveles' deplorable condition in 1787:

> Toward noon I went on shore to the village, which is composed of about forty houses, built of bamboo ... In front of the principal street, there is a large edifice of hewn stone but almost totally in ruins; nevertheless, two brass guns are visible at the windows.... They informed us that this partly decayed house was the habitation of the curate, the church, and the fort, but all these titles had not overawed the moors of the islands to the south ..., who seized it in 1780, burned the village, destroyed ... the parsons house, made slaves of all the indians who were not able to save themselves by flight, and retired with their captives without meeting with any molestation. The inhabitants of the colony had been so terrified by this event that they are afraid to exercise their industry any longer. The lands are almost overgrown with weeds, and the parish so poor that we could purchase no more than a dozen fowls and a small hog ... [the] pastor was a young mulatto indian.... His parish, he told us, consisted of about two hundred persons, of both sexes and every age, ready, at the least warning, to hide themselves in the woods in order to escape the moors who still frequently make their descents upon this coast.[86]

The fear of pursuing one's livelihood was not confined to peasant agriculturalists. The fishermen of Manila Bay, and the firewood gatherers of Bataan province, who harvested the coastal mangrove, were often seized by Iranun in small vessels disguised like those of the locality.[87] Fear of these forays stopped work and led to periodic shortages of fish and firewood in Manila. Iranun raiders also created havoc with Manila's coasting trade, seizing flotillas of small rice-laden vessels from the provinces of Bataan, Pampanga, Bulacan, Tondo, and Cavite. Traders had to travel by the interior rivers to Manila and voyages were far more costly both in time and money.[88]

A Spanish expedition destroyed Mamburao in 1770.[89] The Governor was provoked to take effective action against the Iranun of Mamburao when they seized a large Chinese junk bound for Manila. The unexpected loss of the junk resulted in the Manila galleon *San Joseph* sailing for New Spain with an incomplete cargo. The first expedition sent to Mamburao in July failed because of the difficulties it encountered in finding and entering the river. It was not until October that a second expedition of nine vessels, several Visayan *prahus* and seven hundred troops and artillery arrived at Mamburao. After a siege of twelve hours, the Mexican and Filipino soldiers found the stockade abandoned the following morning. When news of the victory reached Manila, a mass was celebrated at the Cathedral. Later Iranun continued to use the Mamburao river as a temporary haven, but the bases on other islands became more important as Iranun attacks on southern Luzon and the Visayas accelerated.

During the period 1768–1800, the islands surrounding southern Luzon were one massive raiding base. A ring of satellite stations stretched out around the provinces of Tayabas, Camarines, and Albay, and Iranun raiding *prahus* sailed from all of them: Burias, Masbate, Capul, and Catanduanes.[90] Few coastal towns and villages in southern Luzon were spared. Large settlements were the targets of fleets of forty to fifty *prahus*. These fleets usually contained 2,500 to 3,000 armed men and carried heavy artillery to erect shore batteries. Mass attacks took place on towns and villages on both sides of the coast. In 1755, Virac was destroyed; in 1767, Guinyagen was overwhelmed by a fleet of thirty-two *prahus*; in 1781, Majobac was burnt down; in 1793, Obuyon was attacked and levelled by a fleet of seventy-five *prahus;* and in 1798 the towns of Baler, Casiguran, and Palanan were reduced to ashes by a fleet of twenty-five *prahus* from Burias.[91]

Some of the old towns were rebuilt on the original site, or on a new one nearby, but Iranun raids put a decisive end to many villages. The search for security and the fear of starvation and disease drove Filipinos to abandon villages that had existed for generations, after they experienced the forced harvesting and burning of their fields, and the slaughter of their plough animals. The dilemma facing stricken villagers in the aftermath of a large-scale raid was how to resume their original way of life without risking enslavement in the future. Some went to live in larger villages; some looked for new village sites, often on elevated ground; others abandoned the coast altogether for an equally harsh life in the mountain fastness of the interior where sometimes many were reduced to eating grass to survive. The Spanish labelled these fugitives *cimarrones* and *remontados.* On islands like Marinduque, Polillo, and Catanduances, villagers could not readily flee to another area and were forced to stand and fight. The raids knitted the inhabitants of the coastal towns of smaller islands like these together closely for mutual defence.

The Visayas and the northeast coast of Mindanao experienced some of the worst slave raids in the last quarter of the eighteenth century. The Visayan territories were prime Iranun targets with their dense populations and their developed coastal shipping. Through the narrow straits of the Visayan sea flowed much of the traffic of the Philippines. In terms of seaborne warfare, Spanish naval patrols were unable to take up the cudgels against the raiders. Heavily armed Iranun fcotillas wrought havoc on the Philippine coasting trade, and coastal shipping so essential to the prosperity of the Visayas all but collapsed. In 1771, over fifty trading vessels were seized from Bohol, and the people of Samar and Leyte discontinued trade to Manila for decades at a time. Manila's efforts to ban the local construction of coastal junks which frequently fell into the hands of the Iranun failed. The Governor wrote:[92]

> For the past several years moro raiding has been relentless but it is worse now than ever before, because in the past the raiders only used bladed weapons and lance and were unable to approach and board another vessel, but now they have and use (though not with perfect discipline) cannon and muskets on their vessels. They readily seize small junks and *caracaos* which the Visayan *indios* utilize in their trade with this city because the former are slow and unwieldy and the latter are poorly manned and equipped.*

Problems of distance and communication posed grave difficulties to the Spanish, who did not have the power to prevent the Iranun from ranging over the poorly defended coasts and straits of the Visayan sea. The exposure of the Western Visayas, in particular, to Sulu and Mindanao facilitated slave-raiding from the south.

The Spanish were, in fact, too weak to prevent the inland seas of the central Philippines from becoming a "Muslim lake". Control of these waters by the Iranun enabled them to penetrate the hinterlands up to twenty miles on Leyte, Panay, and Negros to attack villages.[93] This aggression was to be the root cause of the migratory movement of Filipinos between Negros, Panay, and Cebu for over half a century. In 1770, two hundred raiding vessels were active on the coasts of Leyte and Samar, and it was rumoured in the country houses and *conventos* of the Augustinian friars that the Sultan of Sulu planned to install his brother-in-law on Leyte to reign over the Visayas.† The remorseless

---

* Nor were European vessels passing through the Visayas spared:"We took the opportunity of favourable weather we now enjoyed to put the ships in a state of defense. The guns were accordingly mounted, a sufficient quantity of powder and ammunition was filled, and every other necessary preparation made, as those seas are infested with numerous bands of pirates. Two very fine ships had lately been taken by them. One of them was the *May,* of 300 tons, and mounting twenty guns, and had been on a trading voyage from Bengal to the coast of Borneo ... the proas from Magindanao and Sooloo issue forth in such swarms, that it becomes dangerous for a weak ship to sail those seas. These proas are manned with a hundred, and sometimes a hundred and fifty men, well armed, and generally mounting pieces of cannon of 6 or 12 pounders.... These people cruise in fleets of 30 or 40 ... proas; ... and though we did not very much apprehend that they would venture to attack two ships, it would have been unpardonable negligence if we had not prepared ourselves...." Meares, *Voyage Made in the Years 1788 and 1789 from China to the Northwest coast of America,* pp.19–20; see also *Journal of the Lydia,* East India Marine Society, Peabody Museum (entries for 22–25 Oct. 1801); Journal of the *Logan,* 656/1837/39L, vol.1, Peabody Museum (entries for 7 May 1837; vol.2, 22 Apr. 1838).

† In this transitional period (1770–75) the reputation the Taosug developed for marauding was attributable to the activities of Iranun sponsored by the Magindanao as well as themselves. The friars already perceived with some exaggeration in 1770 a shift in power from Cotabato to Sulu. El Provincial de Recolectos de Filipinas, a Vuestra Magestad, 5 June 1771, AGI, Filipinas 685.

invasion of Leyte between 1768 and 1772 resulted in the captivity of two thousand Filipinos.[94] In Caraga province it resulted in the destruction of most of the churches and the death of several friars, and the near total collapse of the trade and agriculture of northeast Mindanao.*

The Iranun confronted the frontier villages of the southern Visayas and Mindanao with some of their greatest demonstrations of force. In 1770 the provincial of the Recollects wrote that no part of the Visayan islands had been left unscathed that year; in his province the Iligan *presidio* had staved off an attack by 180 *prahus*,† but the besieged defenders were helpless to prevent the raiders from burning the surrounding villages and church as they withdrew.[95] Few communities on northeast Mindanao could cope with the pace of the onslaught since the beginning of the previous decade when the Iranun had first appeared on an annual basis; all the villages in Caraga had been burned at least once, and in Iligan province they had destroyed the villages of Ipanan, Alilitum, Gompot, Salay, and Sipara. They frequently undertook raids against Camiguin island.[96] Evidence of these attacks is provided by the name of the principal coastal town—Catarman—which means "place of fear".[97] After examining parish documents in 1779, the Bishop of Cebu stated that slave raids were the basic reason for declining parish enrolments and the continued poverty of the churches in Caraga, Iligan, and Panay.[98] The raids continued and the Filipinos' condition grew worse on northeast Mindanao. At the start of the nineteenth century, they could only cultivate their fields, fish, and communicate with neighbouring villages and provinces at great risk.[99]

Gunboats, Watchtowers, and Warring Friars

The success of the slave raiders of the Sulu Sultanate was related to the deteriorating financial and military situation in the Philippines in the eighteenth century. Iranun marauding placed a tremendous burden on the treasury and the Filipinos for the maintenance of coast guard fleets and

---

* Iranun raiding in the period before 1790 often involved wanton destruction of Filipino lands and communities, suggesting that marauding was then viewed as an extension of *jihad,* with political not simply economic motives. This sort of activity was far less common after 1800 when raiding was more organized and slaves were the prime object. No.226, II, AGI, Filipinas 492, p.10; No.28, Expediente del Provincial de Augustinos Recolectos, 10 Oct. 1772, AGI, Filipinas 627.

† The figures reported by Friars and officials on the overall size and composition of raiding flotillas can be deceptive. The Spanish terms *vinta, panco,* or *joanga* were frequently used to refer to any raiding craft (between 30 and 90 feet in length) irrespective of its construction and use. The largest raiding flotillas rarely exceeded forty vessels. Their numbers were often inflated because each vessel either carried or towed an auxilliary dugout canoe for inshore operations. These craft were labelled *kakap, baroto,* or *vinta* by astute Dutch and Spanish observers. Thus, forty *prahus* with their tenders becomes eighty plus.

the upkeep of forts, troops, and cannon.[100] The Government was forced to solicit funds from religious corporations, private institutions, and wealthy individuals to meet the persistent expenditures for the defence of the archipelago.* In this period, financial constraints and the advent of trade between Manila and Jolo prevented the Spanish from undertaking a large-scale campaign against the Sulu Sultanate.[101] Spain chose instead to wage a defensive war in Philippine waters. The official assumption was that cruising, construction of coastal defence works, and the building of *vintas* and *barangayans* deterred raiding; hence the demand that coast guard patrols be maintained and more vessels and forts built. From 1778 to 1793, the Spanish spent over a million and a half pesos to establish fleets of *vintas* and cannon launches to patrol the seas principally near Manila,[102] but very little was spent on village defence. Village friars were expected to organize parishioners to build their own coastal defences and fortify them from village contributions and religious coffers. The obvious "solution" to the raiding problem would have been an offensive against the major centres of marauding and the occupation of Jolo. This tack was apparently not in the best interests of the Manila administration which was in the ironic position of developing a lucrative trade inadvertently predicated on the "piracy" it so religiously decried.

Iranun raiding from 1765 to 1775 highlighted the lack of surveillance—this meant building fast-moving coast guard craft rather than conventional naval vessels.[103] Recognizing that only shallow draught vessels could pursue the slave raiders, Governor Basco Vargas, in 1778, organized "the light navy" to police the 300,000 square miles of seas and its archipelago.[104] A small fleet of *vintas*, armed outriggered craft, was hastily constructed to patrol the waters from Manila to Panay, and an order was sent to military governors, and *alcaldes mayores* making them responsible for the organization and maintenance of *vinta* squadrons in the provinces.[105] By this measure, Governor Basco hoped to establish coast guard flotillas at Cebu, Iligan, and Iloilo without undue expenditure by the Government. Three years later, a fee in kind, called *vinta* in Pampanga and Bulacan and *falua* in other provinces, was introduced by the Government to help finance

---

* In 1773 the Governor Captain General informed the Crown that the 100,000 pesos allotted for defence and expeditions against the Muslims were not enough. As a result of the grave financial situation, he raised more than 250,000 pesos by donation in Manila: 170,000 pesos from the Manila Chinese; 20,000 pesos from the new *Kapitan China* for being confirmed in his appointment; 5,203 pesos from the mestizos of Tondo; 50,000 pesos from the wealthy widow, Dona Maria Israel Gomez de Careaga. The Governor described Dona Maria, who donated more money to "contain" the Muslims than anyone else in Manila, as a "woman of good character and the finest deeds". She also financed privately the construction of a patrol galley, provided weapons and food for the Mamburao expedition, and agreed to supply all rations—food and drink—necessary to support expeditions against the Muslims for a period of five years. Ibid.; No.276, GCG a Senor Secretario de Estado, 16 Jan. 1773, AGI, Filipinas 493.

coastal patrols.[106] Beleaguered provinces could not always raise sufficient funds to support the *vintas*. In 1790, Manila refused to provide the necessary assistance to the *alcalde mayor* of Iloilo, whose province had incurred an alarming series of raids, and temporary relief—a galley and several *vintas*—had to be sent from neighbouring islands.[107]

Within two decades the programme collapsed. Apart from costing the government a minimum of 70,000 pesos a year, the *vintas* had other more serious drawbacks: they only cruised at certain times of the year and then only in good weather; they were stationed in some parts of the archipelago but not others; and, from the beginning, there were never enough *vintas* to carry out Vargas' programme.[108] In 1794, leading military and civilian officials decided to abolish the *vintas* and replace them with six divisions of *faluas* (cannon boats) and *lanchas* (armed, flat boats).[109] The specially built copper-bottomed boats of the anti-piracy force, or *Marina Sutil* also proved inadequate to the task of patrolling such an expanse of water.[110] In 1803, the Spanish had thirty such patrol boats, fifty-five to sixty feet in length, armed with an 18- to 24-pound cannon in the bow and swivel guns at the quarters, and capable of speeds up to six knots in a favourable wind.[111] However, Iranun raiding vessels made eight to nine knots with sails and oar, and with good winds might cover several hundred miles in less than a day.[112]

Further, *falua* crews were not well trained and the officers were of poor calibre, some being English and French seamen conscripted off the Manila docks.* Nor were the marine grenadiers on the *faluas* properly equipped:

> The feluccas in which these soldiers embark are very small and the soldiers go on board in coats, knapsacks, shakos and muskets, too much even when not embarked. The people employed in boats of this kind ought to be able to row as well as to fight—no coats, nor helmets, nor muskets, but (rather) short and thick blunderbusses, hand grenades, and fireballs.[113]

In 1826, the failure of the *Marina Sutil* as a defence against slave raids was pointed out by the Augustinian Provincial, Gregorio Rodriguez, in a frank reply to the Governor-General's request as to whether the addition of four *faluas* and two *lanchas* would suffice to defend the coasts of Panay and Calamianes:

> The general opinion in Iloilo [province] ... is that the *lanchas* ordinarily cause more harm than good. In the nine years of my residence on Panay, I cannot remember ever hearing of the *lanchas* having been victorious; ... they have not

---

* Officers on the gunboats were poorly paid: "They cannot obtain a higher rank than that of Captain, and then they only receive forty dollars which is less pay than an ensign of infantry at Manila. Having no retirement they only think of acquiring if they can some little fortune by trading at the ports to which they are sent for defence. It would be much better to promise them and their crews a sum of money for each *prahu* or pirate they took." Notes translated from the Spanish relative to the pirates on the island of Mindanao, PRO, Admiralty 125/133.

seized a single *panco* or a single muslim, nor have they been able to prevent them from coming and going with impunity; and, despite all the divisions of *lanchas* and *faluas* that presently exist ..., the muslims have the audacity to pass right in front of Corregidor, under the Governor's very nose, and it is only after the *pancos* have gone that the *lanchas* set out in pursuit. It is as though you were sending a tortoise to catch a deer.[114]

The candid letter concludes on a desperate note by suggesting the Government reinstitute the practice of offering a bounty to Filipinos for each raiding vessel and Muslim captured—the friars would administer the head money in the victorious villages.[115]

In desperation, a few friars in villages on wide open coasts were forced to mobilize the inhabitants of several settlements to build and arm their own fleets of *barangayan* to defend themselves.* The most notable example was father Julian Bermejo, the friar of Boljoon on southern Cebu from 1804 to 1836. He established a line of *baluartes*, small forts, that ran from Tanog to Silbonga, created an early warning system that used flags to alert villagers to the approach of Iranun-Samal vessels, and where to congregate to defend themselves, and organized the construction of a fleet of ten *barangayan* by the inhabitants of Argao, Dalaguete, and Sibonga, that were ready to put to sea at a moment's notice.[116] The scheme was so successful that by 1830 the Filipinos of southern Cebu and Bohol employed seventy *barangayan*† to protect their villages and *tripang* fisheries.[117]

The consequence of slave-raiding in the Philippine archipelago was a perennial struggle for life and property, on the part of the Filipinos often one-sided. The *bantay*, the village watchtower, and the *baluarte,* which varied from slit trenches on hill crests to stone block houses, were features of most coastal villages. Manila could not afford to assist all coastal settlements in the islands to fortify themselves and, as a rule, only built *presidios* in or near the provincial capitals. Nevertheless, in 1769, the Government ordered all villages to use their own resources to build stockades.[118] Since Manila had very little to do with village defence, the construction of lookout

---

* The *barangayan* were similar to Iranun raiding *prahus* or *pancos,* and constructed in the same manner, but they did not exceed 55 feet in length, nor 14 feet in width, Bernaldez, *Guerra al Sur,* p.44.

† On the whole it is clear that well-organized and equipped *barangayan* fleets were capable of defending themselves and defeating the Iranun-Samal raiders in coastal waters. The division that was commanded by D. Pedro Esteban of Tabaco in Albay Province was much respected by the raiders for its courage. At the age of 80, the embattled veteran came out of retirement to capture 9 *pancos* and sink 18 smaller boats in 1818. Estaban's career in the coast-guard spanned 36 years: in 1782 he was given the rank of provisional captain in the light navy for having captured 2 Muslim *pancos;* in 1788 he was placed in command of the *vinta* squadron for Albay Province; in 1796 he destroyed 37 *pancos* near Bacacay. Since that time he had lived quietly until he abandoned his fields to command the squadron once more in 1818, No.8, PNA, Ereccion del Pueblo Albay 1772–1831.

towers, palisades, and forts was managed chiefly by village friars with Filipino labour. Comyn observed that Filipinos defended their villages

> by opening ditches and planting a breastwork of stakes and palisades, crowned with watchtowers, or a wooden or stone castle; precautions which sometimes are not sufficient against the nocturnal irruptions and robberies of the moors, more especially when they come in strength with firearms, in general scarce among the natives.[119]

Friars played a critical role in preventing the Iranun from establishing unconditional dominion over the coasts of southern Luzon and Visayan islands. They were at one and the same time priests, soldiers, and technical advisors, skilled not only in the use of artillery but in boatbuilding, navigation, and first aid. As authority figures, they provided the leadership and organization that pulled Filipinos together to form coastguard flotillas and sentinel systems:

> ... In situations of common danger, he is their leader by sea and land; and on account of his superior wisdom and courage, he is looked up to as a strong tower against the invasion and inroads of the Mahometans. It is the prerogative of each missionary in his own parish to issue orders for building or repairing the fort, for providing it with cannon and ammunition, and for the construction of war canoes, which he frequently commands in person. He appoints all subordinate officers, presides over the discipline of the militia, regulates the number of guards, and even directs the sentinel to his proper post.[120]

At the same time, the threat of slave raids significantly enhanced the friar's authority and prestige, enabling him to foster village dependence.

The implementation of village defence rested entirely on the Filipinos themselves. They acted as *telegrafistas,* built and manned the *baluartes,* and served on coastguard vessels against Muslim raiders. Forty-six out of sixty-five villages in the Bishopric of Cebu had a *baluarte* and/or fort (see Appendix N); Filipinos had built all of them. Once erected, the watchtowers, earthworks, and palisades had to be maintained and rebuilt when demolished by typhoons and earthquakes.[121] Gale force winds on southern Luzon not infrequently left a trail of disaster which swept away watchtowers and stockades leaving coastal settlements defenceless, while torrential rains dampened what little gunpowder villages possessed and rusted cannon.[122]

Filipino sentinels stood watch day and night during the southwest monsoon.[123] The belfry of churches and watchtowers on hill-tops furnished some of the best vantage points.* At the slightest alarm a *telegrafista* rang

---

* In some instances, Filipinos who were assigned regularly as *telegrafistas* on offshore islands or in the highlands brought their families to settle at the outpost and formed the nucleus of a new settlement. Women in one such community on Camiguin island passed their time on the hillsides by skeining abaca fibres for weaving local cloth. See Historical Data on San Pascual, HDP, Masbate; Historical Data on Catarman, HDP, Misamis Oriental; Historical Data on Bacacay, HDP, Albay.

the church bell or warned the village by signalling with a big flag waved high in the air during the day and with a torch at night. In 1788, Meares wrote of the Mindoro coast: "the inhabitants not only kept numerous and constant fires along the shores, but had even lighted them on the very summits of the mountains".[124] Besides fire there were other commonly used warning devices to guard against raids; women and children scrambled for refuge at the first sound of the sentry blowing on a shell horn, or beating a gong, drum, or hollowed-out log, while the men assembled to take up their positions in the fort or church.[125]

The presence of a friar could exert a strong influence on the security of a village in face of government neglect. Of the eight communities dispersed by raiding in the Bishopric of Cebu in 1779, only one—Cacub in Caraga province—had either a priest or *baluarte*. Coastal villages that lacked a friar and a *baluarte* ran a substantial risk of being attacked. It was in the interest of such settlements to locate near some sort of natural refuge where Filipinos could flee on first sight of the "moros". Mountains, or any high ground were an obvious choice,[126] but villages in some instances were encircled with plantations of bamboo or thickets of pandan, a plant with a spiny trunk and leaves.[127] On Masbate, cave complexes were fortified and used as transitory dwellings by settlers fearful of returning to the coast.[128]

The appearance of large numbers of slaving *prahus* with overwhelming firepower was a terrifying experience for Filipinos who lacked arms and boats to defend themselves. One of the most outspoken critics of the Government's lack of assistance in village defence was the Bishop of Nueva Caceres whose churches were periodically plundered and burnt. Most of his churches with thick walls and high towers served as fortresses as well as places of worship, and in some villages were the Filipinos' sole security against slave raids. In 1770 the Bishop accused the Government of having forsaken the provinces of Camarines and Albay and urged that revenue from these provinces be made available for their defence:

> In conclusion, your Excellency, the truth of the matter is that Camarines and Albay province don't have a King to protect them, let alone a pistol or sword for their defense. Nevertheless, they pay more in tribute than the combined amount collected from the indios of Bohol, Dapitan and Iligan.[129]

The question of the cost and supply of arms and ammunition was particularly troublesome for the Bishops towards the end of the eighteenth century. Many of their villages had firearms provided by the Church, but were frequently destitute of gunpowder and shot.[130] When communities had powder it was often in insufficient amounts and of poor quality. The religious orders had little difficulty in purchasing cannon, but feared not being able to obtain the more scarce gunpowder. The Bishops had reason to be concerned about purchasing security for their poorly defended parishes. Not only did government officials charge exorbitant prices for gunpowder to clerics but they often ignored or rejected out of hand petitions from newly found villages and others that had been raided to allow them to purclase cannon and gunpowder.[131] No administrator in Manila wanted to be responsible for the decision of supplying Filipinos with arms and ammunition. The Government objected to such a measure for several reasons:

> The first is arming and instructing a subjugated people, the second is that wanting order, leaders, and valour at the least surprise they fly whither they can abandoning their arms and ammunition which fall into the possession of the moros who have in consequence already taken many guns.[132]

In the 1790s, Manila was forced to reconsider its policy towards supplying munitions to coastal villages because of the great harm inflicted on them by slave raids, especially those conducted by Iranun from Burias. By 1799, the central Government felt it expedient that provincial authorities assume more responsibility for defending the coasts of their provinces. The burden of this task fell to the *alcaldes mayores* whom the Government accordingly entrusted with Crown arms and gunpowder.[133] In the following three decades (1800–1830) more than 1,500 cannons were distributed among the coastal villages of the Philippines.[134] Some *alcaldes*, charged with the defence of provinces, particularly on Negros and Panay, took full advantage of the opportunity to further their personal fortunes, and sold government munitions to the Iranun and Samal.[135] In the 1850s, many of these guns were recalled by a government more fearful of awakening nationalist sentiment and the spectre of Filipinos possessing arms than of Samal slave raids.[136] The Balangingi appeared as far north as Mindoro for another twenty years and *La Politica* noted that not infrequently villages had only sharpened sticks and stones to defend themselves as late as 1864.[137]

The Anatomy of Raiding

The Spanish friars had been able to establish over a thousand towns and cities in the island lowlands by 1898. The majority of these communities had less than 2,000 inhabitants; 200 had a population of over 2,000; thirty over 5,000; nine over 10,000.[138] The study of the history of population in the Philippines is just beginning to focus attention on the impact of Iranun-Samal raiding on the development of towns, population growth, and migration within regions and between islands in the late eighteenth and nineteenth centuries. Obviously, raiding concentrated on some islands, provinces, and districts and not others depending on geographic and other variables. A diversity of responses and demographic patterns would be expected to emerge from a study of their population history.[139]

I would like to examine briefly the impact of Iranun-Samal marauding on the population history of one Bishopric on Luzon, namely, Nueva Caceres, with special reference to Tayabas, Camarines, and Albay provinces between 1751 and 1815. I have used two types of social statistics—religious and civil. The principal demographic data are the censuses made at the request of the Spanish Crown by the provincial Bishops.* I have supplemented the censuses with isolated reports of military officials, parish curates, and information on community location, presence, or absence of a priest, frequency of raids, and enumeration of artillery, small arms, boats, and *baluartes* to create a community profile on sixty-six communities listed in the 1780 census for Nueva Caceres.[140]

From a systematic comparison of village population fluctuations with village defensive posture and frequency of raids, it is possible to reconstruct a more substantial picture of settlement patterns of the Hispanized communities of southern Luzon at the end of eighteenth century. Table 3 lists location, frequency of raids and/or destruction of communities, and the population variations between 1751 and 1815 of fifteen communities that were either destroyed or known to have been raided more than once. There is enough evidence to show that the nature of raiding in Nueva Caceres changed between 1755 and 1800 as the Iranun and Samal concentrated their attacks on smaller targets. There was a shift away from frontal assaults and prolonged sieges of *cabecera* (concentrated mission settlements) in Albay and Camarines provinces, to attacks on outlying small villages, *visitas*. The *visitas* of the southern Luzon provinces, more particularly Tayabas, were already common targets in the 1790s.[141] In the nineteenth century, they were to become the principal targets of Balangingi slave raids. This change in strategy by raiding expeditions was related to the growth of towns in certain areas, the acquisition of administrative skills by their local leaders, and the increased organizational strength of coastal defence forces.

With better organization, the exponential growth of population centres became a key factor in deterring raids (see Appendix P). Settlements that

---

* There are considerable problems in using the censuses. Their accuracy is suspect, particularly for analysis of population growth rates, and they must be used with utmost caution by historians. A number of factors are responsible for inaccuracies in the records on which censuses are based. Friar error is one of the most important factors that must be taken into account when considering the reliability of religious records. Population counts in censuses were difficult to tally and reflect the care, neglect, and eccentricities of parish priests who kept them. Some friars with meticulous attention for detail sometimes made errors when copying records for transmission to Manila. Other friars were prevented from reporting current populations of distant villages by illness, poor communication—unnavigable rivers and impassable roads—and fear of the Muslims. Another consideration has been partial destruction or loss of key censuses, or parts thereof, to ravages of war, climate, and to negligence by record-keepers and governments in the past. Comyn, *State of the Philippines in 1810*, pp.1–3; Nicholas P.Cushner, *Spain in the Philippines* (Quezon City: Ateneo de Manila University, 1971), pp.108–12.

Fig. 1. Andahuat, Chief of the "Negros" of Jolo. A pen and ink sketch done by Juan Ravenet, a member of the Malespina expedition, in the early 1790s. Note the simplicity of the man's dress.
(courtesy of the Museo Naval)

Fig. 2. A "negress" of Jolo in Manila. A pen and ink sketch by Juan Ravenet.
(courtesy of the Museo Naval)

Fig. 3. A "Malay Chief" of Jolo whose wealth and power was based on the careful regulation of external trade. He is dressed in high fashion—a headcloth of American or Bengal manufacture, a brightly coloured Chinese silk jacket, embossed and filagreed with gold, satin pants, and several splendid kris— a reflection of his economic status and social prestige. This beautiful illustration was done in the early 1840s.
(courtesy of Frank Marryat, *Borneo and the Indian Archipelago)*

Fig. 4. The dress of a Segai-i warrior of Gunung Tabor beautifully depicted by Frank Marryat.
(courtesy of Frank Marryat, *Borneo and the Indian Archipelago)*

Fig. 5. Entrance to Jolo town in the late 1830s. The trading *prahu* is Taosug or Samal and appears to be crewed by Chinese.

(courtesy of M. Dumont D'Urville, *Voyage au Pole sud et dans L'Oceanie,* vol. 2, 1837–40, pl. 139)

Fig. 6. Zamboanga Town in the early 1790s at the time of the visit of the Malespina Expedition. A fortified watchtower stands prominently at the northern end of the garrison community. There is no palisade erected along the shoreline yet as depicted in figure 8, nearly half a century later when slave raiding against the community had dramatically increased in the late 1830s.

(courtesy of M. Dumont D'Urville, *Voyage au Pole sud et dans L'Oceanie,* vol. 2, 1837–40, pl. 141)

Fig. 7. A street scene in Zamboanga. The houses are built on posts and the ladders taken up at night as the Samal often attacked the inhabitants who occasionally had to seek refuge in the *presidio*.

(courtesy of M. Dumont D'Urville, *Voyage au Pole sud et dans L'Oceanie,* vol. 2, 1837–40)

Fig. 8. A *vigia* or village watchtower at Zamboanga built by the local inhabitants for coastal defence. Such watchtowers were common features of most coastal villages in the Philippines in the late 18th and 19th centuries.

(courtesy of M. Dumont D'Urville, *Voyage au Pole sud et dans L'Oceanie,* vol. 2, 1837–40, pl. 143)

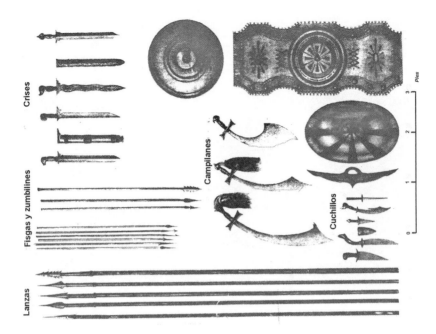

Lanzas Fisgas y zumbilines Crises Campilanes Cuchillos

Pies

◀Fig. 9. An "Iranun" sea-warrior attired in the distinctive thick cotton quilted red vest, and armed with a kris, long spear, and the Kampilan, a long, heavy "lanoon sword" ornamented with human hair.

(courtesy of Frank Marryat, *Borneo and the Indian Archipelago*)

Fig. 10. Taosug weapons ▲ wrought from iron bars and the hoops taken off the bales of English textiles, and worked into artistically and technically superior blades and lance heads; the serpentine kris regarded as the noblest weapon; the bamboo lance with its damascened spearhead; the Zumbline or boarding spear; as protective arms use was made of shields in leather and wood.

(courtesy of Emilio Bernaldez, *Reseña historico de la Guerra a Sur de Filipinas*)

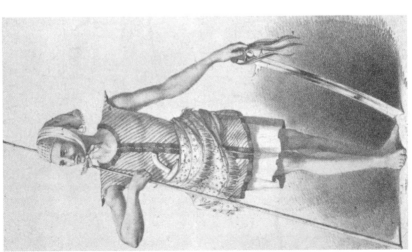

Fig. 11. The Samal Bajau Laut, the maritime nomadic fishers of the Sulu zone, who performed an invaluable role in the Sultanate's economy as gatherers of sea produce.

Fig. 12. The Salisipan (see Appendix A)

(courtesy of the Museo Naval, Rafael Mouleon, *Construccion Navales*)

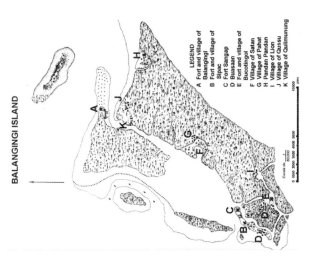

BALANGINGI ISLAND

LEGEND

A Fort and village of
   Balangingi
B Fort and village of
   Sipac
C Fort Sangap
D Buasaan
E Fort and village of
   Bucotingol
F Village of Satan
G Village of Pahat
H Pandan Pandan
I Village of Lion
J Village of Qussu
K Village of Qulimunung

Escala de
1:60,000

0 1000 2000 3000 4000 5000   10000   15000

Fig. 13. A plan of the Samal
kota of Sipak. It was situated on
raised ground, protected by reefs,
mangrove, and a defensive moat,
and defended with heavy cannon.
(courtesy of Emilio Bernaldez,
*Resana historico de la Guerra
a Sur la Filipinas*)

Fig. 14. The Samalese group, home
of the Balangingi. The islands
were fringed with mangrove
swamps and separated from one
another by reefs and channels.
The map notes the location of the
Samal forts and villages in 1848.
(courtesy of Emilio Bernaldez,
*Resana historico de la Guerra
a Sur de Filipinas*)

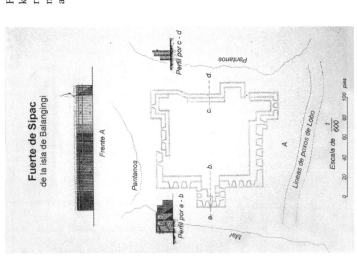

Fuerte de Sipac
de la isla de Balangingi

Frente A

Perfil por a - b

Perfil por c - d

Pantanos

Mar

Pantanos

Pantanos

Líneas de poxos de Lobo

Escala de
1/600

0   20   40   60   80   100 pies

Fig. 15. A Joanga, an Iranun warship of the late 18th century with three banks of oars under full sail. Upward of 100 feet long, these vessels were provided with large bamboo outriggers, both sides were rowed and paddled by more than 190 men.

(courtesy of the Musco Naval, Rafael Mouleon, *Construccion Navales*)

Fig. 16. A Balangingi Garay or panco with two banks oars under full sail.

(courtesy of the Museo Naval, Rafael Mouleon, *Construccion Navales*)

Fig. 17. The Faluas or gunboats of the anti-piracy force were equipped with oars and lanteen sails. Such patrol boats, 55–60 feet in length, were armed with an 18- to 24- pound cannon in the bow, and capable of speeds of up to 6 knots.

(courtesy of the Museo Naval, Rafael Mouleon, *Construccion Navales*)

Fig. 18. The *canonero* was a prefabricated, flat-decked, shallow draught (2 metres) steamer that was rigged as a fore and aft schooner. First introduced in 1860, the *canonero* carried a smooth 24-pound bowgun with swivel guns mounted on the rails. It proved more than a match for Balangingi *garay* in coastal waters and signalled the end of Samal maritime hegemony.

(courtesy of the Museo Naval, Rafael Mouleon, *Construccion Navales*)

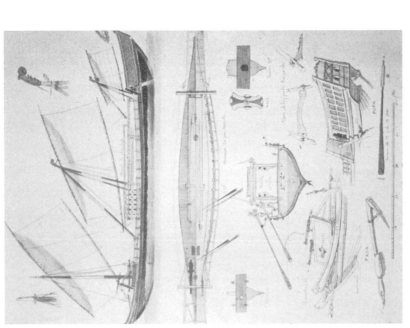

Fig. 20. The Garay (see Appendix A)
(courtesy of the Museo Naval, Rafael
Mouleon, *Construccion Navales*)

Fig. 19. The Lanong (see Appendix A)
(courtesy of the Museo Naval, Rafael
Mouleon, *Construccion Navales*)

TABLE 5
SLAVE RAIDING AND POPULATION VARIATIONS IN NUEVA CACERES (1751–1815)

Pueblos	Location	Number of Recorded Raids				Year Community Destroyed by Raiding	Population in 1751 (or 1780)	Population in 1815 (or 1813)	Population Variation between 1751 and 1815—When Population of 1751 or 1780 =100
		1755–1779	1780–1790	1791–1800	1801–1815				
Tayabas province									
Mayobac	Coast	1	1			1765, 1782	747	0	0
Palanan	Coast			1		1798	1,334	371	27.8
Guinayangan	Coast	3		1		1767, 1791–1800	1,225	382	31.2
Obuyon	Coast	1		1		1793	850	481	56.6
Baler	Coast			1		1798	977	740	75.7
Casiguran de Baler	Coast			1		1798	796	644	80.9
Lupi	Inland	1	1			1759–1761	1,859	1,624	87.4
Catanavan	Coast	2		1			1,585(1780)	1,542	97.3
Pagbilao	Coast	2		1		1759–1761	724	909	125.6
Camarines province									
Capalonga	Coast	2	2			1760	492	301	61.2
Indan	Coast	3	1			1760	2,946	2,446	83.7
Daet	Coast	2					3,074(1780)	2,903	94.0
Albay province									
Sorsogon	Coast	2					6,422	4,008	62.4
Virac	Coast	1	1			1755	3,250	4,981	153.3
Caramoan	Inland	2				1761	771(?)	1,972	255.8

Notes: The information on the frequency of raids and destruction of *pueblos* has been compiled from the following sources: Noticias veridicas de los perjucios, robos, muertes, y cautivietos y otros inhumanidades, que los moros han executada en los anos de 59 y 60 en la Provincia de Tayabas, Camarines, y parages correspondientes a la administracion de los ramos Descalzados de nuestra Santa padre San Francisco y clerigos, perteniezientes a el Obispado de el propio Camarines, AGI, Filipinas 681; El Arzobispo de Manila a Vuestra Magestad, 3 June 1761, AGI, Filipinas 603; Alcalde Mayor de Tayabas a Gobernador y Capitan General de las Islas Filipinas, 20 December 1768, PNA. Ereccion de Pueblo de Tayabas III, Testemonio de Provincial de San Franzisco, Francisco Xavier Estongo in Numero 46, El Gobernador y Capitan General de las Islas Filipinas a Senor Secretario de Estado y del Despacho Universal de Marina y Indias, 17 Aug. 1770, AGI, Filipinas 490; Alcalde Mayor y Capitan de Guerra a Gobernador y Capitan General de las Islas Filipinas, 18 Sept. 1781, PNA. Ereccion de Pueblo Tayabas 217, bundle 1; Numero 20, El Obispo de Nueva Caceres remite a Vuestra Magestad su ultima visita Diocesana de 1791 y 1972, 1 Dec. 1792, AGI, Duplicados del Obispo de Nueva Caceres 1033; Alcalde Mayor de Tayabas a Gobernador y Capitan General de las Islas Filipinas, 2 Dec. 1973, PNA. Ereccion de Pueblo Tayabas, 1793–1857, pt II, Numero 7, El Gobernador y Capitan General de las Islas Filipinas a Senor Secretario de Estado y del Despacho Universal de la Hacienda y las Indias, 4 June 1806, AGI, Filipinas 510; the letter of Don Matheo de Meza Juez, Provisor y Vicario General Inderado de este Obispo vacante de Nueva Caceres en El Arzobispo de Manila a Vuestra Magestad, 15 July 1814, AGI, Ultrama 683.

were formerly potential targets increased in size and strength to a point (1,500+) beyond which the risks became too great for the Iranun under most circumstances. In 1826, the Provincial of the Augustinians was to write:

> As the population increases in the Philippine islands, the *moros* cannot cause the devastation they have in the past when they landed, laid waste to towns and carried off many *indios* into slavery: nowadays there are situated on all coasts sizeable communities that bravely defend themselves, consequently the *moros* don't attack the large population centres.[142]

There was no scaling down of raiding activity in the 1790s—only a change of targets. The new pattern that emerged combined mass attacks with inshore scouring. When mass attacks were successful, results were spectacular, as was the case on the northwestern side of Luzon in 1798 (an estimated 450–500 people were seized from Casiguran, Baler, and Palanan).[143] But such successes appear by then to have been the exception rather than the norm. What made the impact of the new raiding pattern so strongly felt was the laser-like Iranun-Samal concentration in certain places—mainly the Ragay gulf and Camarines Norte—and more widespread use of shallow draught canoes for surprise attacks. Clearly, to pluck unsuspecting fishermen and their families, traders, and travellers from isolated beaches and coasting boats with inshore scouring canoes was easy and safe; and slave raiders, more particularly the Balangingi, came to rely increasingly on the use of this technique for getting captives.*

It is difficult to estimate the annual number of Filipinos directly lost through captivity or death in Nueva Caceres. In 1761 the Bishop was unable to provide an overall figure for the decline in the population of the provinces but conservatively estimated the loss in Camarines between 1759 and 1760 at 800 people.[144] In 1817, the Bishop estimated Sulu marauders captured more than 1,500 people, predominantly boys and girls from the *cabeceras* and *visitas* of Albay, Camarines, and Tayabas.[145] The intensity of Balangingi raiding by 1830, closely tied to Sulu's expanding economy, would tend to support an estimate that on an average 750–1,500 Filipinos were carried off or killed from Nueva Caceres annually; further, that the cumulative totals rose in the first half of the nineteenth century at an annual rate that was greater than in the last quarter of the eighteenth century.†

Despite increased expenditure for coastal defence, the continuing high incidence of raiding on the smaller shore towns that could not be adequately

---

* This is made quite clear in Appendix R which is based on the testimonies of fugitive captives in the years from 1836 to 1864.

† Direct losses from slave raids varied considerably in different parts of the archipelago, Cruikshank estimates that 100 Samarenos were captured or killed annually between 1768 and 1858, Cruikshank, "A History of Samar Island", p.74.

cared for was a cause for alarm. In such settlements, the anxiety of waiting for slave raiders to strike became as great as the actual fear of facing them. Fear itself threatened paralysis of daily life; it disrupted the rhythm of the rice harvest, it prevented fishermen from putting to sea, and more generally, it separated individuals and communities from one another—people did not visit, and babies remained unbaptized for years at a time. One of the most apparent results of the raiding was the destabilizing effect of internal migration motivated by fear. The perennial fear of slave raids and the need for adequate food and shelter forced terrified Filipinos to abandon their villages. Throughout this period (1790–1848), large and small groups were constantly on the move seeking resettlement opportunities. They often remained within their province, flocking to larger urban centres or moving inland. But some never settled down again joining the ranks of *remontados*, beyond the pale of Spanish authority.

8

Slave Raiding in Southeast Asia, 1830–1898

THE BALANGINGI, THE FISHERS OF MEN

The Balangingi Samal lived, along with Iranun and other Samal-speaking groups, in a dozen or more villages scattered along the southern Mindanao coast, the southern shore of Basilan, and on the islands of the Samalese cluster of which Balangingi was dominant. As Sulu's trade expanded at the end of the eighteenth century, Taosug *datus* increasingly retained neighbouring groups of Samal as slave raiders. From Balangingi and related communities on other islands, Samal-speakers voyaged great distances; they swept the coasts from Luzon to Brunei and from Singapore to Menado, capturing slaves. But who were the Balangingi? Although Francisco Combes and Thomas Forrest described the warlike activities and trade of the Samal in earlier periods, there are no historical references to the Balangingi as a separate group before the nineteenth century.[1] In Western sources, marauders are first mentioned as Balangingi rather than Iranun in the area of Singapore and east Malaya in the 1830s.* From that period the label *Balangingi* began to supersede *Illanun* in the European literature as synonymous with "pirate". The Balangingi Samal seem to have acquired ethnic distinction only as they specialized in raiding activity and incorporated an incredible number of non-Samal peoples into their population.

The Samalese group comprised Balangingi island (6 square miles) and Tunkil, a cluster of four islets (9.5 square miles) situated in the centre of the Sulu archipelago, midway between Borneo and Mindanao.[2] The islets were subject to change of size and shape, with tidal variations and modulations in the wind and weather patterns, separating into small parcels of rock when inundated at high tide. They were fringed with mangrove swamps, and separated from neighbouring islands by reefs and winding channels through which swirled strong currents and counter-currents.† With no surface water,

---

* Several "Iranun" *prahus* were destroyed by the steamboat *Diana* on the east coast of Malaya in 1838, and some of the survivors when interrogated called themselves Balangingi after the island which was their home. See Appendix Q.

† In regard to the treacherous character of these currents, Bernaldez wrote: "they usually swirl about at six or seven miles an hour [and] we have seen a steam warship dragging both anchors, after letting out more than 60 fathoms of chain on each anchor in Balangingi waters". Bernaldez, *Guerra al Sur de Filipinas,* pp.15, 153.

and little flora except the ubiquitous coconut palm, they were incapable of providing the subsistence base necessary to support a dense population.[3] On these islands, the Balangingi Samal constructed wells and four forts (Balangingi, Sipac, Bucotingal, Sangap) to guard their villages and *prahus*. The forts (*kota*), situated on raised ground and protected by coral reefs on three sides, were stockades of two, three, and four tiers of stout tree trunks, packed with earth and coral to a height of twenty feet and defended with heavy cannon.[4]

The islands and shallow seas upon which the original Samalan-speaking people of the Balangingi cluster lived placed them in an ecological bind that shaped their character and relationship to the Sulu Sultanate.* The sole orientation of the Samal was, of necessity, towards the sea. From it, as specialists in maritime raiding, boat-building, and marine procurement, they derived their strength, security, and—ultimately—wealth. Lack of self-sufficiency bound the Samal to Jolo. Its proximity to Jolo as an outlet for retailing captives; its dependence on larger, volcanic islands like Jolo and Basilan as sources of rice, fruits, and vegetables, and trade goods; and the natural barriers surrounding it help to explain why Balangingi became the natural home of one of the most feared piratical groups of island Southeast Asia.[5]

In the nineteenth century, the Balangingi were integrated within the Sulu Sultanate by a three-level class system comprising aristocrats, freemen, and *a'ata* (slaves).[6] The Sultan appointed a *panglima* to represent him, but *datus* exercised titular rights and imposed jural authority over specific Samal islands and populations.[7] All *datus* were Taosug, but not infrequently *panglima* were Samal. The Samal paid tribute in *tripang,* pearl shell, and salt;† and as clients of powerful *datus,* they offered their services for slaving expeditions in return for trade opportunities and for protection from rival Taosug.[8] *Datus* who exercised supervision over Samal populations were frequently associated with—if not directly related to—the Sultan, and often resided in or near Jolo. In the first half of the nineteenth century, the most important Taosug patrons of Samal communities were: Datu Dacula (Sipac), Datu Tahel, Datu Molok, and Maharaja Lela (Balangingi).[9]

---

* The captive Francisco Thomas stated: "the inhabitants of these places [the Samalese group] live by piracy and that they have no other means of existence, in fact that piracy is the general vocation of the people". Bonham to Maitland, 28 June 1838, PRO, Admiralty 125/133.

† Chrishaan Soerma, a captive of Datu Molok's served as one of his tribute collectors in the early 1840s. In his statement he lists the customary amounts particular Samal communities payed Datu Molok in tribute: negeri Tawi-Tawi, 200 piculs pearl shell; negiri parang, 125 piculs of pearl shell; Sandakan, 25 piculs bird's nest; Pangutaran, 150 coconut oil lamps, bananas, and coconuts. Verklaring van Chrishaan Soerma, 10 Aug. 1846, ANRI, Menado 50.

An Ethnographic Fiction

To understand the important role played by the Balangingi in the slave trade in Southeast Asia, it is necessary to trace their history as an ethnic group. The only historical work which deals with the Balangingi does not consider their ethnic origins.[10] Avoidance of this question presents a deceptive picture of a static "society" with a homogeneous population. Samal groups in the Sulu archipelago were emergent populations; the success of the Balangingi as slave raiders was due in large measure to their ethnic heterogeneity. Captives' statements present a picture of Samal populations undergoing constant readjustments until 1848. At the beginning of the nineteenth century, there was an infusion of ethnically diverse captive people among the Balangingi—mostly through demands for their labour on raiding *prahus* and in the *tripang* and pearl fisheries—that complicated the identity of the Samal populations.

Many of the captives or slaves who were brought to Balangingi turned Samal—adopting language, religion, and customs. Insufficient data prevents a precise reconstruction of the overall size and origin of Samal populations at that time.[11] What information there is for the nineteenth century has survived in the statements of fugitive captives; these show that the incorporation of foreign elements took place on a large scale, especially in the second and third generation. In 1836 it was estimated that only one tenth of the male population were "true" Balangingi Samal; the remainder were *renegados* (renegades), more particularly Visayan and Tagalog, and other captives.[12]

The Taosug economy was expanding rapidly enough at this time for Samal populations to absorb larger and larger numbers of captives. An apparently conscious recruitment policy of the *datus* changed the numerical structure and ethnic composition of Samal groupings in less than two generations (1820–48). Barth considers a ten per cent rate of incorporation in a generation drastic.[13] By those standards, the flexibility of the Sulu system was incredible. Village populations in 1836 appear to have ranged from just over 300 people with 10–12 raiding *prahus* (*garay*) at Tunkil to more than a thousand people, with 30–40 *prahus,* at Balangingi.[14] In less than a decade, Balangingi's population roughly quadrupled;[*] in 1845 the village had an estimated 4,000 people and 120–150 large vessels.[15] The overall Samal population devoted to slave raiding reached an upper limit, in 1848, of 10,000 people with 200 raiding *prahus.*[16] The consequence of this extraordinary growth was the creation of an "emergent" slave-raiding population within the Sulu Sultanate—the Balangingi.

---

[*] The following fortified villages were located on Balangingi in 1848: Balangingi, Sipac, Sangap, and Bucotingol. Unfortified communities included Suitan, Paliat, Pandan-Pandan, Lion, Qussu, and Qulimunung.

The Social Organization of Raiding

The general importance of the relationship of Balangingi raiders to the history of island Southeast Asia is widely recognized; but thus far scholars have concentrated primarily on the Samal as "pirates", and on their suppression by colonial navies. These explanations of Samal piracy fail to recognize the central relationship of ethnogenesis to Sulu's redistributive economy, its exponential growth, and its dependence on raiding. Clearly, much of the Sultanate's power and much of the rapid growth of the Balangingi population in the first half of the nineteenth century stemmed from the traffic in slaves, and incorporation of them into the society.

For the Taosug, slave-raiding was significantly related to power and wealth. A *datu* who could acquire large numbers of captives could engage more people in procurement activities and trade; and, with the wealth they produced, he could attract others to him. Hunt recognized that the power of the *datus* derived from the number of wealth-producing persons— clients and slaves—in their retinues: "Their principal passion appears to be a lust for power ... and the object of their life is to increase their number of ambas [slaves]".[17] Thus, the principal aim of Taosug-sponsored Iranun/ Balangingi attacks on Southeast Asian villages and *prahu* shipping was the capture of slaves who could be converted into a source of wealth.[18] Slave-raiding in the Sulu Sultanate was highly organized. There were several types of expeditions: some equipped by the Sultan and his kindred; some independently recruited with the encouragement of the Sultan, and some conducted without the sanction of the Sultan. The right to organize raiding expeditions resided at all levels of the Taosug political system; however, the Sultan and certain *datus* on the coast by virtue of their control over foreign trade and their more expansive network of alliances were in the best position to actually carry it out.

The Sultan's main source of wealth was from trade, harbour and market fees, and tribute. His income was supplemented, however, by slaves— given in repayment for commissions to raid, for assistance to raiding parties, and for harbour fees. Hunt charged the Sultan with a principal role in the organization of slave raids, stating that Samal raiders handed over to him and other aristocrats a certain number of captives, on the basis of previous agreement.[19] The statements made by fugitive captives in the 1830s tend to corroborate this allegation.[20] But the disclosures that directly implicate the Sultan as an important backer are contained in the statements of Balangingi prisoners taken on board the H.M.S. *Wolf* after the capture of their *prahus* in east Malayan waters, and at Singapore's Paupers Hospital in 1838:"Orang Kaya Kullul informed us that the Sultan had desired him to plunder and capture all nations save Europeans."[21]

The military and economic activities of Samal populations were closely regulated by their Taosug patrons, who encouraged the Balangingi over a number of generations to become fishers of men. To meet the increased demands for slave labour in the Sulu zone between 1800 and 1848, *datus* not only equipped Samal vessels but also provided credit to the Iranun—with advances in boats, powder and ball, cannon, rice, opium, and additional crew.[22]* Everything was to be repaid in captured slaves.[23] In this context, slaves were considered not only chattels but common purpose currency as well; they provided a valuable medium of exchange that was readily transferable. For example, the value of a slave in the 1850s as an article of barter in transactions between *datu* and Samal raiders was roughly equivalent to 200–300 gantangs (3.1 kilogrammes) of rice. A *prahu* could be purchased for six to eight slaves; boat rental amounted to only two to three slaves. A rifle (often defective) could be rented for five pieces of linen of twenty fathoms; a portable cannon was loaned at the rate of one slave.[24]

Most *datus* lacked the necessary means to equip expeditions on a large scale. The few *datus* who possessed such resources were inevitably involved in Sulu's external trade. Their strict supervision of external trade enabled them to maintain control over the supply and distribution of guns to client military groups. In the first half of the nineteenth century, there was a crucial struggle between the Sultan (and his supporters) and other *datus* to establish exclusive control over the arms trade. By 1842, the Sultan had lost dominance over external trade and particular Samal populations: "The whole power, within the last thirty years, has been usurped by one or two datus, who now have monopolized the ... foreign trade that comes to these islands."[25] Two chiefs emerged paramount from a factional struggle spanning three decades (1810–40): the Datu Molok, the Prime Minister, described in European accounts as an enterprising, intelligent man, owning four trading ships and a large quantity of arms (25 cannon and 100 muskets) and reputed to be worth 150,000 pesos; and Datu Tahel (the son of Datu Emir Bahar), a powerful figure in Sulu's external trade in the 1830s and principal organizer of Balangingi raiding expeditions.[26]

In the political organization of slave raiding the elements responsible for Taosug military efficiency and predominance in the zone can be seen. The Sultan and *datus* formed alliances with *panglimas* to authorize Samal groups to engage in raiding.[27] When permission was given to carry out a raid, the *panglima* acted as the organizer. It was he who obtained from the Taosug *datu* (who received, in return, a share of the captives) the supplies necessary to outfit the expedition. And it was he who appointed the *nakodah* (the *prahu*

---

* Majul (*Muslims in the Philippines,* p.285) fails to recognize the important redistributive role of the Taosug in raiding and its relationship to the economy of the Sulu Sultanate: "All the evidence points to the fact that the Sulu Sultan and chief datus never encouraged or approved of piracy by Samal or Iranun datus, for they were themselves traders having an interest that all shipping lanes be kept safe especially for traders going or coming from Jolo."

commanders). Each *nakodah* was responsible for recruiting his own crew; he mustered them from among his support groups in the village, personal kindred, dependent followers, and others with whom he was allied.* This pyramiding of authority and responsibility in the organization of the raiding was commented on by British officials in 1838: "It is also pretty certain from statements of [the] prisoners ... that the six boats were under the command of Orang Kaja Koollul, [who is] ... reported to be related to Panglima Alip, the local chief of Bangeenge [Balangingi] who is again subordinate to the Sultan of Sulu."[28]

An expedition was commanded by a *panglima* or an *orang kaya*. Each *prahu* had its own *nakodah*; and a large part of the crew would be his kindred, followers, and slaves. The successful execution of a slave-raiding expedition was difficult and dangerous work, and depended largely on the skill of its personnel. Many *renegados* held important positions—*nakodah*, occasionally even squadron commander—in slaving expeditions; in return, they acquired wealth and slaves, who complemented their personal followings. Visayans in particular demonstrated their talent and courage as *nakodah*, and developed a fearful reputation in the Philippines,[29] but captives from other parts of the Malay world, who had knowledge of dialects and of their former localities, proved equally skilful boat commanders.[30]

Once the *panglima* and *nakodahs* determined the course, they rarely left the *prahus* during the voyage. They had several experienced officers to assist them: the *juru mudi* (*julmuri*), of whom there were two or more on each vessel, acted as steersmen and were responsible for the crew (*sakay*) and the maintenance of the boat; the *juru batu* (pilot) tended the anchor and kept watch for reefs, shoals, rocks, trading ships, and the enemy.[31] Accompanying a fleet was at least one *hatib* or *imam,* who read the Koran, led prayer recitation,† and acted as legal arbiter and judge (*hakim*) when

---

* The *panglima* supplied rice to the *nakodah* who in turn fed the crew from the beginning to end of the expedition. Crews were rarely in short supply of chickens, fresh and dried fish, sago flour, and salt. All foodstuffs looted by raiders were divided equally among them. Jansen, "Aantekeningen omtrent Sollok en de Solloksche Zeeroovers", pp.222, 228; Geoghegan, "Balangingi Samal", pp.12, 18, 21.

† Prayer recitation is mentioned in the translation of a statement written by *nakodah* Amzah, one of the rescued captives from a Balangingi fleet destroyed in 1862: "After four days between Karamata and Pulo Datu, they fell in with a Sambas prahu belonging to Haji Bahir, she proved to be from Belitong, loaded with dry fish, sago etc. The pirates captured her and her crew of five men. The whole of the next day they were chased by a war steamer, but they escaped by keeping in shoal waters, and by night falling. Five days afterwards, off Cape Baiong, they fell in with nakodah Daud's prahu, but did not molest her. Three days later they passed Cape Datu [West Borneo] and brought up for two days in Serabang Bay and read the ruah selamat, a prayer of thanksgiving. " S. Baring-Gould and C.A.Bampfylde, *A History of Sarawak under Its Two White Rajas, 1839–1908,* p.276.

disputes arose between the commanders and their crews.[32] In this way, strict discipline was maintained in the fleets. Most vessels appear to have carried several robust youths (12–15 years old), who could provide assistance at the oars in difficult situations as part of their apprenticeship while learning the finer points of raiding technique and navigation. Often there would be an elderly chief (*orang tua*) on board—a man no longer strong enough to be in command, but placing his rich store of experience at the disposal of the expedition.[33] Women rarely went on expeditions, except occasionally as the consort of a commander.

The crew members consisted partly of Balangingi whose task was to fight, partly of trusted slaves who had accompanied the raiders since their youth, and slaves who had been seized on earlier expeditions. The officers and even ordinary crew brought slaves with them to cook, fetch water, and assist them from time to time with their shipboard duties. The slaves were not armed, but were considered an integral part of the crew; it was their job to row, bail, clean, and repair the *prahu*.[34] The size of the crew depended of course upon the size of the vessel. At the end of the eighteenth century, the largest Iranun raiding boats carried from fifty to eighty fighting men and about one hundred rowers. But in the nineteenth century, when slave raiders used smaller craft, the biggest Balangingi Samal *prahus* were only sixty to seventy feet long and carried a complement of no more than a hundred men including slaves. An average size crew numbered about forty men. Smaller, less heavily armed boats carried twenty-five to thirty men.*

The size of the expedition depended not only upon its purpose but also upon complex factors such as the overall length of time of the cruise, the participants' relative familiarity with the target areas, and, more importantly, ability of the organizer to mobilize followers for the venture. Small expeditions could be managed by individual communities; sometimes

* The crew size of two Balangingi fleets which were destroyed in 1838 and 1856 were as follows:

1838		1856	
Officer of Vessel	Crew	Officer of Vessel	Crew
Orang Kaya Kullul (Commander)	46	Si Taup (Commander)	32
Si Damah	30	Si Gading	39
Si Tomboh	23	Si Tanusi	28
Si Dunlines	25	Si Udin	32
Si Putlahs	28	Mas Bud	24
Tala Goa	29	Si Nawan	38

Statement of Angel Custodio, Alex Quijano, and Mariano Sevilla in Exp. 12, 4 Oct. 1836, PNA, Mindanao/Sulu 1803–1890.

whole crews came from a single village. However, composite crews were not uncommon in expeditions of less than ten *prahus*. Balangingi vessels frequently left with a skeleton crew of ten to fifteen men and travelled to neighbouring Samal villages and islands to fill out their complements.[35] It was common for masters to send unaccompanied slaves on these *prahus*, but *nakodahs* were reluctant to take those who objected to their master's wish.[36] Large-scale enterprises entailing thirty, forty, and even fifty *prahus* required the cooperation of many communities on a regional basis.* Organizationally, such expeditions reflected the alliance networks of powerful *datus*. For example, of the twenty-six "Balangingi" vessels that seized Francisco Basilo and 350 other people in 1836, nine were from Balangingi, four from Tunkil, five from Basilan, two from Pilas, and six from Iranun settlements on Mindanao.[37] These groupings did not have any permanence beyond the immediate expedition. Expediency was paramount; leaders and groups of boats were constantly realigned to conduct forays and independent missions patronized by Taosug *datus* and *panglimas*.

Of course, not all Samal populations were loyal to their patrons; Samal islands were sometimes known to have switched their allegiance. Further, there were instances of unsanctioned slave-hunting by Balangingi, and defiant refusals by their *nakodahs* to pay the Sultan's harbour fee—especially after 1836, when the expanding population of the Balangingi Samal, the success of their raiding, and the growing strength and political independence of their *panglimas* began to challenge the influence of the dominant ethnic group, the Taosug.

The Pattern of Balangingi Raiding

The Balangingi visited the Philippines twice annually, once in March and again in October.[38] From 1830 to 1848, repeated reports were made to the Government from *alcaldes mayores,* and published in Manila, of sightings on their coasts, of villages being attacked, and of their inhabitants and fishermen being killed or carried off by the Balangingi.† It was the small settlements far from the *cabeceras* with little or no outside communication or defence, and those situated on offshore islands which could not be protected from the mainland, that were exposed to the greatest danger. On Luzon these

---

* Major changes appear to have occurred in the size of flotillas after 1800, and again in the 1850s. In the period from 1775 to 1795, flotillas contained on average from 10 to 40 large *prahus:* 1800–1856, 6–24 *prahus:* 1856–1878, 1–6 *prahus.*

† A government circular of 17 Feb. 1847 called for provincial leaders to supply the following information: movement of pirates on the coasts of their province, activities of the *Fuerza Sutil;* the number of captives seized by the raiders per month; and the state of the coastal defences.

settlements were found principally on the Pacific coast and, in favourable weather, the Balangingi came from the south up, or went right around the island in a clockwise direction, to attack the weaker ones: Palanan, Polillo, Capalonga, Indan, Daet, and Caramoan.[39] Rapid attacks were made on west coast villages on their way north to the Pacific, and Balangingi appeared on the Zambales coast every year from 1836 to 1841. Villages in the Calamian group, Cuyo, and other adjacent islands, particularly Dumaran and Linpacan, were frequently subject to Samal slave raids in this period by combined fleets of up to a hundred *prahus*.[40] In the central and southern Visayas, the Balangingi continued to attack coastal villages on Panay, Negros, Cebu, Samar, and Mindanao.[41]

In another direction, Brunei was within easy range of the Balangingi, and a squadron hovered about southern Palawan from the middle of March to the end of November to seize Brunei inhabitants and cut off trade to North Borneo.[42] The attacks were an important contributing factor to Brunei's decline. The Balangingi were alleged to have a saying that "It is difficult to catch fish but easy to catch Borneans."[43] In the same manner, the Maluso Samal of Basilan harried the settlers of Zamboanga who attempted to trade with Cotabato.[44] Houses beyond the *presidio* walls were scattered, and the Samal often attacked them at night. Fishermen and other inhabitants sometimes had to leave their huts after dark and seek refuge behind the walls of the *presidio*. In 1842 Wilkes wrote:

> One or two huts which were seen in the neighbourhood of the bay, are built on posts twenty feet from the ground, and into them they ascend by ladders, which are hauled up after the occupants have entered. These, it is said, are the sleeping huts, and are so built for the purpose of preventing surprise [attacks] at night.[45]

The raids made it impossible for townspeople to fish and, ironically, Zamboanga became dependent on its assailants, the Samal of Maluso, for fresh supplies. In the south the Balangingi disputed Buginese rights to control over marine produce and subject people. The Taosug needed slaves to replace divers in the pearl and *tripang* fisheries, and Balangingi raids forced large numbers of Samal Bajau Laut, who were clients of Buginese chiefs in the Berau area, to migrate to Tontoli and Makassar.[46]

The Samal Diaspora

Balangingi fortunes changed in the 1840s and with them the pattern of raiding in Southeast Asia. The destruction of Tempasuk and Marudu by the English in 1845 forced Iranun groups to relocate on the east coast at Tunku. The loss of these confederate communities made it more difficult for the Balangingi to conduct slave raids in the western sector of the archipelago. This event, coupled with the founding of Labuan by James Brooke, and the appearance of steam gunboats on the northwest coast of Borneo, forced them to gradually withdraw from that area and concentrate their activities more and more on the Dutch possessions.[47]

At the same time, the Spanish adopted a far more aggressive policy in the south. Governor Claveria, to protect Spain's claim to sovereignty over the Sulu archipelago from political interference by European powers, authorized an expedition against Balanginggi in 1845, and established a small fort and naval base on Basilan.[48] Although the expedition had been ill-prepared—lacking sufficient troops, artillery, and scaling ladders—and ultimately failed, the Spanish managed for the first time to reconnoitre the Samalese group, and formed a detailed picture of the topography, defences, and population of Balanginggi.[49] Armed with this information, Claveria devoted several years to organizing a formidable expedition comprised of the best trained and equipped colonial troops—an expedition that his honour and patriotism demanded he command himself. As part of his programme to strengthen the military, he ordered several steam vessels from the English, which were to prove indispensable in the campaign against Balanginggi.*

The Governor's expedition, consisting of three war steamers, schooners, transports, brigantines, a detachment of the *Marina Sutil,* and five hundred troops, was secretly fitted out and left Manila for Zamboanga on 27 January 1848.[50] An auxiliary force of Zamboanguenos joined the expedition before the attack. Claveria ordered that no quarter be given as the steamers approached Balanginggi island at dawn on 16 February 1848. The Balanginggi were unprepared for the attack, with more than half the men away on slave cruises, and were terrified by the *kapal api* with its superior firepower and facility of movement. Nevertheless, they fought ferociously, and at Sipac drove the attackers from the walls three times before the Spanish were able to penetrate the outer defences of the *kota* under cover of artillery fire.[51] Once inside, the Spanish found the Balanginggi, who expected no quarter, killing their women and children in desperation. The slaying stopped only after the Spanish commander promised clemency—the men then put down their arms and surrendered.[52]

The horror of the attack at Sipac and the terror inspired by the steam warships is recorded in a *jawi* document found on one of the survivors, a wounded woman named Camarang. She had addressed the letter to her lord, the Sultan of Sulu:

> Behold, I begin to tell as clearly as I am able what has befallen; and I give thanks to God from my heart; and I make obeisance to thee a thousand times, beseeching God to bestow all happiness upon thee.

---

* The Spanish first attempted to purchase a steamer from the English in 1844 with no success. N.100, Vice-Adm. William Parker, to Lord Ellenborough, 12 Jan. 1844, IOL, F/4/2702.

It is a vassal of thine who sends this letter along with Dayda, in the name
of the six persons, men and women, who have here been taken captive by the
Christians....

The black ship fired its guns at us many times until noonday, and we could
no longer bear it.

Then they stayed six days, until they had finished destroying our stronghold.

We have great sorrow, even unto death.

Hear us, who are vassals of the Sultan, and doubt not that from the time of
our forbears nothing so fateful ever befell.

The chief Olancaya therefore said: Let us all bear witness together by our
deaths, for now is the appointed end of our faithful observance.

And Oto, his son, said: There is no help. O Imam Baidola, let us meet death
together, you and I!

And Dina said: Be not afraid, my uncle; let us die bearing witness, and so
depart from this world.

And Donoto made answer: By the life of our grandsires, we must hang back
no longer.

And Binto replied: My father, there is nothing to hold us back; let us die
fighting, and not part company ever again.

To the Sultan of Sulu from the vassal Camarang.[53]

The Balangingi who died in the battle totalled 450, and another 350 men,
women, and children were taken prisoners. The Spanish liberated some 300
slaves from the Philippine provinces and the Dutch islands.[54] In the week
following the assault, the attackers razed to the ground the forts, seven
villages, and 150 vessels, as well as 7,000–8,000 coconut trees, and left
Balangingi desolate, unfit for habitation.[55]

The Spanish transferred whole Samal populations to the Cagayan Valley
in the interior of northern Luzon. The first group of exiles transported to
Luzon after the destruction of Balangingi in 1848 numbered 350. In 1858,
the Spanish seized hundreds of women and children from Balangingi (the
island had been resettled) while the men were away on slaving expeditions.
When the Samal returned with their *prahus* filled with Filipino captives,
they were forced to send negotiators to Zamboanga to arrange for the
recovery of their families. It was through a false promise of immunity that
Julano Taupan, a leading chief, was persuaded to come to Zamboanga to
claim his family, and was imprisoned. Their women and children were
restored to them only upon unconditional obedience to the Spanish; many
Samal were obliged to settle in or near Zamboanga under the watchful eye
of the authorities. The chiefs, Taupan, Dando, and Tumungsuc, and their
families were sent to Cavite and later transferred to Fort Santiago in Manila.
They were kept under close surveillance in prison for some time before the

Governor-General decided to relocate them in Echague (formerly Camarag) in Isabella Province.*

Although many Balangingi were killed, others transported, and their vessels burnt, the Spanish victory was not decisive; more than half the male population had been absent raiding when the attack occurred, and hundreds of others managed to elude their assailants and escape to Sulu.[56] In December 1848, some Samal attempted to reestablish themselves on Balangingi and Tunkil under Julano Taupan, who was away purchasing rice to provision the strongholds when the Spanish attacked. He had taken refuge on Sulu, but had failed to convince the Sultan and the *ruma bichara* to assist him in getting back the survivors' women and children being held prisoners at Zamboanga. The Sultan realized he could no longer defy the Spaniards to the degree that his predecessors had done—not if Taosug trade and regional relationships were to survive. Taupan defied the Sultan and began to resettle his following on Balangingi and Tunkil, but they were quickly dispersed by a second Spanish expedition, which also destroyed Bual several months later.[57] In the years 1848–51, there were few slave raids reported in the

---

* Although some of the first generation exiles and many of their descendants became Christians, I could find nothing in the Dominican Archives (Isabella Province was under Dominican jurisdiction) concerning the deported Samal populations except a brief statement written by Father Buenaventura Campa in 1890: "There is in this town Echague ... a group of moros, the remnant of the prisoners exiled from Balangingi and Jolo after the expeditions of 1848 and 1851 which were commanded by the Governors Claveria and Urbiztondo, those transported a number of years later, and the descendants of the first exiles most of whom have already died...."

At the beginning of the twentieth century, Haji Datu Nuno, the son of one of the exiled chiefs of Simisa, arranged with the American authorities to repatriate the Samal to Mindanao and Sulu. Francisco Boher, a Spanish tobacco planter in Isabella, agreed to send those settlers who wished to go, providing they turned their land and plough animals over to him. In about 1905, a hundred men, women, and children returned to Zamboanga on the S.S. *Mauban*, and Haji Nuno settled them at Taluksangay, Tigboa, and Tupalic.

In 1941, R.Wendover, an American in charge of the "cutch" camps in Zamboanga province, overheard several bark-peelers speaking Ilocano. When he asked how they came to speak this central Luzon dialect, one of the men, Kising, stated that: "He was born at Tumauini, in Isabella, and that his father's name was Damsig and his grandfather's name Insani. Both his father and grandfather, he said, had been taken to Manila aboard a Spanish ship.... Later, along with some two hundred other men, women, and children they were taken to Tumauini and Echague on the Cagayan river. Many of them were christianized and Damsig married ... a Tumauini girl, Kising ... being the first born son."

While none of the original exiles were still alive then, at Taluksangay an old woman, who was a second-generation exile, told her story: "She said her name was No-Jula, the daughter of Kasan, widow of Zalim. She was born in the Echague district about fifty five years ago. She said her father, Kasan, has been captured by the spaniards on Balangingi and had been taken along with the others, first to Zamboanga and then to Cagayan. Some of her relatives had escaped

Philippine archipelago as Samal groupings were generally disorganized and
leaderless.[58] The Samals more than ever before were thrown on their own
economic, social, and political resources owing to the successive Spanish
campaigns. They still had a considerable number of *prahus* in 1850,[59] but the
action of the Spanish cruisers tended to scatter the Balangingi throughout the
Sulu archipelago, and on the coasts of southern Palawan, north Borneo, and
beyond.

Some survivors sought the Sultan's protection and were given permission
to settle on Capual island, on the north side of Jolo, and on Dong Dong and
Patian islands on the south side.[60] The villages of Parang and Bual also
accepted Samal refugees.[61] Other remnants of the Balangingi, manning ten
prahus, found a new home on Palawan under the protection of Datu
Alimudin, the Taosug overlord of the island, who gave them wives and a place
of settlement.[62] Some of the most militant among the Balangingi migrated
with Panglima Taupan to the Tawi-Tawi group and settled at Binadan,
Banaran, Balimbing, and Simunul.[63] Another group was settled on Flores at
Riung (which was perfectly situated for disrupting the Dutch trade of
Sumbawa, Timor, Celebes, and Borneo) where their leader, Samai Garuda,
had made an agreement with the Rajas of Flores.[64] Riung became an

---

from Balangingi and had settled at Taluksangay, which was the reason why she had come here.
Those of her group taken to Cagayan were settled near Echague, among the Ibanogs. They
were at first put to work on the *haciendas* and kept under the surveillance of the government.
The children were apprenticed to various planters to learn tobacco and corn cultivation. After
some years they were given parcels of land and left free to sell their tobacco to buyers. As they
lived in their own communities they were allowed to retain their own religion."

Obviously, the Spanish had been quite successful in turning these maritime people into
tobacco cultivators, and from No-Jula's account they appear to have known nothing about the
sea upon their return to Mindanao. Her memories of Cagayan were fond ones: "One could
always raise tobacco there and we had money and made a good living. Here [Taluksangay]
many of us are landless and living is very hard." In 1941, there were about two hundred
families of the second, third, and fourth generation of Balangingi Samal exiles living around
Zamboanga. Thirty years later, Majul noted that the Christian descendants of the exiles in
Cagayan are still recognizable, and the older ones can remember the *Kalimah* as recited by
their grandparents. This tends to corroborate information given to the author while in the
Philippines in 1974 that small isolated pockets of these people, who are located at some
distance from Echague, still practise the Koran and trace their original settlement in the
area to the transportation of the Balangingi in 1848. Bernaldez, *Guerra al Sur de Filipinas*,
p.168; Fray Buenaventura Campa, "une visita a las Rancherias de Ilongotes", in *El Correo
Sino Annomita o correspondencia de las missiones del Sagrado Orden de Predicadores
en Formosa, China, Tung-King Y Filipinas*. (Manila: Imprenta del Real Colegio de Santo
Tomas, 1891), 25, XXV, p.576; BH-PCL, VI, Paper 162, no.23, Christie, "The Moros of
Sulu and Mindanao", p.55; BH-PCL, VI, Paper 162, no.25; Christie, "The Non Christian
Tribes of the Northern Half of the Zamboanga Peninsula ", p.100; No.816, GCG a Presidente
del Consejo, 21 Sept. 1859, AHN, Ultramar 5172; R.F.Wendover, "The Balangingi Pirates",
pp.325, 337–38; Majul, *Muslims in the Philippines: Past, Present and Future Prospects*, p.15.

important satellite community for the Tawi-Tawi Samal operating in the Java and Banda seas after 1852.

These dispersed Balangingi, who were known in the European records as "Tawi-Tawi pirates", were able to assemble beteen 60 and 100 *prahus* by joining forces with kindred groups in Jolo, and the Iranun of Tunku.[65] By the mid-1850s the Samal had renewed their attacks on the Philippine archipelago and the Moluccas, and their expeditions now preyed on Taosug trade between Borneo and Sulu as well.[66] Once a year the Tawi-Tawi Samal left their villages for the Dutch islands. They concentrated their attacks on Bugis trade on the southeast coast of Borneo, and on the smaller villages of the northern coast of Celebes, from the beginning of January until May, when their flotillas appeared in the vicinity of the Bangka strait. Running before the southwest monsoon they visited the Natunas and Tambelan islands and returned to Tawi-Tawi via the Balabac strait.[67] After 1852, they also began to visit islands which had been left unscathed for years. The most important targets were Ternate and Tidore. In 1854 an estimated three hundred people were seized from these islands,[68] and the following year the Menado residency suffered even more heavily when thirty "Magindanao" *prahus* captured 500–700 people, not only from Menado but also from smaller islands to the south and east, especially Batjan.[69] Wallace mentions their raiding activities in the Aru islands in 1858 after an absence of eleven years: "by thus making attacks at long and uncertain intervals the alarm dies away, and they find a population for the most part unarmed and unsuspicious of dangers". But with the stationing of steamers on the Minahassan coasts in 1857 and the destruction of Riung the following year, Samal attacks lessened; by 1863 official sightings of Samal flotillas on the Celebes coast were becoming a thing of the past. The Sulu *Zeerovers* disappeared from the annual reports of the Menado residency in 1870 but the Indonesians' fear and memory of the Samal slave raiders was to linger for years.[70]

Despite the destruction of Balangingi and the Samal diaspora of 1848–52, slave-raiding continued in the Philippine archipelago for three more decades. As in the past, Samal marauders attacked smaller villages that lacked firearms in Tayabas and Albay provinces, but the greatest number of captives were taken from the coasts of Panay and Negros.[71] In terms of sheer numbers of boats and firepower, the Spanish were now far superior to the Samal, especially after 1860 when steamers were introduced on a large scale in the Philippines. This forced the Samal to reduce drastically the size of their flotillas. Of the new strategem a Spanish naval officer wrote: "Whereas in the past four expeditions of one hundred sail set out, now one hundred expeditions of four sail leave [the Sulu archipelago] and the problem is not destroying them, but locating them."[72] The Samal's total reliance on this mode of evasion was noted by the English Consul in Manila:

Piracy still exists and large numbers are still carried ... from these coasts into
slavery but piracy is now carried on in small bodies of light boats and directed
against the coasts and small craft of contiguous parts of these possessions, and no
longer appears, as formerly, in combined operations of large fleets of proas. ...[73]

The southerly shift of Samal migratory—marauding activity was
intensified by the advent of flotillas of steamers in Philippine waters. In 1860,
under Governor-General Norzagaray, eighteen prefabricated steam gunboats,
(*canonero*) were sent from England (around Cape Horn) and assembled at
the Cavite shipyards *en masse*.* With the arrival of the steamers the Spanish
Navy abandoned cruising among the islands, and deployed the steamers in
key straits in the archipelago through which the Balangingi passed, and at
several stations in the Sulu Sea.[74] The English Vice-Consul at Iloilo reported:

Of the steam gunboats which are replacing throughout the Archipelago the
heavy sailing boats (*faluas*) previously employed, Yloilo has been supplied
with two. These have in some measure promoted ... communication with
neighbouring islands and provinces, and occasionally with Manila, and are
likely to prove much more effectual in repressing piracy than the former
gunboats. Recently they have had several encounters with the pirates of the
Sooloo sea, in the immediate neighbourhood of Yloilo, and have brought
in five pirate *pancos* and other smaller boats, making away with between
two hundred and fifty to three hundred of these habitual depredators of the
Philippine coasts.[75]

The speed, firepower, and manoeuvrability of the *canonero* stemmed Samal
slaving. After 1860 their *prahus* no longer prowled unchallenged. Samal
losses were mounting. In less than three years, four flotillas were destroyed
by the steamers in the Visayas alone.[76] When the *canonero* were encountered
in open sea, the Balangingi were annihilated:

In the channel between Tawi-Tawi and Borneo fifteen *pancos* were sighted.
Their numbers, movements, and course appeared suspicious, and the Taosug
on board, who were experienced in such matters, felt they were Balangingi.
The *canonero Samar* began pursuit. The chase lasted two hours during which
time the pirates made strenuous efforts to reach the security of the Tawi-
Tawi coast. When unable to do so, because we had placed ourselves between
them and the shoreline, the *pancos* hove to as a group to fight. I then gave the
order to sink them; a half an hour was all that was necessary to accomplish it,
during which time the ram and cannon worked in unison to destroy them....
I continued steaming on course towards Borneo amidst the debris and bodies
that strewn the sea.[77]

---

* The little boats were largely subsidized from local community chests throughout the
Philippines.

The port of Isabella on Basilan was fortified by the Spanish and became their principal steamship post in the south. From there and Balabac, nine or more gunboats regularly patrolled the Sulu Sea. The appearance of steam gunboats in the Visayas and the Sulu Sea, and a series of expeditions conducted by the Spanish navy against Samal settlements on Tawi-Tawi from 1860 to 1864,[78] forced the Balangingi to shift their predatory activities away from Philippine waters into the Sulu zone, but Negros Oriental and Surigao suffered attacks along their coasts till 1875, and desultory raiding was still experienced in various parts of the Philippines on the eve of the twentieth century.[79]

The Dutch and English undertook similar measures in a joint venture to protect the coasts of Borneo, Java, and Sumatra in 1862; they placed steam gunboats at fixed stations all along the raiding track of the Samal during the appropriate season.[80] The presence of the British at Labuan, of the Spanish in the Sulu Sea, and the Dutch on the east coast of Borneo made the Sulu zone the final theatre of Balangingi operations. By 1875 they were confined to capturing riverine shore dwellers and Samal Bajau Laut on the north Borneo coast; a combined fleet of Iranun and Samal *prahus* from Tunku and Tawi-Tawi were alleged to have captured 600 people in 1877, and the following year William Pryer heard numerous reports of Tawi-Tawi slave raiders penetrating north Bornean waters with impunity.[81] The future prosperity of the northeast coast under the North Borneo Chartered Company was made secure only after the H.M.S. *Kestrel* bombarded Tunku in 1878, and Dutch steamers took active measures in the Berau region.[82] Tunku's destruction and the presence of Dutch warships on the southern periphery of the zone were responsible for a drastic decline in the size and number of Samal forays on the northeast coast. Raids, however, continued to be made against north Bornean territory until the 1890s.[83] The North Borneo Chartered Company—administratively weak, plagued by a host of financial problems, and concerned about the territorial designs of its Dutch neighbour—was unable to prevent slave-raiding, especially by the Samal in Darvel Bay, or the continued movement of captives from Tawi-Tawi to Bulungan.[84] Small-scale Samal marauding and slavery were only abolished when the Americans closed the slave markets on Sulu and Tawi-Tawi in the first decade of the twentieth century.

9

Slave Marketing in the Sulu Zone, 1768–1878

The impact of the West's commercial intrusion in China towards the end of the eighteenth century had significant bearing on the growth of the slave trade in Southeast Asia. It led to the crystallization of a permanent slave traffic around organized markets and depots in the Sulu zone. Jolo Island, as the centre of a redistributive network encompassing the Sulu zone, became the most important slave centre by 1800.[1] This had not always been the case. Most accounts of the Sulu Sultanate written before 1780 indicate that the internal demand for slaves at Jolo was on a much smaller scale than it was destined to become in the nineteenth century. These early writers reported that it was often more profitable for the Taosug to deliver slaves to the Magindanao and Bugis merchants of Cotabato and Pasir for transhipment to Makassar and Batavia than employ them in their own settlements.[2]

Slaves stopped being re-exported to foreign parts by Taosug when external trade to Sulu escalated and the large-scale use of slave labour in the fisheries, and in raiding *prahus* became essential for the growth of the Taosug state. By 1800, the Sulu Sultanate was the centre of an extensive range of commercial, raiding, and slave dealing activities concentrated at Jolo.[3] To Madi Mahad (Jolo town) the Iranun and Balangingi Samal brought boatloads of captives for barter. In 1814 Hunt described Jolo as the commercial headquarters of the Iranun and Samal:

> Their roving depredations are directed in large fleets of small prows in the Straits of Makassar, among the Moluccas, but more particularly in the southern part of the Philippines; the whole produce is sold at Jolo, which is the grand entrepot.[4]

Jolo town was the most important outlet for the exchange of slaves, but Samal also bartered them directly to *datus* and Chinese in other communities on Jolo island like Bual and Parang. They visited other islands in the Sulu archipelago—Patian, Pangutaran, and Tapian Tana—and went as far south as Simunul to sell slaves before 1846 (see Appendix R). Some Balangingi slavers took their captives to seasonal markets and trading posts situated on Sarangani island, at the southern tip of Mindanao, and to Marudu, Sandakan, and Gunung Tabor on the Bornean coast.[5] Many of the slaves transported to Marudu in repayment for the food, powder, arms, and salt supplied to Balangingi groups under the credit system of Sherif Usman were employed in his swiddens and collected forest produce. If they were Brunei Malays, they could be resold at considerable profit to their relations in Brunei.[6]

It was the fate of other less fortunate captives to be taken farther down the coast for sale. Riverine tribes on the Kinabatangan, Sambakong, Bulungan, and Berau were involved in the slave trade through Taosug merchants and Bugis settlers who had gained a permanent foothold on the east Bornean coast. These Muslim middlemen acquired bird's nest and wax for the external trade at Jolo in return for the captives. The traditional ceremony held among Ida'an, Tidong, and Kenyah groups referred to by European observers of the late eighteenth and nineteenth centuries as "surmungup", a ritual sacrifice, accounted for much of the demand for captives by these interior Bornean tribes.[7] Their religious beliefs required the sacrifice of aliens, which were connected with the taking of heads for *mamat* festivals, and the offering of human sacrifices on the death of a chief or other persons of lesser rank.[8] The development of the slave trade on the Bornean rivers appears to have altered ceremonial practice surrounding ritual sacrifices. In earlier periods preference had been given to killing young warriors or slaves captured from rival tribes in warfare, but the coming of the Taosug traders enabled the widespread purchase of aliens, particularly the elderly and infirm, for ritual purposes. The availability of cheaply priced aliens in large numbers, who could be purchased for forest produce, made popular participation in the ceremonies easier. Now mourning commoners, in remembrance of the deceased, were able to subscribe.[9] The slave was purchased, bound with cloth and tied up, and speared to death. The number of slaves killed at a ceremony was small and varied with the rank of the deceased, from a single individual to a small household.[10] Slaves who were not purchased for ritual purposes fulfilled important economic roles among interior tribal groups. They were absorbed into the slave class and procured forest produce for the coast-hinterland trade. It was estimated that 400–500 people were brought to the Kinabatangan for further distribution each year by Taosug and the Iranun and Balangingi in the first half of the nineteenth century.[11]

Between 1768 and 1848, Sulu had attracted Samal speakers from the surrounding areas, and it remained a focal point of trade for certain Samal raiders after 1852. But as a result of combined colonial interference in the zone in the later period, the area of Samal settlement and trade was broadened, and the independent raiders from Tawi-Tawi and Sibutu frequently took their slaves to Parang, Basilan, Palawan, the Kinabatangan, and Bulungan.[12] Bulungan became the principal market for slaves of the Balangingi once the Spanish inaugurated the blockade of Jolo. Slaves were retailed at villages on southern Tawi-Tawi and moved in Samal *prahus* to Bulungan via Omaddal island. Slave raiding was thoroughly commercial and the Samal brought captive peoples, both "infidel" and Muslim, to be sold there; "All was fish that came into their nets", Governor Treacher wrote, "Bajaus, Bruneis, Manila men, natives of Palawan, and natives of the interior of Magindanao."[13] These slaves replenished the work force of the Sultan of Gunung Tabor's coal mine, and gathered gutta-percha and wax to be loaded on the vessels of William Lingard (the Tom Lingard of Joseph Conrad's novels of the Eastern Seas) and the Singapore Arabs, or were sold for ritual purposes. Several thousand slaves were taken to Bulungan from the Sulu archipelago during the famine in 1879 alone, when owners who could no longer afford to support their slaves were compelled to sell them to get food.[14]

The demand for imports on the west coast was equally great. The owners of Marudu district were unable to prevent their slaves from fleeing to Labuan, and slaves were landed as replacements by the Balangingi in Marudu Bay and at Sulamen and Mengkabong.[15] It became increasingly difficult for the Balangingi to sell their slaves, however, owing to the approach of the Spanish from the north, the British from the southwest, and the Dutch from the southeast. In the 1880s, most Balangingi were forced to give up slave trading as a profession and settled down as suppliers of jungle and sea produce in the Sulu archipelago and north Borneo.[16]

After the Spanish blockade closed Jolo to the Balangingi in 1871, there was a large gap left in the Sultanate's slave supply that was never filled satisfactorily. Now the Magindanao attacked neighbouring people, for sale in Jolo's market, to replace wholesale captures by the Balangingi. The Taosug relied on Magindanao *datus* such as Uto, and the Chinese of Cotabato, Glan, and Lalabuan,* to supply them with slaves from among the upland tribes of eastern Mindanao, predominantly Tiruray and Bilaan,† in exchange for guns to halt the Spanish advance.[17] The movement of slaves to Jolo in this period frequently occurred outside the regular channels of the captive trade. Slave theft and confiscation could and did occur on a large scale between 1878 and 1898 with the decline of the slave trade;[18] there was considerable movement of slaves from one part of the zone to another as they transferred owners under duress or for payment of debts.‡

---

* Hill women were sold to the Cotabato Chinese for more than 50 *pesos* each in the 1880s. The Spanish claimed that most Chinese households in the town had at least fourteen slaves, mostly women and children.

† In 1881, it was said that half a dozen able-bodied Bilaan men could be purchased from Magindanao or Iranun dealers for one picul ($23).

‡ Pryer claimed that many of these slaves were being transported on European vessels: "Stopping the importation of slaves should not be a difficult matter. It is very clear that British ships are in nine cases out of ten, the means by which they are introduced...." Pryer to Treacher, 5 Oct. 1881, CO, 874/229.

Slave Trading

Slave-holding was the primary form of investment for the Taosug. As a form of wealth, slaves were a tangible asset in easily transferable form. They played a major role in the economy both as a unit of production and as a medium of exchange. The accumulation of wealth and the transmission of power and privilege in the Taosug state was facilitated by the ownership of slaves. This was even more the case after the advent of external trade in the Sulu archipelago in the late eighteenth century.

In Sulu a great many factors were taken into consideration when determining the value of individual slaves. The prices varied with sex, age, ethnicity, and personal condition, as well as demand. The highest prices were for young women, who could be offered as wives and concubines to recruit fighting men to a *datu*'s retinue, and youths, who were considered tractable and therefore more readily incorporated into Taosug society than men.[19]

The market price of slaves was apt to be influenced also by the cultural characteristics of their group. The Tagalogs or "Manila men" had great powers of endurance and thus made good rowers, as well as being skilful helmsmen and boatbuilders,* but were prone to escape.[20] Visayans were unsurpassed as divers and considered superior to the Tagalogs as sailors. Papuans and Flores islanders always found a ready sale, particularly the latter who were supposed to be good artificers and uncommonly faithful to their masters.[21] The courageous reputation of the Buginese as traders and soldiers, with a talent for learning the use of arms, made them favoured in the trade. Visayan women were reputed to be superior weavers. Tagalogs were desired for their business ability, and as wives of *datus* were often entrusted with the management of accounts.[22] Most esteemed for their beauty were mestiza Chinese.[23] Women from the Aru islands and Papua were also considered attractive and sold without difficulty at higher than average prices.[24]

Other considerations such as education, high status, or poor health might add or detract from the slave's value. C.Z. Pieters, the captain of the cutter *Petronella,* was seized by the Balangingi in 1838:

> Before I was taken by the pirates I had learnt from persons that had made their escape from them, that whenever they found any of their captives were of superior origin, they sold them for larger prices. On this account I warned my people and slaves, on the day we were sold to be careful not to show me any

---

* Spenser St. John described his Tagalog steersman, who was captured by the Balangingi when a boy and raised as a Muslim: "Musa, though modest and gentle in his manner, was brave as a lion, and would have followed me anywhere. Though very short, he was squarely built, and exceedingly strong, a very powerful swimmer, and good boatman." *Life in the Forests of the Far East,* vol.2, p.163; Bernaldez, *Guerra al Sur,* p.36.

TABLE 6

A LIST OF SLAVES TAKEN ON BOARD THE *SANTA FILOMENA* AT JOLO
AND TAWI-TAWI, SEPTEMBER/OCTOBER 1862

Indios	Time in Captivity	Malays	Time in Captivity
Marimiana	20 yrs	Duman	2 yrs
Salustiani Martinita	10 yrs	Numan	2 yrs
Francisco Mateo	7 yrs	Tiang Lon	1 yr, 2 mths
Feliz Dieznoble	6 yrs	Simayasin	1 yr, 2 mths
Victoriano Pedrosa	6 yrs	Aminudi	1 yr
Ramon Acento	6 yrs	Amat	7 mths
Leonardo Garin	5 yrs	Iadmant	7 mths
Dominga Marcelo	5 yrs	Masikit	7 mths
Laurencio Aguilar	5 yrs	Panacajuan	5 mths
Santiago Sale	5 yrs	Sidi	5 mths
Nicholas Rafael	4 yrs	Aduluman	4 mths
Matio Gomora	4 yrs	Pagarin	4 mths
Hilario Conde	4 yrs	Mohamed	4 mths
Geranimo Marco	4 yrs	Raginul	4 mths
Gregorio Pena	4 yrs	Mananal	3 mths
Alejandro Canonega	4 yrs	Camo	46 days
Marcelo Dugalo	4 yrs	Mojamontanac	46 days
Andres Lampapini	3 yrs	Manaquil	46 days
Floretino Ballot	3 yrs	Alubocal	33 days
Juan Anillo	3 yrs	Sirano	15 days
Martin Malandal	3 yrs		
Pascual Asia	3 yrs		
Marcos Marquis	3 yrs		
Leoncio Eliazar	3 yrs		
Florentino Rivera	2 yrs		
Vincenta Hugate	2 yrs		
Pedro Angel	2 yrs		
Paulino Vico	2 yrs		
Pablo Vinaso	2 yrs		
Eugenio Ballete	2 yrs		
Cristobal Magalun	2 yrs		
Manuel Boson	1 yr		
Ambrosio	1 yr		
Mariano Masancan	2 mths		

Source: This table has been compiled from two sets of statements, No.52, GCG a Senor
Ministro de la Guerra y de Ultramar, 4 Sept. 1862, AHN, Ultramar 5190; No.105,
GCG a Senor Ministro de la Guerra y Ultramar, 25 Oct. 1862, AHN, Ultramar
5192.

marks of respect and not to call me by my real name. They were only to give me the name of Jumaat, or if they should forget that, then that of Domingo.[25]

The major determinants of the composition of slave intake were external forces affecting raiding patterns. Until 1848 a larger percentage of the captives (perhaps as high as 65 per cent) were from the Philippines, particularly southern Luzon and the central Visayas, while the rest came from various parts of the Malay world—the great majority from Celebes (Tontoli, Amurang, Menado, Gorontalo) and the Moluccas.[26]

Table 6 reveals the extent to which the source of Sulu's slave supply changed in the second half of the nineteenth century. Of the 54 captives who escaped to the Spanish warship, 34 were Filipinos principally from the western and southern Visayas, whose period in captivity had ranged from twenty years to two months; 28 out of the 34 slaves had been imported between 1856 and 1860. Only three had been brought to Sulu since 1860. In marked contrast, all 20 "Malays" had been imported within the last year or two. It is clear that as the slave trade to the Sulu Sultanate began to decline at mid-century, an ever larger percentage of imported slaves were brought to Sulu from Celebes, the west coast of Borneo near Pontianak, and Bangka. This trend became more pronounced after 1860 with the stationing of *canonero* flotillas in the Philippine seas.[27] After 1870 most of the people brought by slave mongerers to Sulu were tribal people from the hill regions of eastern Mindanao.[28]

There appears to have been a standard schedule of prices for various categories of slaves, but the basic price level varied according to Sulu's political and economic situation. In 1726 the value of slaves was as follows: a man or woman in excellent health, forty pesos; a man or woman with a weak constitution, thirty pesos; boys and girls, twenty pesos; and small children, ten pesos.[29] By the beginning of the nineteenth century the price of female slaves was much higher than male slaves, indicating the important role they played in the recruitment process and the difficulty in obtaining them: in general, the price of a male slave varied according to his age and qualifications from twenty to thirty pesos; the price of a female slave ranged between sixty to one hundred pesos and occasionally more, according to her age and ability to work, and small children were estimated to be worth half the price of a man.[30]

The value of slaves rose considerably after 1850 as imports to Jolo began to taper off. The most important factors responsible were the Spanish campaigns conducted against the Samal on Tawi-Tawi from 1860 to 1864 and the blockade of Jolo, which had the effect of creating an acute slave shortage in the northern half of the Sulu archipelago in the 1870s. By then the price of slaves in Sulu was as follows: a man, three piculs (a picul was equivalent to $20 to $25 in the 1870s and 1880s); a young woman, three to five piculs; a young couple, seven to eight piculs; a middle-aged person, about 1½ piculs; a middle-aged couple, up to five piculs; a boy, two piculs; and a girl, three to four piculs.[31] Evidently, young couples were most desired to help foster a hereditary slave class on a larger scale than had previously existed once Balangingi traffic dwindled.

The common payment for slaves was a variety of Western trade goods, including opium, iron bars, and Bengal cloth, and natural products of the Sulu Sultanate. Recognized mediums of exchange throughout the zone were used frequently to purchase slaves: bolts of coarse cotton cloth, brassware in the form of *lantanca,* gongs, and trays, and rice.[32] The evidence in Table 7 shows that the price of individual slaves could fluctuate greatly in a short

TABLE 7
SOME PRICES OF FILIPINO SLAVES IN KIND (1822–1847)

Slave	Age	Year of Purchase	Price/goods
Pedro del Remidio	36	1822	20 cavans padi
Augustin Juan	35	1826	10 *lagas* padi
Jose Reales	30	1831	a bundle of coarse cotton cloth
Juan Sabala	48	1834	a *lantaka*
Maria Gertrudiz	35	1834	a *lantaka*
Francisco Feliz	45	1834	5 bundles of Ilocos cloth
Juan Teodoro	56	1834	30 pieces of coarse cotton cloth
Angel Custodio	19	1835	3 balls of opium
Evaristo Pinto	25	1835	70 pieces of coarse cotton cloth
Domingo Francisco	35	1836	3 bundles of coarse cotton cloth, 2 carafes, 2 plates, 2 cups
Juan Salvador		1836	5 pieces of coarse cotton cloth
Manuel de los Santos	27	1836	assorted goods worth 60 pesos
Juan Monico	14	1836	6 lengths of gauze and a Visayan bell
Francisco Xavier	35	1836	5 bundles of coarse cotton cloth
Eusebio de la Cruz	28	1836	2 painted boxes, 3 pieces of coarse cotton cloth & a carafe
Casimiro Santiago	27	1838	a piece of cotton cloth and 100 *chapas*
Lucas Baracel	25	1838	6 pieces of white cotton cloth
Domingo la Cruz	30	1840	5 pieces of cotton cloth
Francisco Aquino	31	1844	109 cavans padi
Eluterio de Juan	15	1845	5 pieces of black cotton cloth
Pedro Gregorio	26	1846	50 cavans padi
Juan Feliz	24	1847	90 cavans padi

Source: This table has been compiled from captive statements in the following sources: Exp.12, 4 Oct. 1836, PNA, Mindanao/Sulu 1803–1890 (see Appendix R); Relacion Jurada de los seis cautivos venidos de Jolo sobre el bergatin Espanol San Vincente in No.1673, Capitania del Puerto de Manila y Cavite a GCG, 14 Jan. 1850, PNA, Piratas 3.

space of time, depending on the preferred market value and scarcity of the objects to be exchanged.

Rice was the most important natural commodity used for purchasing slaves from the Balangingi. Their islands lacked cultivable soil and there was little or no provision made for the storage of rice on them. The Balangingi were forced to rely on the Taosug credit system to sustain their food supply. Rice was either brought directly to the Samal islands in Taosug trading *prahus* or obtained in Jolo at the advanced rate of thirty *cavans* per slave in 1836. The extent to which the Balangingi were at the mercy of their environment is reflected in the annual turnover of large numbers of captives and slaves by them to the Taosug for advances (or payment of previous advances) of rice and war stores. In 1836, Mariano Sevilla estimated that the Balangingi had seized more than a thousand captives by September, of which two-thirds had already been taken to Jolo.[33] Rice and cloth continued to be the principal items exchanged by Taosug for Balangingi slaves in the second half of the nineteenth century. According to Jansen, the Dutch Resident of Menado, the value of a slave, depending on his sex, health, and skills, in 1856 was worth on average ten *kayus* (pieces of coarse cotton cloth twenty fathoms in length), or two bundles of coarse *kain* (*sarongs*), or 200–300 gantangs of rice.[34]

TABLE 8
SLAVES RETAILED FROM *PRAHUS*

Slave's name	Place of origin	Age	Year of captivity	Period of time on board *prahu*
Carlos de los Santos	Cebu	30	1846	2 days at Balangingi
Eulalio Composano	Albay	23	1844	2 days at Balangingi
Angel Manuel	Leyte	45	1841	3 days at Balangingi
Augustin Bernado	Bohol	35	1845	4 days at Balangingi
Juan Pedro	Cebu	40	1846	4 days at Balangingi
Jose de la Cruz	Cebu	42	1844	5 days at Balangingi
Juan Jose	Iloilo	21	1845	6 days at Tunkil
Jacinto Diomeso	Iloilo	37	1846	1 week at Tunkil
Dammaso Soledad	Cuyo	23	1846	1 week at Balangingi
Plieto de la Cruz	Cebu	42	1844	2 weeks at Balangingi
Gabriela Santiago	Ilocos Sur	44	1842	2 weeks at Balangingi
Juan Velano	Iloilo	37	1846	1 month at Tunkil

Source: This table has been compiled from statements of fugitive captives in Relacion Jurada de los cuarenta y cinco cautivos venidos de Jolo sobre el Bergantin Cometa, PNA, Piratas 3; statements of Juan Monico and Francisco Feliz in Exp.12, 4 Oct. 1836, PNA, Mindanao/Sulu 1803–1890.

Generally the Balangingi retailed their slaves at Jolo within weeks of their return to the Sulu archipelago. The statements of the fugitive captives taken on board the Spanish brigantine *Cometa* in 1847 demonstrate the rapid turnover. Of the 44 slaves brought to Balangingi (35) and Tunkil (9), 27 remained in residence less than two weeks before being taken to Jolo; 8 less than a month; 6 less than two months; 3 less than a year; and 2 less than two years.[35]

Further, more than a quarter of the slaves were sold right out of the boats, having spent up to a month on board without ever setting foot on shore at either Balangingi or Tunkil. The slaves were the principal source of wealth for the Balangingi and were used to pay all their outstanding debts.

Taosug *datus,* European traders, Chinese merchants, Visayan *renegados,* and Tidong chiefs all gathered in Jolo's market to purchase captured slaves.[36] In 1774, Cencelli noted that Jolo's slave market operated on a preferential basis, with the Iranun reserving all Spaniards and friars for the Taosug, who also had their pick of the Filipinos before the Chinese and other prospective customers were allowed to purchase their human cargoes.[37] The Taosug involved in trading, procurement activities, and rice cultivation dominated the purchase of slaves in Sulu throughout most of the nineteenth century as well.

Slaves were sold over and over again. *Datus* rarely sold their own followers, but they trafficked extensively in slaves who were given to them in payment of debts or as captives by Iranun and Balangingi. It was not at all uncommon for a slave to have had two, three, or even four masters in his lifetime, to have lived among several ethnic groups in very different parts of the zone, to have fulfilled a variety of economic functions, and experienced varying degrees of hardship and servitude. For example, Si-Ayer was seized by an Iranun squadron in 1847:

> I was ... carried first to Sibat, then to Makawau, two small rivers immediately above Tunku. Makawau, which is between the two others, was the residence of the [Iranun] Raja Muda. I was sold two months after my arrival, to a Lanun who lives at Sooloo, named Matalissi, who made me pull [an oar] in his boat; he was going on a piratical cruise in the neighbourhood of Brune [Brunei] when Matalissi was told that the English had settled in Labuan, and that his intended cruising ground was not safe. He sold me to a man named Sindeko, in part exchange for a boat to make up the price. Nakodah Ursup, a Sambas man, bought me from him, and Mr. Medlrum freed me, and I am his servant for wages.[38]

The fate of Mariano, a Samareno, who was carried off by the Balangingi from a sea coast village in 1853 when he was ten years old is another case in point. He entered upon a career as a slave that spanned twenty-five years and five masters:

I was seized by Balangingi pirates ... while fishing with my father on the bank of the river near our village. My father managed to flee but I was taken prisoner and brought to Jolo where I was sold. After three years on Jolo island my master took me to the Kinabatangan river and sold me to a Taosug called Ujou who in turn, brought me to be sold at Mengkabong on the northwest coast of Borneo. I stayed with my new master Amimudin in Mengkabong for five years. He then took me to Brunei and sold me to a Kadayan called Raja who took me to his household in the interior. I remained in the custody of Raja, my master, for twelve years until I escaped to Labuan.[39]

The ease with which slaves could be moved about the economic system is reflected in these transfers.

TABLE 9

AVERAGE NUMBER OF SLAVES CARRIED ON SAMAL RAIDING *PRAHUS*, 1826–1847

Slave Informant	Year of Captivity	No. of Prahus	No. of Captives	Total Average Figure
Mariano Domingo	1826	15	200	13
Juan Benedicto	1833	10	150	15
Domingo Candelario	1833	8	300	38
Juan Florentino	1835	4	150	38
Mariano Sevilla	1835	6	400	67
Francisco Basilio	1836	26	350	13
Juan de la Cruz	1840	12	80	7
Manuel Molo	1842	6	107	18
Felix Torres	1842	9	100	11
Francisco Vincente	1843	10	50	5
Lucas Felis	1843	2	25	12
Martin de la Cruz	1844	5	70	14
Francisco Aquino	1844	9	108	12
Nicolas Antonio	1844	12	115	10
Pedro Armero	1846	8	300	38
Cerapio Parenas	1846	7	40	6
Satarino Martin	1846	8	100	13
Juan Pablo	1847	2	60	30
Francisco Santiago	1847	2	70	35
Mateo Francisco	1847	2	30	15

Source: This table has been compiled from the following sources: statements of slaves in Exp.12, 4 Oct. 1836, PNA, Mindanao/Sulu 1803–1890; Relacion jurada de los cuarenta y cuatro cautivos venidos sobre el Bergantin Cometa procedente de Joloy Zamboanga, 8 Feb.1848, PNA, Piratas 3.

There are no statistics on the overall number of slaves imported into Jolo in the period under consideration, except the estimates of European observers. These range from 750 to as high as 4,000 captives a year for the Philippines alone from 1775 to 1848.[40] It is possible to reconstruct a clearer picture of the pattern of slave imports to the Sulu Sultanate on the basis of the captive statements and other sources by using a sample of boatloads of slaves to determine the average number carried by an individual *prahu,* and multiplying this figure by the number of raiding *prahus* possessed by Samal and Iranun groups to establish an estimate of the overall number of slaves imported during a particular period. From 1770 to 1835, the raiding populations had 100–150 *prahus*; from 1836 to 1848, 150–200 *prahus*; and from 1852 to 1878, 60–100 *prahus*.[41]

On the basis of the statements of slaves seized between 1826 and 1847 (Table 9) an average of twenty-one slaves were carried on a vessel. This sample supports St. John's calculation of twenty slaves per *prahu* in 1849.[42] Slave imports to the Sulu Sultanate during the first sixty-five years probably averaged between 2,000 and 3,000 a year. The steepest rise in the number of slaves annually brought to Sulu, between 3,000 and 4,000, occurred in the period 1836–48, during which foreign trade was most intense at Sulu. The trade reached its apex in 1848 and slackened considerably in the next two decades, with imports ranging between 1,200 and 2,000 slaves a year until it collapsed in the 1870s.[43] The figures appear to show that between 200,000 and 300,000 slaves were moved in Iranun and Samal vessels to the Sulu Sultanate in the period 1770–1870.*

Demographic Infusion

The first half of the nineteenth century was an important period in the demographic history of the Sulu Sultanate because of the rapid growth of population stemming from the incorporation of slaves and their descendants into Taosug society. The size, composition, and regional distribution of the Sultanate's population were radically altered by 1848. The only source material available for the study of the area's population are the estimates and comments of slaves, colonial officials, and travellers. European accounts of population in Sulu must be used with caution because of variable sensitivity to ethnic distinctions, but they do corroborate the slave testimonies on several points regarding the ethnic composition of the Sultanate in the nineteenth century.

---

* For a precise calculation on slave imports to Sulu between 1770 and 1870 I have used the figure 20.5 slaves per boat, based on the statements of slaves seized between 1826 and 1847 minus 4,800 to 8,000 slaves (1,200 to 2,000 per year) for the period 1848–52. From the calculation it therefore follows that the number of slaves imported over the period 1770–1870 varied from a low estimate of 201,350 to a high estimate of 302,575.

Based on the estimates of Dalrymple and Hunt, the population of Jolo island steadily expanded from 40,000 people in 1770 to about 200,000 people in 1814.[44] Hunt noted a step rise in population after 1800 which coincided with the unprecedented growth of external trade, and slave raiding:

> The population of Sulu (island) as stated in most Gazetteers, is computed at 60,000 souls; however, this might have been the case, there is at this day a very great increase of its population. As I have had an opportunity of inspecting the Sultan's archives, of making enquiries of the chiefs of districts, and of personal observation, I think the following statements from the Sultan's books (149,732) is rather under the truth, than exceeding it, viz two hundred thousand.[45]

In 1773, Cencelli estimated that slaves comprised more than one quarter of the population of the archipelago.[46] On some islands and settlements the slave population was believed to exceed that of the Taosug. For example, the Spanish reported that slaves constituted more than fifty per cent of the population on Jolo island as early as 1773.[47] That estimate seems unduly high for the period, but by 1830 the population edge was definitely in favour of the captives. In a number of the principal towns on Jolo, especially in the interior, the slave class was several times the size of the Taosug communities into which they were being incorporated.

Hunt described the settlement of Jolo:

> .. Sulu town or Soog, the capital, has 3,500 dwelling houses, with a resident population of six thousand Islams and eight hundred Chinese ... a larger population is not reckoned, as more than half the inhabitants are always out on trading voyages, in the pearl and tripang fisheries and collecting of bird's nest....[48]

According to Hunt, slaves constituted the bulk of the town's population in 1814.[49] Commenting on the influx of captives at Jolo and their incorporation Juan de los Santos stated:

> The Taosug do not participate in slave raids but the people from Balangingi, Tunkil, and the other islands in the Samalese group as well as the Iranun come to Jolo to barter large numbers of Christian captives annually. At present in Jolo there are more captives than Taosugs with whom they are easily confused. Many of them have intermarried with the Taosug.[50]

Francisco Feliz confirmed his observation: "... presently [1836] the number of Christian captives in Jolo is at least twice as great as the Taosug population, the vast majority being Visayan".[51] By 1843 Jolo's population had risen to ten thousand, but there were other settlements that were as large, notably Parang.[52]

Parang was a market town for the hinterland of Jolo island, a staging centre for the Balangingi, and a port of call for trading *prahus* bound for the southern part of the archipelago and Borneo. In the 1830s there were "more captives than muslims in Parang". After 1830 this population ratio, vastly in favour of slaves, was paralleled throughout the archipelago; Francisco Mariano—"there are many Christian captives on Tapul, nearly all of them are Visayan"; Juan Florentino—"there are eighty Muslim families on Pilas and at least twice as many Christian captives who live alone in the fields, some of them go raiding with the Balangingi"; Santiago Manuel de Luna—"At Pata there are many Christian captives".[53]

It seems clear that before 1850 the size of the slave population was several times larger than that of the host society. The balance of these slaves were being incorporated into the population of the Sulu Sultanate which included, perhaps, a half a million people by mid-century.[54] It was a dynamic process and manumitted slaves and their descendants were continually being redefined according to the ethnicity of their host communities. After 1850, the ethnic-class structure became more stable, and the proportion of locally born slaves increased every year as raiding declined. By the end of the nineteenth century the Sulu Sultanate had become a nation of birthright Taosug.

Covering the period after the advent of external trade in the late eighteenth century, the primary object of this part of the book is to analyze the significance of the role the Iranun and Balangingi performed in the rise of the Sulu Sultanate, and to define the actual nature and extent of their slave-raiding activities. As the demands of the European and Chinese traders increased, squadrons of Iranun, from Western Mindanao, North Borneo, and Sulu, began hunting on the prevailing monsoon for slaves as far away as New Guinea, and out into the Gulf of Siam to Vietnam. Their vessels of up to 90 or 100 feet long were heavily armed, and their expeditions could last several years before returning to Sulu with slaves to exchange for opium, gunpowder, cloth, and rice. The inexorable regularity of their sweeps in the northern and central parts of the Philippines under Spanish control accounted for many abandoned villages and the disruption of coastal trade for years on end.

Close attention is given to the rise of the Balangingi Samal, one of the least known but most important population groups in nineteenth-century Southeast Asia, and their break-up at the hands of the Spanish navy. The Samal slave-raiding routes are traced and the process of conducting raids is depicted; slave-raiding was a dangerous pursuit and rigorous discipline was maintained on board the vessels. Not only did slaves accompany the Balangingi on expeditions, they also played important roles as boat commanders, gunners, and as impressed warriors. Some renegados even served as squadron commanders. In the second half of the nineteenth century, the Spanish navy gradually curbed the raiding of the Balangingi

Samal, but some spots continued to be major raiding areas; in those villages that were repeatedly preyed upon in the central Visayas and the Moluccas they retained a fearsome reputation until as late as the 1870s.

Slaves also appeared as an important additional commodity in Sulu's trade. The unfortunate—the elderly and infirm—were sent to Borneo. Those left behind were absorbed into Sulu society for work in the fisheries and fields. Sulu chiefs involved in trading, raiding, and procurement activities came to depend on their own household slaves and were quite reluctant to give them away. The astonishing fact, however, is that captives or captives' descendants came to constitute fifty per cent or more of the population of the Sulu archipelago by 1850.

I now want to turn in the last part of this book to the institution of slavery in the Sulu Sultanate. This became an essential element of Sulu society upon which its economic expansion had been predicated.

III

SLAVERY

10

Slavery in the Sulu Sultanate

Slavery in the Sulu Sultanate was not as rigidly defined an institution as in the West where it was historically synonymous with property. Slavery in Sulu, as in other areas of Southeast Asia, was primarily a property relation but not exclusively so, and in this context must be understood to imply several possible statuses of "acquired persons" who have been more or less forcefully transferred from one society to another.[1] A distinction was drawn by Taosug between chattel-slaves (*banyaga, bisaya, ipun, or ammas*) and bond-slaves (*kiapangdilihan*). *Banyaga* were either the victims or the offspring of victims of slave raids; *Kiapangdilihan* were commoner Taosug whose servility was the direct result of personal debt.[2] Between these two categories there was a continuum of status and privilege.

Slaves in non-Western societies were not necessarily defined solely in terms of their status as property. Their social position was also determined by factors often independent of their servile status. In Sulu *banyaga* could have family roles as husband or wife, they could own property, and they often filled a variety of political and economic roles—as bureaucrats, farmers, and raiders, as concubines and traders—by virtue of which they were entitled to certain rights and privileges accorded to other members of the community. It should be noted, however, that servile institutions were quite different among the Iranun, and other Maranao speakers, where chattel-slaves, *bisaya*, had few rights and almost no chance of altering their status.[3]

Slavery was a means of incorporating people into the Taosug social system. *Banyaga* were enrolled in the followings of *datus* for political support and to labour in the fields and fisheries to maintain an expansive redistributional economy. They were predominantly Visayan, Tagalog, Minahassan, and Buginese speakers although almost every major ethnic group of insular Southeast Asia was to be found among their ranks. Some were hereditary. Others were obtained as a form of tax or in fulfilment of debt obligations, but all *banyaga* or their descendants had been seized by slave raiders and retailed in communities throughout the Sulu chain.[4]

215

Debt Slavery

Capture in raiding was the principal mode of Taosug recruitment, but debt and fine obligations among the Taosug themselves provided a significant number of bond-slaves. Conviction for criminal offences such as stealing and acts of sexual impropriety, particularly adultery, were punishable by heavy fines.[5] Inability to pay or offer some form of security for the fine imposed reduced people to the status of *kiapangdilihan*. The enslavement of debtors was widespread in Sulu.[6] In addition to non-payment of fines, debts were incurred by gambling or pawning. Not infrequently a Taosug offered his services voluntarily for a fixed period of time in return for money or goods to meet the expenses of a wedding, a funeral, or to liquidate a debt.

Kiapangdilihan were an integral part of a creditor's following but with a lower status than freemen, who voluntarily attached themselves to a leader. The creditor claimed rights over only a *kiapangdilihan*'s economic services and, in theory, was not allowed to harm him physically. In return for food, clothing, and shelter, a *kiapangdilihan* was obliged to work for his creditor but his services did not generally count towards repayment of his debt. Many *kiapangdilihan* became dependents for life and their families might remain obligated for several generations. Indebtedness enabled *datus* to command the labour of Taosug commoners to ensure the military and labour reserves they required. Slavery for debt was most common in periods of distress (famines or epidemics) when Taosug might pawn themselves to gain subsistence and protection, and when the ranks of a *datu*'s following were apt to be decimated.[7]

Debt bondage as an economic institution in Sulu was most fully developed at the end of the nineteenth century, when the Taosug could no longer rely on Balangingi raids to supply sufficient numbers of *banyaga* for their retinues, by increasing the amount of tribute ordinarily collected from clients, and making the fines in the legal codes prohibitive.[8]

Slaves and the Law

The legal position of a *banyaga* in the Sultanate of Sulu was determined by the Sulu code, a body of law codified from custom and precedent as well as Islamic law.[9] The *Sharia'ah* (Islamic law) recognized the existence of slavery but placed strict conditions on its practice. Its tenets included the humane treatment of slaves and conditions for disassociation. The Taosug did not adhere explicitly to all the provisions of Koranic law with regard to slavery.

In theory, as defined in the Taosug codes, a *banyaga* had no legal personality; the will of a free adult was legitimate but the will of the insane, the child, and the *banyaga* was not; a non-pregnant slave woman was allowed legally to mourn for her husband only half the length of time (two months, five days) as a non-pregnant free woman.[10] The codes left a *banyaga* absolutely in the power and possession of his master: a *banyaga* could not hold property; a *banyaga* could be transferred, bought, or sold at will; and a master held the power of life and death over a *banyaga* who could be punished for the slightest infraction of the law. The legal expression of social distinctions is exemplified in the scale of penalties and fines in the codes for the offences of murder, adultery, theft, and inheritance. Punishments were much more severe for *banyaga* than members of other social classes:

> *Luwaran Code*
> Article 57 — murder
> 1 — If a free man kill another free man or a free woman, or a slave kill another slave, they shall be punished.
> 2 — If a free man killed a slave, the free man shall not be put to death.
> 3 — If a slave or other servant kill a free person, he shall be put to death.[11]

Similarly, if a male *banyaga* had sexual intercourse with a free woman, he could either be killed outright or be severely punished,* and become the property of the woman's husband or family.[12] On the other hand, if a free man had sexual relations with a married female slave he need only pay a fine of twenty lengths of cotton cloth.[13] Less severe penalties for adultery between *banyaga* derived from their inferior social status. The Taosug commonly associated such degrading behaviour with slaves.

Although these laws provide institutional opinion on the debasement of people, and further reflect the low opinion of slaves held by masters, in fact *banyaga* were often socially and economically indistinguishable from freemen and in some respects more secure. The actual life situation of many individual *banyaga* as revealed in their testimonies contradicted their legal status as a group. *Banyaga* were permitted to purchase their freedom and assume a new status and ethnicity; the children of a female *banyaga* and a freeman inherited the status of their father; some *banyaga* could bear arms; any slave could own property which reverted to his master at death.

Master and Slave

The basic difference between slavery among the Taosug and slavery as it was generally understood in the West was the variability of social distance that existed between slave and master. William Pryer stated that on the east

---

* Datu Dacula of Sibuguey in Mindanao killed a *bisaya* who seduced his younger sister, and spared her life only on condition that their baby be killed shortly after birth. No.139, El Gobernador de Zamboanga a GCG, 12 Feb. 1845, PNA, Mindanao/Sulu 1836–1897.

coast of Borneo the relation was that of follower and lord rather than slave and master.[14] The power and wealth of a *datu* was commensurate with the number of slaves he owned. The more slaves a *datu* acquired, the greater was his reputation as personal provider and protector, and the willingness of people to seek security within his settlement in return for services. *Banyaga* were often well clothed, carried fine kris, and were entrusted with long journeys for their masters.[15] The personal and economic ties of slaves in the Sulu Sultanate "provided a sense of security which bound them to their masters and gave them an identity and reason to labour".[16] A slave's individual status was enhanced by the prominent status of an acquiring master. On the other hand, when a powerful slave-holder suffered a serious loss of prestige so did his slaves, as he personified their worth as human beings. It is not surprising then that efforts of colonial administrators to free Taosug slaves were often met with reluctance on the part of the slaves because of their affective loyalty:

> Told Juan he was now a free man, which he seemed to regard from the "heritage of woe" point of view, and seemed very melancholy. Mahomet addressed a few words to him when handing him over and burst into tears. Juan wept and Mohamet's wives howled, altogether it was very affecting.[17]

A master was constrained to feed and clothe his slaves or give them sufficient opportunities to earn a living, otherwise his slaves might demand to be sold.[18] It appears to have been a common practice in the Sulu Sultanate to allow a *banyaga* when he desired, to change masters rather than risk desertion:

> Now that I had returned to my master I again pressed him to sell me ... my master then said, "why do you ask so to be sold? I always treat you as a brother, so that you have nothing to do but cure sick people." In this manner he endeavoured to prevail on me to remain with him, but I said, "if you will not sell me I will make away with myself, or kill some other persons that I may be put to death; be assured that I would rather die than remain longer with you". Very well, he said, "I promise to sell you, but you will repent when you afterwards fall into bad hands." After waiting four days in vain for the fulfilment of the promise I went to the relations of my master hoping that I might learn something of the matter. When they saw me they immediately asked why I had requested my master to sell me, to which I replied that I had a dislike to their country, especially as I have been accustomed at home to eat three times a day and that I never wanted for money there. These persons told my master of what I had said the same evening. The consequence was that on the following day my master asked me where I wished to be sold. I answered "at Solok." "Very well," he replied, "I will take you there."[19]

Nevertheless there are also statements of fugitive slaves and other reports which present a much less "benign" view of the master-slave relationship. In principle, the master's ownership was absolute and his authority unbounded. A *banyaga* could suffer physical cruelty and be put to death; he could be sold, bartered, or given away if it served his master's interests.[20] *Banyaga* who repeatedly tried to escape were put to death, but it was far more common for them to be disposed of to someone else, in most cases to the Segai-i.[21] Masters, such as Datu Tahel, used the threat of disposal to interior Kenyah to prevent the desertion of disaffected slaves. There are cases when *banyaga*, in moments of anger, passion, or drunkenness, provoked their masters to the point of death:

> I was told, his armourer, or blacksmith, a Bisayan captive, being drunk, had dared to affront the Spanish envoy: Rajah Moodo so lost his usual self command, that had it not been for the interposition of his lady, it was though he would have put the miscreant to death on spot.[22]

Pryer noted the ambivalence that existed in the paternalistic relationship between slave and master:

> Masters have the power of beating them [slaves] or even chopping them, but as a rule slavery here [Sandakan Bay and the coastal area] is regarded much as servantism is elsewhere ... but a former Dato here cut one of his slaves to pieces for trying to escape.[23]

While there is evidence of contrasting degrees of benevolence and material deprivation, what is important to ascertain in assessing the system is whether they were modal characteristics of slavery in the Sultanate. The fact that a *datu* defined his power in terms of the number of *banyaga* he possessed, and that *banyaga* were able to flee to another *datu* or to try to escape to Zamboanga or Menado, placed important constraints on his actions. A purely antagonistic relation would little benefit a master's self-interest if only because the successful exploitation of Sulu's natural produce hinged on the large-scale organization of the goodwill and cooperation of the slaves and their dependents. In 1842, an American sailor who accompanied the Wilkes expedition wrote:

> We saw several captives here who had been captured among the islands in the Sooloo Sea [Visayas] or Philippine group. One was taken out of a fishing boat in the harbour of Batavia. They are all kept as slaves until ransomed. This man, who belonged to Batavia, spoke some English, but very imperfectly. He states that they were treated well by their masters, and did not seem anxious to obtain their freedom.[24]

A master was liable to neglect or mistreat a *banyaga* who was remiss in his duties, but their statements and travel accounts of observers reveal that slaves, especially those with knowledge and skills, had good relations with their master and were not easily distinguished among his following.

The Economic Integration of Slaves

Slavery, I have emphasized, became crucial to Sulu's economic and cultural life towards the end of the eighteenth century. The impact of the

West's commercial intrusion in China was a watershed in the formation of the Sulu state. Slaves who were valuable for the variety of their labours essential to the growth of the state came to play a more avowedly important role in Sulu at this time. *Banyaga* were used in trading ventures, in diplomatic negotiations, as slave raiders, as concubines and wet nurses, as tutors to their masters, as craftworkers, and as peasants and fishermen.[25] There was a clear division of labour between the work of male and female *banyaga*. Heavy work was performed generally by male slaves. Physically able men assisted their masters in clearing virgin forest, in ploughing fields, in harvesting timber, in building and maintaining boats, and hauling water.[26] Male *banyaga* also laboured in the fisheries in search of *tripang* and mother of pearl shell, manufactured salt, accompanied their masters on trading expeditions and, when occasion demanded, sailed as crew on Balangingi *prahus*. Included among the major tasks of female *banyaga* were sowing and weeding in rice farming, pounding and threshing of rice, and gathering and preparation of strand products.[27] Female *banyaga* were also included in the entourage of their mistresses as attendants, and some enjoyed positions of trust and some comfort as concubines of leading *datus*.

Slavery played an essential role in the economic and military organization of the Sulu Sultanate. *Banyaga* were encouraged to participate in the economic life of the state through a system of incentives. Some used this to advantage and were able to rise in the social hierarchy:

> At Soung, business seems active, and all, slaves as well as masters, seem to engage in it ..., these circumstances promote the industry of the community, and even that of the slave, for he too as before observed, has a life interest in what he earns.[28]

Banyaga of initiative and energy were entrusted with their masters' property and sent on trading voyages. Hunt noted that the Taosug employed slaves in their *prahus* not only as crewmen but as traders.[29] Slaves regularly traded from Jolo to Balangingi and Palawan on behalf of their masters in the 1830s.[30] The more capable *banyaga* were employed in trading excursions to the northeast coast:

> The most intelligent of them are picked out as traders and perform long journeys sometimes of months duration, trading to different ports without ever thinking of running away. Many of these slaves amass considerable sums of money and have houses and belongings even finer than their masters ....[31]

Aristocratic women were given *banyaga* to assist them in their business activities, primarily local marketing.[32] By the mid-nineteenth century, some of the leading local traders in Sulu were women:

> In Sulu the wives of the chiefs are entrusted with the principal management of accounts, and carry on much of the trade; it is said that they have acquired

considerable knowledge from the Manilla captives, who are often of a superior class.[33]

Ordinarily, the vending of cloth, vegetables, and other trade goods in villages, at the open market, or to foreign vessels was done by *banyaga*. Noble women by virtue of their station lacked the liberty to barter produce, which entailed wandering amongst the houses, visiting the Chinese quarter, or rowing into the Bay to a trading ship. It was common for Taosug women to send one or two Spanish-speaking slaves into the roadstead in small canoes on the arrival of a European vessel.[34] The boats carried fruits, vegetables, coils of *tali lanun* (cheap rope of excellent quality), weapons, and curiosities. In 1834, an American sailor described the boats of slave vendors at Siassi as being full of "poultry, eggs, coconuts, bananas, turtles, monkeys, and parrots".[35] *Banyaga* were instructed to barter a specified minimum amount of produce by evening. They accepted only cups and saucers, scissors, buttons, nails, empty bottles, tobacco, and opium as trade items from European sailors. Slave hawkers were an important source of wealth to their mistresses. It was at the same time an attractive and profitable way of life for many:

> ... one day I was talking to a Malay, of whom I had just bought some coconuts, when he informed me that he also was a captive ..., upon which I enquired why he did not profit by the opportunity to escape, and revisit his country. "Why should I do so?" he replied, "There is something to regret everywhere; here I am well enough, my master treats me as if I were one of his kindred, I am well paid, and could save money if I wished; in my own country I know I could not do better, and perhaps should not fare as well; therefore, I prefer remaining here."[36]

The increased development of a slave mode of production conditioned the integration of the subsistence sector as a major component of the redistributive system. *Banyaga* employed in agriculture contributed towards providing the food supply which maintained the community, and freed a *datu* and his retinue from subsistence pursuits to devote their labour to trading and raiding.[37] Small, dispersed farming communities comprised of *banyaga* dotted the interior of the larger fertile islands, especially on Jolo, Tapul, and Pata. Masters allotted their *banyaga* a bamboo hut large enough to accommodate a single family and farm a plot.[38] The huts were scattered about over large tracts of land. The slave statements suggest that in some cases these subordinate agricultural settlements were homogeneous in language and religion.* Farm slaves were expected to provide for their

---

* Most *banyaga* settled in Datu Tahel's community in the hinterland of Jolo island were Buginese and "Malay". Other communities were settled almost entirely by Visayans. The size of such settlements is not known. Datu Tahel's village had more than a hundred male *banyaga* cultivating corn, rice, and sweet potato. Statement of Pedro Antonio, Exp. 12, 4, Oct. 1836, PNA, Mindanao/Sulu 1830–1890.

own needs from the fields and gardens that had been given to them. They were obligated to remit a fixed minimum portion of produce to their master through the agency of the village headman, who could be of slave or non-slave origin. Farming was their major economic obligation, but *datus* also demanded that villages near the coast collect *tripang* and pearl shell, although for this they received barter goods in exchange. All were liable to be called upon for military services.[39] While opportunities for social advance were few as a farm slave, to many Filipinos the Taosug system of share cropping and reciprocity was a less harsh form of exploitation than the poverty and social injustice they had previously endured under the *tributo* system of the Spanish Government.

The prosperity of the Sulu Sultanate depended to a large extent on the labour of *banyaga* who manned the raiding *prahus*. They augmented the strength of client communities that specialized in slaving, and as hirelings enriched their masters through active participation in raids. Wilkes observed that *datus* "receive a high price ... for the services of their slaves".[40] They exercised an enforceable claim on the wealth (goods or slaves) their *banyaga* received when hired out on raiding vessels.[41] Undoubtedly *datus* were constrained to reward such *banyaga*, otherwise they would have been far more reluctant to participate in such a hazardous undertaking. Raiding seems to have provided such slaves with opportunities for modest social advance, especially if they showed a talent for fighting.* Jadee, a Batak retailed to "Sulu pirates" for trade goods on the east Sumatran coast, was "made at first to row, and bale water out of their *prahus,* [but] he gave such proofs of courage and address, that in a short time they advanced him to the rank of fighting man".[42]

Occupations and Social Mobility

Differences in wealth, status, and privilege among *banyaga* were reflected in the diversity of occupations they pursued. The needs of Taosug *datus* determined the relative value of the services that a *banyaga* might render as a craftsman or specialist. Obviously, *banyaga* of unusual talent

---

* In some instances *banyaga* redeemed themselves by acts of bravery which indebted their master's gratitude to them. *Banyaga* involved in raiding were most apt to receive their freedom under such circumstances.

The following example illustrates the circumstances under which a master might have exercised the right of redemption by a sacred promise to God: "Datu Meldrum of Johor states that he saw Pengeran Mahomet of Brunei wearing a *baju ranti* [chain mail] at Pandassan, in the early fifties. The Pengeran had married an Illanun wife who was settled there and who claimed rule over the river. Pengeran Mahomet said he had been pirating on the coast of China, more than once along with the Illanuns, on one occasion he fell into the sea with his *baju ranti* on but was saved by a slave who dived and fished him up ...." *NBH,* 16 Sept. 1895, p.236.

or considerable ability and training who could not readily be replaced commanded more prestige and rewards than those with few skills. In prominent trading centres like Jolo, Parang, and Bual, where agriculture was of secondary importance, talented *banyaga* engaged in a wide range of activities and included among their numbers bureaucrats, tribute collectors, artisans, musicians, scribes, and commercial agents. The opportunities for social mobility among these slaves stand in marked contrast to those engaged in farming or fishing.

Banyaga recruited by the Sultan as office-holders enjoyed considerable power and prestige. The Sultan appointed them to administer trade and subject people in different parts of the zone to centralize his authority, and thwart the ambitions of rival Taosug. Because of their inferior social status, *banyaga* did not have the political aspirations of the *datu* class, and the Sultan's power was strengthened by the use of such slave administrators. The interests of these *banyaga,* by virtue of their elevation to political office, lay unquestionably with the Sultan, and they made loyal followers. *Banyaga* played leading roles as bureaucrats on the Samal islands, acted as tribute collectors throughout the zone, and manned tariff stations on Bornean rivers.[43] Chrishaan Soerma, a slave of the Datu Molok, commanded a large *prahu* that collected tribute from Parang, Tapul, Tawi-Tawi, and Sandakan Bay in the 1830s.[44] A Chinese seized near Banjermasin by the Iranun (named Banjer), "was a Sultan's man and had once been put on a Bintang Marrow station" to control interior trade on the Kinabatangan river.[45] The Sultan also made use of *banyaga* to exercise control over dependent groups on the northeast coast of Borneo. In 1878 Pryer wrote, "it is not considered particularly degrading to be a slave, most of the leading men here have been so ...".[46] One of the most influential of these slave headmen was Tuan Imam Gelanee who dominated the Samal Bajau Laut on the northeast coast after mid-century:

> Tuan Emum is a Bugis, he was captured when young by Sooloo pirates and taken over by the Sultan himself who finding him to be a man of ability sent him over here, Sandakan then apparently being pretty much in the hands of the Badjus, Emum married the queen of the Badjus, [and] became the headman amongst them.[47]

As Taosug trade became more complex, and the political problems posed by the West grew, so did the amount of work which required literacy. The use of written documents were no longer confined principally to records of the genealogy of the Sultan, the appointment of officials, and the collection of tribute and legal fees. After 1768, writing was required for diplomatic and trade correspondence with the Spanish, Dutch, and English, for recording grants of land and the terms of treaties of various sorts with the West, and to keep track of the accounts of *datus'* commercial enterprises.

Paradoxically, few Taosug aristocrats could read and write and *banyaga* with education who could serve as scribes, interpreters, and language tutors were much sought after:[48] "There are a few [*datus*] who understand a little Arabic; but the greatest number, even amongst the most considerable cannot write."[49] The illiteracy of the *datus,* and their dependence on *banyaga* who surpassed them in education and ability,* was commented upon by Hunt:

> Most of the chiefs at Sulo speak the Malay, but very few can either read or write it .... Many of the Datus speak the Spanish language, and some of them the Chinese fluently; the former they have learnt from the Christian slaves, the latter from the great numbers of that nation, settled all over the Sulo possessions.[50]

Most of the scribes were male slaves drawn from different parts of the Malay world, but female Filipino slaves and the occasional deserter from Zamboanga served as the Sultan's secretary at different times.[51] The negotiator of the treaty between Sulu and Spain in 1805 was a Mexican corporal, Jose Panciano Enriquez, "who finding himself serving a four year term in Zamboanga as a deserter from the King's regiment, escaped to Jolo, where he functioned as secretary of state with the rank and privileges of a datu .... It was not unusual in relations with Jolo to see individuals of the lowest class participating in serious affairs [of state]";[52] at Cotabato the grant of the island of Bunwoot by the Sultan to Thomas Forrest on behalf of the English East India Company was written in Spanish by Abderagani, "a native of Pampanga—once a slave, who, by turning mussalman, had obtained his liberty".[53] While most other slave specialists—artisans and craftsmen—were more or less expendable, the skills of the educated *banyagas* could not easily be mastered by others and were considered indispensable to the business enterprise of *datus* who employed them. *Banyagas* who could speak or write one or more foreign languages were employed as trading agents by *datus*, enabling them to amass considerable personal wealth: "These [educated slaves] are not denied the right of holding property which they enjoy during their lives, but at their death it reverts to their master. Some of them are quite rich ...."[54] Wilkes described such a *banyaga* who appears to have been of some assistance to his expedition:

> All accounts of the Dato of Soung are kept in Dutch, by a young Malay from Ternate, who writes a good hand, and speaks English, and whom we found exceedingly useful to us. He is the slave of the Datu who employs him for this purpose only. He told me he was captured in a brig by the pirates of Basilan,

---

* Wilkes wrote:"Few if any of the Sooloos can write or read, though many talk Spanish. Their accounts are all kept by the slaves. Those who can read and write are, in consequence, highly prized." Wilkes,"Jolo and the Sulus", pp.160–61.

and sold here as a slave, where he is likely to remain for life, although he says the Datu has promised to give him his freedom after ten years.[55]

The number of slave artisans—goldsmiths, silversmiths, blacksmiths, and weavers—was never large, and comprised only a fraction of the total slave population. Gifted *banyaga*, whose raw materials, brought by trade or tribute, were transformed into jewellery, tools, weapons, and armour, were full-time artisans while others who were less talented pursued their occupations on a part-time basis.* Not surprisingly, the arbitrary distribution of *banyaga* left some talents wasted. Jose Ruedas, a silversmith, spent three years as a fisherman and gatherer of pearl shell before being taken by his master to be exchanged for a bundle of cotton cloth at Jolo, where he resumed his craft.[56] While some *banyaga* found their skills superfluous in a particular island's economy, others appear to have had the opportunity to acquire training in critical occupations, especially as blacksmiths and armourers.†

It is clear from the accounts of Forrest, Hunt, D'Urville, and Wilkes that slaves were called upon to perform instrumental music and sing, sometimes in Spanish, or recite Visayan poetry for religious festivals, and when Europeans visited Jolo.[57] Under such circumstances, there was ample opportunity for *banyaga* with musical talent to improve their condition. Furthermore, some *datus* played the flute, violin, or guitar, and all were fond of Spanish songs and dances. Filipino slaves could and did act as their music instructors and entertained them at night while they smoked opium and discussed trade and politics. The *fiola* or violin was the favourite instrument of the aristocrats of Sulu: "The Bisayan slaves play often on the violin, and the Sooloos are fond of European music."[58] Forrest noted also at Cotabato that some slaves doubled as part-time performers: "as he [the Raja Muda] is a performer on the violin, I presented him with two violins, and a German flute: he had a Bisayan, one of his guards, who played tolerably by ear on the violin."[59] *Banyaga* who were talented musicians could expect to be transferred from one office-holder to the next:

---

* Forrest described some of the craftsmen that he met at Cotabato and their varying degrees of skill: "They [the Magindanao] have goldsmiths, who make filligree buttons, earings, and c., pretty well, but not nearly so well as Malays generally do on Sumatra and Java. Their blacksmiths are incapable of making anything that requires more ingenuity than a common nail. Rajah Moodo had several Bisayan slaves; one of them could mend a gunlock; he fitted my rudder irons. Others amongst them were tolerable silversmiths, and those he kept in constant employ; but Mindanoers have almost all their culinary utensils from China, by way of Sooloo ...." Forrest, *Voyage to New Guinea*, p.299.

† For example, Gabriel Francisco worked as a labourer on Tunkil until he was sold in Jolo and apprenticed to his master's blacksmith. Statement of Gabriel Francisco in Exp. 12, 4 Oct. 1836, PNA, Mindanao/Sulu 1803–1890, p.32.

... [Banjer] had been captured by the Illanuns in his youth and taken over by the Sultan of Sooloo who sent him over here [Sandakan Bay] afterwards. The Sultan told him to become [a] musician to Datu Haroun and after Haroun left here when Mohammed Ascalee came ... There were instructions in Mohammed's chop for Banjer to serve him in a similar way.[60]

Chrishaan Soerma was captured by the Balangingi in 1834 and sold at Jolo to the Datu Molok:

Datu Molok agreed at the time of my transfer that I should have a pair of trousers but I went about naked and ill-fed, and was made to carry heavy loads a considerable distance. My lot was a miserable one. After having been there for three months, I was summoned at about eight o'clock one evening by Datu Molok who asked me if I knew how to play the *fiola*. I thought the Raja would provide me with a decent subsistence and security if I could demonstrate my ability to play the instrument, but I feared not being talented enough. He promptly produced an English violin which he had bought from the Captain John Anthony Sommes, who trades regularly at Sulu with a brig, and ordered me to play. Afterwards he said, "Fine, now you no longer will have to do manual labour but only be present in the *rumah bakar* [smoking den] to play the violin." I did this during evening hours whenever the Raja commanded from 7 to 12.30 p.m.[61]

In less than seven years, Chrishaan went on to become a petty trader for the Raja, and ultimately functioned as one of his tribute collectors.

Banyaga with medical knowledge were perhaps most scarce. The experience of Captain C.Z. Pieters among the Balangingi illustrates that slaves who claimed even a rudimentary understanding of medicine and medical practice could enjoy a privileged position:

One day my master and his wife asked me to what kind of work I was accustomed. I said that I could not work and that my former master had only employed me in looking after his goods, accounts and dollars, and giving medicine to sick people. When they learnt this from me, my master went and told everyone that he had a slave who could cure all kinds of sickness. The consequence of this was that on the following day many persons came and asked me to tell them, from looking at their hand, if they were fortunate. I told them that I did not possess this art, but could only feel the pulse, on which they asked me to do this and tell them what was the matter with them. I complied with the request and said that they were in trouble and could eat very little. They acknowledged that I had spoken the truth. Afterwards whenever I visited sick people I generally asked them for a small quantity of sweet potatoes and rice....[62]

As Pieters' reputation as a healer grew, so did his material and social success, but the responsibility and risks increased with the demand for his services in cases of serious illness:

At one time my master Baludin ordered me to prescribe for his teacher, an old man, named Langujang. He was seriously ill and could not walk. His wife asked me if I could cure him, but I said that the sickness was of too serious nature for medicine to do him any good. I said this purposely, as I was afraid if the man died while I was attending him his death might be imputed to my treatment and I might perhaps be punished or killed. Notwithstanding my declaration his wife still besought me to prescribe for her husband ... she promised me that if he recovered ..., she would give me two slaves, with whom I could trade as if I were free, and that I should be at liberty either to remain at Balangingi or return to my own country. She assured me that the customs of the country allowed this. I remained six days in attendance upon the sick man, who soon felt much better, and I did not hesitate to remind him of his promise to give me two slaves, but he would not acknowledge it. I then determined to return to my master Baludin, whom I requested three days later to sell me. Instead of complying with this he ordered me again to take the sick man under my care .... However unwilling, I was obliged to obey his commands.[63]

As concubines (*sandil*), women achieved a high status. Concubinage was an important part of the traditional social structure in Sulu. It was a key means of producing wealth and maintaining rank, for concubines could be offered to men as mistresses or wives to recruit followers. In theory there was no limit to the number of concubines that a Sultan or *datu* could acquire for his retinue.[64] When Forrest visited Cotabato, the Sultan had one wife and fourteen or fifteen concubines.[65] In Sulu *datus* rarely had more than a few concubines. Many of them were *kiapangdilihan*; others were purchased; some were given to the Sultan and leading *datus* as potential wives in the hope of forging political alliances through the kinship bond.[66] Concubines had a recognized status. One who bore a child to her master could expect to be manumitted. The child of a concubine could not inherit the status of the father but was given a lesser title and incorporated into his following.[67] Indicative of their higher status was the fact that some Filipino women, if they had any choice in the matter, would have willingly become concubines. Maria Biermosa, forty years of age and a weaver by trade from Capiz province, stated:

that she was taken to Capuz, a province of the Samals, where she served the daughter of Datu Ume, a nobleman of Jolo, who obtained her as a gift, and in whose country estate she lived for three years, and in Jolo another three ... that five years ago, that is, after her first year of captivity, her master obliged her to marry a fellow slave ... that her appointed tasks were housework and farmwork, which among the Moros were performed only by slaves or indio captives, called by them *uripon* ... that the Moros not only made their slave women do the work she mentioned, but took them for their concubines; but she said, she had not had that good fortune.[68]

The boundaries between segments of the retainer class (freemen who voluntarily attached themselves to *datus*) and slaves were not clear-cut. There was considerable mobility for talented members of inferior status groups within and between all classes and strata. Among the hierarchy of *banyaga,* those who functioned as bureaucrats, craftsmen, scribes, and concubines often had a greater degree of power and privilege than Taosug commoners. Wilkes remarked of such *banyaga*: "some of them are quite rich and are invariably better off than untitled freemen."[69] For the generality of slaves, however, opportunities for advance were modest. Dramatic advance depended largely on historical circumstance, good fortune, skills, and personal character, and were associated with occupations which provided access to wealth and power. There is some evidence[70] illustrating that in rare instances *banyaga* of remarkable talent rose to the rank of *orang kaya* and *datus* as proteges of their masters.*

Disassociation: Manumission, Redemption, and Escape

Manumission was commonly practised in the Sulu Sultanate, and freed slaves were merged into the general population, assuming a new ethnicity and status.[71] For *banyaga,* conversion and/or marriage were prerequisites to manumission. The process of manumission in the Taosug social system (occurring primarily among those *banyaga* in close contact with their masters), tended to be a gradual one in which incorporation was implicit.[72] A Filipino who altered his ethnic identity by becoming a Muslim and was manumitted found a new range of opportunities open to him as a "Taosug" and a free man. It is not clear whether captured Muslim slaves could be manumitted and rise in status more easily than converted Filipinos. The fact that some groups, especially the Buginese, took pride in their cultural heritage could not have helped, since freedom apparently implied going through a process of assimilation.

Manumission was easier for women than men. It was not necessary for a female Filipino slave to renounce her faith to be manumitted. When a freeman married a Filipino slave she became free.[73] Whether or not she adopted Islam,† her children were raised as Muslims and were absorbed into Sulu society as Taosugs. Marriage played an important part in the Sulu system. The provision of wives was a basis on which followings were built and retained. For the upwardly mobile captive, an arranged marriage was closely linked to status advancement or manumission.

A *banyaga* could purchase his freedom in the Sulu Sultanate.[74] This was frequently the case among those *banyaga* who had an aptitude for trade. Their owners often found it best to allow such slaves to acquire property so as to encourage initiative and establish their loyalty. In time

---

* In 1903 Gen. Leonard Wood described Panglima Hassan as "Originally a slave born on Pata island, and little by little has worked up until he is now the most important chieftain in the island of Jolo, next to the Sultan and Datu Jokanien". Leonard Wood Papers, container 3, Diary of Leonard Wood, 18 Aug. 1903.

† According to the Shariaʿah there is only one marriage that is considered invalid—that of a Muslim woman to a non-Muslim.

the *banyaga* might purchase his freedom with his master's backing, having profited from participation in his commercial affairs. Once free, reciprocal obligations continued to bind them—now as a patron and client instead of master and slave. Manumission was an important feature of the Taosug social system. The steady leakage of manumitted slaves swelled the ranks of a *datu*'s retainers and hence increased his political hegemony and prestige. The likelihood of manumission was essentially a function of occupation. *Banyaga* who provided immediate and indispensable services to their masters, who served in their households or on their trading *prahus*, had better chances of manumission than those who laboured in the fields or fisheries.

Redemption

The Iranun and Balangingi sometimes permitted people they seized to redeem themselves by ransom. Often this was done immediately after their seizure, but *banyaga* were also ransomed in the Sulu archipelago from the Taosug, sometimes after having spent a considerable period in captivity. When away on cruises, slave raiders went out of their way to take captives for whom ransoms might be obtained: a *banyaga* was always entrusted to fetch the ransom. Zuniga observed that only certain types of persons could be ransomed:

> The only captives suitable for this kind of barter are wealthy chiefs and religious missionaries; these can be ransomed since their relatives or religious brethren have the ready cash which the Moros require. Because of this the price of a captive has risen enormously. A religious cannot be ransomed for less than 1,000 pesos, nor an indian chief for less than 300 pesos in silver, rice, or other articles .... They are particularly fond of card games, and playing cards constitute one of the items which they accept for the ransom of captives.[75]

In 1785, Iranun vessels arrived at Pasacao, in the Ragay gulf, in the hope of obtaining ransom for a captured Spaniard and a mestizo. The Bishop of Nueva Caceres freed the former but not the latter.[76] Given the magnitude of slavery, it was inconceivable for the Church to ransom Filipino slaves generally. Nevertheless, their villages were sometimes expected to raise the money for the ransom of the friars, and were left impoverished as a result.[77] Nor was it a widespread practice for Malay royalty to obtain the release of their kindred by negotiation and ransom.[78]

There was a standard scale of ransom fees by 1800: a friar was valued at about 2,000 pesos, a European at 300 pesos, and a male Filipino slave at 30 to 50 pesos. Lascars taken from English ships were ransomed at 100 pesos each.[79] The heavy ransoms offered for friars meant that they were especially coveted.[80] In 1769, the Governor of Zamboanga paid 2,200 *kangans* (bolts of cotton cloth) to ransom three Augustinian friars;[81] a priest from Mariveles was ransomed for 1,000 pesos in 1770/71;[82] and in 1823 the Provincial of the Recollects, Pedro de Santa Eulalia, was seized with another friar while making his annual *visita* and the order had to pay a ransom of 10,000 pesos for the two of them.[83] The ransoming of priests and other Europeans at Jolo was a common practice in the eighteenth century, and the Sultan took an active part in such negotiations, especially in cases that involved the Governor of Zamboanga.[84] By 1830, however, the Sultan of Sulu no longer condoned their seizure or ransom. He did not consider it advantageous from the standpoint of trade and politics to permit Europeans, particularly priests, to be brought to Jolo where their presence could become a *cause celebre* and jeopardize relations with Western powers. This became a source of some of the resentment and conflict that developed between the Taosug and Balangingi after 1835. The Balangingi refused to yield the religious and Europeans among their slaves to the Sultan, to be turned over to the Zamboanga authorities, and defiantly pressed for their ransom. Once European captives had become undesirable to the Taosug, they were increasingly put to death by the Balangingi when a ransom could not be found for them:

> A renagado from Cebu, who was one of the pirates, came in secrecy to verify my worst fears. He assured me that he had overheard the chiefs discussing whether it would be more sensible to kill me to avoid the problem of bringing a "white face" to Jolo, since the Sultan would be obliged to surrender me to the governor of Zamboanga, and he might, perhaps turn my captors over to further ingratiate himself with the governor. On the other hand, they could ransom me for a high price to be delivered to a trusted person and I could be set free.[85]

Before 1850, European slaves in Jolo were regularly redeemed by ship captains who traded there:[86]

> I was taken for sale on board the Spanish brig *Leonidas* the captain of which was called Escrebano. As they could only speak Spanish there, we went to the American barque *Minerva*. The master of this vessel was named M.A.Somes.* After Unkud and I had saluted the captain, the latter asked me where I came from and what my name was. I replied that I was from Menado and that my name was Cornelius Zacharias Pieters. As soon as I had said this ... he told me you must not take it ill that I have not shaken hands with you, for if I did that they would ask a large price for you. You had better now go forward and I will speak with this man about your purchase .... After I had remained about

---

* In 1834 Somes was described as the captain of the brig *Luzon*: "Captain S. is a fat and jolly Yankee, but as he has a wife and children at Manilla, he calls himself a Spaniard and sails under Spanish colours. The supercaro of the *Luzon*, I believe, is an Irishman. His name was Windham...." Jacobs, *The Cruise of the Clipper Margaret Oakley*, p.336.

half an hour forward Unkud called me to return home with him, because, as he said, this unbelieving captain would not purchase me. The latter however told me in the English language that Unkud had asked a very high price, and would not take a cent less than a thousand dollars. As I agreed with the captain that the amount was too great and I knew that I would never be able to repay him such a sum, I said that I would return in a couple of days to inform him of my wishes regarding the matter.[87]

Pieters refused to eat during the next several days, and his worsening health and depression was a cause of real concern to his master. Three days after he had begun the hunger strike. Unkud sold him to Captain Somes for 300 pesos.[88] Ship captains took advantage of the fact that they held out the sole opportunity of redemption for Filipinos. Merchant-traders considered them a cheap, convenient source of labour, and redeemed Filipino slaves had to work the ransom price off in passage. As crew members their indenture was apt to last up to a year and take them further and further away from their villages.[89]

Escape

For many *banyaga* among the Taosug and Samal, escape remained their central ambition. Escape was more likely among *los nuevos*, the newly enslaved. This was particularly the case of Filipino men who had been separated from their families, or who clung to their faith.[90] *Banyaga* who retained memories of another home were more prone to escape than slaves who had been seized in their youth and were more easily acculturated to the Taosug social system.[91] Francisco Augustino's case was typical of those whose previous social and cultural ties remained paramount:

> I remained two weeks with my master Capitan Binuang who had seized me, and it was he who brought me to Jolo. The moro Ande purchased me. Although I was well treated by him, I felt that I had to escape to return to my family and village.[92]

It was during the early years of captivity that the desire to escape was greatest. Out of a total of 50 slaves who escaped to the Spanish fleet visiting Jolo in 1836, 38 had been in captivity less than six years; 7 for between six and eight years; and the remainder for more than a decade. The number of newly acquired Filipino slaves who either escaped or were ransomed to the captain of the brigantine *Cometa* in 1847 was even higher; 43 out of the 45 slaves had been in captivity less than six years. Of this number, 25 had been in captivity less than a year, 7 for two years, 8 for three years, and 3 for five years. Similarly, of the 26 Dutch subjects who escaped to Menado by small sailboat between 1845 and 1849, 17 had been in captivity for less than three years.[93]

The condition and treatment of new slaves was similar to that of others, except that they were watched more closely. The Taosug system was such that coercive controls were difficult to apply, and one to two hundred *banyaga* who chafed under oppression fled annually to foreign vessels at Jolo, to the interior of Jolo or some other island in the archipelago, or to Zamboanga and Menado.[94] Once the decision was made to escape, a *banyaga* often sought out another slave from the same ethnolinguistic group or province to make plans. Often such a compact was made between *banyaga* belonging to the same master or ones living in contiguous settlements. Obviously, common heritage was important in maintaining secrecy and cooperation necessary for successful escape.[95] This seems to have especially been so for *banyaga* who attempted the long and difficult journey to Menado. There are rare instances of *banyaga* who yearned to return home but did not risk escape until accidentally meeting their kindred. The Samareno Francisco Aquino stated that:

> he remained two weeks on Balangingi ... and then was taken to Jolo and sold for 109 *cavans* of palay to Lacha whom I served as a slave for four years. That ... having satisfied the full value of his purchase his master had freed him ... and he remained another two years in the village ... that in Jolo he met his brother-in-law and they arranged to escape .... They managed to flee in a small dugout [boat] to Pasanhan [Basilan] in two days and two nights. From there they were sent to Zamboanga and three days later were put on the brigantine *San Ramos* bound for Manila.[96]

Francisco Gamu spent twelve years in captivity on Pata island before accidentally meeting his cousin Lorenzo Gamu. He immediately proposed that they attempt to escape to Zamboanga and ultimately return home. They were picked up by a Spanish naval steamer and an officer described Lorenzo in this manner: "He had a vague sense of being a Christian but had no recollection of his village and could only state that he had been captured when very young."[97]

Escape from Jolo and neighbouring islands to Zamboanga was rather easy. Zamboanga's proximity to, and commercial dependence on, Jolo offered *banyaga* ample opportunities to reach the *presidio* on trading *prahus* or by small canoe. A *banyaga's* chance of escape diminished the further away he was sold from Jolo.[98] This was especially the case for *banyaga* retailed on the northeast coast of Borneo where some waited eighteen years before an opportunity to escape presented itself in the form of a punitive expedition or the visit of a European trading boat.[99]

Escape by small boat to the Visayas of Menado was a hazardous undertaking. Unpredictable winds and strong currents could take a small canoe far from its destination, or it could break up and sink in choppy seas. The voyage to Menado took at least ten days and required an outriggered sailing boat large enough for at least two men, but such attempts often required three to five *banyaga*. The difficult nature of the voyage to northern Celebes is apparent from the small number of slaves that successfully completed it: from 1845 to 1849, 29 slaves reached Menado; in 1855,

15 slaves; in 1857, 21 slaves, in 1858, 7 slaves.[100] The danger of dying from hunger and thirst is evident in the story of the Cebuano fisherman, Relampago, who escaped from Jolo with his wife in a small boat for the western Visayas:*

> In a few days we arrived at Jolo. There the prisoners were allotted, and the master to whose share we fell took us home with him .... Our captivity lasted two years .... My master often took me with him to the banks of a lake in the interior of the island, and there I remained for ... months, separated from ... Theresa ... A circumstance occurred which made me take an audacious step. Theresa became pregnant ... as a slave the thought of becoming a father horrified me .... I had hurt my leg on a previous excursion and this was of much service to me. My master set out one day for the banks of the ... lake, and left me at Jolo, on account of my wound. I profited by this opportunity to execute a long formed plan of escape. The risk was great ... when night came. Theresa set out by one path and I by another and we met on the seashore. There we entered a small canoe .... I shall never forget that flight. We rowed all night, it was very dark and the wind was ... high ... At ... dawn, we distinguished the rocks upon the shore and saw that we were unpursued. Our hopes of escape increased, and we continued our efforts at the oar, guiding our canoe in a northerly direction, where we might find an island inhabited by Christians. We had a few cocoanuts on board, but they were poor nourishment and when we had been for three days without anything to eat, our strength was ... exhausted. We fell upon our knees and prayed to the infant Jesus of Zebou [Cebu]. Then we laid ourselves down in the boat, resigned to die together. Our weakness increased and ... we became insensible. The canoe went at the will of the waves. When we recovered ... consciousness, I know not in how long a time—we found ourselves among Christians [from Negros] who had ... picked us up. We were long in recovering from the sufferings we had undergone .... [101]

Emaciated slaves waiting to die who were picked up at sea by European and native vessels were often dropped at the nearest port along the way, many taking months—even years—to reach home.[102]

A far easier mode of escape for *banyaga* in Jolo, and one which could be accomplished alone, was to swim or row out to a visiting European vessel. The usual plan was "to sneak alongside at night, cling hold of the chain plates, kick the canoe adrift, which they had in all probability stolen, and then make a noise until helped up the side".[103] The timing of the venture was crucial to its success. *Banyaga* escaped to merchant vessels only at the close of the trading season, as their chances of being granted asylum were greater then, when their presence was less apt to become an issue and disrupt trading.[104] Despite such precautions, *banyaga* sometimes were turned

---

* Women were less frequently in a position to escape, and when they did it was usually in the company of their husbands.

away or given by traders—European and Chinese—to another *datu* as a
"gift".[105] In 1834, the American brig, *Margaret Oakley*, was at anchor off
Siassi:

> On the previous night our sentinel had discovered something in the water near
> the stern. Having hailed three times without receiving any reply, he fired his
> rifle .... A ... voice called for help. We picked up a naked Malay, with kreese
> on his hand, and ... he said that he was a slave, ... he begged us to protect
> him and take him to the country whence he had been stolen. Luckily, he was
> not wounded. We did not know whether to believe his story or not, but half
> suspected that he had swam off to steal our boat; if we had anything to do with
> him we might get ourselves in trouble.... We gave him something to eat and
> drink put him in the boat and rowed near the beach where we told him to jump
> overboard. He did so and swam to the shore.[106]

After the 1830s, when Spanish warships began to frequent the area, larger
numbers of *banyaga* risked escape. In contrast to the uncertainties of escape
to trading vessels, fugitives were assured protection on European warships.
More than fifty Filipino slaves from every island group in the archipelago
were taken on board the vessels of the Spanish fleet that visited Jolo in
1836.[107] The longer war vessels remained in the Jolo roadstead, the more
prone *banyaga* were to risk escape. A doctor accompanying a French naval
expedition in 1845 wrote:

> During the night ... we were suddenly awakened by a great tumult on board
> our vessel; the sentinels gave the alarm, and called attention to the ...
> appearance of some individuals who kept swimming round our ships,
> apparently with the wish of coming on board; after having conferred with
> the commander, an officer belonging to the *Cleopatra* gave orders that one
> of these men who had seized upon the chain of the anchor should be
> assisted on board. He was a young Malay, of about 16 or 18, ... and scarcely
> had he set foot upon the deck of the *Cleopatra,* than he fell on his hands and
> knees and made the sign of the cross with ... fervour and piety, and having
> briefly uttered his thanks to God, he informed us that he was a ... Christian
> slave whom Soulouan pirates had taken prisoner on the coast of Manilla,
> and who now sought refuge in the protection of his French brethren ... ropes
> were flung to the rest of the poor unfortunates, all of whom were. taken on
> board ... when ... once more reunited: kneeling at the feet of the officers, they
> implored in most moving terms the compassion which was readily yielded
> them, then embracing and congratulating each other upon their good fortune,
> they gave vent to their feelings in a flood of tears ... for several nights
> following the number of fugitives who thronged around the vessel was very
> considerable; amongst them were a Spaniard and an Indian from the coast of
> Malabar....[108]

When *datus* became aware that once a *banyaga* set foot on board a warship
he was free, they began to take precautions. Newly acquired *banyaga* in
particular were herded together and locked up at night, or marched into the

interior until the departure of a squadron. In 1836, all small canoes were taken off the beaches and sentinels patrolled the shore after dark. *Banyaga* who failed in a bid to escape could be in danger of being beaten or killed, though it was more usual to sell them.[109]

The Second Captivity

Few fates can have been as cruelly deceptive as the one experienced by the *banyaga* who escaped to Zamboanga. Most *banyaga* who fled one form of servitude were forced to remain in Zamboanga and enter another— a "second captivity". It was a standard practice of the Governors of the *presidio* to delay the return of Filipinos to their villages for years at a time in order to exploit their labour.[110] Denied any opportunity to practice a trade in Zamboanga, Filipino fugitives from the Sulu archipelago were integrated into the lowest stratum of Zamboanga society with criminals, deserters, and *deportados,* as a residual source of manpower. Men were forced to labour on the fortifications, manufacture salt, collect firewood, and tend the carabao. They also toiled in the fields beside their women, some of whom were forced to become prostitutes for the garrison and coastguard force.[111]

It is not surprising, therefore, that Zamboanga developed an infamous reputation as a place of refuge among *banyaga* in the Sulu archipelago. Its sole attraction was its proximity. It was a commonly held opinion among Filipino slaves that the nature of the servitude experienced in Zamboanga was far worse than among the Taosug.[112] A group of twenty Filipino women in Jolo confronted a Spanish naval officer, intent on transporting them to Zamboanga, with the following ultimatum:

> Senor Commander if you wish to take us someplace other than Zamboanga we wish to be manumitted; but if we must first go to Zamboanga where we will be assigned to people's houses as domestics while waiting for a boat to repatriate us, and treated worse than slaves, then we prefer to remain as captives among the moros the rest of our lives....[113]

Similarly, when an English frigate picked up a boatload of fugitive slaves mid-way between Jolo and Panay, they begged the captain not to take them to Zamboanga and threatened to throw themselves into the sea if he persisted.[114]

The arrival of so many *banyaga* at Zamboanga gave rise to an interesting social situation. The fugitives established themselves with impoverished Chinese and vagrants in a community situated some distance from the *presidio.* Originating from different parts of the Philippine archipelago and lacking a common language, these *degradados* developed their own Spanish-Creole dialect—Chavacano—to communicate. A large percentage of the surrounding rural population labelled Zamboangueno at the end of the nineteenth century were descendants of fugitive slaves who had lived on the margins of the *presidio* as social outcasts.*[115]

Very little is known about the fate of those Filipinos who actually managed to return to their villages. Published records concerning repatriation are rare. After 1838, the vessels of the *Marina Sutil* and private traders were instructed by the Government to assist fugitive *banyaga* in Zamboanga to reach the Visayas. At the port of their province, they were to be handed over to the *corregidor* or *alcalde mayor* who was responsible for returning them to their villages.[116] The passage scheme was never implemented properly, and fugitive slaves were entirely dependent for their welfare on the goodwill of Spanish administrators and ship captains who did not hesitate to exploit them. Undoubtedly, a Filipino sometimes reached home to find some or all of his family dead, his wife remarried, and outstanding debts and reciprocal obligations unfulfilled.[117] Many who escaped were left to make a new life, the reality of which was more harsh than the one they had fled from as *banyaga* in Sulu.

---

* In the same fashion, the labour of fugitive *banyaga* from Tawi-Tawi, Omaddal, and Bulungan was instrumental in the pioneering efforts of the Chartered Company to build and settle Elopura and Tawau at the end of the 19th century.

11

The Captives

THE ODYSSEY

It is the main purpose of this chapter to combine the testimonies of former *banyaga* with manuscript sources and travel accounts to describe the lives of individuals under slavery in the Sulu Sultanate. The experience of captives from the moment of seizure, and their passage in the slave *prahus*, to their settlement, life, and labour in Sulu emerges from anonymity in the slave testimonies. I want to employ these statements as a source to portray slave culture and life as it was seen from the inside "by documenting important conditions, changes, or relations which are hard to detect in the experience of any particular individual by accumulating the experiences of many individuals".[1] My concern then is to use the technique of collective biography to answer the question "what was it like to be a slave in the Sulu Sultanate?" As a historical source the testimonies of the fugitive *banyaga* of the Sulu Sultanate are both invaluable and neglected. They provide new evidence about the experience of slavery in the Sulu Sultanate that could never be found in more traditional primary sources. Although the evidence is bound to be inadequate to make generalizations, it still enables us to come closer than any previous historical study to the *banyaga*'s own world, and the way in which everyday life intersected with history. These statements represent the voices of the normally inarticulate in history—tens of thousands of Southeast Asians rarely heard from—voices from below.

Most captive statements were taken when *banyaga* escaped to European ships. They contain data on the social status of *banyaga,* their occupations, religion, treatment, and family life. Spanish and Dutch interests required information on the social organization of raiding and ethnic relations in the Sulu zone, and consequently evidence given in interrogations revolved around these issues. Virtually all the statements concern the experiences of *banyaga* who fled from Jolo island, with the exception of a small number furnished by those who managed to escape from Tempasuk, Marudu Bay, and Gunung Tabor. While *banyaga* from Jolo were disproportionately represented, many of them had spent a period of their captivity elsewhere and provided information on their servitude in other parts of the Sulu archipelago, especially on Balangingi. Out of 180 *banyaga* listed in Appendix R, only four were women. Their age at the time of their interrogation ranged from nine to sixty years old, but the servile experience overwhelmingly represented was that of manhood, the period between twenty and fifty years of age.

The Spanish frequently carried two interpreters on their warships who were fluent in Tagalog and Visayan. All Filipino slaves who sought refuge on board Spanish vessels were interrogated immediately. In the rare instance when a Malay speaker escaped to a Spanish ship, the statement was deferred and taken in Malay at Zamboanga. But Filipino slaves who fled to Menado were generally unable to make themselves understood, or answer the very specific questions put to them in Malay or Dutch. As a rule the Spanish sought answers to the following series of questions: What is your name? What is your age? What province and/or village did you come from in Philippines? What activity were you engaged in when seized? Where and when were you seized? Who were the slave raiders? How many vessels were in the flotilla? How many persons had they captured? Were the slave raiders pursued at any time during the course of their cruise by one of our coast guard squadrons? Where were you taken? To whom were you sold? How were you employed and treated? Are there a large number of slaves on Jolo island? Can slaves bear arms? What roles do slaves play in raiding? Do vessels leave from Jolo to go on slave forays? And, is there any other information that you can provide us with in regard to piracy?[2] The Dutch asked fugitive *banyaga* more than thirty questions that focused principally on slave-raiding.[3] The Spanish and Dutch sources complement one another, and together contain analytical information for portraying raiding and slavery in the Sulu Sultanate from within the culture. Because the questions tended to be mechanical, answers could be routine, especially when fugitives were interrogated as a group. In such instances, one *banyaga* was apt to act as the spokesman for the rest, and the others when questioned tended simply to confirm his answers. Nevertheless, important differences in treatment, occupation, and observations on ethnic groups were apt to surface even under these circumstances. In the proper atmosphere, a single question from a sensitive interrogator to an individual *banyaga*, for example, "Why did you escape?" could spur him to pour out his life story in a lengthy response.

Slave Raiding

Banyaga were captured by attacking small native vessels—*prahus,* schooners, junks—and coastal villages. Balangingi and Iranun vessels carried several suits of local sails of the various ethnic groups whose coasts they visited, and in each locality they hoisted the particular sail used there by coastal traders.[4] Under this guise they attacked ill-armed trading boats commanded by Chinese, Arabs, and Buginese. Much of the raiding on coastal settlements was done with sailing canoes that carried up to twenty men. Before a descent was made on a village, the large *prahus* were hidden among the mangrove on an uninhabited stretch of coast, or remained out of sight offshore. The raiding canoes (*kakap, baroto, salisipan*) were used at dawn or dusk, with most of the crew lying concealed on the bottom of the canoe, leaving only two or three men disguised as Filipinos or Chinese to navigate. They picked off fishermen at river mouths, surprised *prahus* travelling to religious festivals at neighbouring villages, and rushed ashore to carry off unsuspecting individuals involved in strand procurement, salt manufacture, or cutting mangrove.* Women and children were taken in preference to men because they fetched higher prices in Sulu. People who attempted to flee were knocked down with a cudgel and if they resisted strenuously were killed. This mode of attack was used to great advantage by the Balangingi to seize coastal people throughout Southeast Asia.[5]

In 1838, statements were taken from the survivors of part of a Balangingi squadron destroyed off the Trengganu coast. The Balangingi had been away for more than seven months raiding in Philippine waters and on the east coast of Malaya, and had used the long canoes repeatedly in their seizures. Francisco Thomas stated:

> I reside at Cavite about two hours sail from ... Manilla, and about seven months since, myself, my father Juan Mateo, Nicholas, Marselo and my younger brother Augustino St Maria ... went out to fish in a sampan, and when after a considerable distance from the land we were attacked and captured by four Illanoun pirates. My father was shot through the head and killed by ... Succum.[6]

Essee, a Siamese woman: "I live at Patani and about half a month since myself, eight other women and a man named Boh Kay How were collecting shellfish on the beach when a number of pirates landed from three sampans and seized the whole party. Boy Kay How was killed by the pirates [and] the females were put on board six large ... prahus"; Omar, about seven years old: "I am a native of Calantan [Kelantan] and sometime ago ... myself and my father named Lebby Ahmad were fishing close to the beach when we were seized ... my father resisted and attempted to escape and in the struggle was killed by the pirates"; Yusof: "I am a native of ... Calantan. About fifteen days since, myself, father and another man called Pak Tigal went out to fish in a sampan when we were captured by the pirates...."; Ahmat: "I reside at Calantan on the east coast of the Malayan Peninsula. That about the third of May instant myself, Alli, Mohammed, and Moonien went out to fish, on reaching the mouth of the river Gunging which is situated a few hours from Calantan, I and my companions were seized by a number of Illanoon who were in a sampan...."[7]

---

* Tibercio Juan stated that in less than three months in 1834 four Balangingi *panco* seized more than 100 fishermen and *tripang* gatherers from the coasts of Masbate, Panay, Negros, and Cebu. Statement of Tibarcio Juan in Exp. 12, 4 Oct. 1836, PNA, Mindanao/Sulu 1803–1890; No.7, GCG a Secretario de Estado, 4 June 1806.

Coastal scouring accounted for the vast majority of seizures after 1800. One unfortunate Filipino was taken captive twice in this manner:

> I was fishing for *tripang* with nine others in a small canoe near Masbate Island when we were pursued by four Balangingi *baroto*.... One of my companions was killed when he resisted seizure ... I was taken along with 150 other captives to Pilas island and allotted. I fell to Candayo, one of the *nakodah.* After two months Candayo sold me at Jolo to the Muslim Siangu with whom I remained for eight years. Last year [1844] I accompanied my master to Palawan on a trading expedition, and while I was fishing two Balangingi *pancos* passed and seized me. I was taken immediately to Pilas and sold.[8]

Although such seizures were considered demographically insignificant at the provincial level by Colonial authorities by the 1830s, inshore raiding with shallow draught canoes made a tragic difference in the lives of individual families in isolated small settlements. The family-oriented nature of subsistence activity provided ample opportunities to seize children, and mothers who could not bear the pain of separation were known to have run to the seashore and begged to be taken with their children as *banyaga.*[9]

At the outset of their passage to the Sulu archipelago, captives were subjected to harsh treatment. When raiders plundered and sunk a *prahu* or seized people from the shore, the captured persons were separated from one another and taken aboard different vessels. Nah Soo Hong, "Lim Kiat was put on one boat and myself on another...": Francisco Thomas, "... myself and brother were put on board one boat and Nicholas and Marselo in others": Yusof, "my father and I were put into one boat.... Pak Tigal was on board a different one": Abdullah, "I was separated from my companions and taken onto one of the *prahus*...": Amat, "on reaching the piratical fleet, myself and companions were put in different boats...."[10] Once on board, they were stripped naked, a rattan ring was put around their necks, and some were tied down to the side of the *prahu.* Others were forced to lie immobile on the bottom of the *prahu* with their hands and feet bound with sharp rattan. A Kelantan Malay stated, "on reaching the piratical [*prahu*] ... my hands were put into a kind of stocks and a rattan collar around my neck...."[11] C.Z.Pieters recalled, "... when I came again to my senses I found that I was stripped naked and bound in a *prahu*.... The commander of the *prahu* in which I was caused me to be tied up by the hands, feet, and neck. The rope by which captives are tied by the neck is taken off in the daytime. At six o'clock in the evening, whether they are inclined to sleep or not, they must lie down and are bound by the feet, hands and neck to the deck of the *prahu,* and the rope by which their necks are confined remains within reach of the pirates who are keeping watch."[12]

In the first stages of the passage captives, particularly robust ones, remained tied up for weeks, even months. They were deliberately caned with a flat piece of bamboo on the elbows and knees and the muscles of the arms and legs so that they could not swim or run away.[13] Younger children were not fettered but caned. In his personal narrative, Ibanez Y. Garcia, a Spanish soldier, described how the Balangingi, compared the exploitation of the Spanish Government with their own social system, when punishing children: "I have seen them cane some boys for recollecting the memory of their parents, telling them at the same time, 'you should be content to be with us, since you will not have to pay the *tributo,* nor perform personal services'."[14] Captives were also ill-fed at this stage of the journey to further weaken their will to resist. Ideally, they were given just enough rice, sago, and water to survive. Ebenezer Edwards, a sailor from the brig *Sarah and Elizabeth,* said, "Our food consisted only of a little rice and water and the rice was generally spoiled and the rations so small that we never had enough of it." For the survivors of a Balangingi squadron destroyed off the Sarawak coast in 1862, nothing had hurt so much as the salt water they were forced to drink: "... they never gave us fresh, but mixed three parts of fresh water with four of salt, and all they gave us to eat was a handful of rice or sago twice a day".[15]

When sufficiently cowed, captured persons were put to the sweeps in gangs, and rowed in relays night and day.[16] There was no respite for them from the back-breaking ordeal when the Balangingi visited uninhabited islets to clean, repair, and provision the vessels:

> ... the sun came out and the storm subsided and we were able to anchor near an island ... for two days we were forced to gather firewood and haul water; as a consequence of this arduous work ... my hands bled and were affected with inflammation; there was no remedy except to bear the pain in silence.[17]

There was a real possibility of dying from the poor diet and rough treatment suffered during the period of captivity on board the raiding *prahu.* Whether a captive's health deteriorated depended on a number of other factors: the state of his physical condition before seizure; the size of the vessel he was placed on board, and the number of captives on it; the length of time spent lashed to the side of the vessel; and whether the vessel was able to touch at islands for any length of time where captives might rest and recuperate. A sixty-foot Balangingi *prahu* would carry between twenty and forty crew and occasionally as many as seventy captives. The victims were packed together, for weeks and even months on end, among the provisions stowed in its cramped bottom or on deck with no shelter from tropical heat and the deluge of rain squalls. Their strength ebbed away.[18] A number died on the voyages from the combined assaults of malnutrition, hard labour at the sweeps, and faecal-borne diseases. Si-Ayer related a chilling account of his passage in an Iranun *prahu* in 1847:

> ... the prisoners were all kept tied, until they showed no symptoms of attempting to escape; ... water and rice [were] given to us very sparingly.

Some died from hunger, some from being handcuffed, some from grief; they untied me after about a month. If prisoners were sick so they could not pull an oar they were thrown overboard.[19]

Juan Apolonio, who was seized by the Balangingi when very young, remembered that many captives had died at sea. Diomicio Francisco was among the 475 captives in thirty-six *prahus* who survived a voyage to Sulu; others had died from hunger or were drowned in passage.[20] The attrition was highest among Europeans who were far less inured to such hardship than Filipinos and Malays; the work at the oar, the continual struggle with the elements, infectious diseases, and a diet of seawater and unwashed sago was too much for most of them.[21] After 1850, dangers faced by the newly-captured came from two sides. Mortality among their ranks in the middle passage rose sharply because of the more frequent encounters by Balangingi with colonial war vessels. In such engagements, no quarter was expected by the Balangingi who, driven to the extremity of death, forced their captives to come up from below and sit on the deck side-by-side to form a human shield, *la muralla de sangre,* or wall of blood. Under these circumstances, Spanish naval officers calculated that to redeem four captives, they had to kill ten.[22] On the inward-bound voyage, captives were sometimes bartered out of necessity between flotillas or to coastal communities for foodstuffs. A seaman from Catanduanes related:

> ... on the following day the Iranun continued sailing towards Polillo where they seized several people, afterwards they rendezvoused at Daet with fourteen Balangingi *panco,* which accompanied them to an island at the edge of the Visayas where the captives were allotted. I was bartered to a Balangingi for a half a cavan of rice.[23]

A Cebuano silversmith stated:

> The Balangingi flotilla sailed towards Dumaguete and then crossed over to the Mindanao coast passing close to the port of Santa Maria, from there they sailed to Boalan where they exchanged some of the captives for rice before the vessels in the squadron separated for Balangingi and Tunkil.[24]

Soesa, a trader from Buntung, stated:"... the fleet belonged to Balangingi and left for that place after the *prahus* were overhauled on Buntung where I was bartered to a Buginese trader".[25]

Occasionally, captives managed to escape by jumping overboard. In 1868, Albert Bickmore, a professor of natural history, wrote in his journal:

> While I was at Kema two Malays appeared at the house of the officer with whom I was residing, and said they were natives of a small village on the Bay of Gorontalo; and that while they were fishing, they were captured by a fleet of [Balangingi] pirates, who soon after set out on their homeward voyage; ... while the fleet was passing Sangir, ... they succeeded in escaping by jumping overboard and swimming a long distance to the shore.[26]

According to one account,* the name of a town in the Cuyo islands, off the northeast coast of Palawan, originated in this way:"Lucbuan comes from the Cuyono word 'Lucbo' meaning 'jump'. Once, a moro ... boat came to that place and captured *indios* to be carried away as slaves. At the point where the old fort now stands, a captive jumped off the boat and escaped. The name Lucbuan was derived from that incident."[27] To deter captives from leaping overboard, the Balangingi had a supply of long barbed bamboo spears ready to throw on an instant's notice. They were capable of throwing one of these pronged spears accurately up to thirty yards, and captives hit by one of them were easily recaptured.†

It was far more common for captives to escape when a squadron touched at an island for some time: Dino, "when the pirates obtained water on Siloeang island, I ran away..."; Sodo, "I was always bound and made to row, but I managed to escape while drawing water on Siloeang island"; Salama, "I ran away while hauling water on Siloeang island";[28] Antonio Juan,

> ... the Balangingi set a course for Quinluban island to approach the Calamian group. But heavy seas and strong winds forced them to put in at Cabra island for shelter where they seized two people. After having been there for two days I fled to the mountainous part of the island and remained in hiding for a week until hunger forced me to return to the coast. I began to build a raft to sail to Quinluban. Several people accidentally stumbled upon me while I was at work on it but fled fearing I was a Moro. After much persuasion they realized I was not a Muslim and returned to help me finish it. These four people had been chased by the Moros and had to abandon their *baroto*, but reached the shore before the pirates could overtake them.[29]

Escape often meant leaving members of one's family behind. Maria Damiani, a fourteen-year-old, recalled with candour:

> I don't remember the year I was captured because I was very young. I had been travelling with my parents in a small sailboat when we were seized by pirates from several Moro *pancos*; my father had the good fortune to escape on an island the flotilla touched at, but we were taken to Tunkil.[30]

---

* Stories of captivity and escape from the "Moros" abound in local oral traditions.

† A Taosug *nakodah* identified one of these spears found on board an Iranun *prahu* from Tunku: "... his attention instantly fixed on an instrument, which we had mistaken for ... a 'fish gig' ... but which we were informed was for taking men! This instrument is bifurcate, with a sufficient spread between the points, which are barbed internally, to include the neck of a man; the weapon is thrown with almost unerring aim, so as to secure the victim by the neck, and jerking it back with a sharp motion, fixes him within the barbs, setting all opposition at defiance." Belcher, *Voyage of the Samarang,* vol.1, 252; see also the Balangingi raiding *prahu* in the Appendix.

The small islands of Bangka and Talisse at the northeastern tip of Celebes were the final place of call for all Balangingi fleets operating in the eastern archipelago before they began the last leg of the journey to Sulu. Here they took on water, repaired the *prahus,* and not infrequently divided their captives: "We were taken on board one of the *prahus* and bound to one another. At Bangka island my companions were allotted among the pirates and only I was retained to be taken to Balangingi."[31] Pieters stated:

> ... I had been bound for eighteen days and nights when we reached the island of Bangka. Off Likupang, the captives who were on board the ten prahus and who amounted to one hundred in number, were divided amongst the pirates. Amongst these captives were natives of Ternate, Tidore, Bouton, Banggai, Sangir, Makassar, and Gorontalo.[32]

Sometimes the distribution of the captives did not take place until after the fleet returned home. In 1833, Francisco Sacarias was seized between Cebu and Bohol by a fleet of eighteen Balangingi *prahus* under the command of Languyang: "On their return to Balangingi they divided the 180 captives who stood beside the men who seized them. An equal number were apportioned to each *prahu,* after which Languyang chose eight captives for himself."[33] Juan Pedro was seized two years later: "... the squadron crossed to Balangingi ... the distribution of the captives was as follows: 10 captives for the commander Tamsi; 5 captives to each *prahu;* 3 captives for each fighting man; and 2 captives for each four pound cannon loaned".[34]

The rules governing the division of the captives were complicated, and information regarding this matter is not altogether clear. According to Jansen, the Dutch resident of Menado, the normal procedure was for the captives to be divided amongst the raiders according to their rank and role. In the initial division of the captives on behalf of the members of the expedition, the commander received the largest number, as many as eight or ten. The *nakodah* of each *prahu* kept at least six of the best captives for himself. The *jurumudi* and *jurubatu* each received two captives. Each crew member received a captive, but distinctions were made between those whose principal task it was to fight and those who sailed the boat. The former were entitled to a larger number of captives than the latter, and they had to be of superior quality—younger, stronger, or women. *Banyaga* who accompanied their masters on expeditions or who were lent or hired out did not receive captives. As crew members their share in the captives reverted to their masters. If the number of captives was so small that after the *panglima* and *nakodah* had taken their share, there was not a sufficient number left to be divided among the *jurumudi, jurubatu,* and the crew, the ranking officers' share was decreased. The *panglima* and *nakodah* received one captive each or three captives together, and the remainder were divided among the members of the expedition; one captive becoming the property of two or three crew members.[35] The distribution of the captives frequently gave rise to altercations among the raiders, especially when more than one person claimed rights to a particular captive. The heads of villages from which the *prahus* originated received a captive for each *prahu* sent by their community.[36] When the *panglima* visited Jolo he was obliged to give the Sultan and the *datus* who fitted out the vessels a proportion of the captives. Languyang gave his patron, Datu Dacula, a minimum of eight captives every year, in addition to repaying him in captives for his support in warstores, and the formal consent to make the slave raid.[37]

The condition of a captive who survived the lengthy passage to Bangka materially improved once he had been allotted.[38] It was in the master's interest to see that he was fed, cared for, and watched over in the final stage of the voyage:

> As long as a new captive has no fixed master, he must each day serve a different person, by whom he is fed. As soon as he is appropriated by one of the pirates he is allowed to eat with the slave of his master, and if his owner is well disposed towards him he received a short baju and a small sarong.[39]

At the time of their disposal captives were apt to be given a new name: "... my master asked me what my name was and I told him it was Jumaat, on which he gave me that of Kantores".[40] While many took Samal names, others were given names associated with the place of their seizure or birth: a fisherman from Buntung, Makoboe, "... while fishing ... I was attacked near Makaboe";[41] a Chinese fisherman seized by the Iranun near Banjermasin was called Banjer;[42] and a Filipino from southern Luzon was named Albay. Pieters described the end of his passage with a slave raiding expedition, and entry into the Sulu world:

> From Bangka we proceeded to Balangingi. During the voyage we had to struggle with strong contrary winds and high seas for eight days. When we reached Balangingi our flag was hoisted and the relations of the pirates hastened on board. They asked us what country and place we belonged to. I answered that I was a native of Murang; they asked where that was and I replied that it lay between Kwandang and Gorontalo. As they seemed to think that Murang and Amurang were the same place, I explained to them that this was not the case, adding that Amurang was inhabited by subjects of the Company. They then asked if these people were Dutchmen, to which I answered that there was properly no distinction between subjects of the Company and Dutchmen.[43]

The Captivity

Many *banyaga* ultimately achieved a status and living standard that, though modest, was still an improvement over their previous social condition under colonial overlords who did not scruple to thrust their own subjects into bondage. Farm slaves often lived alone in separate huts in the fields. Ordinarily they possessed no furniture except a sleeping mat laid on the floor. What household objects they might have owned were mostly cooking utensils made of bamboo, wood, and clay. A *banyaga* who formed part of a *datu*'s retinue often occupied a separate section of his master's house:

> ... they have but one story and that amongst the better sort is divided into two parts. The outer part being hung with chintz or some other cloth and the floor covered with mats is chiefly appropriated to the master's use; whilst the inner part is occupied by the women and slaves.[44]

A minority were able to become wealthy; they maintained their own households in the principal towns living out their lives in a style similar to that of their masters.

The dress of *banyaga* varied with their status. The poorest were said to have gone about naked, some wore grass skirts, but it was far more common for a *banyaga* to have at least a Chinese jacket or *sarong* in coarse white cotton cloth.[45] In 1834, Siassi villagers were described as being "... almost in a state of nudity, except for a nankin shirt or a pair of loose trousers of the same fabric, cut off at the knees. The children were ... naked."[46] Hunt had observed earlier that coarse white and brown cotton cloth "was in universal wear among all classes".[47] Some *banyaga* in the capital, however, managed to make their clothes out of imported silk and satin. At Jolo it was difficult for Europeans to distinguish *banyaga* from Taosug:

> As a head dress, most of the Sulo men prefer the Publicat red handkerchief; a few only the fine Javanese handkerchief ... the middling classes and slaves are however partial to handkerchiefs of the most lively and shewy colours of the French and American patterns ... they also wear the China *baju*, full sleeves without buttons, either of rich gauzes, silk and sattens of all colours from China, or Europe and coast Chintzes of the largest and liveliest patterns; and some wear Manilla grass cloth. The lowest slave, in this respect, vies with the *datu* in splendour of apparel....[48]

Most *banyaga* could expect to have their clothing provided by their masters:

> Through the influence of this woman I was bought the same day by her husband Unkud for a lilla the weight of one picul. Immediately I received from my new master a pair of trousers, a Chinese *baju*, a sarong and a headkerchief.[49]

Status discrepancy was common in nineteenth-century Sulu. Some of these *banyaga*, who were wealthier than most Taosug commoners and even some aristocrats, owned mats, chests, fine clothes, a few brass utensils, weapons, and gongs. A *banyaga* of standing had a *prahu* and owned a few other slaves to do his trading.[50] Of the condition of *banyaga* in Jolo, Manuel de los Santos observed: "... those slaves who wish to marry can do so because there are many women. I have seen some of them bear arms. Others who were slaves formerly, now are wealthy and free"; Jose Ruedas stated, "there are many Christian captives in Jolo some of whom are happily married and wealthy...."[51]

Marriages were arranged for *banyaga* who were looked upon with favour by their masters. On slave marriages at Cotabato Forrest wrote: "Rajah Moodo bestows wives on the Bisayan soldiers in his fort, generally slaves from the same country."[52] Antonio Juan related the proposition that his Balangingi master put to him:

> I was very well treated throughout the period of my captivity so much so that my master tried to convince me to marry a female captive, stating that their society had neither the *tributo* nor personal services, nor could anyone order me about in the same manner as in the Christian villages.[53]

Banyaga who had been married in captivity and managed to escape tended to remain together afterwards:

> Lantana ... was no more than twenty-five years old. He had been born on Cuyo but was unable to recall his Christian name ... He professed the Muslim faith. He stated that his master had married him with another captive also *indio*, ... that the urging of this woman and the ill-treatment of his master had convinced him to escape.[54]

She stated:

> that her master compelled her to marry the slave Lantana ... that she wanted to be transported to her village where she had been married and had two sons, the elder one already had two children when she was seized. Since then she has learned nothing of her family. In regard to her new marriage, she had no qualms ... that if her first husband were still alive she would obtain another wife for him but she was determined not to be separated from the young man.[55]

While *banyaga* were allowed to marry with the consent of their common master, matches where the parties belonged to different masters were rare. The marriage of the *banyaga* of one master to the *banyaga* of another involved compensation, and disputes about such arrangements were a cause of enmity.[56]

Filipino men had to convert to Islam to marry Muslim women. Filipino women could avoid conversion, but could not practise their faith openly. Maria Damiani stated, "with the possible exception of not being able to pray and professing to be a Christian, like all the other female captives in Jolo I had total freedom".[57] Many women remained indifferent, embracing neither faith.[58] Although the Taosug expressly forbade their *banyaga* to practise Christianity, some Filipino men not only clung to their Catholic faith despite ostracism and intimidation but managed to worship in secrecy: "He didn't know the number of Christian captives in Jolo, but they greatly outnumber the Moros; those who refuse to give up their faith are mocked and threatened but they still continue to pray."[59] Adherence to Christianity was less difficult when a *banyaga*'s master was Chinese. "Sa Hua had treated him well ... and had allowed him to practise his religion, not caring whether he prayed or not."[60]

The Taosug ate chicken, eggs, fish, venison, carabao, and rice, but the ordinary diet of a *banyaga* was likely to comprise granulated sago, some rice, fruits and vegetables, with perhaps a small piece of salted fish, meat was rarely eaten. Filipino slaves manufactured chocolate, and Hunt noted that cocoa "has become the common beverage of all the classes". The generality of *banyaga* ate twice a day: "the poorer classes manage two meals a day when they can get it which on shore is generally the case, as there can be seldom any scarcity; and in comparison with the Malays, they may be said to be in affluent circumstances".[61] While *banyaga* on Sulu experienced occasional hunger they rarely starved. During famines they were not necessarily worse off than their masters: "He [the *banyaga,* Juan] is big, strong, patient, and has a good character.... during the recent scarcity of food he went without food for two or three days giving his shares to Mohamets' wives and said nothing about it...."[62]

Banyaga commonly suffered from skin rashes, gastro-intestinal infection, and strains of venereal disease:*

> Almost all the inhabitants are inflicted with cutaneous eruptions; the kurap or ringworm is almost a universal disease, and almost one man in twenty is afflicted with leprosy; some of them in a horrible degree ... the intermittent fever and ... dysentery at some seasons of the year are prevalent, but not considered dangerous ... many complain of what I considered to be ghonorea. The rich apply to the Chinese doctors for assistance, the poor have recourse to approved recipes ... consisting of simple vegetables.[63]

A sizeable number of *banyaga* died from sickness and disease, of which smallpox was the most dreaded. When Dalrymple arrived back in the Sulu archipelago in 1762, he found that a smallpox epidemic had killed more than twenty of the leading *datus* and introduced a famine.[64] In 1808, Jolo again was afflicted: "the smallpox raged so violently at Sulo, that most of the principal inhabitants fled from the capital to avoid the infection".[65] It was difficult for Taosug to control the spread of smallpox throughout the islands,

---

* One commander wrote: "We were not long at Sooloo before our people began to grow sick, most of their complaints indeed were venereals they caught here. In this place venereals are of a very stubborn nature, tis scarce in the power of medicine to eradicate them, numbers of our people from the long use of mercurial medicines were seized with fluxes [diarrhoea, dysentery] which few or none recovered.... the sick were sent ashore to a house the Sultan gave for an hospital but we soon lost our surgeon, a loss that was severely felt by us, as it was soon followed by the death of a number of the sick. Lieutenant Hornbuckle got a China surgeon to attend ... the sick, but ... he did them little good except keeping their sores clean, but he healed none. These sores are very common here among the natives as well as our people, ... and generally break out in the foot or ancle and require a long time in healing, we left several people in Madras hospital [because] of these sores they contracted at Sooloo." Andrew Duncan to President and Council, 21 Oct. 1773, IOL, P/341/39, p.734.

and inadequate containment permitted limited outbreaks to develop into large-scale epidemics. Hunt noticed evidence of this on Jolo:

> The smallpox commits as many ravages here as in any part of the world for the extent of its population. It is held in the greatest fear and dread, and whenever it breaks out the doors and windows of the houses are ordered to be closed up, no persons allowed to go in or its inhabitants to communicate with other inhabitants; if it rages extensively all business is at a stand and the people fly to the other islands. One half of the whole that get the infection die with it; innoculation or vaccination is totally unknown to them and its effects are aggravated by improper treatment.[66]

In addition there was also malaria and cholera to drive up the death rate in particular years. Between November 1863 and January 1864, more than 1,500 people died of cholera in the vicinity of Jolo alone.[67] The higher than average mortality among the slave class that resulted from outbreaks of smallpox, malaria, and cholera were usually offset by the continual stream of captives brought to Jolo by the Balangingi.

Despite the benign aspects of slavery as expressed by many *banyaga,* their ownership was absolute. Masters could at any time sell or barter their *banyaga.* Fear of separation—husbands from wives, parents from children—was always present. *Banyaga* were sold in periods of famine, when the master needed money, or considered them a liability because of old age or infirmity. It was the possibility of being sold to interior people in Borneo and Mindanao, rather than transfer *per se,* that terrified those of slave status:

> ... one of my own men tells me ... as long as the transfer takes place amongst the islands they do not care much but usually the people ... are carried off to distant parts for sale, in many cases for the purpose of being murdered [ritual sacrifice] if of the male sex....[68]

Isidoro Gabo, who had been seized by the Balangingi in 1852 and purchased by a Taosug as a farm slave, spoke movingly of his family of twenty years whom he was forced to desert out of fear of being sold to the interior of Mindanao in a famine period:

> ... In 1857 my master married me with another slave, the daughter of captives born on Jolo, named Abiera. She was a Muslim. I had four sons by this woman of whom two died. The other two boys were alive at the time of my escape. My oldest son Majid was eight years and the other boy Ensami was seven.... When I learned that my master Inoc planned to take me to Mindanao to be sold to hill people, I fled in hope of returning to Cuyo to see if my parents and ten brothers were still alive.[69]

Those first-generation *banyaga* who had been torn away from their home and families, and had experienced the hardships of the Balangingi traffic, had difficulty reconciling themselves to slave status. The initial social isolation created by differences in language, customs, and status exacerbated the loneliness and yearning for the lost past. Some never did find the "indispensable margin of social and psychological space" necessary to overcome the trauma of transition and settle down. They constantly reworked their past lives; the remembrance of their towns or villages, family and companions did not fade away.[70] One can feel in reading the statements of some of the fugitive *banyaga* the sense of desperation and their incredible determination to secure freedom and reknit the fabric of their family and community life. All such *banyaga* lived in expectation of that eventual return:

> The Spaniard had lived for fifteen years in the interior of Soulou, where his master treated him very well, and his only reason for escaping was an unconquerable yearning to behold his native country once again.[71]

By and large, however, it was in the early years of captivity that escape was attempted. The acceptance and incorporation of Tagalog and Visayan children into Taosug society was less difficult. Their cultural assimilation into Taosug and Samal households is understandable. For most children there was no hope of escape, and with the passage of time they forgot their parents, their former locality, and language.[72] As they became immersed in Taosug life, a complete change of identity occurred. Fugitive *banyaga* who had been seized as small children were often bewildered when asked if they recalled their name, age, and village:

> The second [one] could not remember his Christian name. He had no idea of his age or how long he had spent in captivity. He called himself Lantana and claimed to be a Muslim.[73]

The youth, Diego, "he appeared to be about twelve years old. It became apparent after several questions that he didn't know his place of birth, who his parents were, when he was seized, or his age. He only knew that he always had been a fisherman"; a fourteen-year-old boy, "he didn't know his real name but stated that he was called Combo. He knew that he had been seized from Cebu ... but that was all because he was taken when very young"; another boy, about fifteen years old, "he didn't know his Christian name. Here he was called Calagon, According to what he had heard, he was supposed to be a Christian from Surigao. Beyond this he could say nothing because he had lived in Jolo since his childhood."[74]

Family memories were often blurred and the old language lost. In 1876, a *banyaga* standing on the beach signalled the *Samar* by waving a handkerchief and was promptly picked up by the steamer's longboat:

> He stated that he was a Christian and a slave of Marajaji Tantig of Siassi ... that he had spent fifteen years in captivity ... that he was only a child at the time of his seizure and as a result cannot remember much about his past.... He

said he was called Pablo but could not recall his surname ... that his father's name was Isidor and his mother's Anadrea, Simbrea, or something like that ... that he had an uncle called Capitan Oran.[75]

Another captive:

... was ordered to make the sign of the cross, which he did in Spanish. He stated the names of the Gobernadorcillo and parish priest of his village ... according to the Visayan sailors on board the gunboat ... he speaks the dialect of Iloilo, but badly. They attribute this to his long captivity.[76]

Thousands of people chose to abandon their original culture, becoming "moros". The rate of ethnic redefinition among captives in Sulu is difficult to assess, but on an intergenerational basis it must have been rapid: "Murudong is a native of the Philippine islands, captured as a boy and brought up as a Sulu. Anjer is related to the first prisoner but is regarded as a pure Sulu."[77] By the mid-nineteenth century, the process of incorporation and cultural assimilation had fundamentally altered the development of the state and society in Sulu.

In the last part of this book, the concept of slavery in the Sulu Sultanate is broadened to include a range of possible statuses of acquired persons. Most extraordinary was the rate and scale of the incorporation of captives from across the Archipelago into Sulu society. Variables affecting the social mobility of the *banyaga* included the status of the acquiring master, the affective loyalty of the *banyaga,* the sexual status of the *banyaga,* and his/ her occupation in captivity. Responses to slave status in Sulu varied from resistance and repeated attempts at escape to acceptance and voluntary assimilation. Depending on their material and social success in captivity, *banyaga* were frequently accorded some measure of leadership and influence—as bureaucrats, traders, raiders, and as concubines.

The slave testimonies as a historical source provide the fullest, most balanced view of the fate of Southeast Asians who were wrenched from their villages and transported to Sulu, who lived out their lives in captivity, first as *banyaga,* and then as assimilated Taosug or Samal in the first or subsequent generations following captivity. An attempt at reconstructing the odyssey of the slaves of the Sulu Sultanate from these testimonies provides an inside look at the workings of the Sulu system and a rare view of the mechanisms of slave relationships in a non-Western society.

Conclusion

This book has attempted to examine the transformation of a maritime community in modern Southeast Asian History with special focus on social and cultural processes in the Sulu Sultanate as it was affected by European commercial and political expansion. By considering Sulu's development in a regional framework it has been possible to highlight such issues as: the role of external trade in the transformation of the state, the function of redistribution in establishing and maintaining the power of the aristocracy, the important role of "hinterlands" or inland areas in coastal networks of trade and exchange, the dependence of the state for its strength on seafaring populations (mercenary, ally, or dependent) to conduct warfare, and to exploit the resources of the sea, the processes responsible for accomplishing ethnicity among maritime peoples, and the role of servile institutions as the basis for the expansion and reproduction of the state.

The establishment of European and Asian commerce and capital at Sulu in the late eighteenth century on a hitherto unprecedented scale stimulated dramatic increases in commodity production, and demand for labour. Slave labour in the *tripang* and pearl fisheries helped to provide the products introduced into the external trade. Power was predicated on personal following. The competitive activities of ambitious *datus* forced the demand for additional labour up and swelled the flow of external trade.

By the beginning of the nineteenth century, the Jolo market offered British manufactured brassware, glassware, Chinese earthenware and ceramic, fine muslins, silk and satin garments, Spanish tobacco and wines, and opium from India. There was a constant increase not only in the variety but in the quality of these objects of trade. These luxury goods for personal adornment and pleasure and for the household were translated into power and prestige symbols by the aristocracy to form the material basis of their social superiority. It is in this sense that external trade became a vital element in the overall functioning of the Sulu social system.

More importantly, the political and commercial growth of the Sulu Sultanate was reflected in the enormous increase in war stores in the Jolo market at the end of the eighteenth century—lead, iron, shot, gunpowder, and cannon. The Taosug aimed at monopolizing control over the exchange and distribution of these goods which, with slaves, enabled the expansion of the Sultanate and domination of the regional trade network. The European munitions supplied by the external trade enabled coastal Taosug to advance their commercial interests in the intersocietal exchange network, to promote raiding on a large scale and keep the zone free of intruders and competitors.

It is important to emphasize again the inextricable role of slave production in the evolution of this trade-process system. The relationship between trade and slavery in Sulu was reciprocal. Power depended on control of persons (slaves and retainers), which in turn depended on disposable wealth to maintain and attract them. Escalating competition for wealth further fuelled the demand for manpower (more slaves and retainers).

By the dawn of the nineteenth century, slavery and slave-raiding were fundamental to the state. The Taosug aristocracy depended on them for its prosperity on the labour of slaves and sea raiders, who fished for *tripang*, secured pearls, and manned the fleets. Marauding became the exclusive vocation of the Samal speakers of Balangingi and other small islets, as they fused their activities with certain Iranun groups from the north coast of Jolo and Mindanao. Trade created the material and social conditions for the large-scale recruitment of slaves and the exploitation of dependent communities. At the same time, the labour of captive and tributary peoples provided the raw materials for expanding trade. More than anything else it was this source and application of labour that was to give Sulu its distinctive predatory character in the eyes of Europeans—past and present—as a "pirate and slave state".

The second half of the nineteenth century proved to be a critical turning-point in the history of the Sulu Sultanate, as it was in the history of the rest of the non-Western world. Everywhere challenges arose to confront the Sulu state's ability to survive. With increased cooperation among Western colonial navies and more effective use of steam vessels, the Sulu world began to shrink. The destruction of Balangingi and Jolo by the Spanish between 1846 and 1852 placed serious constraints on the ability of the Taosug to retain control over the Balangingi Samal, their principle source of slaves. The Western grooved cannon and gunpowder, which had first attracted the Samal to Jolo as clients and suppliers of captives, were now operating to drive them apart. There was a progressive fragmentation of Samal groups because of Spanish incursions and disruption of the Taosug economy. No longer could their swift fleets expect to find distant coasts unprotected and towns defenceless: the era of long-range slave-raiding in insular Southeast Asia was over.

The total collapse of the system only came with the concerted effort of Spain to end Sulu's autonomy. In the last three decades of the century, the trade was destroyed by the Spanish naval campaign to annihilate systematically all *prahu* shipping in the Sulu archipelago, and by the immigration of large numbers of Straits Chinese to Sulu. Taosug control over the regulation of external trade collapsed with drastic consequences. They were forced to curtail their commercial activities and become dependent on the merchant immigrants with contacts in Singapore. The traditional Taosug redistributive role was taken away, the economic network of the zone disintegrated, and the pattern of their lives was altered by the extinction of slavery. The demise of the trading and raiding system robbed Sulu of its former importance as a major commercial entrepot in the wider island economy and left it confronting severe internal social and economic problems at the beginning of the twentieth century.

J.C. van Leur was among the first to interpret the history of the maritime world from an indigenous perspective in which the sea-oriented populations, not the West, were the major actors in the historical processes of the region. He challenged the static categorizations of colonial history that presented the seventeenth-and eighteenth-century maritime states of Southeast Asia as closed and historically stagnant—in a very real sense, as a-historical. He sharply criticized colonial historians for their imbalance of perspective and confusion surrounding the historical phases and the historical reasons for the varying responses of these societies to the West. Under his lens of historical analysis, the interpretation of Asian elements of change and specific trends for the period as a whole were magnified and broadened. His treatment attempted to transcend the West's static conception of the Southeast Asian past to confront and understand the questions of change. He focused on the transformation of societies like Sulu in terms of their own history and interaction with the West in the early phases of European expansion.

Van Leur argued that it was meaningless to speak of this period of Indonesian history (the seventeenth and eighteenth centuries) as the history of the Dutch East Indies—an approach that could only be taken by disregarding the continuity in the economic significance and political autonomy of indigenous societies and cultures. It was clear to him that in this period the West was not yet economically or militarily dominant. He questioned how much further a revisionist history of the autonomous development of Southeast Asia could be pressed:

> There is a gradually ascending line, a curve throughout the eighteenth century, climbing more rapidly because of the infusion of a stronger trade from Europe in the second half of the century. This line keeps climbing over into the nineteenth century. When does it stop? Was it the turn of affairs in China that had changed the picture? Was it the increasing pressure of modern-capitalistic exports, and the stronger power of modern military apparatus that went to support the "peaceful trade" of Europe everywhere in Asia with threats of intervention.[1]

In less than two decades, Britain had established its authority in the Straits Settlements and had humbled Burma. The Dutch had returned to Java and asserted their hegemony over the island and its people. The period 1830–48 witnessed the expansion of French politico-religious activity in Vietnam. In the wake of the aggressive expansion of the West, it has been common to speak of the nineteenth-century history of the maritime states as a period of economic decline and chronic piracy associated with stagnation and decay. The documentary evidence on the Sulu Sultanate—a segmentary state patterned on a mosaic principle of ethnic segmentation and economic interdependence—constitutes a challenge to this stereotyped historiographical perspective. The power of the Southeast Asian maritime world represented by Aceh in the seventeenth century and Johor in the eighteenth century is continued in the Sulu Sultanate until the eve of the twentieth century.

Equally significant and indicative of the dynamism of non-Western societies is the flexibility of ethnicity. Historians of the region are indebted to Leach, Lehman, and Moerman for their pioneering work on the nature of ethnic identification among Southeast Asian uplanders.[2] Manifest in the work of all these anthropologists is a conscious effort to define the nature of social categories applied to ethnic groups in Southeast Asia across time. Their work has led to a more complete understanding of the nature of ethnicity and the processes involved in its "accomplishment". Historians of island Southeast Asia in particular have been generally inclined to accept "ethnicity" as a fixed premise.[3] Such formulation has hindered the necessary reappraisal of available evidence on the internal workings of non-Western societies. An outstanding example of this is the case of the Balangingi Samal. Before the beginning of the nineteenth century, the Balangingi Samal did not exist. Yet by the 1830s Balangingi Samal slave-raiding activities, which were an important component of the wider island economy of the Sulu Sultanate, had made them a group renowned and feared throughout Southeast Asia. From the point of view of Philippine history and the larger history of island Southeast Asia, it is important to understand the genesis of this particular ethnic group, to know that the infamous reputation Sulu acquired for slave-mongering in the nineteenth century is attributable to the activities of the Balangingi, an "emergent society" increasingly composed of Filipino captives and their descendants who were brought to the Sulu archipelago and, in many cases, assimilated within a single generation to become the predators of their own people.

Finally, the rise of Sulu as the dominant state in articulating the trade of the zone at the end of the eighteenth century conforms to the more general process of state formation and economic integration accelerated by external trade. The Sulu Sultanate's history parallels the evolution of independent states and stateless societies in Asia, Africa, and Meso America where global-local forces for change, including dynamic indigenous relations of kinship, economy, warfare, and polity are bound up in the general history of the emergence and transformation of these societies in the world beyond Europe.

Appendices

Appendix A

The Prahus of the Sulu Zone

The trading and raiding activities which forged the Sulu zone in the late eighteenth and nineteenth centuries were predicated on specialized craft. Three basic *prahu* types were associated with Iranun/Samal maritime activities: *lanong* (*joanga*), the large, heavily-armed Iranun vessel; *garay* (*panco* or *penjajap*) a raiding ship of lighter construction used by the Balangingi as their principal craft; and *salisipan* (*vinta, baroto,* or *kakap*), a canoe-like vessel with or without outriggers employed as an auxiliary craft for inshore raiding.

Boat-building was an art in the Sulu zone. The shell of Iranun and Samal vessels was built up from the keel (a hollowed-out log) without nails.[1] Fibre lashings were used to bind clinkered planks and ribs together to form the hull. Certain communities specialized in building *prahus* and shipwrights transmitted their techniques from one generation to the next. Forrest observed the construction of many *lanong* at Cotabato along the banks of the Pulangi river:

> In that part of the town ... live a few Chinese; but many Magindanao mechanics, vessel builders and merchants. They build their vessels of various dimensions, and employ them in trading from one part of the coast to the other; often in cruising amongst the (Bisayan) Philippine Islands, for slaves and plunder. They cruise also as far as the coast of Java, and the islands of Celebes and Borneo.... These vessels are always very long for the breath, and very broad for their draft of water.[2]

The Magindanao also constructed vessels on the coast of Sibuguey Bay in 1775: "Here [Sibuguey Bay] ... are built many stout vessels, good timber being in great plenty."[3]

By 1790 the centre of boat-building activity in the zone had shifted away from Cotabato to the Sulu archipelago. Basilan and nearby islands were especially rich in shipbuilding materials, and the Samal of Maluso became celebrated boat-builders.[4] Jolo island itself was fairly well supplied with timber, and Parang was the most noted place on the island for making *garay.*[5] The Samal diaspora of 1848–52 forced many boat-builders to move south and relocate on Tawi-Tawi. The transport of excellent hardwood timber from the forests to the bays for *prahu* manufacture was easy on this narrow island. Balimbing, Banaran, and Bilitan on Tawi-Tawi, and

---

[1] Garin, "Memoria sobre el archipelago de Jolo", p.196.

[2] Forrest, *Voyage to New Guinea,* p.184.

[3] Ibid., p.196.

[4] Statement of Mariano Sevilla in Exp. 12, 4 Oct. 1836, PNA, Mindanao/Sulu 1803–1890; Apuntes sobre la Isla de Basilan 1892, SJA, XIV-9, p.32; BH-PCL, vol.1, paper 160, no.1, Livingston, "Constabulary Monograph of the Province of Sulu", p.5.

[5] Statement of Marcelo Teafilo in Exp. 12, 4 Oct. 1836, PNA, Mindanao/Sulo 1803–1890; Van Hoevall, "De Zeerooverijen der Soeloerezen", p.102; BH-PCL, vol.6, paper 162, no.23, Christie, "The Moros of Sulu and Mindanao", p.38.

Sibutu island were highly reputed places for making large *prahus* in the second half of the nineteenth century.[6]

The water-colour sketches of Monleon done in 1890 of the vessels of the Sulu zone are based on models built by indigenous craftsmen that were brought back to Spain by members of scientific and naval expeditions throughout the nineteenth century. The sketches present a wealth of detail concerning the proportions, materials, construction, and type of ships employed by various ethnic groups that is lacking in the literature.

The Lanong

The *lanong* was made for long cruises and it was this ship which composed the flotillas that raided the Straits Settlements under the leadership of the Iranun of Tempasuk and Reteh. The length averaged 80–90 feet, and the hull breadth 20 feet amidship. A dug-out keel formed the lower hull, with sides built up of planks. The stern and bow were built up and overhung the keel. The *lanong* had one large mainsail forward and two tripod sheers that could be raised or lowered on a moment's notice. Much of the main interior was occupied by a fighting platform and cabin. The latter served as the *nakodah*'s quarters and a powder magazine. The vessel depicted carried 34 oars a side; double-banked and steered with two rudders. Armament consisted of a strong bulwark at the bow, mounting a long gun (6–24 pounder) as well as several swivel guns. Shields were fixed along the side of the platform, and many *lanong* carried a boarding bridge. The crew consisted of 150–200 men, with the warrior-sailors occupying the upper platform. A triangular flag of the commander was affixed to the stern. By 1830 the *lanong* had been replaced by the more swift, lightly armed Balangingi *garay*.

The Garay

The Balangingi *garay* was a beautifully built vessel of wood, bamboo, nipa, and rattan. The size of the largest *garay* was 80 feet in length, and the breadth of the beam was 20 feet with a projecting stage of about one foot along the sides. The *garay*, very sharp fore and aft with a great beam, and drew from three to five feet of water. The large beam enabled the vessel to carry an enormous rectangular sail on a tall, collapsible tripod mast of bamboo and move over reef-studded seas at better than ten knots. The *garay* was also oar propelled, and thirty to sixty oars were used on big vessels. The upper tier of rowers sat on the projecting stage. The hold of the *garay* was either open or decked with split cane from stem to stern. The deck of nibong palm was cut into lengths so that any part of it could be taken up. For armament a fixed gun was carried in a bulwark at the bow. The crew of the largest *garay* numbered upward of 100 men and the smallest 25–30 men. Because

[6] Diary of Leonard Wood, 6 Jan. 1906, Leonard Wood Papers, container 3; BH-PCL, vol.1, paper 160, no.1, Livingston, "Constabulary Monograph of the Province of Sulu", p.5; BH-PCL, vol.2, paper 161, no.11, Walker, "Report of the 53rd Census District" (Tawi-Tawi), p.38; Jansen, "Aanteekeningen omtrent Solok en de Solloksche Zeeroovers", p.220; Garin, "Memoria sobre el Archipelago de Jolo", p.196.

the *garay* sailed well and was light enough to be rowed swiftly, it possessed the manoeuvrability and striking power necessary for inshore raiding in the nineteenth century.

The Salisipan

The *salisipan* was an amphibian craft. It was a long, low, narrow, oar-propelled vessel that was easily hauled ashore. It was open, provided with an oar at the stern for steering, and the crew used either oars or sculls. The *salisipan* carried one mast with a single square sail. The largest were 30–35 feet long, and were manned from the crew of the *garay* to which the *salisipan* belonged. One could be sure that when a *salisipan* was encountered, a *garay* was not far off. In calm weather the Balangingi ran along the shore in *salisipan* or ascended small rivers, relying on their rapidity of movement. This craft proved a dangerous enemy for all coastal peoples of Southeast Asia.

Appendix B

List of China Trade Goods and Natural Products of Sulu That Comprised the Cargo of an Amoy Junk, *circa* 1776

		China Price (Spanish $)	Sulu Price (Spanish $)
Textiles			
5,000	Pieces Kompow, white strong linen	¾	1
500	Kangans, 25 in a bundle, called *gandangs,* per *gandang*	7	10
3,000	Pieces black *kowsongs*, a kind of nankeen, per piece	¾	1
200	Pieces of flowered silks	6	10
50	Piculs raw silk	400	600
Ceramic			
	One million of pieces China ware, consisting of small terenes and basins in nests, big and small, plates and basins with red edges for Mindanao, per hundred	1	2
Brass and Iron Manufacture			
200	*Quallis,* an iron thin pan, three foot diameter each	1 1	2 2
500	Nests of *Quallis,* three in a nest	4	8
100	Piculs of iron, in small pieces, line Bengal iron		
2,000	*Galangs*(salvers of brass) seven to a picul	40	70
Sugar candy, a quantity per picul		7	10

Besides tea, cutlery, and other hardware, brasswire, gongs, beads of all colors, like swan shot, and fireworks.

Note: Sensitive to local politics and the market situation, the value of these articles was liable to fluctuate, and Forrest's and Hunt's figures must be considered as relative estimates of the real value and volume of the commerce in China trade goods and natural products of Sulu between 1786 and 1840. The invoices readily reflect, however, the high profit margin of the trade current in the late 18th and 19th centuries, its volume in China goods per vessel, and the variety of imports.

Source: Forrest, *Voyage to New Guinea,* p.325.

List of the United Cargoes of China Trade Goods of 3 Junks (2 Amoy, 1 Iloilo) and a Pontin from Manila in 1814

		China Price (Spanish $)	Sulu Price (Spanish $)
Textiles			
1,000	Gandang Kompow, a broad strong white nankeen	¾ each	1 each
2,000	Gadang Kintai, a narrow cloth of different colors	¼ each	½ each
200	Gandang Kawong, a coarse nankeen	¾ each	1 each
100	Gandang Kangano, a narrow white coarse cloth	7 per gadang	10 per gadang
200	Pieces Hangankin silk	12	35
500	Pieces Baqua silk	—	4–5
250	Pieces Lia silk	—	8
500	Pieces Jawsay, in fine white cloth, flowered, etc.	—	8
500	Pieces Daso, with or without flowers	—	12
200	Pieces Pakan	—	—
100	Pieces Kongtoan	—	45
500	Bundles Tinasua, thread white and black	—	—
100	*Piculs* of raw silk	400	600

Ceramic			
5,000	Nests Kantow coarse china ware	—	—
2,000	Nests Chaichipchoon coarse china ware	—	—
2,000	Nests Chaituatow coarse china ware	—	—
2,000	Nests Pai Tuatow coarse china ware	—	—
2,000	Nests Quetuatow coarse china ware	—	—
2,000	Nests Wago chun coarse china ware	—	—
1,000	Nests Chaigo chun coarse china ware	—	—
2,000	Nests Twasewpua coarse china ware	—	—
2,000	Nests Teongseu coarse china ware	—	—
1,000	Nests Twachewa coarse china ware	—	—
10,000	Nests Tungsi coarse china ware	—	—
2,000	Nests Kimkikowchun coarse china ware	—	—

Brass and Iron Manufactures			
2,000	Pieces Sanghitean, quallies, pans of cast iron	1	2
500	Nests Sanghitean, quallies, three in a nest	1	2
500	Pieces Lisholaktia	—	—
500	Pieces Tihokpe	—	—
500	Piculs of China iron in small pieces	4	8
5,000	Galangs, brass salvers seven to a picul	40	70
	Tonqua(salasa) copper betel boxes	—	—
	Bitnang(salasa) white copper betel boxes	—	—
100	Tubs sugar candy second sort	7	10

Besides boxes of black tea, medicines, parangs, China cutlery and hardware, brass wire, gongs(Javanese gongs preferred), beads of all colors, China shoes, gold thread, China needles, sweet meats, services of glassware, dried fruits, chests and trunks, paper, and laquered ware.

Source: J. Hunt, "Some Particulars Relating to Sulo", pp.56–57.

Appendix C

A Translation of a Letter of Friendship, Protection and Commerce granted by the Sultan of Sulu to Captain Spiers, 1821

This is the seal and mark of faith, truth, honor and respect [seal] and hear from his highness Sultan Mahomed Allie Aldeen [Ali ud-Din] Sultan of Soloo, this favor is granted to Captain Spiers to certify to all his highness' subjects, that his highness has favoured him with his royal protection, friendship, and permission to trade to all those islands immediately under his highness' dominions. His highness also requests and orders, that all respect and protection should be offered to him in the same manner as has been done to him at Soloo. Should the Soloo people meet Captain Spiers whether out to sea or on any land it is his highness' order and request to recognize him immediately as their most particular friend, and aid, and assist him to the utmost of their power, in all necessaries of life and trade, and afford him all protection from injuries.

This certificate is sealed and delivered at the island of Soloo on Wednesday 3rd of Doolcaida Heijara 1237 corresponding to August of the Christian era 1821.

William Patton—Malay interpreter

Source: Lt. W. Spiers to Charles Livingston, 10 Apr. 1822, IOL, F/4/7/4, no. 19495, 14.

Appendix D

A Comparative List of Textile Imports to Sulu, 1761–1835

Extracts from:

Dalrymple's order of goods—1761	Pieces	Hunt's estimated annual consumption 1814	Pieces	Ward's List— potential consumption of American manufactures 1835	Pieces
Muslins, doreas, fine-checked	420	Muslins, doreas, plain, flowered-striped	500		
Madras chintz	200	Madras chintz: red ground large flowers	400	red cotton cloth	1,000
Long blue cloth	800	blue cloth—gd.quality	2,000		
Surat cloth(baftas)	200	white baftas—medium quality	4,000	fine white cotton cloth	8,000
		coarse Patna chintz	4,000	coarse cotton cloth	4,000
		Cuddalore coarse chintz	2,000	coarse white cotton cloth	10,000
Coromandel cloth (moores fine bleached)	200	moores blue and white cloth	20		
Metchlipatan chintz	200	blue Madras salampores	2,000	cotton shawls	500
Flowered betaclas	40	bleached salampores	4,000	Pulicat cloth	500
Striped betaclas	40	Trimularampathan chintz	1,000	red cloth	100
Long cloth—medium quality	200	Cuddalore small palampores	1,000	figured muslins	100

Extracts from:

Dalrymple's order of goods—1761	Pieces	Hunt's estimated annual consumption 1814	Pieces	Ward's List—potential consumption of American manufactures 1835	Pieces
Long cloth—ordinary quality(unspecified)		Cuddalore large palampores	1,000	scarlet cloth	20
		Madras fine palampores	100	silk cloth	1,000
		Madras Camboys red	200	scarlet silk	30
		Madras Tanjams	200	blue figured silk	50
		Madras fine long cloth	50		
		Europe chintz	500		
		Pulicat fine red handkerchiefs	1,000		
		Madras handkerchiefs	1,000		
		Ventepollam handkerchiefs —fine and coarse quality	2,000		
		Java handkerchiefs—fine quality	100		
		embossed cloth	20		
		embossed aurora cloth	20		
		embossed broadcloth	6		
		blue succatoons fine quality	10		

Source: "List of Products of Sulu and Its Immediate Dependencies", in "Memoir of the Sooloogannan Dominions and Commerce", 26 Feb. 1761, PRO, Egremont Papers, 30/4/20/1; "A List of the Annual Consumption of Sulo and Its Dependencies of European and Indian Articles", in Hunt, "Some Particulars Relating to Sulo", pp.46–47; and a list entitled "Goods for Sooloo Market", Ms. included with the log of the ship *Allbree*, 656/1833A, Peabody Museum, Salem.

Appendix E

A Letter Soliciting Trade between the United States and Sulu

To Capt. G.E. Ward
  Navigator of the Spanish Brig Leonidas

[Seal]

Sir,
  I herewith inform you that having consulted with the Sultan and chief Datoos, I find it is the wish of all as well as your humble servant to establish a commercial intercourse Between [Sulu] and the United States of America which I believe will be equally Beneficiall to both parties and as you cannot enter into any contract without the consent of your Gov.^{mt} I am requested to inform you that it is the General wish of all the chief men of Soloo that you return here with a cargo of American produce according to the enclosed list which I am authorized to State will meet with a ready Sale to the extent of fourty or fifty Thousand dollars. Further that you shall have every privelege and protection while in our Port That the most favoured enjoy. Also that if your Govern.^{t} will give you power to form a treaty with us on equitable terms that we Should be much pleased thereat. For we are well acquainted with the Glory that the Americans have gained in their Struggles with other Nations.
  Wishing you a safe and speedy return to the Land of the Brave and the home and embraces of your friends.

I remain your H^{bl} Servant
D' Amilbahar

[Seal]

Soloo —
P.S. We Trust to see you again in eight or nine months with a Cargo that will pay you
  a handsome Profit.

Yours
D' Amilbahar

[Seal]

Source: Papers of William D. Waters, Peabody Museum, Salem.

Appendix F

The Manila-Jolo Trade, 1786–1830

I have developed this statistical series from the *estados* for the port of Manila. These annual records, which contain detailed data on European ships, Chinese junks, and native vessels entering and leaving Manila harbour, were sent to Spain to provide information to the Crown on the current state of the Philippine economy. Recordkeepers in Manila noted the type of sailing craft, its point of origin, the volume and value of the products imported or exported by the vessels, and its destination. There are difficulties involved in the use of the *estados* to establish an index of commercial activity between Manila and Jolo. Besides chronological gaps in the series, the data on the number of vessels leaving Manila for Sulu are not always reliable. In some instances their arrival date from the Sultanate has been recorded but their departure date from Manila in the previous year was not, and vice versa. The names of vessels can cause considerable confusion. Captains provide an abbreviated version of the vessel's name on one voyage and used the actual name at another time or an alias. As a result, the researcher can be misled into exaggerating the number of different vessels that participated in the trade in a particular period. When possible I have noted a vessel's alias with the designation (a). Similarly, when only information on the type of indigenous craft originating in Jolo was supplied (*vinta, panco, pontin*) without the *nakodah*'s name the same problem arises. In addition to the *estados*, other trade related statistics, particularly the *almojarifazgo,* the import-export tax, contain precise information on the quantity and ownership of cargoes. All trade data used in this series are from documents in the AGI. See 1786–1787, Filipinas 976; 1792, Ultramar 659; 1793, Filipinas 502, 977; 1794–1795, Filipinas, 977; 1796, Ultramar 658, Filipinas 977; 1797, Ultramar 658; 1798, Ultramar 658, Filipinas 978; 1802, Ultramar 621, 658; Ultramar 587; 1806–1807, Filipinas 506, Ultramar 587, 682; 1808–1809, Filipinas 506; 1810, Filipinas 506, Ultramar 661; 1811–1812, Filipinas 979, Ultramar 661; 1814, Ultramar 591; 1815, Ultramar 592; 1817–1818, Filipinas 511; 1820–1821, Filipinas 806; 1823, Ultramar 624; 1825, Ultramar 625, Filipinas 811; 1826, Filipinas 811, 814; 1827, Filipinas 814; 1828, Ultramar 625; 1829, Ultramar 625, 664, Filipinas 818; 1830, Filipinas 818.

Appendix F (cont.)

VESSEL/MASTER	DEPARTURE	ARRIVAL	DESTINATION	EXPORT CARGO	VALUE (Pesos)	IMPORT CARGO	VALUE (Pesos)
Panco, *Binta*	Jolo, 1786	Manila, 1786	Manila				8,030
Panco, *Binta*	Jolo, 1787	Manila, 1787	Manila				8,306
Panco, *Labodin*	Manila, 11 Dec. 1792		Jolo	77 quintales of sugar, 25 quintales biscuits	510		
Panco, *Sampaytay*	Manila, 17 Dec. 1792		Jolo	30 quintales of sugar, 20 quintales biscuits	250		
Chinese Pontin, *Nuestra Senora de la Soterrana*	Manila, 22 Dec. 1792		Jolo	206 quintales of salt, 8000 bricks	460		
Panco	Manila, 10 Feb. 1793		Jolo	275 quintales of sugar	687		
Panco, *Guim Pon-am*	Manila, 19 Feb. 1793		Jolo	261 quintales of sugar, 25 quintales biscuits, 50 wooden boxes	940		
Spanish galiot, *Animas*	Manila, 29 Apr. 1793		Jolo	275 quintales of rice, 875 quintales sugar	2,337		
Panco, *Sampaytay*	Manila, 16 Dec. 1793		Jolo	90 piculs of rice, 37 piculs of sugar	204		
Panco, *Coypunman*	Manila, 16 Dec. 1793		Jolo	190 piculs or rice, 189 piculs of sugar	926		
Panco, *Binta*	Manila, 30 Dec. 1793		Kuran (East coast of Borneo)			13 piculs of sugar	92
Spanish Brigantine, *Aventurera*	Manila, 22 Jan. 1794		Jolo	200 piculs of rice	229		
Spanish Frigate, *Dorado*	Manila, 18 Feb. 1794		Brunei	1000 piculs of rice, 400 piculs of sugar, 1000 cavans salt	3,095		3,095
Spanish ship, *Constante*	Manila, 19 Feb. 1794		Jolo	200 piculs rice, 2000 cavans unhusked rice, 20 piculs sugar, 200 cavans salt	880		
Spanish ship, *Constante*		Manila, 23 Aug. 1795	Jolo			Canton goods(natural produce of Jolo)	7,615
Spanish Frigate, *Dorado*		Manila, 2 Oct. 1795	Brunei			Canton goods	41,709

Appendix F (cont.)

VESSEL/MASTER	DEPARTURE	ARRIVAL	DESTINATION	EXPORT CARGO	VALUE (Pesos)	IMPORT CARGO	VALUE (Pesos)
Panco, *Salamat*	Manila, 18 Nov.1795		Jolo	43 piculs sugar, 200 assorted chinese manufactures	243	Canton goods	7,087
Chinese Panco, *Quim Fiang*	Manila, 16 Feb. 1796	Manila, 7 Oct. 1795	Jolo	350 piculs sugar, 20 piculs rice	1,609	Canton goods	19,409
Spanish Frigate, *Concepcion*		Manila, 18 Aug. 1796	Jolo			Canton goods	32,352
Spanish Brigantine, *Santa Cruz*		Manila, 19 Aug. 1796	Jolo			Canton goods	6,227
Spanish galiot, *Nuestra Santa del Refugio*		Manila, 17 Sept. 1796	Jolo			Canton goods	1,407
Portuguese Brigantine, *Maria*		Manila, 8 Oct. 1796	Jolo			European manufactures and Bengal commodities	7,902
Panco, *Caiponan* (Caypunnan)	Manila, 5 Jan. 1797	Manila, Oct. 1796	Jolo	50 piculs of sugar, 15 piculs of sulphur	1,275	Canton goods	15,799
Spanish Brigantine, *Santa Cruz*		Manila, 21 July 1797	Jolo			Canton goods	5,975
Spanish vessel, *La Paz*		Manila, 26 Aug. 1797	Jolo			Canton goods	2,685
Spanish Frigate, *Concepcion*		Manila, 10 Oct. 1797	Jolo			Canton goods	11,731
Panco, *Tinquin*		Manila, 10 Oct. 1797	Jolo			Canton goods	16,238
Panco, *Guing Fin*	Manila, 19 Nov. 1798		Jolo	119 piculs of sugar, 19 quintales indigo	1,205		
Panco, *Guajap*	Manila, 21 Dec. 1798	Manila, 8 July 1798	Jolo	90 piculs of sugar	290	Canton goods	17,120
Panco, *Sing Yap Di*	Manila, 22 Dec. 1798	Manila, 8 Aug. 1798	Jolo	20 piculs of sugar	100	Canton goods	4,165
Junk, *Sin Sin Tay*	Manila, 20 Dec. 1798		Jolo	13 piculs of sugar	65		
Spanish schooner, *San Jose*	Manila, 1798		Jolo(seized in environs of Tawi-Tawi)				
Portuguese Schooner, *Nuestra Senorade Rosario*	Manila, 27 Jan. 1802		Jolo	20 piculs of sugar, 270 leather hides	179		

Appendix F (*cont.*)

VESSEL/MASTER	DEPARTURE	ARRIVAL	DESTINATION	EXPORT CARGO	VALUE (Pesos)	IMPORT CARGO	VALUE (Pesos)
Portuguese Brig	Manila, 28 Apr. 1802	Manila, 30 Sept. 1802	Jolo	980 piculs of sugar	6,860	European manufactures	2,873
Portuguese Frigate, *Sultana*	Manila, 1802		Jolo				
Portuguese Frigate, *Sultan de Jolo*		Manila, 23 July 1802	Jolo			European manufactures	4,955
Spanish Pontin, *San Rafael el Arrogante*		Manila, 23 Sept. 1805				Bengal piece goods, several thousand assorted cloth items, Canton goods, sea cucumber, birds' nest, mother of pearl, wax, camphor, sharks' fin, cacao	20,869
Portuguese Packetboat, *Buen Amigo*	Manila, 31 Jan. 1807	Manila, 16 July 1807	Jolo	200 piculs of sugar	1,400	Canton goods, 9 kinds of sea-cucumber, 166 piculs; pearlshell, 453 piculs; 3 kinds of birds' nest, 27 piculs; wax, 72 piculs, etc.	18,068
Junk, *Jap Son*(a) *San Jose*		Manila, 3 July 1808	Jolo			Wax, sea-cucumber, camphor, cacao, rattans	13,850
Junk, *Sin Sin Juat*		Manila, 25 Aug. 1808	Jolo			Small quantity of Indian cotton stuffs, crystal decanters, earthenware, cured hams from Europe, candlewicks, wax, pepper, birds' nest sharks' fin, sea-cucumber—13 kinds, pearl shell, cinnamon, cacao, sago, rattans	14,620
Panco, *San Fernando*		Manila, 12 Sept. 1808	Jolo			Nests, camphor, seacucumber, wax, pepper, cinnamon, pearl shell, coffee, cloves, cacao	10,145
Panco, *San Carlos*		Manila, 12 Sept. 1808	Jolo			Sea-cucumber, 24 kinds; birds' nest, sharks' fin, pepper, wax, pearl shell	2,012

Appendix F (*cont.*)

VESSEL/MASTER	DEPARTURE	ARRIVAL	DESTINATION	EXPORT CARGO	VALUE (Pesos)	IMPORT CARGO	VALUE (Pesos)
Spanish galiot, *San Antonio*		Manila, 19 Sept. 1808	Jolo			Sea-cucumber, 11 kinds; birds' nest, sharks' fin, cinnamon, cacao, pearl shell	2,030
Spanish Pontin, *Vigilante*	Manila, 21 Apr. 1809		Jolo	3 piculs of sugar, 100 jars of rusk, 100 boxes assorted merchandise	1,012		
Junk, *Sin Sin Juat*		Manila, 1 Mar. 1810	Jolo			Sea-cucumber, sharks' fin, birds' nest, pearl shell, sweets, chocolate, tea, fruit preserves, cinnamon, wax, camphor, cacao, rattans, Chinese notebooks	3,111
Spanish Pontin, *San Josef*	Manila, 3 Mar. 1810		Jolo	100 piculs of sugar, 5 piculs flour, 6 quintales indigo, 60 jars rusks	384		
Spanish Frigate, *Union*		Manila, 4 Sept. 1810	Jolo			Bengal piece goods, 17 different types of fabric—several thousand pieces; cast iron frying pans, earthenware, tea, camphor, wax, birds' nest, sea-cucumber	14,226
Spanish Brigantine, *Modesto*		Manila, 25 Oct. 1810	Jolo			Bengal piece goods, 13 different types of fabric, nests, pearl shell, wax, sea-cucumber, camphor	3,464
Spanish Brigantine, *San Luis*	Manila, 12 Mar. 1811		Jolo	2 piculs rice, 11 jars of rusk	15		
Spanish Pontin, *San Josef*	Manila, 6 Apr. 1811		Jolo	20 piculs of sugar, 9 jars of rusk	52		

Appendix F (cont.)

VESSEL/MASTER	DEPARTURE	ARRIVAL	DESTINATION	EXPORT CARGO	VALUE (Pesos)	IMPORT CARGO	VALUE (Pesos)
Spanish Packetboat, *Victoria*	Manila, 6 Apr. 1811		Jolo				
Chinese Junk	Manila, 27 Jan. 1812		Jolo	53 ½ piculs of sugar, 44 jars of rusk	151		
Junk, *Guing Fin Le* Capt. Lim chong qua	Manila, 27 Jan. 1812		Jolo	52 piculs of sugar, earthenware, 430 ploughs, potatoes, Bengal cloth, 1 ½ piculs sugar, silk, 40 jars rusk	1,427		6,526
Pontin, *San Josef* Capt. Thomas Acong	Manila, 18 Mar. 1812	Manila, 11 Mar. 1812	Jolo		14,101		2,606
Spanish Brigantine, *Jesus, Maria, Y Joseph*, Capt. Miguel Talero	Manila, 7 Apr. 1812		Jolo	Bengal commodities & assorted items	8,833		
Spanish Packetboat, *Nuestra Senora de la Victoria* Capt. Alanzo Blanco	Manila, 13 Apr. 1812		Jolo	Bengal commodities & assorted items	7,198		
Spanish Pontin, *Nuestra Senora del Carmen*		Manila, 14 Sept. 1814	Jolo			Wax, sea-cucumber, camphor, pearl shell, birds' nest, 1 picul of flour, cacao, rattans, sewing scissors(250)	5,900
Spanish Pontin, *Neustra Senora del Carmen*	Manila, 5 Apr. 1815	Manila, 19 Oct. 1815	Mindanao and Jolo	32 piculs of sugar, 23 jars foodstuffs, 35 pieces malabar cloth, 720 plough blades	345	Birds' nest, wax, rattans, sharks' fin, sea-cucumber, coloured paper, cacao, medicines	3,805
Spanish Pontin, *Vigilante*	Manila, 5 Apr. 1815	Manila, 19 Oct. 1815	Jolo	52 piculs of sugar, 92 pieces malabar cloth	240	Pearl shell, sea-cucumber, birds' nest, wax, sharks' fin, rattans, pearls for medicinal use, cacao, cloves, sewing scissors, Bengal piece goods, camphor	

Appendix F (*cont.*)

VESSEL/MASTER	DEPARTURE	ARRIVAL	DESTINATION	EXPORT CARGO	VALUE (Pesos)	IMPORT CARGO	VALUE (Pesos)
Spanish Pontin, *Nuestra Senora del Carmen*	Manila, 5 Apr. 1817	Manila, 3 Oct. 1817	Jolo	15 piculs of sugar, 8 quintales indigo, 202 jars of bread, 950 small ploughs, 114 pieces Bengal cloth	621	Bengal piece goods, Ylocos cloth, sea-cucumber, mother of pearl, wax, birds' nest, sharks' fin, iron, 20 piculs; rattans, cacao, camphor	10, 807
Spanish Pontin, *San Pasqual*	Manila, 28 Apr. 1817	Manila, 22 Sept. 1817	Jolo	300 piculs rice, 1 ½ piculs dried beef, 15 piculs sugar, 338 jars bread, 100 small ploughs, 960 pieces of Bengal cloth	1,830	Bengal piece goods, mother of pearl shell, birds' nest, camphor, sharks' fin, cinnamon, iron bars, 71 piculs, mandarin oranges, wax, cacao, copper jars, spitroons, gold leaf, 50 rolls	10,055
Spanish Brigantine, *Vigilante*		Manila, 22 Sept. 1817	Jolo		1,199	Bengal piece goods, 300 piculs of iron, sea-cucumber, birds' nest, wax, assorted manufactured hardware	4,682
Spanish Brigantine, *San Jose Las Animas*	Manila, 3 May 1818		Jolo	406 pieces of Bengal cloth, 600 ploughs			
Panco, *Juat*	Manila, 22 Aug. 1818		Jolo	2 piculs of sugar, 9 piculs rice, Bengal cloth, 280 small ploughs, 50 jars rusk	192	Birds' nest, sharks' fin, wax, sea-cucumber, mother of pearl, cacao, camphor, 12 Lorikeet (small parrot)	4,773
Panco, *Binta*	Manila, 4 Nov. 1818	Manila, 5 Jun. 1818	Bulungan (est coast of Borneo)	12 piculs of sugar, 1130 kitchen utensils, 420 axes, Bengal cloth	343	Wax, birds' nest, sea-cucumber, pearl shell, camphor, gold, diamonds	6,236
Panco, *Chan*	Manila, 27 Nov. 1818	Manila, 31 Aug. 1818	Jolo	200 small ploughs, 100 large jars rusk	156	Sharks' fin, birds' nest, mother of pearl, sea-cucumber, cacao, cinnamon, 12 Lorikeet	4,757

Appendix F (*cont.*)

VESSEL/MASTER	DEPARTURE	ARRIVAL	DESTINATION	EXPORT CARGO	VALUE (Pesos)	IMPORT CARGO	VALUE (Pesos)
Pontin, *Nuestra de La Concepcion*	Manila, 21 Dec. 1818		Jolo	28 piculs of sugar, 15 piculs Chinese noodle, 7 quintales indigo, 80 ploughs, 300 jars rusk	530		
Panco, *Chan*	Manila, 27 Nov. 1818	Manila, 31 Aug. 1818		200 small ploughs, 100 large jars of biscuits	156	Sharks' fin, wax, birds' nest, mother of pearl, sea-cucumber, cacao, cinnamon, lorikeets	4,757
Spanish Brigantine, *San Jose Las Animas*	Manila, 18 Apr. 1820	Manila, 29 Nov. 1820	Jolo	60 piculs of sugar, 20 leather hides, 174 large jars of rusks, Bengal piece goods, Ilocos cloth	1,684	Bengal piece goods (17 kinds), Canton goods	16,140
Spanish Pontin, *Nuestra Senora del Rosario*	Manila, 27 Apr. 1820	Manila, 23 Dec. 1820	Jolo	200 piculs of rice, 10 piculs of sugar, 12 jars of cocoanut oil, 170 jars of rusks(value 519 pesos) foreign trade goods comprising cargo valued at 7038 pesos	7,557	Mother of pearl shell(731 piculs), cinnamon, sea-cucumber(549 piculs), pepper, birds' nest, sharks' fin, camphor	
Panco, *Cachuruma*	Manila, Nov.Dec.1820?	Manila, 22 Oct. 1820	Bulungan			Sea-cucumber, birds' nest, wax, pearl shell, camphor, pearls	3,801
Panco, *Hong Hong*	"		"				
Panco, *Conting*	"		"				
Panchalang	"		"				
Panchalang	"		"				
Pontin, *Macassar*		Manila, 11 Apr. 1821	"			Sea-cucumber, nests, pepper, camphor, sharks' fin, gold	19,303
Spanish Brigantine, *San Josef*		Manila, 9 May 1821	Jolo			Pearl shell, sharks' fin, sea-cucumber, cacao	885
Spanish Brigantine, *Providencia*		Manila, 5 Oct. 1821	Mindanao			Sea-cucumber, sharks' fin, mother of pearl, precious shells, wax	10,956

Appendix F (*cont.*)

VESSEL/MASTER	DEPARTURE	ARRIVAL	DESTINATION	EXPORT CARGO	VALUE (Pesos)	IMPORT CARGO	VALUE (Pesos)
Spanish Pontin, *Nuestra Senora del Rosario*	Manila, 18 Mar. 1821	Manila, 9 Oct. 1821	Jolo	381 cavanes of rice, 700 cavanes of unhusked rice, Malabar cloth, 10 jars cocoanut oil, 276 jars of rusks	1,747	Bengal cloth, mother of pearl (664 piculs), sea-cucumber (739 piculs), nests, wax, cinnamon, camphor, cacao	35,242
Spanish Brigantine, *San Jose*	Manila, 18 Mar. 1821	Manila, 28 Oct. 1821	Jolo	26 piculs of sugar, 190 cavanes of rice, 150 small ploughs, 129 jars of rusks	1,334	Mother of pearl (552 piculs), sharks' fin, sea-cucumber (764 piculs), nests, wax, camphor	33,103
Spanish Brigantine, *San Josef*	Manila, 24 Mar. 1823	Manila, 8 Aug. 1823	Jolo	80 ploughs, 104 jars of rusks, foreign merchandise	8,865	Assorted foodstuffs and trinkets	265
Spanish Brigantine, *Nuestra Senora de los Dolores*		Manila, 30 Sept. 1823	Zamboanga			Assorted hardwares, small toys	1,337
Spanish Brigantine, *San Josef*		Manila, 11 Oct. 1823	Jolo			Assorted manufactured hardware, foodstuffs	9,627
Spanish Brigantine, *San Jose*		Manila, 11 Oct. 1823	Jolo			Wax, assorted manufactured hardware, foodstuffs	31,372
Spanish Pontin, *Nuestra Senora del Rosario*		Manila, 18 Nov. 1823	Jolo			Wax, mother of pearl, foodstuffs, tradegoods	14,655
Spanish Brigantine, *Nuestra Senora del Rosario*	Manila, 24 Mar. 1823	Manila, 29 Nov. 1823	Jolo	14 piculs of sugar, 250 jars of rusks, 14 jars of oil & lard, foreign merchandise	9,996	Wax, assorted tradegoods, foodstuffs.	5,505
Spanish Frigate, *Nuestra Senora de la Soledad*	Manila, 24 Mar. 1823	Manila, 17 Oct. 1823	Jolo	310 piculs of sugar, 320 pieces of Malabar cloth, 248 jars of rusks, 20 jars of oil & lard, foreign merchandise	12,965	Birds' nest, pearl shell, wax, sharks' fin, sea-cucumber, cinnamon, pepper, camphor	15,294
Spanish Pontin, *San Antonio de Padua*	Manila, 3 May 1823	Manila, 12 Dec. 1823	Jolo	25 piculs of sugar, 392 pieces of Malabar cloth, 30 pieces of Ilocos cloth, 125 Jars of rusks, foreign merchandise	10,591	Sea-cucumber, nests, sharks' fin, cinnamon, wax, mother of pearl, tradegoods	9,252

Appendix F (cont.)

VESSEL/MASTER	DEPARTURE	ARRIVAL	DESTINATION	EXPORT CARGO	VALUE (Pesos)	IMPORT CARGO	VALUE (Pesos)
Pontin, *Bulungan* Spanish Brigantine	Manila, 1823	Manila, 1823	Bulungan			Sea-cucumber, sharks' fin, nests, pepper, wax, camphor, mother of pearl	16,160
Spanish Brigantine, *Amador de Manila*		Manila, 9 May 1825	Jolo			Sea-cucumber, nests mother of pearl, wax, sharks' fin	7,049
Spanish Brigantine, *San Antonio de Padua*		Manila, 10 Oct. 1825	Jolo			Sea-cucumber, nests, shell, sharks' fin	5,047
Spanish Pontin, *San Jose*	Manila, 3 Jan. 1825	Manila, 24 Oct. 1825	Jolo	8½ piculs of Lacsa (vermicelli), Bengal cloth, 50 cured leather hides, foreign merchandise	7,362	Sea-cucumber, nests, shells, mother of pearl, camphor, cinnamon, cow-hides, rattans, cacao, pepper, shellfish, tradegoods	15,432
Small junk, *Quin Son Guan*	Manila, 11 Feb. 1825			21½ piculs of Chinese noodle, 550 cavanes of rice, 287 jars of rusk	2,856		
Spanish Brigantine, *San Antonio de Padua*		Manila, 2 Nov. 1824	Jolo			Sea-cucumber, nests, shells, mother of pearl, wax, camphor, sharks' fin, cacao, pearls	15,792
Spanish Pontin, *San Gabriel*	Manila, 31 Dec. 1825	Manila, 20 June 1826	Jolo	Bengal piece goods	679	Trepang, wax, sharks' fin, cinnamon, nests, shell, cacao	4,419
Spanish Schooner, *San Jose*	Manila, 31 Dec. 1825		Jolo	200 cavanes of rice, Bengal piece goods, 40 jars of rusk	2,183		
Spanish Brigantine, *Nuestra Senora de la Consolacion*	Manila, 4 Apr. 1826	Manila, 7 Jul. 1826	Jolo	Bengal piece goods, 77 jars of rusk, 760 cavanes of rice, 330 cavanes of unhusked rice	7,307	Mother of pearl, sea-cucumber	2,481
Spanish Brigantine, *San Francisco de Asis*		Manila, 7 Oct. 1826	Jolo			Sea-cucumber, shell, nests, sharks' fin, camphor, wax, cinnamon, sago, rattans, 4800 Malay handkerchiefs, 1000 china cups of chocolate	31,889

Appendix F (*cont.*)

VESSEL/MASTER	DEPARTURE	ARRIVAL	DESTINATION	EXPORT CARGO	VALUE (Pesos)	IMPORT CARGO	VALUE (Pesos)
Spanish Brigantine, *Amador de Manila*	Manila, 4 Feb. 1826	Manila, 25 Nov. 1826	Jolo and Mindanao	Bengal piece goods, 32 jars of rusk, 281 galls of red wine	4,987	Shell, nests, sea-cucumber, mother of pearl, sharks' fin, wax, cinnamon, rattans	3,309
Portuguese Frigate, *Basco de Gama*	Manila, 8 Feb. 1826		Jolo				
Portuguese Brigantine, *Feliz*	Manila, 29 June 1826		Jolo				
Portuguese Brigantine, *Esperanza*	Manila, 27 Aug. 1826		Jolo				
Spanish Brigantine, *San Jose*		Manila, 20 Sept. 1826	Jolo			Sea-cucumber, sharks' fin, wax, mother of pearl, camphor, nests, cinnamon, cacao, Bengal goods, manufactured hardware, tradegoods	16,051
Spanish Brigantine, *Consolacion(a) El Caraqueno*		Manila, 21 Oct. 1826	Jolo			Sharks' fin, cinnamon, nests, rattans, mother of pearl, sea-cucumber, wax, camphor, cacao, Bengal goods, books for Chinese record keeping, trade stores	22,351
Portuguese Frigate, *Carolina*	Manila, 20 Nov. 1826		Jolo				
Portuguese Brigantine, *El Nuevo Viajante*	Manila, 24 Nov. 1826		Jolo				
Spanish Brigantine, *Asumpcion*	Manila, 7 Dec. 1826		Jolo and Ternate		24,989		
Spanish Brigantine, *Consolacion(a) La Maria*	Manila, 9 Dec. 1826		Jolo and Menado		24,449		
Spanish Brigantine, *San Jose las Animas*	Manila, 25 Jan. 1827		Jolo	346 piculs of sugar, hams, red pepper, tar, Bengal piece goods, a horse carriage, shoes	9,637		

Appendix F (cont.)

VESSEL/MASTER	DEPARTURE	ARRIVAL	DESTINATION	EXPORT CARGO	VALUE (Pesos)	IMPORT CARGO	VALUE (Pesos)
Spanish Pontin, *San Pedro Advincula*		Manila, 16 Jan. 1827	Jolo			Nests, sea-cucumber, shell, pepper, camphor	1,046
Spanish Brigantine, *Amador de Manila*		Manila, 15 Feb. 1827	Jolo and Moluccas			Mother of pearl, sea-cucumber, nests, shells, sharks' fin, camphor, cacao, tradegoods,	4,522
Spanish Frigate, *Primero de Marzo*	Manila, 23 Mar. 1827	Manila, 19 Oct.1827		Tar, Bengal piecegoods, 1,000 cavanes of rice, 1,370 cavanes of unhusked rice, 377 axes, 3184 cutting knives	8,506	Sea-cucumber, wax,pepper, sharks' fin, shell, cinnamon, camphor, primary textiles	17,313
Spanish Brigantine, *San Jose*		Manila, 15 Sept. 1827	Jolo			Sea-cucumber, nests, wax, manufactured hardware, tradegoods	3,979
Spanish Brigantine, *San Antonio de Padua*	Manila, 12 Apr. 1827	Manila, 3 Nov. 1827	Jolo	430 cavanes of rice, 300 cutting knives, foreign merchandise	7,161	Shells, nests, foodstuffs, tropical birds	2,728
Spanish Brigantine, *Amador*		Manila, 17 Nov. 1827	Timor, Moluccas and Jolo			99 piculs of wax, 114 bottles of cajuput oil, tradegoods	4,381
Spanish Brigantine, *Nuestra Senora de la Consolacion(a) La Estrella*		Manila, 30 Nov. 1827	Jolo			Shell, mother of pearl, sharks' fin, wax, cacao, sea-cucumber, camphor, Bengal piece goods, manufactured hardwares, tradegoods, foodstuffs	11,438
Spanish Pontin, *Salvador*	Manila, 13 Dec. 1827		Jolo	1,100 cutting knives, foreign merchandise			
Spanish Pontin, *San Jose*		Manila, 5 Jan. 1828	Mindanao			Sea-cucumber, wax	1,744
Spanish Brigantine, *Asuncion*	Manila, 17 May 1828	Manila, 8 Oct. 1828	Jolo	15 piculs of sugar, 570 cavanes of rice, 100 ploughs, 400 cutting knives, 9 jars of rusk, 800 cavanes of unhusked rice, foreign merchandise	13,308	Nests, shell, camphor, sea-cucumber, wax, mother of pearl, cacao, manufactured hardware, tradegoods	6,116

Appendix F (*cont.*)

VESSEL/MASTER	DEPARTURE	ARRIVAL	DESTINATION	EXPORT CARGO	VALUE (Pesos)	IMPORT CARGO	VALUE (Pesos)
Spanish Brigantine, *San Luiz*	Manila, 23 June 1828		Jolo	67½ piculs of sugar, 265 cavanes of rice, 1½ picos of Chinese noodle, 150 jars of rusk, foreign merchandise	12,514		
Chinese Panco, *Con Tuan*		Manila, 17 Oct. 1828	Jolo			Wax and cacao	277
Spanish Frigate, *Rita*	Manila, 24 June 1828	Manila, 22 Oct. 1828	Jolo	108 piculs of sugar, 800 cavanes of rice, 116 jewellery cases, 1,200 cavanes unhusked rice, foreign merchandise	8,489	Shell, camphor, nests, sea-cucumber, cacao, tradegoods	13,442
Spanish Frigate, *Maria*		Manila, 4 Nov. 1828	Jolo			Wax, Bengal piecegoods, tradegoods	9,496
Spanish Pontin, *Nuestra Senora de la Merced*		Manila, 10 Nov. 1828	Jolo			Wax, sago, cacao, tradegoods	268
Spanish Pontin *Nuestra Senora de la Merced*	Manila, 24 Dec. 1828		Iloilo and Jolo	10 ploughs, 735 cutting knives, foreign merchandise	13,036		
Spanish Brigantine, *San Luis Gonzaga*	Manila, 27 Dec. 1828		Ternate, Menado and Jolo	520 cates of vermicelli, 50 cane hats, foreign merchandise	1,854		
Spanish Brigantine, *San Juan Nepo Muceno,* (Capt. D.R.Cordero)	Manila, 10 Feb. 1829		Negros and Jolo	100 cavanes of rice, 190 jars of cocoanut oil, 600 gallons of red wine, 150 ploughs, large quantity textiles, 17,500 pieces of earthenware pottery, 350 cavanes of salt, 47 sets of china, foreign merchandise			
Spanish Brigantine, *Nuestra Senora del Rosario,* (Capt. D. Manuel Nobleza)	Manila, 27 Feb. 1829	Manila, 6 Oct. 1829	Jolo	Bengal piece goods, 2,300 fish-hooks, cowhides & foreign merchandise	10,644	Wax, shell, nests, tradegoods	4,918

Appendix F (cont.)

VESSEL/MASTER	DEPARTURE	ARRIVAL	DESTINATION	EXPORT CARGO	VALUE (Pesos)	IMPORT CARGO	VALUE (Pesos)
Spanish Brigantine, *San Antonio de Padua*	Manila, 18 Mar. 1829	Manila, 25 Sept. 1829	Jolo	625 cavanes of rice, 28 cutting knives, foreign merchandise	6,676	Cinnamon, wax, shell, tradegoods	1,812
Spanish Brigantine, *Consolacion*, (Capt. D.Vincente Florentino)	Manila, 4 Apr. 1829					Shell, nests, mother of pearl, wax, pepper, camphor, cacao, European handkerchiefs, tradegoods	7,729
Spanish Brigantine, *Diligente*, (Capt. D. Rafael Laguillema)	Manila, 23 May 1829	Manila, 27 Dec. 1829	Jolo	Bengal piece goods, earthenware, 80 ploughs, silk garments, articles for Chinese community at Jolo, foreign merchandise	10,644	Wax, cinnamon, camphor, shell, nests	3,197
Spanish Brigantine Schooner, *Soledad*, (Capt, D.Jose Maria Morgado)		Manila, 25 Sept. 1829	Jolo			Nests, sea-cucumber, shell, rattans, sharks' fin, tobacco, camphor	
Spanish Brigantine, *Nuestra Senora del Rosario*	Manila, 20 Mar. 1830	Manila, 14 Sept. 1830	Jolo	900 cavanes of rice, foreign merchandise	1,707	Mother of pearl, wax, nests, tradegoods	727
Spanish Brigantine, *Nuestra Senora de los Dolores*	Manila, 21 Mar. 1830	Manila, 30 Nov. 1830	Jolo	600 cavanes of rice, foreign merchandise	2,361	Nests, sea-cucumber, wax, mother of pearl, sharks' fin, foodstuffs	1,753
Spanish Brigantine, *Alerta*	Manila, 23 Mar. 1830	Manila, 12 Oct. 1830	Jolo	1,410 cavanes of rice, 1,050 cutting knives, 50 iron axes, foreign merchandise	32,016	Rattans, sharks' fin, nests, shell, wax, mother of pearl, tradegoods	17,954
Spanish Pontin, *San Pedro Advincula de Arruada*		Manila, 1830	Jolo			Shell and wax	6,349
Pontin, *Macassar*	Manila, 29 Nov. 1830		Bulungan				
Schooner, *Matayo*	Manila, 29 Nov. 1830	Manila, 11 May 1830	Bulungan			Nests, shell, sea-cucumber, mother of pearl	7,723

The Manila–Moluccas Trade, 1820–1830

VESSEL/MASTER	DEPARTURE	ARRIVAL	DESTINATION	EXPORT CARGO	VALUE (Pesos)	IMPORT CARGO	VALUE (Pesos)
Spanish Pontin, *San Jose*		Manila, 27 Sept. 1820	Ternate			Nests, shell, sea-cucumber	642
Spanish Pontin, *San Josef*		Manila, 31 Oct. 1821	Ternate			Nests, shell, mother of pearl, sea-cucumber, sharks' fin, wax, cacao	6,424
Spanish Brigantine	Manila, 1824		Timor				
Spanish Brigantine	"		Timor				
Spanish Brigantine	"		Ternate				
	"		Moluccas				
Spanish Brigantine, *San Jose Constante del Mar*		Manila, 4 July 1825	Moluccas			Shell, sea-cucumber, nests, sharks' fin, cacao	5,424
Spanish Brigantine, *San Jose y las Animas*		Manila, 18 Oct. 1825	Moluccas			Mother of pearl, sea-cucumber, nests, sharks' fin	31,523
Spanish Pontin, *San Jose*		Manila, 11 Feb. 1826	Ternate			Sea-cucumber, mother of pearl, wax, sharks' fin, shell, cacao, foodstuffs	11,767
Spanish Brigantine, *Asumpcion*	Manila, 7 Dec. 1826		Jolo and Ternate				
Spanish Brigantine, *Consolacion*, (a) *La Maria*	Manila, 9 Dec. 1826		Jolo and Menado				
Spanish Brigantine, *San Jose*, (a) *El Pumbalobo*		Manila, 24 Oct. 1826	Menado			Nests, shell, sea-cucumber, sharks' fin, cacao	17,575
Spanish Brigantine, *Amador de Manila*		Manila, 15 Feb. 1827	Moluccas and Jolo			Mother of pearl, sea-cucumber, nests, shell, sharks' fin, camphor, cacao, tradegoods	4,552

Appendix G (*cont.*)

VESSEL/MASTER	DEPARTURE	ARRIVAL	DESTINATION	EXPORT CARGO	VALUE (Pesos)	IMPORT CARGO	VALUE (Pesos)
Spanish Pontin, *San Jose*		Manila, 15 Sept. 1827	Ternate			Sea-cucumber, sharks' fin, mother of pearl, nests	3,658
Spanish Brigantine *Amador*		Manila, 17 Nov. 1827	Timor, Moluccas and Jolo			99 piculs wax, 114 bottles of cajeput oil, tradegoods	4,381
Spanish Brigantine, *San Jose y Las Animas*		Manila, 19 Nov. 1827	Ternate			Sea-cucumber, nests, shell, mother of pearl, wax, cacao, sharks' fin, tradegoods	11,213
Spanish Brigantine, *Ascuncion*		Manila, 12 May 1828	Ternate			Wax, cacao, shell, sharks' fin, rattans, Madras handkerchiefs, tradegoods	11,771
Spanish Brigantine, *San Luis Gonzaga*	Manila, 27 Dec. 1828		Ternate, Menado and Jolo	520 cates vermicelli, 50 cane hats, foreign merchandise	1,854		
Spanish Brigantine, *San Jose Las Animas*		Manila, 10 Nov. 1829	Ternate			Shell, nests, sharks' fin, mother of pearl	
Spanish Brigantine, *Nuestra Senora del Rosario*	Manila, Jan. 1829		Ternate	Paper, books, 25,000 dishes, cups & saucers, 5,700 common European plates, brooms, foreign merchandise			
Spanish Brigantine, *Bartsina Lugre*, (Capt. Tomas Tonson)	Manila, 1 Mar. 1829		Moluccas	740 piculs of Sapanwood, Bengal piecegoods, 55, axes, 2,000 bricks, foreign merchandise			
Spanish Frigate, *Rita*		Manila, 10 Oct. 1830	Ternate			Shell, nests, sharks' fin, mother of pearl	
Spanish Pontin, *Nuestra Senora del Rosario*		Manila, 1 Nov. 1830				Shell, sharks' fin	

Source: All trade data used in this series are from documents in the AGI. See 1820–1821, Filipinas 806; 1824, Ultramar 624, 625; 1826, Filipinas 811, 814; 1827, Filipinas 814, 625; 1828–1829, Ultramar 624, 625; 1830, Filipinas 818.

Appendix H

The Prahu Trade from Brunei to Manila, 1796–1812

VESSEL/MASTER	DEPARTURE	ARRIVAL	DESTINATION	EXPORT CARGO	VALUE (Pesos)	IMPORT CARGO	VALUE (Pesos)
Panco, *canaycan*	Manila, 19 Nov. 1796	Manila, 14 Sept. 1796	Brunei	10 piculs of sugar, sundries	1,150	Canton goods	11,668
Panco, *Ylot*	Manila, 1802	Manila, 1802	Brunei				
Panco, *Nazarudin*	"	"	Brunei				
Panco, *Canaycan*	"	"	Brunei				
Panco, *Galela*	"	"	Brunei				
Panco, *Famago*, Naquodah Pangaronamong	Manila, 18 Oct. 1811	Manila, 28 Sept. 1811	Brunei		1,174		2,589
Panco, *Prao*, Naquodah Saly	Manila, 20 Oct. 1812	Manila, 15 Sept. 1812	Brunei	Several hundred bundles of textiles, 200 ord. plates, 14 cavanes rice, 16 piculs of salt, etc.	1,907		3,576
Panco, *Naroc Simpen*, Naquodah Suda Nangindra	Manila, 22 Oct. 1812	Manila, 22 Sept. 1812	Brunei	141 bundles of textiles, 19 boxes of cloth, 200 plates, 15 cavanes of rice, 15 piculs of salt	3,877		6,106
Panco, *Prao*	Manila, 6 Dec. 1814		Brunei	1 picul of cotton			

Source: All trade data used in this series are from documents in the AGI, 1796, Ultramar 658, Filipinas 506; 1802, Ultramar 621; 1811–1812, Filipinas 979.

Appendix I

James Brooke's Letter of Introduction to the Sultan of Sulu

From the Honourable Lieutenant Colonel W.G. Butterworth companion of the most honourable the military order of Bath, Governor of Prince of Wales Island, Singapore and Malacca to His Highness Mohumed Tadlal Kahier, Sultan of the Sooloo Islands.

It is a long time since I received my friends letter expressing his desire for the suppression of piracy, but that letter assured me of my friends earnestness to cooperate with the British Government in putting down these enemies of all mankind, and I have therefore not troubled my friend further on the subject. My present letter is to disclaim all participation in the late proceedings of other nations against Sooloo, and to introduce to my friend His Excellency Sir James Brooke, Knight Commander of the most honourable order of Bath, the plenipotentiary of Her Majesty the Queen of Great Britain and Ireland in these seas, and the Governor of the new colony of Labuan who is anxious to make my friends acquaintance and to consolidate the good understanding between my friend and the British nation. His Excellency Sir James Brooke, K.C.B. will probably be known to my friend by the high character which he has secured for himself as the English Rajah of Sarawak in which principality he has caused order, regularity and happiness to prevail where anarchy, confusion, and misery obtained. He is now the representative of Her Majesty the Queen of Great Britain and Ireland in these parts, and as such I request my friend to receive him.

W.G. Butterworth

Source: Governor of the Straits Settlements to the Sec. of the Government of India, 8 July 1848, IOL, F/4/2331(121955), 5.

Appendix J

The Treaty of Sir James Brooke with the Sultan of Sulu

Agreement

Her Majesty, the Queen of the United Kingdom of Great Britain and Ireland, desirous of encouraging commerce between her subjects and those of the independent princes in the Eastern seas, and of putting an end to the piracy which has up to this time hindered said commerce; and his Highness the Sultan Mohammed Pulalun who occupies the throne and governs the territories of Sulu, animated by like sentiments and desirous of co-operating in the measures which may be necessary for the achievement of the objects mentioned; have resolved to place on record their determination on these points by an agreement which contains the following articles:

Article 1. From now on there shall be peace, friendship, and good understanding between her Majesty the Queen of Great Britain and Ireland and his Highness Mohammed Pulalun, Sultan of Sulu, and between their respective heirs and successors, and between their subjects.

Article 2. The subjects of her Britannic Majesty shall have complete liberty to enter, reside, carry on business, and pass with their merchandise through all parts of the dominions of his Highness the Sultan of Sulu, and they shall enjoy in them all the privileges and advantages with respect to commerce or in connection with any other matter whatever which are at this time enjoyed by, or which in the future may be granted to, the subjects or citizens of the most favoured nation; and the subjects of his Highness the Sultan of Sulu shall likewise be free to enter, reside, carry on business, and pass with their merchandise to all parts of the dominions of her Britannic Majesty, in Europe as well as in Asia, as freely as the subjects of the most favoured nation, and they shall enjoy in said dominions all the privileges and advantages with respect to commerce and in connection with other matters which are now enjoyed by, or which in the future may be granted to, the subjects or citizens of the most favoured nation.

Article 3. British subjects shall be permitted to buy, lease, or acquire in any lawful way whatever all kinds of property within the dominions of His Highness the Sultan of Sulu, and his Highness extends, as far as lies within his power, to every British subject who establishes himself in his dominions, the enjoyment of entire and complete protection and security to person and to property—as well as any property which in the future may be acquired, as that which has already been acquired prior to the date of this agreement.

Article 4. His Highness the Sultan of Sulu offers to allow the war vessels of her Britannic Majesty and those of the India Company to enter freely the ports, rivers, and inlets situarted within his dominions and to permit said vessels to supply themselves, at reasonable prices, with the goods and provisions which they may need from time to time.

Article 5. If any English vessel should be lost on the coasts of the dominions of his Highness the Sultan of Sulu the latter promises to lend every aid in his power for the recovery and delivery to the owners of every thing that can be saved from said vessels; and his Highness also promises to give entire protection to the officers and crew and to every person who may be aboard the shipwrecked vessel, as well as to their property.

Article 6. Therefore, her Majesty the Queen of the United Kingdom of Great Britain and Ireland, and the Sultan of Sulu, bind themselves to adopt such measures as lie within their power to suppress piracy within the seas, islands, and rivers under their respective jurisdiction or influence, and his Highness the Sultan of Sulu binds himself not to harbour or protect any person or vessel engaged in enterprises of a piratical nature.

Article 7. His Highness the Sultan of Sulu, for the purpose of avoiding in the future any occasion for disagreement, promises to make no cession of territory within his dominions to any other nation, nor to subjects or citizens thereof, nor to acknowledge vassalage or feudality to any other power without the consent of her Britannic Majesty.

Article 8. This treaty must be ratified, and the ratification will therefore be exchanged in Jolo within two years from date. Home Copy-Brooke-Approved, etc.—Signed and sealed May 29, 1849.

Source: Governor of the Straits Settlements to the Sec. of the Government of India, 6 July 1849, IOL, F/4/2363(125401); Saleeby, *History of Sulu*, pp.222–228.

Appendix K

Treaty of 30 April 1851 between Spain and the Sultan of Sulu

SULTANATE OF SULU

Act of Incorporation into the Spanish Monarchy, April 30, 1851

Solemn declaration of incorporation and adhesion to the Sovereignty of Her Catholic Majesty Isabel II, constitutional Queen of Spain, and of submission to the Supreme Government of the Nation, made by His High Excellency the Sultan of Sulu, Mohammed Pulalun, Datus Mohammed Buyuk, Muluk, Daniel Amil Bahar, Bandahala, Muluk Kahar, Amil Badar, Tumanggung, Juhan, Sanajahan, Na'ib, Mamancha and Sharif Mohammed Binsarin, in the name and in representation of the whole island of Sulu, to Colonel José Maria de Carlos y O'Doyle, politico-military Governor of the Province of Zamboanga, islands of Basilan, Pilas, Tonkil, and those adjacent thereto, as Plenipotentiary specially authorized by His Excellency Antonio de Urbiztondo, Marquis of Solana, Governor and Captain-General of the Philippine Islands.

Article 1.   His Excellency the Sultan of Sulu, for himself, his heirs and descendants, Datus Mohammed Buyuk, Muluk, Daniel Amil Bahar, Bandahala, Muluk Kahar, Amil Badar, Tumanggung, Juhan, Sanajahan, Na'ib, Mamancha and Sharif Mohammed Binsarin, all of their own free will, declare: That, for the purpose of making amends to the Spanish nation for the outrage committed against it on the first of January of this year, they desire and request that the island of Jolo and all its dependencies be incorporated with the Crown of Spain, which for several centuries has been their only sovereign and protectress, making on this day a new solemn declaration of adhesion and submission and recognizing Her Catholic Majesty Isabel II, constitutional Queen of Spain, and those who may succeed her in this supreme dignity, as their rightful Sovereign Lords and Protectors, in virtue of the treaties made in old times, of the treaty of 1836 and the additions made thereto by the present governor of Zamboanga in August, and also and very particularly of the recent conquest of Jolo on the 28th of February of the present year by Captain-General Antonio Urbiztondo, Marquis of Solana and Governor-General of the Philippine Islands.

Article 2.   The Sultan and Datus solemnly promise to maintain the integrity of the territory of Sulu and all its dependencies as a part of the Archipelago belonging to the Spanish Government.

Article 3.   The island of Sulu and all its dependencies having been incorporated with the Crown of Spain, and the inhabitants thereof being part of the great Spanish family which lives in the vast Philippine Archipelago, the Sultan and Datus shall not be empowered to make or sign treaties, commercial agreements or alliances of any kind with European powers, companies, persons or corporations, and Malayan sultans or chiefs, under pain of nullity; they declare all treaties made with other powers to be null and void if they are prejudicial to the ancient and indisputable rights held by Spain over the entire Sulu Archipelago as part of the Philippine Islands, and they ratify, renew and leave in force all documents containing clauses favourable to the Spanish Government that may have been drawn up before this date, however old they may be.

285

Article 4.   They renew the solemn promise not to carry on piracy or allow anybody to carry on piracy within the dominions of Sulu, and to run down those who follow this infamous calling, declaring themselves enemies of all islands that are enemies of Spain and allies of all her friends.

Article 5.   From this day forth the island of Sulu shall fly the Spanish national flag in its towns and on its ships, and the Sultan and other constituted authorities shall use the Spanish war flag, under the principles in use in other Spanish possessions, and shall use no other either on land or on sea.

Article 6.   The island of Sulu and its dependencies having been declared an integral part of the Philippine Archipelago, which belongs to Spain, commerce under the Spanish flag in all the ports of the Sultanate shall be free and unmolested, as it is in all the ports belonging to the Nations.

Article 7.   The Sultan and Datus of Sulu, having recognized the sovereignty of Spain over their territory, which sovereignty is now strongly established, not only by right of conquest but by the clemency of the conqueror, they shall not erect fortifications of any kind in the territory under their command without express permission of His Excellency the Governor-General of these Islands; the purchase and use of all kinds of firearms shall be prohibited except with a licence issued by the same supreme authority, and craft found with arms other than the edged weapons which have from time immemorial been in use in the country shall be considered as enemies.

Article 8.   The Spanish Government as an unequivocal proof of the protection which it grants the Sulus, will give the Sultan and Datus adequate royal titles establishing their authority and their rank.

Article 9.   The Spanish Government guarantees with all solemnity to the Sultan and other inhabitants of Sulu the free exercise of their religion, with which it will not interfere in the slightest way, and it will also respect their customs.

Article 10.   The Spanish Government also guarantees the right of succession to the present Sultan and his descendants in the order established and as long as they observe these agreements, and equally guarantees the rank and dignities of the privileged classes, which shall retain all their rights.

Article 11.   Sulu ships and goods shall enjoy in Spanish ports, without any distinction whatever, the same privileges and advantages granted the natives of the Philippine Islands.

Article 12.   Except in the case of Spanish ships, the duties that constitute the income with which the Sultan and Datus maintain their respective ranks shall remain in force, so that they may continue to keep up the proper splendour and decorum of their station; for this purpose said duties shall be paid by all ships coming to their ports; other measures will be taken later on to enhance their dignity and increase their prestige.

Article 13.   For the purpose of assuring and strengthening the authority of the Sultan, and also of promoting a regular trade which may enrich the island of Sulu, a trading post, garrisoned by Spanish forces, shall be established as soon as the Government so orders, and in accordance with Article 3 of the Treaty of 1836; for the building of the trading post the Sultan, Datus and natives shall give all the assistance in their power and furnish native labour, which will be paid for, and all necessary materials, which they will charge at the regular market prices.

Article 14.   The trading post shall be established at the place called Daniel's Kuta, next to the roadstead, as it is the most suitable place; but care shall be taken not to encroach in any way on the native cemetery, which has to be religiously respected, and no buildings whatever shall be erected in said cemetery, so as to avoid the trouble that would ensue to those who might build there.

Article 15.   The Sultan of Sulu may issue passports to all persons within
his dominions that may request them, and fix the amount of the fees; he is also
authorised to countersign or place his seal on the passports of Spaniards visiting his
place of residence.

Article 16.   In view of the Sultan's declarations regarding the losses suffered by
him in the destruction by fire of his forts and palace, and convinced of the reality of
the losses, the Spanish Government grants him an annuity of 1,500 pesos in order
to indemnify him in a certain way for these losses and at the same time to help him
to maintain, with proper splendour, the decorum due his person and his rank. The
same considerations induce the Spanish Government to grant Datu Mohammed
Buyuk, Muluk, and Datu Daniel Amil Bahar 600 pesos per annum each, and 360
pesos to Sharif Mohammed Binsarin on account of his good services to the Spanish
Government.

Article 17.   The Articles contained in this solemn Act shall go this day into full
effect, subject however to the superior approval of His Excellency the Governor-
General of these Philippine Islands. Any doubt which may arise in regard to the text
of this Act shall be resolved by adhering to the literal meaning of the Spanish text.

Signed at Jolo on the 19th of April 1851. Seal of the Sultan. Seals of Datus Muluk
Kahar; Tumanggung; Sanajahan; Mamancha; Muluk Bendahala; Amil-Badar; Juhan
Na'ib and signature of Sharif Mohammed Binsarin. The politico-military Governor
of the province of Zamboanga, etc.: José Maria de Carlos y O'Doyle.

I, Don Antonio de Urbiztondo y Eguia, Marquis de la Solana, Knight Grand
Cross of the Royal American Order of Isabel the Catholic, Knight of the Royal
Order of San Fernando of the first and third class, and of that of San Hermenegildo,
Lieutenant-General of the National Forces, Governor and Captain-General of the
Philippine Islands, President of the Royal Audiencia of the Philippine Islands, Judge-
Subdelegate of Post Office Revenues, Vice-Royal Patron, and Director-General of
the troops, etc., approved, confirmed and ratified this capitulation in the name of Her
Majesty Isabel II.

Manila, April 30, 1851. —Antonio de Urbiztondo.

True copy. —Seal of the Captain-General of the Philippines.

Source: BIA, File 3671–2, No.27; Saleeby, *History of Sulu,* pp.107–111.

Appendix L

Regulations Declaring all Muslim Shipping Illegal in the Sulu Sea

Office of the Commander General of the Navy
on the Philippine Station

Don Juan Antequera y Bobadilla, Rear Admiral, Commander General of the squadron and the naval station of the Philippines.

I have hereby to make known that the Sultanate (Sultania) of Sooloo having been declared to be in open rebellion, and the conciliatory means made use of hitherto to reduce the Sultan to obedience having been ineffective, the protection afforded by the authority of the said Sultan to navigation by his vessels in the Archipelago becomes, consequently, null and void. In order to prevent the depredations which the said vessels commit on our coasts, I have arranged, in concert with the Captain General Superior Governor of these Islands, that, from this date, the following regulations be observed.

1st. Every vessel coming from the Sooloo Archipelago and manned by Moors shall be destroyed, and its crew and passengers destined to labour on public works on the northerly islands of the Archipelago.

2nd. If the vessels referred to in the former article be armed, they shall, as our laws direct, be held as pirates and their crews be tried by court martial according to the provisions of the Penal Code.

3rd. Every vessel, although it may not be manned, belonging to Moors of the islands of Sooloo and Tawi Tawi, shall be destroyed by the cruisers.

4th. Vessels referred to in the former articles, which do not acknowledge the authority of the Sultan and do not carry on piracy, shall, when they endeavour to sail from other islands than those of Sooloo and Tawi Tawi, be conducted by the cruisers to the islands whence they had come.

5th. In the islands whence the vessels referred to in the previous article may proceed, fishing will be permitted under restrictions deemed desirable by the Commander of the Division.

Manila, 2nd August 1873.

Juan Antequera.

Source: *Singapore Daily Times*, 4 Sept. 1873.

Appendix M

Official Letter of the General Government Prohibiting the Chinese from Trading in the Interior of Mindanao

To the Politico-Military Governor of Cottabatto

July 9, 1890.

The most Excellent the Governor-General has seen fit to direct, in reply to the enquiry made by your most Illustrious self in your communication of the 18th of June last, that you be informed that the restrictions placed upon the Chinese in order to prevent them from passing beyond the lines of the military posts and travelling into the interior of the rancherias of the moros or infidels for the purpose of commerce, extend to all persons wearing Chinese dress, whether they be *Mestizos* or not, and in general, to all persons, of whatever class they be, who purpose to carry on the said unlawful commerce to the prejudice of the interest of the state; for the principal object of this measure is to prevent anyone from disturbing, under the pretext of commerce, our relations with those tribes by penetrating into territory where the action of the Government does not yet extend in a direct manner.

Which, by direction of the said Superior Authority, I communicate to your lordship for proper action.

Official Letter of the General Government Prohibiting the Commerce in Copper for the Reasons that the Moros Use It in the Manufacture of Arms

To the Politico-Military Governor of Cottabatto

November 25, 1891.

In view of the fact that copper is one of the metals used by the moros in the manufacture of various arms, the most excellent the Governor-General has seen fit to declare under this date that the buying or selling of the said metal in your District is prohibited.

Which I communicate to your lordship in answer to the inquiry made by you in the premises, in a communication of the 7th instant, addressed to this office.

Source: BIA, FIle 3671-2.

The Coastal Defences of the Bishopric of Cebu, 1779

COMMUNITY	LOCATION	PRESENCE OF PRIEST	CHURCH AS FORTIFICATION	*BALUARTE* (Stone towers, block houses, Palisades) CONSTRUCTED BY *INDIOS*	FORT CONSTRUCTED BY *INDIOS*	GARRISON OF *BALUARTE/* FORT	*PRESIDIO* AND COMPLEMENT	NATURAL DEFENSE	COMMUNITIES DISPERSED BY RAIDING
CEBU PROVINCE									
Talibon	Coast		Wood Church	Wood *Baluarte*	Stone Fort	—			
Loon	Coast	Priest	Wood Church	Stone *Baluarte*	Stone Fort	—			
Malabohoe	—	Priest			Stone Fort	*Indios* and priest			
Tagbilaran	Coast	Priest	Stone Church		Stone Fort	*Indios and* priest			
Baclayon	Coast	Priest	Stone Church	Stone *Baluarte*	Stone Fort	*Indios* and priest			
Loay	Coast	Priest	Wood Church	Stone *Baluarte*	Stone Fort	*Indios*			
Dimiao	Coast	Priest	Wood Church	Wood Palisade	Stone Fort	*Indios* and priest			
Hagna	Coast	Priest	Wood Church	Stone *Baluarte*	Stone Fort	*Indios* and priest			
Davis	Coast	Priest	Stone Church	Stone *Baluarte*	Stone Fort	*Indios*			
Danao	Coast	Priest	Stone Church	Wood Palisade	Stone Fort	*Indios* and priest			
Catmon	Coast		Wood Church	Wood *Baluarte*	Wood Fort	*Indios*			
Dinabongan			Wood Church	Stone *Baluarte*		—			
Loboc	Inland	Priest	Stone Church	Stone *Baluarte*	Stone Fort	*Indios* and priest			
Malabago	Inland		Wood Church		Stone Fort	*Indios*			
CALAMIANES PROVINCE									
Tatay	Coast	Priest	Wood Church		Stone Fort	*Indios* and priest			

Appendix N (*cont.*)

COMMUNITY	LOCATION	PRESENCE OF PRIEST	CHURCH AS FORTIFICATION	BALUARTE (Stone towers, block houses, Palisades) CONSTRUCTED BY INDIOS	FOR CONSTRUCTED BY INDIOS	GARRISON OF BALUARTE FORT	PRESIDIO AND COMPLEMENT	NATURAL DEFENSE	COMMUNITIES DISPERSED BY RAIDING
Dumaran	Coast		Wood Church	Wood Baluarte	Wood Fort	—			
Silanga	Coast	Priest	Wood Church		Wood Fort	Indios and priest			
Culion	Coast	Priest	Wood Church	Stone Baluarte	Stone Fort	Indios and priest			
Linapacan	Coast		Wood Church	Wood Baluarte		Indios			
Bintoan	Coast		Wood Church						
Carong	Coast							Mountains	
Agutaya	Coast	Priest	Stone Church	Stone Baluarte	Stone Fort	Indios and priest		Mountains	Dispersed
Cuyo *PANAY PROVINCE*	Coast	Priest	Stone Church	Stone Baluarte	Stone Fort				
Romblon	Coast	Priest	—	Stone Baluarte		Indios and priest			
Sibuyan	Coast		Wood Church	Stone Baluarte		Indios			
Tablas	Coast		Wood Church	Stone Baluarte		Indios			
Banton	Coast	Priest	Wood Church	Wood Palisade	Wood Fort	Indios and priest			
Mambusao	Inland	Priest	Stone Church						
Batang *CARAGA PROVINCE*	Inland		Wood Church						
Tandag	Coast	Priest	Stone Church		Stone Fort		73		
Marihatog	Coast		Wood Church					Mountains	Dispersed
Liangan	Coast							Mountains	Dispersed
Paniquian	Coast			Wood Baluarte		Indios			Dispersed
Bayuyo	Coast		Wood Church						Dispersed

Appendix N (*cont.*)

COMMUNITY	LOCATION	PRESENCE OF PRIEST	CHURCH AS FORTIFICATION	*BALUARTE* (Stone towers, block houses, Palisades) CONSTRUCTED BY *INDIOS*	FORT CONSTRUCTED BY *INDIOS*	GARRISON OF *BALUARTE* FORT	*PRESIDIO* AND COMPLEMENT	NATURAL DEFENSE	COMMUNITIES DISPERSED BY RAIDING
Catel	Coast	Priest	Wood Church	Stone *Baluarte*			number unknown		Dispersed
Bagangoa	Coast		Wood Church						Dispersed
Bislig	Coast								
Hinatuan	Coast								
Surigao	Coast	Priest	Wood Church	Wood *Baluarte*		*Indios* and soldiers			
Cabungbungan	Coast		Wood Church	Wood *Baluarte*		*Indios*			
Hiraquet	Coast		Wood Church	Wood *Baluarte*		*Indios*			
Cacub	Coast			Wood *Baluarte*		*Indios*			Dispersed
Butuan	Inland	Priest	Stone Church	Wood *Baluarte*		*Indios* and priest			
Hinago	Inland				Wood Fort	*Indios*			
Tubay	Inland		Wood Church					Mountains	
Habongan	Inland							Mountains	
Mainit	Inland							Mountains	
Talacoban	Inland		Wood Church						
Linao	Inland			Wood Palisade		*Indios*	number unknown		
ILIGAN PROVINCE									
Iligan	Coast	Priest	Wood Church	Stone *Baluarte*		—	78		
Initao	Coast		Wood Church	Wood *Baluarte*		*Indios*	20		
Dapitan	Coast		Wood Church	Wood *Baluarte*			20		
Misamis	Coast	Priest	Wood Church		Stone Fort	*Indios* and soldiers	68		
Cagayan	Coast	Priest	Stone Church	Stone *Baluarte*			20		
Tagoloan	Coast		Wood Church						
Alilutum	Coast		Wood Church		Wood Fort	*Indios*			

Appendix N (*cont.*)

COMMUNITY	LOCATION	PRESENCE OF PRIEST	CHURCH AS FORTIFI-CATION	*BALUARTE* (Stone towers, block houses, Palisades) CONSTRUCTED BY *INDIOS*	FORT CON-STRUCTED BY *INDIOS*	GARRISON OF *BALUARTE* FORT	*PRESIDIO* AND COMPLE-MENT	NATURAL DEFENSE	COMMUNITIES DISPERSED BY RAIDING
Salay	Coast		Wood Church						Dispersed
Cugman	Coast		Wood Church					Mountains	
Mambahao	Coast	Priest	Wood Church	Wood *Baluarte*		*Indios* and priest		Mountains	
Guinsiliban	Coast		Wood Church	Wood *Baluarte*					
Zamboanga	Coast	Priest	Wood Church	Stone *Baluarte*	Stone Fort	*Indios*	370		
Ilaga	Inland		Wood Church						
Lubungan	Inland	Priest	—	Stone *Baluarte*		*Indios* and priest			
Bagug	Inland	Priest	Wood Church	Wood *Baluarte*		*Indios* and priest			
Hiponan	Inland		Wood Church	Wood *Baluarte*		*Indios*			

Notes: Blank—implies that characteristic not present in the community.
Dash—no information

Source: This table was compiled from the following source: Pasa reveremente los testemonios que refiere sobre el estado de los Yglesias y Bienes de la administracion de los religiosos Franciscanos y Augustanos Descalzos: con lo demas que expone en orden a las otras respectivos de su jurisdiccion, El Obispo de Zebu, Don Matheo Joachim Rubio de Aravelo a vuestra Magestad, December 21, 1779, AGI, Filipinas 1027.

Appendix O

An Inventory of the Land and Sea Defences of Albay Province, 1799

PUEBLOS	LANCHAS AND VINTAS	PANCOS	CANNON						RIFLES
			8 POUND	6 POUND	4 POUND	2 POUND	1 POUND	½ POUND	
Albay	1				1	3	1(?)		12
Palanas		1			2	6	2		18
Virac		1			1	3	2		6
Bato-Bato						2	2		4
Caramoan		1			1		1	2	12
Payo		1			1	1	3	2	4
Tambongan		1					1	2	
Biga		1			1	1	3	2	12
Pandan		1			1		1	2	4
Bagamonac					1		3		6
Tabgon							3		3
Caramoan						3	3		6
Laganoy		1				8			12
Tiui	1				5	4			18
Malinao	1				1	1	4		12
Tabaco			1			1	1		12
Bagacay	1				2	4	2		6
Libac		1				2	2		6
Bulusan	2					7	2		24
Gubat	2				5				
Casiguran	2					4			18
Luban		1			10	6	2		34
Bacon	1		2		3	4			24
Sorsogon		1	2	1		2			40
Quipia					2	4	2		12
Donzol	1			1	2	2	2		6
San Jacinto	1					2			8
Mobo	1				5	6	6	4	14
Baleno		1			2	2	2	2	6
	15	12	5	2	47	78	50	18	345

Source: In several instances the number of cannon do not correspond to the sum total because of damage to parts of the document. See Numero 8, Junta celebradas por los gobernadorcillos y principales de la provincia de Albay sobre la necesidad de vintas, lanchas, canones, polvara, y balas para perseguir los moros y, contener sus hostilidades, May 15, 1799, PNA, Ereccion del Pueblo Albay, 1799–1864.

Appendix P

Population Variations in Nueva Caceres Between 1751/1780 and 1815

POPULATION FOR 1751/1780 EQUALS 100

	1751	1780	1782	1786	1790	1794	1798	1801	1815
CAMARINES PROVINCE									
Tabuco		100.0	65.5	81.8	86.1	82.7	*	10.6	143.2
Santa Cruz		100.0	63.1	75.9	90.6	77.0	*	4.4	68.6
Daet		100.0	112.2	150.9	106.4	114.9	*	105.3	*
Indan	100.0	24.9	*	60.4	90.4	*	70.2	*	83.7
Paracale		100.0	184.8	250.5	388.9	*	127.0	*	133.3
Mambulao		100.0	*	*	*	*	*	260.0	281.3
Capalonga	100.0	97.2	64.8	67.9	49.4	54.0	*	45.1	61.2
Naga		100.0	115.5	107.8	94.2	111.6	110.9	163.3	201.3
Camaligan		100.0	101.4	84.8	99.0	125.4	116.4	134.8	150.4
Canaman		100.0	78.3	131.4	112.7	113.2	127.0	132.9	154.6
Magarao		100.0	174.5	200.4	218.2	246.5	272.1	291.8	258.7
Guipao		100.0	99.2	105.2	92.3	92.2	214.5	79.2	105.3
Bombon		100.0	103.7	112.7	99.2	105.9	*	114.8	123.3
Calabanga		100.0	101.8	135.3	144.9	115.1	183.1	154.5	161.2
Libmanan		100.0	101.6	117.8	127.2	122.7	134.7	138.5	163.3
Milanor		100.0	104.5	119.8	118.0	114.8	122.7	129.8	120.2
Bada		100.0	113.6	117.2	99.7	102.7	136.1	140.2	140.6
Bula		100.0	97.2	120.2	124.7	182.5	133.6	127.9	183.2
Nabula		100.0	114.3	147.1	159.3	147.4	148.4	155.9	204.4
Batto		100.0	101.6	101.6	106.1	113.3	121.8	113.6	180.3
Iraga		100.0	95.2	109.9	120.7	106.1	135.1	144.2	204.9
Buxi		100.0	113.7	118.6	117.4	132.6	116.9	155.9	225.2
Polangi		100.0	101.7	102.9	104.4	104.3	117.2	123.5	106.2
Libon		100.0	104.1	80.7	109.8	101.5	96.6	122.8	204.1
Das		100.0	101.9	102.4	112.3	108.8	106.8	112.4	157.8
Ligao		100.0	99.8	102.7	115.6	99.8	102.5	108.0	113.1
Guinobatan		100.0	74.1	91.0	108.7	108.7	104.3	106.5	83.7
Camarines		100.0	80.3	78.4	78.8	72.0	78.9	82.0	87.8
Cagsava		100.0	79.1	82.5	71.4	63.1	56.2	53.1	58.1
ALBAY PROVINCE									
Albay		100.0	50.5	92.6	125.5	126.4	110.5	*	100.1
Ligbog		100.0	184.2	90.6	*	75.8	*	90.5	165.5
Bagacay		100.0	92.9	97.5	105.3	95.4	*	105.9	123.6
Tabaco		100.0	204.6	188.5	179.3	179.0	*	217.0	210.3
Malinao		100.0	101.2	89.5	92.0	119.7	*	134.1	132.9
Tivi		100.0	111.1	118.5	143.8	110.6	*	188.8	166.1
Lagonoy		100.0	111.4	114.0	97.3	*	*	209.6	262.9

295

Appendix P (*cont.*)

Caramoan	100.0	125.2	197.1	197.9	179.4	189.2	155.0	*	255.8
Biga		100.0	76.6	*	88.5	87.2	*	97.2	71.3
Birac	100.0	103.6	80.6	101.4	143.4	135.8	*	126.7	153.3
Bulusan		100.0	96.8	79.4	108.8	111.3	*	104.5	127.3
Gubat		100.0	102.1	110.9	130.8	118.2	*	137.5	195.4
Galte		100.0	79.9	451.4	106.8	*	*	132.8	*
Casiguran		100.0	96.3	112.6	113.1	112.1	*	131.2	172.5
Luban		100.0	85.0	79.6	74.4	63.0	*	56.1	65.3
Sorsogon	100.0	20.6	29.7	31.1	30.1	33.0	*	33.8	62.4
Bacon		100.0	104.9	101.5	125.4	120.9	*	137.4	202.2
TAYABAS PROVINCE									
Tayabas		100.0	104.7	108.7	112.4	107.7	116.6	138.2	203.1
Mauban		100.0	97.6	104.8	109.0	119.9	125.6	137.2	158.5
Lucban		100.0	98.3	89.0	86.3	94.3	99.7	96.3	113.3
Pagbilao	100.0	79.1	85.8	71.8	85.1	90.2	109.3	128.2	125.6
Sadjaja		100.0	*	106.0	109.2	133.1	150.0	151.2	207.0
Polillo		100.0	94.9	108.1	118.0	102.6	122.9	130.0	144.5
Lampon (Binangonan)		100.0	102.6	130.4	117.8	124.6	153.0	164.9	199.0
Casiguran(De Baler)	100.0	142.3	70.7	76.9	77.3	92.2	107.7	70.1	80.9
Atimonan		100.0	192.4	209.9	201.8	218.2	220.0	252.1	349.1
Gumaca		100.0	101.5	120.9	130.2	128.2	129.8	148.7	186.0
Mayobac	100.0	54.1	*	*	*	*	*	*	*
Guinayangan	100.0	21.9	*	*	*	*	*	*	31.2
Catanavan		100.0	87.6	84.0	55.1	76.2	*	60.8	97.3
Obuyon	100.0	29.4	24.4	26.1	*	*	*	31.8	56.6
Baler	100.0	70.7	49.1	64.0	69.8	76.9	78.0	88.1	75.7
Palanan	100.0	93.6	61.3	*	38.8	38.8	44.9	26.1	27.8
Lupi	100.0	126.5	*	*	*	*	*	42.2	87.4
Manguirin		100.0	27.4	32.4	32.4	45.6	35.8	*	49.5
Goa		100.0	62.5	55.5	77.1	105.3	*	134.6	133.7
Tigaon		100.0	120.9	123.5	*	160.4	*	134.0	211.2

Notes: Formula Used Variation = $(\frac{\text{Population–base}}{\text{Base}} \times 100) + 100$

Where 'Base' is the population for either 1751 or 1780
No data is shown by an asterisk

Appendix Q

Statements of Balangingi Prisoners, 1838

1 *Statement of Silammkoom*

I am a native of one of the Sooloo Isles called Ballongningkin [Balanguingui] and I usually reside there. I sometimes trade in a small way such as selling Padi at Basilon and Mindanao. The Sultan lives at Sooloo proper. The principal Chief at Ballongningkin is Panglima Alip, it is well inhabited and there are large fleets of boats which are employed in collecting sea weed, tortoiseshell, [and] trepang, ... on account of the Sultan who gives the people in return, cloth or any other article he may think proper. Our fleet consisting of six prahus came from Ballongningkin and left that place about 3 months since. The fleet was commanded and under the sole direction of Orang Kaja Kullul, who is a relation of Panglima Alip. Orang Kaja Kullul informed us that the Sultan had desired him to plunder and capture all nations save Europeans. I have never seen the Sultan of Sulu, this is my first voyage to the east coast of the Malayan Peninsula, but for many years I have cruized in the vicinity of Manillas, Macassar and other places on which occasion Orang Kaja Kullul took any boats he happened to meet.

2 *Statement—Prisoner Mah roon alias Mah sandar*

I am a native of Ujang Pandan (? Pandars) Makassar—I was captured about two years since by a forminable Illanoon fleet consisting of 23 prahus—When I was taken I was proceeding to Mandas in company with 2 of my countrymen named Sindrah and Pannsil. After cruizing about for some time the piratical fleet went to Ballongningkin where I was treated as a slave and compelled to perform all kinds of work. Panglima Alip is the chief of Ballongningkin, and Orang Kaja Kullul is considered the second person in authority. The Sultan lives at Sooloo proper— We left Ballongningkin about 3 months since. The fleet consisted of six prahus— the whole under the command of Orang Kaja Kullul. I did not voluntarily join the pirates. I was compelled to go, two other of my countrymen (Sookut and Pula Nea) are in a similar position as myself. Ballongningkin is well peopled and I think there are about 200 prahus of the same size as the one destroyed by the steamer.

3 *Statement made by Daniel*

By birth I am an Illanun and for years have resided at Ballongningkin—for six years I have been pirating near Macassar, Myungka, Yan Le Lah, Seah-Seah, Tambulan, and other places. Panglima Alip is the chief of Ballongningkin, he is under the Sultan of Sulu. I cannot pretend to say whether the Sultan and Panglima Alip give any directions touching the fitting out of piratical fleets, but the fact is save 'Mangoorays' (pirating) we have scarcely any other means of getting a livelihood. Six boats left Ballongningkin under the command of Orang Kaja Kullul... Talagoa was panglima of our boat ... we had a crew of 29 men, six of whom were killed and several wounded.

4 *Statement of Tala Goa*

I live at Ballongningkin with my family. I occasionally magoorap(pirating)[and] at other times[I am] making salt, planting Paddy, [or] collecting tortoise shell. I am a follower of Orang Kaja Kullul and I am compelled to do and act as he may direct. Panglima Alip is the chief of Ballongningkin, he of course, was aware of the subject of the cruize and Orang Kaja Kullul received instructions not to molest trading boats to and from the ports of Singapore and Tringanoo. I can say nothing positively relative to the Sultan of Sooloo. I am not a panglima, I was placed in charge of one of the boats by Orang Kaja Kullul who had exclusive control of the six prahus—the persons in charge of the several prahus were besides myself, See Deman, See Tambie, See Tundine, and See Puttah. Ballongningkin was destroyed by a force from Manilla when I was quite a youth.

Source: Bonham to Maitland, June 28, 1838, PRO, Admiralty 125/133.

Appendix R

Statements of the Fugitive Captives of the Sulu Sultanate, 1836–1864

The statements have been compiled and ordered as a series from the following sources:

XVIII. 1 Declaraciones de todos los cautivos fugados de Jolo y acogidos a los buques de la expresada divicion, con objeto de averiguar los puntos de donde salen los pancos piratas, la clase de gente que los tripulan, la forma en que se hacen los armamentos y otros particulares que arrojan las mismas declaraciones, Expediente 12, October 4, 1836, PNA, Mindanao/Sulu 1803–1890.

XVIII. 2 Relacion jurada de los cuarenta y cinco cautivos venidos de Jolo sobre el bergantin Espanol *Cometa,* March 19, 1847, PNA, Piratas 3.

XVIII. 3 Relacion jurada de los cuarenta y cuatro cautivos venidos de Jolo sobre el bergantin Espanol *Cometa*, February 8, 1848 (statements 1–10); Relacion jurada de los individuos cautivos venidos en la Fragata de guerra Inglesa *Samarang,* procedente de Jolo, March 15, 1845 (statements 11–14); Relacion jurada de los cuatro cautivos venidos en el navio Ingles de guerra *Agincourt,* procedente de la Isla de Borneo, December 11, 1845 (statements 15–18); Relacion jurada de los dos individuos cautivos venidos en la corbeta de guerra Francesa *Salina,* September 17, 1845 (statements 19–20); Relacion jurada de los cinco cautivos venidos en la Falua de la division de la isla del corregidor, August 23, 1845 (statements 21–24); Relacion jurada de los seis cautivos venidos de Jolo sobre el bergantin Espanol *San Vincente,* January 14, 1850 (statements 25–30). The remaining captives were brought to Manila on the following vessels: the steamer, *Elcano* (31); Brigantine, *San Ramos* (32–33); Frigate, *Magnolia* (34); Brigantine, *Cometa* (35–39); steamer, *Reyno de Castilla* (40–41), PNA, Piratas 3.

XVIII.4 Relacion de los cautivos rescatados y evadidos del poder de los moros dentro del presente ano que se embarcan con esta fecha en la goleta de S.M.*Animosa,* July 22, 1864, PNA, Piratas 3.

XVIII.5 Verklaringen van ontvlugten personen uit den handen der zeeroovers van 1845–1849, ANRI, Menado 37.

XVIII.6 Verklaringen van ontvlugten personen uit den handen der zeeroovers van 1845–1849, ANRI, Menado 37.

Appendix R

Statements of the Fugitive Captives of the Sulu Sultanate, 1836–1864

	CAPTIVE	MASTER	PERSON SOLD TO	PLACE	PRICE	YEAR OF CAPTIVITY	AGE
1	Mariano de la Cruz	Tusan(Tunkil)	Datu Mhd. Buyo	Jolo	5 bundles of Ilocos cloth	1836	21
2	Francisco Feliz		Amanang	Jolo	3 bundles of cotton cloth, 2 glass water bottles, 2 plates, 2 cups	1834	45
3	Domingo Francisco	Visayan Renegade(Tunkil)	Chinese mestizo merchant	Jolo		1836	35
4	Juan Salvador	Balangingi Samal	A Taosug	Jolo	5 pieces of cotton cloth	1836	
5	Manuel de los Santos	Balangingi Samal	A Taosug merchant	Jolo	Assorted goods to the value of 60 pesos	1836	27
6	Esmerald Francisco	Visayan Renegade(Balangingi)	Tiboral	Jolo		1836	50
7	Maria Gertudiz	Balangingi Samal	Tiglam	Jolo	Bronze Lantanca (cannon)	1834	35
8	Marcelo teofilo	Maluso man		Parang	25 pieces of cotton cloth		43
9	Tibarcio Juan	Balangingi Samal	Datu Mende	Jolo		1834	41
10	Juan Monico	Balangingi Samal	A Taosug	Jolo	6 lengths of gauze (cotton or silk?) and a Visayan bell	1836	14
11	Maria Damiana	Tunkil Samal	Chinese-Intiao	Jolo			14
12	Domingo Candelario	Balangingi Samal	Man from Laminosa—resold in Jolo 6 months later	(Basilan)		1833	28
13	Francisco Mariano	Balangingi Samal	Sold at Parian Batang—escaped then sold at Tapul island—escaped, seized and sold to a Muslim trader (Jolo)	Jolo		1826	40
14	Juan de los Santos	Tunkil Samal	Suyan—retainer of Datu Sadula	Jolo		1829	21
15	Juan Florentino	Pilas man	A Taosug	Zamboanga		1835	35
16	Pedro Santiago	Basilan-BagBagon[2](village)	A Visayan Renegade	Jolo		1835	16
17	Agapito de la Cruz	Balangingi Samal	Escaped—seized by a Taosug from Guimba	Interior of Jolo		1831	29
18	Juan de la Cruz	Balangingi Samal	Sold at Jolo, then at Siassi	Jolo		1826	25
19	Manuel Feliz	Balangingi Samal	A Taosug	Interior of Jolo		1831	26
20	Vizcente Remigio	Balangingi Samal	Datu Tael	Jolo		1833	31
21	Juan Santiago	Balangingi Samal					
22	Juan Sabala	Balangingi Samal	Datu Molo	Jolo	Bronze Lantanca	1834	40
23	Augustin Juan	Balangingi Samal	Datu Tael	Jolo	10 lagas of unhusked rice	1826	35

Appendix R (*cont.*)

	CAPTIVE	MASTER	PERSON SOLD TO	PLACE	PRICE	YEAR OF CAPTIVITY	AGE
24	Pedro Antonio	Balangingi Samal	Samal Fishermen	Babaon village		1828	24
25	Jose German Reales	Visayan renegade (Tunkil)	Datu Daniel	Jolo	A bundle of cotton cloth and 3 balls of opium	1831	30
26	Angel Custodio	Balangingi Samal	A village headman(Balangingi)			1835	19
27	Anastacio Caullo	Balangingi Samal	A Muslim from Sandacan			1826	36
28	Francisco Agustin	Iranun	Muslim trader			1832	23
29	Alexo Quijano	Balangingi Samal	Datu Bendahara	Jolo		1828	33
30	Matias de la Cruz	Balangingi Samal	Datu Mhd.Buyo	Jolo	30 pieces of cotton cloth	1825	33
31	Juan Teodoro	Balangingi Samal	A Chinese	Jolo	70 pieces of cotton cloth	1834	56
32	Evaresto Pinto	Balangingi Samal	Antonio—Visayan renegade	Jolo		1835	25
33	Santiago Manuel de Tuna	Balangingi Samal	Pata	Jolo		1828	50
34	Francisco Gregorio	Balangingi Samal	Datu Bendahara	Jolo		1829	28
35	Francisco Sereno	Sipac Samal	A Muslim—Sagio	Jolo		1834	28
36	Mariano de la Cruz	Balangingi Samal		Jolo		1836	28
37	Juan de la Cruz	Balangingi Samal	Datu Salipasan	Jolo		1830	57
38	Francisco Sacarias	Balangingi Samal	Datu Molo	Jolo		1833	25
39	Juan Apolonio	Balangingi Samal	Datu Mhd.Buyo	Jolo		1831	25
40	Matias Domingo	Balangingi Samal	Datu Daniel	Jolo		1834	18
41	Francisco Basilio	Balangingi Samal	Aamiang	Jolo		1836	30
42	Juan Pedro	Renegade—tumol(Balangingi)	Salane	Jolo		1835	26
43	Diomicio Francisco	Balangingi	Amanan	Jolo		1836	28
44	Francisco Augustino	Binuong-Balangingi	Ande			1836	
45	Francisco Xaiver	Tunkil Samal	A Chinese	Jolo	5 bundles of cotton cloth	1836	35
46	Eusebio de la Cruz	Balangingi Samal	A Chinese merchant	Jolo	2 red boxes, 3 pieces of cotton cloth, 1 glass water bottle	1836	28
47	Pedro Francisco	Balangingi Samal	A Chinese merchant—Sa Hua	Jolo		1832	
48	Vizcente Santiago	Balangingi Samal	A Muslim merchant	Pangutaran island		1832	38
49	Gabriel Francisco	Tukil Samal	A Taosug merchant			1833	45
50	Mariano Sevilla	Balangingi Samal	Ransomed by the Spanish captain of the schooner *Soledad*			1835	40

Appendix R (cont.)

	NAME	PROVINCE	AGE	STATUS	ACTIVITY WHEN SEIZED	NO. OF RAID VESSELS	RETAILING POINT	PERIOD OF RESIDENCE AT RETAILING POINT	PERSON SOLD TO AT JOLO	MEANS OF MANUMISSION	YEAR OF CAPTIVITY
1	Lorenzo Sixto	Surigao	33	Married	Fishing—4 others	8 Pancos	Balangingi	2 weeks	Sinden	Ransomed for 40 pesos	1845
2	Alejandro Valuenzuela	Tondo	47	Single	Trading	3 Pancos	Balangingi	1 week	William Wyndham	Ransomed	1844
3	Pedro Flores	Capiz	30	Married	Trading	5 Pancos	Balangingi	3 days	Simindo	Baroto—to *Cometa*	1844
4	Pedro Ysidoro	Capiz	40	Married	Fishing	4 Pancos	Balangingi	3 weeks	Sumaran	Baroto—to *Cometa*	1844
5	Simon Ylario	Cebu	19	Married	Fishing—7 others	8 Pancos	Balangingi	1 month	Utu	escaped	1846
6	Angel Manuel	Leyte	45	Widow	Fishing—1 other	3 Pancos	Balangingi	3 days	Vay-Chinese	—came with his master to Manila	1841
7	Alejandro Juan	Leyte	18	Single	Fishing	5 Pancos	Balangingi	1½ years	William Wyndham	escaped to the *Cometa*	1845
8	Damaso Soledad	Cuyo	23	Married	Trading	3 Pancos	Balangingi	1 week	Sandiasan	escaped	1846
9	Angustin Bernardo	Cebu	35	Married	Trading	3 Pancos	Balangingi	4 days	Datu Mirasan	ransomed by W. Wyndham	1845
10	Manuel Valdez	Samar	30	Single	Fishing—1 other	8 Pancos	Balangingi	1 week	Camunug	escaped to *Cometa*	1846
11	Alberto de la Cruz	Negros	30	Single	Trading—19 others	?	Tunkil	1 month	Datu Sisi	escaped to *Cometa*	1846
12	Juan Pedro	Cebu	40	Married	Fishing—5 others	3 Pancos	Balangingi	4 days	Alm'ain	escaped to *Cometa*	1846
13	Vincente Remigio	Cebu	28	Married	Fishing—5 others	3 Pancos	Balangingi	4 days	Datu Abdula	escaped to *Cometa*	1846
14	Toribio de la Cruz	Mindoro	26	Single	Fishing—2 others	2 Baroto	Balangingi	8 days	Barit	escaped to *Cometa*	1845
15	Jose de la Cruz	Cebu	42	Married	Fishing—3 others	8 Pancos	Balangingi	5 days	Sacan	escaped to *Cometa*	1844
16	Manuel Francisco	Leyte	28	Single	Cutting Nipa—3 others	4 Pancos	Balangingi	1 week	Undin	escaped to *Cometa*	1846
17	Pedro Apolinario	Negros	30	Married	Delivering a church despatch	3 Salisipan	Tunkil	1 month	Panguindayan	escaped to *Cometa*	1844
18	Yngacio Francisco	Leyte	19	Single	Fishing—1 other	2 Pancos	Balangingi	2 months	Ymban	escaped to *Cometa*	1842

Appendix R (cont.)

	NAME	PROVINCE	AGE	STATUS	ACTIVITY WHEN SEIZED	NO.OF RAID VESSELS	RETAILING POINT	PERIOD OF RESIDENCE AT RETAILING POINT	PERSON SOLD TO AT JOLO	MEANS OF MANUMISSION	YEAR OF CAPTIVITY
19	Gregoria de la Concepcion	Albay	48	Widow	Travelling	6 Pancos	Balangingi	2 years	Machadi	escaped to *Cometa*	1838
20	Pliesto de la Cruz	Zambales	20	Single	Trading	3 Pancos	Balangingi	2 weeks	Datu Ayut	escaped to *Cometa*	1842
21	Juan Francisco	Cebu	30	Married	Trading	9 Pancos	Balangingi	2 weeks	Vincente Chinese	came with his master to Manila	1846
22	Ambrosio Magno	Ylocos Sur	25	Married	Fishing—2 others	7 Pancos	Balangingi	1 month	Balatjan	escaped to *Cometa*	1844
23	Antonio Francisco	Albay	30	Single	Travelling	8 Pancos	Tunkil	1 month	A Muslim	ransomed for 40 pesos	1846
24	Carlos de los Santos	Cebu	30	Married	Fishing—2 others	8 Pancos	Balangingi	2 nights	Damblod	ransomed for 35 pesos	1846
25	Fernando Francisco	Cebu	36	Single	Trading	9 Pancos	(Sipac)	11 days	Bala	ransomed for 60 pesos	1846
26	Francisco Eusebio	Cebu	25	Married	Fishing—1 other	8 Pancos	Balangingi	1 month	William Wyndham	W.Wyndham sent to Manila	1845
27	Eulalio Composano	Albay	23	Single	Trading	5 Pancos	Balangingi	2 days	Daut then to William Wyndham	W.Wyndham sent to Manila	1844
28	Gelacio Gabriel	Illocos Sur	55	Married	Trading	3 Pancos	Balangingi	5 days	Datu Maasi	ransomed for 15 pesos	1846
29	Pedro Sabado	Illocos Sur	45	Married	Trading	3 Pancos	Balangingi	5 days	Datu Maasi	ransomed for 15 pesos	1846
30	Gabriela Santiago	Illocos Sur	44	Married	Fishing—5 others	3 Pancos	Balangingi	2 weeks	Ynban	escaped to *Cometa*	1842
31	Juan Velano	Yloylo	35	Married	Fishing	4 Pancos	Tunkil	month		ransomed to *Cometa*	1846
32	Celedonio Justo	Yloylo	36	Married	Fishing—2 others	3 Pancos	Tunkil	month	Bairo	ransomed to *Cometa*	1846
33	Francisco Salvador	Leyte	17	Single	Travelling—19 others	5 Pancos	Balangingi	week	Abdumanel	escaped to *Cometa*	1844
34	Francisco de Leon	Cebu	36	Married	Trading	9 Pancos	Balangingi	2 weeks		ransomed by Capt. *Cometa*	1846
35	Geronimo Ibanez	Samar	21	Single	Trading	8 Pancos	Balangingi	2 months		ransomed by Capt. *Cometa*	1846
36	Juan Jose	Yloylo	21	Single	Travelling—6 others	4 Pancos	Tunkil	6 days	Uray then to W.Wyndham	W.Wyndham sent to Manila	1845

Appendix R (*cont.*)

	NAME	PROVINCE	AGE	STATUS	ACTIVITY WHEN SEIZED	NO. OF RAID VESSELS	RETAILING POINT	PERIOD OF RESIDENCE AT RETAILING POINT	PERSON SOLD TO AT JOLO	MEANS OF MANUMISSION	YEAR OF CAPTIVITY
37	Jacinto Diomeso	Yloylo	37	Married	Seized in Camarin	5 Barotos	Tunkil	week	Majumat	ransomed by Capt. *Cometa*	1846
38	Vincente Ferrer	Yloylo	40	Married	Travelling—14 others	1 Panco	Amian Island	2 months	W. Wyndham	W. Wyndham sent to Manila	1845
39	Jose Bruno	Yloylo	25	Single	Travelling	3 Pancos	Balangingi		W. Wyndham	W. Wyndham sent to Manila	1846
40	Juan Gregorio	Yloylo	43	Married	Fishing—3 others	3 Pancos	Tunkil	week	Datu Camalic	Freed by Capt. *Cometa*	1846
41	Clemente Tranquilino	Albay	32	Married	Travelling	8 Pancos	Sipac	3 months	Sibotoc	Freed by Capt. *Cometa*	1846
42	Jose Manacio	Camarines Sur	19	Single	Trading	8 Pancos	Balangingi	2 months	Capt. of *Cometa*		1846
43	Martino Antonio	Yloylo	22	Single	Fishing	1 Panco	Balangingi	3 days	sold on Basilan	escaped from Basilan to Zamboanga	1846
44	Fausto Francisco	Negros	9	Single	Fishing—6 others	3 Pancos	Tunkil	2 months	Capt. of *Cometa*		1846
45	Juan Miguel	Negros	10	Single	Fishing—6 others	3 Pancos	Tunkil	2 months	Capt. of *Cometa*		1846

Appendix R (*cont.*)

	NAME	PROVINCE	AGE	STATUS	ACTIVITY WHEN SEIZED	NO.OF RAID VESSELS	RETAILING POINT	PERIOD OF RESIDENCE AT RETAILING POINT	PERSON SOLD TO	PLACE	PRICE OF SALE	MEANS OF MANUMISSION	YEAR OF CAPTIVITY
1	Martin de la Cruz	Mindoro	55	Widow	Fishing	5 Pancos	Balangingi	3 days	Buto	Jolo		Escaped 1846	1844
2	Francisco Santiago	Misamis	20	Single	Travelling	2 Pancos	Sipac	6 days				Escaped to Zamboanga	1847
3	Manuel Molo	Leyte	55	Married	Travelling	6 Pancos	Balangingi	5 days		Catifan Island		Escaped to *Cometa*—1847	1842
4	Pedro Armero	Cebu	25	Single	Fishing—1 other	8 Pancos	Balangingi	3 days		Tapiantana		Escaped to Pasanhan & Zamboanga	1846
5	Ambrosio Mision	Bohol	28	Married	Fishing—5 others	8 Pancos	Balangingi	3 days		Jolo		Escaped to Zamboanga	1847
6	Pedro Francisco	Bohol	18	Single	Trading	8 Pancos	Balangingi	1 day	Sapdula	Jolo		Escaped to *Cometa*	1847
7	Cerapio Parenas	Ilocos Sur	40	Married	Fishing	7 Pancos	Balangingi	month		Jolo		Escaped to *Cometa*	1846
8	Mateo Francisco	Cebu	19	Single	Fishing—1 other	2 Salisipan	Tunkil			Jolo		Escaped to *Cometa*	1847
9	Juan Francisco	Cebu	22	Married	Trading—7 others	2 Pancos	Balangingi	2 days	Datu Abu	Jolo		Escaped by baroto to *Cometa*	1847
10	Saturnino Martin	Capiz	18	Single	Fishing—2 others	8 Pancos	Balangingi	4 days	Sipay	Jolo		Escaped to *Cometa*	1846
11	Francisco Anostacio	Yloylo	18		Fishing	Salisipan	Balanging	1 year	Ahmat-trader	Jolo		Escaped by baroto to *Samarang*	1843
12	Jacinto Pedro	Yloylo	50	Married	Fishing	Salisipan Baroto	Tunkil		Bua	Jolo		Escaped by baroto to *Samarang*	1843
13	Fragido San Juan	Zamboanga	23	Married	Constructing a lime kiln		Tapiantana	7 days		Gunong Tabur		Capt. Belcher negotiates freedom	1842
14	Mateo San Francisco	Camarines Sur	20		Fishing	9 Pancos	Tunkil		Chinese	Jolo		Escaped to *Samarang*	1842

Appendix R (cont.)

	NAME	PROVINCE	AGE	STATUS	ACTIVITY WHEN SEIZED	NO.OF RAID VESSELS	RETAILING POINT	PERIOD OF RESIDENCE AT RETAILING POINT	PERSON SOLD TO	PLACE	PRICE OF SALE	MEANS OF MANUMISSION	YEAR OF CAPTIVITY
15	Juan Benedicto	Yloylo	27		Trading	10 Pancos	Balangingi	1 month		Malludu		Escaped to English expedition	1883
16	Mariano Domingo	Yloylo	25	Single	Fishing	15 Pancos	Balangingi	1 year		Malludu		Escaped to English expedition	1821
17	Francisco Vincente	Cebu	40	Married	Fishing	10 Pancos	Balangingi	3 months		Malludu		Escaped to English expedition	1843
18	Juan de la Cruz	Yloylo	31	Single	Cutting wood	12 Pancos	Tampasuk			Malludu		Escaped to English expedition	1840
19	Felix Torres	Albay	23	Married	Travelling	9 Barotos	Balangingi	3 years				Escaped to English expedition	1842
20	Juan Florentino	Yloylo	40	Married	Fishing	4 Pancos	Pilas	2 months	Siangui			Recaptured by *Balangingi*	1835
21	Antonio Juan	Calamianes		Single	Fishing	2 Barotos	Balangingi	1 year				Escaped from Marauding expedition	1844
22	Domingo Apolinario	Mindoro			Travelling	2 Barotos	Balangingi	6 years				Escaped from Marauding expedition	1841
23	Nazario de la Cruz	Albay			Travelling	7 Pancos	Visayan Is.			Balangingi		Escaped from Marauding expedition	1840
24	Severino Santiago	Zamboanga			Fishing	2 Pancos	Basilan		Datu Molok	Jolo		Escaped from Marauding expedition	1845
25	Casimiro Santiago	Capiz	27	Single	Trading—18 others	12 Pancos	Balangingi	1 day	Adul Jaman	Jolo	1000 pieces of Chinese coin 1 piece of white cotton cloth	Baroto to *San Vincente*	1838
26	Pedro Gregorio	Capiz	26	Married	Trading—4 others	3 Pancos	Tunkil	2 weeks	Datu Maribajal	Jolo	50 cavanes of unhusked rice	Escaped to *San Vincente*	1846

Appendix R (*cont.*)

	NAME	PROVINCE	AGE	STATUS	ACTIVITY WHEN SEIZED	NO. OF RAID VESSELS	RETAILING POINT	PERIOD OF RESIDENCE AT RETAILING POINT	PERSON SOLD TO	PLACE	PRICE OF SALE	MEANS OF MANUMISSION	YEAR OF CAPTIVITY
27	Domingo de la Cruz	Yloylo	30	Married	Fishing	3 Pancos	Tunkil	1 month	Majaradia	Jolo	5 pieces of white cotton cloth	Escaped by baroto to *San Vincente*	1840
28	Juan Feliz	Leyte	24	Single	Travelling	5 Pancos	Sipac	2 months	Guichay	Jolo	90 cavanes of unhusked rice	Ransomed by Capt. *San. Vincente*	1847
29	Elevterio de Juan	Yloylo	15	Single	Fishing	2 Pancos	Tunkil	2 days	Datu Buyog	Jolo	5 large pieces of black cotton cloth	Escaped to *San Vincente*	1845
30	Lucas Barcarcel	Pangasinan	25	Single	Trading	6 Pancos	Balangingi	month	Eman Said	Jolo	6 pieces of white cotton cloth	Escaped to *San Vincente*	1838
31	Pedro del Remedio	Cebu	36	Single	Trading	20 Pancos	Balangingi	2 years	Datu Labuan	Jolo	20 cavanes of unhusked rice	Escaped by baroto to *Elcano*	1823
32	Francisco Mariano	Samar	45	Married	Trading	5 Pancos	Balangingi		Gaya			Escaped to Pasanhan	1847
33	Francisco Aquino	Samar	31	Married	Trading	9 Pancos	Balangingi	2 weeks	Lacha		109 cavanes of unhusked rice	Escaped to Pasanhan	1846
34	Ignasio Ambrocio	Bohol	25		Trading	8 Pancos	Sipace	6 months	Chambit			Escaped to Windham's vessel	1848
35	Nicolas Antonio	Albay	30		Trading	12 Pancos	Balangingi	3 months	Datu Salabansajasin			Escaped to *Cometa*	1844
36	Lucas Felis	Yloylo	27	Single	Fishing	2 Pancos	Tunkil	1 month	Olo			Escaped to *Cometa*	1843
37	Estaban Escribano	Yloylo	60	Married	Trading	4 Pancos	Balangingi	2 weeks	Digno			Escaped to *Cometa*	
38	Gaspar Regulacion	Samar	20	Single	Fishing	2 Barotos	Balangingi	1 month	Tampin			Escaped to *Cometa*	1846
39	Juan Tubis	Samar	40	Married	Trading		Balangingi	1 night	Anti			Escaped to *Cometa*	1846
40	Juan Fernando	Capiz	28		Travelling	4 Pancos	Balangingi	1 week	Buso			Escaped by *Banca* to *Zamboanga*	1845
41	Dionieso Fernando	Capiz	15		Travelling	4 Pancos	Balangingi	1 week	Esmo			Escaped by *Banca* to *Zamboanga*	1845

Appendix R (cont.)

NAME	PROVINCE	COMMUNITY	AGE	STATUS	ACTIVITY WHEN SEIZED	NO. OF RAID VESSELS	RETAILING POINT	PERIOD OF RESIDENCE AT RETAILING POINT	PERSON SOLD TO	PLACE	MEANS OF MANU-MISSION	YEAR OF CAPTIVITY
1 Andres Reyes	Yloylo	Molo	12	Single						Tunkil	Rescued by Navy expedition to Tunkil	1860
2 Maria Hermigia	Yloylo	Yloylo	30	Married			Tawi²-1860			Patian Island—Jolo	Escaped to Zamboanga	1864
3 Paduman, Malay	Moluccas	Macassar	30	Single			Tawi²				Escaped to Zamboanga	1860
4 Tuyo, Malay	Moluccas	Macassar	28	Single			Tawi²			Tawi²	Escaped	1862
5 Vincente Andunday	Samar	Bobon	40	Married			Carondong			Patian Island—Jolo	Escaped to Zamboanga	1860
6 Gregorio Arawa	Tayabas	Gumaca	40	Married			Punuan			Punuan—Jolo	Escaped to Zamboanga	1859–1860
7 Anastielo Francisco	Yloylo	Yloylo	19	Single			Balangingi			Jolo	Escaped to Zamboanga	1862
8 Tomas Meiguelleno	Cebu	San Nicolas	30	Single			Balangingi		Taupan	Jolo	Escaped to Zamboanga	1844
9 Eulogio Dano	Cebu	San Nicolas	23	Single			Balangingi			Jolo	Escaped to Zamboanga	1847
10 Sebero Munez	Cebu	San Nicolas	43	Married			Balangingi			Jolo	Escaped to Zamboanga	
11 Julian Domingo	Capiz	Capiz	30	Married			Lom² Island near Jolo		Datu Asivi	Jolo	Escaped to Zamboanga	1860
12 Teodora de los Santos	Romblon	Capidiocan	32	Married			Balangingi		Datu Asivi	Jolo	Escaped to Zamboanga	1861
13 Marcos de la Cruz	Cebu	Talisay	20	Single			Tunkil		Yting	Tawi²	Escaped to Zamboanga	
14 Lorenzo Debulgndo	Yloylo	Dumangas	13	Single						Caboncol		

Appendix R (cont.)

	NAME	PLACE OF RESIDENCE	AGE	ACTIVITY WHEN SEIZED	NO.OF RAID VESSELS	RETAILING POINT	PERSON SOLD TO	PLACE	EMPLOYMENT IN CAPTIVITY	MEANS OF MANU-MISSION	YEAR OF CAPTIVITY	NO.OF YEARS IN CAPTIVITY
1	Tongua			Travelling	8 large pancos 4 salisipan 4 vintas	Balangingi	A woman	Jolo	Trader in cloth with Chinese	Escaped in a small sailing craft	1838	7
2	Omia			Travelling	8 large pancos, 4 salisipan 4 vintas	Balangingi	Retained by Samal Master-Mintas	Pilas	Domestic work	Escaped in a small sailing craft	1838	7
3	Hajati	Gorontalo		Travelling	24 pancos 24 salisipan	Balangingi	Agas	Gunong Bara	Agricultural work	Escaped in a small sailing craft	1835	10
4	Paulino Josebeo	Batangas		Fishing	6 large pancos		Retained by Master	Balangingi	Restored vessels		1845	1
5	Diaminie	Tontoli		Fishing	3 large pancos, 3 small vantas	Balangingi	Retained by Master	Balangingi		Escaped from marauding fleet at night to the shore in small baroto	1845	1
6	Rapar	Tombaririe	30		4 large pancos 4 small vintas	Balangingi	Salie	Jolo	Domestic workporter	Escaped in a small sailing craft with a Sangirnese captive	1843	3
7	Sadai	Makassar		Trading	3 pancos	Balangingi	Yakie	Bual	Agricultural work for Yakie's mother	Escaped with 3 other Makassarese captives to Chiauw by small sailing craft	1842	4
8	Sarenko	Boeton		Fishing	3 large pancos	Balangingi	Saha	Jolo	Agricultural & domestic work	Escaped with 3 other Makassarese captives to Chiauw by small sailing craft	1843	3

Appendix R (cont.)

	NAME	PLACE OF RESIDENCE	AGE	ACTIVITY WHEN SEIZED	NO. OF RAID VESSELS	RETAILING POINT	PERSON SOLD TO	PLACE	EMPLOYMENT IN CAPTIVITY	MEANS OF MANU-MISSION	YEAR OF CAPTIVITY	NO. OF YEARS IN CAPTIVITY
9	Lasado	Boni		Fishing	5 vintas	Balangingi	Yakie	Bual	Agricultural work	Escaped with 3 other Makassarese captives to Chiauw by small sailing craft	1834	12
10	Hatibi Soleman	Bangai		Travelling	6 large pancos, 6 small vintas	Balangingi	Yakie	Bual	Agricultural work	Escaped with 3 other Makassarese captives to Chiauw by small sailing craft	1843	3
11	Kilapon	Amoerang	20		4 small pancos	Balangingi		Balangingi		Escaped with another in a small sailing craft to an island near Tontoli	1843	3
12	Mootalo	Kwandang		Travelling	4 large pancos, 2 small vintas	Balangingi	Retained by Master	Balangingi	Domestic work	Escaped while collecting firewood & water for marauding fleet	1846	1
13	Tabaronc	Sangir Island	30	Travelling	4 large pancos	Balangingi		Balangingi	Domestic work	Escaped from marauding fleet at Lembelsland near Kema	1843	3
14	Kadasa	Hila Island	15	Fishing	1 small panco	Sipac	Ganadoan Iranun	Patian	Agricultural & domestic work	Escaped with 3 others from Patian Island by small sailing craft	1843	3
15	Abdul	Gonong	25	Fishing	6 large & 5 small pancos	Sipac	Gondorico— a blacksmith	Patian	Agricultural & domestic work	Escaped with 3 others from Patian Island by small sailing craft	1845	1

Appendix R (*cont.*)

	NAME	PLACE OF RESIDENCE	AGE	ACTIVITY WHEN SEIZED	NO.OF RAID VESSELS	RETAILING POINT	PERSON SOLD TO	PLACE	EMPLOYMENT IN CAPTIVITY	MEANS OF MANU-MISSION	YEAR OF CAPTIVITY	NO.OF YEARS IN CAPTIVITY
16	Njow	Kilbat	30	Travelling	4 large pancos	Balangingi	Sakajang	Patian	Fishing and domestic work	Escape with 3 others from Patian Island by small sailing craft	1845	1
17	Francis Mariano	Manila	45	Collecting tripang & nests	3 large pancos	Sipac	Uming	Parang	Fishing and domestic work	Escaped with 5 others in a small sailing craft to Menado	1837	10
18	Francisco Basiiio Basilio	Cebu	28	Trading	7 pancos	Sipac	Uming	Parang	Agricultural work	Escaped with 5 others in a small sailing craft to Menado	1842	5
19	Siado	Bolang	25	Fishing	3 large pancos, 3 small vintas	Balangingi	Sawadi	Sulu	Agricultural work	Escaped with 5 others in a small sailing craft to Menado	1844	3
20	Jacob Estephanus	Taboekan	50	Fishing	1 large panco 1 small vinta	Balangingi	Uming	Parang	Agricultural work	Escaped with 5 others in a small sailing craft to Menado	1827	20
21	Pedro Francisco	Leyte	30	Travelling	5 large pancos	Basilan	Uming	Sulu	Agricultural work	Escaped with 5 others in a small sailing craft to Menado	1843	4
22	Kawase	Goron	45	Travelling	6 large pancos	Balangingi	Bajang	Balangingi	Agricultural work	Escaped with 3 others in a sailing craft	1846	1
23	Madi	Tumbuka	30	Collecting sago	3 large pancos	Balangingi	Ybie	Balangingi	Agricultural work	Escaped with 3 others in a sailing craft	1844	3

Appendix R (*cont.*)

	NAME	PLACE OF RESIDENCE	AGE	ACTIVITY WHEN SEIZED	NO.OF RAID VESSELS	RETAILING POINT	PERSON SOLD TO	PLACE	EMPLOYMENT IN CAPTIVITY	MEANS OF MANU- MISSION	YEAR OF CAPTIVITY	NO.OF YEARS IN CAPTIVITY
24	Ramaka	Ratahan	40	Fishing	3 large pancos	Balangingi	Arik	Ubian	Agricultural work	Escaped with Madja to Gorontalo in a small sailing craft	1846	1
25	Abdul	Djupandang	30	Fishing	1 large panco 1 small	Balangingi	Tallaga	Tapiantana	Fishing and domestic work	Escaped to Zamboanga in small sailing craft then sailed on a Sulu brig to Menado	1841	6
26	Sendie	Dongala	30	Trading	3 large pancos 2 small vintas	Sipac		Pangalmata	Agricultural work		1844	3
27	Sirua	Kalumpang	40	Fishing	3 large & 3 small pancos	Basilan then Sipac	Idris	Pangalmata	Agricultural work	Escaped in small sailing craft to Taboekan with Sendie	1841	6
28	Benonko	Lacasan Isl.	50	Trading	4 large & 4 small pancos	Tunkil	Hassan	Tunkil	Agricultural work— Salt manufacture	Escaped with 2 others in small sailing craft	1847	1
29	Abdulla	Pontianak	40	Trading	9 large & 1 small pancos pancos	Tunkil	Suiding	Tunkil	Agricultural work— Salt manufacture	Escaped with 2 others in small others in small sailing craft		
30	Pedro Juan	Yloylo	50	Trading	3 large pancos	Balangingi	Suiding	Tunkil	Domestic work— Salt manufacture	Escaped with 2 others in small sailing craft	1813	35

Appendix R (*cont.*)

NAME	PLACE OF RESIDENCE	AGE	NO. OF PERSONS SEIZED	FLEET SIZE	ARMAMENT OF EACH VESSEL	COMMANDER OF VESSEL	CREW PER VESSEL	WHERE MARAUDING FLOTILLA ORIGINATED	WHO OUTFITTED AND EQUIPPED THE FLOTILLA	ISLANDS USED FOR OBTAINING WATER	ISLANDS USED FOR CAREENING, CAULKING ETC	TIME OF YEAR WHEN VESSEL PUT TO SEA	YEAR OF CAPTIVITY
1 Tongua				8 pancos 4 salisipan 4 vintas			50	Balangingi	Datus of Sulu	Kassaputang River near Kaydipang	Unknown island near Kottaboona		1838
2 Omai			2	8 pancos 4 salisipan 4 vintas			10*	Balangingi	Datus of Sulu	Kadoga-Sulu Islands			1838
3 Hajati	Gorontalo		2-voyage	24 pancos 24 salisipan	8 brass cannon		30*	Balangingi	Inhabitants of Balangingi	Cham-Sangir Islands	During voyage vessels brought ashore		1835
4 Paulino Josebo	Batangas—(Philippines)		3-fishing	6 large pancos	3 lella (brass cannon)	Marthinos (a Manilaman)	40	Balangingi	Inhabitants of Balangingi	Talissie		November	1845
5 Diaminie	Tontoli		1-fishing	3 large pancos 3 small vintas	3-1 pound cannon			Balangingi	Panglimas at Balangingi	Banka Island & 3 Brother Islands	On one of the 3 Brothers Islands		1845
6 Rapar	Tombaririe	30	6	4 pancos 4 small vintas	Rantanka (brass cannon)		40 10*	Balangingi	Inhabitants of Balangingi	Banka & Menado Tua	Banks Island	West Monsoon	1843
7 Sadai	Makassar		2-voyage	3 pancos	5 rantanka		20*	Balangingi		Small islands south & west Celebes	Places where water is obtained		1842
8 Sarenko	Boeton		2-fishing	3 large pancos	1 rantanka	Samau'uh	50	Balangingi		Monde Island			1843
9 Lasado	Boni		4-fishing	5 vintas				Balangingi					1834
10 Hatibi Soleman	Bangai		4-voyage	6 large pancos 6 small vintas	1 lella			Balangingi			At Balangingi on their return		1843
11 Kilapon	Amoerang	20	3	4 small pancos	2 brass cannon		6*	Balangingi	Inhabitants of Balangingi				1843

* = Number of crew on a small craft.

Appendix R (cont.)

	NAME	PLACE OF RESIDENCE	AGE	NO. OF PERSONS SEIZED	FLEET SIZE	ARMAMENT OF EACH VESSEL	COMMANDER OF VESSEL	CREW PER VESSEL	WHERE MARAUDING FLOTILLA ORIGINATED	WHO OUTFITTED AND EQUIPPED THE FLOTILLA	ISLANDS USED FOR OBTAINING WATER	ISLANDS USED FOR CAREENING, CAULKING ETC	TIME OF YEAR WHEN VESSEL PUT TO SEA	YEAR OF CAPTIVITY
12	Moetala	Kwandang		2-voyage	4 large pancos 2 small vintas	Lella	Dangie and Manalompo	30 10*	Balangingi	Inhabitants of Balangingi	Telisa and Lembe—near Kema	Salua-Buaya Island near Gorontalo		1846
13	Taborong	Sangir Isl.	30	19-voyage	4 large pancos	Lella Rantanka & leela	Padawi and Sabitong	30 50	Balangingi	Inhabitants of Balangingi	Talise Island			1843
14	Kadasa	Hila Island (Ambon)	15	8-fishing	1 small panco			6*	Sipac	Inhabitants of Sipac	Pulsu Tudju	Batu Kapul-near Lembu Island	West Monsoon	1843
15	Abdul	Gonong (under Banda)	25	1-fishing	6 large & 5 small pancos	2 lella	Malutop (a Makassar-man)	30 6*	Balangingi	Inhabitants of Balangingi				1845
16	Njow	Banda) Kilbat	30	3-voyage	4 large pancos	5 brass cannons		50–60	Balangingi	On Mindanao by those who trade with Balangingi	Obie Island		West Monsoon	1845
17	Francis Mariano	Manila	45	3-Tripang nests	3 large pancos	3-1 pound cannons	Inam Tarawie	50	Sipac	Imam Tarawie & Kapitan Rajah	Sugut Island	Binur Bulan Island	West Monsoon	1837
18	Francisco Basilio	Cebu	28	6-voyage	7 pancos	6 cannons in large prahu, 2 cannons in small prahu	Sapan (a Manila-man)	50 30*	Balangingi	Inhabitants of Balangingi	Tinunajan Island	Birik Island		1842
19	Siado	Bolang(Simoi)	25	1-fishing	3 large pancos 3 small vintas	5 cannons in large prahu, 3 cannons in small prahu	Lumujul		Balangingi		Banka Island			1844

* = Number of crew on a small craft.

Appendix R (*cont.*)

NAME	PLACE OF RESIDENCE	AGE	NO. OF PERSONS SEIZED	FLEET SIZE	ARMAMENT OF EACH VESSEL	COMMANDER OF VESSEL	CREW PER VESSEL	WHERE MARAUDING FLOTILLA ORIGINATED	WHO OUTFITTED AND EQUIPPED THE FLOTILLA	ISLANDS USED FOR OBTAINING WATER	ISLANDS USED FOR CAREENING, CAULKING ETC	TIME OF YEAR WHEN VESSEL PUT TO SEA	YEAR OF CAPTIVITY
20 Jacob Estephanus	Taboekan	50	2-fishing	1 large panco 1 small vinta	4 cannons in large prahu 1 cannon in small prahu	Sarip Mie	30 10*	Balangingi	Sherifs on Balangingi	Kawio Island near Mindanao		West Monsoon	1827
21 Pedro Francisco	Leyte	30	2-voyage	5 large pancos	5 rantanka	Palain(a Manila-man)	50	Sipac		Kaibirang Isl. near Manila	Kalanbaman-small islands	West Monsoon	1843
22 Kawase	Goron (under Ceram)	45	11-voyage	6 large pancos	2 lella	Sangie	30	Balangingi		an island near Gorontalo	At Balangingi on their return		1846
23 Madi	Tumbuka (under Ternate)	30	5-collecting sago	3 large pancos	1 lella	Leso	20	Balangingi	Inhabitants of Balangingi	the Bugis coast	Kabina Island	West Monsoon	1844
24 Ramaka	Ratahan (Menado)	40	alone-fishing	3 large pancos	1 brass cannon		50	Balangingi	Inhabitants of Balangingi				1846
25 Abdul	Djupandang (Makassar)	30	6-fishing	1 large panco 1 small vinta	3 rantanka	Lasama	30	Balangingi	Mangindanao people	Tandjongtola near Gorontalo	At Balangingi on their return		1841
26 Sendie	Dongala (Bugis)	30	2-voyage	3 large pancos 2 small vintas	1 large rantanka	Sibaugay (a Bangai islander)	40 10*	Sipac	Inhabitants of Balangingi		Dongala		1844
27 Sirua	Kalumpang (Tontoli)	40	7-fishing	3 large & 3 small pancos	1 large cannon 2 rantanka	Utap		Sipac	Inhabitants of Balangingi			West Monsoon	1841
28 Benonko	Lacasan Island	50	9-voyage	4 large & 4 small pancos	4 rantanka 4 lella	Hassan	40 10*	Tunkil	Panglima Hassan				1847
29 Abdulla	Pontianak	40	4-voyage	9 large & 1 small pancos	4 lella	Hassan	40	Tunkil	Panglima Hassan				
30 Pedro Juan	Yloylo	50	10-voyage	3 large pancos	1 large cannon	Hassan	40	Tunkil	Panglima Hassan		Balangingi		1813

* = Number of crew on a small craft.

Notes

Preface

[1] See J.C. van Leur, *Indonesian Trade and Society.*

[2] Notable exceptions are the significant studies that have been published in the past decade on the Sultanates of Aceh (1607–36) and Johor (1641–1728) which use an impressive array of sources to portray the cosmopolitan urbanism of ruler and merchant in the maritime Malay world of the 17th century. See Denys Lombard, *Le Sultanat d'Atjeh au tempo d'Iskander Muda, 1607–1636;* and Leonard Andaya, *The Kingdom of Johor, 1641–1728.* Another important contribution is Ileto's study of the Magindanao (Cotabato) Sultanate—Reynaldo Clemena Ileto, *Magindanao, 1860–1888: The Career of Datu Uto of Buayan;* See also Carl A. Trocki, *Prince of Pirates: The Temenggongs and the Development of Johor and Singapore, 1784–1885.*

[3] Van Leur, *Indonesian Trade and Society,* p.153.

[4] See Nicholas Tarling, *Piracy and Politics in the Malay World; Sulu and Sabah: A Study of British Policy towards the Philippines and North Borneo from the Late Eighteenth Century;* Lennox A. Mills, *British Malaya, 1824–1867,* pp.323–24, 328–29; Leigh R. Wright, *The Origins of British Borneo,* pp.5, 39; and Cesar A. Majul, *Muslims in the Philippines.*

[5] Nathan Wachtel, *The Vision of the Vanquished: The Spanish Conquest of Peru Through Indian Eyes, 1530–1750* (Sussex: Harvester Press, 1977), p.2.

[6] Suzanne Miers and Igor Kopytoff, *Slavery in Africa: Historical and Anthropological Perspectives* (Madison, Wis., 1977), pp.11–12, 76–78.

[7] Extensive ethnological research has been conducted among the Taosug by Thomas Kiefer; among the Balangingi Samal by William Geoghegan; among the Samal of Cagayan de Sulu and Palawan by Eric Casino; among the Samal Laut by Harry Nimmo, Clifford Sather, and Carol Warren; among the Yakan by Carol Molony; among the Maranao by Melvin Mednick and David Barradas; and among the Subanun by Charles Frake.

[8] *Tarling, Piracy and Politics,* pp.20, 146–85; *Sulu and Sabah,* p.4; Tarling has been sharply criticized for this imbalance of perspective in relation to Sulu by Reber and Kiefer. See Anne Lyndsey Reber, "The Sulu World in the Eighteenth and Early Nineteenth Centuries: A Historiographical Problem in British Writings on Malay Piracy"; Thomas Kiefer, "The Sultanate of Sulu: Problems in the Analysis of a Segmentary State", pp.46–51.

[9] Najeeb M. Saleeby, *The History of Sulu; Majul Muslims in the Philippines,* pp.107–316.

Introduction to the First Edition

[1] Extensive ethnological research on the Taosug (Tausug, Tawsug, Suluk, Su'ug) conducted by Thomas Kiefer principally in the years 1966–68 has been published in numerous articles and several monographs. See Thomas Kiefer, *The Tausug: Violence and Law in a Philippine Moslem Society;* idem, "The Tausug Polity and the Sultanate of Sulu: A Segmentary State in the Southern Philippines".

[2] Alexander Spoehr, *Zamboanga and Sulu: An Archeological Approach to Ethnic Diversity*, p.22.

[3] For a cogent discussion of the advent of Islam in Mindanao and Sulu, and its relationship to Southeast Asian Islam until the coming of the Spaniards, see ch.2 of Majul's *Muslims in the Philippines*.

[4] Kiefer, *The Tausug*, p.10.

[5] For a complete description of the ecology of the strand environment, see David E. Sopher, *The Sea Nomads: A Study Based on the Literature of the Maritime Boat People of Southeast Asia*, pp.1–47.

[6] Spoehr, *Zamboanga and Sulu*, p.23; William Geoghegan, "Balangingi Samal", p.1.

[7] See Reynaldo Clemena Ileto, *Magindanao, 1860–1888*.

[8] The idea of a distant assemblage of islands constituting the hinterland of a port town was developed by Spoehr in the context of contemporary culture change in the Pacific Islands. Alexander Spoehr, "Port Town and Hinterlands in the Pacific Islands", *American Anthropologist* 62 (1960): 568–92.

[9] This perspective was adopted by Eric Casino in a paper presented at the seminar on Mindanao and Sulu Cultures held in Jolo in 1972. Gerard Rixhon, "Coordinated Investigation of Sulu Culture, Jolo, Sulu", p.20. The inherent advantages of this approach in an upland agricultural context are readily apparent in E.R. Leach's pioneering work on the political systems of Highland Burma. In discussing the historic record of political instability in the Kachin hills area, he states:

> these [documents] show clearly that during the last one hundred and thirty years the political organization of the area has been very unstable ... there have been violent and very rapid shifts in the overall distribution of power. It is therefore methodologically unsound to treat the different varieties of political system which we now find in the area as independent types; they should clearly be thought of as part of a larger total system in flux.

E.R. Leach, *Political Systems of Highland Burma: A Study of Kachin Social Structure* (London, 1954), p.6. See also Robert F. Berkhofer, *A Behavioural Approach to Historical Analysis* (New York, 1969), pp.188–90.

[10] This section relies heavily on the anthropological studies of Kiefer and also acknowledges the pioneering work of Gullick and Mednick concerned with the historical reconstruction of traditional Muslim political systems in Southeast Asia; Kiefer, *The Tausug*, pp.104–12; idem, "The Taosug Polity and the Sultanate of Sulu", pp.19–64; idem, "The Sultanate of Sulu: Problems in the Analysis of a Segmentary State", pp.46–50; John Gullick, *Indigenous Political Systems of Western Malaya;* Melvin Mednick, "Some Problems of Moro History and Political Organization", pp.39–52. See also Donald Brown, *Brunei: The Structure and History of a Bornean Malay Sultanate.*

[11] Kiefer, "The Taosug Polity and the Sultanate of Sulu", p.23.

[12] Clifford A. Sather, Introduction to *Traditional States of Borneo and the Southern Philippines,* ed. Clifford Sather, p.45.

[13] For a basic discussion of segmentary systems and the inherent difficulties involved in their classification, see Aidan Southall, "A Critique of the Typology of States and Political Systems", *Political Systems and the Distribution of Power,* ed. Michael Banton (London, 1965), pp.126–29; Georges Balandier, *Political Anthropology,* trans. A.M. Sheridan Smith (London, 1970), pp.72–77.

[14] Kiefer, *The Tausug*, p.105.

[15] J.Hunt, "Some Particulars relating to Sulo in the Archipelago of Felicia" (1st ed. 1837), p.37.

[16] Kiefer, "The Tausug Polity and the Sultanate of Sulu", p.26.

[17] Ibid., p.48.

[18] Kiefer, *The Tausug*, pp.110–11.

[19] Ibid., p.109.

[20] Cesar Majul, "Political and Historical Notes on the old Sulu Sultanate", p.28.

[21] Kiefer, "The Tausug Polity and the Sultanate of Sulu", p.30.

[22] For a good discussion of the more formal ceremonial and linguistic correlates of stratification in the Brunei Sultanate, see Brown, *Brunei*, pp.20–26.

[23] Kiefer, *The Tausug*, p.107.

[24] AGI, Filipinas 510; Vincente Barrantes, *Guerras Piraticas de Filipinas contra Mindanaos y Joloanos*, p.168.

[25] Kiefer, *The Tausug*, p.109; Balandier, *Political Anthropology*, pp.140–42.

PART I

Chapter 1

[1] "Historical Sketch of the Circumstances Which Led to the Settlement of Penang and of the Trade to the Eastward Previous to and Since That Period", in Mr. Graham to Mr. Dundas, 29 May 1795, IOL, H/Misc/437/6, p.149.

[2] Edgar Wickberg, *The Chinese in Philippine Life, 1850–1898*, p.88.

[3] "A Memoir on the Sooloogannon Dominion and Commerce", Alexander Dalrymple, 26 Feb. 1761, PRO, Egremont Papers, 30/47/20/1.

[4] Hunt, "Some Particulars Relating to Sulo", p.46.

[5] John Crawford, *History of the Indian Archipelago*, vol.3, p.184.

[6] Hunt, "Some Particulars Relating to Sulo", p.46.

[7] Ibid., Wilkes, "Jolo and the Sulus", p.169.

[8] Hunt, "Some Particulars Relating to Sulo", p.46.

[9] AGI, Filipinas 510.

[10] Hunt, "Some Particulars Relating to Sulo", p.46.

[11] Ibid.

[12] IOL, G/4/1, p.355.

[13] Jose Maria Halcon a GCG, "Memoria sobre Mindanao y demas puntos del Sur", 31 Dec.1837, AUST, seccion Folletos, Tomo 117.

[14] Dalrymple, "Essays towards an Account of Sooloo", p.567.

[15] Hunt, "Some Particulars Relating to Sulo", p.46.

[16] Dalrymple, "Essays towards an Account of Sooloo", p.567; Forrest, *Voyage to New Guinea*, p.325; Tomas de Comyn, *State of the Philippines in 1810*, p.124; Hunt, "Some Particulars Relating to Sulo", p.46; William Milburn, *Oriental Commerce*, vol.2, p.425, Wilkes, "Jolo and the Sulus", p.169.

[17] Hunt, "Some Particulars Relating to Sulo", p.46.

[18] Dalrymple, "Essays towards an Account of Sooloo", pp.563–66; Forrest, *Voyage to New Guinea*, p.325; Comyn, *State of the Philippines in 1810*, p.124; Hunt, "Some Particulars Relating to Sulo", p.46; Wilkes, "Jolo and the Sulus", p.169.

[19] Forrest, *Voyage to New Guinea*, p.324; see App. B.

[20] Milburn, *Oriental Commerce*, vol.2, p.513.

[21] Mr. Graham to Mr.Dundas, 29 May 1795, IOL, H/Misc/437/6, p.149.

[22] Hunt, "Some Particulars Relating to Sulo", p.46.

[23] D. MacDonald, *A Narrative of the Early Life and Services of Captain D. MacDonald, R.N.*, 3rd ed., p.200.

[24] Spoehr, *Zamboanga and Sulu*, p.214.

[25] There are numerous references in the literature of the first half of the 19th century to the intelligence, enterprise, and spirit of commercial adventure of these maritime people. See D.H. Kolff, *Voyage of the Dutch Brig of War Dourga through the Southern and Little Known Parts of the Moluccan Archipelago and the Previously Unknown Southern Coast of New Guinea Performed During the Years 1825 and 1826*, trans. George Windsor Earl, p.11; MacDonald, *A Narrative of the Early Life and Services of Captain D. MacDonald*, p.217; J. Dalton, "On the Present State of Piracy", p.29.

[26] Alexander Dalrymple to Mr. Orme, 12 Apr. 1762, IOL, Orme Collection, vol.67, p.115.

[27] Alexander Dalrymple to the court of Directors, 1 February 1764, IOL, H/Misc/771/2, p.71; No.15, 31 July 1777, AGI, Filipinas 360; No.157, 1 December 1779, AGI, Filipinas 494.

[28] Thomas Forrest, *A Voyage from Calcutta to the Mergui Archipelago Lying on the East Side of the Bay of Bengal*, p.83.

[29] J.R. Wortman, "The Sultanate of Kutai, Kalimantan Timur: A Sketch of the Traditional Political Structure", p.53.

[30] H. Van Dewall, "Aanteekeningen omtrent de Noordoostkust van Borneo", p.456.

[31] Dr. Leyden, "Sketch of Borneo", in Moor, *Notices of the Indian Archipelago*, p.97.

[32] J. Dalton, "Remarks on the Bugis Campong Semerindan", ibid., p.70.

[33] Ibid., p.69.

[34] "A Memoir on the Sooloogannan Dominion and Commerce", 26 Feb. 1761, PRO, Egremont Papers, 30/47/20/1.

[35] No.4, Manuel de la Cruz a GCG, 25 Apr. 1838, PNA, Mindanao/Sulu 1816–98; Jose Maria Halcon a GCG. 31 Dec. 1837, AUST, seccion Folletos, Tomo 117, p.43; Sir Edward Belcher, *Narrative of the Voyage of H.M.S. Samarang, During the Years 1843–1846*, vol.2, pp.123–24; Van Dewall, "Aanteekeningen omtrent de Noordoostkust van Borneo", p.426.

[36] Alexander Dalrymple to the Hon. Court of Directors, 30 October 1769, IOL, H/Misc/771/2, p.209.

[37] "A Memoir on the Sooloogannan Dominion and Commerce", 26 Feb.1761, PRO, Egremont Papers, 30/47/20/1.

[38] Expediente, 15 July 1765, AGI, Filipinas 611; No.2, 9 May 1767, AGI, Filipinas 669; Barrantes, *Guerras Piraticas*, p.44.

[39] Alexander Dalrymple to Mr. Orme, 12 Apr.1762, IOL, Orme Collection, vol.67, p.115; "A Memoir on the Sooloogannan Dominion and Commerce", 26 Feb.1761, PRO, Egremont Papers, 30/47/20/1.

[40] Alexander Dalrymple to George Pigot, 22 Mar. 1762, IOL, H/Misc/771/2, p.31.

[41] IOL, H/Misc/795/11, p.47; David Woodward, *The Narrative of Captain David Woodward and Four Seamen*, 1st ed. (1804), p.85; "Some Notices of the Northern or Dutch Half of Celebes", *JIAEA* II, (1848), p.677.

[42] Presgrave to Murchison, 5 Dec. 1828, PRO, Admiralty 125/133.

[43] Commissioners Chad and Bonham to Murchison, 11 Sept. 1836, PRO, Admiralty 125/144.

[44] "Makassar, the Advantages of Making It a Free Port", in Moor, *Notices of the Indian Archipelago*, p.73.

[45] No.2, 9 May 1767, AGI, Filipinas 669; No.4, 5 July 1814, AGI, Filipinas 810; AR, Kolonien Archief 2922, p.667; Felix Renouard, *Voyage Commercial et Politique aux Indes Orientales*, vol.2, p.275; Barrantes, *Guerras Piraticas*, pp.160–61; Montero y Vidal, *Historia General de Filipinas*, vol.2, p.369.

[46] No.2, 9 May 1767, AGI, Filipinas 669; No.9, 19 Dec. 1775, AGI, Filipinas 359; No.7, 5 July 1814, AGI, Filipinas 810; Barrantes, *Guerras Piraticas,* p.44.

[47] No.2, 9 May 1767, AGI, Filipinas 669; No.29, 2 July 1777, AGI, Filipinas 687, p.36.

[48] Abdullah bin Abdul Kadir, *The Hikayat Abdullah,* an annotated trans., A.H. Hill, *JMBRAS* XXVIII, 3 (1955), pp.161–62.

[49] AR, Kolonien Archief, 3281, pp.165–66; AR, Kolonien Archief 3337, pp.316–17; Forrest, *Voyage to New Guinea,* p.35.

[50] Forrest, *Voyage to New Guinea,* p.330.

[51] Jose Maria Halcon a GCG, 31 Dec. 1837, AUST, seccion Folletos, Tomo 117, p.43; No.40, AHN, Ultramar 5162, p.8.

[52] Dr.Leyden, "Sketch of Borneo", p.105.

[53] Jose Maria Halcon a GCG, 31 Dec. 1837, AUST, seccion Folletos, Tomo 117, p.43.

Chapter 2

[1] C. Northcote Parkinson, *Trade in the Eastern Seas, 1793–1813,* p.89; Micheal Greenberg, *British Trade and the Opening of China, 1800–1842,* p.9.

[2] Elisa A. Julian, "British Projects and Activities in the Philippines, 1795–1805" (Ph.D. diss., University of London, 1963), p.2.

[3] Mr. Graham to Mr. Dundas, 29 May 1795, IOL, H/Misc/437/6, p.181.

[4] Robert R. Reed, "The Primate City in Southeast Asia: Conceptual Definitions and Colonial Origins", p.308.

[5] The career of Alexander Dalrymple as visionary civil servant, explorer, pioneering hydrographer, and author is carefully explored in a recent biography. See Howard Fry, *Alexander Dalrymple and the Expansion of British Trade.*

[6] Extract of the general letter from Fort St. George, 17 Apr. 1762, IOL, H/Misc/771/2, p.47.

[7] IOL, H/Misc/771/12, pp.123–24.

[8] Extract to an establishment at Balambangan, IOL, G/4/1, p.310.

[9] Fry, *Alexander Dalrymple and the Expansion of British Trade,* p.90.

[10] Extract of a general letter to Bencoolen, 7 May 1771, IOL, H/Misc/771/4, p.739.

[11] Fry, *Alexander Dalrymple and the Expansion of British Trade.* pp.90-91: Quiason, English *"Country Trade" with the Philippines, 1644–1765,* pp.126–33; Nicholas Tarling, *Sulu and Sabah: A Study of British Policy towards the Philippines and North Borneo from the Late Eighteenth Century;* Vincent T. Harlow, *The Founding of the Second British Empire, 1763–1793,* vol.1, pp.92–97. Harlow and Tarling discuss the ill-fated Balambangan settlement from 1773 to 1775, but principally trace the course of Herbert's altercations with and deception of the Company in trade. For a pioneering study which stresses the importance of Dalrymple's writings for the reconstruction of the Sultanate's historical experience, see Reber, "The Sulu World in the Eighteenth and Nineteenth Centuries".

[12] Letter from Chief at Balambangan to the President and Governor in Council, 25 Aug. 1772, IOL, P/2/1, pp.712–13.

[13] Ibid., pp.718, 722.

[14] Ibid., p.716.

[15] John Knight to John Herbert, 17 Jan. 1774, IOL, P/2/6, p.78.

[16] John Herbert to the Governor and Council of Fort William, 18 Feb. 1774, IOL, P/2/6, p.30.

[17] Governor and Council at Fort William to John Herbert, 13 June 1774, IOL, P/2/6, p.130.

[18] Chief and Council at Balambangan to Governor and Council at Fort William, 31 Dec. 1774, IOL, P/2/10, p.547.

[19] Draught from the Directors to the Chief and Council at Balambangan, IOL, H/Misc/771, p.563.

[20] Draught from the Directors to the Chief and Council at Balambangan, IOL, H/Misc/771, p.567.

[21] Wilkes, "Jolo and the Sulus", pp.153–54; St.John, *Life in the Forest of the Far East,* pp.11, 176, 189; Sir Edward Belcher, *Narrative of the Voyage of H.M.S. Samarang, During the Years 1843–46,* vol.1, p.206; Dr. Melchior Yvan, *Six Months among the Malays and a Year in China,* p.247.

[22] "Memoir of the Sooloogannan Dominions and Commerce", 26 Feb. 1761, PRO, Egremont Papers, 30/47/20/1.

[23] Thomas Forrest, *A Voyage from Calcutta to the Mergui Archipelago, Lying on the East Side of the Bay of Bengal,* p.85.

[24] John Meares, *Voyages made in the Years 1788 and 1789 from China to the Northwest Coast of America,* p.42.

[25] Singh's estimate of 30 to 40% profit in the opium trade is far too low. S.B. Singh, *European Agency Houses in Bengal, 1783–1833,* p.145.

[26] Extract of Bengal Secret Consultations, 7 Mar. 1783, the letter of Capt. Thomas Forrest, 1 Feb. 1782, IOL, H/Misc/169/16, pp.479–80.

[27] Spenser St.John, *Life in the Forrest of the Far East,* vol.1, p.403.

[28] Jules Sebastien Cesar Dumont d'Urville, *Voyage au Pole Sud et dans L'Oceanie Sur Les Corvettes L'Astrolobe et La Zelee pendant Les annees 1837, 1838, 1839, 1840* (Paris, 1841–54), vol.7, p.199.

[29] "Memoir of Sooloo", IOL, Orme Collection, vol.67, p.100 (emphasis added).

[30] Pierre Vicomte De Pages, "Travels Round the World in the Years 1767, 1768, 1769, 1770, 1771", in *Travel Accounts of the Islands, 1513–1787* (Manila: Filipiniana Book Guild, 1971), p.157.

[31] "Memoir of the Sooloogannan Dominions and Commerce", 26 Feb. 1761, PRO, Egremont Papers, 30/47/20/1.

[32] Alexander Dalrymple to the Court of Directors, 8 Aug. 1770, IOL, H/Misc/771/2, p.309.

[33] "Memoir of the Sooloogannan Dominions and Commerce", 26 Feb. 1761, PRO, Egremont Papers, 30/47/20/1.

[34] Forrest, *A Voyage to New Guinea,* p.187; Hunt "Some Particulars Relating to Sulo", p.58.

[35] President and Council at Balambangan to the Governor and Council of Fort William, 18 Feb. 1774, IOL, P/2/6, pp.40–41.

[36] Chief and Council at Balambangan to President and Council at Fort William, 31 Dec. 1774, IOL, P/2/10, p.540.

[37] No.380, 12 July 1774, AGI, Filipinas 686.

[38] El Provincial de Recolectos de Filipinas a vuestra magestad, 15 June 1771, AGI, Filipinas 685.

[39] No.226, Tomo 2, 1772, AGI, Filipinas 492, p.2.

[40] No.228, 18 July 1772, AGI, Filipinas 492; No.265, 12 Jan. 1773, AGI, Filipinas 493.

[41] No.165, 16 Jan. 1772, AGI, Filipinas 491; No.263, 12 Jan. 1773, AGI, Filipinas 493.

[42] No.29, 28 Feb. 1773, AGI, Filipinas 687, p.22.

[43] Ibid.

[44] No.380, 12 July 1774, AGI, Filipinas 686.

[45] Ibid.

[46] "A Memoir on the Sooloogannan Dominion and Commerce", 26 Feb. 1761, PRO, Egremont Papers, 30/47/20/1.

[47] IOL, H/Misc/771/2, p.123.

[48] Extract from a letter (copy) from Mr.Andrew Majendei, 23 Dec. 1771, IOL, P/1/51, p.434.

[49] Extract of a letter from the President and Council at Fort William, 1 Mar. 1773, IOL, H/Misc/108/3, p.190; see also a copy of a letter from Sultan Mutzammad Israel to Mr. Andrew Majendei, 23 Dec.1771, IOL, P/1/51, p.435.

[50] Capt.Savage Trotter to the Court of Directors, 24 Dec. 1769, IOL, H/Misc/102/4, pp.353–55; Alexander Dalrymple to the secret committee of the Court of Directors, 1 Feb. 1764, IOL, H/Misc/771/2, pp.71–72; Harlow, The Founding of the Second British Empire, vol.1, pp.90–91.

[51] James Rochford to Chairman of the East India Company, 14 Mar. 1771, IOL, H/Misc/105/4, pp.49–50; extract of the Company's separate letter to Bombay, 12 June 1771, IOL, H/Misc/116, pp.627–28.

[52] Draught from Directors to Chief and Council at Balambangan, IOL, H/Misc/771, pp.517, 535.

[53] No.228, 18 July 1772, AGI, Filipinas 492.

[54] Sultan Mahamed Isreil to the President and Council, 4 Dec. 1773, IOL, P/341/39, pp.718–19.

[55] AR, Kolonien Archief 3281, p.166.

[56] Ibid.

[57] AR, Kolonien Archief 3281, p.165.

[58] No.29, 28 Feb. 1773, AGI, Filipinas 687.

[59] Ibid.

[60] For an in-depth study of how this imperial rivalry unfolded as it related to the Spanish Philippines, see Julian, "British Projects and Activities in the Philippines, 1795–1805".

[61] For statements of fugitive captives which provided the Spanish with some of the earliest information on the activity of the English at Balambangan, see No.276, 9 July 1772, AGI, Filipinas 492.

[62] No.29, 28 Feb. 1773, AGI, Filipinas 687. Incidents related to the disruption of junk traffic in Philippine waters by Magindanao-Iranun raiders are detailed in: No.70, 28 Dec. 1770, AGI, Filipinas 491; No.99, 10 July 1771, AGI, Filipinas 491, pp.1–3.

[63] No.325, 20 Dec. 1778, AGI, Filipinas 686.

[64] Extract of a letter from the Chief and Council at Balambangan to the Court of Directors of the East India Company, 15 Sept. 1774, IOL, H/Misc/116/10, pp.663–65.

[65] No.325, 20 Dec. 1773, AGI, Filipinas 687.

[66] Ibid.

[67] Ibid.

[68] Coronel Juan Cencelli a Senor Conde Aranda, 16 Apr. 1774, AHN, Estado 2845, caja 2.

[69] Ibid.; extract of a letter from the Chief and Council at Balambangan to the Bombay Council, 17 Aug. 1774, IOL, H/Misc/115/14, pp.317–18.

[70] Coronel Juan Cencelli a Senor Conde de Aranda, 16 Apr. 1774, AHN, Estado 2845, caja 2.

[71] Ibid.

[72] Diario de la expedicion del mando de Don Juan Cencelli, 16 Apr. 1774, AHN, Estado 2845, caja 2.

[73] For a discussion of the concept of shame and its relation to reciprocity and revenge in Taosug culture, see Kiefer, The Tausug, pp.67–70.

[74] No.2, Memorandum, Papers relating to the loss of Balambangan, IOL, H/Misc/165/28, pp.306–11.

[75] For a detailed list of the enormous booty captured at Balambangan by the Taosug which included a brig, several smaller vessels, opium, textiles, and specie worth over 900 thousand Mexican dollars, see Extract of a letter from Mr. John Jesse, resident at Borneo proper, 3 May 1775, IOL, H/Misc/165/28, pp.355–56; No.455, 4 July 1775, AGI, Filipinas 686; Barrantes, *Guerras Piraticas,* p.100.

[76] John Herbert and Thomas Palmer to James Barton, 31 May 1775, IOL, H/Misc/165/28, p.360.

Chapter 3

[1] See Holden Furber, *John Company at Work: A Study of European Expansion in India in the Late Eighteenth Century,* p.160; Parkinson, *Trade in the Eastern Seas, 1793–1842,* p.141; Greenberg, *British Trade and the Opening of China, 1800–1842,* p.16; see also Singh, *European Agency Houses in Bengal, 1783–1833,* pp.1–3.

[2] Several articles have been written about the expansion of country trade along the coast of Malaya and in the Straits of Malacca. See D.K. Bassett, "British Commercial and Strategic Interests in the Malay Peninsula During the Late Eighteenth Century", pp.121–40; Diane Lewis, "Growth of the Country Trade to the Straits of Malacca, 1760–1777", pp.114–30.

[3] Furber, *John Company at Work,* pp.160–61; Singh, *European Agency Houses in Bengal, 1783–1833,* pp.1–3, 131–32.

[4] Ibid., pp.9, 20.

[5] AR, Kolonien Archief 3144, 1623–24; AR, Kolonien Archief 3205, 2188.

[6] Extract of a general letter from Bengal, 10 Jan. 1772, IOL, H/Misc/771/4, p.749; President and Council at Bombay to President and Council at Fort William, 30 July 1771, IOL, P/341/35, p.781.

[7] A copy of a letter from Sultan Mutzammad Izrael to Mr. Andrew Majendei, 23 Dec. 1771, IOL, P/1/51, p.435.

[8] El Goberanador de Zamboanga a GCC, 19 Oct. 1780, PNA, Mindanao/Sulu 1780–1890.

[9] No.414, 6 May 1781, AGI, Filipinas 498.

[10] Log kept aboard the packet *Fox* by Capt. Jonathan Court (25 July 1782–2 Aug. 1782), IOL, L/MAR/B/4561. See entries for 7 May 1782 to 12 May 1782.

[11] Log kept aboard the packet *Antelope* (31 Dec. 1781 to 5 June 1783), IOL, L/MAR/B/570A. See entries between 21 Apr. 1783 and 16 May 1783.

[12] A Copy of a letter from Sultan Mutzammad Israel to Mr. Andrew Majendie, 23 Dec. 1771, IOL, P/1/51, p.435.

[13] W.H. Coates, *The Old "Country Trade" of the East Indies,* p.104.

[14] President and Council at Bombay to President and Council at Fort William, 30 July 1771, IOL, P/341/35.

[15] Capt. George Smith to Josiah Webb, 27 May 1798, IOL, P/242/5, p.1600.

[16] Capt. George Smith to Messrs. Roebuck, Abbot & Co., 10 Oct. 1797, IOL, P/242/5, p.1817.

[17] Lt. W. Spiers to Chief Sec. to Government at Fort William, 10 Apr. 1822, IOL, F/4/714, no.19495.

[18] Alexander Dalrymple to the Court of Directors, 8 Aug. 1770, IOL, H/Misc/771/2, p.308.

[19] Ibid., p.310.

[20] Capt. Savage Trotter to the Court of Directors, 24 Dec. 1769, IOL, H/Misc/102/4, p.351.

[21] "Memoir of the Sooloogannan Dominions and Commerce", 26 Feb. 1761, PRO, Egremont Papers, 30/47/20/1.

[22] Capt. Savage Trotter to the Court of Directors, 24 Dec. 1769, IOL, H/Misc/162/4, p.351.

[23] Forrest, *Voyage to New Guinea,* p.281.

[24] Amasa Delano, *A Narrative of Voyages and Travel in the Northern and Southern Hemispheres: Comprising Three Voyages Round the World; Together with a Voyage of Survey and Discovery, in the Pacific Ocean and Oriental Islands,* 1st ed. (1817), p.173.

[25] Milburn, *Oriental Commerce,* vol.2, p.425.

[26] "Memoir of the Sooloogannan Dominions and Commerce", 26 Feb. 1761, PRO, Egremont Papers, 30/47/20/1.

[27] Parkinson, *Trade in the Eastern Seas, 1793–1813,* pp.348–49.

[28] James Horsburgh, *India Directory of Directions for Sailing to and from the East Indies, China, Australia, Cape of Good Hope, Brazil, and Other Adjacent Ports,* p.460.

[29] The Court of Directors to the Governor and Council of Fort St. George, 19 Feb. 1766, IOL, H/Misc/771/2, p.102.

[30] Letter from Xolo and Balambangan received from Mr.Majindei, 16 Oct. 1772, IOL, H/Misc/107/3, p.33.

[31] "Memoir of the Sooloogannan Dominions and Commerce", 26 Feb. 1761, PRO Egremont Papers, 30/47/20/1.

[32] Meares, *Voyage Made in the Years 1788 and 1789 from China to the North-West Coast of America,* p.289.

[33] "Memoir of the Sooloogannan Dominions and Commerce", 26 Feb. 1761, PRO, Egremont Papers, 30/47/20/1; Delano, *Voyages and Travel in the Northern and Southern Hemispheres,* p.169.

[34] Singh, *European Agency Houses in Bengal,* p.145.

[35] Ibid.

[36] Mr. J. Hunt to the Lt. Governor in Council Java, 1 Sept. 1814, IOL, G/21/26, p.1204 (emphasis added).

[37] G. King to Messrs. Jardine Matheson & Co., 2 July 1835, Cambridge University Library, Jardine Matheson Archive, file B1/99 East Indies 1835 July–Dec.For information about King, see A. Van Marle, "De Rol van de Buitenlandse Avonturier", p.36.

[38] Capt. George Smith to Josiah Webb, 27 May 1798, IOL, P/242/5, p.1599, and *passim.*

[39] Extract of a letter from Mr. J.F. Sykes to Mr. Benjamin Roebuck, 26 Dec. 1797, IOL, P/242/5, p.1818.

[40] Ibid., pp.1818–20.

[41] Capt. George Smith to Josiah Webb, 27 May 1798, IOL, P/242/5, p.1603.

[42] Mr. Benjamin Roebuck to Josiah Webb, IOL, P/242/5, p.1811.

[43] Translation of a letter from the Sultan of Sooloo to the Governor of Madras, in Col. D. Burr to Josiah Webb, 29 Nov. 1800, IOL, P/254/69, p.1195 and *passim;* for a different version of the events surrounding Capt. Pavin's death, see Hunt, "Some Particulars Relating to Sulo", p.24.

[44] Lt. W. Spiers to Chief Sec. to Government at Fort William, 10 Apr. 1822, IOL, F/4/714, no.19495, p.14.

[45] Ibid.; the translated copy of the Sultan's letter of friendship, protection, and commerce is included as well as a brief letter of recommendation from the Datu Amir Bahar. See App. C.

[46] Lt. W. Spiers to Chief Sec. to Government at Fort William, 10 Apr. 1822, IOL, F/4/714, no.19495, p.19.

[47] Robert Farquhar to Lord Wellesley, 16 Feb. 1804, IOL, P/166.

[48] These sources are a "List of products of Sulu and its immediate dependencies", in "Memoir of the Sooloogannan Dominions and Commerce", 26 Feb. 1761, PRO, Egremont Papers, 30/47/20/1; "a list of the annual consumption of Sulo and its dependencies of European and Indian articles", in Hunt, "Some Particulars Relating to Sulo", pp.46–47; and a list entitled "Goods for Sooloo Market", MS included with the log of the ship *Allbree*, 656/1833A, Peabody Museum, Salem.

[49] Hunt, "Some Particulars Relating to Sulo", p.47.

[50] "Goods for Soloo Market", MS Peabody Museum. Figures are lacking for the earlier period, but the value for the gunpowder alone which is in excess of the total worth of Dalrymple's order, shows expansion.

[51] Dumont d'Urville, *Voyage,* vol.7, p.198.

[52] Robert Farquhar to Lord Wellesley, 16 Feb. 1804, IOL, P/166.

[53] Thomas Raffles to Lord Minto, Gov.-Gen. of India, 20 Sept. 1811, IOL, EUR.F.148/7, par.67.

[54] J. Dalton, "On the Present State of Piracy, Amongst These Islands, and the Best Method of Its Suppression", in Moor, *Notices of the Indian Archipelago,* p.26.

[55] Ibid.

[56] George Windsor Earl, *The Eastern Seas, or Voyages and Adventures in the Indian Archipelago in 1832, 1833, 1834,* p.444.

[57] Log kept aboard the brig *Leonidas* (8 Feb. 1836–25 Sept. 1836), 656/1835A, Peabody Museum. No entries are listed in the log between 5 Mar. and 31 Aug. when the vessel was conducting trade at Sulu.

[58] Letter soliciting trade between the United States and Sooloo, Papers of William D. Waters, Peabody Museum. See App. E.

[59] Wilkes, "Jolo and the Sulus", p.171.

[60] No.293, Gobierno Militar de la plaza de Zamboanga a GCG, 23 Aug. 1847, PNA, unclassified Mindanao/Sulu bundle.

[61] St. John, *Life in the Forests of the Far East,* vol.2, p.203.

[62] Henry Keppel, *A Visit to the Indian Archipelago, in H.M. Ship Macander,* p.59.

[63] Dorothy Shineberg, "The Sandalwood Trade in Melanesian Economics, 1841–65", p.132.

[64] G.W. Hubbell to John Quincy Adams, Sec. of State, 31 Dec. 1823, U.S. National Archives, Consular Despatches, Manila, 1817–1840.

[65] No.234, 12 Apr. 1829, AGI, Ultramar 664, p.818.

[66] *The Stratis Times and Singapore Journal of Commerce,* 19 Jan. 1848, vol.4, no.242.

[67] No.293, Gobierno Militar de la plaza de Zamboanga a GCG, 23 Aug. 1847, PNA, unclassified Mindanao/Sulu bundle; no.30, 5 Nov. 1847, AHN Ultramar 5159.

[68] No.228, 18 July 1772, AGI, Filipinas 492.

[69] Ibid.

[70] No.29, Sargento Mayor Manuel Alvarez a GCG, AGI, Filipinas 687.

[71] GCG a Sultan Muhammed Israel, 9 Nov. 1773, AGI, Filipinas 686.

[72] GCG a Secretario de Estado 20 Dec. 1773, AGI, Filipinas 686.

[73] No.415, GCG a Secretario de Estado, 6 May 1781, AGI, Filipinas 498.

[74] Ibid.

[75] No.415, GCG a Secretario de Estado, 6 May 1781, AGI, Filipinas 498.

[76] Maria Lourdes Diaz Trechuelo Spinola, *La Real Compania De Filipinas,* p.342.

[77] Estado, No.339, 9 June 1788, AGI Filipinas 976.

[78] The work of Pierre and Huguette Chauna, *Seville et L'Atlantique, 1504–1650,* has demonstrated the significance of Spanish archival sources for the study of European expansion, the development of world trade, and Spanish economic history. In a more recent book, Pierre Chaunu applied the same mode of analysis to document the trade from the Philippines to Mexico between 1586 and 1790. Part of the importance of Chaunu's work rests in the fact that it affirms the potential of Spanish documents for the reconstruction of trade patterns in the non-Western world, but particularly the Philippines, in the 16th, 17th, and 18th centuries. The use of the manuscript material in the Archives of Spain (principally Seville) and the Philippines is a prerequisite to any effort at examining the contours of the trade of China, Japan, and several Southeast Asian realms with Manila. See Huguette and Pierre Chaunu, *Seville et L'Atlantique, 1504–1650, Ports—Routes—Trafics;* Pierre Chaunu, *Les Philippines et le Pacifique des Iberiques (XVI, XVII, XVIII siecles),* Introduction methodologique et indices d'activite, Ports—Routes—Trafics, 11, Ecole Pratique des Hautes Etudes, VI section, Centre de Recherches Historiques.

[79] For an important article which discusses quantification in history from the standpoint of Spanish sources, see Juan J. Linz, "Five Centuries of Spanish History: Quantification and Comparison", pp.177, 261; See App. F.

[80] Numero 339, Ciracao Gonzalez Caravajal a Senor Marques de Sonora, 9 June 1788, AGI, Filipinas 976.

[81] Estados, No.305, 11 June 1806, AGI, Ultramar 659; AGI, Filipinas 502; No.73, 22 July 1794, AGI, Filipinas 977.

[82] Estado, AGI, Filipinas 977.

[83] Estado, No.127, AGI, Filipinas 818.

[84] Estado, AGI, Filipinas 978.

[85] Tomas de Comyn, *State of the Philippines in 1810,* p.119.

[86] Estado, No.52, AGI, Ultramar 624.

[87] Estado, No.122, AGI, Filipinas 811.

[88] Estado, MN, Coleccion Enrile VII, Documento 15, p.55.

[89] Robert MacMicking, *Recollections of Manila and the Philippines during 1848, 1849, and 1850,* p.149. For a general discussion of the Manila-Jolo trade by contemporaries of MacMicking, see Rafael Dias Arenas, *Memoria sobre el comercio y la Navegacion de las Islas Filipinas,* pp.7–14, Jean Bassilan de Mallat, *Les Philippines; histoire, geographie, moeurs, agriculture, industrie et commerce des colonies espagnoles dans L'Oceanie,* vol.2, pp.321–26; J. Lannoy, *Iles Philippines,* pp.107–8.

[90] 656/1835A, Log of Brig *Leonidas* (8 Feb. 1836 to 23 Sept. 1836), Peabody Museum, entry for 17 Feb. 1836.

[91] Dias Arenas, *Memoria,* p.12.

[92] Ibid., p.14; MacMicking, *Recollections of Manila and the Philippines,* p.153.

[93] "Camba's Report on Commerce with Sulu", in Saleeby, *The History of Sulu,* p.219.

[94] Wickberg, *The Chinese in Philippine Life,* p.89.

[95] Ibid.

[96] No.3, Testimonio de los Duros de Subvencion-ano 1811, AGI, Filipinas 979, pp.58–68.

[97] Quaderno No.3, AGI, Filipinas 979, p.25.

[98] See Jose Maria Halcon, a GCG, 31 Dec. 1837, AUST, Seccion Folletos, Tomo 117, p.43.

[99] Diario de Navegacion del Capitan, MN, Ms.211.

[100] Dias Arenas, *Memoria,* p.12; MacMicking, *Recollections of Manila and the Philippines,* pp.149–50.

[101] Diario de Navegacion del Capitan, MN, Ms.211, pp.87–88.

[102] No.8, 9 Nov. 1837, PNA, Mindanao/Sulu 1816–1898.

[103] Dias Arenas, *Memoria,* p.12.

[104] Dias Arenas, *Memoria,* p.10; MacMicking, *Recollections of Manila and the Philippines,* p.151.

[105] Ibid.

[106] Dias Arenas, *Memoria,* p.13.

[107] Hunt, "Some Particulars Relating to Sulo", p.48.

[108] Estado, No.9, AGI, Filipinas, 806.

[109] Hunt, "Some Particulars Relating to Sulo", p.47.

[110] Dias Arenas, *Memoria,* p.13.

[111] Jose Maria Halcon a GCG 31 Dec. 1837, AUST, seccion Folletos, Tomo 117, p.43.

[112] MacDonald, *A Narrative of the Early Life and Services of Captain D. MacDonald,* p.200.

[113] Jose Maria Halcon a GCG, 31 Dec. 1837, AUST, seccion Folletos, Tomo 117, p.44.

[114] Ibid., p.46.

[115] Diario de Navegacion del Capitan, MN, Ms.211; Montero y Vidal, *Historia General de Filipinas,* vol.2, p.556.

[116] Wickberg, *The Chinese in Philippine Life,* pp.83-84.

[117] Estado, MN, Coleccion Enrile VII, Documento 15, 55; MacMicking, *Recollections of Manila and the Philippines,* p.149.

[118] Pierre Sonnerat, *A Voyage to the East Indies and China; Performed by the Order of Lewis XV Between the Years 1774 and 1781,* trans. Francis Magnus, vol.3, p.131.

[119] No.7, GCG a Senor Secretario de Estado, 4 June 1806, AGI, Filipinas 510, p.58.

Chapter 4

[1] Ethnographic studies of the Samal Bajau Laut, spanning nearly a decade, have been conducted in the environs of Tawi-Tawi. See Harry Arlo Nimmo, "The Structure of Bajau Society" (Ph.D. diss., University of Hawaii, 1969), p.49; idem, *The Sea People of Sulu: A Study of Social Change in the Philippines.*

[2] H.A. Nimmo, "Social Organization of the Tawi-Tawi Badjaw", p.436.

[3] No.139, El Gobernador de Zamboanga a GCG, 12 Feb. 1845, PNA, Mindanao/Sulu 1836–97.

[4] Ibid.

[5] Wernstedt and Spencer, *The Philippine Island World,* p.595.

[6] Hunt, "Some Particulars Relating to Sulo", pp.54–59.

[7] Dalrymple, *Oriental Repertory,* p.530; Belcher, *Voyage of the Samarang,* vol.1, p.280.

[8] Van Capellan, "Berigt Aangaande den Togt van L.M. Schoener Egmond, naar Berow", p.84.

[9] Hageman, "Aanteekeningen", p.94; Van Dewall, "Aanteekeningen omtrent de Noordoostkust", p.446.

[10] Sopher, *The Sea Nomads,* p.246.

[11] "List of Goods to be Had at Soloo", MS, included with the log of the ship *Albree,* 656/1833A, Peabody Museum.

[12] Forrest, *Voyage to New Guinea*, p.221; Hunt, "Some Particulars Relating to Sulo", p.44; Garin, "Memoria sobre El Archipielago de Jolo", p.198.

[13] Dalrymple, *Oriental Repertory*, p.520.

[14] Wu Ching-Long, *A Study of References to the Philippines in Chinese Sources from Earliest Times to the Ming Dynasty*, p.110.

[15] Dalrymple, "Account of Some Natural Curiosities at Sooloo", p.1

[16] Ibid., pp.13–14; "A Memoir on the Sooloogannan Dominion and Commerce", 26 Feb. 1761, PRO, Egremont Papers, 30/47/20/1.

[17] Dalrymple, *Oriental Repertory*, p.525.

[18] Dalrymple, "Account of Some Natural Curiosities at Sooloo", p.11; Hunt, "Some Particulars Relating to Sulo", p.59; St. John, *Life in the Forests of the Far East*, vol.2, p.180.

[19] Dalrymple, *Oriental Repertory*, p.504.

[20] Comision Reservada a Borneo y Jolo 1881–1882, bound MS. Biblioteca de Palacio, p.38.

[21] Dalrymple, "Account of Some Natural Curiosities at Sooloo", pp.13–14.

[22] Ibid., p.3.

[23] Ibid., p.12.

[24] Hunt, "Some Particulars Relating to Sulo", p.59.

[25] Dalrymple, "Account of Some Natural Curiosities at Sooloo", p.12; Forrest, *Voyage to New Guinea*, p.328.

[26] Forrest, *Voyage to New Guinea*, p.328.

[27] Dalrymple, "Account of Some Natural Curiosities at Sooloo", p.11.

[28] Forrest, *Voyage to New Guinea*, p.328.

[29] Dalrymple, "Account of Some Natural Curiosities at Sooloo", p.11.

[30] A.J.F. Jansen, "Aanteekeningen Omtrent Sollok en de Solloksche Zeeroovers", p.217.

[31] Dalrymple, *Oriental Repertory*, p.527.

[32] Hunt, "Some Particulars Relating to Sulo", p.53.

[33] "Memoir of the Sooloogannan Dominion and Commerce", 26 Feb. 1761. PRO, Egremont Papers, 30/47/20/1.

[34] No.276, GCG a Senor Secretario de Estado, 9 July 1771, AGI, Filipinas 492.

[35] Thomas Raffles to Lord Minto, 20 Sept. 1811, IOL, EUR/148/7, par.55.

[36] Barrantes, *Guerras Piraticas*, p.160.

[37] The original jawi letter from the Sultan of Brunei to the Governor of Manila is in the Philippine National Archive. See PNA, Isla de Borneo (2).

[38] Barrantes, *Guerras Piraticas*. p.180.

[39] R.T. Farquhar to Lord Wellesley, 18 July 1805, IOL, P/166.

[40] Capt. Graham to Charles Assey, 15 Nov. 1813, IOL, G/21/40, 10.

[41] Jose Maria Halcon a GCG, 31 Dec. 1837, AUST, seccion Folletos, Tomo 117, p.45.

[42] St. John, *Life in the Forests of the Far East,* vol.2, p.192.

[43] Bulwer to the Earl of Granville, 28 May 1872, CO, 144/36.

[44] Carlos Cuarteron, prefecto apostolico, a GCG, 27 Oct. 1857, PNA, Isla de Borneo (1).

[45] Relacion jurada de los cuatro cautivos benidos en el navio Yngles de Guerra Agincort, 11 Dec. 1845, PNA, Piratas (3); P.P.H.C., 1851, vol.56, pt.1, "Historical Notices upon the Piracies Committed in the East Indies....", pp.135–36.

[46] Carlos Cuarteron, prefecto apostolico, a GCG, 27 Oct. 1857, PNA, Isla de Borneo (1).

[47] Pretymann's Diary, 14 May 1879, CO, 874/71.

[48] Treacher to Sir Rutherford Alcock, 3 Mar. 1886, CO, 874/240.

[49] Hunt, "Some Particulars Relating to Sulo", p.53.

[50] Ibid.

[51] Dalrymple, *Oriental Repertory,* p.534; Hunt, "Some Particulars Relating to Sulo", p.54.

[52] Dalrymple, *Oriental Repertory*, p.534; Hunt, "Sketch of Borneo", *Notices of the Indian Archipelago and Adjacent Countries,* p.29.

[53] Rattan collecting was despised by those who were forced to cut it because of its great bulk. St. John, *Life in the Forests of the Far East,* vol.1, p.403; Pretymann's Diary, 16 May 1879, CO, 874/71.

[54] Dalrymple, *Oriental Repertory,* p.534.

[55] Hunt, "Sketch of Borneo", p.29.

[56] "Memoir of the Sool'oogannan Dominion and Commerce", 26 Feb. 1761, PRO, Egremont Papers, 30/47/20/1.

[57] Hunt, "Sketch of Borneo", p.29.

[58] St. John, *Life in the Forests of the Far East,* vol.1, p.398.

[59] Hunt, "Some Particulars Relating to Sulo", p.54.

[60] St. John, *Life in the Forests of the Far East,* vol.1, p.398.

[61] Hunt, "Sketch of Borneo", p.29.

[62] Hunt, "Some Particulars Relating to Sulo", p.54.

[63] Diary of William Pryer, 3 June 1879, CO, 874/68.

[64] Ibid.; 2, 21 Mar. 1878, CO, 874/67.

[65] Hunt, "Some Particulars Relating to Sulo", p.54.

[66] Ibid.

[67] Mr. J. Hunt to Thomas Raffles, 1 Sept. 1814, IOL, G/21/26, p.1211.

[68] Hunt, "Some Particulars Relating to Sulo", p.54.

[67] Ibid., p.55.

[70] Hunt, "Some Particulars Relating to Sulo", p.54.

[71] Hunt, "Some Particulars Relating to Sulo", p.55.

[72] Ibid.

[73] Hunt, "Some Particulars Relating to Sulo", p.56.

[74] Ibid.; Dalrymple, *Oriental Repertory,* p.531.

[75] Hunt, "Some Particulars Relating to Sulo", p.56.

[76] Dalrymple, *Oriental Repertory,* p.527; Hunt, "Some Particulars Relating to Sulo", p.56.

[77] Le Bar (ed.), *Ethnic Groups of Insular Southeast Asia,* vol.1, p.168.

[78] Dr. Leyden, "Sketch of Borneo", pp.93, 107; Carl Bock, *The Headhunters of Borneo: A Narrative of Travel up the Mahakam and down the Barito; Also Journeyings in Sumatra,* pp.133, 218–19.

[79] Rodney Needham, "Penan", *Ethnic Groups of Insular Southeast Asia,* ed. Le Bar, vol.1, pp.176–80; J.Hageman, "Aanteekeningen", p.93; Van Dewall, "Aanteekeningen Omtrent de Noordoostkust", pp.434–35, 443, 454–55.

[80] Hageman, "Aanteekeningen", pp.86, 97; Van Dewall, "Aanteekeningen Omtrent de Noordoostkust", p.429.

[81] Hunt, "Sketch of Borneo", p.29.

[82] Hunt, "Some Particulars Relating to Sulo", p.56.

[83] Forrest, *Voyage to New Guinea,* p.16.

[84] Hunt, "Some Particulars Relating to Sulo", p.57.

[85] Van Dewall, "Aanteekeningen Omtrent de Noordoostkust", pp.438–42.

[86] "Berigten omtrent den Zeeroof in den Nederlandsch-Indischen Archipel, 1858", *TBG* XX (1873), p.306.

[87] Hunt, "Some Particulars Relating to Sulo", p.57.

[88] Van Dewall, "Aanteekeningen Omtrent de Noordoostkust", p.426.

[89] "Memo of a visit to Bulungun", in Alec Cook to Sir Rutherford Alcock, 10 Sept. 1887, CO, 874/243.

[90] Hageman, "Aanteekeningen", p.78.

[91] Van Dewall, "Aanteekeningen Omtrent de Noordoostkust", p.436.

[92] Dalrymple, "Account of Some Natural Curiosities at Sooloo", p.18.

[93] Forrest, *Voyage to New Guinea,* p.375.

[94] Hageman, "Aanteekeningen", p.79.

[95] Van Dewall, "Aanteekeningen Omtrent de Noordoostkust", pp.436, 443.

[96] Ibid., p.426; Alec Cook to Sir Rutherford Alcock, 10 Sept. 1887, CO, 874/243.

[97] Hageman, "Aanteekeningen", p.78.

[98] No.77, Estado, 13 Aug. 1819, AGI, Filipinas 511.

[99] Dr. Leyden, "Sketch of Borneo", p.97.

[100] Van Dewall, "Aanteekeningen Omtrent de Noordoostkust", p.429.

[101] Hunt, "Some Particulars Relating to Sulo", p.57.

[102] Hageman, "Aanteekeningen", 94; see also Van Capellan, "Berigt Aangaande den Togt van L.M. Schoener Egmond, naar Berow, op de Oostkust van Borneo, in het najaar van 1844", p.83.

[103] Hageman, "Aanteekeningen", 94; see also copie verslag van C. Notte, 24 Feb. 1827, AR, Kolonien Archief 3200.

[104] J. Dalton, "Remarks on the Exports of Coti", *Notices of the Indian Archipelago,* p.56.

[105] Van Dewall, "Aanteekeningen Omtrent de Noordoostkust", p.436.

[106] Ibid., pp.447–49.

[107] Le Bar (ed.), *Ethnic Groups of Insular Southeast Asia,* vol.1, pp.170, 172.

[108] Van Dewall, "Aanteekeningen Omtrent de Noordoostkust", p.450.

[109] Van Dewall, "Aanteekeningen Omtrent de Noordoostkust", p.450.

[110] Diary of William Pryer, 20 May 1878, CO, 874/67; William Pryer to Malcolm Brown, 10 Feb. 1885, CO, 874/238; William Pryer, "On the Natives of North Borneo", p.229.

[111] Van Dewall, "Aanteekeningen Omtrent de Noordoostkust", pp.443, 445, 451.

[112] Ibid., p.424; Hageman, "Aanteekeningen", p.75.

[113] The ruins of the forts were discovered in 1938 by a district officer on the east coast. See J. Valera, "The Old Forts of Semporna", pp.40–41.

[114] Van Dewall, "Aanteekeningen Omtrent de Noordoostkust", pp.424, 445; Hageman, "Aanteekeningen", p.75.

[115] William Pryer to Malcom Brown, 10 Feb. 1885, CO, 874/238.

[116] Diary of William Pryer, 12 Oct. 1878, CO, 874/68; Treacher to Alfred Dent, 26 Oct. 1881, CO, 874/228.

[117] "Memoir of the Sooloogannan Dominion and Commerce", 26 Feb. 1761, PRO, Egremont Papers, 30/47/20/1.

[118] Kiefer, *The Tausug,* pp.14–15.

[119] Dalrymple, *Oriental Repertory,* p.512; Forrest, *A Voyage to New Guinea,* p.322; Hunt, "Some Particulars Relating to Sulo", 43; F.A.A. Gregori, *Aanteekeningen en Beschouwingen betrekkelijk de Zeeroovers en hunne Rooverijen Magindanao en de Soolo-Archipel* (1844), p.329.

[120] Jose Maria Halcon a GCG, 31 Dec. 1837, AUST, Seccion Folletos, Tomo 117, p.47.

[121] Wernstedt and Spencer, *The Philippine Island World,* p.545.

[122] Forrest, *Voyage to New Guinea,* p.279.

[123] Ibid., p.278. See also Christie, "The Non-Christian Tribes of the Northern Half of the Zamboanga Peninsula", p.96.

[124] Forrest, *Voyage to New Guinea,* p.279.

[125] BH-PCL, vol.6, Paper 162, No.23, Emerson Brewer Christie, "The Moros of Sulu and Mindanao", p.58. For the conduct of Magindanao–Tiruray relations involving the use of ritually approved muslim traders and peddlers, and the establishment of local trade pacts with specific Tiruray communities, see Schlegel, "Tiruray-Magindanaon Ethnic Relations", pp.25–28, Ileto, *Magindanao, 1860–1888,* pp.24–25.

[126] Jose Maria Halcon a GCG, 31 Dec. 1837, AUST, Seccion Folletos, Tomo 117, p.8.

[127] Forrest, *Voyage to New Guinea,* p.328.

[128] Ibid., p.281.

[129] Jose Maria Halcon a GCG, 31 Dec. 1837, AUST, Seccion Folletos, Tomo 117, p.48; Milburn, *Oriental Commerce,* vol.2, p.424.

[130] No.4, Manuel de la Cruz a GCG, 25 Apr. 1838, PNA, Mindanao/Sulu 1816–1898.

[131] Recent ethnolinguistic studies of Yakan Culture undertaken by Charles Frake and Carol Maloney remain unpublished to date. See Charles Frake "Struck by Speech", pp.146–47; J. Wulf, "Features of Yakan Culture", pp.52–72.

[132] Kiefer, *The Tausug,* p.110.

[133] Hunt, "Some Particulars Relating to Sulo", pp.58–59.

[134] Marian Lourdes Diaz Trechuelo Spinola, *Arquitectura Espanola en Filipinas, 1565–1800,* p.363.

[135] Expediente 591, El Gobierno Militar y Politico de Zamboanga a GCG, 8 Apr. 1838, PNA, Mindanao/Sulu 1838–1890.

[136] El Gobierno Militar y Politico de Zamboanga, undated letter, PNA, Mindanao/Sulu 1838–1891.

[137] For an account of the dishonest and arbitrary means used by the Governors of Zamboanga to engross the local trade to themselves, see Diario de la Expedicion del mando de Don Juan Cencelli, 16 Apr. 1774, AHN, Estado 2845, caja 2; Meares, *Voyages Made in the Years 1788 and 1789,* pp.288–90.

[138] Ibid., p.44.

[139] Expediente 591, El Gobierno Politico y Militar del Zamboanga a GCG, 8 Apr. 1838, PNA, Mindanao/Sulu, 1838–1890, p.9.

[140] Ibid.

[141] Expediente 14, El Gobierno Politico y Militar del Zamboanga a GCG, 15 Nov. 1847, PNA, Mindanao/Sulu, 1838–1885.

[142] Ibid.

[143] Cesar Majul, "Chinese Relationships with the Sultanate of Sulu", *The Chinese in the Philippines, 1570–1770,* ed. A. Felix, p.155.

[144] The trade was worth 21,435 pesos in the years between 1832 and 1836. The annual value of the trade in pesos was as follows: 1832–4,033; 1833–3,841; 1835–4,056; 1836–5,870. See No.12, Estado de los Productos de la Aduana por el comercio del Sur en el ultimo quinquenio, PNA, Memoria de Zamboanga.

[145] Jose Maria Halcon a GCG, 31 Dec. 1837, AUST, Seccion Folletos, Tomo 117, p.47.

[146] Jose Maria Halcon a GCG, 31 Dec. 1837, AUST, Seccion Folletos, Tomo 117.

Chapter 5

[1] Bulwer to the Earl of Carnarvon, 9 May 1878, CO, 144/42.

[2] For a detailed account of Brooke's mission to Sulu, see Governor of Prince of Wales Island, Singapore and Malacca, to Sec. to the Government of India, 6 July 1849, IOL, F/4/2363 (125401), pp.4–5.

[3] Saleeby, *The History of Sulu,* 226; Governor of Prince of Wales Island, Singapore and Malacca, to Sec. to the Government of India, 6 July 1849, IOL, F/4/2363 (125401).

[4] Bulwer to the Earl of Carnarvon, 9 May 1874, CO, 144/42.

[5] Governor of the Straits Settlements to the Sec. to the Government of India, 4 Apr. 1851, IOL, F/4/2450 (13571), pp.10–11; Saleeby, *History of Sulu,* p.104.

[6] Enclosure 2, No.10, in Farren to Palmerston, 16 Mar. 1851, CO, 144/8.

[7] Bulwer to the Earl of Granville, 29 Dec. 1871, CO, 144/35.

[8] Majul, "Chinese Relationships with the Sultanate of Sulu", p.156.

[9] W. Napier to Early Grey, 20 Mar. 1849, CO, 144/3.

[10] Rodney Mundy, *Narrative of Events in Borneo and Celebes, Down to the Occupation of Labuan,* vol.1, p.380.

[11] Lt. Governor Scott to Earl Grey, 25 Mar. 1851, CO, 144/7.

[12] No.73, Letter of Capt. Thomas Massie, 24 Jan. 1852, National Maritime Museum, Greenwich, MAS/7.

[13] Lt. Governor Scott to Earl Grey, 25 Mar. 1851, CO, 144/7; Edwards to Colonial Office, 8 Dec. 1856, CO, 144/13.

[14] Estado, No.6, *Balanza General Del Comercio de Las Islas Filipinas* (Manila, 1853).

[15] Bulwer to Earl of Carnarvon, 9 May 1874, CO, 144/42.

[16] Bulwer to the Earl of Kimberley, 23 Sept. 1873, CO, 144/41.

[17] Edwardes to Colonial Office, 8 Dec. 1856, CO, 144/13.

[18] Bulwer to Earl of Kimberley, 23 Sept. 1873, CO, 144/41.

[19] Edwardes to Colonial Office, 8 Dec. 1856, CO, 144/13.

[20] Bulwer to the Earl of Carnarvon, 9 May 1874, CO, 144/42.

[21] Edwardes to the Duke of Newcastle, 6 June 1861, CO, 144/19.

[22] Bulwer to the Earl of Carnarvon, 30 Sept. 1874, CO, 144/43.

[23] Low to the Duke of Buckingham and Chandos, 15 Oct. 1867, CO, 144/26; Bulwer to the Earl of Granville 28 May 1872, CO, 144/36.

[24] Low to Earl of Derby, 3 Jan. 1876, CO, 144/46.

[25] Pope Hennesey to the Duke of Buckingham and Chandos, 17 Aug. 1868, CO, 144/27.

[26] Ibid.

[27] Pope Hennesey to the Earl of Granville, 31 Mar. 1867, CO, 144/29.

[28] Pope Hennesey to Duke of Buckingham and Chandos, 16 Feb. 1868, CO, 144/27.

[29] Statement of Ong Kiat, enclosure 2 in despatch no.1, Bulwer to the Earl of Kimberley, Jan. 1874, CO, 144/42.

[30] Statement of Mr. Howard, enclosure 2 in despatch no.1, Bulwer to the Earl of Kimberley, Jan. 1874, CO, 144/42.

[31] Statement of Chin Sing, ibid.

[32] Statement of Ong Kiat, ibid.

[33] Bulwer to the Earl of Kimberley, 6 Jan. 1873, CO, 144/42.

[34] Statement of Lee Cheng Hok, enclosure 2 in despatch number 1, Bulwer to the Earl of Kimberley, January 1874, CO, 144/42.

[35] Pope Hennesey to Duke of Buckingham and Chandos, 17 Aug. 1868, CO, 144/42.

[36] Ibid.

[37] Callaghan to Edward Cardwell, 22 Apr. 1865, CO, 144/24.

[38] Callaghan to Colonial Office, 1 Apr. 1865, 144/24.

[39] Callaghan to Edward Cardwell, 22 Apr. 1865, CO, 144/24.

[40] Callaghan to Colonial Office, 1 Apr. 1865, CO.144/24.

[41] Bulwer to the Earl of Carnarvon, 27 July 1874, CO, 144/42.

[42] Bulwer to the Earl of Carnarvon, 4 July 1874, CO, 144/42.

[43] Governor of Straits Settlements to Sec. to the Government of India, 23 Oct. 1863, FO, 71/1.

[44] Statement of John Dill Ross, enclosure 2 in despatch no.1, Bulwer to Earl of Kimberley, Jan. 1874, CO, 144/42.

[45] Bulwer to the Earl of Carnarvon, 4 July 1874, CO, 144/42, CO, 144/42; Pope Hennesey to the Earl of Granville, 25 Jan. 1870, CO, 144/31.

[46] Pryer to Dent, 7 June 1880, CO, 874/192.

[47] Bulwer to the Earl of Kimberley, 29 Dec. 1871, CO, 144/35.

[48] Pope Hennesey to the Duke of Buckingham and Chandos, 16 Feb. 1868, CO, 144/27.

[49] Bulwer to the Earl of Kimberley, 3 Nov. 1873, CO, 144/71.

[50] Bulwer to the Earl of Kimberley, 23 Sept. 1873, CO, 144/41.

[51] Bulwer to the Earl of Carnarvon, 9 May. 1874, CO, 144/42.

[52] Bulwer to the Earl of Granville, 23 Sept. 1873, CO.144/41.

[53] Bulwer to the Earl of Kimberley, 6 Jan. 1873, CO.144/42.

[54] Report of the Committee of Council on the Opium and Tobacco Farms of the Colony, enclosure no.1 in despatch no.1, in Bulwer to the Earl of Kimberley, Jan. 1874, CO, 144/42.

[55] Statement of Chin Sing in enclosure 2, no.1, Bulwer to the Earl of Kimberley, Jan. 1874, CO, 144/42.

[56] Treacher to Dent, 8 Dec. 1881, CO, 874/228.

[57] Statement of Chang Siang Kiat in enclosure 2, no.1, Bulwer to the Earl of Kimberley, Jan. 1874, CO, 144/42; see also the statement of the Chinese trader Soo-Ning who was the partner of the Pengiran Temonggong of Brunei.

[58] Bulwer to the Earl of Carnarvon, 9 May 1874, CO, 144/42.

[59] Statement of Choa Bok Song in enclosure 2, no.1, Bulwer to the Earl of Kimberley, Jan. 1874, CO, 144/42.

[60] Bulwer to the Earl of Kimberley, Jan. 1874, CO, 144/42.

[61] Bulwer to the Earl of Carnarvon, 7 July 1874, CO, 144/42.

[62] Bulwer to the Earl of Carnarvon, 25 June 1874, CO, 144/42.

[63] Speech of Pope Hennesey to the Legislative Council of Labuan, 17 Oct. 1868, CO, 144/28.

[64] For a good collection of price current circulars and market reports for Syme & Co., Jose D'Almeida & Sons, Paterson Simon & Co., and Behn Meyer & Co. relevant to the activities of the Straits traders in this period, see Papers of the Jardine, Matheson & Co., CL/14, Straits, Batavia 1845–1863, 1860–1864, 1860–1866, Cambridge University Library.

[65] Lt. de Crespigny to the Sec. of the Admiralty, 15 Oct. 1858, CO, 144/15.

[66] No.838, GCG a Senor Presidente del consejo de ministros, 7 Oct. 1859, AHN Ultramar 5182.

[67] Ibid.

[68] Extract from the Journal of the barque *Osprey*, in Col. Cavanagh to Sec. to the Government of India, 28 Jan. 1863, FO, 71/1.

[69] Ibid.

[70] BH-PCL, vol.1, paper 160, no.2; Stephenson, *Constabulary Monograph of the Districts of Tawi-Tawi,* p.28.

[71] Comision Reservada a Borneo y Jolo, 1881–1882, pp.123–200.

[72] Bulwer to the Earl of Kimberley, 26 Jan. 1873, CO, 144/42; Bulwer to the Earl of Carnarvon, 4 July 1874, CO, 144/42.

[73] Bulwer to the Earl of Carnarvon, 14 July 1874, CO, 144/42.

[74] Bulwer to the Earl of Carnarvon, 25 June 1874, CO, 144/42.

[75] Comision Reservada a Borneo y Jolo, 1881–1882, p.124.

[76] Bulwer to the Earl of Carnarvon, 4 July 1878, CO, 144/42.

[77] H.M.Consul Farren, Circular to Manila merchants, 6 June 1855, FO, 72/876.

[78] Bulwer to the Earl of Granville, 29 Dec. 1871, CO, 144/35.

[79] Bulwer to the Earl of Carnarvon, 30 Sept. 1874, CO, 144/43.

[80] Spenser St. John to the Earl of Malmsbury, 32 May 1859, FO, 12/26.

[81] Acuerdos de las communicaciones sobre la ocupacion de Tulayan asi como acerca del cambio de Secretario de Sultan de Jolo, 20 Jan. 1859, PNA, Unclassified Mindanao/Sulu bundle.

[82] Extract from the Straits Settlement Government Gazette in Bulwer to the Earl of Granville, 23 Mar.1873, CO, 144/40.

[83] See Ch.2 in L.R. Wright, *The Origins of British Borneo.*

[84] No.41, GCG a Senor Ministro de Ultramar, 1 Feb. 1873, AHN, Ultramar 5217.

[85] Bulwer to the Earl of Granville, 12 June 1872, CO, 144/37.

[86] Ricketts to the Earl of Granville, 1 Nov. 1871, FO, 72/1283; Bulwer to the Earl of Granville, 12 June 1872, CO, 144/37.

[87] E. St. John Hart, "The Strange Story of a Little Ship", *The Wide World Magazine* (1906), pp.350–51.

[88] Bulwer to the Earl of Carnarvon, 17 July 1874, CO, 144/42.

[89] Comision Reservada a Borneo y Jolo, 1881–1882, p.124; no.75, Carlos Cuarteron, Prefecto Apoltolico a GCG, 19 Sept. 1872, PNA, Mindanao/Sulu 1857–1895, pp.11–12; Comandancia General de Marina del Apostadero de Filipinas a GCG, 4 Nov. 1875, PNA, Isla de Borneo (2).

[90] St. John Hart, "The Strange Story of a Little Ship", p.353.

[91] Ibid., p.351.

[92] Commander Buckle to Vice Admiral Ryder, 28 Feb. 1875, CO, 144/45.

[93] Bulwer to the Earl of Granville, 12 June 1872, CO, 144/37.

[94] D. Santiago Patero, *Sistema que Conviene Adoptar para Acabar con La Pirateria: que Los Mahometanos de La Sultania de Jolo Ejercen en el Archipielago Filipino,* pp.39–42.

[95] Ibid., p.9.

[96] Bulwer to the Earl of Carnarvon, 30 Sept. 1874, CO, 144/43.

[97] Bulwer to the Earl of Kimberley, 7 Nov. 1873, CO, 144/41.

[98] Capt.Knorr to Imperial Admiralty, Berlin, 24 May 1875, in the Earl of Derby to Lord Odo Russel, 12 Feb. 1876, CO, 144/46.

[99] Statement of Datu Jemulano, 10 Jan. 1875, in Report of Commander Buckle on the State of the Sulu Archipelago, CO, 144/45.

[100] Bulwer to the Earl of Carnarvon, 30 Sept. 1874, CO, 144/43.

[101] Ibid.

[102] Ibid.

[103] Acting Consul General Low to the Earl of Derby, 3 Jan. 1876, CO, 144/46.

[104] Bulwer to the Earl of Carnarvon, 30 Sept. 1874, CO, 144/43.

[105] Bulwer to the Earl of Carnarvon, 25 June 1874, CO, 144/42.

[106] Meade to Tenterden, 2 Sept. 1873, FO, 71/3.

[107] Bulwer to the Earl of Kimberley, 14 Jan. 1874, CO, 144/42.

[108] Commander Buckle to Vice-Adm.Ryder, 28 Feb. 1875, CO, 144/45.

[109] Ibid.

[110] Commander Buckle to Vice-Adm.Ryder, 28 Feb. 1875, CO, 144/45.

[111] St. John Hart, "The Strange Story of a Little Ship", p.352.

[112] Bulwer to the Earl of Carnarvon, 30 Sept. 1874, CO, 144/43.

[113] Expediente 6, Secretaria de la Sultania de Jolo a Gobernador Militar y Politico de Mindanao 27 Feb. 1867, PNA, Mindanao/Sulu 1839–1898.

[114] Translation from the *Diario de Manila* in Bulwer to the Earl of Granville, 29 Dec. 1871, CO, 144/35.

[115] Alfred Marche, *Luzon and Palawan,* p.272.

[116] Commander Buckle to Vice-Adm. Ryder, 28 Feb. 1875, CO, 144/45.

[117] Ag. Consul-General Low to the Earl of Derby, 15 July 1875, in Bulwer to the Earl of Carnarvon, 16 July 1875, CO, 144/44.

[118] Ag.Consul-General Low to the Earl of Derby, 8 May 1875, CO, 144/44.

[119] Ag.Consul-General Low to the Earl of Derby, 29 Feb. 1876, CO, 144/46.

[120] Ag.Consul-General Low to the Earl of Derby, 26 May 1876, CO, 144/46.

[121] Ag.Consul-General Low to the Earl of Derby, 25 Nov. 1875, CO, 144/45.

[122] Ibid.

[123] Report by Consul Palgrave on the Island and Archipelago of Sulu and their relations with Spain, 24 Jan. 1877, FO, 572/4.

[124] For a copy of the text of this Protocol, see Saleeby, *History of Sulu*, pp.239–41.

[125] Palgrave to the Earl of Derby, 7 Sept. 1877, FO, 72/1477.

[126] Saleeby, *History of Sulu*, p.124; Majul, *Muslims in the Philippines*, pp.242–98; Tarling, *Sulu and Sabah*, pp.95–143.

[127] The full text of both the Spanish and Taosug translations are found in Saleeby, *History of Sulu*, pp.124–29.

Chapter 6

[1] Hunt, "Some Particulars Relating to Sulo", pp.47–50.

[2] Several European observers in the first part of the 19th century would comment on the poverty of the Chinese of Jolo. See Hunt, "Some Particulars Relating to Sulo", pp.44–50; D'Urville, *Voyage au Pole Sud et dans L'Oceanie Sur Les Corvettes L'Astrolobe et La Zelee*, vol.7, p.184; Wilkes, "Jolo and the Sulus", p.168.

[3] Hunt, "Some Particulars Relating to Sulo", pp.49–50.

[4] Oficios del Gobernador con las diligencias practicadas sobre el establicimeiento de los Ingleses en la Ysla de Balambangan 1804–1805, PNA, Mindanao/Sulu 1774–1887, p.55.

[5] J. Hunt to Thomas Raffles, 1 Sept. 1814, IOL, G/21/26, p.213.

[6] Comyn, *State of the Philippines*, p.3.

[7] Wilkes, "Jolo and the Sulus", pp.147, 155–56; D'Urville, *Voyage au Pole Sud et dans L'Oceanie Sur Les Corvettes L'Astralobe et La Zelee*, vol.7, p.310.

[8] GCG a Secretario de Estado, 18 July 1772, AGI, Filipinas 492; MacDonald, *A Narrative of the Early Life and Services of Captain D. MacDonald, R.N.*, p.200; in this period the Chinese in Jolo filled in Taosug society what Wertheim has called an "occupational gap". See W.F. Wertheim, *East-West Parallels: Sociological Approaches to Modern Asia* (The Hague: Van Hoeve, 1964), pp.43–74.

[9] St. John, *Life in the Forests of the Far East*, vol.2, p.187.

[10] Jansen, "Aanteekeningen omtrent Sollok en de Solloksche Zeeroovers", p.217.

[11] Extract from the journal of the British barque *Osprey*, in Col. Cavanagh to Sec. to the Government of India, 28 Jan. 1863, FO, 71/1.

[12] Bulwer to the Earl of Granville, 29 Dec. 1871, CO, 144/35.

[13] Consul-General Low to the Earl of Derby, 8 May 1875, CO, 144/44.

[14] Statement of Chinese trader Ko Pic to Hugh Low, 3 Dec. 1872, in the Earl of Derby to Lord Odo Russel, 12 Feb. 1876, CO, 144/46.

[15] Statement of Wyndham in Commander Buckle's report on the State of the Sulu Archipelago, Confidential Print, 2604, CO, 144/45.

[16] Consul-General Low to the Earl of Derby, 15 July 1875, in Bulwer to the Earl of Carnarvon, 16 July 1875, CO, 144/44.

[17] The career of this remarkable Magindanao overlord is carefully traced in Ileto's fine study of Cotabato, *Magindanao, 1860–1888: The Career of Datu Uto of Buayan*.

[18] See the following letters of Carlos Cuarteron detailing the sale of arms and ammunition to Taosug and Chinese and foreign ship movements. Carlos Cuarteron, Prefecto Apostolico a GCG, 27 Mar. 1877, 25 Sept. 1877, 7 July 1879, PNA, Isla de Borneo (1); No.129, el Governador Politico y Militar de Jolo a GCG, 4 Dec. 1881, AHN, Ultramar 5331.

[19] Garin, 'Memoria sobre el Archipelago de Jolo', p.206; Montero y Vidal, *Historia de la Pirateria Malayo-Mohometena en Mindanao, Jolo y Borneo*, p.77.

[20] Wickberg, *The Chinese in Philippine Life*, p.92.

[21] Ileto, *Magindanao, 1860–1888*, p.31.

[22] "Comision Reservada Borneo y Jolo", p.75; Wickberg, *The Chinese in Philippine Life*, pp.92–93.

[23] Crocker to Sir Rutherford Alcock, 30 Apr. 1887, CO, 874/243; in the PNA there is enormous documentation of Arolas' administration as well as that of his predecessor.

[24] PNA, Chinos, Cotabato, Davao, Jolo, Misamis 1878–1898.

[25] For the full text of these decrees, see the official letter prohibiting Chinese from trading in the interior, 9 July 1890, BIA, 3671–2; No.45, Gobierno Politico y Militar de la Isla de Mindanao a GCG 19 Mar. 1891, PNA, Mindanao/Sulu 1862–1898; Garin, "Memoria sobre el Archipielago de Jolo", p.173; see also Appendix M.

[26] Saleeby, *History of Sulu*, p.26.

[27] *BHN*, 1 Sept. 1892, p.282.

[28] Ibid.

[29] Saleeby, *The History of Sulu*, p.21.

[30] Wright, *The Origins of British Borneo*, pp.148–54; see also K.G. Tregonning, *A History of Modern Sabah, 1881–1963*, pp.13–29.

[31] Pringle, *Rajahs and Rebels*, p.2.

[32] Tregonning, *A History of Modern Sabah*, p.197.

[33] Diary of William Pryer, 12 Feb. 1878, CO, 874/67.

[34] Diary of William Pryer, 15 Oct. 1878, CO, 874/68.

[35] "Observations of the North Coast of Borneo", in Joseph Hatton, *The New Ceylon*, p.182.

[36] Ethnographic fieldwork has been conducted among the Jama Mapun by Eric Casino. See *The Jama Mapun: A Changing Samal Society in the Southern Philippines;* idem, "Jama Mapun Ethnocology", pp.1–32.

[37] Bulwer to the Earl of Kimberley, 30 Nov. 1872, CO, 144/38.

[38] Diary of William Pryer, 17–19 Feb. 1878, CO, 874/67.

[39] No.372, Gobierno Politico y Militar de Jolo a GCG, 11 June 1889, PNA, Mindanao/Sulu 1877–1895.

[40] Dean Worcester, *The Philippine Islands and Their People*, p.124.

[41] No.570, Gobierno Politico y Militar de Jolo a GCG, 27 Oct. 1886, PNA, Mindanao/Sulu 1862–1898; see also Commandancia General de Marina a GCG, 25 Sept. 1886, PNA, Mindanao/Sulu 1864–1898.

[42] No.372, Gobierno Politico y Militar de Jolo a GCG, 11 June 1889, PNA, Mindanao/Sulu 1877–1895.

[43] Birch to Martin 4 Feb. 1903, CO, 874/271.

[44] *NBH*, 1 Aug. 1894, p.193.

[45] *NBH*, 1 Jan. 1895, p.4. This trade persisted into the 20th century, and the Jama Mapun would be labelled "smugglers" by the Americans who replaced the Spanish in the Philippines. Diary of Leonard Wood, 21–26 July 1904, Library of Congress, Papers of General Leonard Wood, container 3; Hugh Scott to Government Colonial Sec., 6 July 1905, Library of Congress. Papers of Hugh Scott, container 56; Birth to Martin, 4 Feb. 1903, 874/271.

[46] "Historical Data Papers for Palawan", HDP, National Library of the Philippines, p.1.

[47] Ibid.

[48] Carlos Cuarteron, Prefecto Apostolico a GCG, 27 Oct. 1857, PNA, Isla de Borneo (1); Bulwer to the Earl of Kimberley, 23 Sept. 1873, CO, 144/41; Bulwer to the Earl of Carnarvon, 30 Sept. 1874, CO, 144/42.

[49] Treacher to Sir Rutherford Alcock, 14 Apr. 1884, CO, 874/236; 26 July 1884, CO, 874/237.

[50] Treacher to Sir Rutherford Alcock, 27 Dec. 1884, CO, 874/237.

[51] Ibid.; Treacher to Sir Rutherford Alcock, 5 July 1883, CO, 874/234; 1 June 1886, CO, 874/241.

[52] Treacher to Sir Rutherford Alcock, 27 Dec. 1884, CO, 874/243.

[53] Donop to Sir Rutherford Alcock, 15 Mar. 1887, CO, 174/243.

[54] Agents of Darby and Company to Consular Agent, Sandakan, 29 June 1906, CO, 874/268.

[55] Warren, *The North Borneo Chartered Company's Administration of the Bajau*, pp.65–70.

[56] Warren, *The North Borneo Chartered Company's Administration of the Bajau*, pp.52–61, 70–78.

[57] Pryer to J.Brown, 15 Jan. 1886, CO, 874/240.

[58] Treacher to Sir Rutherford Alcock, 3 July 1904, CO, 874/237.

[59] Treacher to Sir Rutherford Alcock, 15 July 1885, CO, 874/239.

[60] Diary of William Pryer, 4 May 1879, CO, 874/68; Pryer to J. Brown, 10 Feb. 1885, CO, 874/238.

[61] Treacher to Sir Rutherford Alcock, 28 Apr. 1885, CO, 874/238.

[62] Treacher to Sir Rutherford Alcock, 3 Mar. 1886, CO, 874/240.

[63] *NBH*, 1 July 1886, p.122; 16 July 1936, p.183; Warren, *The North Borneo Chartered Company's Administration of the Bajau*, pp.56–58.

[64] William Treacher, "Sketches of Brunei, Sarawak, Labuan and North Borneo", p.100.

[65] *NBH*, 1 July 1886, p.122.

[66] *NBH*, 1 Oct.1886, p.209; Treacher, "British Borneo", p.100.

[67] Crocker to Sir Rutherford Alcock, 14 May 1887, CO, 874/243; NBH, 1 June 1887, p.120; the founding of Semporna is discussed at length in Warren, *The North Borneo Chartered Company's Administration of the Bajau*, pp.61–64.

[68] Crocker to Sir Rutherford Alcock, 30 Apr.1887, CO, 874/243.

[69] Crocker to Sir Rutherford Alcock, 7 May 1887, CO, 874/243.

[70] Crocker to Sir Rutherford Alcock, 14 May 1887, CO, 874/243.

[71] Donop to Crocker, 22 July 1887, CO, 874/243; Callaghan to Crocker, 14 Nov.1887, Co, 874/244.

[72] Pryer to Creagh, 14 June 1888, CO, 874/245; Creagh to Sir Rutherford Alcock, 13 Sept. 1888, CO, 874/246. BH-PCL, vol.1, paper 160, no.2, Stephenson, "Constabulary Monograph of Tawi-Tawi", p.55; *Handbook of the State of North Borneo: With a Supplement of Statistical and other useful Information* (London: British North Borneo Chartered Company, 1934), p.106.

[73] Dunlop to Ag. Colonial Sec., 15 Aug. 1892, CO, 874/253; *NBH,* 1 Jan. 1893, p.25; 1 June 1893, p.25; 1 May 1895, p.111; Cook to Martin, 5 Oct. 1899, CO, 874/264.

[74] Treacher to Sir Rutherford Alcock, 31 Dec. 1882, CO, 874/232; *NBH,* 1 June 1892, p.171.

PART II

[1] In these Euro-centred histories, which dwell on the activity of the Iranun and Balangingi at length, the term "piracy" is conspicuously present in the titles. Barrantes, *Guerras Piraticas de Filipinas contra Mindanaos y Joloanos;* Emilio Bernaldez, *Resana historica de la guerra a Sur de Filipinas, sostenida por las armas Espanoles contra los piratas de aquel Archipelago,*

desde la conquista hasta nuestras dias; Montero y Vidal, *Historia de la Pirateria Malayo Mahometana en Mindanao, Jolo y Borneo;* Tarling *Piracy and Politics in the Malay World.*

² Ann L.Reber, "The Sulu World in the Eighteenth and Early Nineteenth Centuries: A Historiographical Problem in British Writings on Malay Piracy" (M.A. diss., Cornell University, 1966); in fact, as Reber points out, Raffles could have reached very different conclusions regarding the subject of piracy and the Sulu Sultanate. He seems to have been unaware of the accurate published accounts, and manuscript material (written by Alexander Dalrymple, Thomas Forrest, and James Rennel at the end of the 18th century; and available in the archives of the East India Company) on the Sulu world.

³ Lennox A.Mills, *British Malaya, 1824–1867,* pp.323–24, 328–29; Tarling, *Piracy and Politics in the Malay World,* pp. 20, 146; Tregonning, *A History of Modern Sabah,* p.186; Wright, *The Origins of British Borneo,* pp.5, 39; Majul, *Muslims in the Philippines,* chs.7, 8.

⁴ See Blake to Maitland, 13 Aug. 1838, PRO, Admiralty 125/133; Declaraciones de todos los cautivos fugados de Jolo y acogidos a los Buques de la expresada Divicion, con objeto de averiguar los puntos de donde salen los pancos piratas, la clase de gente que los tripulan, la forma en que se hacen los armamentos y otros particulares que arrogan las mismas declaraciones, Jolo, 4 Oct. 1836, PNA, Mindanao/Sulu 1803–1890, pp.1–72; Relacion de los cautivos venidos de Jolo sobre el Bergantin Espanol *Cometa,* 19 Mar. 1847, PNA, Piratas 3; Verklaringen van ontvlugten personen uit de handen der Zeeroovers van 1845–1849, ANRI, Menado 37. Freed captives and captive marauders expressed their own attitudes toward raiding in numerous statements and interrogations, recorded over several decades. These were occasionally published in Dutch scholarly journals: see A.J.F. Jansen, "Aanteekeningen omtrent Sollok en de Solloksche Zeeroovers", pp.212–43; "Berigten omtrent den Zeeroof in den Nederlandsch-Indischen Archipel, 1857", *TBG* XVIII (1868–1872): 435–57; "Berigten omtrent den Zeeroof in den Nederlandsch-Indischen Archipel, 1858", *TBG* XX (1873): 302–26; W.R. van Hoevell, "De Zeerooverijen der Soloerezen", pp.99–105.

Chapter 7

¹ Edward Kuder, "The Moros in the Philippines", p.123.
² Admiralty to Under-Sec. to State, 14 July 1862, PRO, FO, 12/30; Mr. W. Stanton to Admiralty, 27 Sept. 1862, PRO, FO, 12/30.
³ BH-PCL, vol.2, Paper 161, Saleeby, "The Moros", p.11.
⁴ Ibid., p.10; see introductory chapters of Mednick, "Encampment of the Lake: The Social Organisation of a Moslem Philippine People", (Ph.D. diss., University of Chicago, 1965).
⁵ Ibid., p.18; personal communication, David Barradas, 7 Feb. 1974.
⁶ Capt. William Dampier, *Dampier's Voyages,* vol.1, ed. John Masfield, p.333.
⁷ Forrest, *Voyage to New Guinea,* pp.192–93; see also Mednick, "Some Problems of Moro History", p.43.
⁸ Mednick, "Encampment of the Lake", p.47.
⁹ Personal communication, David Barradas, 7 Feb. 1974; Van Hoevell, "De Zeerooverijen der Soloerezen", p.100.
¹⁰ Mednick, "Encampment of the Lake", pp.30–31.
¹¹ Majul, *Muslims in the Philippines,* p.365.
¹² Forrest, *Voyage to New Guinea,* pp.193, 237–38.
¹³ Ibid., p.230; Juan Cencelli a Senor Conde de Aranda, 16 Apr. 1774, AHN, Estado 2845, Caja 2.

[14] Personal communication, Jeremy Beckett, 17 Jan. 1975.

[15] Comyn, *State of the Philippines in 1810*, p.132; Saleeby, *Studies in Moro History, Law and Religion*, p.15.

[16] No.7, GCG a Senor Secretario de Estado, 4 June 1806, AGI, Filipinas 510; Forrest described the harbour of Tubug as the chief point for the assemblage of marauding flotillas. Forrest, *Voyage to New Guinea*, p.193.

[17] Maj. James Rennell, "Journal of a Voyage to the Sooloo Islands and the Northwest Coast of Borneo, from and to Madras, With Descriptions of the Islands", Apr. 1762–Feb. 1763, British Museum, Add. 19299, p.38; BH-PCL, vol.1, Paper 160, no.1, Livingston, "Constabulary Monograph of the Province of Sulu", 15 Nov. 1915, p.7; Forrest, *Voyage to New Guinea*, p.322.

[18] No.7, GCG a Senor Secretario de Estado, 4 June 1806, AGI, Filipinas 510; Barrantes, *Guerras Piraticas*, pp.159–61; Montero y Vidal, *Historia de Filipinas*, vol.2, p.372.

[19] GCG a Senor Secretario de Estado, 18 July 1772, AGI, Filipinas 492; Blake to Maitland, 13 Aug. 1838, PRO, Admiralty 125/133, p.7.

[20] GCG a Senor Secretario de Estado, 12 Jan. 1773, AGI, Filipinas, p.493.

[21] Barrantes, *Guerras Piraticas*, p.181.

[22] Rennell, "Journal of a Voyage to the Sooloo Islands and the Northwest coast of Borneo", p.38.

[23] Forrest, *Voyage to New Guinea*, p.322.

[24] Juan Cencelli a Senor Conde de Aranda, 16 Apr. 1774, AHN, Estado 2845, caja 2; No.7, GCG a Senor Secretario de Estado, 4 June 1806, AGI, Filipinas 510; Montero y Vidal, *Historia de Filipinas*, vol.2, p.311.

[25] BH-PCL, vol.6, Paper 162, no.23, Christie, "The Moros of Sulu and Mindanao", p.43.

[26] J. Dalton, "On the Present State of Piracy, Amongst These Islands, and the Best Method of Its Suppression", in Moor, *Notices of the Indian Archipelago*, p.18.

[27] Blake to Maitland, 13 Aug. 1838, PRO, Admiralty 125/133, p.8.

[28] Jansen, "Aanteekeningen omtrent Sollok en de Solloksche Zeeroovers", p.231; Extract from *Singapore Free Press*, 6 Apr. 1847, in PRO, Admiralty 125/133.

[29] Dalrymple, *Oriental Repertory*, p.553.

[30] Ibid., p.507.

[31] Gregori, "Aanteekeningen en Beshouwingen betrekkelijk de Zeeroovers en hunne rooverijen in den Indischen Archipel, alsmede aagaande Magindanao en de Sooloo-Archipel", pp.305–6.

[32] AR, Archief Kolonien 4168.

[33] Extract from Mr. Presgraves' report on the subject of piracy, 5 Dec. 1828, PRO, Admiralty 125/133; No.7, GCG a Senor Secretario de Estado, 4 June 1806, AGI, Filipinas 510; Barrantes, Guerras Piraticas, pp.159–60.

[34] Personal communication, Clifford Sather, 6 Apr. 1972.

[35] Barrantes, *Guerras Piraticas*, p.160.

[36] Extracts from Mr. Presgraves' report on the subject of piracy, 5 Dec. 1828, PRO, Admiralty 125/133.

[37] Francis Light to Consul at Fort William, 13 Dec. 1786, IOL, Straits Settlement Factory Records/1355; Maj. Kyd to John Thornhill, 26 Dec. 1795, IOL, P/4/39, p.302; Mr. Graham to Mr. Dundas, 29 May 1795, IOL, H/Misc/437/6, p.153.

[38] Light to Consul at Fort William, 16 July 1789, IOL, Straits Settlement Factory Records/2.

[39] Light to Consul at Fort William, 5 Dec. 1790, IOL, Straits Settlement Factory Records/2.

[40] Light to Consul at Fort William, 5 Jan. 1791, IOL, Straits Settlement Factory Records/2.

[41] Kommisar te Palembang, aan dem Gouveneur General van Nederlandsch Indien, 25 May 1818, AR, Archief Kolonien, 4168.

[42] Thomas Horsfield, "Report on the Island of Banca", pp.318–24.

[43] "The Piracy and Slave Trade of the Indian Archipelago", *JIAEA* 3 (1849): 587.

[44] *Singapore Chronicle,* 18 Apr. 1833; T.J. Newbold, "Outline of Political Relations with the Native States on the Eastern and Western Coasts, Malayan Peninsula", in Moor, *Notices of the Indian Archipelago,* p.90.

[45] *Singapore Chronicle,* 25 Aug. 1831.

[46] Testimony of Raja Akil in Kommisar te Palembang, aan de Gouveneur General van Nederlandsch Indien, 25 May 1818, AR, Archief Kolonien 4168; No.115, De Resident van Banka, aan der Gouveneur General over Nederlandsch Indien, 29 Jan. 1831, AR, Archief Kolonien 4168.

[47] No.115, De Resident van Banka aan der Gouveneur General over Nederlandsch Indien, 29 Jan. 1831, AR, Archief Kolonien 4168.

[48] "Historical Notices upon the Piracies Committed in the East Indies, and upon the Measures Taken for Suppressing Them, by the Government of the Netherlands, within the Last Thirty Years". Abstracted from articles by Cornet de Groot in the Moniteur des Indes, P.P.H.C., 1851, vol.56, pt.1 (1390): 94–95.

[49] "Piracy and Slave Trade of the Indian Archipelago", *JIAEA* 4 (1850): 619.

[50] G. Bushby to W. Macnaghten, 24 July 1835, IOL, P/13/13.

[51] "Piracy and Slave Trade of the Indian Archipelago", *JIAEA* 4 (1850): 626; Tarling, *Piracy and Politics in the Malay World,* pp.75–111.

[52] "Piracy and Slave Trade of the Indian Archipelago", *JIAEA* 3 (1849): 586; "Berigten omtrent den Zeeroof in den Nederlandsch-Indischen Archipel, 1858", p.322.

[53] No.839, 8 June 1955, AR, Schaarsbergen Kolonien 5873.

[54] Vosmaer aan den Gouveneur General van Nederlandsch Indien, 25 Nov. 1833, AR, Archief Kolonien 4168; N.842, 29 Jan. 1872, AR-Schaarsbergen, Kolonien 2496.

[55] Jansen, "Aantekeningen omtrent Sollok en de Solloksche Zeeroovers", p.232.

[56] Vosmaer aan den Gouveneur General van Nederlandsch Indien, 25 Nov. 1833, AR, Kolonien Archief 4168.

[57] Van Dewall, "Aanteekeningen Omtrent de Noordoostkust", p.442.

[58] Beright en Bijlagen Nopens de Manadose Commissie beginnende den 21 Oct. 1780 tot 21 Dec. 1780, ANRI, Ternate 138; Barrantes, *Guerras Piraticas,* p.108.

[59] Forrest, *Voyage to New Guinea,* p.228.

[60] Ibid., p.229.

[61] Farquhar to Col. Oliver, 1 June 1802, IOL, P/2–5/18.

[62] IOL, G/21/1, p.367; F.W. Stapel (ed.), *Corpus Diplomaticum Neerlands-Indicum,* vol.6, p.437.

[63] Farquhar to Lord Clive, 1 Jan. 1802, IOL, P/242/42, 2551.

[64] Col. Oliver to Lord Clive, 6 Mar. 1802, IOL, P/242/42, 2612.

[65] Kolf, *Voyages of the Dutch Brig of War Dourga,* vol.11.

[66] Charles Court, to Marquis Wellsley, 30 June 1801, IOL, P/165/76.

[67] Col. Oliver to Lord Clive, 6 Mar. 1802, IOL, P/242/42, 2612.

[68] Farquhar to Lord Clive, 1 Jan. 1802, IOL, P/242/42, 2560.

[69] John Hayes, commander of the Company ship *Swift,* to the resident at the Molucca islands, 21 Aug. 1801, IOL, P/242/42.

[70] Hunt, "Some Particulars Relating to Sulo", p.51.

[71] Van Hoevell, "De Zeerooverijen der Soloerezen", p.51.

[72] Kommisar te Palembang, aan Gouveneur General van Nederlandsch Indien, 25 May 1818, AR, Archief Kolonien 4168.

[73] Ibid.; Vosmaer aan der Gouveneur General van Nederlandsch Indien, 25 Nov. 1833, AR, Archief Kolonien 4168.

[74] Testimony of Pangeran Syed Hassan Habassy, 15 Oct. 1830, AR, Archief Kolonien 4168.

[75] "Aantekenengin nopens den staat en tegenwoordige gesteldheid der Moluksche Eilanden", AR, Kolonien Archief 2954 [c. 1818].

[76] Resident van Manado, aan Den Gouveneur der Moluksche eilanden, no.11, 6 Jan. 1846; No.155, 14 Mar. 1846; No.565, 10 Aug. 1846, ANRI, Manado 50.

[77] AR, Archief Kolonien 3089.

[78] No.46, GCG a Secretario de Estado, 17 Aug. 1770, AGI, Filipinas 790; Alexander Dalrymple to Secret Committee, 7 Feb. 1764, IOL, G/4/1, pp.402–3.

[79] No.28, GCG a su Magestad, 1 Aug. 1765, AGI, Filipinas 611, p.4.

[80] Memoir of Sooloo, IOL, Orme Collection, vol.67, p.100.

[81] No.28, GCG a su Magestad, 1 Aug. 1765, AGI, Filipinas 611, p.4.

[82] No.99, GCG a Secretario de Estado, 10 July 1771, AGI, Filipinas 491, pp.1–3.

[83] Forrest, *Voyage to New Guinea,* p.302.

[84] No.165, GCG a Secretario de Estado, 16 Jan. 1772, AGI, Filipinas 491; No.226, AGI, Filipinas 492, p.4.

[85] No.482, GCG a Senor Secretario de Estado, 31 Mar. 1775, AGI, Filipinas 360.

[86] J.F. de la Perouse, *A Voyage Round the World in the Years 1785, 1787, and 1788,* 3 vols. (London, 1798) in *Travel Accounts of the Islands, 1513–1787,* pp.365–66.

[87] No.7, GCG a Senor Secretario de Estado, 4 June 1806, AGI, Filipinas 510, p.51; No.226, AGI, Filipinas 492, p.4; Joachim Martinez de Zuniga, *Estadismo de las Filipinas; o mis Viajez por este Pais,* p.495.

[88] No.70, GCG a Secretario de Estado, AGI, Filipinas 491; No.1, 10 Oct. 1772, AGI, Filipinas 626.

[89] No.70, GCG a Secretario de Estado, 26 Dec. 1770, AGI, Filipinas 491; No.105, GCG a Secretario de Estado, 12 July 1771, AGI, Filipinas 491; No.1, Consejo de las Indias, 10 Oct. 1772, AGI, Filipinas 626.

[90] No.482, GCG a Senor Secretario de Estado, 31 Mar. 1775, AGI, Filipinas 360; No.7, GCG a Senor Secretario de Estado, 4 June 1806, Filipinas 510, pp.61, 95; No.46, GCG a Senor Secretario de Estado, 17 Aug. 1770, AGI, Filipinas 490; Comyn, *State of the Philippines in 1810,* p.119.

[91] Alcalde Mayor de Tayabas a GCG, 20 Dec. 1768, PNA, Ereccion de Pueblo, Tayabas III; Alcalde Mayor de Tayabas a GCG, 18 Sept. 1781, PNA, Ereccion de Pueblo, Tayabas 217; Alcalde Mayor de Tayabas a GCG, 2 Dec. 1793, PNA, Ereccion de Pueblo, Tayabas 99 (1793–1857 pt.II); No.7, GCG a Senor Secretario de Estado, 4 June 1806, AGI, Filipinas 510; Montero y Vidal, *Historia de Filipinas,* p.377.

[92] El Provincial de Recolectos de Filipinas informa Vuestra Magestad de el estado de las Islas, 15 June 1771, AGI, Filipinas 685; see also, Expediente sobre la falta de trafico y comercio con aquellas capital de los naturales de las Provincias de Catbolonga, Leyte y Samar, en las Visayas, Consejo de las Indias, 1 Aug. 1780, AGI, Filipinas 645; No.248, GCG a Senor Secretario de Estado, 8 June 1773, AGI, Filipinas 493; No.165, GCG a Senor Secretario de Estado 16 Jan. 1772, AGI, Filipinas 491.

[93] No.46, GCG a Senor Secretario de Estado, AGI, Filipinas 490, p.32.

[94] Expediente de Fray Bernando Suarez Provincial de Augustinos Calzados de las Islas Filipinas, 18 May 1772, AGI, Filipinas 627.

[95] El Provincial de Recollectos, a vuestra magestad, 5 June 1771, AGI, Filipinas 685.

[96] No.226, II, AGI, Filipinas 492, p.10.

[97] Historical Data on Catarman, HDP Misamis Oriental, p.45.

[98] El Obispo de Zebu, a su Magestad, 21 Dec. 1779, AGI, Filipinas 1027.

[99] No.4, 5 July 1814, AGI, Filipinas 510.

[100] No.234, GCG a Senor Secretario de Estado, 12 December 1772, AGI, Filipinas 493; No.265, GCG a Senor Secretario de Estado y del Despacho Universal de Marina y Indias, 12 January 1773, AGI, Filipinas 493.

[101] No.7, GCG a Senor Secretario de Estado, 4 June 1806, AGI, Filipinas 510.

[102] Notes translated from the Spanish relative to the pirates on Mindanao, PRO, Admiralty 125/133.

[103] No.31, GCG a Senor Secretario de Estado, 11 Jan. 1770, AGI, Filipinas 489; No.226, I, AGI, Filipinas 492, p.25.

[104] GCG a Senor Secretario de Estado, 20 Dec. 1778, AGI, Filipinas 687; No.7, GCG a Secretario de Estado, 4 June 1806, AGI, Filipinas 510.

[105] No.125, GCG a Secretario de Estado, 22 May 1779, AGI, Filipinas 494; MN, Coleccion Guillen, Tomo V, Documento 33; No.7, GCG a Secretario de Estado, 4 June 1806, AGI, Filipinas 510.

[106] Eliodoro Robles, *The Philippines in the Nineteenth Century,* p.73; in 1829, the *vinta* was replaced with a tax on the coasting trade called *cabotaje,* but it was revived shortly afterwards and was in force until 1851. Montero y Vida, *Historia de Filipinas,* vol.3, p.154.

[107] No.7, GCG a Secretario de Estado, 4 June 1806, AGI, Filipinas 510.

[108] Ibid.; No.4, Ventura de los Reyes a Secretario de Estado, 5 July 1814, AGI, Filipinas 510.

[109] No.7, GCG a Senor Secretario de Estado, 4 June 1806, AGI, Filipinas 510.

[110] Notes translated from the Spanish relative to the pirates on the island of Mindanao, PRO, Admiralty 125/133.

[111] R. Farquhar to the Marquis Wellesley, 6 Jan. 1804, IOL, P/166; Bernaldez, *Guerra al Sur,* pp.36, 143.

[112] MN, Coleccion Guillen, Tomo V, Documento 33; Bernaldez, *Guerra al Sur,* p.143.

[113] R. Farquhar to the Marquis Wellesley, 16 Jan. 1804, IOL, P/166.

[114] Montero y Vidal, *Historia de Filipinas,* vol.2, p.500.

[115] Ibid., p.505; for other comments on the offering of head money and issuing letters of marque, *ordenanzo de corso,* see No,10, 15 July 1777, AGI, Filipinas 636; No.13, Consejo de las Indias, 31 July 1777, AGI, Filipinas 360.

[116] For a brief sketch of his life, see Elviro J. Perez, *Catalogo Bio-Bibliografico de las Reliogiosos Augustinos de la Provincia del Santisimo Nombre de Jesus de las Islas Filipinas desde su fundacion hasta nuestros dias,* pp.376–78; Montero y Vidal, *Historia de Filipinas,* vol.2, pp.501–4.

[117] MN, Coleccion Enrile, Tomo XVII, documento 16; Francisco Osario, a GCG, 3 Aug. 1834, MN, Coleccion Guillen, Tomo XIII, Ms. 1740, p.132.

[118] No.46, GCG a Senor Secretario de Estado, 7 Aug. 1770, AGI, Filipinas 490.

[119] Comyn, *State of the Philippines in 1810,* p.120.

[120] Pierre Viscomte de Pages, *Travels Round the World in the Years 1767, 1768, 1769, 1770, 1771,* p.148.

[121] There are ample references to the destruction of coastal defences by natural forces. For earthquakes, see Historical Data on Oslob, HDP, Cebu; Historical Data on Pasacao, HDP, Camarines Sur, 4; by volcanic eruption, Historical Data on Libog, HDP, Albay; by typhoon and hurricane, No.27, GCG a Senor Secretario de Estado, 5 Dec. 1844, AHN, Ultramar 5157; No.11, GCG a Presidente del Consejo de Ministros, 11 Feb. 1852, AHN, Ultramar 5163. Notices of the rebuilding of watchtowers and *baluarte* were sometimes placed in the Manila newspapers: "A *telegrafo* has been built in the pueblo of Lingayen, Pangasinan province to replace the one destroyed in a storm." *Estrella de Manila,* 15 July 1848.

[122] MN, Coleccion Enrile XIII, Documento 9.

[123] No.7, GCG a Secretario de Estado, 4 June 1806, AGI, Filipinas 510.

[124] Meares, *Voyages Made in the Years 1788 and 1789 from China to the Northwest coast of America,* p.21.

[125] For the difficulties in using fire as a warning signal, see MN, Coleccion Enrile, Tomo XIII, documento 2, p.1; for information on the use of flags and torches, see Historical Data on Oslob, HDP, Cebu; Historical Data on Boto, HDP, Catanduan 3; for shell horns and drums,

see Historical Data on Alo Guinsan, HDP, Cebu; Historical Data on Badajoz, HDP, Romblon; Historical Data on San Remigio, HDP, Cebu; Pierre Viscomte de Pages, *Travels Round the World in the Years 1767, 1768, 1769, 1770, 1771,* p.146.

[126] Historical Data on Numancia, HDP, Suriagao; Historical Data on Libon, HDP, Albay; Historical Data on Bugao, HDP, Catanduanes; Historical Data on Mamperao (Camarines Sur), HDP, Zamboanga del Sur; Historical Data on Tarangoran, HDP, Samar, vol.8, 10; Historical Data on Culasi, HDP, Antique.

[127] Historical Data on Bato, HDP, Catanduanes; Historical Data on Pandan, HDP, Catanduanes.

[128] Historical Data on Uson, HDP, Masbate.

[129] No.46, GCG a Secretario de Estado, 17 Aug. 1770, AGI, Filipinas 490.

[130] El Provincial de Recolects de Filipinas a Vuestra Magestad, 15 June 1771, AGI, Filipinas 685; No.43, 16 Oct. 1785, PNA, Ereccion de Pueblo Camarines Sur, 1786–1837, VII; No.7, 4 June 1806, AGI, Filipinas 510.

[131] No.14, Alcalde Mayor de Tayabas a GCG, 23 Dec. 1794, PNA, Ereccion de Pueblo Tayabas, 1793–1857, pt.II: see also No.7, GCG a Senor Secretario de Estado 1806, AGI, Filipinas 510.

[132] Notes translated from the Spanish relative to Pirates on the Island of Mindanao, PRO, Admiralty 125/133.

[133] No.8, 15 May 1799, PNA, Ereccion del Pueblo Albay, 1799–1864.

[134] Notes translated from the Spanish relative to Pirates on the Island of Mindanao, PRO, Admiralty 125/133; see Appendix O for an inventory of the land and sea defences of Albay Province in 1799.

[135] Ibid.; No.7, GCG Secretario de Estado, 4 June 1806, AGI, Filipinas 510; MN, Coleccion Enrile, Tomo XIII, Documento 9.

[136] No.2042, 31 Dec. 1851, PNA, Ereccion de Pueblo Albay, 1834–1864.

[137] No.1035, 7 Nov. 1864, AHN, Ultramar 5197; Jagor, *Travels in the Philippines,* p.164.

[138] Reed, "The Primate City in Southeast Asia", pp.310–11.

[139] For a detailed discussion of the impact of Iranun-Samal raiding on Samar Island, see Bruce Cruikshank, "A History of Samar Island, the Philippines, 1768–1898" (Ph.D. diss., University of Wisconsin, 1975), pp.60–82; for Albay province, see Norman G. Owen, "Kabikolan in the Nineteenth Century: Socio-Economic Change in the Provincial Philippines" (Ph.D. diss., University of Michigan, 1976), pp.13, 34–47.

[140] For demographic data, see AGI, Filipinas 323; the first census for Nueva Caceres known to have survived is for 1780: see AGI, indiferente General 1527; for 1782, 1783, 1785, 1786, 1787, AGI, indiferente General 1527; 1789, 1790, AGI, Ultramar 661; 1794, AGI, Duplicados del Obispo de Nueva Cazeres 1033; 1795, AGI, Ultramar 682; 1800, 1801, 1803, AGI, Duplicados del Obispo de Nueva Caceres 1033; 1813, AGI, Ultramar 683; for 1815, AGI, Ultramar 684. See also the Franciscan returns for 1793, AGI, Ultramar, 666; 1796, AGI, Ultramar 699. Much of the information on community location and defence has been assembled from a number of key sources: No.20, 1 Dec. 1792, AGI, Duplicados del Obispo de Nueva Caceres; No.8, 15 May 1799, PNA, Ereccion del Pueblo Albay 1799–1864; and a map, Plano Geografico y Ydrografico de la Provincia de Camarines ano de 1823, AGI, M. y P. Filipinas 134. See Appendix P.

[141] No.57, 14 Nov. 1793; 2 Dec. 1793, PNA, Ereccion de pueblo 1793–1857, pt.2; No.7, 4 June 1806, AGI, Filipinas 510.

[142] Cited in Montero y Vidal, *Historia de Filipinas,* vol.2, 501; see also MN, Coleccion Enrile, Documento 9.

[143] No.7, 4 June 1806, AGI, Filipinas 510.

[144] AGI, Filipinas 681; El Arzobispo de Manila a Vuestra Magestad, 31 June 1761, AGI, Filipinas 603; No.46, 17 Aug. 1770, AGI, Filipinas 490, II.

[145] El Obispo de Nueva Caceres a Vuestra Magestad, 14 May 1817, AGI, Ultramar 684.

Chapter 8

[1] Combes, *Historia de las Islas de Mindanao, Jolo y sus adyacentes.* cols.28–32; Forrest, *Voyage to New Guinea,* pp.372–74; Geoghegan, "Balangingi Samal", p.4.

[2] *Gazetteer of the Philippine Islands* (Washington, 1902), vol.1, p.318; El Gobierno Politico y Militar del Zamboanga a GCG, 30 May 1842, PNA, Mindanao/Sulu 1838–1885; Bernaldez, *Guerra al Sur de Filipinas,* p.153; Geoghegan, "Balangingi Samal", p.4.

[3] El Gobierno Politico y Militar del Zamboanga a GCG, 30 May 1842, PNA, Mindanao/Sulu 1838–1885.

[4] Bernaldez, *Guerra al Sur de Filipinas,* p.153.

[5] El Gobierno Politico y Militar de Zamboanga a GCG, 30 May 1842, PNA, Mindanao/Sulu 1838–1885; statements of Francisco Gregario, Diomicio Francisco, and Mariano Sevilla in Exp.12, Declaraciones de todos los cautivos fugados de Jolo, 4 Oct. 1836, PNA, Mindanao/Sulu 1803–1890 [Exp.12, unless otherwise specified, will hereafter refer to this set of Declaraciones]; J. Farren to Viscount Palmerston, 29 Feb. 1848, PRO, FO, 72/749.

[6] Geoghegan, "Balangingi Samal", p.22.

[7] Kiefer, "The Taosug Polity and the Sultanate of Sulu", p.51; Majul, "Political and Historical Notes on the old Sulu Sultanate", pp.28, 39–40.

[8] Statement of Jose Ruedas in Exp.12, 4 Oct. 1836, PNA, Mindanao/Sulu 1803–1890, p.32; statement of Silammkoom in Bonham to Maitland, 28 June 1838, PRO, Admiralty 125/133.

[9] Statements of Juan de la Cruz and Jose Ruedas in Exp.12, 4 Oct. 1836, PNA, Mindanao/Sulu 1803–1890; Van Hoevell, "De Zeerooverijen der Soloerezen", p.102.

[10] Tarling, *Piracy and Politics in the Malay World,* pp.146–85.

[11] Rennell and Forrest only make passing references to the Samal islands. Rennell, *Journal of a Voyage to the Sooloo Islands and the Northwest Coast of Borneo,* p.54; Forrest, *A Voyage to New Guinea,* pp.21–22.

[12] Statements of Angel Custodio, Juan Salvador, Domingo Candelario, and Juan Santiago in Exp.12, 4 Oct. 1836, PNA, Mindanao/Sulu 1803–1890; Diary of William Pryer, 9 Mar. 1879, CO, 874/68.

[13] Barth, *Ethnic Groups and Boundaries,* p.22.

[14] Statements of Jose Ruedas, Gabriel Francisco, and Matias de la Cruz in Exp.12, 4 Oct. 1836, PNA, Mindanao/Sulu 1803–1890.

[15] El Gobierno Politico y Militar de Zamboanga a GCG, 30 May 1842, PNA, Mindanao/Sulu 1838–1885; Exp.12, 17 Feb. 1845, PNA, Mindanao/Sulu 1836–1897.

[16] Information obtained by Charles Grey at Singapore from Wyndham relating to Sulo, 24 Feb. 1847, PRO, Admiralty 125/133; Van Hoevell, "De Zeerooverijen der Soloerezen", p.102.

[17] Hunt, "Some Particulars Relating to Sulo", p.40.

[18] Blake to Maitland, 8 Aug. 1838, PRO, Admiralty 125/133; Jansen, "Aanteekeningen omtrent Sollok de Soloksche Zeeroovers", pp.217, 229.

[19] Hunt, "Some Particulars Relating to Sulo", 3537, pp.50–51.

[20] See the statement of Juan de la Cruz in particular, in Exp.12, 4 Oct. 1836, PNA, Mindanao/Sulo 1803–1890.

[21] The Statement of Silammkoom, 31 May 1838, in Bonham to Maitland, 28 June 1838, PRO, Admiralty 125/133.

[22] Statements of Matias Domingo and Juan de la Cruz in Exp.12, 4 Oct. 1836, PNA, Mindanao/Sulu 1803–1890; extract from *Singapore Free Press,* Apr. 1847, PRO, Admiralty 125/133.

[23] Statement of Juan de la Cruz in Exp.12, 4 Oct. 1836, PNA, Mindanao/Sulu 1803–1890; El Gobierno Politico y Militar de Zamboanga a GCG, 30 May 1842, PNA, Mindanao/Sulu 1838–1885.

[24] Jansen, "Aanteekeningen omtrent Sollok en de Solloksche Zeeroovers", pp.216, 227.

[25] Wilkes, "Jolo and the Sulu", p.180.

[26] Dumont d'Urville, *Voyage au pole sud et dans l'Oceanic sur les Corvettes L'Astrolobe et La Zelee*, vol.7, pp.179, 303, 307–8; Belcher, *Narrative of the Voyage of N.M.S. Samarang, during the Years 1843–1846*, p.270; Statements of Juan Santiago, Juan Sabala, Pedro Antonio, Vicente Remigio, and Francisco Zacarias, in Exp.12, 4 Oct. 1836, PNA, Mindanao/Sulu 1803–1890.

[27] Statement of Juan de la Cruz in Exp.12, 4 Oct. 1836, PNA, Mindanao/Sulu 1803–1890; Bonham to Maitland, 28 June 1838, PRO, Admiralty 125/133.

[28] Bonham to Maitland, 28 June 1838, PRO, Admiralty 125/133.

[29] Statements of Juan Florentino, Manuel Feliz, Diomicio Francisco, and Mariano Sevilla, in Exp.12, 4 Oct. 1836, PNA, Mindanao/Sulu 1803–1890; Extracts from *Singapore Free Press*, 6 Apr. 1847, PRO, Admiralty 125/133; No.137, Carlos Cuarteron, prefecto apostolico, a GCG, 12 Aug. 1878, PNA, Isla de Borneo (2); Comyn, *State of the Philippines in 1810*, p.124; Barrantes, *Guerras Piracticas*, pp.108, 161, 265–66.

[30] Statements of Abdul and Sendie in Verklaringen van ontvlugten personen uit de handen der Zeeroovers van 1845–1849, ANRI, Menado 37; Jansen, "Aanteekeningen omtrent Sollok en de Solloksche Zeeroovers", p.225.

[31] Ibid., pp.223–24.

[32] Ibid., p.215.

[33] Jansen, "Aanteekeningen omtrent Sollok en de Solloksche Zeeroovers", p.222.

[34] Ibid., p.222; Bonham to Maitland, 28 June 1838, PRO, Admiralty 125/133.

[35] Statements of Mariano Sevilla and Juan Santiago in Exp.12, 4 Oct. 1836, PNA, Mindanao/Sulu 1803–1890.

[36] Statements of Alex Quijano, Domingo Candelario, and Mariano Sevilla in Exp.12, 4 Oct. 1836, PNA, Mindanao/Sulu 1803–1890; statement of Mah roon, 2 June 1838, in Bonham to Maitland, 28 June 1838, PRO, Admiralty 125/133.

[37] Statement of Francisco Basilo and Mariano Sevilla in Exp.12, 4 Oct. 1836, PNA, Mindanao/Sulu 1803–1890.

[38] Extracts from *Singapore Free Press*. 6 Apr. 1847, PRO. Admiralty 125/133.

[39] MN, Coleccion Enrile XIII, documento 9, II, p.32, No.82, Corregidor de Camarines Sur a GCG, 4 Sept. 1834, PNA, Ereccion de Pueblo, Camarines Sur 1831–1832, XI; Corregidor de Albay a GCG, 18 May 1836, PNA Ereccion de Pueblo Albay, 1772–1885, pt. I; No.15, GCG a Secretario de Estado, 26 May 1838, AHN, Ultramar 5155; No.70, Gobernador Politico y Militar de Albay a GCG, 12 May 1841, PNA, Ereccion del Pueblo Albay, 1854–1891; No.7, GCG a Secretario de Estado, 31 Dec. 1846, AHN, Ultramar 5159; GCG a Secretario de Estado, 20 Oct. 1847, AHN, Ultramar 5161.

[40] No.75, Alcaldia Mayor de la Provincia de Zambales a GCG, 1 July 1843, PNA, Ereccion de Pueblo Zamblaes, 1801–1844, pt. I; No.135, GCG a Senor Secretario de Estado, 20 Oct. 1836, AHN, Ultramar 5153; J.Farren to John Bidwell, 7 Oct. 1847, PRO, FO, 72/732; GCG a Secretario de Estado, 7 Dec. 1827, AGI, Filipinas 515; Farren to the Earl of Aberdeen, 10 Dec. 1844, PRO, FO, 72/663.

[41] No.38, GCG a Secretario de Estado, 20 Aug. 1838, AHN, Ultramar 5155; No.49, GCG a Secretario De Estado, AHN, Ultramar 5155.

[42] N.100, Maj. Eales to the Sultan of Sooloo, 16 Jan. 1804, IOL, P/154.

[43] Enclosure 2, James Brooke to the Earl of Aberdeen, 31 Mar. 1845, in P.P.H.C., 1851, vol.56, pt.1, pp.134–36.

346 NOTES TO PAGES 191–195

44 No.7, partes pasados a la Capitania General sobre acontecimientos de Moros, PNA, Mindanao/Sulu, unclassified bundle; Manuel Baron a D. Jose Maria Halcon, 21 Oct. 1836, PNA, Mindanao/Sulu, 1836–1897; Exp.591, El Gobierno Militar y Politico de Zamboanga a GCG, 8 Apr. 1838, PNA, Mindanao/Sulu 1838–1890, 17; Exp.34, El Gobernador de Zamboanga a GCG, 15 Feb. 1838, PNA, Mindanao/Sulu 1838–1885.

45 Wilkes, "Jolo and the Sulus", pp.140–41.

46 Hagemann, "Aanteekeningen", p.103; van Dewall, "Aanteekeningen omtrent de Noordoostkust", pp.446–47.

47 No.173, GCG a Secretario de Estado, 15 Oct. 1846, AHN, Ultramar 5159.

48 Expediente 12, Jayme Simo, subteniente de Marina Sutil, a GCG, 17 Feb. 1845, PNA, Mindanao/Sulu 1836–1897; J. Farren to the Earl of Aberdeen, 22 Mar. 1845, PRO, FO, 72/684, pp.184–86; Bernaldez, Guerra al Sur de Filipinas, pp.151–53; Exp.7, Gobierno Militar y Politico de Zamboanga a GCG, 27 Aug. 1846, PNA, Mindanao/Sulu 1838–1885; Farren to Palmerston, 27 Dec. 1849, PRO, FO, 72/761.

49 Exp.12, Sobre haber salido la expedicion contra Balangingi, 17 Feb. 1845, PNA, Mindanao/Sulu 1836–1897.

50 J. Farren to Viscount Palmerston, 10 Jan. 1848, PRO, FO, 72/749; Bernaldez, *Guerra al Sur de Filipinas*, p.155.

51 J. Farren to Viscount Palmerston, 29 Feb. 1848, PRO, FO, 72/749; Bernaldez, *Guerra al Sur de Filipinas*, pp.156–62.

52 Bernaldez, *Guerra al Sur de Filipinas*, pp. 156–62.

53 Spanish copies of the letter are found in Montero y Vidal, *Historia de Filipinas*, vol.3, pp.128–30; Bernaldez, *Guerra al Sur de Filipinas*, p.238; the translation is from Horatio de la Costa, *Readings in Philippine History*, p.208.

54 Bernaldez, *Guerra al Sur de Filipinas*, p.163; *Extract from Straits Times*, 7 Mar. 1848, in J. Plumridge to H.Ward, 24 Mar. 1848, PRO, Admiralty 125/133.

55 Extract from the *Straits Times*, 7 Mar. 1848, in J. Plumridge to H. Ward, 24 Mar. 1848, PRO, Admiralty 125/133.

56 J. Farren to Viscount Palmerston, 29 Feb. 1848, PRO, FO, 72/749. J. Farren to Viscount Palmerston, 28 Jan. 1848, PRO, FO, 72/761; Diario de mi Comission a Jolo en el Vapor Magellenes, Jose Maria Penaranda, 19 Mar. 1848, PNA, Mindanao/Sulu, unclassified bundle.

57 Gobierno Militar y Politico de Zamboanga a GCG, 21 Nov. 1849, PNA, Piratas (3); J. Farren to Viscount Palmerston, 26 Mar. 1849, PRO, FO, 72/761.

58 GCG a Senor Secretario de Estado, 24 June 1851, AHN, Ultramar 5162.

59 Jansen, "Aanteekeningen omtrent Sollok en de Solloksche Zeeroovers", p.231.

60 Diario de mi Commission a Jolo en el vapor Magallenes, Jose Maria Penaranda, 19 Mar. 1848, PNA, Mindanao/Sulu, unclassified bundle; No.64, GCG a Senor Secretario de Estado, 28 June 1850, AHN, Ultramar 5162; Spenser St. John, *Life in the Forests of the Far East,* vol.2, pp.171–73, 187, 225–26.

61 Van Hoevell, "De Zeerooverijen der Soloerezen", p.102.

62 Carlos Cuarteron, prefecto apostolico, a GCG, 27 Oct. 1857, PNA, Isla de Borneo (1); Hugh Low to Scott, 10 Apr. 1851, in Scott to Earl of Gray, 27 June 1851, CO, 144/7.

63 No.7, Mariano Oscariz, a GCG, 28 Mar. 1858, AHN, Ultramar 5172; Treacher to Earl of Derby, 11 Aug. 1877, CO, 144/49.

64 "Berigten omtrent den Zeeroof in den Nederlandsch—Indischen Archipel, 1858", pp.308, 319–21.

65 Extract from Journal of the barque *Osprey* in Col. Cavanagh to Sec. of the Government of India, 28 Jan. 1863, PRO, FO, 71/1; Jansen, "Aanteekeningen omtrent Sollok en de Solloksche Zeeroovers", p.231.

66 For interethnic conflict between the Balangingi and the Taosug after 1850, see Antonio de Mora a Commandante General del Apostadero de Filipinas, 18 Aug. 1862, AHN, Ultramar

5159; No.3, El Comandante de la Goleta "Santa Filomena" a Commandancia General del Apostadero de Filipinas, 23 July 1862, AHN, Ultramar 5190; Callaghan to the Duke of Newcastle, 10 Nov. 1862, CO, 144/21.

[67] Callaghan to the Duke of Newcastle, 10 Nov. 1862, CO, 144/21.

[68] No.15, Exp. relativo a la repression de la pirateria en aquella Islas, AHN, Ultramar 5167.

[69] No.839, 8 June 1855, AR-Schaarsbergen, Kolonien 5873; Politick Verslag der Residentie Menado over het jaar 1855, ANRI, Menado 166; Nota van den Minister van Marine voor den Minister van Buitenlandsche Zaken over de Expeditie van Sooloo met England, 4 Apr. 1862, AR, Ministerie van Buitenlanden Zaken 3268; Alfred Russel Wallace, *The Malay Archipelago*, p.261.

[70] Wallace, *The Malay Archipelago*, p.334; Politick Verslag der Residentie Menado over het jaaren 1856–1857, ANRI; Politick Verslag der Residentie Menado over het jaar 1863. ANRI; No.1028/23, Den Gouveneur General van Nederlandsche Indien aan der Minister van Kolonien, 6 Dec. 1869, AR-Schaarsbergen, Kolonien 2290.

[71] GCG a Senor Ministro del Consejo, 20 July 1861, AHN, Ultramar 5184; Loney to Farren, 10 July 1861, PRO, FO, 72/1017.

[72] Concas y Palau, "Nuestras Relaciones con Jolo. Discourso pronunciado en la Sociedad geografica en 12 de Febrero de 1884", *Revista General de Marina* 16 (Feb. 1895): 204.

[73] Farren to the Earl of Clarendon, 9 Mar. 1854, PRO, FO, 72/663.

[74] No.229, GCG a Ministro de Guerra y Ultramar, 20 June 1860, AHN, Ultramar 5179; Concas y Palau, "Nuestras Relaciones con Jolo", pp.203–5.

[75] Loney to Farren, 10 July 1861, PRO, FO, 72/1017.

[76] No.236, GCG a Ministro de la Guerra y de Ultramar, 17 Aug. 1861, AHN, Ultramar 5182; see also No.192, 2 July 1861; Numero 164, 5 June 1861, AHN, Ultramar 5182.

[77] No.3, El Comandante de la Goleta, *Santa Filomena,* a Commandancia General del Apostadero de Filipinas, 23 July 1862, AHN, Ultramar 5190.

[78] El Comandante de la Goleta, *Santa Filomena* a Commandancia General del Apostadero de Filipinas, 18 July 1862, AHN, Ultramar 5190; GCG a Senor Ministro de la Guerra y de Ultramar, 4 Sept. 1862, AHN, Ultramar 5290; El Sultan de Jolo a D.Vincente Roca, 21 Sept. 1862, AHN, Ultramar 5193; GCG a Senor Ministro de la Guerra y de Ultramar, 25 Oct. 1862, AHN, Ultramar 5192; GCG a Senor Presidente del Consejo de Ministros, 20 May 1863, AHN, Ultramar 5194; Colonel Cavanagh to Sec. to the Government of India, 28 Jan. 1863, PRO, FO, 71/1.

[79] Mr.Ricketts to the Earl of Clarendon, 27 June 1870, PRO, FO, 72/1246; Gobierno Politico y Militar de la Isla de Mindanao a GCG, 28 July 1872, PNA, Pirates (1); Ricketts to the Earl of Derby, 28 Jan. 1875, PRO, FO, 72/1423; No.179, Gobierno Politico y Militar de la Isla de Mindanao a GCG, 2 Dec. 1877, PNA, Mindanao/Sulu 1858–1897; No.34, Gobierno Politico y Militar de Misamis a Gobernador Politico y Militar de Mindanao, 19 Nov. 1880, PNA, Mindanao/Sulu 1860–1898.

[80] John Hay to Lord Clarence Paget, 25 Mar. 1862, PRO, FO, 12/30; H.A.Reilly to Vice-Adm. Sir John Hope, 3 Feb. 1862, AR, Ministeria van Buitenlandsch Zaken 3268; No.842, Kommandant der Zeemagt Uhlenbeck aan de Gouveneur General van Nederlandsch Indie, 29 Jan. 1872, AR-Schaarsbergen, Kolonien 2496; Captain Corbett to Rear-Adm. Kuper, 21 Mar. 1863, CO, 144/22; Webb to Lord Russel, 24 Oct. 1864, PRO, FO, 71/1; Pope Hennesey to Earl of Clarendon, 6 July 1869, CO, 144/29. *The Straits Times Overland Journal* 20, N.471, 30 Sept. 1879; Pryer to Treacher, 5 Oct. 1881, CO, 874/229.

[81] Ibid.; Treacher to the Earl of Derby, 11 Aug. 1877, CO, 144/49; Diary of William Pryer, 21 Mar. 1878, CO, 874/67; 7 Apr. 1878, CO, 874/187; 12 Oct. 1878, CO, 874/68; and 17 Oct. 1878, CO, 874/68; Pryer to Treacher, 5 Oct. 1861, CO, 874/229.

[82] *The Straits Times Overland Journal* 20, N.471, 30 Sept. 1879. Den Gouveneur General van Nederlandsche Indie aan den Minister van Kolonien, 22 Feb. 1873, AR-Schaarsbergen,

Kolonien 2565; Kommandant der Zeemagt aan zijne Excellentie der Gouveneur General van Nederlandsch Indie, 9 Aug. 1879, ANRI; Rapport van den Resident der Zuider en Ooster afdeeling van Borneo aan den Gouveneur General van Nederlandsche Indie, 21 Apr. 1880, in besluit No.30, 3 June 1880, ANRI.

[83] Governor of North Borneo to Governor of Sulu, 9 Jan. 1892, in El Gobernador Politico y Militar de Jolo a GCG, 4 Sept. 1890, PNA, Mindanao Sulu 1862–1898; C.V. Creagh to his Excellency the Governor of Sulu, 27 Dec. 1894, PNA, Isla de Borneo (2).

[84] Warren, *The North Borneo Chartered Company's Administration of the Bajau*, pp.52–58, 70–78.

Chapter 9

[1] Comyn, *State of the Philippines in 1810*, pp.123–24.

[2] No.9, El Consejo de las Indias, 19 Dec. 1775, AGI, Filipinas 359; Pierre Vicomte de Pages, *Travels Round the World in the Years 1767, 1768, 1769, 1770, 1771*, p.156; Renouard, *Voyage Commercial et Politique aux Indes Orientales*, vol.2, p.275; Forrest, *Voyage to New Guinea*, p.330; Barrantes, *Guerras Piraticas*, pp.160–61; Montero y Vida, *Historia de Filipinas*, vol.2, p.369.

[3] El Gobierno Politico y Militar de Zamboanga a GCG, 30 May 1842, PNA, Mindanao/Sulu 1838–1885; Extracts from *Singapore Free Press*, 6 Apr. 1847, PRO, Admiralty 125/133.

[4] Hunt, "Some Particulars Relating to Sulo", p.50; Bonham to Maitland, 2 June 1838, PRO, Admiralty 125/133.

[5] Statements of Juan Santiago and Anastacio Casillo in Exp.12, 4 Oct. 1836, PNA, Mindanao/Sulu 1803–1890; Relacion jurada de los cuatros cautivos venidos en el navio Ingles de guerra Agincourt, procedente de la Isla de Borneo, 11 Dec. 1845, PNA, Piratas 3; Relacion jurada de los individuas cautivos venidos en la Fragata de guerra Inglesa Samarang procedente de Jolo, 15 Mar. 1845, PNA, Piratas 3; Numero 55, GCG a Senor Secretario de Estado y Despacho de Marina, Comercio, y Gobernacion de Ultramar, 12 Apr. 1845, AHN, Ultramar, 5157; Farren to the Earl of Aberdeen, 4 Dec. 1844, IOL, F/S/2146 (102773), p.7; P.P.H.C., 1851, LVI, pt.I, pp.135–36; Jansen, "Aanteekeningen omtrent Sollok en de Solloksche Zeeroovers", p.216.

[6] P.P.H.C., 1851, LVI, pt.I, pp.135–36.

[7] No.7, GCG a Secretario de Estado 4 June 1806, AGI, Filipinas, p.510; William Brownrigs to the British Consul or any European merchant in Sooloo or Manila, 10 Sept. 1844, in encl.1, Farren to the Foreign Office, 8 Dec. 1844, FO, 72/663; Dalrymple, *Oriental Repertory*, pp.559, 564; Forrest, *Voyage to New Guinea*, pp.368–69; Barrantes, *Guerras Piraticas*, p.161.

[8] Dalrymple, *Oriental Repertory*, pp.559, 561; Bruno Lasker, *Human Bondage in Southeast Asia*, p.27; Le Bar (ed.), *Ethnic Groups of Insular Southeast Asia*, vol.1, p.172.

[9] Forrest, *Voyage to New Guinea*, pp.368–69; Pryer to Treacher, 5 Oct. 1881, CO, 874/229.

[10] Lasker, *Human Bondage in Southeast Asia*, pp.26–27.

[11] No.7, GCG a Secretario de Estado, 4 June 1806, AGI, Filipinas, p.510; Barrantes, *Guerras Piraticas*, p.161.

[12] Alcalde Mayor de Zamboanga a Senor Gobernador General de Mindanao 9 Nov. 1868, PNA, unclassified Mindanao/Sulu bundle; No.180, El Gobernador Politico y Militar de las Isla de Mindanao, a GCG, 28 July 1872, PNA, Piratas 1; *Straits Times Overland Journal* 20, 31 Oct. 1879.

[13] Treacher, "British Borneo", p.90.

[14] Diary of William Pryer, 6 Apr. 1878, CO, 874/67; Diary of William Pryer, 16 Aug. 1878, 9 March 1879, CO, 874/68; Pryer to Treacher, 5 Oct. 1881, CO, 874/229; Bock, *The Headhunters of Borneo: A Narrative of Travel up the Mahakam and down the Barito*, p.201; Joseph Hatton, *The New Ceylon*, p.91.

[15] No.151, Carlos Cuarteron, prefecto apostalico, a GCG, 25 Dec. 1878, PNA, Isla de Borneo 1; Willi to Treacher, Nov. 1881, CO, 874/229; Treacher to Chairman British North Borneo Company, 8 May 1882, CO, 874/230.

[16] Pryer to Treacher, 5 Oct. 1881, CO, 874/229; Treacher, "British Borneo", p.91.

[17] Govierno Politico y Militar de Cotabato a GCG, 3 Sept. 1884, PNA, Mindanao/Sulu 1875–1899; Wickberg, *The Chinese in Philippine Life*, p.92; Ileto, *Magindanao, 1860–1888*, p.31. Witti to Treacher, Nov. 1881, CO, 874/229.

[18] Diary of William Pryer, 14 Mar. 1878, CO, 874; Diary of William Pryer, 23–26 Nov. 1878; 30 Nov. 1878, 27 Dec. 1878, 3 Mar. 1879, 27 June 1879, CO, 874/68; Diary of William Pryer, 17 Aug. 1879, 20 Aug. 1879, 3 Nov. 1880, CO, 874/69; Pryer to Treacher, 5 Oct. 1881, CO, 874/229; Gobernador Politico Militar de Jolo, 27 Mar. 1885, PNA, Unclassified Mindanao/Sulu bundle; No.68, Gobierno Politico y Militar de las Isla de Mindanao a GCG, 14 July 1892, PNA, Mindanao/Sulu 1864–1898; Gobierno Politico y Militar del 6 districo de Mindanao a Gobernador General Politico y Militar de Mindanao, 20 Apr. 1896, PNA, Mindanao/Sulu 1875–1899.

[19] Extract from *Singapore Free Press*, 6 Apr. 1847, PRO, Admiralty 125/133.

[20] U.S. Senate Documents, vol.15, document 218, p.26.

[21] Kolff, *Cruise of the Dutch Warship Dourga*, p.300; "Short Accounts of Timor, Rotti, Savu, Solor", in Moor, *Notices of the Indian Archipelago*, p.11.

[22] Hunt, "Some Particulars Relating to Sulo", p.37; U.S. Senate Documents, vol.15, document 218, p.64; St. John, *Life in the Forrests of the Far East*, vol.1, p.250.

[23] El Obispo de Zebu a Senor Don Joseph Galvez, 22 May 1779, AGI, Filipinas p.687.

[24] Kolff, *Cruise of the Dutch Warship Dourga*, p.300.

[25] "Adventures of C.Z. Pieters Among the Pirates of Magindanao", *JIAEA* (1858): 303.

[26] Exp.12, 4 Oct. 1836, PNA, Mindanao/Sulu 1803–1890; see statements of Evaristo Pinto and Francisco Xavier as well as Appendix R.

[27] For a shorter list of captives (14) that reinforces the trend in the table but concentrates on the pre-1855 period, see Gobierno Politico militar de la provincia de Zamboanga, 26 Mar. 1853, AHN, Ultramar 5172; No.56, 20 Apr. 1854, AHN, Ultramar 5165.

[28] Witti to Treacher, 1 Nov. 1881, CO, 874/229.

[29] No.7, GCG a Senor Secretario de Estado, 4 June 1806, AGI, Filipinas 510, p.27.

[30] Extracts from *Singapore Free Press*, 6 Apr. 1847, PRO, Admiralty 125/133.

[31] Witti to Treacher, Nov. 1881, CO, 874/229.

[32] Cautivos rescatados en el Rio de Pandasan por la mision de Labuan y Borneo, 18 Nov. 1877, PNA, Isla de Borneo 2; Forrest, *Voyage to New Guinea*, p.229; "Adventures of C.Z. Pieters Among the Pirates of Magindanao", p.309.

[33] Statements of Domingo Candelario, Augustin Juan, Mariano Sevilla, and Juan Santiago in Exp.12, 4 Oct. 1836, PNA, Mindanao/Sulu 1803–1890; Exp.2, El Gobierno Politico y Militar del Zamboanga a GCG, 30 May 1842, PNA, Mindanao/Sulu 1838–1885.

[34] Jansen, "Aanteekeningen omtrent Sollok en de Solloksche Zeeroovers", p.224.

[35] Relacion Jurada de los cuarenta y cinco cautivos venidos de Jolo sobre el Bergantin Espanol Cometa, 19 Mar. 1847, PNA, Piratas 3.

[36] See Appendix R, particularly the statements of Evaristo Pinto, Pedro Santiago, and Vincente Remigio in Exp. 12, 4 Oct. 1836, PNA, Mindanao/Sulu 1803–1890; "Adventures of C.Z. Pieters among the Pirates of Magindanao", pp.309–10.

[37] Juan Cencelli a Senor Conde Aranda, 16 Apr. 1774, AHN, Estado 2845, caja 2.

[38] Encl.12, deposition of Si-Ayer in St. John to Viscount Palmerston, 19 Feb. 1852, P.P.H.C., XXXI, Borneo Piracy, p.487.

[39] Carlos Cuarteron, 10 Nov. 1878, PNA, Isla de Borneo 1; statement of Simona Plasa in Exp.34, Gobernador Militar y Politico de la Provincia de Zamboanga a GCG, 1 Feb. 1852, PNA, Mindanao/Sulu 1838–1885; Verklaring van Chrishaan Soerma, 10 Aug. 1846, ANRI, Menado 50.

[40] Most of the estimates ranged from 750 to 1,500 slaves a year. No.9, El Consejo de las Indias, 19 Dec. 1775, AGI, Filipinas 359; Farren to the Earl of Aberdeen, 20 Jan. 1846, PRO, FO, 72/708; Webb to Lord Russel, 24 Oct. 1864, FO, 71/1; Hunt, "Some Particulars Relating to Sulo", pp.51–52; Bernaldez, *Guerra al Sur,* p.147; J.Montano, "Une Mission aux iles Malaises", *Bulletin, Society de geographic* (1881), p.472.

[41] El Gobernador Politico y Militar de Zamboanga a GCG, 30 May 1842, PNA, Mindanao/Sulu 1838–1885; Exp.12 sobre haber salido la expedicion contra Balanginqi, 17 Feb. 1845, PNA, Mindanao/Sulu 1836–1897; information obtained by Charles Grey at Singapore from Mr.Wyndham relating to Sulo, 24 Feb. 1847, PRO, Admiralty 125/133; Van Hoevell, "De Zeerooverijen der Soloerezen", p.102.

[42] Spenser St. John, "Piracy in the Indian Archipelago", p.258.

[43] Farren to Palmerston, 16 Mar. 1851, CO, 144/8.

[44] Extract of a letter from Mr. Archedekin, 30 Nov. 1770, IOL, P/341/35, p.778; Hunt, "Some Particulars Relating to Sulo", p.41; information obtained by Charles Grey at Singapore from Mr. Wyndham relating to Sulo, 24 Feb. 1847, PRO, Admiralty 125/133.

[45] Hunt, "Some Particulars Relating to Sulo", p.41.

[46] Juan Cencelli a Senor Conde Aranda, 16 Apr. 1774, AHN, Estado 2845, caja 2.

[47] No.29, Manuel Alvarez, a GCG, 28 Feb. 1773, AGI, Filipinas 687.

[48] Hunt, "Some Particulars Relating to Sulo", p.41.

[49] Ibid., p.50.

[50] Statement of Juan de los Santos in Exp.12, 4 Oct. 1836, PNA, Mindanao/Sulu 1803–1890.

[51] Statement of Francisco Feliz in Exp.12, 4 Oct. 1836, Mindanao/Sulu 1803–1890.

[52] Gregori, "Aanteekeningen en Beschouwingen betrekkelijk de Zeeroovers en hunne rooverijen en den Indeschen Archipel, alsmede aagaande Magindanao en de Soolo-Archipel", p.330.

[53] Statements of Marcelo Teafilo, Francisco Mariano, Juan Florentino, and Santiago Manuel de Luna in Exp.12, 4 Oct. 1836, PNA, Mindanao/Sulu 1803–1890.

[54] For population calculations, see the earlier part of this chapter and Chapter 4; Kiefer, "The Taosug Polity and the Sultanate of Sulu", p.23.

Chapter 10

[1] For an important article on the problems of defining slavery, see E.R. Leach, "Caste, Class and Slavery—the Taxonomic Problem", *Comparative Approaches,* pp.12–13; see also Miers and Kopytoff, *Slavery in Africa.*

[2] Mednick, "Encampment of the Lake", pp.60–61, Kiefer, "The Tausug Polity and the Sultanate of Sulu", p.30.

[3] Mednick, "Encampment of the Lake", p.61.

[4] Diary of William Pryer, 25 Nov. 1878; 26 June 1879, CO, 874/68.

[5] BH-PCL, VI, paper 162, no.16, Gunther, "Correspondence, Papers and Reports Relating to the Sulu Moros", pp.10–12; paper 162, no.25, Christie, "The Non Christian Tribes of the Northern Half of the Zamboanga Peninsula", p.87; paper 162, no.28, L.W.V. Kennon, David P. Barrows, John Pershing, and C. Smith, "Census Report Relating to the District of Lanao Mindanoo", p.4; Saleeby, *Studies in Moro History, Law and Religion*, pp.92–93.

[6] For a general discussion of debt bondage in Southeast Asia, see Lasker, *Human Bondage in Southeast Asia*, pp.113–16.

[7] During the famine of 1878–1879 Pryer wrote: "Man offered to sell himself to me for twenty dollars as he was starving." Diary of William Pryer, 4 April 1879, CO, 874/68.

[8] Scott to Governor, 30 June 1904, H.L. Scott Papers, Container 55; Otis to Bates, 11 July 1899, U.S. Senate Documents, vol.9, Otis to Bates, 11 July 1899, U.S. Senate Documents, vol.9, document 136, p.15; Saleeby, *Studies in Moro History, Law and Religion,* p.94.

[9] Saleeby, *Studies in Moro History, Law and Religion,* pp.65, 81, 89.

[10] Ibid., pp.76, 86–87.

[11] Ibid., pp.74, 86; Majul, "Political and Historical Notes on the Old Sulu Sultanate", p.39.

[12] Saleeby, *Studies in Moro History, Law and Religion,* pp.71, 83, 93.

[13] Saleeby, *Studies in Moro History, Law and Religion,* p.93.

[14] Diary of William Pryer, 14 Mar. 1878, CO, 874/68.

[15] William Pryer, "Notes on North Eastern Borneo and the Sulu Islands", pp.92–93.

[16] John Keith Reynolds, "Towards an Account of Sulu and Its Bornean Dependencies, 1700–1878" (M.A. diss., University of Wisconsin, 1970), p.81.

[17] Diary of William Pryer, 15 Oct. 1878, CO, 874/68; see also Diary of William Pryer, 16 Aug. 1879; 27 Feb. 1880, CO, 874/69; U.S. Senate Documents, vol.15, no.218, p.70; BHPCL, VI, Paper 162, no.25; Christie, "The Non Christian Tribes of the Northern Half of the Zamboanga Peninsula", p.78; Paper 162, No. 26, Williamson, "The Moros between Buluan and Punta Flecha", p.103.

[18] Pryer, "Notes on North Eastern Borneo and the Sulu Islands", p.92.

[19] Pieters, "Adventures of C.Z. Pieters Among the Pirates of Magindanao", p.308; statements of Fragedo San Juan and Mateo San Francisco in Relacion jurada de los individuos cautivos venidos en la Fragata de guerra Ynglesa Samarang procedente de Jolo, 15 Mar. 1845, PNA, Piratas 3; the statement of Augustin Bernado in Relacion jurada de los cuarenta y cinco cautivas venidos de Jolo sobre el Bergantin Espanol Cometa, 19 March 1847, PNA, Piratas 3; Diary of William Pryer, 23 Mar. 1878, CO, 874/67.

[20] Forrest, *Voyage to New Guinea,* p.330.

[21] Witti to Treacher, Nov. 1881, CO, 874/229.

[22] Forrest, *Voyage to New Guinea,* p.291.

[23] Diary of William Pryer, 14 Mar. 1878, CO, 874/68.

[24] William Briskoe, Journal, vol.2, entry for 5 Feb. 1842, statement of Vincente Santiago in Exp.12, 4 Oct. 1836, PNA, Mindanao/Sulu 1803–1890.

[25] Wilkes, "Jolo and the Sulus", p.165; Hunt, "Some Particulars Relating to Sulo", p.37; Jansen, "Aanteekeningen omtrent Sollok en de Solloksche Zeeroovers", p.224.

[26] Statements of Mariano de la Cruz and Francisco Gregorio in Exp.12, 4 Oct. 1836, PNA, Mindanao/Sulu 1803–1890; El Gobierno Politico y Militar del Zamboanga a GCG, 9 June 1847, PNA, Mindanao/Sulu 1838–1885.

[27] Extracts from *Singapore Free Press,* 6 Apr. 1847, PRO, Admiralty 125/133; BH-PCL, VI, Paper 162, no.26, Williamson, "The Moros between Buluan and Punta Flecha", p.103; Mednick, "Encampment of the Lake", p.62.

[28] Wilkes, "Jolo and the Sulus", p.168.

[29] Hunt, "Some Particulars Relating to Sulo", p.37.

[30] Statements of Alex Quijano, Francisco Sacarias, and Domingo Francisco in Exp.12, 4 Oct. 1836, PNA, Mindanao/Sulu 1803–1890; statement of Juan Florentino in Relacion jurada

de los dos individuos cautivos venidos en la corbetta de guerra Francesa Salina procedente de Sumalasan en la Archipelago de Jolo. PNA, Piratas 3; Treacher to Sir Rutherford Alcock, 3 July 1884, CO, 874/237.

[31] Pryer to Treacher, 5 Oct. 1881, CO, 874/229; Pryer, "Notes on North Eastern Borneo and the Sulu Islands", p.92.

[32] Pryer, "Notes on North Eastern Borneo and the Sulu Islands", 93.

[33] St. John, *Life in the Forests of the Far East,* vol.2, p.250.

[34] Statements of Anastacio Carillo and Ignacio Valero in Exp.12, 4 Oct. 1836, PNA, Mindanao/Sulu 1803–1890; Robinson, Journal, 4 Feb. 1842; St. John, *Life in the Forests of the Far East,* vol.2, p.193.

[35] Thomas Jefferson Jacobs, *Scenes, Incidents and Adventures in the Pacific Ocean, or the Islands of the Australasian Seas, during the cruise of the clipper Margaret Oakley,* p.335.

[36] Melchior Yvan, *Six Months among the Malays and a Year in China,* pp.258–59.

[37] Farren to Palmerston, 17 Jan. 1851, CO, 144/8; Corbett to the Sec. of the Admiralty, 6 Oct. 1862, FO, 71/1.

[38] Statements of Pedro Antonio Vincente Remigio, and Francisco Augustino in Exp.12, 4 Oct. 1836, PNA, Mindanao/Sulu 1803–1890; Witti to Treacher, Nov. 1881, CO, 874/229.

[39] Statements of Vicente Remigio, Francisco Augustino and Juan Saballa in Exp.12, 4 Oct. 1846, PNA, Mindanao/Sulu 1803–1890.

[40] Wilkes, "Jolo and the Sulus", p.181.

[41] Statement of Alex Quijano in Exp.12, 4 Oct. 1836, PNA, Mindanao/Sulu 1803–1890.

[42] Sherard Osborn, *My Journal in Malayan Waters* (3rd edition, London: Routledge, Warne nd Routledge, 1861), p.41; Witti to Treacher, Nov. 1881, CO, 879/229; Majul, "Political and Historical Notes on the Old Sulu Sultanate", pp.35–36; Kiefer, *The Taosug,* p.41.

[43] Statements of Matias de la Cruz and Francisco Sacarias in Exp.12, 4 Oct. 1836, PNA, Mindanao/Sulu 1803–1890; Verklaring van Chrishaan Soerma, 10 Aug. 1846, ANRI, Menado 50; William Pryer, "Diary of a Trip up the Kinabatangan", p.119.

[44] Verklaring van Chrishaan Soerma, 10 Oct. 1846, ANRI, Menado 50.

[45] Pryer, "Diary of a Trip up the Kinabatangan", p.119.

[46] Diary of William Pryer, 14 Mar. 1878, CO, 874/67.

[47] Ibid.

[48] Briskoe, Journal, vol.2, 5 Feb. 1842; Diario de mi Comision a Jolo en el Vapor Magallenes, 19 Mar. 1848, PNA, Mindanao/Sulu unclassified bundle; Jansen, "Aanteekeningen omtrent Sollok en de Solloksche Zeeroovers", p.214.

[49] Dalrymple, *Oriental Repertory,* p.552.

[50] Hunt, "Some Particulars Relating to Sulo", p.38.

[51] D.Patricio de la Escosura, *Memoria sobre Filipinas y Jolo redactada en 1863 y 1864,* p.371; Diary of William Pryer, 8 Mar. 1879, CO, 874/68.

[52] Montero y Vidal, *Historia de Filipinas,* vol.2, p.382.

[53] Forrest, *Voyage to New Guinea,* pp.251, 292.

[54] Wilkes, "Jolo and the Sulus", p.166; D'Urville, *Voyage au pole sud et dans l'Oceanie sur les Corvettes l'Astrolobe et la Zelee,* vol.7, p.170.

[55] Wilkes, "Jolo and the Sulus", p.161.

[56] Statement of Jose Ruedas in Exp.12, 4 Oct. 1836, PNA, Mindanao/Sulu 1803–1890, p.32.

[57] Forrest, *Voyage to New Guinea,* p.330; Hunt, "Some Particulars Relating to Sulu", p.40; D'Urville, *Voyage au pole sud et dans l'Oceanie sur les Corbettes l'Astrolobe et le Zelee,* vol.7, pp.308, 313; Wilkes, "Jolo and the Sulus", p.165.

[58] Forrest, *Voyage to New Guinea,* p.330; See also Hunt, "Some Particulars Relating to Sulo", p.40.

[59] Ibid., p.296.

[60] Diary of William Pryer, 25 Nov. 1878, CO, 874/68.

[61] Verklaring van Chrishaan Soerma, 10 Aug. 1846, ANRI, Menado 50.

[62] Pieters, "Adventures of C.Z. Pieters among the Pirates of Magindanao", p.305.

[63] Ibid., pp.305–7.

[64] Garin, "Memoria sobre el Archipielago de Jolo", p.175.

[65] Forrest, *Voyage to New Guinea,* p.247.

[66] Escosura, *Memoria sobre Filipinas y Jolo,* 371; Kiefer, "The Tausug Polity and the Sultanate of Sulu", p.37.

[67] Diary of William Pryer, 3 Feb. 1879, CO, 874/68; BH-PCL, I, Paper 160, no.1, Livingston, "Constabulary Monograph of the Province of Sulu", p.14.

[68] Escosura, *Memoria sobre Filipinas y Jolo,* p.375.

[69] Wilkes, "Jolo and the Sulus", p.166.

[70] Montero y Vidal, *Historia de la Pirateria Malayo-Mahometana en Mindanao Jolo y Borneo,* p.69.

[71] Mednick, "Some Problems of Moro History and Political Organisation", p.48.

[72] Statement of Francisco Enriquez in Escosura, *Memoria sobre Filipinas y Jolo,* p.373.

[73] Witti to Treacher, Nov. 1881, CO, 874/229; Alfred Guillaume, *Islam* (Baltimore: Penguin Books, 1954), p.173.

[74] BH-PCL, VI, Paper 163, no.34, Scott and Brown, "Ethnography of the Magindanaos of Parang", p.16; Garin, "Memoria sobre el Archiepelago de Jolo", p.171.

[75] Zuniga, *Estadismo de las Filipinas,* vol.1, pp.118–20.

[76] No.43, El Obispo de Nueva Caceres a GCG, 16 Oct. 1785, PNA, Ereccion de Pueblo, Camarines Sur, 1786–1837, VII.

[77] No.226, AGI, Filipinas 492, p.22.

[78] Extracts from *Singapore Free Press,* 6 Apr. 1847, PRO, Admiralty 125/133.

[79] Robinson, Journal, 31 Jan. 1842; 4 Feb. 1842.

[80] Memoir of Sooloo, IOL, Orme Collection, vol.67, p.128.

[81] El Gobernador de Zamboanga a GCG, 12 Apr. 1769, PNA, Varias Provincias, Zamboanga; No.226, II, AGI, Filipinas 492.

[82] No.226, II, AGI, Filipinas 492, p.11.

[83] Montero y Vidal, *Historia de las Filipinas,*vol.2, 482.

[84] Sultan Muyamad Alimudin a Gobernador D.Juan de Mir, 13 May 1781, PNA, Mindanao/Sulu 1769–1898; Barrantes, *Guerras Piraticas,* p.162.

[85] Luis de Ibanez y Garcia, *Mi Cautiverio; carta que con motivo del que sufrio entre los Moros piratas Joloano Samales en 1857,* p.10.

[86] Robinson, Journal, 4 Feb. 1842; No.338, Secretaria de Gobierno, 20 Aug. 1863, PNA, Piratas 3; No.12, 31 May 1845, AR, Kolonien 2669; No.31, 24 Mar. 1847, Kolonien 2692.

[87] Pieters, "Adventures of C.Z. Pieters among the Pirates of Magindanao", pp.310–11.

[88] Pieters, "Adventures of C.Z. Pieters among the Pirates of Magindanao", p.312.

[89] Statement of Ignacio Ambrocio, 29 Aug. 1850, PNA, Piratas 3; Extracts from the Journal of the barque *Osprey* in Col. Cavanagh to the Sec. of the Government of India, 28 Jan. 1863, FO, 71/1; No.12, 31 May 1845, AR, Kolonien 2669; No.31, 24 Mar. 1847, Kolonien 2692.

[90] See the statements in Relacion jurada de los individuos cautivos venidos en la Fragata de guerra Inglesa Samarang, 15 Mar. 1845, PNA, Piratas 3; Hunt, "Some Particulars Relating to Sulo", p.50.

[91] Jansen, "Aanteekeningen omtrent Sollok en de Solloksche Zeeroovers", p.225.

[92] Statement of Francisco Augustino in Relacion jurada de los individuos cautivos venidos en la Fragata de guerra Inglesa Samarang, 15 Mar. 1845, PNA, Piratas 3.

[93] Exp.12, 4 Oct. 1836, PNA, Mindanao/Sulu 1803–1890; Relacion jurada de los cuarenta y cinco cautivos venidos de Jolo sobre el Bergantin Espanol *Cometa,* 18 Mar. 1847, PNA, Piratas 3; Verklaringen van ontvlugten personen uit de handen der Zeeroovers van 1845–1849, ANRI, Menado 37.

[94] GCG a Presidente del Consejo de Ministro, 9 Dec. 1858, AHN, Ultramar 5184; Hunt, "Some Particulars Relating to Sulo", p. 50.

[95] Statements of Pedro Flores and Pedro Isidoro in Relacion jurada de los cuarenta y cinco cautivos venidos de Jolo sobre el Bergantin Espanol *Cometa,* 19 Mar. 1847, PNA, Piratas 3; statements of Francisco Anastacio and Jacinto Pedro in Relacion jurada de los individuos cautivos venidos en la Fragata de guerra Inglesa Samarang, 15 Mar. 1845, PNA, Piratas 3; "Berigten omtrent den Zeeroof in den Nederlandsch-Indischen Archipel, 1857", pp.440, 445; "Berigten omtrent den Zeeroof in den Nederlandsch-Indischen Archipel, 1858", p.304.

[96] Statement of Francisco Aquino, PNA, Piratas 3.

[97] No.508, Gobierno Politico y Militar a GCG, 16 Aug. 1876, PNA, Mindanao/Sulu 1862–1898.

[98] Statements of Domingo Apolinario and Antonio Juan in Relacion jurada de los cincos cautivos venidos en la falua de la division de la isla del corregidor, 23 Aug. 1845, PNA, Piratas 3.

[99] Statements in Relacion de los cuatros cautivos venidos en el Navio Ingles de Guerra Agincourt, procedente de la Isla Borneo, 11 Dec. 1845, PNA, Piratas 3.

[100] Verklaringen van ontvlugten personen uit de handen der Zeeroovers van 1845–1849, ANRI, Menado 37; Politick Verslag der Residentie Manado over het jaaren 1855, 1857, 1858, ANRI, Menado 166.

[101] Paul de la Gironiere. *Twenty Years in the Philippines,* pp.69–70.

[102] *Singapore Chronicle and Commercial Register,* vol.3, 24 Oct. 1833; P.P.H.C., 1851, LVI, pt.I, p.97.

[103] Henry Keppel, *A Visit to the Indian Archipelago in H.M.S. Maeander,* p.69.

[104] See log kept aboard the brig *Leonidas,* 656/1835A, Peabody Museum, entry for 31 Aug. 1836,

[105] Statement of Juan Santiago in Exp.12, 4 Oct. 1836, PNA, Mindanao/Sulu 1803–1890, p.22.

[106] Jacob, *The Cruise of the Clipper Margaret Oakley,* p.340.

[107] See Appendix R; El Gobernador de Zamboanga a GCG, 13 Feb. 1846, PNA, Mindanao/Sulu 1836–1897, p.20; extract from the *Straits Times,* 11 July 1848, in Governor of the Straits Settlements to the Sec. of the Government of India, 5 July 1848, IOL, F/4/2331 (121954), pp.13–14; No.5, El Gobernador Politico y Militar de Zamboanga a GCG, 26 Mar. 1853, AHN, Ultramar 5172.

[108] Yvan, *Six months among the Malays and a Year in China,* pp.225–58; Belcher, *Narrative of the Voyage of H.M.S.Samarang, During the Years 1843–1846,* vol.1, p.260.

[109] Statements of Vincente Remigio, Anastacio Carillo, Ignacio Valero, Juan Apolonio, Francisco Sereno, Juan de la Cruz in Exp.12, 4 Oct. 1836, PNA, Mindanao/Sulu 1803–1890; Keppel, *A Visit to the Indian Archipelago in H.M.S. Maeander,* pp.68–69; Escosura, *Memoria sobre Filipinas y Jolo,* p.374; statement of Juan Apolonio in Exp.12, 4 Oct. 1836, PNA, Mindanao/Sulu 1803–1890; Diario de mi Comision a Jolo en el Vapor Magallenes, 19 March 1848, unclassified Mindanao/Sulu bundle; statement of Francisco Mariano in Exp.12, 4 Oct. 1836, PNA, Mindanao/Sulu 1803–1890, p.14.

[110] El Gobernador de Zamboanga a GCG, 17 May 1795, PNA, Mindanao/Sulu 1774–1887; Exp.591, El Gobierno Militar y Politico del Zamboanga a GCG, 9 Apr. 1838, PNA, Mindanao/Sulu 1838–1890.

[111] Fr. Guillermo Agudo a GCG, 28 June 1839, PNA, unclassified Mindanao/Sulu bundle; Jose Maria Halcon a GCG, 31 Dec. 1837, AUST, seccion Folletos, Tomo 117, p.29; Exp.36, El

Gobernador de Zamboanga a GCG, 31 Dec. 1837, PNA, Mindanao/Sulu 1816–1898; Mariano de Goecoecha a GCG, 24 Apr. 1838, PNA, unclassified Mindanao/Sulu bundle.

[112] Fr. Guillermo Agudo a GCG, 28 June 1839, PNA, unclassified Mindanao/Sulu bundle.

[113] No.15, Gobierno Militar y Politico de Zamboanga a GCG, 6 Feb. 1860, PNA, varias provincias, Zamboanga.

[114] Jose Maria Halcon a GCG, 31 Dec. 1837, AUST, seccion Folletos, Tomo 117.

[115] No.142, Carlos Cuarteron, prefecto apostolico, a GCG, 31 Oct. 1878, PNA, Isla de Borneo 2; various memoranda of William Pryer, CO, 874/216; Dunlop to Ag. Colonial Sec., 15 Aug. 1892, CO, 874/253; Cook to Martin, 5 Oct. 1899, CO, 874/264; *NBH,* 1 Jan. 1893, p.25; 1 June 1893, p.25; 1 May 1895, p.111.

[116] Mariano de Goecoechea a GCG, 24 Apr. 1838, PNA, unclassified Mindanao/Sulu bundle.

[117] No.133, Carlos Cuarteron, prefecto apostolico, a Senor Gobernador Politico y Militar de Jolo, 3 Dec. 1878, PNA, Isla de Borneo.

Chapter 11

[1] Charles Tilly, "Quantification in History, As Seen from France", p.94.

[2] See Exp.12, 4 Oct. 1836, PNA, Mindanao/Sulu 1803–1890.

[3] Verklaringen van ontvlugten personen uit de handen der Zeeroovers van 1845–1849, ANRI, Menado 37.

[4] No.38, GCG a Secretario de Estado, 20 Aug. 1838, AHN, Ultramar 5155; W.Stanton to Admiralty, 27 Sept. 1862, FO, 12/30; Extracts from *Singapore Free Press,* 6 Apr. 1847, PRO, Admiralty 125/133; Barrantes, *Guerras Piraticas,* p.265; Bernaldez, *Guerra al Sur,* p.43.

[5] Extracts from *Singapore Free Press,* 6 Apr. 1847, PRO, Admiralty 125/133; W. Stanton to Admiralty, 27 Sept. 1862, FO, 12/30; Statements of Mateo Francisco in Relacion de los individuos cautivos venidos en la Fragata de guerra Inglesa Samarang; Felix Torres in Relacion jurada de los dos individuos cautivos venidos en la corbeta de guerra Francesa Salina; Domingo Apolinario in Relacion jurada de los cinco cautivos venidos en la falua de la Division de la isla del Corregidor, PNA, Piratas 3; AGI, Filipinas 510; Extract from *Singapore Free Press,* 6 Apr. 1847, PRO, Admiralty 125/133; Jansen, "Aanteekeningen omtrent Sollok en de Solloksche Zeeroovers", p.226.

[6] Statement of Francisco Thomas in Bonham to Maitland, 28 June 1838, PRO, Admiralty 125/133.

[7] Statements of Essee, Omar, Yusof, and Ahmat, ibid.

[8] Statement of Juna Florentino in Relacion jurada de los dos individuos cautivos en la corbeta de Guerra Francesa Salina 1845, PNA, Piratas 3.

[9] No.49, GCG a Secretario de Estado, 15 December 1838, AHN, Ultramar 5155; see also Ibanez y Garcia, *Mi Cautiverio,* p.21.

[10] Statements of Nah Soo Hong, Francisco Thomas, Yusof, Abdullah and Amat in Bonham to Maitland, 28, June 1838, PRO, Admiralty 125/133.

[11] Church to Wise, 1 July 1847, CO, 144/2; statement of Amat, in Bonham to Maitland, 28 June 1838, PRO, Admiralty 125/133.

[12] Pieters, "Adventures of C.Z.Pieters among the Pirates of Magindanao", p.302; also Ibanez y Garcia, *Mi Cautiverio,* p.8.

[13] Jansen, "Aanteekeningen omtrent Sollok en de Solloksche Zeeroovers", p.224; *Times,* 16 July 1862, in CO, 144/22.

[14] Ibanez y Garcia, *Mi Cautiverio*, p.21.

[15] Jansen, "Aanteekeningen omtrent Sollok en de Solloksche Zeeroovers", p.224; Ibanez y Garcia, *Mi Cautiverio*, p.14; P.P.H.C., 1851, vol.56, pt.1, p.160; *Times*, 16 July 1862, in CO, 144/22; Ibanez y Garcia, *Mi Cautiverio*, p.10.

[16] Statement of Francisco Thomas in Bonham to Maitland, 28 June 1838, PRO, Admiralty 125/133; *Times*, 16 July 1862, in CO, 144/22.

[17] Ibanez y Garcia, *Mi Cautiverio*, p.12. See statement of Jacinto Pedro in Relacion jurada de los individuos cautivos venidos en la fragata de guerra Inglesa Samarang; and Antonio Juan in Relacion jurada de los cinco cautivos venidos en la falua de la Isla de Corregidor, PNA, Piratas 3.

[18] Ibanez y Garcia, *Mi Cautiverio*, p.21; Jansen, "Aanteekeningen omtrent Sollok en de Solloksche Zeeroovers", p.22.

[19] Encl.12, deposition of Si-Ayer, in St. John to Viscount Palmerston, 19 Feb. 1852, P.P.H.C., 31, p.487.

[20] Statements of Juan Apolonio and Diomicio Francisco, Exp.12, 4 Oct. 1836, PNA, Mindanao/Sulu 1803–1890.

[21] Jagor, *Travels in the Philippines*, 87; Ibanez y Garcia, *Mi Cautiverio*, p.16.

[22] Concas y Palau, *Nuestra Relaciones con Jolo*, p.204; extract of a letter from John Hayes to the resident at the Molucca Islands, 21 Aug. 1801, IOL, P/242/42; Charles Gray to Samuel Hood Ingelfield, 31 May 1847, IOL, F/4/2262 (114837), p.179; *Times*, 16 July 1862, in CO, 144/22.

[23] Statement of Nazario de la Cruz in Relacion jurada de los cinco cautivos venidos en la falua de la division de la Isla del Corregidor, 23 Aug. 1845, PNA, Piratas 3.

[24] Statement of Jose Ruedas in Exp.12, 4 Oct. 1836, PNA, Mindanao/Sulu 1803–1890.

[25] "Berigten omtrent den Zeeroof in den Nederlandsch-Indischen Archipel, 1857", p.439.

[26] Albert Bickmore, *Travels in the East Indian Archipelago*, pp.320–21.

[27] Historical data on Lucbuan, HDP, Palawan.

[28] "Berigten omtrent den Zeeroof en den Nederlandsch-Indischen Archipel, 1858", pp.304, 305.

[29] Statement of Antonio Juan in Relacion jurada de los cinco cautivos venidos en la falua de la division de la Isla del Corregidor, 23 Aug. 1845, PNA, Piratas 3; see also No.242, El Corregidor de Albay a GCG, 9 Aug. 1836, PNA, Ereccion del Pueblo, Albay 1772–1831.

[30] Statement of Maria Damiani in Exp.12, 4 Oct. 1836, PNA, Mindanao/Sulu 1803–1890.

[31] Verklaring van Chrishaan Soerma, 10 Aug. 1846, ANRI, Menado 50.

[32] Pieters, "Adventures of C.Z. Pieters among the Pirates of Magindanao", p.303; P.P.H.C., 56, pt.1, p.110.

[33] Statement of Francisco Sacarias in Exp.12, 4 Oct. 1836, PNA, Mindanao/Sulu 1803–1890.

[34] Statement of Juand Pedro, ibid.

[35] Jansen, "Aanteekeningen omtrent Sollok en de Solloksche Zeeroovers", p.229; Extracts from *Singapore Free Press*, 6 Apr. 1847, PRO, Admiralty 12/133.

[36] Jansen, "Aanteekeningen omtrent Sollok en de Solloksche Zeeroovers", p.231.

[37] Statement of Francisco Sacarias in Exp.12, 4 Oct. 1836, PNA, Mindanao/Sulu 1803–1890.

[38] Jansen, "Aanteekeningen omtrent Sollok en de Solloksche Zeeroovers", pp.224, 228.

[39] Pieters, "Adventures of C.Z. Pieters among the Pirates of Magindanao", pp.302–303.

[40] Ibid.

[41] "Berigten omtrent den Zeeroof in den Nederlandsch-Indischen Archipel, 1858", p.436.

[42] Diary of William Pryer, 11 Mar. 1878, CO, 874/67.

[43] Pieters, "Adventures of C.Z. Pieters among the Pirates of Magindanao", p.303.

[44] Rennell, *Journal of a Voyage to the Sooloo Islands and the Northwest Coast of Borneo*, p.34.

[45] Briskoe, Journal, II, entry for 5 Feb. 1842.

[46] Jacobs, *The Cruise of the Clipper Margaret Oakley,* p.332.

[47] Hunt, "Some Particulars Relating to Sulo", p.46.

[48] Ibid., p.39.

[49] Pieters, "Adventures of C.Z. Pieters among the Pirates of Magindanao", p.310.

[50] Witti to Treacher, Nov.1881, CO, 874/229.

[51] Statement of Manuel de los Santos and Jose Ruedas, in Exp.12, 4 Oct. 1836, PNA, Mindanao/Sulu 1803–1890.

[52] Forrest, *Voyage to New Guinea,* p.299.

[53] Statement of Antonio Juan in Relacion jurada de los cincos cautivos venidos en la falua de la Division de los Isla del Corregidor, 23 Aug. 1845, PNA, Piratas 3.

[54] Escosura, *Memoria sobre Filipinas y Jolo redactada en 1863 y 1864,* p.374.

[55] Ibid., p.375.

[56] BH-PCL, VI, paper 162, no.25, Christie, "The Non Christian Tribes of the Northern Half of the Zamboanga Peninsula", pp.75–76.

[57] Statement of Maria Damiani in Exp.12, 4 Oct. 1836, PNA, Mindanao/Sulu 1803–2890.

[58] Montero y Vidal, *Historia de la Pirateria Malaya-Mohometana en Mindanao, Jolo y Borneo,* p.69.

[59] Statement of Francisco Mariano in Exp.12, 4 Oct. 1836, PNA, Mindanao/Sulu 1803–1890.

[60] Statement of Pedro Francisco, in Exp.12, 4 Oct. 1836, PNA, Mindanao/Sulu 1803–1890.

[61] Rennell, *Journal of a Voyage to the Sooloo Islands and the Northwest Coast of Borneo,* p.37; D'Urville, *Voyage au pole sud et dans L'Oceanie sur les Corvettes L'Astrolobe et La Zelee,* vol.7, p.308; Hunt, "Some Particulars Relating to Sulo", pp.40, 44.

[62] Diary of William Pryer, 15 Oct. 1878, CO, 874/68.

[63] Hunt, "Some Particulars Relating to Sulo", p.52.

[64] Account of Sooloo by Mr. Dalrymple to the East India Company, IOL, Orme Collection, vol.88, pp.2–3, 6–7.

[65] Hunt, "Some Particulars Relating to Sulo", pp.35–36.

[66] Ibid., p.52.

[67] No.19, Gobierno Politico y Militar de Mindanao a GCG, 27 Jan. 1864, PNA, Mindanao/Sulu 1861–1899; No.70, Gobierno Politico y Militar de Mindanao a GCG, 1 May 1864, PNA, Mindanao/Sulu 1861–1899; Zamboanga Questionario Geografico y Estadistico, PNA, Memoria de Zamboanga; Letter from Father Pablo Cavalleria to Father Francisco Sanchez, 31 Dec. 1886, *BRPI* 33, p.261.

[68] Pryer to Treacher, 5 Oct. 1881, CO, 874/229.

[69] Declaration de un cautivo Christiano Isidoro Gabo, 13 June 1878, taken before Carlos Cuarteron. PNA, Islas de Borneo I.

[70] BH-PCL, VI, paper 163, no.34, Oscar J.W. Scott and Ira C. Brown, "Ethnography of the Magandanaos of Parang", p.187; Mednick, "Some Problems of Moro History and Political Organization", p.48; Elkins, "Slavery and Its Aftermath in the Western World", p.200; Hunt, "Some Particulars Relating to Sulo", p.50.

[71] Y van, *Six months among the Malays and a Year in China,* p.258.

[72] "Comision Reservada a Jolo y Borneo", p.19.

[73] Escosura, *Memoria sobre Filipinas y Jolo redactada en 1863 y 1864,* p.374.

[74] Statement of Diego, Combo, and Calagon in Exp.12, 4 Oct. 1836, PNA, Mindanao/Sulu 1803–1890.

[75] No.508, Gobierno Politico y Militar de Jolo a GCG, 16 Aug. 1867, PNA, Mindanao/ Sulu 1862–1898.

[76] Ibid.

[77] Pryer to Treacher, 1883, CO, 874/233.

Conclusion

[1] Van Leur, *Indonesian Trade and Society,* pp.283–84.

[2] See E.R. Leach, *The Political Systems of Highland Burma* and "The Frontiers of Burma", pp.49–68; F.K. Lehman, *The Structure of Chin Society* and "Ethnic Categories in Burma and the Theory of Social Systems", pp.93–124; M. Moerman, "Who are the Lue?", pp.1215–30 and "Accomplishing Ethnicity", pp.54–68. For general articles relating to the genesis and persistence of ethnic boundaries, the incorporation of ethnic groups, and the organization of interethnic relations in polyethnic social systems, see F.Barth (ed.), *Ethnic Groups and Boundaries* (Boston: Little, Brown, 1969), and L.A. Despres (ed.), *Ethnicity and Resource Competition in Plural Societies* (The Hague: Mouton, 1975).

[3] A noteworthy exception is Robert Pringle's well-documented study of the Ibans of Western Borneo and the Brooke regime. See *Rajahs and Rebels,* pp.xvi–xx, 17–20.

Glossary

Alcalde mayor. Governor of a Province
Almojarifazgo. Import-export duty
Baluarte. Fort of wood, stone, or earthwork
Baju. Shirt or clothes
Baju rantai. Chain-armour
Banyaga. A chattel-slave who was either the victim or the off-spring of victims of slave raids
Barangayan. A Philippine sailing vessel up to 55 feet in length
Brigantine. Two-masted vessel with square-rigged foremast and fore-and-aft rigged mainmast
Buitengewesten. Dutch term for the "outer islands"; area beyond Java
Cabecera. A town or the capital of a parish
Chapa. Small Chinese brass coin commonly used as a form of currency throughout Southeast Asia
Contrabandista. Smuggler
Corregidor. Politico-military governor of a Province that had not been completely pacified or whose location was of strategic consequence
Dammar. Resin obtained from a tree especially of genus *agathis* or *thorea*
Datu. Chief or aristocrat
Degredados. The degraded ones
Deportado. An individual who has been deported or banished
Duro. Spanish dollar
Estado. A report or account
Gutta Percha. Greyish-black plastic substance obtained from the latex of various Bornean trees
Haji. Honorific title for one who has made the pilgrimage to Mecca
Indio. Term used by the Spaniards to refer to the inhabitants of the Philippines
Jihad. Holy war
Kadi. Muslim judge
Kampong ayer. Stilted village built out over the water
Kangan. A bolt of coarse cotton cloth from China
Kapal api. Steam ship
Kapitan China. Headman of a Chinese community
Kiapangtilihan. Bond slaves
Kora-Kora. A long vessel used in the Moluccas with a high prow and higher stern, large deck house, outriggers, and propelled by oar and sail
Kota. Fort
Lantanca. Long, heavy brass swivel cannon which were esteemed as symbols of wealth and social status
Laxamana. Malay title for admiral of the Royal fleet
Marina Sutil. "The light navy" or anti-piracy force
Mestiza. People of Spanish-Filipino or Chinese-Filipino ancestry
Moro. A term used by the Spaniards in the Philippines to refer to the Muslims
La Muralla de Sangre. The Wall of Blood
Nakodah. Master of a sailing craft
Orang Kaya. A commoner and a man of means

Padi. Unhusked rice

Padron. Tribute roll

Paduakan. Bugis sailing vessel of between 20 and 50 tons burden, broad beamed with high sides

Panco. Spanish term used to refer to the largest type of Muslim raiding craft (between 50 to 90 feet in length)

Panglima. A high-ranking noble

Peso. The official Spanish currency in the Philippines

Polo. A system of forced labour service

Pontin. Undecked cargo boat

Prahu. Malay for sailing craft

Presidio. A garrisoned post; also a penal settlement

Pueblo. A municipal district

Raja. Generic term of Hindu origin for"Ruler"

Raja muda. "Vice-King" or prince and heir apparent to the throne

Remontado. Person with no fixed habitation. In the nineteenth century the term was used to describe people who fled to the mountains

Renegado. Renegade

Ruma Bichara. The Sultanate's loosely organised council of ministers, composed of Royal datus and high ranking aristocrats

Sarong. A piece of cloth the ends of which have been sewn together

Sherif. Religious figure claiming descent from the prophet

Servicio Personal. Personal labour service

Telegrafista. Sentry and / or signal man who manned the watch-towers in Philippine coastal towns

Tripang. Malay for sea cucumber

Ulama. A Muslim scholar

Vinta. Outriggered sailing vessel of the Philippines varying in length from 15 to upward of 50 feet

Visita. Ecclesiastical term for a small village serviced by a non-resident priest

Bibliography

OFFICIAL RECORDS

I Spain

    A. Records of the Archivo de Indias, Seville

    Seccion — Audiencia de Filipinas

    323   — Expediente sobre el numero de religiosos, pueblos, y Iglesias que tener las Religiones de Santo Domingo, San Francisco, y San Augustin 1751–1753

    324   — Expediente sobre el numero de religiosos, pueblos, y Iglesias que tener las Religiones de Santo Domingo, San Francisco y San Augustin 1753–1754

    359–368   — Consultos, Decretos, Ordenes Originales 1770–1850

    370   — Remisiones el Consejo y Ministros 1775

    390   — Gobierno del Capitan General Don Simon Anda 1769–1780

    391   — Gobiernos de los Capitanes Generales D.Jose Vasco y Vargas y D. Felix Berenguer de Marquina 1776–1787

    489-521   — Duplicados de Gobernador 1769–1850

    Cartas y Expedientes 1751–1800:

    602   — Inventario de Cartas y Expedientes, 603A—1751–1761; 603B—1751–1761; 610—1765; 611—1765; 618—1768; 621—1769; 626—1770; 627—1770; 632—1772; 633—1772; 634—1773; 635—1773; 636—1774; 641—1777; 645—1777; 645—1779; 651—1782; 654—1785; 660—1790

    Expedientes Diarios 1700–1800:

    667   — Inventario de Expedientes Diarios; 669—1765–1767

    Expedientes y Instancias de Partes 1700–1800:

    681   — 1761–1764; 685—1773–1775; 686—1776–1778; 687—1779–1780; 688—1781–1783; 690—1784–1785; 697—Ynstancias sin curso 1800–1849

    700   — Duplicados de Autoridades Particulares 1731–1759

    860, 811, 829   — Duplicados de Superintendentes y Yntendentes de Ejercito y Real Hacienda 1821–1832

    976–979   — Expediente del Consular y Comercio 1788–1832

    1027   — Duplicados del Obispo de Cebu 1718–1830

    1031   — Duplicados del Obispo de Nueva Segovia 1757–1829

    1033   — Duplicados del Obispo de Nueva Cazeras 1715–1830

    Seccion — Ministerio de Ultramar

    557   — Indices de consultados, ordenes y representationes que dividen los Gobernadores Capitanes Generales 1787–1822

    558   — Indices de consultados, ordenes y representaciones que divigen los Gobernadores Capitanes Generales 1823–1835

    559   — Indices de consultados, ordenes y representaciones que divigen los Gobernadores Capitanes Generales 1836–1850

    Expedientes y Instancias del partes 1769-1870;

    587   — 1809–1810; 591—1815–1816; 592—1816–1817; 599—1825–1826; 604—1831–1870

    Expediente del Real Hacienda:

624—1825–1827; 625—1828–1830
650—Expedientes de Marina 1802–1825
657–664—Expedientes de Navegacion, Industria y Comercio 1772–1835
682–684—Cartas y Expedientes de los Arbispos y Cabildos 1773–1833
Seccion—Indiferente
1527—Indiferente General
B.   Records of the Archivo Historico Nacional, Madrid
Seccion—Ultramar, Gobierno de Filipinas
Legajos 4542, 5153, 5155, 5157, 5159, 5161, 5162, 5163, 5164, 5165, 5166, 5167,
   5172, 5173, 5180, 5182, 5184, 5186, 5188, 5190, 5191, 5192, 5193, 5194, 5195,
   5197, 5198, 5199, 5200, 5217
Seccion—Estado
Estado 2845, caja 2
Estado 8461
C.   Records of the Archivo de Ministerio de Asuntos Exteriores, Madrid
Correspondencia Consulados Singapore 1848–1920
Legajo 2067—1848–1880; 2068—1881–1920
D.   Records of the Museo Naval, Madrid
Coleccion Enrile
Tomo VII, Documento 14, folio 53–54; Documento 15, folio 55; Documento 16, folio
   56
Tomo XIII, Documento 2, folios 27–39; Documento 9, folios 73–82; Documento 10,
   folios 83–88; Documento 13, folios 93–94
Tomo XVIII, Documento 31, folio 213
Coleccion Guillen
Tomo V, Documento 18; Documento 19, folios 40–43; Documento 26, folios 118–133;
   Documento 33, folios 167–185
Tomo VI, Documento 6, folios 80–91
Tomo XIII, Ms. 1740
Ms. 211. Diario de Navegacion del Capitan de Frigata de la Real Armada D. Jose
   Maria Halcon en su Navegacion de Manila a Jolo con la Galeota de S.M. 'La
   Olosea' y una division de Faluas. Comprende desde 10 Junio de 1836 y abraza
   noticias peculiares a comision extraordinaria que en calidad de plenipotenciario
   desenipeno cerca del Sultan de Jolo
Ms. 823. Pancos y otros embarcaciones de Filipinas por Nicolas Enrile, 1834
II England
A.   Records of the East India Company, India Office Library, London
Bengal Public Consultations
P/1/51, P/2/1, P/2/6, P/2/10, P/2/14, P/4/39, P/4/43, P/5/11, P/6/7, P/8/25, P/12/51,
   P/12/58, P/13/13, P/13/17, P/13/20, P/13/25
Bengal Secret Consultations
P/140, P/154, P/166, P/167, P/236
Bengal Foreign Consultations
P/165/76
Bombay Public Consultations
P/341/33, P/341/35, P/341/37, P/341/38, P/341/39, P/341/40, P/341/41
Madras General Consultations
P/242/42
Madras Military Consultations
P/254/69, P/255/18
Madras Military and Secret Proceedings

P/251/51
Factory Records, Borneo (1648–1814)
G/4/1
Factory Records, Java
G/21/1, G/21/17, G/21/24, G/21/25, G/21/26, G/21/27, G/21/28, G/21/37, G/21/40, G/21/41, G/21/42
Factory Records, Straits Settlements
Vols. 1–3
Home Miscellaneous Series
Vols. 102, 105, 107, 108, 115, 116, 118, 119, 122, 128, 146, 165, 166, 169, 437, 795, 815
Marine Records
L/Mar/6/98C, L/Mar/6/456I and J, L/Mar/6/456T, L/Mar/6/537A and 537B, L/Mar/6/556E, L/Mar/6/570A, L/Mar/6/570B
Orme Collection
Vol.67, 88
Board's Collections
19495 (714) Vol.96, P.231; 77129 (1841) Vol.25, p.1374; 86974 (1978) Vol.34, p.138; 95244 (2072) Vol.42, p.788; 10277 (2146) Vol.50, p.805; 113126 (2245) Vol.58, p.329; 114837 (2262) Vol.59, p.705; 121954 (2331) Vol.64, p.670;121955 (2331) Vol.64, p.670; 124781 (2358) Vol.66, p.676; 125401 (2363) Vol.67, p.597; 135371, 135372 (2450) Vol.75, p.1021; 140594 (2489) Vol.79, p.1160
Raffles Minto Collection
EUR.F. 148/3, EUR.F. 148/5, EUR.F. 148/7, EUR.F. 148/37
Raffles Family Collection
Mss. EUR.D. 742/1, Mss. EUR.D. 742/45
B. Public Records Office
Colonial Office Records
C.O. 144. Labuan, Original Correspondence, 1844–1906, Vols. 1–81
C.O. 874. British North Borneo Papers 1878–1915
Foreign Office Records
F.O. 12. Borneo, 1842–1875
F.O. 71. Sulu, 1848–1888, Vols. 1–19
F.O. 72. Spain, 72/663, 72/684, 72/708, 72/732, 72/749, 72/761, 72/761, 72/795, 72/812, 72/853, 72/876, 72/904, 72/927, 72/1017, 72/1070, 72/1193, 72/1246, 72/1221, 72/1283, 72/1423, 72/1477
Admiralty Records
Adm. 125/133—Sulu Piracy
Adm. 125/144—Borneo Piracy
State Papers—Spain
S/P/94/197, S/P/94/198
Egremont Papers
PRO, 30/47/20/1
C. National Maritime Museum, Greenwich
MAS/7. A series of 83 numbered letters received and written by Massie, captain of H.M.S. *Cleopatra* at Hong Kong and Singapore, from 15th August 1851—9th March 1852
MAS/22. Journal of H.M.S. *Cleopatra* in East Indies kept by Massie while in command as captain 1851–1853
D. Jardine Matheson Archives, Cambridge University Library
East Indies, B1/99, 100, 101, B4/4, C1/14

E.   British Museum, London
     James Rennell, Journal of a Voyage to the Sooloo Islands and the Northwest Coast of
     Borneo, from and to Madras with descriptions of the islands, 1762–1763
F.   Parliamentary Papers, House of Commons
     1850. Vol.L V (238), p.3. Malay Piracy
     1851. Vol.L VI, Pt. 1 [1390], p.1. 'Historical notices upon the piracies committed
     in the East Indies, and upon the measures taken for suppressing them, by the
     Government of the Netherlands, within the last thirty years'. Abstracted from
     articles by Cornets de Groot in the *Moniteur des Indes*
     1851. Vol.L VI, Pt. 1 [1351], p.123. Papers respecting the Operations against the
     pirates on the Northwest coast of Borneo
     1852. Vol.XXXI [1538], p.473. Borneo Piracy
     1852–1853. Vol.L XI (55), p.235. Burn's schooner *Dolphin*

III   Netherlands
A.   Records of the Algemeen Rijksarchief, The Hague
     Kolonien Archief-Overgekomen Brieven
     No.2922, 3144, 3205, 3259, 3281, 3283, 3315, 3337, 3341
     Kolonien
     No.1393, 1594, 2597, 2669, 2675, 2692, 2703, 2710, 3200, 3089, 4168, 4351
     De Archieven van het Department van Buitenlandsche Zaken
     No.3268. Correspondentie over de bestrijding der Zeerooverijen in den Soeloe (Solok)
     Archipel. 1862 April 1—1868, July 25.
B.   Records of Auxiliary Repository, Schaarsbergen
     Ministrie van Kolonien
     No.1398, 2166, 2290, 2434, 2450, 2496, 2565, 3378, 5873, 6000, 6001
C.   Papers of Het Koningklyk Instituut voor-taal-en Volkenkunde, Leiden
     Ligtvoet Collection
     H609A-III-Ligtvoet (A) Bestuur sambtenaar (aantekiningen omtrent Z.W. Celebes)

IV   The United States
A.   Records of the United States National Archive, Washington, D.C.
     The Papers of the Bureau of Insular Affairs
     File 2689. Slavery and Slave Trade in the Philippine Islands (1901–1936)
     File 3671. 'Protocols, Capitulations, Official Letters, Decrees, and Correspondence
     relating to Jolo and Mindanao, 1751–1896'
     The Department of State
     Consular Despatches, Manila 1817–1840
     The Department of the Navy
     Journal of Lieutenant Charles Wilkes aboard the *Vincennes* and the *Porpoise,* Volume
     3 (April 6, 1841—May 15, 1842)
     Journal of William Briskoe, Armorer, aboard the *Relief* and the *Vincennes* (August 18,
     1838—March 23, 1842)
     Journal kept aboard the *Vincennes,* probably by R.P. Robinson, Purser's Clerk (April 6,
     1841—May 15, 1842)
B.   The Library of Congress, Washington, D.C.
     The Leonard Wood Papers
     Container 3: Diary, May, 1902—January 31, 1906
     Containers 32–35: General Correspondence, 1903–1904
     Containers 191, 192, 216, 239: Personal Correspondence
     The Hugh L. Scott Papers
     Containers 55–56: Official letters January 1900–1905

C.   The Philips Library, Salem Peabody Museum, Salem, Massachusetts
     Ships' logs
     656/1792/3, *Britannide*. Journal of a voyage from England to Port Jackson New South
          Wales in the years 1792, 1793 and 1794, and in 1795 in the ship *Britannide,* kept by
          K. Murray
     656/1833A, *Albree*. Abstract log from Boston towards Calcutta, 16 July 1833—
          September 11, 1833, kept by Gamaliel E. Ward. Included also: Memo of goods
          obtainable at Sooloo and a list of goods for the Sooloo Market
     656/1835A, *Leonidas* Brig. Log of Brig *Leonidas* from February 8, 1836 to September
          23, 1836; departure from Manila to neighbouring ports and return
     656/1837/39, *Logan*. Journal kept on board the ship *Logan* 1837–1838 kept by Mrs
          Alonzo Fallonsbee
     Papers of William D. Waters
     10654/*Leonidas*, Letter: soliciting trade between United States and Sooloo [no date]
     Papers of James Devereux
     10654/container 6
     East India Marine Society
     Lydia (barque), Journal of Salem vessel from Manila to Samboangue [Zamboanga]
          and Guam from October 20, 1801 to February 1804 kept by William Haswell
D.   *United States Senate Documents,* United States Congress
     1899–1900. 56th Congress. 1st Session, Vol.IX No.136, Treaty with the Sultan of
          Sulu
     1900–1901. 56th Congress. 2nd Session, Vol.XV, No.218, The People of the
          Philippines

V   The Philippines
A.   The Records of the Philippine National Archives, Manila
     Mindanao y Sulu
     Bundles 1769–1898, 1774–1887, 1780–1898, 1803–1890, 1816–1898, 1836–1897,
          1838–1885, 1838–1890, 1838–1891, 1839–1898, 1842–1897, 1847–1898, 1857–
          1895, 1857–1897, 1858–1897, 1860–1897, 1860–1898, 1861–1893, 1861–1896,
          1861–1897, 1861–1899, 1862–1898 (2 bundles), 1864–1898, 1877–1895, 15
          unclassified bundles
     Piratas
     Bundles I-III
     Isla de Borneo
     Bundles I-II
     Chinos
     Padron de Chinos, Jolo—1892, 1893, 1894
     Padron de Zamboanga—1892
     Cotabato, Davao, Jolo, Misamis 1878–1898
     Varias Provincias
     One bundle—Zamboanga
     Memorias
     Memoria de Zamboanga
     Ereccion del Pueblo
     Albay, 1772–1831, 1772–1885, 1799–1864, 1841–1891, 1843–1846
     Camarines Sur, 1781–1809, 1786–1837, 1797–1859, 1799–1820, 1831–1882, bundle
          67, No.1–28
     Tayabas, bundles 1, 2, 3, 1793–1857, pt. II
     Zambales, 1804–1844, pt. I
     Negros, 1854–1857

B.   The Records of the Archives of the University of Santo Tomes, Manila 'Memoria sobre Mindanao y demas puntos del Sur', Seccion Folletos, Tomo 117

C.   Society of Jesus Archives of the Philippine Province, Quezon City
     Series XIV—Zamboanga and Jolo
     XIV—9 Isabella
     XIV—10 Jolo
     XIV—23 Zamboanga Residence (1)

D.   National Library of the Philippines
     Republic of the Philippines, Bureau of Public Schools, 'Historical Data Papers, unpublished MS'
     Historical Data Papers for Albay, Vols. I–IV; Camarines sur, Vols. I–IV; Camarines Norte; Catanduanes; Masbate, I–III; Romblon; Antique; Cebu; Vols. I–IV; Bohol, Vols. I–II; Samar, Vol.VIII; Palawan; Surigao; Misamis Oriental; Zamboanga del Norte; Zamboanga del Sur

VI   Arsip Nasional Republik Indonesia, Jakarta
     Menado
     Files 37, 50, 166
     Riouw
     File 20/3
     Besluit, August 9, 1879, N. 22
     Besluit, June 3, 1880, No.30

COLLECTIONS

A.   Beyer-Holleman collection of Original sources in Philippine Customary Law. Typescript, Library of Congress, Washington, D.C. and Philippine Studies Program, University of Chicago
     Paper No.159, Vol. I. General Introduction to the Papers on Moro Customary Law
     Paper No.160, Vol. I, No.1. Major Charles Livingston, 'Constabulary Monograph of Sulu' (1915)
     Paper No.160, Vol. I, No.2. 1st Lieutenant A. Bruce Stephenson, 'Constabulary Monograph of the District of Tawi-Tawi' (1916)
     Paper No.161, Vol. II, No.8. Najeeb Saleeby, 'The Moros' (1906)
     Paper No.161, Vol. II, No.10. Howard Hickok, 'Report of the 52nd Census District' (1903)
     Paper No.161, Vol. II, No.11. K. Walker, 'Report of the 53rd Census District' (1903)
     Paper No.162, Vol. VI, No.16. Adolf Gunther, 'Correspondence and Reports relating to the Sulu Moros' (Jolo and Manila, 1901–1903)
     Paper No.162, Vol. XI, No.19. John Whitaker, 'Notes on the Yakan Moros' (1902)
     Paper No.162, Vol. VI, No.21. J. Mahoney, 'Report of the Census of the Island of Basilan' (1903)
     Paper No.162, Vol. VI, No.23. Emerson B. Christie, 'The Moros of Sulu and Mindanao'
     Paper No.162, Vol. VI, No.25. Emerson B.Christie, 'The non Christian Tribes of the Northern half of the Zamboanga Peninsula' (1903)
     Paper No.162, Vol. VI, No.26. F.P. Williamson, 'The Moros between Buluan and Punta Flecha' (1903)

Paper No.163, Vol. VI, No.28. L.W.V. Kennon, David P. Barrows, John Pershing and C. Smith, 'Census Report relating to the District of Lanao, Mindanao' (1903)

Paper No.163, Vol. VI, No.34. Oscar J.W. Scott and Ira C. Brown, 'Ethnography of the Magandanaos of Parang' (1908)

Paper No.164, Vol. VI, No.49. The Bates Treaty with the Sultan of Sulu

Paper No.164, Vol. VI, No.50. Conference of the Philippine Commission with the Sultan of Sulu and his adviser (July 19, 20 and 26, 1904)

Paper No.164, Vol. VI, No.51. John J. Pershing, Leonard Wood and others, 'Correspondence and Papers relating to the status of the Sultan of Sulu' (1904–1913)

Paper No.164, Vol. VI, No.65. Vicente T. Zago, 'The Sovereign Personality of the Sultan of Sulu' (1919)

Paper No.165, Vol. VI, John Garvan, 'Papers on the Pagan People of Mindanao'

Paper No.167, Vol. VI, John Garvan, 'Ethnography of the Manobo people of Eastern Mindanao'

B. John Neilson Conrad Collection, Oamaru, New Zealand

Reed Papers

Papers of the late Dr J.G. Reed of Perak, Malaysia, relating to his research into the life of Joseph Conrad. Two notebooks,1950–1951 correspondence, record of April 13, 1951 interview with Mrs C.C. Oehlers (Nelli Lingard) in Singapore, navigation charts and photographs

C. Haverschmidt Collection, Heerlen, Netherlands

Haverschmidt Papers

Records compiled 1951–1952 in Berau, Kalimantan Timor, Indonesia by Mr R. Haverschmidt, late manager, N.V. Steenkolen Maatschappij Parapattan, Teluk Bajur, Berau. Interviews with elderly local residents (Sultan of Sambaliung, the Ratu of Gunung Tabor, Anang Dachlan Akay, Adji Bagian, Raden Ajub, and Kang Si Gok) in 'Statements of Residents'; a copy of 1904 deed of sale of Lingard house; a copy of chronology of events in Berau from 1800–1926 based on the chronicle of the Sultan of Gunung Tabor; copies of Netherlands government documents 1879–1933 pertaining to the Berau district

NEWSPAPERS

British North Borneo Herald and Official Gazette, 1883–1915 (Sandakan)

La Estrella de Manila, January–December 1848 (Manila)

Makassarsch Handelsblad, May 1868–1883 (Makassar)

Overland Singapore Free Press, 1847 (Singapore)

Singapore Chronicle, 1827, 1830–1833 (Singapore)

Singapore Chronicle and Commercial Register, 7 January 1837–30 September 1838 (Singapore)

Singapore Free Press and Mercantile Advertiser, February 1836–September 1838 (Singapore)

Singapore Daily Times, 1837 (Singapore)

Straits Times Overland Journal (1879), (Singapore)

Straits Times and Singapore Journal of Commerce, 1848, 1851–1853, 1883 (Singapore)

DISSERTATIONS

Ahmat bin Adam. "A Descriptive Account of the Malay Letters sent to Thomas Stamford Raffles in Malacca in 1810 and 1811 by the Rulers of the Indigenous States of the Malay Archipelago". M.A. diss., University of London, 1971.

Cheong, W.E. "Some Aspects of British Trade and Finance in Canton, With Special Reference to the Role of Anglo-Spanish Trade in the Eastern Seas, 1784–1834". Ph.D. diss., University of London, 1963.

Cruikshank, R.B. "A History of Samar Island, the Philippines, 1768–1898". Ph.D. diss., University of Wisconsin, 1975.

de Jesus, Edilberto C. "The Tobacco Monopoly in the Philippines, 1782–1882". Ph.D. diss., Yale University, 1973.

Frake, Charles O. "Social Organisation and Shifting Cultivation among the Sindangan Subanun". Ph.D. diss., Yale University, 1955.

Hunter, S.C. "English, German, Spanish Relations on the Sulu Question, 1871–1877". M.Sc. diss., University of London, 1963.

Julian, Elisa A. "British Projects and Activities in the Philippines, 1795–1805". Ph.D. diss., University of London, 1963.

Matheson, Virginia. "Tuhfat al Nafis". Ph.D. diss., Monash University, 1973.

Mednick, Melvin. "Encampment of the Lake: the Social Organisation of a Moslem Philippine (Moro) People". Ph.D. diss., University of Chicago, 1965.

Nimmo, Harry Arlo. "The Structure of Bajau Society". Ph.D. diss., University of Hawaii, 1969.

Owen, Norman G. "Kabikolan in the Nineteenth Century: Socio-Economic Change in the Provincial Philippines. Ph.D. diss. University of Michigan, 1976.

Reber, Anne L. "The Sulu World in the 18th and Early 19th Centuries: A Historiographical Problem in British Writings on Malay Piracy". M.A. diss., Cornell University, 1966.

Reynolds, John Keith. "Towards an Account of Sulu and Its Bornean Dependencies, 1700–1878". M.A. diss., University of Wisconsin, 1970.

Surojo, A.M. Djuliati. "Perbudakan di Indonesia pada abad XIX". Skripsi Sardjana (M.A.) Universitas Gadjah Mada, 1969.

Warren, Carol A. "Bajau Consciousness in Social Change: The Transformation of a Malaysian Minority Community". M.A. diss., Australian National University, 1977.

BOOKS

Abdullah bin Abdul Kadir. *The Hikayat Abdullah,* trans. A.H.Hill, *Journal Malaysian Branch Royal Asiatic Society* 28, no.3 (1955).

Allen, Jerry. *The Sea Years of Joseph Conrad.* London: Methuen, 1967.

Almeida, Anna. *A Lady's Visit to Manila and Japan.* London: Hurst & Blackett, 1863.

Andaya, Leonard. *The Kingdom of Johor, 1641–1728.* Kuala Lumpur: Oxford University Press, 1975.

Anderson, John. *Mission to the East Coast of Sumatra in 1823.* London: Oxford University Press, 1971.

Arenas, Rafael Dias. *Memoria sobre el Comercio y Navegacion de Las Islas Filipinas.* Cadiz: Imprenta de D. Feros, 1838.

Balandier, Georges. *Political Anthropology.* trans. A.M. Sheridan Smith. London: Penguin Press, 1970.

Balanza General del Comercio de las Islas Filipinas. Manila, 1853.

Balanza General del Comercio de las Islas Filipinas en 1845. Manila, 1854.

Balanza Mercantil de las Islas Filipinas correspondiente al ano de 1858. Manila, 1861.

Banton, Michael, ed. *Political Systems and the Distribution of Power.* London: Tavistock Publications, 1965.

Baring-Gould, S., and Bampfylde, C.A. *A History of Sarawak under Its Two White Rajahs, 1839–1908.* London: Southeran, 1909.

Barrantes, Vicente. *Guerras Piraticas de Filipinas contra Mindanaos y Joloanos.* Madrid: Imprenta de Manuel H. Hernandez, 1878.

Barth, F., ed. *Ethnic Groups and Boundaries.* Boston, Little, Brown, 1969.

Belcher, Edward. *Narrative of the Voyage of H.M.S. Samarang, during the Years 1843–1846.* 2 vols. London: Reeve, Benham & Reeve, 1848.

Berkhofer, Robert. *A Behavioural Approach to Historical Analysis.* New York: Free Press, 1969.

Bernaldez, Emilio. *Resana historico de la guerra a Sur de Filipinas, sostenida por las armas Espanoles contra los piratas de aquel archipielago, desde la conquista hasta nuestros dias.* Madrid: Imprenta del Memorial de Ingenieros, 1857.

Bickmore, Albert. *Travels in the East Indian Archipelago.* London: John Murray, 1868.

Blair, E.H., and Robertson, J.A. *The Philippine Islands, 1493–1898.* 55 vols. Cleveland: A.H. Clark Co., 1903–1919.

Blalock, Hubert M. *Toward a Theory of Minority Group Relations.* New York: John Wiley & Sons, 1967.

Bock, Carl. *The Headhunters of Borneo: A Narrative of Travel up the Mahakkam and down the Barito; Also Journeyings in Sumatra.* London: Sampson Low, 1882.

Bowring, John. *The Philippine Islands.* London: Smith, Elder & Co., 1859.

Broersma, R. *Handel en Bedrijf in Zuid-en Oost Borneo.* The Hague: G. Noeff, 1927.

Brown, Donald. *Brunei: The Structure and History of a Bornean Malay Sultanate.* Brunei: Brunei Museum, 1970.

Brown, W. *Useful Plants of the Philippines.* 3 vols. Manila: Bureau of Printing, 1951.

Buckley, Charles B. *An Anecdotal History of Old Times in Singapore, 1819–1867.* Kuala Lumpur: University of Malaya Press, 1965.

Casino, Eric. *Ethnographic Art of the Philippines: An Anthropological Approach.* Manila: 1973.

Casino, Eric. *The Jama Mapun: A Changing Samal Society in the Southern Philippines.* Quezon City: Ateneo de Manila University Press, 1976.

Chaunu, Huguette and Pierre. *Seville et L'Atlantique, 1504–1650, Ports-Routes-Trafics.* 7 vols. Paris: Colin, 1955.

Chaunu, Pierre. *Les Philippines et le Pacifique des Iberiques (XVI, XVII, XVIII siecles).* Paris: Seupen, 1960.

Coates, W.H. *The Old "Country Trade" of the East Indies.* London: Imray, Laurie, Narie & Wilson, 1911.

Cohen, Ronald, and Service, Elman R., eds. *Origins of the State the Anthropology of Political Evolution.* Philadelphia: Institute for the Study of Human Issues, 1978.

Combes, Francisco S.J. *Historia de las Islas de Mindanao y Jolo.* Madrid, 1667.

Comyn, Tomas de. *State of the Philippines in 1810, Being an Historical, Statistical and Descriptive Account of the Interesting Portion on the Indian Archipelago.* Trans. with notes and preliminary discourse by William Walton. Manila: Filipiniana Book Guild, 1969.

Cook, Oscar. *Borneo: The Stealer of Hearts.* London: Hurst & Blackett, 1924.

Cooper-Cole, Fay. *The Wild Tribes of Davao District, Mindanao.* Chicago: Field Museum of Natural History, Anthropological Series, vol.12, no.2, 1913.

Cooper-Cole, Fay. *The Bukidnon of Mindanao.* Chicago: Natural History Museum, 1956.

Costa, Horacio de la. *Readings in Philippine History.* Manila: Bookmark, 1965.

Crawfurd, John. *History of the Indian Archipelago, Containing an Account of the Languages, Religions, Institutions and Commerce of Its Inhabitants.* 3 vols. Edinburgh, 1820.

Crawfurd, John. *A Descriptive Dictionary of the Indian Islands and Adjacent Countries.* London: Bradbury & Evans, 1856.

Cuadro General del Comercio Exterior de Filipinas con la Metropoli potencias extrangeras de Europa, America, Asia y Colonias de la Oceania en 1856. Manila, 1859.

Cushner, Nicholas. *Landed Estates in the Colonial Philippines.* New Haven: Yale Southeast Asian Studies, 1976.

Dalton, George, ed. *Primitive, Archaic and Modern Economies.* Garden City, N.Y.: Anchor Books, 1968.

Dalrymple, Alexander. *Oriental Repertory.* 2 vols. London, 1808.

Dampier, William. *A New Voyage Round the World.* 2 vols. Edited by John Masfield. London: E.Grant Ricardo, 1960.

Delano, Amasa. *A Narrative of Voyages and Travel in the Northern and southern Hemispheres, Comprising Three Voyages Round the World; Together with a Voyage of Survey and Discovery, in the Pacific Ocean and Oriental Islands.* Boston: E.G. House, 1817.

Despres, L.A., ed. *Ethnicity and Resource Competition in Plural Societies.* The Hague: Mouton, 1975.

Diaz-Trechuelo Spinola, M. L. *Arquitectura Espanola en Filipinas, 1565–1800.* Seville, 1959.

Diaz-Trechuelo Spinola, M.L. *La Real Compania de Filipinas.* Seville, 1965.

Dobby, E.H. *Southeast Asia.* London: University of London Press, 1969.

Dumont D'Urville, Jules Sebastian Cesar. *Voyages au pole sud et dans L'Oceanie sur les corvettes l'Astrolobe et la Zelee ... pendant les annees 1837–1838–1839–1840.* 23 vols., Atlas, 7 vols. Paris: Gide et J. Baudry, 1841–1854.

Earl, George Windsor. *The Eastern Seas or Voyages and Adventures in the Indian Archipelago in 1832, 1833, 1834, Comprising a Tour of the Island of Java—Visits to Borneo, the Malay Peninsula, Siam, Also an Account of the Present State of Singapore with Observations on the Commercial Resources of the Archipelago.* London: W.H. Allen & Co., 1837.

El-Correo-Sino-Annamita o correspondencia de las Misiones del Sagrado Orden de Predicadores en Formosa, China, Tung-King y Filipinas. Vol.25. Manila: Imprenta Del Real Colegio de Santo Tomas.

Escosura, Patricio de la. *Memoria sobre Filipinas y Jolo redactada en 1863 y 1864.* Madrid: Imprenta de Manuel G. Hernandez, 1882.

Espina, Miguel Angel. *Apuntos para hacer un libro sobre Jolo, entresacados de los escrito por Barrantes, Bernaldez, Escosura, Grancia, Giraudier, Gonzales, Parrado, Pagos y otros varios.* Manila: Imprenta de M. Perez, hijo, 1889.

Estadistica General del Comercio Exterior de las Islas Filipinas del ano de 1888. Manila, 1890.

Finley, John P., and Churchill, William. *The Subanun: Studies of a sub-Visayan mountain folk of Mindanao.* Washington, D.C.: Carnegie Institution of Washington, Publication No.184, 1913.

Fischer, David Hackett. *Historians' Fallacies: Toward a Logic of Historical Thought.* New York: Harper & Row, 1970.

Foreman, John. *The Philippine Islands.* 2nd ed. New York: Charles Scribners, 1899.

Forrest, Thomas. *A Voyage to New Guinea and the Moluccas from Balambangan: Including an Account of Magindano, Sooloo and Other Islands.* London: G. Scott, 1779.

Forrest, Thomas. *A Voyage from Calcutta to the Mergui Archipelago Lying on the East Side of the Bay of Bengal.* London, 1792.

Fry, Howard. *Alexander Dalrymple and the Expansion of British Trade.* Royal Commonwealth Society, Imperial Studies No.29, London: Cass, 1970.

Furber, Holden. *John Company at Work: A Study of European Expansion in India in the Late Eighteenth Century.* Cambridge: Harvard University Press, 1951.

Gainza, Francisco. *Memoria y antecedentes sobre las espediciones de Balangingi y Jolo.* Manila: Establecimiento tipografico del Colegio de Santo Tomas, 1851.

Garcia, Luiz de Ibanez. *Mi Cautiverio; carto que con motivo del que sufrio entre los moros piratas Joloanos y Samales en 1857.* Madrid: G. Allhambra, 1859.

Garvan, John M. *The Manobos of Mindanao.* Memorial of the National Academy of Science, vol.23, 1st Memoir. Washington, D.C., 1931.

Gazetteer of the Philippine Islands. 2 vols. Washington, D.C., 1902.

Gowing, Peter, and McAmis, Robert D., eds. *The Muslim Filipinos.* Manila: Solidarid Publishing House, 1974.

Greenberg, Michael. *British Trade and the Opening of China, 1800–1842.* London: Cambridge University Press, 1951.

Gregori, F.A.A. *Aanteekeningen en Beshouwingen betrekkelijk de Zeeroovers en hunn rooverijen in den Indischen Archipel, alsmede aagaande Magindanao en de Soolo-Archipel,* 1844.

Guia de Forasteros en las Yslas Filipinas por el ano de 1843. Manila: Imprenta D. Miguel Sanchez, 1843.

Guia de Forasteros en las Yslas Filipinas Para el ano de 1846. Manila: Imprenta de los Amigos del Pais, 1846.

Guia de Forasteros en las Yslas Filipinas Para el ano de 1856. Manila: Imprenta de los Amigos del Pais, 1856.

Guia de Forasteros en las Yslas Filipinas Para el ano de 1857. Manila: Imprenta de los Amigos del Pais, 1857.

Guillaume, Alfred. *Islam.* Baltimore: Penguin, 1954.

Guillelmard, F.H.H. *The Cruise of the Marchesa to Kamschatka and New Guinea, With Notices of Formosa, Liu-Kiu and Other Various Islands of the Malay Archipelago.* 2 vols. London: John Murray, 1886.

Gullick, J.M. *Indigenous Political Systems of Western Malaya.* London School of Economics Monographs on Social Anthropology No.17. London: Athlone Press, 1958.

Handbook of the State of North Borneo, With a supplement of Statistical and Other Useful Information. London: British North Borneo Chartered Co., 1934.

Hanks, Lucien M. *Rice and Man: Agricultural Ecology in Southeast Asia.* Chicago: Aldine, Atherton, 1972.

Hardy, Charles. *Register of Ships Employed in the Service of the Honourable United East India Company, 1707–1760.* London, 1799.

Harlow, Vincent T. *The Founding of the Second British Empire, 1773–1793.* 2 vols. London: Longmans & Green Co., 1952.

Harrison, Tom and Barbara. *The Prehistory of Sabah.* Kota Kinabalu: Sabah Society, 1971.

Hatton, Joseph. *The New Ceylon, Being a Sketch of British North Borneo or Sabah.* London: Chapman & Hall, 1881.

Horsburgh, James. *India Directory of Directions for Sailing to and from the East Indies, China, Australia, Cape of Good Hope, Brazil and the Interjacent Ports, Compiled Chiefly from the Original Journals of the Company Ships, and from the Observations and Remarks made during Twenty-one Years Experience Navigating in Those Seas.* 4th ed. London, 1836.

Hudson, A.B. *Padju Epat: The Ma'anyan of Indonesian Borneo.* New York: Holt Rinehart & Winston, 1972.

Hutterer, Karl L., ed. *Economic Exchange and Social Interaction in Southeast Asia: Perspectives from Prehistory, History and Ethnography.* Michigan Papers on South and Southeast Asia. Ann Arbor: 1978.

Ileto, Reynaldo Clemena. *Magindanao, 1860–1888: The Career of Dato Uto of Buayan.* Data Paper No.82. Southeast Asia Program, Cornell University. Ithaca, N.Y., 1971.

Irwin, Graham. *Nineteenth Century Borneo: A Study in Diplomatic Rivalry.* Verhandelingen van het Koningklijk Instituut voor Taal-land-en Volkenkinde. deel XXV. The Hague: Martinus Nijhoff, 1955.

Jacobs, Thomas Jefferson. *Scenes, Incidents and Adventures in the Pacific Ocean, or the Islands of the Australasian Seas, during the Cruise of the Clipper Margaret Oakley under Captain Benjamin Morrell.* New York: Harper & Bros., 1844.

Jagor, Fedor. *Travels in the Philippines.* Manila: Filipiniana Book Guild, 1965.

Keppel, Henry. *The Expedition to Borneo of H.M.S. Dido for the Suppression of Piracy, With Extracts from the Journal of James Brooke, Esq., of Sarawak.* 3rd ed., 2 vols. London: Chapman & Hall, 1847.

Keppel, Henry. *A Visit to the Indian Archipelago in H.M.S. Maeander, With Portions of the Private Journal of Sir James Brooke, K.C.B.* London: Richard Bentley, 1853.

Kiefer, Thomas. *Tausug Armed Conflict: The Social Organisation of Military Conflict in a Philippine Modern Society.* Philippine Studies Program, Research Series No.7, University of Chicago. Chicago, Ill., 1969.

Kiefer, Thomas. *The Tausug: Violence and Law in a Philippine Moslem Society.* New York: Holt Rinehart & Winston, 1972.

Kolf, D.H. *Voyages of the Dutch Brig of War Dourga, through the Southern and Little Known Parts of the Moluccan Archipelago and the Previously Unknown Southern Coast of New Guinea Performed during the Years 1825 and 1826.* Trans. George Windsor Earl. London: James Madden, 1840.

La Gironiere, Paul de. *Twenty Years in the Philippines.* Trans. and abridged by Frederick Hardman. London: Brown, Green, & Longmans, 1853.

Lannoy, P.J. *Iles Philippines De Luer situation Ancienne et Actualle.* Bruxelles: Delevingue et Callevaert, 1849.

Lasker, Bruno. *Human Bondage in Southeast Asia.* Chapel Hill: University of North Carolina Press, 1950.

Leach, E.R. *Political Systems of Highland Burma: A Study of Kachin Social Structure.* London: London School of Economics and Political Science, 1954.

Le Bar, Frank M., ed. *Ethnic Groups of Insular Southeast Asia.* Vol.I. New Haven: Human Relations Area Files Press, 1972.

Le Bar, Frank M., ed. *Ethnic Groups of Insular Southeast Asia.* Volume II: *The Philippines and Formosa.* New Haven: Human Relations Area Files Press, 1975.

Lehman, F.K. *The Structure of Chin Society.* Urbana: University of Illinois Press, 1963.

Lenski, Gerhard E. *Power and Privilege: A Theory of Social Stratification.* New York: McGraw-Hill, 1966.

Lombard, Denys. *Le Sultanate d'Atjeh au temps d'Iskander Muda, 1607–1636.* Paris, 1967.

Low, Hugh. *Sarawak; Its Inhabitants and Productions, Being Notes During a Residence in That Country with H.H. the Rajah Brooke.* London: Richard Bentley, 1848.

MacDonald, D. *A Narrative of the Early Life and Services of Captain D. MacDonald R.N. Embracing on Unbroken Period of Twenty-two Years Extracted from His Journal, and Other Official Documents.* 3rd ed., Weymouth, 1843.

MacMicking, Robert. *Recollections of Manila and the Philippines During 1848, 1849 and 1850.* Manila: Filipiniana Book Guild, 1967.

Majul, Cesar A. *Muslims in the Philippines: Past, Present and Future Prospects.* Manila: Convislam, 1971.

Majul, Cesar A. *Muslims in the Philippines.* Quezon City: University of the Philippines Press, 1973.

Mallat, J. *Archipel de Soulou, ou description des groupes des Basilan, de Soulou et de Tawi-Tawi, suivie d'un vocabularie francais-malaise.* Paris: Imprimerie Pollet et compagnie, 1844.

Mallat, J. *Les Philippines; historie, geografie, moeurs, agriculture, industrie et commerce des colonies Espagnoles dans L'Oceanie*. 2 vols. Paris, 1846.

Marche, Alfred. *Luzon and Palawan*. Manila: Filipiniana Book Guild, 1970.

Marryat, Frank. *Borneo and the Indian Archipelago*. London: Longman, Brown, Green & Longman, 1848.

Mas, Sinibaldo de. *Estado de las Islas Filipinas en 1842*. 2 vols. Madrid: Imprenta de I. Sancha, 1843.

Meares, John. *Voyage Made in the Years 1788 and 1789 from China to the North-West Coast of America*. New York: N. Israel/Amsterdam Da Capo Press, 1967.

Meilink-Roelofsz, M.A.P. *Asian trade and European Influence in the Indonesian Archipelago Between 1500 and about 1630*. The Hague: Martinus Nijhoff, 1962.

Milburn, William. *Oriental Commerce; Containing a Geographical Description of the Principal Places in the East Indies, China and Japan, with Their Produce, Manufactures, and Trade, Including the Coasting or Country Trade from Port to Port; Also the Rise and Progress of the Trade of the Various European Nations with the Eastern World, Particularly That of the English East India Company from the Discovery of the Passage Round Cape of Good Hope to the Present Period; With an Account of the Company's Establishments, Revenues, Debts, Assets, at Home and Abroad*. 2 vols. London: Black, Parry & Co., 1813.

Mills, L.A. *British Malaya, 1824–1867*. Kuala Lumpur: Oxford University Press, 1966.

Montero y Vidal, Jose. *Historia de la Pirateria Malayo Mahometano en Mindanao, Jolo y Borneo*. 2 vols. Madrid: Imprenta de M.Tello, 1888.

Montero y Vidal, Jose. *Historia General de Filipinas desde el descubrimiento de dichas Islas hasta nuestras dias*. 3 vols. Madrid: 1894-1895.

Moor, J.H., ed. *Notices of the Indian Archipelago and Adjacent Countries, Being a Collection of Papers Relating to Borneo, Celebes, Bali, Java, Sumatra, Nias, the Philippine Islands, Sulus, Siam, Cochin China, Malayan Peninsula*. London: Cass, 1967 [first edition 1837].

Mouleon, Rafael. *Construccion Naveles: bajo un aspecto artestico por el restangador del Museo Naval, Catalogo descriptivo dos tomos*. 3 vols. Madrid, 1890.

Mundy, Rodney. *Narrative of Events in Borneo and Celebes down to the Occupation of Labuan, from the Journals of James Brook, esq., Together with a Narrative of the Operations of H.M.S. Iris by Capt. Rodney Mundy, R.N.* London: John Murray, 1848.

Nimmo, Harra A. *The Sea People of Sulu: A Study of Social Change in the Philippines*. San Francisco: Chandler Publishing Co., 1972.

Olsen, Marvin, ed. *Power in Societies*. London: Macmillan, 1970.

Orosa, Sixto. *The Sulu Archipelago and Its People*. 2nd ed. Manila: New Mercury Printing Press, 1970.

Osborn, Sherard. *My Journal in Malayan Waters; or the Blockade of Quedah*. 3rd ed. London: Routledge, Warne & Routledge, 1861.

Parkinson, C. Northcote. *Trade in the Eastern Seas, 1793–1813*. London: Cambridge University Press, 1937.

Parkinson, C. Northcote, ed. *The Trade Winds: A Study of British Overseas Trade during the French Wars, 1793–1815*. London: George Allen & Unwin, 1948.

Patero, Santiago. *Sistema que conviene adoptor para acabar con la pirateria que los mahometanos del Sultania de Jolo ejercen en el Archipielago Filipino por el capitan de la armada D. Santiago Paterno*. Madrid: Imprenta de Miguel Ginesta, 1872.

Pazos y Vela-Hidalgo, Pio A. de. *Jolo: Relato historico-militar desde descubrimiento por los Espanoles en 1578 a nuestros dias*. Burgos: Imprenta y esteotipia de Polo, 1879.

Perez, Elviro J. *Catalogo Bio-Bibliografico de las Religiosos Agustinos de la Provincia del Santisimo Nombre de Jesus de las Islas Filipinas desde su fundacion hasta nuestros dias*. Manila: Santo Tomas, 1901.

Phelan, John Leddy. *The Hispanization of the Philippines, Spanish Aims and Filipino Responses, 1565–1700*. Madison: University of Wisconsin Press, 1967.

Polanyi, Karl. Arensburg, Conrad M.; and Pearson, Harry W., eds. *Trade and Market in Early Empires.* Glencoe: The Free Press, 1957.

Polanyi, Karl. *Dahomey and the Slave Trade.* Seattle: University of Washington Press, 1966.

Pringle, Robert. *Rajahs and Rebels: The Ibans of Sarawak under Brooke Rule, 1841–1941.* Ithaca, N.Y.: Cornell University Press, 1970.

Quiason, Serafin D. *English "Country Trade" with the Philippines, 1644–1765.* Quezon City: University of the Philippines Press, 1966.

Renouard, Felix de Sainte-Croix. *Voyage Commercial et Politique aux Indes Orientales, aux Iles Philippenes, a la Chine, avec des nations Sur la Cochin chine et le Touquin, pendant les annees 1803, 1804, 1805, 1806 et 1807.* 3 vols. Paris: Clement, 1810.

Resink, G.J. *Indonesia's History between the Myths: Essays in Legal and Historical Theory.* The Hague: Van Hoeve, 1968.

Reuk, Anthony de, and Knight, Julie, eds. *Caste and Race: Comparative Approaches.* London: J. & A. Churchill, 1967.

Robles, Eliodaro G. *The Philippines in the Nineteenth Century.* Quezon City: Malaya Books, 1969.

Ross, John Dill. *Sixty Years Life and Adventures in the Far East.* 2 vols. London: Hutchinsons, 1911.

Roth, Dennis, *The Friar Estates of the Philippines.* Albuquerque: University of New Mexico Press, 1977.

Ruibing, A.H. *Ethnologische studie betreffende de Indonesische Slavernij als Maatschappelijk verschijnsel.* Zutphen: W.J. Thieme & Co., 1937.

Saleeby, Najeeb M. *Studies in Moro History, Law and Religion.* Dept. of the Interior, Ethnological Survey Publications. Vol.4, pt. 1. Manila: Bureau of Public Printing, 1905.

Saleeby, Najeeb M. *The History of Sulu.* Manila: Filipiniana Book Guild, 1963.

Service, Elman R. *Primitive Social Organization: An Evolutionary Perspective.* New York: Random House, 1962.

Sherry, Norman. *Conrad's Eastern Sea.* Cambridge: Cambridge University Press, 1966.

Singh, S.B. *European Agency Houses in Bengal, 1783–1833.* Calcutta: K.L. Mukhopadhyay, 1966.

Sonnerat, Pierre. *An Account of a Voyage to the Spice Islands, and New Guinea.* Paris: Bury St. Edmunds, Green, 1781.

Sonnerat, Pierre. *A Voyage to the East Indies and China Performed by Order of Lewis XV between the Years 1774 and 1781.* Trans. Francis Magnus. Calcutta: Stuart & Cooper, 1788.

Sopher, David E. *The Sea Nomads: A Study Based on the Literature of the Maritime Boat People of Southeast Asia.* Memoir of the National Museum, No.5. Singapore, 1965.

Sotoca, Maria Carmen Garcia. *Expedicion de Malespina: Catalogo de Grabados de la expedicion de Malespina.* Madrid, 1966.

Spoehr, Alexander. *Zamboanga and Sulu: An Archeological Approach to Ethnic Diversity.* Ethnology Monograph No.1., Dept. of Anthropology, University of Pittsburgh, Pittsburgh, 1973.

St. John, Horace. *The Indian Archipelago: Its History and Present State.* 2 vols. London: Longman, Brown, Green & Longman, 1853.

St. John, Spenser. *Life in the Forests of the Far East.* 2 vols. London: Smith Elder & Co., 1862.

Stapel, F.W., ed. *Corpus Diplomaticum Neerlands-Indicum.* Vol.6. The Hague: Martinus Nijhoff, 1955.

Steinberg, David J., ed. *In Search of Southeast Asia: A Modern History.* New York: Praeger, 1971.

Tarling, Nicholas. *Piracy and Politics in the Malay World: A Study of British Imperialism in Nineteenth-Century Southeast Asia.* Singapore: Donald Moore, 1963.

Tarling, Nicholas. *Britain, the Brookes and Brunei.* London: Oxford University Press, 1971.

Tarling, Nicholas. *Sulu and Sabah: A Study of British Policy towards the Philippines and North Borneo from the Late Eighteenth Century.* Kuala Lumpur: Oxford University Press, 1978.

Tobing, PH.O.L. *Hukum Pelajaran dan Perdagangan Ammana Gappa.* Jajasan Kebudajaan Sulawesi Selatan dan Tenggara. Makassar, 1961.

Travel accounts of the Islands 1513–1787, by Tomes Pires, Pedro Ordenez de Cevallos, Francois Pyrard, Josis van Speilbergen, Pedro Cubero Sebastion, William Dampier,

Alexander Dalrymple, Pierre de Pages, Captain Crozet, Guillaume Raynal, Thomas Forrest and De la Perouse. Manila: Filipiniana Book Guild, 1971.

Tregonning, K.G. *A History of Modern Sabah, 1881–1963.* Singapore: University of Malaya Press, 1965.

Tripathi, Amales. *Trade and Finance in the Bengal Presidency, 1793–1833.* Calcutta: Orient Longmans, 1956.

Trocki, Carl A. *Prince of Pirates: The Temenggongs and the Development of Johor and Singapore, 1784–1885.* Singapore: Singapore University Press, 1977.

Van Leur, J.C. *Indonesian Trade and Society.* The Hague: Van Hoeve, 1967.

Veth, P.J. *Borneo's Wester-Afdeeling, Geographisch, Statistisch, Historisch, voorafgegaan door eene algemeene schets des ganschen eilands.* 2 vols. Norman, Zaltbommel, 1854–1856.

Wallace, Alfred Russel. *The Malay Archipelago: The Land of the Orang-Utan, and the Bird of Paradise. A Narrative of Travel with Studies of Man and Nature.* 2 vols. London: Macmillan, 1869.

Warren, James Francis. *The North Borneo Chartered Company's Administration of the Bajau, 1878–1909.* Papers in International Studies, Southeast Asia Series, No.22. Athens, Ohio: Ohio University Center for International Studies, 1971.

Wernstedt, Frederick L., and Spencer, J.E. *The Philippine Island World: A Physical, Cultural and Regional Geography.* Berkeley: University of California Press, 1967.

Wertheim W.F. *Indonesian Society in Transition: A Study of Social Change.* The Hague: Van Hoeve, 1959.

Wickberg, Edgar. *The Chinese in Philippine Life, 1850–1898.* New Haven and London: Yale University Press, 1965.

Wolters, O.W. *The Fall of Srivijaya in Malay History.* Ithaca, N.Y.: Cornell University Press, 1970.

Woodward, David. *The Narrative of Captain David Woodward and Four Seamen.* London: Dawsons, 1969.

Worcester, Dean C. *The Philippine Islands and Their People.* New York: Macmillan, 1898.

Wright, Leigh R. *The Origins of British Borneo.* Hong Kong: Hong Kong University Press, 1970.

Wrigley, E.A. *Population and History.* London: Weidenfeld & Nicolson, 1969.

Wu, C.L. *A Study of References to the Philippines in Chinese Sources from Earliest Times to the Ming Dynasty.* Quezon City: University of the Philippines, 1959.

Yvan, Melchior. *Six months among the Malays and a Year in China.* London: James Blackwood, 1855.

Zuniga, Joachim Martinez de. *Estadismo de las Filipinas; a mis viajez por este pais.* 2 vols. Madrid: M.Minuesa de los Rios, 1893.

ARTICLES

Abdul Latif bin Haji Ibrahim. "Padian, Its Market and the Women Vendors", *The Brunei Museum Journal* 2, no.1 (1970): 39–51.

"Adventures of C.Z.Pieters among the Pirates of Magindanao", *Journal of the Indian Archipelago and Eastern Asia* (1858), pp.301–12.

Andre, E.M. "Slavery and Polygamy in the Sulu Archipelago", *The Independent,* pp.3220–22.

Appell, G.N. "Social and Medical Anthropology of Sabah: Retrospect and Prospect", *Sabah Society Journal* 3, no.7 (1968): 246–86.

Appell, G.N. "Studies of the Tausug (Suluk) and Samal-Speaking populations of Sabah and the Southern Philippines", *Borneo Research Bulletin* 1, no.2 (1969): 21–22.

Appel, G.N. "Ethnographic Notes on the Iranon Maranao (Illanun) of Sabah", *Sabah Society Journal* 5, no.2 (1970): 77–82.

Asri J. Abubakar. "Muslim Philippines, With Reference to the Sulus, Muslim-Christian Contradictions, and the Mindanao Crisis", *Asian Studies* 11, no.1 (1973): 112–27.

Baradas, David. "Some Implications of the Okir Motif in Lanao and Sulu Art", *Asian Studies* 6, no.2 (1968): 129–68.

Barth, Frederick. "Ecologic Relationships of Ethnic Groups in Swat, North Pakistan", *American Anthropologist* 58 (1956): 1079–89.

Basset, D.K. "British Commercial and Strategic Interests in the Malay Peninsula During the late Eighteenth Century", in *Malayan and Indonesian Studies,* ed. J. Bastin and R. Roolvink. London: Oxford University Press, 1964.

Benda, Harry J. "The Structure of Southeast Asian History: Some Preliminary Observations", *Journal of Southeast Asian History* 3, no.1 (1962): 106–38.

"Berigten omtrent den Zeeroof in den Nederlandsch-Indischen Archipel, 1857", *Tijdschrift voor Indische Taal-, Land-en Volkenkunde, uitgegeven door het (Koninklijk) Bataviaasch Genootschap van Kunsten en Wetenschappen* 20 (1873): 302–26.

"Berigten omtrent den Zeeroof in den Nederlandsch-Indischen Archipel, 1857", *Tijdschrift voor Indische Taal-, Land-en Volkenkunde, uitgegeven door het (Koninklijk) Bataviaasch Genootschap van Kunsten en Wetenschappen* 18 (1868–1872): 435–57.

Black, I.D. "The Political Situation in Sabah on the Eve of Chartered Company Rule", *Borneo Research Bulletin* 3, no.2 (1971): 62–65.

Blummentritt, Ferdinand. "Los Moros del Filipinas", *Boletin de la Sociedad geografica de Madrid* 23 (1892): 106–112.

Brassey, Lord. "North Borneo", *Nineteenth Century* (1887): 248–56.

Brown, D.E. "Brunei and the Bajau", *Borneo Research Bulletin* 3, no.2 (1971): 55–58.

Butcher, John. "Recent Research in Southeast Asian History, and Another Look at the Question of Perspective", *Time Remembered* 2 (1978): 57–68.

Casino, Eric. "Jama Mapun Ethnoecology", *Asian Studies* 5 (1967): 1–32.

Casino, Eric. "Some Notes on Sociopolitical Change among the Jama Mapun", *Borneo Research Bulletin* 3, no.2 (1971):65–66.

Cheong, W.E. "Changing the Rules of the Game (The India-Manila Trade: 1785–1809)", *Journal of Southeast Asian Studies* 1, no.2 (1970): 1–19.

Concas y Palau, Victor M. "Ocupacion de Tataan en la Isla de Taui-Taui", *Boletin de la Sociedad geografica de Madrid* 16 (1883): 307–10.

Concas y Palau, Victor M. "Conferencia sobre las relaciones de Espana con Jolo", *Boletin de la Sociedad geografica de Madrid* 16 (1884): 400–424.

Concas y Palau, Victory M. "Nuestras relaciones con Jolo. Discurso pronunciado en la Sociedad geografica en 12 de Febrero de 1884", *Revista general de Marina* 16 (1884): 153–82.

Concas y Palau, Victory M. "Nuestras relaciones con Jolo. Discurso pronunciado en la Sociedad geografica en 12 de Febrero de 1884", *Revista general de Marina* 16 (1885): 55–70 (1885): 199–213.

Curtin, Philip. "Field Techniques for Collecting and Processing Oral Data", *Journal of African History* 9, no.3 (1968): 367–85.

Dalrymple, Alexander. "Account of Some Natural Curiosities at Sooloo", in *An Historical Collection of the Several Voyages and Discoveries in the South Pacific Ocean,* vol.I. London, 1770.

Dalton, George. "Economic Anthropology", *American Behavioural Scientist* 20, no.5 (1977): 635–56.

Dalton, George. "Karl Polanyi's Analysis of Long Distance Trade and His Wider Paradigm", in *Ancient Civilizations and Trade,* ed. J.A. Sabloff and C.C. Lamberg-Karlovsky. Albuquerque: University of New Mexico Press, n.d.

Dalton, J. "Remarks on the Exports of Coti", in *Notices of the Indian Archipelago and Adjacent Countries,* ed. J.H. Moor. London: Cass, 1967.

Dalton, J. "On the Present State of Piracy, amongst These Islands, and the Best Method of Its Suppression", in *Notices of the Indian Archipelago and Adjacent Countries*, ed. J.H. Moor. London: Cass, 1967.

Dalton, J. "Remarks on the Bugis Campong Semerindan", in *Notices of the Indian Archipelago and Adjacent Countries*, ed. J.H. Moor. London: Cass, 1967.

Dalton, J. "Makassar, The Advantages of Making It a Free Port", in *Notices of the Indian Archipelago and Adjacent Countries*, ed. J.H. Moor. London: Cass, 1967.

Damsani, Maduh; Efren Alawi, and Rixhon, Gerard. "Four Folk Narratives from Mullung, a Tausug Storyteller", *Sulu Studies* 1 (1972): 191–255.

Elkins, Stanley. "Slavery and Its Aftermath in the Western World", in *Caste and Race: Comparative Approaches*, ed. Anthony de Reuck and Julie Knight. London: J. and A. Churchill, 1967.

Frake, C.O. "The Eastern Subanun of Mindanao", in *Social Structure of Southeast Asia*, ed. G.P.Murdock. Viking Fund Publications in Anthropology No.29. New York, 1960.

Frake, C.O. "Cultural Ecology and Ethnography", *American Anthropologist* 63 (1962): 113–32.

Frake, C.O. "Struck by Speech", in *Law in Culture and Society*, d. L. Nader. Chicago, 1969.

Fried, Morton H. "On the Evolution of Social Stratification and the State", in *Culture in History*, ed. S. Diamond. New York: Columbia University Press, 1960.

Garin y Sociats, Arturo. "Memoria sobre el Archipielago de Jolo", *Boletin del la Sociedad geografica de Madrid* 10 (1881): 110–33, 161–97.

Geoghegan, William. "Balangingi Samal", in *Ethnic Groups of Insular Southeast Asia*, vol.2, ed. Frank M. Le Bar. New Haven: Human Relations Area Files Press, forthcoming.

Hageman, J. "Aanteekeningen omtrent een gedeelte der Oostkust van Borneo", *Tijdschrift voor Indische Taal-, Land-en Volkenkunde, uitgegeven door het (Koninklijk) Bataviaasch Genootschap van Kunsten en Wetenschapen* 4 (1855): 71–106.

Harrison, Barbara. "Bird Caves of Idahan", *The Straits Times Annual* (1969): 91–94.

Harrison, Tom. "The Unpublished Rennell Ms.A Borneo Philippine Journey, 1762–1763", *Journal Malaysian Branch, Royal Asiatic Society* 39, pt.1 (1966): 92–136.

Harrison, Tom. "The Rennell Manuscript in the Brunei Museum", *Brunei Museum Journal* 1 (1969): 157–65.

Horsfield, Thomas. "Report on the Island of Banka", *Journal of the Indian Archipelago and Eastern Asia* 2 (1848): 299–336, 373–427, 705–25, 779–824.

Hunt, J. "Some Particulars Relating to Sulo in the Archipelago of Felicia", in *Notices of the Indian Archipelago and Adjacent Countries*, ed. J.H. Moor. London: Cass, 1967.

Hunt, J. "Sketch of Borneo or Sulo Kalamantan, Communicated by J. Hunt Esq. in 1812, to the Honorable Sir T.S. Raffles, Late Lieut. Governor of Java", in *Notices of the Indian Archipelago and Adjacent Countries*, ed. J.H. Moor, London: Cass, 1967.

Hunt, J. "Sketch of Borneo or Pulo Kalamantan, Communicated by J. Hunt Esq. in 1812 to the Honorable Sir T.S. Raffles, Late Lieut. Governor of Java", in *Notices of the Indian Archipelago and Adjacent Countries*, ed. J.H. Moor. London: Cass, 1967.

Jansen, A.J.F. "Aanteekeningen omtrent Sollok en de Solloksche Zeeroovers", *Tijdschrift voor Indische Taal-, Land-en Volkenkunde, uitgegeven door het (Koninklijk) Bataviaasch Geenootschap van Kunsten en Wetenschapen* 7 (1858): 212–39.

Kiefer, T.M. "Power, Politics and Guns in Jolo: The Influence of Modern Weapons on Tausug Legal and Economic Institutions", *Philippine Sociological Review* 15 (1967): 21–29.

Kiefer, T.M. "Institutionalized Friendship and Warfare among the Tausug of Jolo", *Ethnology* 7 (1968): 225–44.

Kiefer, T.M. "Reciprocity and Revenge in the Philippines: Some Preliminary Remarks about the Tausug of Jolo", *Philippine Sociological Review* 16 (1968): 124–31.

Kiefer, T.M. "Modes of Social Action in Armed Combat: Affect, Tradition, and Reason in Tausug Private Warfare", *Journal of the Royal Anthropological Institute* 5 (1970): 586–96.

Kiefer, T.M. "The Sultanate of Sulu: Problems in the Analysis of a Segmentary State", *Borneo Research Bulletin* 3, no.2 (1971): 46–51.

Kiefer, T.M. "The Tausug Polity and the Sultanate of Sulu: A Segmentary State in the Southern Philippines", *Sulu Studies* 1 (1972): 19–64.

Kiefer, T.M. "Parrang Sabbil: Ritual Suicide among the Tausug of Jolo", *Bidjdragen Tot de Taal, Land–en Volkenkunde* 129 (1973): 108–23.

Kottak, Conrad P. "Ecological Variables in the Origin and Evolution of African States: The Buganda Example", *Comparative Studies in Society and History* 14, no.31 (1972): 351–80.

Kuder, Edward M. "The Moros in the Philippines", *Far Eastern Quarterly* 4, no.2 (1945): 119–26.

Lapian, Adrian B. "The Sealords of Berau and Mindanao: Two Responses to the Colonial Challenge", *Masyarakat Indonesia* 1, no.2 (1974): 143–54.

Larkin, John. "The Place of Local History in Philippine Historiography", *Journal of Southeast Asian History* 8, no.2 (1977): 306–17.

Leach, E.R. "The Frontiers of Burma", *Comparative Studies in Society and History* 3 (1962): 48–67.

Leach, E.R. "Caste, Class and Slavery: The Taxonomic Problem", in *Caste and Race: Comparative Approaches,* ed. Anthony de Reuck and Julie Knight. London: J. and A. Churchill, 1967.

Lehman, F.K. "Ethnic Categories in Burma and the Theory of Social Systems", in *Southeast Asian Tribes, Minorities and Nations,* vol.1, ed. P. Keinstader. Princeton: Princeton University Press, 1967.

Lenski, Gerhard E. "The Dynamics of Distributive Systems", in *Power in Societies,* ed. Marvin Olsen. London: Macmillan, 1970.

Lewis, Diane. "Growth of the Country Trade to the Straits of Malacca, 1760–1777", *Journal of the Malaysian Branch, Royal Asiatic Society* 47, no.2 (1970): 114–30.

Leyden, Dr. "Sketch of Borneo", in *Notices of the Indian Archipelago and Adjacent Countries,* ed. J.H. Moor. London: Cass, 1967.

Linz, Juan J. "Five Centuries of Spanish History: Quantification and Comparison", in *The Dimensions of the Past: Materials, Problems and Opportunities for Quantitative Work in History,* ed. Val R. Lorwin and Jacob M. Price. New Haven: Yale University Press, 1972.

Macknight, C.C. "The Nature of Early Maritime Trade: Some Points of Analogy from the Eastern Part of the Indonesian Archipelago", *World Archeology* 5, no.2 (1973): 198–208.

Majul, Cesar A. "Political and Historical Notes on the Old Sulu Sultanate", *Journal of the Malaysian Branch, Royal Asiatic Society* 38, pt.1 (1965): 23–43.

Majul, Cesar A. "Succession in the Old Sulu Sultanate", *Philippine Historical Review* 1 (1965): 252–71.

Majul, Cesar A. "The Role of Islam in the History of the Filipino People", *Asian Studies* 4 (1966): 303–15.

Majul, Cesar A. "Islamic Influence in the Southern Philippines", *Journal of Southeast Asian History* 7 (1976): 61–73.

Majul, Cesar A. "Chinese Relationships with the Sultanate of Sulu", in *The Chinese in the Philippines, 1570–1770,* ed. Alfonso Felix. Manila: Solidaridad Publishing House, 1966.

Medhurst, W. "British North Borneo", *Royal Colonial Institute* 16 (1884/85): 273–307.

Medina, Isagani R. "American Logbooks and Journals in Salem, Massachusetts on the Philippines, 1796–1897", *Asian Studies* 11, no.1 (1973): 179–98.

Moerman, M. "Who are the Lue?", *American Anthropologist* 67 (1965): 1215–30.

Moerman, M. "Accomplishing Ethnicity", in *Ethnomethodology,* ed. R.Turner. London: Penguin Books, 1974.

Montano, J. "Une Mission aux Iles Malaise", *Societe Geographic Bulletin* (1881): 465–83.

Montero y Gay, Claudio. "Conferencias sobre las Filipinas, pronunciados en 3 de Junie y 7 de Octubre de 1876", *Boletin de Sociedad geografica de Madrid* 1 (1876): 297–338.

Mednick, Melvin. "Some Problems of Moro History and Political Organisation", *Philippine Sociological Review* 5 (1957): 39–52.

Needham, Rodney. "Penan", in *Ethnic Groups of Insular Southeast Asia,* vol.1, ed. Frank le Bar. New Haven: Human Relations Area Files Press, 1972.

Newbold, T.J. "Outline of Political Relations with the Native States on the Eastern and Western Coasts, Malayan Peninsular", in *Notices of the Indian Archipelago and Adjacent Countries,* ed. by J.H. Moor. London: Cass, 1967.

Nimmo, Harry A. "Social Organisation of the Tawi–Tawi Badjaw", *Ethnology* 4 (1965): 421–47.

Nimmo, Harry A. "The Sea Nomads: Description and Analysis", *Philippine Studies* 15 (1967): 209–12.

Nimmo, Harry A. "Reflections on Badjau History", *Philippine Studies* 17 (1968): 32–59.

"The Piracy and Slave Trade of the Indian Archipelago", *Journal of the Indian Archipelago and Eastern Asia* 3 (1849): 581–88, 629, 636; 4 (1850): 45–52, 144, 162, 400–410, 617–28, 734–46; 5 (1851): 374–82.

Prentice, D.J. "The Linguistic Situation in Northern Borneo", in *Pacific Linguisitic Studies in Honour of Arthur Capell,* ed. S.A. Wurm and D.C. Laycock. Pacific Linguistics. Canberra: Australian National University, 1970.

Pryer, William. "Notes on Northeastern Borneo and the Sulu Islands", *Royal Geographical Society Proceedings* 5 (1883): 90–96.

Pryer, William. "On the Natives of North Borneo", *Royal Anthropological Institute of Great Britain and Ireland* 16 (1887): 230–36.

Pryer, William. "Diary of a Trip up the Kinabatangan", *Sabah Society Journal* 5, no.2 (1970): 117–26.

Reed, Robert T. "The Primate City in Southeast Asia: Conceptual Definitions and Colonial Origins", *Asian Studies* 10, no.3 (1972): 283–321.

Resink, G.J. "De Archipel voor Joseph Conrad", *Bijdragen tot de Taal–Land–en Volkenkunde* 115, pt.II (1959): 192–208.

Resink, G.J. "The Eastern Archipelago Under Joseph Conrad's Western Eyes", in *Indonesia's History Between the Myths,* ed. G.J. Resink. The Hague: Van Hoeve, 1968.

Rixhon, Gerard. "Ten Years of Research in Sulu, 1961–1971", *Sulu Studies* 1 (1972): 1–17.

Rixhon, Gerard. "Mullung: A Taosug Storyteller", *Sulu Studies* 1 (1972): 172–90.

Rixhon, Gerard. "Coordinated Investigation of Sulu Culture, Jolo, Sulu", *Borneo Research Bulletin* 5, no.1 (1973): 19–21.

Sather, Clifford. "Social Rank and Marriage Payments in an Immigrant Moro Community in Malaysia", *Ethnology* 6 (1967): 97–102.

Sather, Clifford, ed. "Traditional States of Borneo and the Southern Philippines", *Borneo Research Bulletin* 3, no.2 (1971): 45–46.

Sather, Clifford. "Sulu's Political Jurisdiction over the Bajau Laut", *Borneo Research Bulletin* 3, no.2 (1971): 58–62.

Sather, Clifford. "Tidong", in *Ethnic Groups of Insular Southeast Asia,* vol.1, ed. Frank le Bar. New Haven: Human Relations Area Files Press, 1972.

Schlegel, Stuart. "Tiruray—Maguindanaon Ethnic Relations: An Ethnohistorical Puzzle", *Solidarity* 7, no.4 (1972): 25–30.

Scott, James C. "The Erosion of Patron-Client Bonds and Social Change in Rural Southeast Asia", *Journal of Asian Studies* 32, no.1 (1972): 5–39.

Shineberg, Dorothy. "The Sandalwood Trade in Melanesian Economics, 1841–1865", *Journal of Pacific History* 1 (1966): 129–46.

"Short accounts of Timor, Rotti, Savu, Solor", in *Notices of the Indian Archipelago and Adjacent Countries,* ed. J.H.Moor. London: Cass, 1967.

Skertchly, Ethelbert Forbes. "Cagayan Sulu: Its Customs, Legends and Superstitions", *Asiatic Society of Bengal Journal* 65, pt.3: 47–53.

Smail, John. "On the Possibility of an Autonomous History of Modern Southeast Asia", *Journal of Southeast Asian History* 2, no.2 (1971): 72–102.

Soeri Soerato. "Tindjuan Singkat Tentang Pertumbuhan Badjak Laut Sulu", *Buletin Sastra Universitas Gajah Mada* 1 (1970): 97–117.

Spoehr, Alexander. "An Archeological Approach to Ethnic Diversity in Zamboanga and Sulu", *Sulu Studies* 2 (1973): 95–101.

Stone, Richard L. "Intergroup Relations among the Taosugs, Samal, and Badjaw of Sulu", *Philippine Sociological Review* 10 (1962): 107–33.

St. John, Spenser. "Piracy in the Indian Archipelago", *Journal of the Indian Archipelago and Eastern Asia* 3 (1849): 251–60.

St. John Hart, E. "The Strange Story of a Little Ship", *The Wide World Magazine* (1906): 347–54.

"Sulu", *The Journal of the Indian Archipelago and Eastern Asia* 3, no.7 (1849): 412.

Tarling, Nicholas. "British Policy in Malayan Waters in the 19th Century", in *Papers on Malayan History*, ed. K.G. Tregonning. Singapore, 1962.

Tarling, Nicholas. "Consul Farren and the Philippines", *Journal of the Malaysian Branch, Royal Asiatic Society* 38, pt.2 (1966): 258–73.

Tarling, Nicholas. "The Entrepot at Labuan and the Chinese". Reprinted from *Studies in the Social History of China and Southeast Asia*, ed. J. Chen and N. Tarling. London: Cambridge University Press, 1970, *Sabah Society Journal* 5, no.2 (1970): 101–16.

Terray, Emmanuel, "Long-Distance Exchange and the Formation of the State: The Case of the Abron Kingdom of Gyaman". *Economy and Society* 3 (1974): 315–45.

Tilly, Charles. "Quantification in History, as Seen from France", in *The Dimensions of the Past: Materials, Problems, and Opportunities for Quantitative Work in History*, ed. Val R. Lorwin and Jacob M. Price. New Haven: Yale University Press, 1972.

Treacher, William. "Sketches of Brunei, Sarawak, Labuan and North Borneo", *Journal of the Straits Branch, Royal Asiatic Society* 20 (1889): 13–74; 21 (1890): 19–122.

Valera, J. "The Old Forts of Semporna", *Sabah Society Journal* 1, no.2 (1972): 40–41.

Van Capellan. "Berigt Aangaande den togt van Z.M. Schoener Egmond naar Berow, op de Oostkust van Borneo, in het najaar 1844", in *Bijdragen tot Kennis der Nederlandsche en vreemde Kolonien betrekklijk der vrijlating der slaven, 1844–1847*. Utrecht: Vanderpost, 1844–1847.

Van Dewall, H. "Aanteekeningen omtrent de Noordoostkust van Borneo", *Tijdschrift voor Indische Taal-, Land-en Volkenkunde, uitgegeven door het (Koninklijk) Bataviaasch Kunsten en Wetenschappen* 4 (1885): 423–58.

Van Hoevell, W.R. "Laboean, Serawak, de Noord-oostkust van Borneo en de Sulthan van Soeloe", *Tijdschrift voor Nederlandsche Indie* 11, pt.1 (1849): 66–83.

Van Hoevell, W.R. "De Zeerooverijen der Soeloerezen", *Tijdschrift voor Nederlandsch Indie* 2 (1850): 99–105.

Van Marle, A. "De Rol van de Buitenlandse Avonturier", *Bijdragen en Mededelingen Betreffende de Geschiedenis Der Nederlanden* 86, pt.1 (1971): 32–39.

Van Sina, Jan. "Once Upon a Time: Oral Traditions as History in Africa", *Daedalus* (1971): 442–68.

Van Verschuer, F.H. "De Badjoo", *Nederlandsch Aadrijksckundig Genootschap* 7 (1883): 1–7.

Vidrovitch, C. Coquery. "An African Mode of Production". *Critique of Anthropology* 4 (1975): 37–71.

Warren, J. "Balambangan and the Rise of the Sulu Sultanate, 1772–1775", *Journal of the Malaysian Branch, Royal Asiatic Society* 50, pt.I (1977): 73–93.

Warren, J. "Sino-Sulu Trade in the Late Eighteenth and Nineteenth Centuries", *Philippine Studies* 25 (1977): 50–79.

Warren, J. "Slave Markets and Exchange in the Malay world: The Sulu Sultanate, 1770–1878", *Journal of Southeast Asian Studies* 8, no.2 (1977): 112–75.

Warren, J. "Joseph Conrad's Fiction as Southeast Asian History: Trade and Politics in East Borneo in the Late Nineteenth Century", *The Brunei Museum Journal* (1977): 21–34.
Warren, J. "Who were the Balangingi Samal? Slave Raiding and Ethnogenesis in Nineteenth–Century Sulu", *Journal of Asian Studies* 37, no.3 (1978): 477–90.
Warren, J. "The Sulu Zone: Commerce and the Evolution of a Multi-Ethnic Polity, 1768–1898", *Archipel.* 18 (1979): 223–29.
Wendover, R.F. "The Balangingi Pirates", *Philippine Magazine* 38, no.8 (1941): 323–38.
Wheatley, Paul. "Satjantra in Suvarnadvipa from Reciprocity to Redistribution in Ancient Southeast Asia", in *Ancient Civilisations and Trade,* ed. J.A. Sabloff and C.C. Lamberg-Karlovsky. Albuquerque: University of New Mexico Press.
Wickberg, Edgar. "Spanish Records in the Philippine National Archives", *Archivinia* 1, no.1 (1968): 15–20, 30.
Windsor, G.E. "The Trading Ports of the Indian Archipelago", *Journal of the Indian Archipelago and Eastern Asia* 2 (1850): 283–51, 380–99, 483–93, 530–51.
Wortmann, J.R. "The Sultanate of Kutai, Kalimantan–Timur: A Sketch of the Traditional Political Structure", *Borneo Research Bulletin* 3, no.2 (1971): 51–55.
Wulf, J. "Features of Yakan Culture", *Folk* 6 (1964): 52–72.

BIBLIOGRAPHICAL AND ARCHIVAL GUIDES

Guia de los Archivos De Madrid: prologo del tenor D. Francisco Sintes y Obrador. Madrid: Direccion, General de Archivos y Bibliotecas Servicio De Publicaciones del Ministerio de Educacion Nacional, 1952.
Jaquet, F.G.P. *Gids van in Nederland aanivezige Bronnen betreffende de geschiedenis van Asie en Oceanie, 1796–1949;* Vols.I–VII. Leiden: Konink-Lyk Instituut voor Taal-, Landen Volkenkunde, 1968–1973.
Jaquet, F.G.P. "Dutch Archive Material Relating to the History of Asia, 1769–1949", *Southeast Asian Archives* 8 (1975): 10–36.
Lanzas torres, Pedro. *Relacion Descriptivo de los Mapos, Planos, etc. de Filipinas existentes en Archivo de Indias.* Madrid, 1897.
Medina, Isagani. *Filipiniana Materials in the National Library.* Quezon City: University of the Philippines Press, 1972.
Retana, Wenceslao Emilio. *Bibliografia de Mindanao.* Madrid: Viuda de M.Minuesa de los Rios, 1894.
Retana, Wenceslao Emilio. *Aparato Bibliografico de la Historia General de Filipinas.* 3 vols. Madrid, 1906.
Robertson, James Alexander. *Bibliography of the Philippine Islands; Printed and Manuscript; Preceded by a Descriptive Account of the Most Important Archives and Collections Containing Philipiniana.* Cleveland, Ohio: Arthur H. Clark Co., 1908.
Roessingh, M.P.H. "Dutch Relations with the Philippines: A Survey of Sources in the General State Archives, The Hague, Netherlands", *Asian Studies* 5, no.2 (1967):377–407.
Sanchez Belda, Luis. *Guia del Archivo Historico Nacional,* Madrid, 1958.
Tello leon, Pilar. *Mapos, Planos, y Dibujos de la Seccion de Estado del Archivo Historico Nacional.* Madrid: Direccion General de Archivos y Bibliotecas, 1969.
Tiamson, Aldfredo T.*Mindanao-Sulu Bibliography containing Published, Unpublished Manuscripts and Works in-Progress, A Preliminary Survey.* Davao City: Ateneo de Davao, 1970.
Van Der Chijs, J.A.*Inventaris van Stands Archief te Batavia (1602–1816).* Batavia: Landsdrukery, 1882.

Index

Abdullah, Munshi: on Bugis slave traffic at Singapore, 14

Agricultural slaves, 221–23, 244–45

Alimudin (Sultan of Sulu), 27

Alimudin (datu of southern Palawan), 107–8; and trade to Labuan, 138; accepts Balangingi refugees, 194

Alvarez, Sgt. Maj. Manuel, 25, 30; diplomatic mission to Jolo, 32, 53

Ammas, *See* Slavery

Ammunition: *See* Gunpowder

Amurong, Iranun slave raids against, 161, 165

Anda y Salazar, Simon de (Governor Captain General of the Philippines), 25–26; encourages trade with Sulu, 53

Arms, *See* Firearms

Assumpcion, Father Sebastion de la (Provincial of the Recollect Order), 24

Balangingi (island): description of, 182–83; location of Samal villages of, xlii; salt manufacture in, 71; Spanish attack on, 104, 191–92

Balangingi Samal (ethnic group) of Sulu Archipelago, xvi; no historical references to, 182; history of, as an ethnic group, 184; as an "emergent" society, 254; integration of, within Sulu Sultanate, 183; in slave raiding, xviii; transfer of, to Cagayan Valley, 192–94; *See also* Sipac and Tawi-Tawi Samal

Balangingi: role in marine procurement, 67; role in salt manufacture, 74; slave raiding, pattern of, 180; slave raiding, decline in, 200; rivalry with Taosug, 107, 189, 230; diaspora, 190–97, 252; prisoners, statements of, 297–98

Balambangan (island): cession of, 18; trade in firearms on, 22–23; and trade to Cotabato Sultanate, 29; arms traffic and intensification of slave raiding on, 25; destruction of settlement on, 34–35; and rise of the Sulu Sultanate, 37

Bantilan (Sultan of Sulu): and trade in firearms, 23; list of Sulu products for export by, 43, 48; and rivalry with sultanates of Cotabato and Brunei, 27

Banyaga, *See* Slavery

Basco y Vargas, Jose (Governor Captain General of the Philippines): encourages Sulu trade with Manila, 54; organizes the "light navy", 172

Basilan (island): location of Samal communities on, xlii; lumber from, exported for trade, 8; rice from, exported to Sulu, 99; establishment of Spanish naval base on, 191

Beeswax, *See* Wax

Berau (region): immigrant Bugis assimilated into host society in, 10; as focal point of Taosug-Bugis trade, 14, 88; and trade to Manlia, 55

Bermejo, Father Julian: scheme for coastal defence on Cebu, 174

Bird's nests: as trade item for Chinese cuisine, xxi, 6, 8; Sulu export of, to Manila, 62; exchanged for opium, 21; from Gomantan caves of Sandakan bay, 82; Taosug-Bugis trade in, 14; struggle over, in Bulungan region, 88, 90; traffic in, via Omaddal island, 139–40

Bisaya, *See* Slavery

Bishopric of Nueva Caceres, *See* Nueva Caceres

Blacksmiths, slaves as, 225; *See also* Iranun

Gold, mining of, *See* Punan
Guns, *See* Firearms
Gunpowder, xxii; Taosug manufacture of, 23; traffic in, at Jolo, 48–49; as Bugis trade item, 11–12; trade in, at Balambangan, 22; exported from Singapore, 63; scarcity of, in Filipino villages, 176–77; Spanish officials traffic in, 177
Gutta-percha: imported to Labuan, 109

Halcon, Capt. Jose Maria (Spanish naval officer expert in Sulu affairs), 101
Head Money: for pirates, 173–74
Health: effect of diet of slaves on, 247; *See also* Disease
Herbert, John (East India Company factor), 19; and conduct of Sulu trade, 20
Historiography: periodization in, 253–54; the "trade and empire approach" in, xvii; of Sulu as a pirate and slave state, xx, 252; approach emphasizing religious rivalries in, xx–xxi; of the Sulu Zone, necessity of a regional framework in, xlii–xliii; ethnicity as a fixed premise in, 254; and East India Company's relations with Sulu, 19; significance of slave testimonies to, 236
Human sacrifice: slaves as, in east Borneo, 199
Hunt, J.: report on Sulu by, xliv, 7, 9; on profits of country trade at Sulu, 45
Hunting and gathering societies, *See* Punan, and Samal Bajau Laut
Hussin, Sherif (east Bornean river chief), of the Sugut, 79

I-Lanaw-en (Magindanao term), 149
Illanun (as an ethnic label), 149
Internal trade: of Sulu Zone, 67–102; role of Straits Chinese in, 128–29
Ipun, *See* Slavery
Iranun (ethnic group) of Mindanao: principal mooring sites of, on

Mindanao, 151; influence of Magindanao on, 151; known as "Magindanao" in Celebes, 161; as blacksmiths, 151; slavery among, 215; crippling of local shipping by, 25, 32–33, 159; in the Moluccas and Celebes, 160–65; in the Philippines, 165–81
Iranun: immigrant communities in Sulu, 151–53; trade at Jolo, 34; trade in opium, 22; rivalry with Taosug, 32, 152; satellite communities, 155–56; slave raids in the Malacca Straits, 156–60
Iron: trade in, at Sulu, 49
Islam: and the Sultan of Sulu, xliv; and slavery, 216
Israil, Mohammed (Sultan of Sulu): attitude of, towards Balambangan settlement, 27–28; statecraft of, 30

Jama Mapun (ethnic group) of Cagayan de Sulu: and trade to Labuan and Sandakan, 136–37; *See also* Cagayan de Sulu, and Copra
Jihad: Magindanao raiding as an extension of, xxi, 171
Jolo (capital of Sulu Sultanate), xli

Kadis, xlv
Kassim (datu of southern Palawan): Spanish attack on prahu of, 118; attempt by, to control trade of southern Palawan, 118
Kema: Iranun slave raids against, 161
Kenyah–Kayan–Kayang (culture complex) of east Borneo, 84–85
Khutbah, xlvi
Kiefer, Thomas: on factional politics of Taosug society, xliv; on rights and duties associated with Taosug political office, xlv
Kinabatangan (Taosug market town), 83
Kinabatangan (river): significance of, in procurement trade, 75, 82; slave trade to, 199

Omaddal (island): importance of, in trade of east Borneo, 139; expedition against, 140

Opium: market for in Southeast Asia, 17; Taosug-Bugis traffic in, 14, 49; profits from, 44; trade at Balambangan, 19–20; country trade cargoes, 41; trade at Labuan, 107, 109, 111–112

Opium smoking, addiction of Taosug Datus, 20–21, 225–26

Outcastes, fugitive slaves in Zamboanga, 234–35

Outsiders, slaves as, 231, 248–49

Paduakan, Bugis trading boat, 11

Paitan river, 75; *See* Camphor

Palawan (island), pattern of Taosug settlement, 137; rice exported to Sulu, 99

Pariah, *See* Samal Bajau Laut

Pasir, Bugis trading community, 10; country trade to, 40; outfitting of Iranun *prahus*, 161

Pata (island), x1

Patero, Santiago (Spanish naval officer), architect of cruising system, 118, 252

Pawning, in periods of distress, 216; *See* Debt Bondage

Pearl Diving, hazards of, 73; *See* Fisheries

Pearl Fisheries, *See* Fisheries

Piracy, historiographical problems of writings on, xxi–xxii, 252

Political Power, related to ownership of slaves, xix, xli, 201, 271–18, 251

Population, increase in Sulu, xix, xxii, 53; and slavery, xix–xx, 208–211; and slave raiding in the Philippines, 177–181; in the Moluccas, 165; estimates of Chinese in the Philippines, 127

Porcelain, Chinese tradeware, 6, 8

Portuguese, trade from Macao to Sulu, 40, 55, 63

Powder, *See* Gunpowder

Prahus, use of compass on Sulu, 42

Prestige, and ownership of slaves, xxi, 217–18

Prices, of slaves, 13, 200–1, 203–5, 218; in equivalents of rice, 98, 205; in cloth, gold and wax, 91; in pearl shell, 121; in slaves, 186

Products exported from Sulu, 65; *See also* Bird's nest, Gutta-percha, Mother-of-pearl, pearls, salt, tripang, and coax

Pryer, William (pioneer administrator of North Borneo Chartered Co.), 135–36

Punan (ethnic group) of east Borneo, 85; mining gold, 87

Raffles, Sir Stamford: on Sulu and slave raiding, xx, xliv, 147; on Salem traders, 50

Ransom, *See* Redemption

Rattans: collection of, for export, 79–80; monopoly of trade in, on northeast coast of Borneo, 115; trade in, from Palawan, 138

Reber, Anne Lyndsey, xxiii; on historiography and the Sulu world, 147

Redistributive system: as dominant economic pattern of Sulu Zone, 3, 17

Regional framework: of interpretation and analysis, xlii–xliii, 251

Renegados: and Balangingi Samal population, 184; role of, in slave raiding, 151–52, 161, 187, 210

Reteh (Iranun satellite community), 157, 159–60

Rice: in the economy of the Sulu Sultanate, 95–102; in trade at Jolo, 6; in Bugis trade to Sulu, 11, 14; in Magindanao trade to Sulu, xlii; exported from Marudu to Sulu, 77, 79; Tidong export of, to Sulu, 87; in the Manila-Jolo trade, 60; Sulu's self-sufficiency in, 121; Philippine export of, to China, 64; exchanged for slaves, 204–5